GILBERT KEITH CHESTERTON

CHESTERTON'S MONUMENT DESIGNED BY ERIC GILL

GILBERT KEITH CHESTERTON

by

Maisie Ward

New York

SHEED & WARD

1943

MANUFACTURED IN THE UNITED STATES OF AMERICA
BY BURR PRINTING HOUSE, INC., NEW YORK

Contents

81158

Contents

Illustrations

Chiefly Concerning Sources

THE MATERIAL FOR this book falls roughly into two parts: spoken and written. Gilbert Chesterton was not an old man when he died and many of his friends and contemporaries have told me incidents and recalled sayings right back to his early boyhood. This part of the material has been unusually rich and copious so that I could get a clearer picture of the boy and the young man than is usually granted to the biographer.

The book has been in the making for six years and in three countries. Several times I laid it aside for some months so as to be able to get a fresh view of it. I talked to all sorts of people, heard all sorts of ideas, saw my subject from every side; I went to Paris to see one old friend, to Indiana to see others, met for the first time in lengthy talk Maurice Baring, H. G. Wells and Bernard Shaw; went to Kingsland to see Mr. Belloc; gathered Gilbert's boyhood friends of the Junior Debating Club in London and visited "Father Brown" among his Yorkshire moors.

Armed with a notebook, I tried to miss none who had known Gilbert well, especially in his youth: E. C. Bentley, Lucian Oldershaw, Lawrence Solomon, Edward Fordham. I had ten long letters from Annie Firmin, my most valuable witness as to Gilbert's childhood. For information on the next period of his life, I talked to Monsignor O'Connor, to Hilaire Belloc, Maurice Baring, Charles Somers Cocks, F. Y. Eccles and others, besides being now able to draw on my own memories. Frances I had talked with on and off about their early married years ever since

I had first known them, but she was, alas, too ill and consequently too emotionally unstrung during the last months for me to ask her all the questions springing in my mind. "Tell Maisie," she said to Dorothy Collins, "not to talk to me about Gilbert. It makes me cry."

For the time at Beaconsfield, out of a host of friends the most valuable were Dr. Pocock and Dr. Bakewell. Among priests, Monsignors O'Connor and Ronald Knox, Fathers Vincent McNabb, O.P. and Ignatius Rice, O.S.B. were especially intimate.

Dorothy Collins's evidence covers a period of ten years. That of H. G. Wells and Bernard Shaw is reinforced by most valuable letters which they have kindly allowed me to publish.

Then too Gilbert was so much of a public character and so popular with his fellow journalists that stories of all kinds abound: concerning him there is a kind of evidence, and very valuable it is, that may be called a Boswell Collective. It is fitting that it should be so. We cannot picture G.K. like the great lexicographer accompanied constantly by one ardent and observant witness, pencil in hand, ready to take notes over the teacups. (And by the way, in spite of an acquaintance who regretted in this connection that G.K. was not latterly more often seen in taverns, it *was* over the teacups, even more than over the wine glasses, that Boswell made his notes. I have seen Boswell's signature after wine—on the minutes of a meeting of The Club—and he was in no condition then for the taking of notes. Even the signature is almost illegible.) But it is fitting that Gilbert, who loved all sorts of men so much, should be kept alive for the future by all sorts of men. From the focussing of many views from many angles this picture has been composed, but they are all views of one man, and the picture will show, I think, a singular unity. When Whistler, as Gilbert himself once said, painted a portrait he made and destroyed many sketches—how many it did not matter, for all, even of his failures, were fruitful—but it would have mattered frightfully if each time he looked up he found a new subject sitting placidly for his portrait. Gilbert was fond of asking in the *New Witness* of people who expressed admiration for Lloyd George: "Which George do you mean?" for, chameleon-like, the politician has worn many colours and the portrait painted in 1906 would have had to be torn up in 1916. But gather the Chesterton portraits: read the files when he first grew into fame: talk to Mr. Titterton who worked with him on the *Daily News* in 1906 and on *G.K.'s Weekly* in 1936, collect witnesses from his boyhood to his old age, from Dublin to Vancouver: individuals who knew him, groups who are endeavoring to work out his ideas: all will agree on the ideas and on the man as making one pattern throughout, one developing but integrated mind and personality.

Gathering the material for a biography bears some resemblance to interrogating witnesses in a Court of Law. There are good witnesses and bad: reliable and unreliable memories. I remember an old lady, a friend of my mother's, who remarked with candour after my mother had confided to her something of importance: "My dear, I must go and write that down immediately before my imagination gets mixed with my memory." One witness must be checked against another: there will be discrepancies in detail but the main facts will in the end emerge.

Just now and again, however, a biographer, like a judge, meets a totally unreliable witness.

One event in this biography has caused me more trouble than anything else: the Marconi scandal and the trial of Cecil Chesterton for criminal libel which grew out of it. As luck would have it, it was on this that I had to interrogate my most unreliable witness. I had seen no clear and unbiased account so I had to read the many pages of Blue Book and Law Reports besides contemporary comment in various papers. I have no legal training, but one point stuck out like a spike. Cecil Chesterton had brought accusations against Godfrey Isaacs not only concerning his own past career as a company promoter, but also concerning his dealings with the government over the Marconi contract, in connection with which he had also fiercely attacked Rufus Isaacs, Herbert Samuel and other ministers of the Crown. But in the witness box he accepted the word of the very ministers he had been attacking, and declared that he no longer accused them of corruption: which seemed to me a complete abandonment of his main position.

Having drafted my chapter on Marconi, I asked Mrs. Cecil Chesterton to read it, but more particularly to explain this point. She gave me a long and detailed account of how Cecil had been intensely reluctant to take this course, but violent pressure had been exerted on him by his father and by Gilbert who were both in a state of panic over the trial. Unlikely as this seemed, especially in Gilbert's case, the account was so circumstantial, and from so near a connection, that I felt almost obliged to accept it. What was my amazement a few months later at receiving a letter in which she stated that after "a great deal of close research work, re-reading of papers, etc." (in connection with her own book *The Chestertons*) and after a talk with Cecil's solicitors, she had become convinced that Cecil had acted as he had because "the closest sleuthing had been unable to discover any trace" of investments by Rufus Isaacs in English Marconis. "For this reason Cecil took the course he did—not through family pressure. That pressure, *I still feel*,* was exerted, though possibly not until the trial was over."

It was, then, the lady's feelings and not facts that had been offered to me as evidence, and it was the merest luck that my book had not appeared before Cecil's solicitors had spoken.

The account given in Lord Birkenhead's *Famous Trials* is the Speech for the Prosecution. Mrs. Cecil Chesterton's chapter is an impressionist sketch of the court scene by a friend of the defendant. What was wanted was an impartial account, but I tried in

---

* Italics mine.

vain to write it. The chronology of events, the connection between the Government Commission and the Libel Case, the connection between the English and American Marconi companies —it was all too complex for the lay mind, so I turned the chapter over to my husband who has had a legal training and asked him to write it for me.

The Chestertons is concerned with Gilbert and Frances as well as with Cecil; and the confusion between memory and imagination—to say nothing of reliance on feelings unsupported by facts—pervades the book. It can only be called a Legend, so long growing in Mrs. Cecil's mind that I am convinced that when she came to write her book she firmly believed in it herself. The starting-point was so ardent a dislike for Frances that every incident poured fuel on the flame and was seen only by its light. When I saw her, the Legend was beginning to shape. She told me various stories showing her dislike: facts offered by me were either denied or twisted to fit into the pattern. I do not propose to discuss here the details of a thoroughly unreliable book. Most of them I think answer themselves in the course of this biography. With one or two points I deal in Appendix C. But I will set down here one further incident that serves to show just how little help this particular witness could ever be.

For, like Cecil's solicitors, I spoilt one telling detail for her. She told me with great enthusiasm that Cecil had said that Gilbert was really in love not with Frances but with her sister Gertrude, and that Gertrude's red hair accounted for the number of red-headed heroines in his stories. I told her, however, on the word of their brother-in-law, that Gertrude's hair was not red. Mr. Oldershaw in fact seemed a good deal amused: he said that Gilbert never looked at either of the other sisters, who were "not his sort," and had eyes only for Frances. Mrs. Cecil however would not relinquish this dream of red hair and another love. In her book she wishes "red-gold" hair on to Annie Firmin, because in the *Autobiography* Gilbert had described her golden plaits. But unluckily for this new theory Annie's hair was yellow,* which is quite a different colour. And Annie, who is still alive, is also amused at the idea that Gilbert had any thought of romance in her connection.

When Frances Chesterton gave me the letters and other documents, she said: "I don't want the book to appear in a hurry: not for at least five years. There will be lots of little books written about Gilbert; let them all come out first. I want your book to be the final and definitive Biography."

The first part of this injunction I have certainly obeyed, for it will be just seven years after his death that this book appears. For the second half, I can say only that I have done the best that in me lies to obey it also. And I am very grateful to those who have preceded me with books depicting one aspect or another of my subject. I have tried to make use of them all as part of my material, and some are "little" merely in the number of their pages. I am especially grateful to Hilaire Belloc, Emile Cammaerts, Cyril Clemens and "Father Brown" (who have allowed me to quote with great freedom). I want to thank Mr. Seward Collins, Mr. Cyril Clemens and the University of Notre Dame for the loan of books; Mrs. Bambridge for the use of a letter from Kipling and a poem from *The Years Between*.

Even greater has been the kindness of those friends of my own and of Gilbert Chesterton's who have read this book in manuscript and made very valuable criticisms and suggestions: May Chesterton, Dorothy Collins, Edward Connor, Ross Hoffman, Mrs. Robert Kidd, Arnold Lunn, Mgr. Knox, Father Murtagh, Father Vincent McNabb, Lucian Oldershaw, Beatrice Warde, Douglas Woodruff, Monsignor O'Connor.

Most of the criticisms were visibly right, while even those with which I could not concur showed me the weak spot in

---

* See G.K.'s letter to her daughter, p. 633.

my work that had occasioned them. They have helped me to improve the book—I think I may say enormously.

One suggestion I have not followed—that one name should be used throughout: either Chesterton or Gilbert or G.K., but not all three. I had begun with the idea of using "Chesterton" when speaking of him as a public character and also when speaking of the days before I did in fact call him "Gilbert." But this often left him and Cecil mixed up: then too, though I seldom used "G.K." myself, other friends writing to me of him often used it. I began to go through the manuscript unifying—and then I noticed that in a single paragraph of his *Bernard Shaw* Gilbert uses "GBS," "Shaw," "Bernard Shaw" and "Mr. Shaw." Here was a precedent indeed, and it seemed to me that it was really the natural thing to do. After all we do talk of people now by one name, now by another: it is a matter of slight importance if of any, and I decided to let it go.

As to size, I am afraid the present book is a large one—although not as large as Boswell's *Johnson* or *Gone With the Wind*. But in this matter I am unrepentant, for I have faith in Chesterton's own public. The book is large because there is no other way of getting Chesterton on to the canvas. It is a joke he would himself have enjoyed, but it is also a serious statement. For a complete portrait of Chesterton, even the most rigorous selection of material cannot be compressed into a smaller space. I have first written at length and then cut and cut.

At first I had intended to omit all matter already given in the *Autobiography*. Then I realised that would never do. For some things which are vital to a complete Biography of Chesterton are not only told in the *Autobiography* better than I could tell them, but are recorded there and nowhere else. And this book is not merely a supplement to the *Autobiography*. It is the Life of Chesterton.

The same problem arises with regard to the published books and I have tried to solve it on the same lines. There has rung in my mind Mr. Belloc's saying: "A man is his mind." To tell the story of a man of letters while avoiding quotation from or reference to his published works is simply not to tell it. At Christopher Dawson's suggestion I have re-read all the books *in the order in which they were written,* thus trying to get the development of Gilbert's mind perfectly clear to myself and to trace the influences that affected him at various dates. For this reason I have analysed certain of the books and not others—those which showed this mental development most clearly at various stages, or those (too many alas) which are out of print and hard to obtain. But whenever possible in illustrating his mental history I have used unpublished material, so that even the most ardent Chestertonian will find much that is new to him.

For the period of Gilbert's youth there are many exercise books, mostly only half filled, containing sketches and caricatures, lists of titles for short stories and chapters, unfinished short stories. Several completed fairy stories and some of the best drawings were published in *The Coloured Lands.* Others are hints later used in his own novels: there is a fragment of *The Ball and the Cross,* a first suggestion for *The Man Who Was Thursday,* a rather more developed adumbration of *The Napoleon of Notting Hill.* This I think is later than most of the notebooks; but, after the change in handwriting, apparently deliberately and carefully made by Gilbert around the date at which he left St. Paul's for the Slade School, it is almost impossible to establish a date at all exactly for any one of these notebooks. Notes made later when he had formed the habit of dictation became difficult to read, not through bad handwriting, but because words are abbreviated and letters omitted.

Some of the exercise books appear to have been begun, thrown aside and used again later. There is among them one only of real biographical importance, a book deliberately used for the development of a philosophy of life, dated in two places, to which I devote a chapter and which I refer to as *the* Notebook. This book

is as important in studying Chesterton as the Pensées would be
for a student of Pascal. He is here already a master of phrase
in a sense which makes a comparison with Pascal especially apt.
For he often packs so much meaning into a brilliant sentence or
two that I have felt it worth while, in dealing especially with
some of the less remembered books, to pull out a few of these
sentences for quotation apart from their context.

Other important material was to be found in *G.K.'s Weekly*,
in articles in other periodicals, and in unpublished letters. With
some of the correspondences I have made considerable use of
both sides, and if anyone pedantically objects that that is unusual
in a biography I will adapt a phrase of Bernard Shaw's which
you will find in this book, and say, "Hang it all, be reasonable!
If you had the choice between reading me and reading Wells
and Shaw, wouldn't you choose Wells and Shaw."

GILBERT KEITH CHESTERTON

Chapter I

Background for Gilbert Keith Chesterton

I T IS USUAL to open a biography with some account of the subject's ancestry. Chesterton, in his *Browning*,* after some excellent foolery about pedigree-hunting, makes the suggestion that middle-class ancestry is far more varied and interesting than the ancestry of the aristocrat:

The truth is that aristocrats exhibit less of the romance of pedigree than any other people in the world. For since it is their principle to marry only within their own class and mode of life, there is no opportunity in their case for any of the more interesting studies in heredity; they exhibit almost the unbroken uniformity of the lower animals. It is in the middle classes that we find the poetry of genealogy; it is the suburban grocer standing at his shop door whom some wild dash of Eastern or Celtic blood may drive suddenly to a whole holiday or a crime.

This may provide fun for a guessing game but is not very useful to a biographer. The Chesterton family, like many another, had had the ups and downs in social position that accompany the ups and downs of fortune. Upon all this Edward Chesterton, Gilbert's father, as head of the family possessed many interesting documents. After his death, Gilbert's mother left his papers undisturbed. But when she died Gilbert threw away, without examination, most of the contents of his father's study, including all family records. Thus I cannot offer any sort of family tree. But it is possible to show the kind of family and the social atmosphere into which Gilbert Chesterton was born.

* Pp. 7–8.

Some of the relatives say that the family hailed from the village of Chesterton—now merged into Cambridge, of which they were Lords of the Manor, but Gilbert refused to take this seriously. In an introduction to a book called *Life in Old Cambridge,* he wrote:

I have never been to Cambridge except as an admiring visitor; I have never been to Chesterton at all, either from a sense of unworthiness or from a faint superstitious feeling that I might be fulfilling a prophecy in the countryside. Anyone with a sense of the savour of the old English country rhymes and tales will share my vague alarm that the steeple might crack or the market cross fall down, for a smaller thing than the coincidence of a man named Chesterton going to Chesterton.

At the time of the Regency, the head of the family was a friend of the Prince's and (perhaps as a result of such company) dissipated his fortunes in riotous living and incurred various terms of imprisonment for debt. From his debtors' prisons he wrote letters, and sixty years later Mr. Edward Chesterton used to read them to his family: as also those of another interesting relative, Captain George Laval Chesterton, prison reformer and friend of Mrs. Fry and of Charles Dickens. A relative recalls the sentence: "I cried, Dickens cried, we all cried," which makes one rather long for the rest of the letter.

George Laval Chesterton left two books, one a kind of autobiography, the other a work on prison reform. It was a moment of enthusiasm for reform, of optimism and of energy. Dickens was stirring the minds of Englishmen to discover the evils in their land and rush to their overthrow. Darwin was writing his *Origin of Species,* which in some curious way increased the hopeful energy of his countrymen: they seemed to feel it much more satisfying to have been once animal and have become human than to be fallen gods who could again be made divine. Anyhow, there were giants in those days and it was hope that made them so.

When by an odd confusion the *Tribune* described G. K. Chesterton as having been born about the date that Captain Chesterton published his books, he replied in a Ballade which at once saluted and attacked:

> I am not fond of anthropoids as such,
> I never went to Mr. Darwin's school,
> Old Tyndall's ether, that he liked so much
> Leaves me, I fear, comparatively cool.
> I cannot say my heart with hope is full
> Because a donkey, by continual kicks,
> Turns slowly into something like a mule—
> I was not born in 1856.
>
> .   .   .   .
>
> Age of my fathers: truer at the touch
> Than mine: Great age of Dickens, youth and yule:
> Had your strong virtues stood without a crutch,
> I might have deemed man had no need of rule,
> But I was born when petty poets pule,
> When madmen used your liberty to mix
> Lucre and lust, bestial and beautiful,
> I was not born in 1856.*

Both *Autobiography* and *Prison Life* are worth reading.† They breathe the "Great Gusto" seen by Gilbert in that era. He does not quote them in his *Autobiography*, but, just mentioning Captain Chesterton, dwells chiefly on his grandfather, who, while George Laval Chesterton was fighting battles and reforming prisons, had succeeded to the headship of a house agents' business in Kensington. (For, the family fortunes having been dissipated, Gilbert's great-grandfather had become first a coal merchant and then a house agent.) A few of the letters between this ancestor and his son remain and they are interesting, confirming Gilbert's description in the *Autobiography* of his grandfather's feeling that he himself was something of a landmark in

* Quoted in *G. K. Chesterton. A criticism.* Alston Rivers (1908) pp. 243–244.
† See Appendix A.

Kensington and that the family business was honourable and important.

The Chestertons, whatever the ups and downs of their past history, were by now established in that English middle-class respectability in which their son was to discover—or into which he was to bring—a glow and thrill of adventurous romance. Edward Chesterton, Gilbert's father, belonged to a serious family and a serious generation, which took its work as a duty and its profession as a vocation. I wonder what young house-agent today, just entering the family business, would receive a letter from his father adjuring him to "become an active steady and honourable man of business," speaking of "abilities which only want to be judiciously brought out, of course assisted with your earnest co-operation."

Gilbert's mother was Marie Grosjean, one of a family of twenty-three children. The family had long been English, but came originally from French Switzerland. Marie's mother was from an Aberdeen family of Keiths, which gave Gilbert his second name and a dash of Scottish blood which "appealed strongly to my affections and made a sort of Scottish romance in my childhood." Marie's father, whom Gilbert never saw, had been "one of the old Wesleyan lay-preachers and was thus involved in public controversy, a characteristic which has descended to his grandchild. He was also one of the leaders of the early Teetotal movement, a characteristic which has not." *

When Edward became engaged to Marie Grosjean he complained that his "dearest girl" would not believe that he had any work to do, but he was in fact much occupied and increasingly responsible for the family business.

There is a flavour of a world very remote from ours in the packet of letters between the two and from their various parents, aunts and sisters to one another during their engagement. Edward illuminates poems "for a certain dear good little child,"

* *Autobiography*, pp. 11–12.

sketches the "look out from home" for her mother, hopes they did not appear uncivil in wandering into the garden together at an aunt's house and leaving the rest of the company for too long. He praises a friend of hers as "intellectual and unaffected, two excellent things in woman," describes a clerk sent to France with business papers who "lost them all, the careless dog, except the Illustrated London News."

A letter to Marie from her sister Harriette is amusing. She describes her efforts at entertaining in the absence of her mother. The company were "great swells" so that her brother "took all the covers off the chairs himself and had the wine iced and we dined in full dress—it was very awful—considering myself as hostess." Poor girl, it was a series of misfortunes. "The dinner was three-quarters of an hour late, the fish done to rags." She had hired three dozen wine-glasses to be sure of enough, but they were "brought in in twos and threes at a time and then a hiatus as if they were being washed which they were not."

In the letters from parents and older relatives religious observances are taken for granted and there is an obvious sincerity in the many allusions to God's will and God's guidance of human life. No one reading them could doubt that the description of a dying relative as "ready for the summons" and "going home" is a sincere one. Other letters, notably Harriette's, do not lack a spice of malice in speaking of those whose religion was unreal and affected—a phenomenon that only appears in an age when real religion abounds.

Doubtless her generation was beginning to see Christianity with less than the simplicity of their parents. They were hearing of Darwin and Spencer, and the optimism which accompanied the idea of evolution was turning religion into a vague glow which would, they felt, survive the somewhat childish dogmas in which our rude ancestors had tried to formulate it. But with an increased vagueness went also, with the more liberal—and the Chestertons were essentially liberal both politically and theologically—an increased tolerance. In several of his letters, Edward Chesterton mentions the Catholic Church, and certainly with no dislike. He went on one occasion to hear Manning preach and much admired the sermon, although he notes too that he found in it "no distinctively Roman Catholic doctrine." He belonged, however, to an age that on the whole found the rest of life more exciting and interesting than religion, an age that had kept the Christian virtues and still believed that these virtues could stand alone, without the support of the Christian creed.

The temptation to describe dresses has always to be sternly resisted when dealing with any part of the Victorian era, so merely pausing to note that it seems to have been a triumph on the part of Mrs. Grosjean to have cut a *short* skirt out of 8½ yards of material, I reluctantly lay aside the letters at the time when Edward Chesterton and Marie were married and had set about living happily ever after.

These two had no fear of life: they belonged to a generation which cheerfully created a home and brought fresh life into being. In doing it, they did a thousand other things, so that the home they made was full of vital energies for the children who were to grow up in it. Gilbert recollects his father as a man of a dozen hobbies, his study as a place where these hobbies formed strata of exciting products, awakening youthful covetousness in the matter of a new paint-box, satisfying youthful imagination by the production of a toy-theatre. His character, serene and humorous as his son describes him, is reflected in his letters. Edward Chesterton did not use up his mental powers in the family business. Taught by his father to be a good man of business, he was in his private life a man of a thousand other energies and ideas. "On the whole," says his son,* "I am glad he was never an artist. It might have stood in his way in becoming an

* *Autobiography*, p. 35.

amateur. It might have spoilt his career; his private career. He could never have made a vulgar success of all the thousand things he did so successfully."

Here, Gilbert sees a marked distinction between that generation of business men and the present in the use of leisure; he sees hobbies as superior to sport. "The old-fashioned Englishman, like my father, sold houses for his living but filled his own house with his life. A hobby is not merely a holiday. . . . It is not merely exercising the body instead of the mind, an excellent but now largely a recognised thing. It is exercising the rest of the mind; now an almost neglected thing." Edward Chesterton practised "water-colour painting and modelling and photography and stained glass and fretwork and magic lanterns and mediaeval illumination." And, moreover, "knew all his English literature backwards."

It has become of late the fashion for any one who writes of his own life to see himself against a dark background, to see his development frustrated by some shadow of heredity or some horror of environment. But Gilbert saw his life rather as the ancients saw it when *pietas* was a duty because we had received so much from those who brought us into being. This Englishman was grateful to his country, to his parents, to his home for all that they had given him.

I regret that I have no gloomy and savage father to offer to the public gaze as the true cause of all my tragic heritage; no pale-faced and partially poisoned mother whose suicidal instincts have cursed me with the temptations of the artistic temperament. I regret that there was nothing in the range of our family much more racy than a remote and mildly impecunious uncle; and that I cannot do my duty as a true modern, by cursing everybody who made me whatever I am. I am not clear about what that is; but I am pretty sure that most of it is my own fault. And I am compelled to confess that I look back to that landscape of my first days with a pleasure that should doubtless be reserved for the Utopias of the Futurist.*

* G. K. Chesterton. *Autobiography,* pp. 22–3.

Chapter II

Childhood

GILBERT KEITH CHESTERTON was born on May 29, 1874 at a house in Sheffield Terrace, Campden Hill, just below the great tower of the Waterworks which so much impressed his childish imagination. Lower down the hill was the Anglican Church of St. George, and here he was baptised. When he was about five, the family moved to Warwick Gardens. As old-fashioned London houses go, 11 Warwick Gardens is small. On the ground floor, a back and front room were for the Chestertons drawing-room and dining-room with a folding door between, the only other sitting-room being a small study built out over the garden. A long, narrow, green strip, which must have been a good deal longer before a row of garages was built at the back, was Gilbert's playground. His bedroom was a long room at the top of a not very high house. For what is in most London houses the drawing-room floor is in this house filled by two bedrooms and there is only one floor above it.

Cecil was five years younger than Gilbert, who welcomed his birth with the remark, "Now I shall always have an audience," a prophecy remembered by all parties because it proved so singularly false. As soon as Cecil could speak, he began to argue and the brothers' intercourse thenceforward consisted of unending discussion. They always argued, they never quarrelled.

There was also a little sister Beatrice who died when Gilbert was very young, so young that he remembered a fall she had

8

from a rocking-horse more clearly than he remembered her death, and in his memory linked with the fall the sense of loss and sorrow that came with the death.

It would be impossible to tell the story of his childhood one half so well as he has told it himself. It is the best part of his *Autobiography.* Indeed, it is one of the best childhoods in literature. For Gilbert Chesterton most perfectly remembered the exact truth, not only about what happened to a child, but about how a child thought and felt. What is more, he sees childhood not as an isolated fragment or an excursion into fairyland, but as his "real life; the real beginnings of what should have been a more real life; a lost experience in the land of the living."

I was subconsciously certain then, as I am consciously certain now, that there was the white and solid road and the worthy beginning of the life of man; and that it is man who afterwards darkens it with dreams or goes astray from it in self-deception. It is only the grown man who lives a life of make-believe and pretending; and it is he who has his head in a cloud.*

Here are the beginnings of the man's philosophy in the life and experience of the child. He was living in a world of reality, and that reality was beautiful, in the clear light of "an eternal morning," which "had a sort of wonder in it, as if the world were as new as myself." A child in this world, like God in the moment of creation, looks upon it and sees that it is very good. It was not that he was never unhappy as a child, and he had his share of bodily pain—"I had a fair amount of toothache and especially earache." But the child has his own philosophy and makes his own proportion, and unhappiness and pain "are of a different texture or held on a different tenure."

What was wonderful about childhood is that anything in it was a wonder. It was not merely a world full of miracles; it was a miraculous world. What gives me this shock is almost anything I really recall; not the things I should think most worth recalling. This is

* *Autobiography*, p. 49.

where it differs from the other great thrill of the past, all that is connected with first love and the romantic passion; for that, though equally poignant, comes always to a point; and is narrow like a rapier piercing the heart, whereas the other was more like a hundred windows opened on all sides of the head.*

These windows opening on all sides so much more swiftly for the genius than for the rest of us, led to a result often to be noted in the childhood of exceptional men: a combination of backwardness and precocity. Gilbert Chesterton was in some ways a very backward child. He did not talk much before three. He learnt to read only at eight.

He loved fairy tales: as a child he read them or had them read aloud to him: as a big boy he wrote and illustrated a good many, some of which are printed in *The Coloured Lands*. I have found several fragments in praise of Hans Andersen written apparently in his schooldays. In the chapter of *Orthodoxy* called "The Ethics of Elfland" he shows how the truth about goodness and happiness came to him out of the old fairy tales and made the first basis for his philosophy. And George Macdonald's story *The Princess and the Goblin* made, he says, "a difference to my whole existence, which helped me to see things in a certain way from the start." It is the story of a house where goblins were in the cellar and a kind of fairy godmother in a hidden room upstairs. This story had made "all the ordinary staircases and doors and windows into magical things." It was the awakening of the sense of wonder and joy in the ordinary things always to be his. Still more important was the realization represented by the goblins below stairs, that "When the evil things besieging us do appear, they do not appear outside but inside." In life as in this story there is

. . . a house that is our home, that is rightly loved as our home, but of which we hardly know the best or the worst, and must always wait for the one and watch against the other. . . . Since I first read

* *Autobiography*, pp. 31–32.

CHESTERTON AT THE AGE OF SIX
From an oil-painting by Baccari (1881).

that story some five alternative philosophies of the universe have come to our colleges out of Germany, blowing through the world like the east wind. But for me that castle is still standing in the mountains, its light is not put out.*

All this to Gilbert made the story the "most real, the most realistic, in the exact sense of the phrase the most like life" of any story he ever read—then or later! Another recurrent image in books by the same author is that of a great white horse. And Gilbert says, "To this day I can never see a big white horse in the street without a sudden sense of indescribable things." *

Of his playmates, "one of my first memories," he writes in the *Autobiography*, "is playing in the garden under the care of a girl with ropes of golden hair; to whom my mother afterwards called out from the house, 'You are an angel'; which I was disposed to accept without metaphor. She is now living in Vancouver as Mrs. Robert Kidd."

Mrs. Kidd, then Annie Firmin, was the daughter of a girlhood friend of Mrs. Chesterton's. She called her "Aunt Marie." She and her sister, Gilbert says in the *Autobiography*, "had more to do with enlivening my early years than most." She has a vivid memory of Sheffield Terrace where all three Chesterton children were born and where the little sister, Beatrice, whom they called Birdie, died. Gilbert, in those days, was called Diddie, his father then and later was "Mr. Ed" to the family and intimate friends. Soon after Birdie's death they moved to Warwick Gardens. Mrs. Kidd writes:

. . . the little boys were never allowed to see a funeral. If one passed down Warwick Gardens, they were hustled from the nursery window at once. Possibly this was because Gilbert had such a fear of sickness or accident. If Cecil gave the slightest sign of choking at dinner, Gilbert would throw down his spoon or fork and rush from the room. I have seen him do it so many times. Cecil was fond of

---

* Introduction to *George Macdonald and His Wife.*

animals. Gilbert wasn't. Cecil had a cat that he named Faustine, because he wanted her to be abandoned and wicked—but Faustine turned out to be a gentleman!

Gilbert's story-telling and verse-making began very early, but not, I think, in great abundance; his drawing even earlier, and of this there is a great deal. There is nothing very striking in the written fragments that remain, but his drawings even at the age of five are full of vigour. The faces and figures are always rudimentary human beings, sometimes a good deal more, and they are taken through lengthy adventures drawn on the backs of bits of wall paper, of insurance forms, in little books sewn together, or sometimes on long strips glued end to end by his father. These drawings can often be dated exactly, for Edward Chesterton, who later kept collections of press-cuttings and photographs of his son, had already begun to collect his drawings, writing the date on the back of each. With the earlier ones he may, one sometimes suspects, have helped a little, but it soon becomes easy to distinguish between the two styles.

Edward Chesterton was the most perfect father that could have been imagined to help in the opening of windows on every side. "My father might have reminded people of Mr. Pickwick, except that he was always bearded and never bald; he wore spectacles and had all the Pickwickian evenness of temper and pleasure in the humours of travel." He had, as his son further notes in the *Autobiography*, a power of invention which "created for children the permanent anticipation of what is profoundly called a 'Surprise.'" The child of today chooses his Christmas present in advance and decides between Peter Pan and the Pantomime (when he does not get both). The Chesterton children saw their first glimpses of fantasy through the framework of a toy-theatre of which their father was carpenter, scene-painter and scene-shifter, author and creator of actors and actresses a few inches high. Gilbert's earliest recollection is of one of these figures in a golden crown carrying a golden key, and his father was all through his childhood a man with a golden key who admitted him into a world of wonders.

I think Gilbert's father meant more to him than his mother, fond as he was of her. Most of their friends seem to feel that Cecil was her favorite son. "Neither was ever demonstrative," Annie Firmin says, "I never saw either of them kiss his mother." But in some ways the mother spoilt both boys. They had not the training that a strict mother or an efficient nurse usually accomplishes with the most refractory. Gilbert was never refractory, merely absent-minded; but it is doubtful whether he was sent upstairs to wash his hands or brush his hair, except in preparation for a visit or ceremonial occasion ("not even then!" interpolates Annie). And it is perfectly certain that he ought to have been so sent several times a day. No one minded if he was late for meals; his father, too, was frequently late and Frances during her engagement often saw his mother put the dishes down in the fireplace to keep hot, and wait patiently—in spite of Gilbert's description of her as "more swift, relentless and generally radical in her instincts" than his father. Annie Firmin's earlier memories fit this description better. Much as she loved her "aunt," she writes:

Aunt Marie was a bit of a tyrant in her own family! I have been many times at dinner, when there might be a joint, say, and a chicken—and she would say positively to Mr. Ed. "Which will you have, Edward?" Edward: "I think I'd like a bit of chicken!" Aunt M. fiercely: "No, you won't, you'll have mutton!" That happened so often. Sometimes Alice Grosjean, the youngest of Aunt M.'s family, familiarly known as "Sloper," was there. When asked her preference she would say, diffidently, "I think I'll take a little mutton!" "Don't be a fool, Alice, you know you like chicken,"—and chicken she got.

Visitors to the house in later years dwell on Mrs. Chesterton's immense spirit of hospitality, the gargantuan meals, the eager desire that guests should eat enormously, and the wittiness of her conversation. Schoolboy contemporaries of Gilbert say that although immensely kind, she alarmed them by a rather forbidding appearance—"her clothes thrown on anyhow, and blackened and protruding teeth which gave her a witchlike appearance. . . . The house too was dusty and untidy." She called them always by their surnames, both when they were little boys and after they grew up, "Oldershaw, Bentley, Solomon."

"Not only," says Miss May Chesterton, "did Aunt Marie address Gilbert's friends by their surnames, but frequently added darling to them. I have heard her address Bentley when a young man thus: 'Bentley darling, come and sit over here,' to which invitation he turned a completely deaf ear as he was perfectly content to remain where he was!'

"Indiscriminately, she also addressed her maids waiting at table with the same endearment."

A letter written when Gilbert was only six would seem to show that Mrs. Chesterton had not yet become so reckless about her appearance, and was still open to the appeal of millinery. ("She always was," says Annie.) The letter is from John Barker of High Street, Kensington, and is headed in handwriting, "Drapery and Millinery Establishment, Kensington High Street, September 21, 1880."

MADAM,

We are in receipt of instructions from Mr. Edward Chesterton to wait upon you for the purpose of offering for your selection a Bonnet of the latest Parisian taste, of which we have a large assortment ready for your choice; or can, if preferred, make you one to order.

Our assistant will wait upon you at any time you may appoint, unless you would prefer to pay a visit to our Millinery department yourself.

Mr. Chesterton informs us that as soon as you have made your selection he will hand us a cheque for the amount.

We are given to understand that Mr. Chesterton proposes this transaction as a remembrance of the anniversary of what, he instructs us to say, he regards as a happy and auspicious event. We have accordingly entered it in our books in that aspect.

In conveying, as we are desired to do, Mr. Chesterton's best wishes for your health and happiness for many future anniversaries, may we very respectfully join to them our own, and add that during many years to come we trust to be permitted to supply you with goods of the best description for cash, on the principle of the lowest prices consistent with excellence of quality and workmanship.

We have the honour to be
Madam
Your most obedient Servants
JOHN BARKER & Co.

The order entered in their books "under that aspect," the readiness to provide millinery "for cash," convinces you (as G.K. himself says of another story) that Dick Swiveller really did say, "When he who adores thee has left but the name—in case of letters and parcels." Dickens *must* have dictated the letter to John Barker. After all, he was only dead ten years.

"Aunt Marie used to say," adds Annie Firmin, "that Mr. Ed married her for her beautiful hair, it was auburn, and very long and wavy. He used to sit behind her in Church. She liked pretty clothes, but lacked the vanity to buy them for herself. I have a little blue hanging watch that he bought her one day—she always appreciated little attentions."

The playmates of Gilbert's childhood are not described in the *Autobiography* except for Annie's "long ropes of golden hair." But in one of the innumerable fragments written in his early twenties, he describes a family of girls who had played with him when they were very young together. It is headed, "Chapter I. A Contrast and a Climax," and several other odd bits of verse and narrative introduce the Vivian family as early and constant playmates.

One of the best ways of feeling a genuine friendly enthusiasm for persons of the other sex, without gliding into anything with a shorter name, is to know a whole family of them. The most intellectual idolatry at one shrine is apt to lose its purely intellectual character, but a genial polytheism is always bracing and platonic. Besides, the

Vivians lived in the same street or rather "gardens" as ourselves, and were amusing as bringing one within sight of what an old friend of mine, named Bentley, called with more than his usual gloom and severity of expression, "the remote outpost of Kensington Society."

For these reasons, and a great many much better ones, I was very much elated to have the family, or at least the three eldest girls who represent it to the neighbourhood, standing once more on the well-rubbed lawn of our old garden, where some of my earliest recollections were of subjecting them to treatment such as I considered appropriate to my own well-established character of robber, tying them to trees to the prejudice of their white frocks, and otherwise misbehaving myself in the funny old days, before I went to school and became a son of gentlemen only. I have never been able, in fact I have never tried, to tell which of the three I really liked best. And if the severer usefulness and domesticity of the eldest girl, with her quiet art-colours, and broad, brave forehead as pale as the white roses that clouded the garden, if these maturer qualities in Nina demanded my respect more than the levity of the others, I fear they did not prevent me feeling an almost equal tide of affection towards the sleepy acumen and ingrained sense of humour of Ida, the second girl and book-reader for the family: or Violet, a veritably delightful child, with a temper as formless and erratic as her tempest of red hair.

"What old memories this garden calls up," said Nina, who like many essentially simple and direct people, had a strong dash of sentiment and a strong penchant for being her own emotional pint-stoup on the traditional subjects and occasions. "I remember so well coming here in a new pink frock when I was a little girl. It wasn't so new when I went away."

"I certainly must have been a brute," I replied. "But I have endeavoured to make a lifetime atone for my early conduct." And I fell to thinking how even Nina, miracle of diligence and self-effacement, remembered a new pink frock across the abyss of the years. . . . Walking with my old friends round the garden, I found in every earth-plot and tree-root the arenas of an active and adventurous life in early boyhood. . . .*

Edward Chesterton was a Liberal politically and what has been called a Liberal Christian religiously. When the family went to church—which happened very seldom—it was to listen

* Unpublished fragment.

to the sermons of Stopford Brooke. Some twenty years later, Cecil was to remark with amusement that he had as a small boy heard every part of the teaching now (1908) being set out by R. J. Campbell under the title, "The New Religion." The Chesterton Liberalism entered into the view of history given to their children, and it produced from Gilbert the only poem of his childhood worth quoting. I cannot date it, but the very immature handwriting and curious spelling mark it as early.

Probably most children have read, or at any rate up to my own generation, had read, Aytoun's *Lays of the Scottish Cavaliers*, and played at being Cavaliers as a result. But Gilbert could not play at being a Cavalier. He had learned from his father to be a Roundhead, as had every good Liberal of that day. What was to be done about it? He took the *Lays* and rewrote them in an excellent imitation of Aytoun, but on the opposite side. In view of his own later developments such a line as "Drive the trembling Papists backwards" has an ironic humour. But one wonders what Aytoun himself would have made of a small boy who took his rhythm and sometimes his very words, turned his hero into a traitor ("false Montrose") and his traitor Argyll into a hero! I have left the spelling untouched.

> Sing of the Great Lord Archibald
> Sing of his glorious name
> Sing of his covenenting faith
> And his evelasting fame.
>
> One day he summoned all his men
> To meet on Cruerchin's brow
> Three thousand covenenting chiefs
> Who no master would allow
>
> Three thousand Knights
> With clamores drawn
> And targets tough and strong
> Knights who for the right
> Would ever fight
> And never bear the wrong.

And he creid (his hand uplifted)
"Soldiers of Scotland hear my vow
Ere the morning shall have risen
I will lay the trators low
Or as ye march from the battle
Marching back in battle file
Ye shall there among the corpses
Find the body of Argyll.

Soldiers Soldiers onward onward
Onward soldiers follow me
Come, remember ye the crimes
Of the fiend of fell Dundee
Onward let us draw our clamores
Let us draw them on our foes
Now then I am threatened with
The fate of false Montrose.

Drive the trembling Papists backwards
Drive away the Tory's hord
Let them tell thier hous of villians
They have felt the Campbell's sword."

And the next morn he arose
And he girded on his sword
They asked him many questions
But he answered not a word.
And he summoned all his men
And he led them to the field
And We creid unto our master
That we'd die and never yield.
That same morn we drove right backwards
All the servants of the Pope
And Our Lord Archibald we saved
From a halter and a rope
Far and fast fled all the trators
Far and fast fled all the Graemes
Fled that cursed tribe who lately
Stained there honour and thier names.

CHAPTER III

School Days

CURIOUSLY ENOUGH Gilbert does not in the *Autobiography* speak of any school except St. Paul's. He went however first to Colet Court, usually called at that time Bewsher's, from the name of the Headmaster. Though it is not technically *the* preparatory school for St. Paul's, large numbers of Paulines do pass through it. It stands opposite St. Paul's in the Hammersmith Road and must have been felt by Gilbert as one thing with his main school experience, for he nowhere differentiates between the two.

St. Paul's School is an old city foundation which has had among its scholars Milton and Marlborough, Pepys and Sir Philip Francis and a host of other distinguished men. The editor of a correspondence column wrote a good many years later in answer to an enquirer: "Yes, Milton and G. K. Chesterton were both educated at St. Paul's school. We fancy however that Milton had left before Chesterton entered the school." In an early life of Sir Thomas More we learn of the keen rivalry existing in his day between his own school of St. Anthony and St. Paul's, of scholastic "disputations" between the two, put an end to by Dean Colet because they led to brawling among the boys, when the Paulines would call those of St. Anthony "pigs" and the pigs would call the Paulines "pigeons"—from the pigeons of St. Paul's Cathedral. Now, however, St. Anthony's is no more, and St. Paul's School has long moved to the suburbs and lies about seven minutes' walk along the Hammersmith Road from Warwick Gardens. Gilbert Chesterton was twelve when he entered

St. Paul's (in January 1887) and he was placed in the second
Form.

His early days at school were very solitary, his chief occupa-
tion being to draw all over his books. He drew caricatures of
his masters, he drew scenes from Shakespeare, he drew prominent politicians. He did not at first make many friends. In the
Autobiography he makes a sharp distinction between being a
child and being a boy, but it is a distinction that could only be
drawn by a man. And most men, I fancy, would find it a little
difficult to say at what moment the transformation occurred.
G.K. seems to put it at the beginning of school life, but the fact
that St. Paul's was a day-school meant that the transition from
home to school, usual in English public-school education,* was
never in his case completely made. No doubt he is right in
speaking in the *Autobiography* of "the sort of prickly protection like hair" that "grows over what was once the child," of the
fact that schoolboys in his time "could be blasted with the horrible revelation of having a sister, or even a Christian name."
Nevertheless, he went home every evening to a father and
mother and small brother; he went to his friends' houses and
knew their sisters; school and home life met daily instead of
being sharply divided into terms and holidays.

This fact was of immense significance in Gilbert's development. Years later he noted as the chief defect of Oxford that it
consisted almost entirely of people educated at boarding-schools.
For good, for evil, or for both, a boy at a day-school is educated
chiefly at home.

* The terminology for English schools came into being largely before the
State concerned itself with education. A Private School is one run by an
individual or a group for private profit. A Public School is not run for private
profit; any profits there may be are put back into the school. Mostly they are
run by a Board of Governors and very many of them hold the succession to
the old monastic schools of England (e.g. Charterhouse, Westminster, St.
Paul's). They are usually, though not necessarily, boarding schools, and the
fees are usually high. Elementary schools called Board Schools were paid for
out of local rates and run by elected School Boards. They were later replaced
by schools run by the County Councils.

In the atmosphere of St. Paul's is found little echo of the dogma
of the Head Master of Christ's Hospital. "Boy! The school is your
father! Boy! The school is your mother." Nor, as far as we know has
any Pauline been known to desire the substitution of the august
abstraction for the guardianship of his own people. Friendships
formed in this school have a continual reference to home life, nor
can a boy possibly have a friend long without making the acquaintance and feeling the influence of his parents and his surroundings.
. . . The boys' own amusements and institutions, the school sports,
the school clubs, the school magazine, are patronised by the masters,
but they are originated and managed by the boys. The play-hours of
the boys are left to their several pleasures, whether physical or intellectual, nor have any foolish observations about the battle of Waterloo
being won on the cricket-field, or such rather unmeaning oracles, yet
succeeded in converting the boys' amusements into a compulsory
gymnastic lesson. The boys are, within reasonable limits, free.*

Gilbert calls the chapter on his school days, "How to be a
Dunce," and although in mature life he was "on the side of his
masters" and grateful to them "that my persistent efforts not to
learn Latin were frustrated; and that I was not entirely successful even in escaping the contamination of the language of
Aristotle and Demosthenes," he still contrasts childhood as a time
when one "wants to know nearly everything" with "the period
of what is commonly called education; that is, the period during
which I was being instructed by somebody I did not know about
something I did not want to know."

The boy who sat next to him in class, Lawrence Solomon
(later Senior Tutor of University College, London), remembered him as sleepy and indifferent in manner but able to master
anything when he cared to take the trouble—as he very seldom
did. He was in a class with boys almost all his juniors. Lucian
Oldershaw, who later became his brother-in-law, says of Gilbert's own description of his school life that it was as near a pose
as Gilbert ever managed to get. He wanted desperately to be

* MS. *History of J.D.C.* written about 1894.

the ordinary schoolboy, but he never managed to fulfill this ambition. Tall, untidy, incredibly clumsy and absent-minded, he was marked out from his fellows both physically and intellectually. When in the later part of his school life some sort of physical exercises were made compulsory, the boys used to form parties to watch his strange efforts on the trapeze or parallel bars. In these early days, he was (he says of himself) "somewhat solitary," but not unhappy, and perfectly good-humoured about the tricks which were inevitably played on a boy who always appeared to be half asleep.

"He sat at the back of the room," says Mr. Fordham, "and never distinguished himself. We thought him the most curious thing that ever was." His schoolfellows noted how he would stride along, "apparently muttering poetry, breaking into inane laughter." The kind of thing he was muttering we learn from a sentence in the *Autobiography*: "I was one day wandering about the streets in that part of North Kensington, telling myself stories of feudal sallies and sieges, in the manner of Walter Scott, and vaguely trying to apply them to the wilderness of bricks and mortar around me."

"I can see him now," wrote Mr. Fordham, "very tall and lanky, striding untidily along Kensington High Street, smiling and sometimes scowling as he talked to himself, apparently oblivious of everything he passed; but in reality a far closer observer than most, and one who not only observed but remembered what he had seen." It was only of himself that he was really oblivious.

Mr. Oldershaw remembers that on one occasion on a very cold day they filled his pockets with snow in the playground. When class reassembled, the snow began to melt and pools to appear on the floor. A small boy raised his hand: "Please Sir, I think the laboratory sink must be leaking again. The water is coming through and falling all over Chesterton."

The laboratory sink was an old offender and the master must have been short-sighted. "Chesterton," he said, "go up to

Mr. —— and ask him with my compliments to see that the trouble with the sink is put right immediately." Gilbert, with water still streaming from both pockets, obediently went upstairs, gave the message and returned without discovering what had happened.

The boys who played these jokes on him had at the same time an extraordinary respect, both for his intellectual acquirements and for his moral character. One boy, who rather prided himself in private life on being a man about town, stopped him one day in the passage and said solemnly, "Chesterton, I am an abandoned profligate." G.K. replied, "I'm sorry to hear it." "We watched our talk," one of them said to me, "when he was with us." His home and upbringing were felt by some of his schoolfellows to have definitely a Puritan tinge about them, although on the other hand the more Conservative elements regarded them as politically dangerous. Mr. Oldershaw relates that his own father, who was a Conservative in politics and had also joined the Catholic Church, seriously warned him against the Agnosticism and Republicanism of the Chesterton household. But even at this age his schoolfellows recognised that he had begun the great quest of his life. "We felt," said Oldershaw, "that he was looking for God."

I suppose it was in part the keenness of the inner vision that produced the effect of external sleepiness and made it possible to pack Gilbert's pockets with snow; but it was also the fact that he was observing very keenly the kind of thing that other people do not bother to observe. I remember my mother telling me, when I first came out, that she had almost ceased trying to draw people's characters and imaginatively construct their home lives, because for the first time in her life she was trying to notice how they were dressed. She was not noticeably successful. Gilbert Chesterton never even tried to see what everyone else saw. All the time he was seeing qualities in his friends, ideas in literature and possibilities in life. And all this world of imagination had, on his own theory, to be carefully concealed from his masters. In the *Autobiography* he describes himself walking to school fervently reciting verses which he afterwards repeated in class with a determined lack of expression and wood-enness of voice; but when he assumes that this is how all boys behave, he surely attributes his own literary enthusiasms far too widely. One would rather gather that he supposed the whole of St. Paul's School to be in the conspiracy to conceal their love of literature from their masters! Such of his own schoolboy papers as can be found show an imagination rare enough at any age, and an enthusiasm not commonly to be found among school-boys. A very early one, to judge by the handwriting, is on the advantages for an historical character of having long hair, illus-trated by the history of Mary Queen of Scots and Charles the First. In the contrast he draws between Mary and Elizabeth, appear qualities of historical imagination that might well belong to a mature and experienced writer.

. . . As in the cause of the fleeting heartless Helen, the Trojan War is stirred up, and great Ajax perishes, and the gentle Patroclus is slain, and mighty Hector falls, and godlike Achilles is laid low, and the dun plains of Hades are thickened with the shades of Kings, so round this lovely giddy French princess, fall one by one the haughty Dauphin, the princely Darnley, the accomplished Rizzio, the terrible Bothwell, and when she dies, she dies as a martyr before the weeping eyes of thousands, and is given a popular pity and regret denied to her rival, with all her faults of violence and vanity, a greater and a purer woman.

It must indeed have been a terrible scene, the execution of that unhappy Queen, and it is a scene that has been described by too many and too able writers for me to venture on a picture of it. But the continually lamented death of Mary of Scotland seems to me happy compared with the end of her greater and sterner rival. As I think on the two, the vision of the black scaffold, the grim headsman, the serene captive, and the weeping populace fades from me and is replaced by a sadder vision: the vision of the dimly-lighted state-bedroom of Whitehall. Elizabeth, haggard and wild-eyed has flung herself prone upon the floor and refuses to take meat or drink, but lies there, surrounded by ceremonious courtiers, but seeing with that terrible insight that was her curse, that she was alone, that their homage was a mockery, that they were waiting eagerly for her death to crown their intrigues with her successor, that there was not in the whole world a single being who cared for her: seeing all this, and bearing it with the iron fortitude of her race, but underneath that invincible silence the deep woman's nature crying out with a bitter cry that she is loved no longer: thus gnawed by the fangs of a dead vanity, haunted by the pale ghost of Essex, and helpless and bitter of heart, the greatest of Englishwomen passed silently away. Of a truth, there are prisons more gloomy than Fotheringay and deaths more cruel than the axe. Is there no pity due to those who undergo these?

It is surprising to read the series of form reports written on a boy who at fifteen or sixteen could do work of this quality. Here are the half-yearly reports made by his Form Masters from his first year in the school at the age of thirteen to the time he left at the age of eighteen.

December 1887. Too much for me: means well by me, I believe, but has an inconceivable knack of forgetting at the shortest notice, is consequently always in trouble, though some of his work is well done, when he does remember to do it. He ought to be in a studio not at school. Never troublesome, but for his lack of memory and absence of mind.

July 1888. Wildly inaccurate about everything; never thinks for two consecutive moments to judge by his work: plenty of ability, perhaps in other directions than classics.

December 1888. Fair. Improving in neatness. Has a very fair stock of general knowledge.

July 1889. A great blunderer with much intelligence.

December 1889. Means well. Would do better to give his time to "Modern" subjects.

July 1890. Can get up any work, but originates nothing.

December 1890. Takes an interest in his English work, but otherwise has not done well.

July 1891. He has a decided literary aptitude, but does not trouble himself enough about school work.

December 1891. Report missing.

July 1892. Not on the same plane with the rest: composition quite futile, but will translate well and appreciate what he reads. Not a quick brain, but possessed by a slowly moving tortuous imagination. Conduct always admirable.

What is much clearer from the mass of notebooks and odd sheets of paper belonging to these years than from the *Autobiography* is the degree to which the two processes of resisting and absorbing knowledge were going on simultaneously. At school he was, he says, asleep but dreaming in his sleep; at home he was still learning literature from his father, going to museums and picture galleries for enjoyment, listening to political talk and engaging in arguments, writing historical plays and acting them, and above all drawing.

To most of his early writing it is nearly impossible to affix a date—with the exception of a "dramatic journal," kept by fits and starts during the Christmas holidays when he was sixteen. G.K. solemnly tells the reader of this diary to take warning by it, to beware of prolixity, and it does in fact contain many more words to many fewer ideas than any of his later writings. But it is useful in giving the atmosphere of those years. Great part is in dialogue, the author appearing throughout as Your Humble Servant, his young brother Cecil as the Innocent Child.

The first scene is the rehearsal of a dramatic version of Scott's *Woodstock.* This has been written by Your Humble Servant who is at the same time engaged on a historic romance. At intervals in the languid rehearsing, endless discussions take place: between Oldershaw and G.K. on Thackeray, between Oldershaw, his father and G.K. on Royal Supremacy in the Church of England. The boys, walking between their two houses, "discuss Roman Catholicism, Supremacy, Papal *v.* Protestant Persecutions. Your Humble Servant arrives at 11 Warwick Gardens to meet Mr. Mawer Cowtan, Master Sidney Wells and Master William Wells. Conversation about Frederick the Great,

Voltaire and Macaulay. Cheerful and enlivening discourse on Germs, Dr. Koch, Consumption and Tuberculosis."

"Conservative" Oldershaw regards his friend as a "red hot raging Republican" and it is interesting to note already faint foreshadowings of Gilbert's future political views. His parents had made him a Liberal but it seemed to him later, as he notes in the *Autobiography*, that their generation was insufficiently alive to the condition and sufferings of the poor. Open-eyed in so many matters, they were not looking in that particular direction. And so it was only very gradually that he himself began to look.

Your Humble Servant read Oldershaw Elizabeth Browning's "Cry of the Children," which the former could scarcely trust himself to read, but which the latter candidly avowed that he did not like. Part and parcel of Oldershaw's optimism is a desire not to believe in pictures of real misery, and a desire to find out compensating pleasures. I think there was a good deal in what he said, but at the same time I think that there is real misery, physical and mental, in the low and criminal classes, and I don't believe in crying peace where there is no peace.

Of his brother, Gilbert notes, "Innocent Child's fault is not a servile reverence for his elder brother, whom he regards, I believe, as a mild lunatic." And Oldershaw recalls his own detestation of Cecil, who would insist on monopolising the conversation when Gilbert's friends wanted to talk to him. "An ugly little boy creeping about," Mr. Fordham calls him. "Cecil had no vanity," writes Mrs. Kidd, "and thoroughly appreciated the fact that he was not beautiful; when he was about 14 he said at dinner one day: 'I think I shall marry X (a very plain cousin); between us we might produce the missing link.' Aunt Marie was shocked!"

Many of the games arise from the skill in drawing of both Gilbert and his father. A long history of two of the Masters drawn by Gilbert shows them in the Salvation Army, as Christy

Minstrels, as editors of a new revolutionary paper, "La Guillotine," as besieged in their office by a mob headed by Lord Salis-
bury, the Archbishop of Canterbury and other Conservative
leaders. Getting tired at last of the adventures of these two mild
scholars, Gilbert starts a series of Shakespeare plays drawn in
modern dress—

Shylock as an aged Hebrew vendor of dilapidated vesture, with
a tiara of hats, Antonio as an opulent and respectable city-merchant,
Bassanio as a fashionable swell and Gratiano as his loud and disreputable "pal" with large checks and a billy-cock hat. Portia was
attired as a barrister in wig and gown and Nerissa as a clerk with a
green bag and a pen behind his ear. This being much appreciated,
Your Humble Servant questions what portion of the Bard of Avon
he shall next burlesque.

The little group seems certainly at this date to be living in a
land in which 'tis always afternoon. In one house or another tea-
time goes on until signs of dinner make their appearance. The
boys only move from one hospitable dining-room to another, or
adjourn to their own bedrooms where Gilbert piles book on book
and reduces even neat shelves to the same chaos that reigns in
his own room.

The Christmas holidays to which the "dramatic journal"
belongs came a few months after the founding of the Junior
Debating Club, which became so central in Gilbert's life and
which he treated with a gravity, solemnity even, such as he
never showed later for any cause, a gravity untouched by
humour. It was a group of about a dozen boys, started with the
idea that it should be a Shakespeare Club, but immediately
changed into a general discussion club. They met every week
at the home of one or other and after a hearty tea some member
read a paper which was then debated.

At the age of twenty, when he had left school two years,
G.K. wrote a solemn history of this institution in which the
question of whether it was right or wrong to insist on penny

fines for rowdy behaviour is canvassed with passionate feeling! One boy who was expelled asked to be readmitted, saying, "I feel so lonely without it." Gilbert's enthusiasm over this incident could be no greater had he been a bishop welcoming the return of an apostate to the Christian fold. I suppose it was partly because of his early solitary life at school, partly because of the general trend of his thought, partly that at this later date he was under the influence of Walt Whitman and cast back upon his earlier years a sort of glow or haze of Whitman idealism. Anyhow, the Junior Debating Club became to him a symbol of the ideal friendship. They were Knights of the Round Table. They were Jongleurs de Dieu. They were the Human Club through whom and in whom he had made the grand discovery of Man. They were his youth personified. The note is still struck in the letters of his engagement period, and it was only forty years later, writing his *Autobiography,* that he was able to picture with a certain humorous detachment this group of boys who met to eat buns and criticise the universe.

A year after their first meeting, the energy of Lucian Oldershaw produced a magazine called *The Debater*. At first it was turned out at home on a duplicator—the efficiency of the production being such that the author of any given paper was able occasionally to recognise a few words of his own contribution. Later it was printed and gives a good record of the meetings and discussions. It shows the energy and ardour of the debaters and also their serious view of themselves and their efforts. At first they are described as Mr. C, Mr. F, etc. Later the full name is given. Besides the weekly debates, they started a Library, a Chess Club, a Naturalists' Society and a Sketching Club, regular meetings of which are chronicled.

"The Chairman [G.K.C.] said a few words," runs a record, after some months of existence, "stating his pride at the success of the Club, and his belief in the good effect such a literary institution might have as a protest against the lower and unworthy phases of school life. His view having been vehemently corroborated, the meeting broke up."

In one fairly typical month papers were read on "Three Comedies of Shakespeare," "Pope," and "Herodotus," and when no paper was produced there was a discussion on Capital Punishment. In another, the subjects were "The Brontës," "Macaulay as an Essayist," "Frank Buckland" (the naturalist) and "Tennyson." A pretty wide range of reading was called for from schoolboys in addition to their ordinary work, even though on one occasion the Secretary sternly notes that the reading of the paper occupied only three and one-half minutes. But they were not daunted by difficulties or afraid of bold attempts.

Mr. Digby d'Avigdor on one occasion "delivered a paper entitled 'The Nineteenth Century: A Retrospect.' He gave a slight resumé of the principal events, with appropriate tribute to the deceased great of this century."

Mr. Bertram, reading a paper on Milton, "dealt critically with his various poems, noting the effective style of 'L'Allegro,' giving the story of the writing of 'Comus' and cursorily analysing 'Paradise Lost,' and 'Paradise Regained.'"

"After discussing the adaptability of *Hamlet* to the stage, Mr. Maurice Solomon"—who may have been quite fifteen—"passed on to review the chief points in the character of the Prince of Denmark, concluding with a slight review of the other characters which he did not think Shakespeare had given much attention to."

In a discussion on the new humorists, we find the Secretary "taking grievous umbrage at certain unwarrantable attacks which he considered Mr. Andrew Lang had lately made on these choice spirits." This discussion arose from a paper by the Chairman on the new school of poetry "in which, in spite of its good points, he condemned the absence of the sentiment of the moral, which he held to be the really stirring and popular element in literature."

Evidently some of his friends tended towards a youthful cynicism for in a paper on Barrie's *Window in Thrums* Gilbert apologises to "such of you as are much bitten with the George Moore state of mind."

The book which describes the rusty emotions and toilsome lives of the Thrums weavers will always remain a book that has given me something, and the fact that mine is merely the popular view and that what I feel in it can be equally felt by the majority of fellow-creatures, this fact, such is my hardened and abandoned state, only makes me like the book more. I have long found myself in that hopeless minority that is engaged in protecting the majority of mankind from the attacks of all men. . . .

In this sentiment we recognise the G.K. that is to be, but not when we find him seconding Mr. Bentley in the motion that "a scientific education is much more useful than a classic."

"Mr. M," reading a paper on Herodotus, "gave a minute account of the life of the historian, dwelling much upon the doubt and controversy surrounding his birth and several incidents of his history"; while "Mr. F. read a paper on Newspapers, tracing their growth from the Acta Diurna of the later Roman Empire to the hordes of papers of the present day."

Perhaps best of all these efforts was that of Mr. L.D. who "after describing the governments of England, France, Russia, Germany and the United States, proceeded to give his opinion on their various merits, first saying that he personally was a republican."

Of the boys that appear in *The Debater*, Robert Vernède was killed in the Great War; Laurence Solomon at his death in 1940 was Senior Tutor of University College, London; his brother Maurice who became one of the Directors of the General Electric Company is now an invalid. I read a year or so ago an interesting *Times* obituary of Mr. Bertram, who was Director of Civil Aviation in the Air Ministry; Mr. Salter became a Principal in the Treasury, having practised as a solicitor up to the War; Mr.

Fordham, a barrister, was one of the Legal Advisers to the Ministry of Labour and has now retired.

The two outstanding "debaters" in G.K.'s life were Lucian Oldershaw who became his brother-in-law and will often reappear in these pages, and Edmund Clerihew Bentley, his friend of friends. Closely united as was the whole group, Lucian Oldershaw once told me that they were frantically jealous of one another: "We would have done anything to get the first place with Gilbert."

"But you know," I said, "who had it."

"Yes," he replied, "our jealousy of Bentley was overwhelming."

Mr. Bentley became a journalist and was for long on the editorial staff of the *Daily Telegraph,* but he is best known for his detective stories—especially *Trent's Last Case*—and as the inventor of a special form of rhyme, known from his second name as the Clerihew. He wrote the first of these while still at school, and the best were later published in a volume called *Biography for Beginners,* which G.K. illustrated. Everyone has his favourite. My own is:

> Sir Christopher Wren
> Said "I am going to dine with some men,
> If anybody calls
> Say I'm designing St. Paul's."

Or possibly:

> The people of Spain think Cervantes
> Equal to half-a-dozen Dantes,
> An opinion resented most bitterly
> By the people of Italy.

Bentley was essentially a holiday as well as term-time companion and when they were not together a large correspondence between the two boys gives some idea of how and where Gilbert spent his summer holidays. They are very much schoolboy letters and not worth quoting at full length, but it is interesting

CHESTERTON AGED ABOUT THIRTEEN

to compare both style and content with the later letters. All the letters begin "Dear Bentley." The first use of his Christian name only occurs after both had left school.

Austria House
Pier Street
Ventnor, Isle of Wight
(undated, probably 1890)

Although you dropt some hints about Paris when you were last in our humble abode, I presume that this letter, if addressed to your usual habitation, will reach you at some period. Ventnor, where, as you will perceive we are, is, I will not say built upon hills, but emptied into the cracks and clefts of rocks so that the geography of the town is curious and involved. . . .

. . . My brother is intent upon "The Three Midshipmen" or "The Three Admirals" or the three coal-scuttles or some other distinguished trio by that interminable ass Kingston. I looked at it today and wondered how I ever could have enjoyed his eternal slave schooners and African stations. I would not give a page of "Mansfield Park" or a verse of "In Memoriam" for all the endless fighting of blacks and boarding of pirates through which the three hypocritical vagabonds ever went. I am getting old. How old it will shortly be necessary for me to state precisely, for, as you doubtless know there is going to be a Census. . . .

"I have been trying to knock into shape a story, such as we spoke about the other day, about the first introduction of Tea, and I should be glad of your assistance and suggestions. I think I shall lay the scene in Holland where the merits of tea were first largely agitated, and fill the scene with the traditional Dutch figures such as I sketch. I find in Disraeli's "Curiosities of Literature" which I consulted before coming away that a French writer wrote an elaborate treatise to prove that tea merchants were always immoral members of society. It would be rather curious to apply the theory to the present day. . . .

11, Warwick Gardens,
Kensington.
(undated.)

I direct this letter to your ancient patrimonial estate unknowing whether it will reach you or where it will reach you if it does;

whether you are shooting polar bears on the ice-fields of Spitzbergen or cooking missionaries among the cannibals of the South Pacific. But wherever you are I find some considerable relief in turning from the lofty correspondence of the secretary (with no disparagement of my much-esteemed friend, Oldershaw) to another friend (ifelowmecallimso as Mr. Verdant Greene said) who can discourse on some other subjects besides the Society, and who will not devote the whole of his correspondence to the questions of that excellent and valuable body. The Society is a very good thing in its way (being the President I naturally think so) but like other good things, you may have too much of it, and I have had. . . .

As I said before, I don't know where you are disporting yourself, beyond some hurried remark about Paris which you dropped in our hurried interview in one of the "brilliant flashes of silence" between those imbecile screams and yells and stamping, which even the natural enthusiasm at the prospect of being "broken up" cannot excuse.

> 6, The Quadrant,
> North Berwick, Haddington,
> Scotland.
> (? 1891.)

You will probably guess that as far as personal taste and instincts are concerned, I share all your antipathy to the noisy Plebian excursionist. A visit to Ramsgate during the season and the vision of the crowded, howling sands has left in me feelings which all my Radicalism cannot allay. At the same time I think that the lower orders are seen unfavorably when enjoying themselves. In labour and trouble they are more dignified and less noisy. Your suggestion as to a series of soliloquies is very flattering and has taken hold of me to the extent of writing a similar ballad on Simon de Montfort. The order in which they come is rather incongruous, particularly if I include the list I have in mind for the future thus—Danton, William III, Simon de Montfort, Rousseau, David and Russell. . . . I rejoice to say that this is a sequestered spot into which Hi tiddly hi ti, etc. and all the ills in its train have not penetrated.

In these last two letters there are sentences of a kind not to be found anywhere else in Chesterton. The disparagement of

Lucian Oldershaw's excessive enthusiasm for the Junior Debating Club, the solemn reprobation of the "imbecile screams and yells and stamping" of the last day at school before the summer holidays, the antipathy expressed for the rowdy enjoyments of the lower orders—these things are not in the least like either the Chesterton that was to be or the Chesterton that then was. But they are very much like Bentley. He was two years younger than Chesterton, but far older than his years and seemed indeed to the other boys (and perhaps to himself) like an elderly gentleman smiling a remote amused smile at the enthusiasms of the young. I get the strongest feeling that at this stage Chesterton not only admired him—as he was to do all his life—but wanted to be like him, to say the kind of thing he thought Bentley would say. This phase did not last, as we shall see; it had gone by the time Chesterton was at the Slade School.

> 6, The Quadrant,
> North Berwick
> Haddington, Scotland.
> (undated, probably 1891.)

DEAR BENTLEY,

We have been here three days and my brother loudly murmurs that we have not yet seen any of "the sights." For my part I abominate sights, and all people who want to look at them. A great deal more instruction, to say nothing of pleasure is to be got out of the nearest haystack or hedgerow taken quietly, than in trotting over two or three counties to see "the view" or "the site" or the extraordinary cliff or the unusual tower or the unreasonable hill or any other monstrosity deforming the face of Nature. Anybody can make sights but nobody has yet succeeded in making scenery. (Excuse the unaccountable pencil drawing in the middle which was drawn unconsciously on the back of the unfinished letter.) . . .

> 9, South Terrace,
> Littlehampton, Sussex.
> (undated.)

. . . I agree with you in your admiration for Paradise Lost, but consider it on the whole too light and childish a book for persons of our age. It is all very well, as small children to read pretty stories about Satan and Belial, when we have only just mastered our "Oedipus" and our Herbert Spencer, but when we grow older we get to like Captain Marryat and Mr. Kingston and when we are men we know that Cinderella is much better than any of those babyish books. As regards one question which you asked, I may remark that the children of Israel [presumably the Solomons] have not gone unto Horeb, neither unto Sittim, but unto the land that is called Shropshire they went, and abode therein. And they came unto a city, even unto the city that is called Shrewsbury, and there they builded themselves an home, where they might abide. And their home was in the land that was called Castle Street and their home was the 25th tabernacle in that land. And they abode with certain of their own kin until their season be over and gone. And lo! they spake unto me by letter, saying, "Heard ye aught of him that is called Bentley? Is he in the house of his fathers or has he come unto a strange land?" Here endeth the 2nd Lesson.

> Hotel de Lille & d'Albion,
> 223, Rue St. Honoré,
> Paris.
> (undated, probably 1892.)

. . . They showed us over the treasures of the Cathedral, among which, as was explained by the guide, who spoke a little English, was a cross given by Louis XIV to "*Meess*" Lavallière. I thought that concession to the British system of titles was indeed touching. I also thought, when reflecting what the present was, and where it was and then to whom it was given, that this showed pretty well what the religion of the Bourbon regime was and why it has become impossible since the Revolution.

> Grand Hotel du Chemin de Fer,
> Arromanches (Calvados)
> (undated)

. . . Art is universal. This remark is not so irrelevant and Horace Greeley-like as it may appear. I have just had a demonstration of its truth on the coach coming down here. Two very nice little French boys of cropped hair and restless movements were just in front of us and my pater having discovered that the book they had with them was a prize at a Paris school, some slight conversation arose. Not thinking my French altogether equal to a prolonged interview, I took out a scrap of paper and began, with a fine carelessness to draw a picture of Napoleon I, hat, chin, attitude, all complete. This, of course, was gazed at rapturously by these two young inheritors of France's glory and it ended in my drawing them unlimited goblins to keep for the remainder of the interview.

In May 1891, the Chairman of the J.D.C. attained the maturity of seventeen.

The Secretary then rose and in a speech in which he extolled the merits of the Chairman as a chairman, and mentioned the benefit which the Junior Debating Club received on the day of which this was the anniversary, viz., the natal day of Mr. Chesterton, proposed that a vote wishing him many happy returns of the day and a long continuance in the Chair of the Club should be passed. This was carried with acclamations. The Chairman replied after restoring order. . . .

Naturally this question of order among a crowd of boys loomed large. At the beginning a number of rules were passed giving great powers to the Chairman, "which that gentleman," he says of himself, "lenient by temperament and republican by principles, certainly would never have put in force. . . . It was seldom enough," he continues:

that a boy of fifteen * found himself in the position of the Chairman, an attitude of command and responsibility over a body of his friends and equals, and it was not to be expected that they would easily take to the state of things. Nor was the Chairman himself, like the Secretary, protected and armed by any personal aptitude for practical proceedings. But solely by the certain degree of respect entertained for his character and acquirements. This respect, sincere and even excessive as it frequently was, contrasted somewhat humorously with the common inattentior to questions of order, nor could anything be more noisy than the loyalty of Fordham and Langdon Davies, with the exception of their interruptions. It may then fairly

* He was, in fact, sixteen when the J.D.C. began.

be said that the troubles and discussions of the first months of the Club's existence centred practically round the question of order, the first of the great difficulties of this most difficult enterprise. How boys who could scarcely be got to behave quietly under the strictest schoolmasters could ever be brought to obey the rebuke of their equal and schoolfellow: how a heterogeneous pack of average schoolboys could organise themselves into a self-governing republic, these were problems of real and stupendous difficulty. The fines of a penny and of twopence, which were instituted at the first meeting, were found hopelessly incompetent to cope with the bursts of oblivious hilarity. Fordham in particular, whose constant breaches of order threatened to exhaust even the extensive treasury of that spoilt and opulent young gentleman, soon left calculation far behind, nor can the story be better or more brightly told than by himself. "Mr. F.," he wrote, "at one time, after considerable calculation found that he was in debt to the extent of some 10 or 11 shillings; but as he felt that by refusing to pay the sum he would be striking a blow for the liberty of the subject, he manfully held out against what he considered an unjust punishment for such diminutive frivolities as he had indulged in." . . . At times incidents of a disturbing and playful nature have roused the wrath of the Chairman and Secretary to a pitch awful to behold. At one time Mr. H. (a member who soon resigned) spent a considerable part of a meeting under the table, till he found himself used as a public footstool and a doormat combined. At another as Mr. Bentley was departing from the scene of chaos a penny bun of the sticky order caressingly stung his honoured cheek, sped upon its errand of mercy by the unerring aim of Mr. F.*

Mr. Fordham well remembers how G.K. one day took him aside at the Oldershaws' house and told him that he really must be less exhuberant. This historic occasion was always alluded to later as "the day on which the Chairman spoke seriously to Mr. F."

After various resignations order was restored, and a little later two of the chief recalcitrants asked to be received back into the Club. "I feel so lonely without it," one of them had remarked;

* MS. *History of the J.D.C.*

and G.K. comments, "This has always appeared to the present writer one of the most important speeches in the history of the Club. . . . The Junior Debating Club had come through its moments of difficulty and was a fact and an establishment."

Nor was the circulation of *The Debater* long confined to members of the Club and their own circle of friends and relatives. Some of the boys had no doubt a regular allowance, but probably a small one. Gilbert himself says in his diary that he had no income "except errant sixpences." And printers' bills had to be paid. Moreover in the first number the editor Lucian Oldershaw confessed frankly that one reason for the paper's existence was "that the Society may not degenerate into the position of a mutual admiration Society by totally lacking the admiration of outsiders." The staff were able immediately to note, "Any apprehensions we may have felt on the morning of the publication of *The Debater* were speedily dispelled, when by nightfall we had disposed of all our copies." Of a later issue the energetic editor sold sixty-five copies in the course of the summer holidays. Masters, too, began to read it and at last a copy was laid on the table of the High Master, Mr. Walker. Cecil Chesterton describes the High Master as a gigantic man with a booming voice. Some Paulines believed he had given Gilbert the first inspiration for the personality of "Sunday" in *The Man Who Was Thursday*. Another contemporary says that he was reputed to take no interest in anything except examination successes, and that the boys were amazed at the effect on him of reading *The Debater*. Reading in the light of his future, one sees qualities in Gilbert's work not to be found in that of the other contributors, but it is worth noting that the J.D.C. members were in fact a quite unusually able group. Almost every one of them took brilliant scholarships to Oxford or Cambridge; the High Master had never boasted of so many scholarships from one set of boys. And in reading *The Debater* (an enjoyment I wish others could share) one has to bear in mind the relative ages of the contributors. It is, I think, striking that all these boys should have recognised Gilbert's quality and accepted his leadership, for they were all a year or so younger than he was and yet were in the same form. They knew that this was only because G.K. would not bother to do his school work; still, I think that at that age they showed insight by knowing it.

Gilbert's work is to be found in every number of *The Debater* —usually verse as well as prose. Both Fordham and Oldershaw remember most vividly the effect of reading a fanciful essay on Dragons in the first number. "The Dragon" it began, "is the most cosmopolitan of impossibilities." And the boys, rolling the words on their tongues, murmured to one another, "This is literature."

Except for a very occasional flash the one element not yet visible in these *Debater* essays is humour. This is curious, because some of his most brilliant fooling belongs to the same period. In a collection made after his death, *The Coloured Lands*, is an illustrated jeu d'esprit of 1891 *Half Hours in Hades*: "an elementary handbook of demonology" which is as amusing a thing as he ever wrote. The drawings he made for it show specimens of the evolution of various types of devil into various types of humans: the devils themselves are carefully classified— the common or garden serpent (Tentator Hortensis), the red devil (Diabolus Mephistopheles) the blue devil (Caeruleus Lugubrius) etc. Mr. J. Milton's "specimen" is discussed and various methods of pursuing observations in supernatural history which "possesses an interest which will remain after health, youth and even life have departed."

There is nothing of this kind in *The Debater*. Besides the historical soliloquies mentioned in the letter to Bentley, there are poems in which he is beginning to feel after his religious philosophy. One of these in a very early number shows considerable power for a boy not yet seventeen.

ADVENIAT REGNUM TUUM

Not that the widespread wings of wrong brood o'er a moaning earth,
Not from the clinging curse of gold, the random lot of birth;
Not from the misery of the weak, the madness of the strong,
Goes upward from our lips the cry, "How long, oh Lord, how long?"
Not only from the huts of toil, the dens of sin and shame,
From lordly halls and peaceful homes the cry goes up the same;
Deep in the heart of every man, where'er his life be spent,
There is a noble weariness, a holy discontent.
Where'er to mortal eyes has come, in silence dark and lone,
Some glimmer of the far-off light the world has never known,
Some ghostly echoes from a dream of earth's triumphal song,
Then as the vision fades we cry, "How long, oh Lord, how long?"
Long ages, from the dawn of time, men's toiling march has wound
Towards the world they ever sought, the world they never found;
Still far before their toiling path the glimmering promise lay,
Still hovered round the struggling race, a dream by night and day.
Mid darkening care and clinging sin they sought their unknown
    home,
Yet ne'er the perfect glory came—Lord, will it ever come?
The weeding of earth's garden broad from all its growths of wrong,
When all man's soul shall be a prayer, and all his life a song.
Aye, though through many a starless night we guard the flaming oil,
Though we have watched a weary watch, and toiled a weary toil,
Though in the midnight wilderness, we wander still forlorn,
Yet bear we in our hearts the proof that God shall send the dawn.
Deep in the tablets of our hearts he writes that yearning still,
The longing that His hand hath wrought shall not his hand fulfil?
Though death shall close upon us all before that hour we see,
The goal of ages yet is there—the good time yet to be:
Therefore, tonight, from varied lips, in every house and home,
Goes up to God the common prayer, "Father, Thy Kingdom come." *

Gilbert's prose work in *The Debater* must have been little
less surprising to any master who had merely watched him
slumbering at a desk. His historical romance "The White
Cockade" is immature and unimportant. But essays on Spenser,

* *The Debater,* Vol. I. March–April, 1891.

Milton, Pope, Gray, Cowper, Burns, Wordsworth, "Humour in Fiction," "Boys' Literature," Sir Walter Scott, Browning, the English Dramatists, showed a range and a quality of literary criticism alike surprising. Perhaps most surprising, however, is the fact that all this does not seem to have made clear to either masters or parents the true nature of Gilbert's vocation. He suffered at this date from having too many talents. For he still went on drawing and his drawings seemed to many the most remarkable thing about him, and were certainly the thing he most enjoyed doing.

Even now his school work had not brought him into the highest form—called not the Sixth, as in most schools, but the Eighth: the highest form he ever reached was 6B. But in the Summer Term of 1892 he entered a competition for a prize poem, and won it. The subject chosen was St. Francis Xavier. I give the poem in Appendix A. It is not as notable as some other of his work at that time: what is interesting is that in it this schoolboy expresses with some power a view he was later to explode yet more powerfully. He might have claimed for himself what he said of earlier writers—it is not true that they did not see our modern difficulties: they saw through them. Never before had this contest been won by any but an Eighth Form boy, and almost immediately afterwards Gilbert was amazed to find a short notice posted on the board: "G. K. Chesterton to rank with the Eighth.—F. W. Walker, High Master."

The High Master at any rate had travelled far from the atmosphere of the form reports when Mrs. Chesterton visited him in 1894 to ask his advice about her son's future. For he said, "Six foot of genius. Cherish him, Mrs. Chesterton, cherish him."

Chapter IV

Art Schools and University College

WHEN ALL GILBERT'S friends were at Oxford or Cambridge, he used to say how glad he was that his own choice had been a different one. He never sighed for Oxford. He never regretted his rather curious experiences at an Art School—two Art Schools really, although he only talks of one in the *Autobiography*, for he was for a short time at a School of Art in St. John's Wood (Calderon's, Lawrence Solomon thought), whence he passed to the Slade School. He was there from 1892 to 1895 and during part of that time he attended lectures on English Literature at University College.

The chapter on the experiences of the next two years is called in the *Autobiography*, "How to be a Lunatic," and there is no doubt that these years were crucial and at times crucifying in Gilbert's life. During a happily prolonged youth (he was now eighteen and a half) he had developed very slowly, but normally. Surrounded by pleasant friendships and home influences he had never really become aware of evil. Now it broke upon him suddenly—probably to a degree exaggerated by his strong imagination and distorted by the fact that he was undergoing physical changes usually belonging to an earlier age.

Towards the end of his school life Gilbert's voice had not yet broken. His mother took him to a doctor to be overhauled and was told that his brain was the largest and most sensitive the doctor had ever seen. "A genius or an idiot" was his verdict on the probabilities. Above all things she was told to avoid for him any sort of shock. Physically, mentally, spiritually he was

43

on a very large scale and probably for that reason of a slow rate of development. The most highly differentiated organisms are the slowest to mature, and without question Gilbert did mature very late. He was now passing through the stage described by Keats: "The imagination of a boy is healthy and the mature imagination of a man is healthy; but there is a space of life between"—a period unhealthy or at least ill-focussed.

Intellectually Gilbert suffered at this time from an extreme scepticism. As he expressed it he "felt as if everything might be a dream" as if he had "projected the universe from within." The agnostic doubts the existence of God. Gilbert at moments doubted the existence of the agnostic.

Morally his temptations seem to have been in some strange psychic region rather than merely physical. The whole period is best summarised in a passage from the *Autobiography,* for looking back after forty years Gilbert still saw it as deeply and darkly significant: as both a mental and moral extreme of danger ·

There is something truly menacing in the thought of how quickly I could imagine the maddest, when I had never committed the mildest crime . . . there was a time when I had reached that condition of moral anarchy within, in which a man says, in the words of Wilde, that "Atys with the blood-stained knife were better than the thing I am." I have never indeed felt the faintest temptation to the particular madness of Wilde, but I could at this time imagine the worst and wildest disproportions and distortions of more normal passion; the point is that the whole mood was overpowered and oppressed with a sort of congestion of imagination. As Bunyan, in his morbid period, described himself as prompted to utter blasphemies, I had an overpowering impulse to record or draw horrible ideas and images; plunging deeper and deeper as in a blind spiritual suicide.*

Two of his intimate friends, finding at this time a notebook full of these horrible drawings, asked one another, "Is Chesterton going mad?"

* Pp. 88–9.

He dabbled too in spiritualism until he realised that he had reached the verge of forbidden and dangerous ground:

I would not altogether rule out the suggestion of some that we were playing with fire; or even with hell-fire. In the words that were written for us there was nothing ostensibly degrading, but any amount that was deceiving. I saw quite enough of the thing to be able to testify, with complete certainty, that something happens which is not in the ordinary sense natural, or produced by the normal and conscious human will. Whether it is produced by some subconscious but still human force, or by some powers, good, bad, or indifferent, which are external to humanity, I would not myself attempt to decide. The only thing I will say with complete confidence, about that mystic and invisible power, is that it tells lies. The lies may be larks or they may be lures to the imperilled soul or they may be a thousand other things; but whatever they are, they are not truths about the other world; or for that matter about this world.*

He told Father O'Connor some years later † that "he had used the planchette freely at one time, but had to give it up on account of headaches ensuing . . . 'after the headaches came a horrid feeling as if one were trying to get over a bad spree, with what I can best describe as a bad smell in the mind.'"

Idling at his work he fell in with other idlers and has left a vivid description in a *Daily News* article called, "The Diabolist," of one of his fellow students.

. . . It was strange, perhaps, that I liked his dirty, drunken society; it was stranger still, perhaps, that he liked my society. For hours of the day he would talk with me about Milton or Gothic architecture; for hours of the night he would go where I have no wish to follow him, even in speculation. He was a man with a long, ironical face, and close red hair; he was by class a gentleman, and could walk like one, but preferred, for some reason, to walk like a groom carrying two pails. He looked like a sort of super-jockey; as if some archangel had gone on the Turf. And I shall never forget the half-hour in which he and I argued about real things for the first and last time.

* *Autobiography*, p. 77.
† *Father Brown on Chesterton*, p. 74.

. . . He had a horrible fairness of the intellect that made me despair of his soul. A common, harmless atheist would have denied that religion produced humility or humility a simple joy; but he admitted both. He only said, "But shall I not find in evil a life of its own? Granted that for every woman I ruin one of those red sparks will go out; will not the expanding pleasure of ruin . . ."

"Do you see that fire?" I asked. "If we had a real fighting democracy, some one would burn you in it; like the devil-worshipper that you are."

"Perhaps," he said, in his tired, fair way. "Only what you call evil I call good."

He went down the great steps alone, and I felt as if I wanted the steps swept and cleaned. I followed later, and as I went to find my hat in the low, dark passage where it hung, I suddenly heard his voice again, but the words were inaudible. I stopped, startled; but then I heard the voice of one of the vilest of his associates saying, "Nobody can possibly know." And then I heard those two or three words which I remember in every syllable and cannot forget. I heard the Diabolist say, "I tell you I have done everything else. If I do that I shan't know the difference between right and wrong." I rushed out without daring to pause; and as I passed the fire I did not know whether it was hell or the furious love of God.

I have since heard that he died; it may be said, I think, that he committed suicide; though he did it with tools of pleasure, not with tools of pain. God help him, I know the road he went; but I have never known or even dared to think what was that place at which he stopped and refrained.*

Revulsion from the atmosphere of evil took Gilbert to no new thing but to a strengthening of old ties and a mystic renewal of them. The J.D.C. was idealised into a mystical city of friends:

A List

I know a friend, very strong and good. He is the best friend in the world,
I know another friend, subtle and sensitive. He is certainly the best friend on earth.

* Quoted in *G. K. Chesterton: A Criticism.* Alston Rivers Ltd. 1908, pp. 20–22.

G. K. CHESTERTON AT SIXTEEN

I know another friend: very quiet and shrewd, there is no friend so good as he.

I know another friend, who is enigmatical and reluctant, he is the best of all.

I know yet another: who is polished and eager, he is far better than the rest.

I know another, who is young and very quick, he is the most beloved of all friends,

I know a lot more and they are all like that.

Amen.

The Cosmic Factories

What are little boys made of?

Bentley is made of hard wood with a knot in it, a complete set of Browning and a strong spring;

Oldershaw of a box of Lucifer matches and a stylographic pen;

Lawrence of a barrister's wig: files of Punch and salt,

Maurice of watch-wheels, three riders and a clean collar.

Vernède is made of moonlight and tobacco,

Bertram is mostly a handsome black walking-stick.

Waldo is a nice cabbage, with a vanishing odour of cigarettes,

Salter is made of sand and fire and an university extension ticket.

But the strongest element in all can not be expressed; I think it is a sort of star.*

There are fragments of a Morality Play entitled "The Junior Debating Club," of a modern novel in which everyone of the Debaters makes his appearance, of a mediaeval story called "The Legend of Sir Edmund of the Brotherhood of the Jongleurs de Dieu." Notes, fragments, letters, all show an intense individual interest that covered the life of each of his friends. If one of them is worried, he worries too; if one rejoices, he rejoices exceedingly. They write to him about their ideas and views, their relations with one another, their reactions in the world of Oxford life, their love affairs. "I am in need of some literary tonic or blood-letting," says Vernède, "which you alone can supply."

* From *The Notebook.*

"I only hope," writes Bertram, "you may be as much use in the world in future as you have been in the past to your friends."

"Most of the absent Club," writes Salter separated from the others, "lie together in my pocket at this moment." And Gilbert writes in *The Notebook*:

AN IDYLL

Tea is made; the red fogs shut round the house but the gas burns.
I wish I had at this moment round the table
A company of fine people.
Two of them are at Oxford and one in Scotland and two at other
    places.
But I wish they would all walk in now, for the tea is made.

Gilbert was devoted to them all. But as we have seen, Bentley's was the supreme friendship of his youth. It was a friendship in foolery as we are told by the dedication of *Greybeards at Play*:

> He was through boyhood's storm and shower
> My best my nearest friend,
> We wore one hat, smoked one cigar
> One standing at each end.

It was a deeply serious friendship as we are told in the dedication of *The Man Who Was Thursday*. With Bentley alone he shared the

Doubts that drove us through the night as we two talked amain,
And day had broken on the streets ere it broke upon the brain.

Most young men write or at least begin novels of which they are themselves the heroes. Gilbert wrote and illustrated a fairy story about a boyish romance of Lucian Oldershaw's while two unfinished novels have Bentley for hero. He is, too, in the mediaeval story, Sir Edmund of the Brotherhood of the Jongleurs de Dieu. Gilbert sings, like all young poets, of first love—but it is Bentley's not his own: he was as much excited about a girl

Bentley had fallen in love with as if he had fallen in love with her himself. And where a London street has a special significance one discovers it is because of a memory of Bentley's. To Bentley then, with whom all was shared, Gilbert wrote, when through friendship and the goodness of things he had come out again into the daylight. The second thought that had saved him had largely grown out of the first. The J.D.C. meant friendship. Friendship meant the highest of all good things and all good things called for gratitude. As he gave thanks he drew near to God.

> Dunedin Lodge
> Forth Street
> North Berwick.
> (undated, but probably Long Vac., 1894.)

Your letter was most welcome: in which, however, it does not differ widely from most of your letters. I read somewhere in some fatuous Complete Letter-writer or something, that it is correct to imitate the order of subjects, etc. observed by your correspondent. In obedience to this rule of breeding I will hurriedly remark that my holiday has been nice enough in itself; we walk about; lie on the sand; go and swim in the sea when it generally rains; and the combination gets in our mouths and we say the name of the Professor in the "Water Babies." Inwardly speaking, I have had a funny time. A meaningless fit of depression, taking the form of certain absurd psychological worries came upon me, and instead of dismissing it and talking to people, I had it out and went very far into the abysses, indeed. The result was that I found that things when examined, necessarily *spelt* such a mystically satisfactory state of things, that without getting back to earth, I saw lots that made me certain it is all right. The vision is fading into common day now, and I am glad. The frame of mind was the reverse of gloomy, but it would not do for long. It is embarrassing, talking with God face to face, as a man speaketh to his friend.

And in another letter:

A cosmos one day being rebuked by a pessimist replied, "How can you who revile me consent to speak by my machinery? Permit me

to reduce you to nothingness and then we will discuss the matter."
Moral. You should not look a gift universe in the mouth.

Another powerful influence in the direction of mental health
was the discovery of Walt Whitman's poetry. "I shall never
forget," Lucian Oldershaw writes, "reading to him from the
Canterbury Walt Whitman in my bedroom at West Kensington. The séance lasted from two to three hours, and we were
intoxicated with the excitement of the discovery."

For some time now we shall find Gilbert dismissing belief in
any positive existence of evil and treating the universe on the
Whitman principle of jubilant and universal acceptance. He
writes, too, in the Whitman style. By far the most important of
his notebooks is one which, by amazing good fortune, can be
dated, beginning in 1894 and continuing for several years. In
its attitude to man it is Whitmanesque to a high degree, yet it is
also most characteristically Chestertonian. Whitman is content
with a shouting, roaring optimism about life and humanity.
Chesterton had to find for it a philosophical basis. Heartily as
he disliked the literary pessimism of the hour, he was not content simply to exchange one mood for another. For whether he
was conscious of it at the time or not, he did later see Walt
Whitman's outlook as a mood and not a philosophy. It was a
mood, however, that Chesterton himself never really lost, solely
because he did discover the philosophy needed to sustain it.
And thereby, even in this early Notebook, he goes far beyond
Whitman. Even so early he knew that a philosophy of man
could not be a philosophy of man only. He already *feels* a presence in the universe:

It is evening
And into the room enters again a large indiscernable presence.
Is it a man or a woman?
Is it one long dead or yet to come?
That sits with me in the evening.

This again might have been only a mood—had he not found the philosophy to sustain it too. It is remarkable how much of this philosophy he had arrived at in The Notebook, before he had come to know Catholics. Indeed The Notebook seems to me so important that it needs a chapter to itself with abundant quotation.

Meanwhile, what was Gilbert doing about his work at University College? Professor Fred Brown told Lawrence Solomon that when he was at the Slade School he always seemed to be writing and while listening to lectures he was always drawing. It is probably true that, as Cecil Chesterton says, he shrank from the technical toils of the artist as he never did later from those of authorship; and none of the professors regarded him as a serious art student. They pointed later to his illustrations of *Biography for Beginners* as proof that he never learnt to draw. Yet how many of the men who did learn seriously could have drawn those sketches, full of crazy energy and vitality? I know nothing about drawing, but anyone may know how brilliant are the illustrations to *Greybeards at Play* or *Biography for Beginners*, and later to Mr. Belloc's novels. And anyone can see the power of line with which he drew in his notebooks unfinished suggestions of humanity or divinity. Anyone, too, can recognise a portrait of a man, and faces full of character continue to adorn G.K.'s exercise books. Of living models he affected chiefly Gladstone, Balfour, and Joe Chamberlain. In hours of thought he made drawings of Our Lord with a crown of thorns or nailed to a cross —these suddenly appear in any of his books between fantastic drawings or lecture notes. As the mind wandered and lingered the fingers followed it, and as Gilbert listened to lectures, he would even draw on the top of his own notes. He had always had facility and that facility increased, so that in later years he often completed in a couple of hours the illustrations to a novel of Belloc's. Nor were these drawings merely illustrations of an already completed text, for Mr. Belloc has told me that the characters were often half suggested to him by his friend's drawings.

On one, at any rate, of his vacations, Gilbert went to Italy, and two letters to Bentley show much of the way his thoughts were going:

                                        Hotel New York
                                        Florence.
                                        (undated, probably 1894.)

DEAR BENTLEY,

I turn to write my second letter to you and my first to Grey [Maurice Solomon], just after having a very interesting conversation with an elderly American like Colonel Newcome, though much better informed, with whom I compared notes on Botticelli, Ruskin, Carlyle, Emerson and the world in general. I asked him what he thought of Whitman. He answered frankly that in America they were "hardly up to him." "We have one town, Boston," he said precisely, "that has got up to Browning." He then added that there was one thing everyone in America remembered: Whitman himself. The old gentleman quite kindled on this topic, "Whitman was a real Man. A man who was so pure and strong that we could not imagine him doing an unmanly thing anywhere." It was odd words to hear at a table d'hôte, from your next door neighbour: it made me quite excited over my salad.

You see that this humanitarianism in which we are entangled asserts itself where, by all guidebook laws, it should not. When I take up my pen to write to you, I am thinking more of a white-moustached old Yankee at an hotel than about the things I have seen within the same 24 hours: the frescoes of Santa Croce, the illuminations of St. Marco; the white marbles of the tower of Giotto; the very Madonnas of Raphael, the very David of Michael Angelo. Throughout this tour, in pursuance of our theory of travelling, we have avoided the guide: he is the death-knell of individual liberty. Once only we broke through our rule and that was in favour of an extremely intelligent, nay impulsive young Italian in Santa Maria Novella, a church where we saw some of the most interesting pieces of mediaeval painting I have ever seen, interesting not so much from an artistic as from a moral and historical point of view. Particularly noticeable was the great fresco expressive of the grandest mediaeval conception of the Communion of Saints, a figure of Christ surmounting a crowd of all ages and stations, among whom were not only Dante, Petrarca, Giotto, etc., etc., but Plato, Cicero, and best of all, Arius. I said to the guide, in a tone of expostulation, "Heretico!" (a word of impromptu manufacture). Whereupon he nodded, smiled and was positively radiant with the latitudinarianism of the old Italian painter. It was interesting for it was a fresh proof that even the early Church united had a period of thought and tolerance before the dark ages closed around it. There is one thing that I must tell you more of when we meet, the tower of Giotto. It was built in a square of Florence, near the Cathedral, by a self-made young painter and architect who had kept sheep as a boy on the Tuscan hills. It is still called "The Shepherd's Tower."

What I want to tell you about is the series of bas-reliefs, which Giotto traced on it, representing the creation and progress of man, his discovery of navigation, astronomy, law, music and so on. It is religious in the grandest sense, but there is not a shred of doctrine (even the Fall is omitted) about this history in stone. If Walt Whitman had been an architect, he would have built such a tower, with such a story on it. As I want to go out and have a good look at it before we start for Venice tomorrow, I must cut this short. I hope you are enjoying yourself as much as I am, and thinking about me half as much as I am about you.

Your very sincere friend,
GILBERT K. CHESTERTON.

No one would have enjoyed more than Gilbert rereading this letter in after years and noting the suggestion that the fifteenth century belonged to the early church and preceded the Dark Ages. And I think, too, that even in Giotto's Tower, he might later have discovered some roots of doctrine.

Grand Hotel De Milan
(undated)

DEAR BENTLEY,

I write you a third letter before coming back, while Venice and Verona are fresh in my mind. Of the former I can really only discourse viva voce. Imagine a city, whose very slums are full of palaces, whose every other house wall has a battered fresco, or a gothic bas-

relief; imagine a sky fretted with every kind of pinnacle from the great dome of the Salute to the gothic spires of the Ducal Palace and the downright arabesque orientalism of the minarets of St. Mark's; and then imagine the whole flooded with a sea that seems only intended to reflect sunsets, and you still have no idea of the place I stopped in for more than 48 hours. Thence we went to Verona, where Romeo and Juliet languished and Dante wrote most of "Hell." The principal products (1) tombs: particularly those of the Scala, a very good old family with an excellent taste in fratricide. Their three tombs (one to each man I mean: one man, one grave) are really glorious examples of three stages of Gothic: of which more when we meet. (2) Balconies: with young ladies hanging over them; really quite a preponderating feature. Whether this was done in obedience to local associations and in expectation of a Romeo, I can't say. I can only remark that if such was the object, the supply of Juliets seemed very much in excess of the demand. (3) Roman remains: on which, however, I did not pronounce a soliloquy beginning, "Wonderful people . . ." which is the correct thing to do. Just as I get to this I receive your letter and resolve to begin another sheet of paper. I did read Rosebery's speech and was more than interested; I was stirred. The old order (of parliamentary forms, peerages, Whiggism and right honourable friends) has changed, yielding place to the new (of industrialism, county council sanitation, education and the Kingdom of Heaven at hand) and, whatever the Archbishop of Canterbury may say, God fulfils himself in many ways, even by local government. . . .

Several things in your letter require notice. First the accusation levelled against me of being prejudiced against Professor Huxley, I repel with indignation and scorn. You are not prejudiced against cheese because you like oranges; and though the Professor is not Isaiah or St. Francis or Whitman or Richard le Gallienne (to name some of those whom I happen to affect) I should be the last person in the world to say a word against an earnest, able, kind-hearted and most refreshingly rational man: by far the best man of his type I know. As to what you say on education generally, I am entirely with you, but it will take a good interview to say how much. As for the little Solomons, I am prepared to [be] fond of all of them, as I am of all children, even the grubby little mendicants that run these Italian streets. I am glad you and Grey have pottered. Potter again.

I have had such a nice letter from Lawrence. It makes me think it is all going "to be the fair beginning of a time."

Had the months of art study only developed in Gilbert Chesterton his power of drawing, they might still have been worthwhile. But they gave him, too, a time to dream and to think which working for a University degree would never have allowed. His views and his mind were developing fast, and he was also developing a power to which we owe some of his best work—depth of vision.

Most art criticism is the work of those who never could have been artists—which is possibly why it tends to be so critical. Gilbert, who could perhaps have been an artist, preferred to appreciate what the artist was trying to say and to put into words what he read on the canvas. Hence both in his *Watts* and his *Blake* we get what some of us ask of an art critic—the enlargement of our own powers of vision. This is what made Ruskin so great an art critic, a fact once realised, today forgotten. He may have made a thousand mistakes, he had a multitude of foolish prejudices, but he opened the eyes of a whole generation to see and understand great art.

G.K. was to begin his published writings with poetry and art criticism—in other words with vision. And this vision he partly owed to the Slade School. Here is a letter (undated) to Bentley containing a hint of what eight years later became a book on Watts:

On Saturday I saw two exhibitions of pictures. The first was the Royal Academy, where I went with Salter. There was one picture there, though the walls were decorated with frames very prettily. As to the one picture, if you look at an Academy catalogue you will see "Jonah": by G. F. Watts, and you will imagine a big silly picture of a whale. But if you go to Burlington House you will see something terrific. A spare, wild figure, clad in a strange sort of green with his head flung so far back that his upper part is a miracle of foreshortening, his hands thrust out, his face ghastly with ecstasy, his dry lips

yelling aloud, a figure of everlasting protest and defiance. And as a background (perfect in harmony of colour) you have the tracery of the Assyrian bas-reliefs, such as survive in wrecks in the British Museum, a row of those processions of numberless captives bowing before smiling Kings: a cruel sort of art. And the passionate energy of that lonely screaming figure in front, makes you think of a great many things besides Assyrians: among others of some words of Renan: I quote from memory: "But the trace of Israel will be eternal. She it was who alone among the tyrannies of antiquity, raised her voice for the helpless, the oppressed, the forgotten."

But this only expresses a fraction of it. The only thing to do is to come and look at this excited gentleman with bronze skin and hair that approaches green, his eyes simply white with madness. And Jonah said, "Yea, I do well to be angry: even unto death."

He had learnt to look at colour, to look at line, to describe pictures. But far more important than this, he could now create in the imagination gardens and sunsets and sheer colour, so as to give to his novels and stories pictorial value, to his fantasies glow, and to his poetry vision of the realities of things. In his very first volume of Essays, *The Defendant,* were to be passages that could be written only by one who had learnt to draw. For instance, in "A Defence of Skeletons":

The actual sight of the little wood, with its grey and silver sea of life is entirely a winter vision. So dim and delicate is the heart of the winter woods, a kind of glittering gloaming, that a figure stepping towards us in the chequered twilight seems as if he were breaking through unfathomable depths of spiders' webs.

In the year 1895, in which G.K. left art for publishing, he came of age "with a loud report." He writes to Bentley:

Being twenty-one years old is really rather good fun. It is one of those occasions when you remember the existence of all sorts of miscellaneous people. A cousin of mine, Alice Chesterton, daughter of my Uncle Arthur, writes me a delightfully cordial letter from Berlin, where she is a governess; and better still, my mother has received a most amusing letter from an old nurse of mine, an exceptionally nice and intelligent nurse, who writes on hearing that it is my twenty-first birthday. Billy (an epithet is suppressed) gave me a little notebook and a little photograph frame. The first thing I did with the notebook was to make a note of his birthday. The first thing I shall do with the frame will be to get Grey to give me a photograph of him to put into it. Yes, it is not bad, being twenty-one, in a world so full of kind people. . . .

I have just been out and got soaking and dripping wet; one of my favourite dissipations. I never enjoy weather so much as when it is driving, drenching, rattling, washing rain. As Mr. Meredith says in the book you gave me, "Rain, O the glad refresher of the grain, and welcome water-spouts of blessed rain." (It is in a poem called "Earth and a Wedded Woman," which is fat.) Seldom have I enjoyed a walk so much. My sister water was all there and most affectionate. Everything I passed was lovely, a little boy pickabacking another little boy home, two little girls taking shelter with a gigantic umbrella, the gutters boiling like rivers and the hedges glittering with rain. And when I came to our corner the shower was over, and there was a great watery sunset right over No. 80, what Mr. Ruskin calls an "opening into Eternity." Eternity is pink and gold. This may seem a very strange rant, but it is one of my "specimen days." I suppose you would really prefer me to write as I feel, and I am so constituted that these daily incidents get me that way. Yes, I like rain. It means something, I am not sure what; something freshening, cleaning, washing out, taking in hand, not caring-a-damn-what-you-think, doing-its-duty, robust, noisy, moral, wet. It is the Baptism of the Church of the Future.

Yesterday afternoon (Sunday) Lawrence and Maurice came here. We were merely infants at play, had skipping races round the garden and otherwise raced. ("Runner, run thy race," said Confucius, "and in the running find strength and reward.") After that we tried talking about Magnus, and came to some hopeful conclusions. Magnus is all right. As for Lawrence and Grey, if there is anything righter than all right, they are that. . . .

There is an expression in Meredith's book which struck me immensely: "the largeness of the evening earth." The sensation that the Cosmos has all its windows open is very characteristic of evening, just as it is at this moment. I feel very good. Everything out of the window looks very, very flat and yellow: I do not know how else to describe it.

It is like the benediction at the end of the service.

CHAPTER V

The Notebook

I AM WRITING THIS chapter at a table facing Notre Dame de
Paris in front of a café filled with arguing French workmen
—in the presence of God and of Man; and I feel as if I understood the one hatred of G.K.'s life: his loathing of pessimism.
"Is a man proud of losing his hearing, eyesight or sense of smell?
What shall we say of him who prides himself on beginning as
an intellectual cripple and ending as an intellectual corpse?" *

SOME PROPHECIES

Woe unto them that keep a God like a silk hat, that believe
    not in God, but in a God.

Woe unto them that are pompous for they will sooner or
    later be ridiculous.

Woe unto them that are tired of everything, for everything
    will certainly be tired of them.

Woe unto them that cast out everything, for out of every-
    thing they will be cast out.

Woe unto them that cast out anything, for out of that thing
    they will be cast out.

Woe unto the flippant, for they shall receive flippancy.

Woe unto them that are scornful for they shall receive scorn.

Woe unto him that considereth his hair foolishly, for his
    hair will be made the type of him.

Woe unto him that is smart, for men will hold him smart
    always, even when he is serious.†

A pessimist is a man who has never lived, never suffered:
"Show me a person who has plenty of worries and troubles and

* From *The Notebook*.   † *Ibid.*

58

I will show you a person who, whatever he is, is not a pessimist."

This idea G.K. developed later in the *Dickens*, dealing with the alleged over-optimism of Dickens—Dickens who if he had learnt to whitewash the universe had learnt it in a blacking factory, Dickens who had learnt through hardship and suffering to accept and love the universe. But that he wrote later. The quotations given here come from the Notebook begun in 1894 and used at intervals for the next four or five years, in which Gilbert wrote down his philosophy step by step as he came to discover it. The handwriting is the work of art that he must have learnt and practised, so different is it from his boyhood's scrawl. Each idea is set down as it comes into his mind. There is no sequence. In this book and in *The Coloured Lands* may be seen the creation of the Chesterton view of life—and it all took place in his early twenties. From the seed-thoughts here, *Orthodoxy* and the rest were to grow—here they are only seeds but seeds containing unmistakably the flower of the future:

> They should not hear from me a word
> Of selfishness or scorn
> If only I could find the door
> If only I were born.

He makes the Unborn Babe say this in his first volume of poems. And in the Notebook we see how the babe coming into the world must keep this promise by accepting life with its puzzles, its beauty, its fleetingness: "Are we all dust? What a beautiful thing dust is though." "This round earth may be a soap-bubble, but it must be admitted that there are some pretty colours on it." "What is the good of life, it is fleeting; what is the good of a cup of coffee, it is fleeting. Ha Ha Ha."

The birthday present of birth, as he was later to call it in *Orthodoxy*, involved not bare existence only but a wealth of other gifts. "A grievance," he heads this thought:

> Give me a little time,
> I shall not be able to appreciate them all;
> If you open so many doors
> And give me so many presents, O Lord God.

He is almost overwhelmed with all that he has and with all that is, but accepts it ardently in its completeness.

> If the arms of a man could be a fiery circle
>   embracing the round world,
> I think I should be that man.

Yet in the face of all this splendour the pessimist dares to find flaws:

> The mountains praise thee, O Lord!
> But what if a mountain said,
>   "I praise thee;
> But put a pine-tree halfway up on the left
> It would be much more effective, believe me."
>
> It is time that the religion of prayer gave
>   place to the religion of praise.

If the mountains must praise God, if the religion of praise expresses the truth of things, how much more does it express the truth of humanity—or rather of men, for he saw humanity not as an abstraction but as the sum of human and intensely individual beings:

> Once I found a friend
> "Dear me," I said, "he was made for me."
> But now I find more and more friends
> Who seem to have been made for me
> And more and yet more made for me,
> Is it possible we were all made for each other
>   all over the world?

And on another page comes perhaps the most significant phrase in the book: "I wonder whether there will ever come a time when I shall be tired of any one person." Hence a fantastic thought of a way of making the discovery of more people to know and to like:

The Human Circulating Library Notes

Get out a gentleman for a fortnight, then change him for a lady, or your ticket. No person to be kept out after a fortnight, except with the payment of a penny a day. Any person morally or physically damaging a man will be held responsible. The Library omnibus calls once a week leaving two or three each visit. Man of the season—old standard man.

Or better still:

My great ambition is to give a party at which everybody should meet everybody else and like them very much.

An Invitation

Mr. Gilbert Chesterton
requests the pleasure
Of humanity's company
to tea on Dec. 25th 1896.
Humanity Esq., The Earth, Cosmos E.

G.K. liked everybody very much, and everything very much He liked even the things most of us dislike. He liked to get wet. He liked to be tired. After that one short period of struggle he liked to call himself "always perfectly happy." And therefore he wanted to say, "Thank you."

You say grace before meals
      All right.
But I say grace before the play and the opera,
And grace before the concert and pantomime,
And grace before I open a book,
And grace before sketching, painting,
Swimming, fencing, boxing, walking, playing, dancing;
And grace before I dip the pen in the ink.

Each day seemed a special gift; something that might not have been:

EVENING

Here dies another day
During which I have had eyes, ears, hands
And the great world round me;
And with tomorrow begins another.
Why am I allowed two?

THE PRAYER OF A MAN WALKING

I thank thee, O Lord, for the stones in the street
I thank thee for the hay-carts yonder and for the
      houses built and half-built
That fly past me as I stride.
But most of all for the great wind in my nostrils
As if thine own nostrils were close.

THE PRAYER OF A MAN RESTING

The twilight closes round me
My head is bowed before the Universe
I thank thee, O Lord, for a child I knew seven
      years ago
And whom I have never seen since.

Praised be God for all sides of life, for friends, lovers, art, literature, knowledge, humour, politics, and for the little red cloud away there in the west—

For, if he was to be grateful, to whom did he owe gratitude? Here is the chief question he asked and answered at this time. At school he was looking for God, but at the age of 16 he was, he tells us in *Orthodoxy,* an Agnostic in the sense of one who is not sure one way or the other. Largely it was this need for gratitude for what seemed personal gifts that brought him to belief in a personal God. Life was personal, it was not a mere drift; it had will in it, it was more like a story.

A story is the highest mark
For the world is a story and every part of it
And there is nothing that can touch the world
    or any part of it
That is not a story.

And again, with the heading, "A Social Situation."

We must certainly be in a novel;
What I like about this novelist is that he takes
    such trouble about his minor characters.

The story shapes from man's birth and it is as he meets the other characters that he finds he is in the right story.

A Man Born On the Earth

Perhaps there has been some mistake
How does he know he has come to the right place?
But when he finds friends
He knows he has come to the right place.

You say it is a love affair
Hush: it is a new Garden of Eden
And a new progeny will people a new earth
God is always making these experiments.

Life is a story: who tells it? Life is a problem: who sets it?

The world is a problem, not a Theorem
And the word of the last Day will be Q.E.F.

God sets the problem, God tells the story, but can those know Him who are characters in His story, who are working out His problem?

Have you ever known what it is to walk along a road in such a frame of mind that you thought you might meet God at any turn of the path?

For this a man must be ready, against this he must never shut the door.

There is one kind of infidelity blacker than all
    infidelities,
Worse than any blow of secularist, pessimist,
    atheist,
It is that of those persons
Who regard God as an old institution.

Voices

The axe falls on the wood in thuds, "God, God."
The cry of the rook, "God," answers it
The crack of the fire on the hearth, the voice of
    the brook, say the same name;
All things, dog, cat, fiddle, baby,
Wind, breaker, sea, thunderclap
Repeat in a thousand languages—
    God.

Next in his thought comes a point where he hesitates as to
the meeting place between God and Man. How and where can
these two incommensurates find a meeting place? What is Incarnation? The greatness and the littleness of Man obsessed Chesterton as it did Pascal; it is the eternal riddle:

Two Strands

Man is a spark flying upwards. God is everlasting.
Who are we, to whom this cup of human life has
    been given, to ask for more? Let us love mercy
    and walk humbly. What is man, that thou re-
    gardest him?
Man is a star unquenchable. God is in him in-
    carnate.
His life is planned upon a scale colossal, of which
    he sees glimpses. Let him dare all things,
    claim all things: he is the son of Man, who
    shall come in the clouds of glory.
    saw these two strands mingling to make the re-
    ligion of man.

"A scale colossal, of which he sees glimpses." This, I think, is the first hint of the path that led Gilbert to full faith in Our Lord. In places in these notes he regards Him certainly only as Man—but even then as *The* Man, the *Only* Man in whom the colossal scale, the immense possibilities, of human nature could be dreamed of as fulfilled. Two notes on Marcus Aurelius are significant of the way his mind was moving.

MARCUS AURELIUS

A large-minded, delicate-witted, strong man,
Following the better thing like a thread between
  his hands.
Him we cannot fancy choosing the lower even by
  mistake; we cannot think of him as wanting
  for a moment in any virtue, sincerity, mercy,
  purity, self-respect, good manners.
Only one thing is wanting in him. He does not
  command me to perform the impossible.

THE CARPENTER

The Meditations of Marcus Aurelius.
Yes: he was soliloquising, not making something.
Do not the words of Jesus ring
Like nails knocked into a board
          In his father's workshop?

On two consecutive pages are notes showing how his mind is wrestling with the question, the answer to which would complete his philosophy:

XMAS DAY

Good news: but if you ask me what it is, I know not;
It is a track of feet in the snow,
It is a lantern showing a path,
It is a door set open.

The Grace of Our Lord Jesus Christ

I live in an age of varied powers and knowledge,
Of steam, science, democracy, journalism, art·
But when my love rises like a sea,
I have to go back to an obscure tribe and a slain man
To formulate a blessing.

Julian

"Vicisti Galilæe," he said, and sank conquered
After wrestling with the most gigantic of powers,
　　　A dead man.

The Crucified

On a naked slope of a poor province
A Roman soldier stood staring at a gibbet,
Then he said, "Surely this was a righteous man,"
And a new chapter of history opened,
Having that for its motto.

Parables

There was a man who dwelt in the east centuries ago,
And now I cannot look at a sheep or a sparrow,
A lily or a cornfield, a raven or a sunset,
A vineyard or a mountain, without thinking of him;
If this be not to be divine, what is it?

Cecil Chesterton tells us Gilbert read the Gospels partly because he was not forced to read them: I suppose this really means that he read them with a mature mind which had not been dulled to their reception by a childhood task of routine lessons. But I do not think at this date it had occurred to him to question the assumption of the period: that official Christianity, its priesthood especially, had travestied the original intention of Christ. This idea is in the *Wild Knight* volume (published in 1900) and more briefly in a suggestion in the Notebook for a proposed drama:

Gabriel is hammering up a little theatre and the
child looks at his hands, and finds them torn
with nails.
Clergyman. The Church should stand by the
powers that be.
Gabriel. Yes? . . . That is a handsome crucifix
you have there at your chain.

That the clergy, that the Christian people, should have settled
down to an acceptance of a faulty established order, should not
be alert to all that Our Lord's life signified, was one of the problems. It was, too, a matter of that cosmic loyalty which he analyses more fully in *Orthodoxy.* Here he simply writes:

It is not a question of Theology,
It is a question of whether, placed as a sentinel
of an unknown watch, you will whistle or not.

Sentinels do go to sleep and he was coming to feel that this
want of vigilance ran through the whole of humanity. In "White
Wynd," a sketch written at this time,* he adumbrates an idea
to which he was to return again in *Manalive* especially, and in
Orthodoxy—that we can by custom so lose our sense of reality
that the only way to enjoy and be grateful for our possessions is
to lose them for a while. The shortest way home is to go round
the world. In this story of "White Wynd" he applies the parable
only to each man's life and the world he lives in. But in *Orthodoxy* he applies it to the human race who have lost revealed
truth by getting so accustomed to it that they no longer look
at it. And already in the Notebook he is calling the attention of
a careless multitude to "that great Empire upon which the sun
never sets. I allude to the Universe."

Most of the quotations about Our Lord come in the later part
of the book: in the earlier pages he dreams that "to this age it
is given to write the great new song, and to compile the new
Bible, and to found the new Church, and preach the new

* It is published in *The Coloured Lands.*

Religion." And in one rather obscure passage he seems to hint at the thought that Christ might come again to shape this new religion.

Going round the world, Gilbert was finding his way home; the explorer was rediscovering his native country. He himself has given us all the metaphors for what was happening now in his mind. Without a single Catholic friend he had discovered this wealth of Catholic truth and he was still travelling. "All this I felt," he later summed it up in *Orthodoxy*, "and the age gave me no encouragement to feel it. And all this time I had not even thought of Catholic theology."

CHAPTER VI

Towards a Career

A CURIOUS LITTLE incident comes towards the end of Gilbert's time at the Slade School. In a letter he wrote to E. C. Bentley we see him, on the eve of his 21st birthday, being invited to write for the *Academy*:

Mr. Cotton is a little bristly, bohemian man, as fidgetty as a kitten, who runs round the table while he talks to you. When he agrees with you he shuts his eyes tight and shakes his head. When he means anything rather seriously he ends up with a loud nervous laugh. He talks incessantly and is mad on the history of Oxford. I sent him my review of Ruskin and he read it before me (Note. Hell) and delivered himself with astonishing rapidity to the following effect: "This is very good: you've got something to say: Oh, yes: this is worth saying: I agree with you about Ruskin and about the Century: this is good: you've no idea: if you saw some stuff: some reviews I get: the fellows are practised but of all the damned fools: you've no idea: they know the trade in a way: but such infernal asses: as send things up: but this is very good: that sentence does run *nicely*: but I like your point: make it a little longer and then send it in: I've got another book for you to review: you know Robert Bridges? Oh very good, very good: here it is: about two columns you know: by the way: keep the Ruskin for yourself: you deserve that anyhow."

Here I got a word in: one of protest and thanks. But Mr. Cotton insisted on my accepting the Ruskin. So I am really to serve Laban. Laban proves on analysis to be of the consistency of brick. It is such men as this that have made our Cosmos what it is. At one point he said, literally dancing with glee: "Oh, the other day I stuck some pins into Andrew Lang." I said, "Dear me, that must be a very good game." It was something about an edition of Scott, but I was told that Andrew "took" the painful operation "very well." We sat up horribly late together talking about Browning, Afghans, Notes, the Yellow Book, the French Revolution, William Morris, Norsemen and Mr. Richard Le Gallienne. "I don't despair for anyone," he said suddenly. "Hang it all, that's what you mean by humanity." This appears to be a rather good editor of the *Academy*. And my joy in having begun my life is very great. "I am tired," I said to Mr. Brodribb, "of writing only what I like." "Oh, well," he said heartily, "you'll have no reason to make that complaint in journalism."

But here is a mystery. Nowhere in the *Academy* columns for 1895 or 1896 are to be seen the initials G.K.C., yet at that date all the reviews are signed. Mr. Eccles, who was writing for it at the time, told me that he had no recollection of G.K. among the contributors—and later he came to know him well when both were together on the *Speaker*. In any case, the idea of reviewing for no reward except the book reviewed would scarcely appeal to a more practical man than Gilbert as a hopeful beginning. Perhaps the mystery is solved by the fact that soon after the date of this letter Mr. Cotton got an appointment in India. To Mr. Eccles it appeared somewhat ironical that the unpaid contributors to the *Academy* were circularised with a suggestion of contributions of money towards a parting present for their late editor.

The actual beginning of G.K.'s journalism was in *The Bookman*; and in the *Autobiography* he insists that it was a matter of mere luck: "these opportunities were merely things that happened to me." While still at the Slade School, he was, as we have seen, attending English lectures at University College. There he met a fellow-student, Ernest Hodder Williams, of the family which controlled the publishing house of Hodder & Stoughton. He gave Chesterton some books on art to review for *The Bookman*, a monthly paper published by the firm. "I need not say," G.K. comments, "that having entirely failed to learn how to draw or paint, I tossed off easily enough some criticisms of the weaker points of Rubens or the misdirected talents of Tintoretto. I had discovered the easiest of all professions, which I have pursued ever since." But neither in the art criticism he wrote for *The Bookman* nor in the poems he was to publish in *The Outlook* and *The Speaker* was there a living. He left the Slade School and went to work for a publisher.

Mr. Redway, in whose office Gilbert now found himself, was a publisher largely of spiritualist literature. Gilbert has described in his *Autobiography* his rather curious experience of ghostly authorship, but he relates nothing of his office experience, which is described in another undated letter to Mr. Bentley:

I am writing this letter just when I like most to write one, late at night, after a beastly lot of midnight oil over a contribution for a Slade Magazine, intended as a public venture. I am sending them a recast of that "Picture of Tuesday."

Like you, I am beastly busy, but there is something exciting about it. If I must be busy (as I certainly must, being an approximately honest man) I had much rather be busy in a varied, mixed up way, with half a hundred things to attend to, than with one blank day of monotonous "study" before me. To give you some idea of what I mean. I have been engaged in 3 different tiring occupations and enjoyed them all. (1) Redway says, "We've got too many MSS; read through them, will you, and send back those that are too bad at once." I go slap through a room full of MSS, criticising deuced conscientiously, with the result that I post back some years of MSS to addresses, which I should imagine, must be private asylums. But one feels worried, somehow. . . .

(2) Redway says, "I'm going to give you entire charge of the press department, sending copies to Reviews, etc." Consequence is, one has to keep an elaborate book and make it tally with other elaborate books, and one has to remember all the magazines that exist and what sort of books they'd crack up. I used to think I hated responsibility: I am positively getting to enjoy it. (3) There is that confounded "Picture of Tuesday" which I have been scribbling at the whole evening, and have at last got it presentable. This sounds like mere amusement, but, now that I have tried other kinds of hurry and bustle, I solemnly pledge myself to the opinion that there is no

work so tiring as writing, that is, not for fun, but for publication. Other work has a repetition, a machinery, a reflex action about it somewhere, but to be on the stretch *inventing things,* making them out of nothing, making them as good as you can for a matter of four hours leaves me more inclined to lie down and read Dickens than I ever feel after nine hours ramp at Redway's. The worst of it is that you always think the thing so bad too when you're in that state.

I can't imagine anything more idiotic than what I've just finished.

Well, enough of work and all its works. By all means come on Monday evening, but don't be frightened if by any chance I'm not in till about 6.30, as Monday is a busy day. Of course you'll stop to dinner . . . what an idiotically long time 8 weeks is. . . .

This letter does not seem to bear out the suggestion in Cecil's book* of Gilbert's probable uselessness to the publishers for whom he worked. After all, literacy is more needful to most publishers than automatic practicality, because it is so very much rarer. Probably G.K. would have been absolutely invaluable had he been a little less kind-hearted. His dislike of sending back a manuscript and making an author unhappy would have been a bar to his utility as a reader. But there are lots of other things to do besides rejecting manuscripts, and two later letters show how capable Gilbert was felt to be in doing most of them.

The exact date at which he left Redway's for the publishing firm of Fisher Unwin (of 11 Paternoster Buildings) I cannot discover, but it was fairly early and he was several years with Fisher Unwin, only gradually beginning to move over into journalism.

"He did nothing for himself," says Lucian Oldershaw, "till we [Bentley and Oldershaw] came down from Oxford and pushed him."

The following letters belong to 1898, being written to Frances when they were already engaged, but I put them here as they give some notion of the work he did for his employer.

. . . The book I have to deal with for Unwin is an exhaustive and I am told interesting work on "Rome and the Empire" a kind

* *G. K. Chesterton: A Criticism,* see p. 23.

of realistic, modern account of the life of the ancient world. I have got to fix it up, choose illustrations, introductions, notes, etc., and all because I am the only person who knows a little Latin and precious little Roman history and no more archaeology than a blind cat. It is entertaining, and just like our firm's casual way. The work ought to be done by an authority on Roman antiquities. If I hadn't been there they would have given it to the office boy.

However, I shall get through it all right: the more I see of the publishing world, the more I come to the conclusion that I know next to nothing, but that the vast mass of literary people know less. This is sometimes called having "a public-school education." *

*   *   *

I have a lot of work to do, as Unwin has given the production of an important book entirely into my hands, as a kind of invisible editor. It is complimentary, but very worrying, and will mean a lot of time at the British Museum.†

11 Paternoster Bldgs.
(Postmark, December 1898)

. . . For fear that you should really suppose that my observations about being busy are the subterfuges of a habitual liar, I may give you briefly some idea of the irons at present in the fire. As far as I can make out there are at least seven things that I have undertaken to do and everyone of them I ought to do before any of the others.

1st. There is the book about Ancient Rome which I have to do for T.F.U.—arrange and get illustrations etc. This all comes of showing off. It is a story with a moral (Greedy Gilbert: or Little Boys Should be Seen and not Heard). A short time ago I had to read a treatise by Dean Stubbs on "The Ideal Woman of the Poets" in which the Dean remarked that "all the women admired by Horace were wantons." This struck me as a downright slander, slight as is my classical knowledge, and in my report I asked loftily what Dean Stubbs made of those noble lines on the wife who hid her husband from his foes.

Splendide mendax et in omne virgo
Nobilis aevum

* Extract from undated letter (postmarked, Aug. 11, 1898).
† Extract from undated letter (postmarked, Aug. 29, 1898).

One of the purest and stateliest tributes ever made to a woman. (The lines might be roughly rendered "A magnificent liar and a noble lady for all eternity"; but no translation can convey the organ-voice of the verse, in which the two strong and lonely words "noble" and "eternity" stand solitary for the last line.) In consequence of my taking up the cudgels against a live Dean for the manly moral sense of the dear old Epicurean, the office became impressed with a vague idea that I know something about Latin literature—whereas, as a matter of fact I have forgotten even the line before the one I quoted. However, in the most confidential and pathetic manner I was entrusted with doing with "Rome et l'Empire" work which ought to be done by a scholar. . . .

2nd. Then there is Captain Webster. You ask (in gruff, rumbling tones) "Who is Captain Webster?" I will tell you.

Captain Webster is a small man with a carefully waxed moustache and a very Bond Street get up, living at the Grosvenor Hotel. Talking to him you would say: he is an ass, but an agreeable ass, a humble, transparent honourable ass. He is an innocent and idiotic butterfly. The interesting finishing touch is that he has been to New Guinea for four years or so, and had some of the most hideous and extravagant adventures that could befall a modern man. His yacht was surrounded by shoals of canoes full of myriads of cannibals of a race who file their teeth to look like the teeth of dogs, and hang weights in their ears till the ears hang like dogs' ears, on the shoulder. He held his yacht at the point of the revolver and got away, leaving some of his men dead on the shore. All night long he heard the horrible noise of the banqueting gongs and saw the huge fires that told his friends were being eaten. Now he lives in the Grosvenor Hotel. Captain Webster finds the pen, not only mightier than the sword, but also much more difficult. He has written his adventures and we are to publish them and I am translating the honest captain into English grammar, a thing which appals him much more than Papuan savages. This means going through it carefully of course and rewriting many parts of it, where relatives and dependent sentences have been lost past recovery. I went to see him, and his childlike dependence on me was quite pathetic. His general attitude was, "You see I'm such a damned fool." And so he is. But when I compare him with the Balzacian hauteur and the preposterous posing of many of our Fleet Street decadent geniuses, I feel a movement of the blood which declares that perhaps there are worse things than War. (Between ourselves, I have a sneaking sympathy with fighting: I fought horribly at school. It is well you should know my illogicalities.)

3rd. There is the selection of illustrations for the History of China we are producing. I know no more of China than the Man in the Moon (less, for he has seen it, at any rate), except what I got from reading the book, but of course I shall make the most of what I do know and airily talk of La-o-tsee and Wu-sank-Wei, criticise Chungtang and Fu-Tche, compare Tchieu Lung with his great successor, whose name I have forgotten, and the Napoleonic vigour of Li with the weak opportunism of Woo. Before I have done I hope people will be looking behind for my pig-tail. The name I shall adopt will be Tches-Ter-Ton.

4th. A MS to read translated from the Norwegian: a History of the Kiss, Ceremonial, Amicable, Amatory, etc.—in the worst French sentimental style. God alone knows how angry I am with the author of that book. I am not sure that I shall not send up the brief report. "A snivelling hound."

5th. The book for Nutt [*Greybeards at Play*], which has reached its worst stage, that of polishing up for the eye of Nutt, instead of merely rejoicing in the eye of God. Do you know this is the only one of the lot about which I am at all worried. I do not feel as if things like the Fish poem are really worth publishing. I know they are better than many books that are published, but Heaven knows that is not saying much. In support of some of my work I would fight to the last. But with regard to this occasional verse I feel a humbug. To publish a book of my nonsense verses seems to me exactly like summoning the whole of the people of Kensington to see me smoke cigarettes.

Macgregor told me that I should do much better in the business of literature if I found the work more difficult. My facility, he said, led me to undervalue my work. I wonder whether this is true, and those silly rhymes are any good after all.

6th. The collection of more serious poems of which I spoke to you. You shall have a hand in the selection of these when you get back.

7th. The Novel—which though I have put it aside for the present, yet has become too much a part of me not to be constantly having chapters written—or rather growing out of the others.

And all these things, with the exception of the last one, are supposed to be really urgent, and to be done immediately. . . . Now I hope I have sickened you forever of wanting to know the details of my dull affairs. But I hope it may give you some notion of how hard it really is to get time for writing just now. For you see they are none of them even mechanical things: they all require some thinking about.

I am afraid . . . that if you really want to know what I do, you must forgive me for seeming egoistic. That is the tragedy of the literary person: his very existence is an assertion of his own mental vanity: he must pretend to be conceited even if he isn't. . . .

Beginning to publish, beginning to write, and still developing mentally at a frantic rate—this is a summary of the years 1895–8.

As the Notebook shows, Gilbert was reflecting deeply at this time on the relations both between God and man and between man and his fellow man. The realisation that their relations had gone very far wrong was necessarily followed—for Gilbert's *mind* was an immensely practical one—by the question of what the proposed remedies were worth. He has told us that he became a Socialist at this time only because it was intolerable not to be a Socialist. The Socialists seemed the only people who were looking at conditions as they were and finding them unendurable. Christian Socialism seemed at first sight, for anyone who admired Christ, to be the obvious form of Socialism, and, in a fragment of this period, G.K. traces the resemblance of modern collectivism to early Christianity.

The points in which Christian and Socialistic collectivism are at one are simple and fundamental. As, however, we must proceed carefully in this matter, we may state these points of resemblance under three heads.

(1) Both rise from the deeps of an emotion, the emotion of compassion for misfortune, as such. This is really a very important point. Collectivism is not an intellectual fad, even if erroneous, but a passionate protest and aspiration: it arises as a secret of the heart, a

dream of the injured feeling, long before it shapes itself as a definite propaganda at all. The intellectual philosophies ally themselves with success and preach competition, but the human heart allies itself with misfortune and suggests communism.

(2) Both trace the evil state of society to "covetousness," the competitive desire to accumulate riches. Thus, both in one case and the other, the mere possession of wealth is in itself an offence against moral order, the absence of it in itself a recommendation and training for the higher life.

(3) Both propose to remedy the evil of competition by a system of "bearing each other's burdens" in the literal sense, that is to say, of levelling, silencing and reducing one's own chances, for the chance of your weaker brethren. The desirability, they say, of a great or clever man acquiring fame is small compared with the desirability of a weak and broken man acquiring bread. The strong man is a man, and should modify or adapt himself to the hopes of his mates. He that would be first among you, let him be the servant of all.

These are the three fountains of collectivist passion. I have not considered it necessary to enter into elaborate proof of the presence of these three in the Gospels. That the main trend of Jesus' character was compassion for human ills, that he denounced not merely covetousness but riches again and again, and with an almost impatient emphasis, and that he insisted on his followers throwing up personal aims and sharing funds and fortune entirely, these are plain matters of evidence presented again and again, and, in fact, of common admission.

Yet that uncanny thing in Gilbert which always forced him to see facts, mutinied again at this point and produced another fragment in which he has moved closer to Christianity and thereby further away from modern Socialism. The world he lived in contained a certain number of Christians who were, he found, highly doubtful about the Christian impulse of Socialism. And most of his Socialist friends had about them a tone of bitterness and an atmosphere of hopelessness utterly unlike the tone and the atmosphere of Christianity. Just as atheists were the first people to turn Gilbert from Atheism towards dogmatic

Christianity, so the Socialists were now turning him from Socialism.

The next fragment is rather long, but it was never published
and I think it so important, as showing how his mind was moving, that it cannot well be shortened. It is a document of capital
importance for the biography of Chesterton.

Now, for my own part, I cannot in the least agree with those who
see no difference between Christian and modern Socialism, nor do I
for a moment join in some Christian Socialists' denunciations of those
worthy middle-class people who cannot see the connection. For I
cannot help thinking that in a way these latter people are right. No
reasonable man can read the Sermon on the Mount and think that
its tone is not very different from that of most collectivist speculation
of the present day, and the Philistines feel this, though they cannot
distinctly express it. There is a difference between Christ's Socialist
program and that of our own time, a difference deep, genuine and
all important, and it is this which I wish to point out.

Let us take two types side by side, or rather the same type in the
two different atmospheres. Let us take the "rich young man" of the
Gospels and place beside him the rich young man of the present day,
on the threshold of Socialism. If we were to follow the difficulties,
theories, doubts, resolves, and conclusions of each of these characters,
we should find two very distinct threads of self-examination running
through the two lives. And the essence of the difference was this:
the modern socialist is saying, "What will society do?" while his
prototype, as we read, said, "What shall I do?" Properly considered,
this latter sentence contains the whole essence of the older Communism. The modern socialist regards his theory of regeneration as
a duty which society owes to him, the early Christian regarded it
as a duty which he owed to society; the modern socialist is busy
framing schemes for its fulfilment, the early Christian was busy considering whether he would himself fulfil it there and then; the ideal
of modern socialism is an elaborate Utopia to which he hopes the
world may be tending, the ideal of the early Christian was an actual
nucleus "living the new life" to whom he might join himself if he
liked. Hence the constant note running through the whole gospel,
of the importance, difficulty and excitement of the "call," the indi-

SELF CARICATURE
SLADE SCHOOL PERIOD

vidual and practical request made by Christ to every rich man, "Sell all thou hast and give to the poor."

To us Socialism comes speculatively as a noble and optimistic theory of what may [be] the crown of progress, to Peter and James and John it came practically as a crisis of their own daily life, a stirring question of conduct and renunciation.

We do not therefore in the least agree with those who hold that modern socialism is an exact counterpart or fulfilment of the socialism of Christianity. We find the difference important and profound, despite the common ground of anti-selfish collectivism. The modern socialist regards Communism as a distant panacea for society, the early Christian regarded it as an immediate and difficult regeneration of himself: the modern socialist reviles, or at any rate reproaches, society for not adopting it, the early Christian concentrated his thoughts on the problem of his own fitness and unfitness to adopt it: to the modern socialist it is a theory, to the early Christian it was a call; modern socialism says, "Elaborate a broad, noble and workable system and submit it to the progressive intellect of society." Early Christianity said, "Sell all thou hast and give to the poor."

This distinction between the social and personal way of regarding the change has two sides, a spiritual and a practical which we propose to notice. The spiritual side of it, though of less direct and revolutionary importance than the practical, has still a very profound philosophic significance. To us it appears something extraordinary that this Christian side of socialism, the side of the difficulty of the personal sacrifice, and the patience, cheerfulness, and good temper necessary for the protracted personal surrender is so constantly overlooked. The literary world is flooded with old men seeing visions and young men dreaming dreams, with various stages of anti-competitive enthusiasm, with economic apocalypses, elaborate Utopias and mushroom destinies of mankind. And, as far as we have seen, in all this whirlwind of theoretic excitement there is not a word spoken of the intense practical difficulty of the summons to the individual, the heavy, unrewarding cross borne by him who gives up the world.

For it will not surely be denied that not only will Socialism be impossible without some effort on the part of individuals, but that Socialism if once established would be rapidly dissolved, or worse still, diseased, if the individual members of the community did not make a constant effort to do that which in the present state of human nature must mean an effort, to live the higher life. Mere state systems could not bring about and still less sustain a reign of unselfishness, without a cheerful decision on the part of the members to forget selfishness even in little things, and for that most difficult and at the same time most important personal decision Christ made provision and the modern theorists make no provision at all. Some modern socialists do indeed see that something more is necessary for the golden age than fixed incomes and universal stores tickets, and that the fountain heads of all real improvement are to be found in human temper and character. Mr. William Morris, for instance, in his "News from Nowhere" gives a beautiful picture of a land ruled by Love, and rightly grounds the give-and-take camaraderie of his ideal state upon an assumed improvement in human nature. But he does not tell us how such an improvement is to be effected, and Christ did. Of Christ's actual method in this matter I shall speak afterwards when dealing with the practical aspect, my object just now is to compare the spiritual and emotional effects of the call of Christ, as compared to those of the vision of Mr. William Morris. When we compare the spiritual attitudes of two thinkers, one of whom is considering whether social history has been sufficiently a course of improvement to warrant him in believing that it will culminate in universal altruism, while the other is considering whether he loves other people enough to walk down tomorrow to the market-place and distribute everything but his staff and his scrip, it will not be denied that the latter is likely to undergo certain deep and acute emotional experiences, which will be quite unknown to the former. And these emotional experiences are what we understand as the spiritual aspect of the distinction. For three characteristics at least the Galilean programme makes more provision; humility, activity, cheerfulness, the real triad of Christian virtues.

Humility is a grand, a stirring thing, the exalting paradox of Christianity, and the sad want of it in our own time is, we believe, what really makes us think life dull, like a cynic, instead of marvellous, like a child. With this, however, we have at present nothing to do. What we have to do with is the unfortunate fact that among no persons is it more wanting than among socialists, Christian and other. The isolated or scattered protest for a complete change in social order, the continual harping on one string, the necessarily jaundiced contemplation of a system already condemned, and above all, the haunting pessimistic whisper of a possible hopelessness of overcoming the giant forces of success, all these impart undeniably to the modern socialist a tone excessively imperious and bitter. Nor can we reasonably blame the average money-getting public for their impatience with the monotonous virulence of men who are constantly reviling them for not living communistically, and who after all, are not doing it themselves. Willingly do we allow that these latter enthusiasts think it impossible in the present state of society to practise their ideal, but this fact, while vindicating their indisputable sincerity, throws an unfortunate vagueness and inconclusiveness over their denunciations of other people in the same position. Let us compare with this arrogant and angry tone among the modern Utopians who can only dream "the life," the tone of the early Christian who was busy living it. As far as we know, the early Christians never regarded it as astonishing that the world as they found it was competitive and unregenerate; they seem to have felt that it could not in its pre-Christian ignorance have been anything else, and their whole interest was bent on their own standard of conduct and exhortation which was necessary to convert it. They felt that it was by no merit of theirs that they had been enabled to enter into the life before the Romans, but simply as a result of the fact that Christ had appeared in Galilee and not in Rome. Lastly, they never seem to have entertained a doubt that the message would itself convert the world with a rapidity and ease which left no room for severe condemnation of the heathen societies.

With regard to the second merit, that of activity, there can be little doubt as to where it lies between the planner of the Utopia and the convert of the brotherhood. The modern Socialist is a visionary, but in this he is on the same ground as half the great men of the world, and to some extent of the early Christian himself, who rushed towards a personal ideal very difficult to sustain. The visionary who yearns toward an ideal which is practically impossible is not useless or mischievous, but often the opposite; but the person who is often useless, and always mischievous, is the visionary who dreams with the knowledge or the half-knowledge that his ideal is impossible. The early Christian might be wrong in believing that by entering the brotherhood men could in a few years become perfect even as their Father in Heaven was perfect, but he believed it and acted flatly and fearlessly on the belief: this is the type of the higher visionary. But all the insidious dangers of the vision; the idleness, the procrastination, the mere mental aestheticism, come in when the vision is indulged, as half our socialistic conceptions are, as a mere humour or fairy-tale, with a consciousness, half-confessed, that it is beyond practical politics, and that we need not be troubled with its immediate fulfilment. The visionary who believes in his own most frantic vision is always noble and useful. It is the visionary who does not believe in his vision who is the dreamer, the idler, the Utopian. This then is the second moral virtue of the older school, an immense direct sincerity of action, a cleansing away, by the sweats of hard work, of all those subtle and perilous instincts of mere ethical castle-building which have been woven like the spells of an enchantress, round so many of the strong men of our own time.

The third merit, which I have called cheerfulness, is really the most important of all. We may perhaps put the comparison in this way. It might strike many persons as strange that in a time on the whole so optimistic in its intellectual beliefs as this is, in an age when only a small minority disbelieve in social progress, and a large majority believe in an ultimate social perfection, there should be such a tired and blasé feeling among numbers of young men. This, we think, is due, not to the want of an ultimate ideal, but to that of any immediate way of making for it: not of something to hope but of something to do. A human being is not satisfied and never will be satisfied with being told that it is all right: what he wants is not a prediction of what other people will be hundreds of years hence, to make him cheerful, but a new and stirring test and task for himself, which will assuredly make him cheerful. A knight is not contented with the statement that his commander has laid his plans so as to insure victory: what the knight wants is a sword. This demand for a task is not mere bravado, it is an eternal and natural part of the higher optimism, as deep-rooted as the foreshadowing of perfection.

I do not know whether Gilbert would yet have actually called himself a Christian. He was certainly tending towards the more Christian elements in his surroundings. It seems pretty clear from all he wrote and said later that he did not hold that transformation to have been fully effected until after his meeting with Frances, to whom he wrote many years later:

Therefore I bring these rhymes to you
Who brought the Cross to me.

These papers are undated and are arranged in no sequence. It is possible this last one was written after their first meeting. Certain it is that in it he had begun feeling after a more Christian arrangement of society than Socialism offered—and particularly after an arrangement better suited to the nature of man. This thought of man's nature as primary was to remain the basis of his social thinking to the end of his life.

Chapter VII

Incipit Vita Nova

In the Notebook may be seen Gilbert's occasional thoughts about his own future love story.

Suddenly in the Midst

Suddenly in the midst of friends,
Of brothers known to me more and more,
And their secrets, histories, tastes, hero-worships,
Schemes, love-affairs, known to me
      Suddenly I felt lonely.
Felt like a child in a field with no more games to play
Because I have not a lady
      to whom to send my thought at that hour
      that she might crown my peace.

Madonna Mia

About Her whom I have not yet met
      I wonder what she is doing
      Now, at this sunset hour,
Working perhaps, or playing, worrying or laughing,
Is she making tea, or singing a song, or writing,
    or praying, or reading
Is she thoughtful, as I am thoughtful
      Is she looking now out of the window
      As I am looking out of the window?

But a few pages later comes the entry:

F.B.

You are a very stupid person.
I don't believe you have the least idea how nice you are.

F.B. was Frances, daughter of a diamond merchant some time dead. The family was of French descent, the name de Blogue having been somewhat unfortunately anglicised into Blogg. They had fallen from considerable wealth into a degree of poverty that made it necessary for the three daughters to earn a living. Frances was never strong and Gilbert has told how utterly exhausted she was at the end of each day's toil—"she worked very hard as secretary of an educational society in London." * The family lived in Bedford Park, a suburb of London that went in for artistic housing and a kind of garden-city atmosphere long before this was at all general. Judging by their photographs the three girls must all have been remarkably pretty, and young men frequented the house in great numbers, among them Brimley Johnson who was engaged to Gertrude, and Lucian Oldershaw who later married Ethel. Some time in 1896, Oldershaw took Gilbert to call and Gilbert, literally at first sight, fell in love with Frances.

To My Lady

> God made you very carefully
> He set a star apart for it
> He stained it green and gold with fields
> And aureoled it with sunshine
> He peopled it with kings, peoples, republics
> And so made you, very carefully.
> All nature is God's book, filled with his rough sketches
>   for you.†

When almost forty years later Gilbert was writing his *Autobiography*, Frances asked him to keep her out of it. The liking they both had for keeping private life private made him call it "this very Victorian narrative." Nevertheless he tells us something of the early days of their acquaintance. Gilbert had mentioned the moon:

* *Autobiography*, p. 153.   † *The Notebook.*

She told me in the most normal and unpretentious tone that she hated the moon. I talked to the same lady several times afterwards; and found that this was a perfectly honest statement of the fact. Her attitude on this and other things might be called a prejudice; but it could not possibly be called a fad, still less an affectation. She really had an obstinate objection to all those natural forces that seemed to be sterile or aimless; she disliked loud winds that seemed to be going nowhere; she did not care much for the sea, a spectacle of which I was very fond; and by the same instinct she was up against the moon, which she said looked like an imbecile. On the other hand, she had a sort of hungry appetite for all the fruitful things like fields and gardens and anything connected with production; about which she was quite practical. She practised gardening; in that curious cockney culture she would have been quite ready to practise farming; and on the same perverse principle, she actually practised a religion. This was something utterly unaccountable both to me and to the whole fussy culture in which she lived. Any number of people proclaimed religions, chiefly oriental religions, analysed or argued about them; but that anybody could regard religion as a practical thing like gardening was something quite new to me and, to her neighbours, new and incomprehensible. She had been, by an accident, brought up in the school of an Anglo-Catholic convent; and to all that agnostic or mystic world, practising a religion was much more puzzling than professing it. She was a queer card. She wore a green velvet dress barred with grey fur, which I should have called artistic, but that she hated all the talk about art; and she had an attractive face, which I should have called elvish, but that she hated all the talk about elves. But what was arresting and almost blood-curdling about her, in that social atmosphere, was not so much that she hated it, as that she was entirely unaffected by it. She never knew what was meant by being "under the influence" of Yeats or Shaw or Tolstoy or anybody else. She was intelligent, with a great love of literature, and especially of Stevenson. But if Stevenson had walked into the room and explained his personal doubts about personal immortality, she would have regretted that he should be wrong upon the point; but would otherwise have been utterly unaffected. She was not at all like Robespierre, except in a taste for neatness in dress; and yet it is only in Mr. Belloc's book on Robespierre that I have ever found any words that describe the unique quality that cut her off from the current culture and saved her from it. "God had given him in his mind a stone tabernacle in which certain great truths were preserved imperishable.*

A letter to a friend, Mildred Wain, who was now engaged to Waldo d'Avigdor, makes the future tolerably easy to foresee.

. . . My brother wishes me to thank you with ferocious gratitude for the music, which he is enjoying tremendously. It reminds me rather of what Miss Frances Blogg—but that is another story.

In your last letter you enquired whether I saw anything of the Bloggs now. If you went and put that question to them there would be a scene. Mrs. Blogg would probably fall among the fire-irons, Knollys would foam in convulsions on the carpet, Ethel would scream and take refuge on the mantelpiece and Gertrude faint and break off her engagement. Frances would—but no intelligent person can affect an interest in what she does.

Lawrence Solomon told me that Mrs. Edward Chesterton did not approve of the rather arty-crafty atmosphere of Bedford Park—that earliest of Garden Cities, so conventionally unconventional—where Frances lived. She did not like her son's friendship with the Bloggs and she had chosen for him a girl who she felt would make him an ideal wife: "Very open air," Mr. Solomon said. "Not booky, but good at games and practical." He was not sure whether Gilbert realised this, but personally I believe that Gilbert realised everything.

"Of course you know," Annie Firmin wrote to me, "that Aunt Marie never liked Frances? Or Bentley?" Annie was the girl chosen by Gilbert's mother. She was very much a member of the family.

"Did Gilbert ever speak to you," she wrote to me recently, "of the old Saturday night parties at Barnes, at the home of the grandparents—every Saturday night the family, or as many of it as could, used to go down to Barnes to supper, and the 'boys' and Tom Gilbert, Alice Chesterton's husband, used to sing round the supper table. Many a one I went to when I was stay-

* *Autobiography*, pp. 151-3.

ing at Warwick Gardens. We used to go on a red Hammersmith bus, before the days of motor cars."

On a longer trip they stayed at Berck in Belgium, and Cecil had a strange idea, apparently regarded by him as humorous, which measures the family absence of a Christian sense at this date. "Cecil urged me to sit at the foot of the big Crucifix in the village street and let him photograph me as Mary Magdalen! I *didn't,* and I don't know how he thought he'd get away with the modern clothing."

Whatever Gilbert's mother may have planned for them, neither she nor Gilbert had any romantic feeling for each other. Indeed Cecil was definitely her favourite and she believed him the favourite of both parents also. "He had more heart," she says, "than the more brilliant Gilbert." Anyhow, his heart was shown more openly to her.

"Cecil was not much given to versifying," she wrote in another letter, "he sent me the enclosed when my son was born. I value it so much." Headed "To Annie" the poem is a long one. It begins with the "ancient comradeship, loyal and unbroken" in which they had "first seen life together."

> Shining nights, tumultuous days,
> Joy swift caught in sudden ways,
> All the laughter, love and praise,
>   All the joys of living
>
> These we shared together dear,
>   Plot and jest and story,
> This is hid, shut off, unknown,
> Seeing that to you alone
> Is the wondrous Kingdom shown
>   And the power and Glory!

Annie's thoughts, then, and Cecil's were not greatly on the elder brother, who was pursuing his own romance with a heart that seems to have been fairly adequate in its energies.

Most mothers have watched their sons through one or more experiences of calf love: Gilbert indicates in the *Autobiography* —and I knew it, too, from some jokes he and Frances used to make—that he had had one or two fancies before the coming of Reality. He must then convince his mother that Reality had come: he must overcome a prejudice avowed by neither: he must call on the deeps of a mother's feelings so effectively that it would never now be avowed, that it might indeed be swept away.

And so, sitting at a table in a seaside lodging, as his mother sat in the same room or moved about making cocoa for the family, Gilbert tried to express what even for him was the inexpressible.

> 1 Rosebery Villas
> Granville Road
> Felixstowe.

MY DEAREST MOTHER,

You may possibly think this a somewhat eccentric proceeding. You are sitting opposite and talking—about Mrs. Berline. But I take this method of addressing you because it occurs to me that you might possibly wish to turn the matter over in your mind before writing or speaking to me about it.

I am going to tell you the whole of a situation in which I believe I have acted rightly, though I am not absolutely certain, and to ask for your advice on it. It was a somewhat complicated one, and I repeat that I do not think I could rightly have acted otherwise, but if I were the greatest fool in the three kingdoms and had made nothing but a mess of it, there is one person I should always turn to and trust. Mothers know more of their son's idiocies than other people can, and this has been peculiarly true in your case. I have always rejoiced at this, and not been ashamed of it: this has always been true and always will be. These things are easier written than said, but you know it is true, don't you?

I am inexpressibly anxious that you should give me credit for having done my best, and for having constantly had in mind the way in which you would be affected by the letter I am now writing. I do hope you will be pleased.

About eight years ago, you made a remark—this may show you

that if we "jeer" at your remarks, we remember them. The remark applied to the hypothetical young lady with whom I should fall in love and took the form of saying "If she is good, I shan't mind who she is." I don't know how many times I have said that over to myself in the last two or three days in which I have decided on this letter.

Do not be frightened; or suppose that anything sensational or final has occurred. I am not married, my dear mother, neither am I engaged. You are called to the council of chiefs very early in its deliberations. If you don't mind I will tell you, briefly, the whole story.

You are, I think, the shrewdest person for seeing things whom I ever knew: consequently I imagine that you do not think that I go down to Bedford Park every Sunday for the sake of the scenery. I should not wonder if you know nearly as much about the matter as I can tell in a letter. Suffice it to say however briefly (for neither of us care much for gushing: this letter is not on Mrs. Ratcliffe lines) that the first half of my time of acquaintance with the Bloggs was spent in enjoying a very intimate, but quite breezy and Platonic friendship with Frances Blogg, reading, talking and enjoying life together, having great sympathies on all subjects; and the second half in making the thrilling, but painfully responsible discovery that Platonism, on my side, had not the field by any means to itself. That is how we stand now. No one knows, except her family and yourself.

My dearest mother, I am sure you are at least not unsympathetic. Indeed we love each other more than we shall either of us ever be able to say. I have refrained from sentiment in this letter—for I don't think you like it much. But love is a very different thing from sentiment and you will never laugh at that. I will not say that you are sure to like Frances, for all young men say that to their mothers, quite naturally, and their mothers never believe them, also, quite naturally. Besides, I am so confident, I should like you to find her out for yourself. She is, in reality, very much the sort of woman you like, what is called, I believe, "a Woman's Woman," very humorous, inconsequent and sympathetic and defiled with no offensive exuberance of good health.

I have nothing more to say, except that you and she have occupied my mind for the last week to the exclusion of everything else, which must account for my abstraction, and that in her letter she sent the following message: "Please tell your mother soon. Tell her

I am not so silly as to expect her to think me good enough, but really I will try to be."

An aspiration which, considered from my point of view, naturally provokes a smile.

Here you give me a cup of cocoa. Thank you.

Believe me, my dearest mother,

Always your very affectionate son

GILBERT.

What exactly Gilbert meant by saying they were "not engaged" it is hard to surmise, in view of Frances's message to her future mother-in-law. Of his sensations when proposing Gilbert gives some idea in the *Autobiography*:

It was fortunate, however, that our next most important meeting was not under the sign of the moon but of the sun. She has often affirmed, during our later acquaintance, that if the sun had not been shining to her complete satisfaction on that day, the issue might have been quite different. It happened in St. James's Park; where they keep the ducks and the little bridge, which has been mentioned in no less authoritative a work than Mr. Belloc's Essay on Bridges, since I find myself quoting that author once more. I think he deals in some detail, in his best topographical manner, with various historic sites on the Continent; but later relapses into a larger manner, somewhat thus: "The time has now come to talk at large about Bridges. The longest bridge in the world is the Forth Bridge, and the shortest bridge in the world is a plank over a ditch in the village of Loudwater. The bridge that frightens you most is the Brooklyn Bridge, and the bridge that frightens you least is the bridge in St. James's Park." I admit that I crossed that bridge in undeserved safety; and perhaps I was affected by my early romantic vision of the bridge leading to the princess's tower. But I can assure my friend the author that the bridge in St. James's Park can frighten you a good deal.*

Now, with Frances promised to him, Gilbert could enjoy everything properly, could execute, verbally at least, a wild fantasia. Among the first of his friends to be written to was Mildred Wain, because, as he says in a later letter, he felt towards her

* *Autobiography*, pp. 154-5.

deep gratitude "for forming a topic of conversation on my first visit to a family with which I have since formed a dark and shameful connection."

DEAR MILDRED,

On rising this morning, I carefully washed my boots in hot water and blacked my face. Then assuming my coat with graceful ease and with the tails in front, I descended to breakfast, where I gaily poured the coffee on the sardines and put my hat on the fire to boil. These activities will give you some idea of my frame of mind. My family, observing me leave the house by way of the chimney, and take the fender with me under one arm, thought I must have something on my mind. So I had.

My friend, I am engaged. I am only telling it at present to my real friends: but there is no doubt about it. The next question that arises is—whom am I engaged to? I have investigated this problem with some care, and, as far as I can make out, the best authorities point to Frances Blogg. There can I think be no reasonable doubt that she is the lady. It is as well to have these minor matters clear in one's mind.

I am very much too happy to write much; but I thought you might remember my existence sufficiently to be interested in the incident.

Waldo has been of so much help to me in this and in everything, and I am so much interested in you for his sake and your own, that I am encouraged to hope our friendship may subsist. If ever I have done anything rude or silly, it was quite inadvertent. I have always wished to please you.

To Annie Firmin he wrote:

I can only think of the day, one of the earliest I can recall of my life, when you came in and helped me to build a house with bricks. I am building another one now, and it would not have been complete without your going over it.

To others he wrote such sentences as he could put together in the whirlwind of his happiness. For himself he stammered in a verse that grew with the years into his great love poetry.

God made thee mightily, my love,
He stretched his hands out of his rest
And lit the star of east and west
Brooding o'er darkness like a dove.
God made thee mightily, my love.

God made thee patiently, my sweet,
Out of all stars he chose a star
He made it red with sunset bar
And green with greeting for thy feet.
God made thee mightily, my sweet.

Chapter VIII

To Frances

THIS CHAPTER CAN be written only by Gilbert himself. It might seem that he had no words left for an emotion heightened beyond the love of his friends and the joyous acceptance of existence. But in these letters he shows the truth of his own theory, that to love each thing separately strengthens the power of loving, to have tried to love everyone is, as he tells Frances, no bad preparation for loving her. The emotion of falling in love had both intensified his appreciation of all things and cast for him a vivid light on past, present and future, so that in the last of these letters he sketches his life down to the moment when a new life begins.

". . . I am looking over the sea and endeavouring to reckon up the estate I have to offer you. As far as I can make out my equipment for starting on a journey to fairyland consists of the following items.

"1st. A Straw Hat. The oldest part of this admirable relic shows traces of pure Norman work. The vandalism of Cromwell's soldiers has left us little of the original hat-band.

"2nd. A Walking Stick, very knobby and heavy: admirably fitted to break the head of any denizen of Suffolk who denies that you are the noblest of ladies, but of no other manifest use.

"3rd. A copy of Walt Whitman's poems, once nearly given to Salter, but quite forgotten. It has his name in it still with an affectionate inscription from his sincere friend Gilbert Chesterton. I wonder if he will ever have it.

"4th. A number of letters from a young lady, containing everything good and generous and loyal and holy and wise that isn't in Walt Whitman's poems.

"5th. An unwieldy sort of a pocket knife, the blades mostly having an edge of a more varied and picturesque outline than is provided by the prosaic cutler. The chief element however is a thing 'to take stones out of a horse's hoof.' What a beautiful sensation of security it gives one to reflect that if one should ever have money enough to buy a horse and should happen to buy one and the horse should happen to have a stone in his hoof—that one is ready; one stands prepared, with a defiant smile!

"6th. Passing from the last miracle of practical foresight, we come to a box of matches. Every now and then I strike one of these, because fire is beautiful and burns your fingers. Some people think this waste of matches: the same people who object to the building of Cathedrals.

"7th. About three pounds in gold and silver, the remains of one of Mr. Unwin's bursts of affection: those explosions of spontaneous love for myself, which, such is the perfect order and harmony of his mind, occur at startlingly exact intervals of time.

"8th. A book of Children's Rhymes, in manuscript, called the 'Weather Book' about ¾ finished, and destined for Mr. Nutt.* I have been working at it fairly steadily, which I think jolly creditable under the circumstances. One can't put anything interesting in it. They'll understand those things when they grow up.

"9th. A tennis racket—nay, start not. It is a part of the new régime, and the only new and neat-looking thing in the Museum. We'll soon mellow it—like the straw hat. My brother and I are teaching each other lawn tennis.

"10th. A soul, hitherto idle and omnivorous but now happy enough to be ashamed of itself.

* *Greybeards at Play.*

"11th. A body, equally idle and quite equally omnivorous, absorbing tea, coffee, claret, sea-water and oxygen to its own perfect satisfaction. It is happiest swimming, I think, the sea being about a convenient size.

"12th. A Heart—mislaid somewhere. And that is about all the property of which an inventory can be made at present. After all, my tastes are stoically simple. A straw hat, a stick, a box of matches and some of his own poetry. What more does man require? . . ."

". . . The City of Felixstowe, as seen by the local prophet from the neighbouring mountain-peak, does not strike the eye as having anything uncanny about it. At least I imagine that it requires rather careful scrutiny before the eerie curl of a chimney pot, or the elfin wink of a lonely lamp-post brings home to the startled soul that it is really the City of a Fearful Folk. That the inhabitants are not human in the ordinary sense is quite clear, yet it has only just begun to dawn on me after staying a week in the Town of Unreason with its monstrous landscape and grave, unmeaning customs. Do I seem to be raving? Let me give my experiences.

"I am bound to admit that I do not think I am good at shopping. I generally succeed in getting rid of money, but other observances, such as bringing away the goods that I've paid for, and knowing what I've bought, I often pass over as secondary. But to shop in a town of ordinary tradesmen is one thing: to shop in a town of raving lunatics is another. I set out one morning, happy and hopeful with the intention of buying (a) a tennis racket (b) some tennis balls (c) some tennis shoes (d) a ticket for a tennis ground. I went to the shop pointed out by some villager (probably mad) and went in and said I believed they kept tennis rackets. The young man smiled and assented. I suggested that he might show me some. The young man looked positively alarmed. 'Oh,' he said, 'We haven't got any—not got

any here.' I asked 'Where?' 'Oh, they're out you know. All
round,' he explained wildly, with a graphic gesture in the direction of the sea and the sky. 'All out round. We've left them all
round at places.' To this day I don't know what he meant, but
I merely asked when they would quit these weird retreats. He
said in an hour: in an hour I called again. Were they in now?
'Well not in—not *in,* just yet,' he said with a sort of feverish
confidentialness, as if he wasn't quite well. 'Are they still—all
out at places?' I asked with restrained humour. 'Oh no!' he said
with a burst of reassuring pride. 'They are only out there—out
behind, you know.' I hope my face expressed my beaming comprehension of the spot alluded to. Eventually, at a third visit, the
rackets were produced. None of them, I was told by my brother,
were of any first-class maker, so that was outside the question.
The choice was between some good, neat first-hand instruments
which suited me, and some seedy-looking second-hand objects
with plain deal handles, which would have done at a pinch. I
thought that perhaps it would be better to get a good-class
racket in London and content myself for the present with econ-
omising on one of these second-hand monuments of depression.
So I asked the price. '10/6' was the price of the second-hand
article. I thought this large for the tool, and wondered if the
first-hand rackets were much dearer. What price the first-hand?
'7/6' said the Creature, cheery as a bird. I did not faint. I am
strong.

"I rejected the article which was dearer because it had been
hallowed by human possession, and accepted the cheap, new
crude racket. Except the newness there was no difference between them whatever. I then asked the smiling Maniac for
balls. He brought me a selection of large red globes nearly as big
as Dutch cheeses. I said, 'Are these tennis-balls?' He said, 'Oh
did you want tennis-balls?' I said Yes—they often came in handy
at tennis. The goblin was however quite impervious to satire,
and I left him endeavouring to draw my attention to his wares

in general, particularly to some zinc baths which he seemed to think should form part of the equipment of a tennis-player.

"Never before or since have I met a being of that order and degree of creepiness. He was a nightmare of unmeaning idiocy. But some mention ought to be made of the old man at the entrance to the tennis ground who opened his mouth in parables on the subject of the fee for playing there. He seemed to have been wound up to make only one remark, 'It's sixpence.' Under these circumstances the attempt to discover whether the sixpence covered a day's tennis or a week or fifty years was rather baffling. At last I put down the sixpence. This seemed to galvanise him into life. He looked at the clock, which was indicating five past eleven and said, 'It's sixpence an hour—so you'll be all right till two.' I fled screaming.

"Since then I have examined the town more carefully and feel the presence of something nameless. There is a claw-curl in the sea-bent trees, an eye-gleam in the dark flints in the wall that is not of this world.

"When we set up a house, darling (honeysuckle porch, yew clipt hedge, bees, poetry and eight shillings a week), I think you will have to do the shopping. Particularly at Felixstowe. There was a great and glorious man who said, 'Give us the luxuries of life and we will dispense with the necessities.' That I think would be a splendid motto to write (in letters of brown gold) over the porch of our hypothetical home. There will be a sofa for you, for example, but no chairs, for I prefer the floor. There will be a select store of chocolate-creams (to make you do the Carp with) and the rest will be bread and water. We will each retain a suit of evening dress for great occasions, and at other times clothe ourselves in the skins of wild beasts (how pretty you would look) which would fit your taste in furs and be economical.

"I have sometimes thought it would be very fine to take an ordinary house, a very poor, commonplace house in West Ken-

sington, say, and make it symbolic. Not artistic—Heaven—O
Heaven forbid. My blood boils when I think of the affronts put
by knock-kneed pictorial epicures on the strong, honest, ugly,
patient shapes of necessary things: the brave old bones of life.
There are aesthetic pottering prigs who can look on a saucepan
without one tear of joy or sadness: mongrel decadents that can
see no dignity in the honourable scars of a kettle. So they concentrate all their house decoration on coloured windows that
nobody looks out of, and vases of lilies that everybody wishes
out of the way. No: my idea (which is much cheaper) is to
make a house really *allegoric*: really explain its own essential
meaning. Mystical or ancient sayings should be inscribed on
every object, the more prosaic the object the better; and the
more coarsely and rudely the inscription was traced the better.
'Hast thou sent the Rain upon the Earth?' should be inscribed
on the Umbrella-Stand: perhaps on the Umbrella. 'Even the
Hairs of your Head are all numbered' would give a tremendous
significance to one's hairbrushes: the words about 'living water'
would reveal the music and sanctity of the sink: while 'Our God
is a consuming Fire' might be written over the kitchen-grate, to
assist the mystic musings of the cook—Shall we ever try that
experiment, dearest. Perhaps not, for no words would be golden
enough for the tools you had to touch: you would be beauty
enough for one house. . . ."

". . . By all means let us have bad things in our dwelling
and make them good things. I shall offer no objection to your
having an occasional dragon to dinner, or a penitent Griffin to
sleep in the spare bed. The image of you taking a sunday school
of little Devils is pleasing. They will look up, first in savage
wonder, then in vague respect; they will see the most glorious
and noble lady that ever lived since their prince tempted Eve,
with a halo of hair and great heavenly eyes that seem to make the
good at the heart of things almost too terribly simple and naked

for the sons of flesh: and as they gaze, their tails will drop off, and their wings will sprout: and they will become Angels in six lessons. . . .

"I cannot profess to offer any elaborate explanation of your mother's disquiet but I admit it does not wholly surprise me. You see I happen to know one factor in the case, and one only, of which you are wholly ignorant. I know you . . . I know one thing which has made me feel strange before your mother—I know the value of what I take away. I feel (in a weird moment) like the Angel of Death.

"You say you want to talk to me about death: my views about death are bright, brisk and entertaining. When Azrael takes a soul it may be to other and brighter worlds: like those whither you and I go together. The transformation called Death may be something as beautiful and dazzling as the transformation called Love. It may make the dead man 'happy,' just as your mother knows that you are happy. But none the less it is a transformation, and sad sometimes for those left behind. A mother whose child is dying can hardly believe that in the inscrutable Unknown there is anyone who can look to it as well as she. And if a mother cannot trust her child easily to God Almighty, shall I be so mean as to be angry because she cannot trust it easily to me? I tell you I have stood before your mother and felt like a thief. I know you are not going to part: neither physically, mentally, morally nor spiritually. But she sees a new element in your life, wholly from outside—is it not natural, given her temperament, that you should find her perturbed? Oh, dearest, dearest Frances, let us always be very gentle to older people. Indeed, darling, it is not they who are the tyrants, but we. They may interrupt our building in the scaffolding stages: we turn their house upside down when it is their final home and rest. Your mother would certainly have worried if you had been engaged to the Archangel Michael (who, indeed, is bearing his disappointment very well): how much more when you are engaged to an aimless, tactless, reckless, unbrushed, strange-hatted, opinionated scarecrow who has suddenly walked into the vacant place. I could have prophesied her unrest: wait and she will calm down all right, dear. God comfort her: I dare not. . . ."

". . . Gilbert Keith Chesterton was born of comfortable but honest parents on the top of Campden Hill, Kensington. He was christened at St. George's Church which stands just under that more imposing building, the Waterworks Tower. This place was chosen, apparently, in order that the whole available water supply might be used in the intrepid attempt to make him a member of Christ, a child of God and an inheritor of the Kingdom of Heaven.

"Of the early years of this remarkable man few traces remain. One of his earliest recorded observations was the simple exclamation, full of heart-felt delight, 'Look at Baby. Funny Baby.' Here we see the first hint of that ineffable conversational modesty, that shy social self-effacement, which has ever hidden his light under a bushel. His mother also recounts with apparent amusement an incident connected with his imperious demand for his father's top-hat. 'Give me that hat, please.' 'No, dear, you mustn't have that.' 'Give me that hat.' 'No, dear—' 'If you don't give it me, I'll say 'At.' An exquisite selection in the matter of hats has indeed always been one of the great man's hobbies.

"When he had drawn pictures on all the blinds and table-cloths and towels and walls and windowpanes it was felt that he required a larger sphere. Consequently he was sent to Mr. Bewsher who gave him desks and copy-books and Latin grammars and atlases to draw pictures on. He was far too innately conscientious not to use these materials to draw on. To other uses, asserted by some to belong to these objects, he paid little heed. The only really curious thing about his school life was that he had a weird and quite involuntary habit of getting French prizes.

They were the only ones he ever got and he never tried to get them. But though the thing was quite mysterious to him, and though he made every effort to avoid it, it went on, being evidently a part of some occult natural law.

"For the first half of his time at school he was very solitary and futile. He never regretted the time, for it gave him two things, complete mental self-sufficiency and a comprehension of the psychology of outcasts.

"But one day, as he was roaming about a great naked building land which he haunted in play hours, rather like an outlaw in the woods, he met a curious agile youth with hair brushed up off his head. Seeing each other, they promptly hit each other simultaneously and had a fight. Next day they met again and fought again. These Homeric conflicts went on for many days, till one morning in the crisis of some insane grapple, the subject of this biography quoted, like a war-chant, something out of Macaulay's Lays. The other started and relaxed his hold. They gazed at each other. Then the foe quoted the following line. In this land of savages they knew each other. For the next two hours they talked books. They have talked books ever since. The boy was Edmund Clerihew Bentley. The incident just narrated is the true and real account of the first and deepest of our hero's male connections. But another was to ensue, probably equally profound and far more pregnant with awful and dazzling consequences. Bentley always had a habit of trying to do things well: twelve years of the other's friendship has not cured him of this. Being seized with a peculiar desire to learn conjuring, he had made the acquaintance of an eerie and supernatural young man, who instructed him in the Black Art: a gaunt Mephistophelian sort of individual, who our subject half thought was a changeling. Our subject has not quite got over the idea yet, though for practical social purposes he calls him Lucian Oldershaw. Our subject met Lucian Oldershaw. 'That night,' as Shakespeare says, 'there was a star.'

"These three persons soon became known through the length and breadth of St. Paul's School as the founders of a singular brotherhood. It was called the J.D.C. No one, we believe, could ever have had better friends than did the hero of this narrative. We wish that we could bring before the reader the personality of all the Knights of that eccentric round table. Most of them are known already to the reader. Even the subject himself is possibly known to the reader. Bertram, who seemed somehow to have been painted by Vandyck, a sombre and stately young man, a blend of Cavalier and Puritan, with the physique of a military father and the views of an ethical mother and a soul of his own which for sheer simplicity is something staggering. Vernède with an Oriental and inscrutable placidity varied every now and then with dazzling agility and Meredithian humour. Waldo d'Avigdor who masks with complete fashionable triviality a Hebraic immutability of passion tried in a more ironical and bitter service than his Father Jacob. Lawrence and Maurice Solomon, who show another side of the same people, the love of home, the love of children, the meek and malicious humour, the tranquil service of a law. Salter who shows how beautiful and ridiculous a combination can be made of the most elaborate mental cultivation and artistic sensibility and omniscience with a receptiveness and a humility extraordinary in any man. These were his friends. May he be forgiven for speaking of them at length and with pride? Some day we hope the reader may know them all. He knew these people; he knew their friends. He heard Mildred Wain say 'Blogg' and he thought it was a funny name. Had he been told that he would ever pronounce it with the accents of tears and passion he would have said, in his pride, that the name was not suitable for that purpose. But there are οὐκ ἐφ' ἡμῖν. . . .

"He went for a time to an Art School. There he met a great many curious people. Many of the men were horrible blackguards: he was not exactly that: so they naturally found each other interesting. He went through some rather appalling discoveries about human life and the final discovery was that there is no Devil—no, not even such a thing as a bad man.

"One pleasant Saturday afternoon Lucian said to him, 'I am going to take you to see the Bloggs.' 'The what?' said the unhappy man. 'The Bloggs,' said the other, darkly. Naturally assuming that it was the name of a public-house he reluctantly followed his friend. He came to a small front-garden; if it was a public-house it was not a businesslike one. They raised the latch—they rang the bell (if the bell was not in the close time just then). No flower in the pots winked. No brick grinned. No sign in Heaven or earth warned him. The birds sang on in the trees. He went in.

"The first time he spent an evening at the Bloggs there was no one there. That is to say there was a worn but fiery little lady in a grey dress who didn't approve of 'catastrophic solutions of social problems.' That, he understood, was Mrs. Blogg. There was a long, blonde, smiling young person who seemed to think him quite off his head and who was addressed as Ethel. There were two people whose meaning and status he couldn't imagine, one of whom had a big nose and the other hadn't. . . . Lastly, there was a Juno-like creature in a tremendous hat who eyed him all the time half wildly, like a shying horse, because he said he was quite happy. . . .

"But the second time he went there he was plumped down on a sofa beside a being of whom he had a vague impression that brown hair grew at intervals all down her like a caterpillar. Once in the course of conversation she looked straight at him and he said to himself as plainly as if he had read it in a book: 'If I had anything to do with this girl I should go on my knees to her: if I spoke with her she would never deceive me: if I depended on her she would never deny me: if I loved her she would never play with me: if I trusted her she would never go back on me: if I remembered her she would never forget me. I may never see her again. Goodbye.' It was all said in a flash: but it was all said. . . .

"Two years, as they say in the playbills, is supposed to elapse. And here is the subject of this memoir sitting on a balcony above the sea. The time, evening. He is thinking of the whole bewildering record of which the foregoing is a brief outline: he sees how far he has gone wrong and how idle and wasteful and wicked he has often been: how miserably unfitted he is for what he is called upon to be. Let him now declare it and hereafter for ever hold his peace.

"But there are four lamps of thanksgiving always before him. The first is for his creation out of the same earth with such a woman as you. The second is that he has not, with all his faults, 'gone after strange women.' You cannot think how a man's self-restraint is rewarded in this. The third is that he has tried to love everything alive: a dim preparation for loving you. And the fourth is—but no words can express that. Here ends my previous existence. Take it: it led me to you."

Chapter IX

A Long Engagement

GILBERT SYMPATHISED WITH his future mother-in-law's anxiety at Frances's engagement to "a self-opinionated scarecrow," but I doubt if it at all quickly occurred to him that the basis of that anxiety was the fact that he was earning only twenty-five shillings a week! Frances herself, Lucian Oldershaw, and the rest of his friends believed he was a genius with a great future and this belief they tried to communicate to Frances's family. But even if they succeeded, faith in the future did not pay dividends in a present income on which to set up house. A widow, considering her daughter's future, might well feel a little anxiety. But one can see wheels within wheels of family conclaves and matters to perplex the simple which drew another letter from Gilbert to Frances:

. . . It is a mystic and refreshing thought that I shall never understand Bloggs.

That is the truth of it . . . that this remarkable family atmosphere . . . this temperament with its changing moods and its everlasting will, its divine trust in one's soul and its tremulous speculations as to one's "future," its sensitiveness like a tempered sword, vibrating but never broken: its patience that can wait for Eternity and its impatience that cannot wait for tea: its power of bearing huge calamities, and its queer little moods that even those calamities can never overshadow or wipe out: its brusqueness that always pleases and its over-tactfulness that sometimes wounds: its terrific intensity of feeling, that sometimes paralyses the outsider with conversational responsibility: its untranslatable humour of courage and poverty and its unfathomed epics of past tragedy and triumph—all this glorious confusion of family traits, which, in no exaggerative sense, make the Gentiles come to your light and the folk of the nations to the brightness of your house—is a thing so utterly outside my own temperament that I was formed by nature to admire and not understand it. God made me very simply—as he made a tree or a pig or an oyster: to perform certain functions. The best thing he gave me was a perfect and unshakable trust in those I love. . . .

Gilbert's sympathy with his future mother-in-law may have been put to some slight strain by an incident related by Lucian Oldershaw. Mrs. Blogg begged him to talk to Gilbert about his personal appearance—clothes and such matters—and to entreat him to make an effort to improve it. One can imagine how much he must have disliked the commission! Anyhow, he decided it would be better to do it away from home and he suggested to Gilbert a trip to the seaside. Arrived there he broached the subject. Gilbert, he says, was not the least angry, but answered quite seriously that Frances loved him as he was and that it would be absurd for him to try to alter. It was only out of a later and deeper experience of women that he was able to write "A man's friends like him but they leave him as he is. A man's wife loves him and is always trying to change him."

A good many things happened in the course of this long engagement. Frances and Gilbert were both young and long engagements were normal at that period, when the idea of a wife continuing to earn after marriage was unheard of. There were obvious disadvantages in the long delay before marriage but also certain advantages. The two got to know each other with a close intimacy: they were comrades as well as lovers and carried both these relationships into married life. For the biographer the advantage has been immense, since every separation between the pair meant a batch of letters. The discerning will have noted that there are in these letters considerable excisions: parts Frances would not show even to the biographer. But they are the richest quarry from which to dig for the most important period of any man's life: the period richest in mental development and the shaping of character. It is, too, the only period of his adult life when Gilbert wrote letters at all, unless they were absolutely unavoidable.

Even in a small family two members will tend to draw together more closely than the rest, and this was so with Frances and her sister Gertrude. They adored one another and Frances offered her to Gilbert as a sister, with especially confident pride. He had never had a sister since babyhood and he enjoyed it. The happiness of the engagement was terribly broken into by the sudden death of Gertrude in a street accident. Frances was absolutely shattered. The next group of letters belongs to the months after Gertrude's death, when Gilbert was still trying to be a publisher, but, urged on by Frances, beginning also to be a writer. During part of this time she had gone abroad for rest and recovery after the shock. Gilbert pictures her reading his letters "under the shadow of an alien cathedral."

None of these letters are dated but most of them have kept their postmarks.

11, Paternoster Buildings
(postmarked July 8, 1899)

. . . I am black but comely at this moment: because the cyclostyle has blacked me. Fear not. I shall wash myself. But I think it my duty to render an accurate account of my physical appearance every time I write: and shall be glad of any advice and assistance. . . .

I have been reading Lewis Carroll's remains, mostly Logic, and have much pleasure in enlivening you with the following hilarious query: "Can a Hypothetical, whose protasis is false, be legitimate? Are two Hypotheticals of the forms, *If A, then B,* and *If A then not B* compatible?" I should think a Hypothetical could be, if it tried hard. . . .

To return to the Cyclostyle. I like the Cyclostyle ink; it is so inky. I do not think there is anyone who takes quite such a fierce pleasure in things being themselves as I do. The startling wetness of water excites and intoxicates me: the fieriness of fire, the steeliness of steel,

the unutterable muddiness of mud. It is just the same with people.
. . . When we call a man "manly" or a woman "womanly" we
touch the deepest philosophy.

I will not ask you to forgive this rambling levity. I, for one have
sworn, I do not hesitate to say it, by the sword of God that has struck
us, and before the beautiful face of the dead, that the first joke that
occurred to me I would make, the first nonsense poem I thought of I
would write, that I would begin again *at once* with a heavy heart at
times, as to other duties, to the duty of being perfectly silly, perfectly extravagant, perfectly trivial, and as far as possible, amusing.
I have sworn that Gertrude should *not* feel, wherever she is, that
the comedy has gone out of our theatre. This, I am well aware, will
be misunderstood. But I have long grasped that whatever we do we
are misunderstood—small blame to other people; for, we know ourselves, our best motives are things we could neither explain nor defend. And I would rather hurt those who can shout than her who is
silent.

You might tell me what you feel about this: but I am myself
absolutely convinced that gaiety that is the bubble of love, does not
annoy me: the old round of stories, laughter, family ceremonies,
seems to me far less really inappropriate than a single moment of
forced silence or unmanly shame. . . .

I have always imagined Frances did not know of her mother's
efforts to tidy Gilbert, but very early in their engagement she
began her own abortive attempts to make him brush his hair, tie
his tie straight and avoid made-up ones, attend to the buttons
on his coat, and all the rest. It would seem that for a time at
any rate he made some efforts, but evidently simply regarded
the whole thing as one huge joke.

11 Warwick Gardens
(Postmarked July 9th, 1899)

. . . I am clean. I am wearing a frockcoat, which from a superficial survey seems to have no end of buttons. It must be admitted
that I am wearing a bow-tie: but on careful research I find that these
were constantly worn by Vikings. A distinct allusion to them is made
in that fine fragment, the Tryggvhessa Saga, where the poet says, in
the short alliterative lines of Early Norse poetry:

> Frockcoat Folding then
> Hakon Hardrada
> Bow-tie Buckled
> Waited for war

(Brit. Mus. Mss. CCCLXIX lines 99981–99985)

I resume. My appearance, as I have suggested, is singularly exemplary. My boots are placed, after the fastidious London fashion, on the feet: the laces are done up, the watch is going, the hair is brushed, the sleeve-links are inserted, for of such is the Kingdom of Heaven. As for my straw hat, I put it on eighteen times consecutively, taking a run and a jump to each try, till at last I hit the right angle. I have not taken it off for three days and nights lest I should disturb that exquisite pose. Ladies, princes, queens, ecclesiastical processions go by in vain: I do not remove it. That angle of the hat is something to mount guard over. As Swinburne says—"Not twice on earth do the gods do this."

It is at present what is, I believe, called a lovely summer's night. To say that it is hot would be as feeble a platitude as the same remark would be in the small talk of Satan and Beelzebub.

If there were such a thing as *blue*-hot iron, it would describe the sky tonight. I cannot help dreaming of some wild fairy-tale in which the whole round cosmos should be a boiling pot, with the flames of Purgatory under it, and that soon I shall have the satisfaction of seeing such a thing as boiled mountains, boiled cities, and a boiled moon and stars. A tremendous picture. Yet I am perfectly happy as usual. After all, why should we object to be boiled? Potatoes, for example, are better boiled than raw—why should we fear to be boiled into new shapes in the cauldron? These things are an allegory.

. . . I am so glad to hear you say . . . that, in your own words "it is good for us to be here"—where you are at present. The same remark, if I remember right, was made on the mountain of the Transfiguration. It has always been one of my unclerical sermons to myself, that that remark which Peter made on seeing the vision of a single hour, ought to be made by us all, in contemplating every panoramic change in the long Vision we call life—other things superficially, but this always in our depths. "It is good for us to be here— it is good for us to be here," repeating itself eternally. And if, after many joys and festivals and frivolities, it should be our fate to have

to look on while one of us is, in a most awful sense of the words,
"transfigured before our eyes": shining with the whiteness of death—
at least, I think, we cannot easily fancy ourselves wishing not to be
at our post. Not I, certainly. It was good for me to be there.

*   *   *   *

11 Warwick Gardens
(postmarked July 11, 1899.)

. . . The novel, after which you so kindly enquire, is proceeding
headlong. It received another indirect stimulus today, when Mr.
Garnett insisted on taking me out to lunch, gave me a gorgeous re-
past at a restaurant, succeeded in plucking the secret of my private
employment from my bosom, and made me promise to send him
some chapters of it. I certainly cannot complain of not being sym-
pathetically treated by the literary men I know. I wonder where the
jealous, spiteful, depreciating man of letters we read of in books has
got to. It's about time he turned up, I think. Excuse me for talking
about these trivialities. . . .

I have made a discovery: or I should say seen a vision. I saw it
between two cups of black coffee in a Gallic restaurant in Soho: but
I could not express it if I tried.

But this was one thing that it said—that all good things are one
thing. There is no conflict between the gravestone of Gertrude and
a comic-opera tune played by Mildred Wain. But there is everlasting conflict between the gravestone of Gertrude and the obscene
pomposity of the hired mute: and there is everlasting conflict between the comic-opera tune and any mean or vulgar words to which
it may be set. These, which man hath joined together, God shall
most surely sunder. That is what I am feeling . . . now every hour
of the day. All good things are one thing. Sunsets, schools of philosophy, babies, constellations, cathedrals, operas, mountains, horses,
poems—all these are merely disguises. One thing is always walking
among us in fancy-dress, in the grey cloak of a church or the green
cloak of a meadow. He is always behind, His form makes the folds
fall so superbly. And that is what the savage old Hebrews, alone
among the nations, guessed, and why their rude tribal god has been
erected on the ruins of all polytheistic civilisations. For the Greeks
and Norsemen and Romans saw the superficial wars of nature and

made the sun one god, the sea another, the wind a third. They were not thrilled, as some rude Israelite was, one night in the wastes, alone, by the sudden blazing idea of all being the same God: an idea worthy of a detective story.

> 11, Paternoster Buildings
> (postmarked July 14, 1899.)

. . . costume slightly improved. The truth is that a mystical and fantastic development has taken place. My clothes have rebelled against me. Weary of scorn and neglect, they have all suddenly come to life and they dress me by force every morning. My frockcoat leaps upon me like a lion and hangs on, dragging me down. As I struggle my boots trip me up—and the laces climb up my feet (never missing a hole) like snakes or creepers. At the same moment the celebrated grey tie springs at my throat like a wild cat.

I am told that the general effects produced by this remarkable psychical development are superb. Really the clothes must know best. Still it is awkward when a mackintosh pursues one down the street. . . .

. . . There is nothing in God's earth that really expresses the bottom of the nature of a man in love except Burns' songs. To the man not in love they must seem inexplicably simple. When he says, "My love is like the melody that's sweetly played in tune," it seems almost a crude way of referring to music. But a man in love with a woman feels a nerve move suddenly that Dante groped for and Shakespeare hardly touched. What made me think of Burns, however, was that one of his simple and sudden things, hitting the right nail so that it rings, occurs in the song of "O a' the airts the wind can blaw," where he merely says that there is nothing beautiful anywhere but it makes him think of the woman. That is not really a mere aesthetic fancy, a chain of sentimental association—it is an actual instinctive elemental movement of the mind, performed automatically and instantly. . . .

> Felixstowe (undated)

. . . I have as you see, arrived here. I have done other daring things, such as having my hair shampooed, as you commanded, and also cut. The effect of this is so singularly horrible that I have found further existence in London impossible. Public opinion is too strong for me. . . . There are many other reasons I could give for being

pleased to come: such as that I have some time for writing the novel;
that I can make up stories I don't intend to write . . . that there
are phosphorescent colours on the sea and a box of cigarettes on the
mantelpiece.

Some fragments of what I felt [about Gertrude's death] have struggled out in the form of some verses which I am writing out for you.
But for real strength (I don't like the word "comfort") for real peace,
no human words are much good except perhaps some of the unfathomable, unintelligible, unconquerable epigrams of the Bible. I
remember when Bentley had a burning boyish admiration for Professor Huxley, and when that scientist died some foolish friend
asked him quite flippantly in a letter what he felt about it. Bentley
replied with the chapter and verse reference to one of the Psalms,
alone on a postcard. The text was, "Precious in the sight of the Lord
is the death of one of his saints." The friend, I remember, thought
it "a curious remark about Huxley." It strikes me as a miraculous
remark about anybody. It is one of those magic sayings where every
word hits a chain of association, God knows how.

"Precious"—we could not say that Gertrude's death is happy or
providential or sweet or even perhaps good. But it is something.
"Beautiful" is a good word—but "precious" is the only right word.

It is this passionate sense of the *value* of things: of the richness
of the cosmic treasure: the world where every star is a diamond,
every leaf an emerald, every drop of blood a ruby, it is this sense of
preciousness that *is* really awakened by the death of His saints.
Somehow we feel that even their death is a thing of incalculable
value and mysterious sweetness: it is awful, tragic, desolating, desperately hard to bear—but still "precious." . . . Forgive the verbosity
of one whose trade it is to express the inexpressible.

The verses he speaks of in this letter, Frances treasured
greatly. She showed them to me, in a book which opens with a
very touching prayer in her own writing. In a later chapter I
quote the lines in which Gilbert writes of his own tone-deafness,
and of how he *saw* what music meant as he watched his wife's
face. Something of the same effect is produced on me by these
verses. Gilbert was not of course tone-deaf to this tragedy, yet
it was chiefly in its effect on Frances that it affected him.

> The sudden sorrow smote my love
> That often falls twixt kiss and kiss
> And looking forth awhile she said
> Can no man tell me where she is.

And again

> Stricken they sat: and through them moved
> My own dear lady, pale and sweet.
>
> This soul whose clearness makes afraid
> Our souls: this wholly guiltless one—
> No cobweb doubts—no passion smoke
> Have veiled this mirror from Thy sun.

In letters to Frances he could enter so deeply into her grief as to make it his own. But when he wrote verse and spoke as it were to himself or to God, the reflected emotion was not enough. These verses could never rank with his real poetry.

It was not possible in fact for a man so happily in love to dwell lastingly on any sorrow. And I cannot avoid the feeling that, quite apart from any theory, cheerfulness was constantly "breaking in." For Gilbert was a very happy man. Across the top of one of his letters is written: "You can always tell the real love from the slight by the fact that the latter weakens at the moment of success; the former is quadrupled."

The next of his letters is a mingling of the comic and the fantastic, very special to G.K.C.

> 11, Paternoster Buildings
> (postmarked Sept. 29, 1899.)

. . . I fear, as you say, that my letters do not contain many practical details about myself: the letters are not very long to begin with, as I think it better to write something every day than a long letter when I have leisure: and when I have a little time to think in, I always think of the Kosmos first and the Ego afterwards. I admit, however, that you are not engaged to the Kosmos: dear me! what a time the Kosmos would have! All its Comets would have their hair brushed every morning. The Whirlwind would be adjured not to walk about when it was talking. The Oceans would be warmed with hot-water pipes. Not even the lowest forms of life would escape the crusade of tidiness: you would walk round and round the jellyfish, looking for a place to put in shirt-links.

Under these circumstances, then, I cannot but regard it as fortunate that you are only engaged to your obedient Microcosm: a biped inheriting some of the traits of his mother, the Kosmos, its untidiness, its largeness, its irritating imperfection and its profound and hearty intention to go on existing as long as it possibly can.

I can understand what you mean about wanting details about me, for I want just the same about you. You need only tell me "I went down the street to a pillar-box," I shall know that you did it in a manner, blindingly, staggeringly, crazily beautiful. It is quite true, as you say, that I am a person wearing *certain* clothes with a *certain* kind of hair. I cannot get rid of the impression that there is something scorchingly sarcastic about the underlining in this passage. . . .

. . . as to what I do every day: it depends on which way you want it narrated: what we all say it is, or what it really is.

What we all say happens every day is this: I wake up: dress myself, eat bacon and bread and coffee for breakfast: walk up to High St. Station, take a fourpenny ticket for Blackfriars, read the Chronicle in the train, arrive at 11, Paternoster Buildings: read a MS called "The Lepers" (light comedy reading) and another called "The Preparation of Ryerson Embury"—you know the style—till 2 o'clock. Go out to lunch, have—(but here perhaps it would be safer to become vague), come back, work till six, take my hat and walking-stick and come home: have dinner at home, write the Novel till 11, then write to you and go to bed. That is what, we in our dreamy, deluded way, really imagine is the thing that happens. What really happens (but hist! are we observed?) is as follows.

Out of the starless night of the Uncreated, that was before the stars, a soul begins to grope back to light. It gropes its way through strange, half-lighted chambers of Dreams, where in a brown and gold twilight, it sees many things that are dimly significant, true stories twisted into new and amazing shapes, human beings whom it knew long ago, sitting at the windows by dark sunsets, or talking in dim meadows. But the awful invading Light grows stronger in the dreams, till the soul in one last struggle, plunges into a body, as into a house and wakes up within it. Then he rises and finds himself in a wonderful vast world of white light and clear, frankly coloured shapes, an inheritor of a million stars. On enquiry he is informed that his name is Gilbert Keith Chesterton. This amuses him.

He goes through a number of extraordinary and fantastic rituals; which the pompous elfland he has entered demands. The first is that he shall get inside a house of clothing, a tower of wool and flax; that he shall put on this foolish armour solemnly, one piece after another and each in its right place. The things called sleevelinks he attends to minutely. His hair he beats angrily with a bristly tool. For this is the Law. Downstairs a more monstrous ceremony attends him. He has to put things inside himself. He does so, being naturally polite. Nor can it be denied that a weird satisfaction follows.

He takes a sword in his hand (for what may not befall him in so strange a country!) and goes forth: he finds a hole in the wall. a little cave wherein sits One who can give him the charm that rules the horse of water and fire. He finds an opening and descends into the bowels of the earth. Down, among the roots of the Eternal hills, he finds a sunless temple wherein he prays. And in the centre of it he finds a lighted temple in which he enters. Then there are noises as of an earthquake and smoke and fire in the darkness: and when he opens the door again he is in another temple, out of which he climbs into another world, leagues and leagues away. And when he asks the meaning of the vision, they talk gibberish and say, "It is a train."

So the day goes, full of eerie publishers and elfin clerks, till he returns and again puts things inside him, and then sits down and makes men in his own head and writes down all that they said and did. And last of all comes the real life itself. For half-an-hour he writes words upon a scrap of paper, words that are not picked and chosen like those that he has used to parry the strange talk of the folk all day, but words in which the soul's blood pours out, like the body's blood from a wound. He writes secretly this mad diary, all his passion and longing, all his queer religion, his dark and dreadful gratitude to God, his idle allegories, the tales that tell themselves in his head; the joy that comes on him sometimes (he cannot help it!) at the sacred intoxication of existence: the million faults of idleness and recklessness and the one virtue of the unconquered adoration of goodness, that dark virtue that every man has, and hides deeper than all his vices!—He writes all this down as he is writing it now. And he knows that if he sticks it down and puts a stamp on it and drops it into the mouth of a little red goblin at the corner of the street—he knows that all this wild soliloquy will be poured into the soul of one wise and beautiful lady sitting far away beyond seas and rivers and cities, under the shadow of an alien Cathedral. . . . This is not all so irrelevant as you may think. It was this line of feeling that taught me, an utter Rationalist as far as dogma goes, the lesson of the entire Spirituality of things—an opinion that nothing has ever shattered since. I can't express myself on the point, nobody can. But it is *only* the spirituality of things that we are sure of. That the eyes in your face are eyes I do not know: they may have other names and uses. I know that they are *good* or beautiful, or rather spiritual. I do not know on what principle the Universe is run, I know or feel that it is *good* or spiritual. I do not know what Gertrude's death was—I know that it was beautiful, for I saw it. We do not feel that it is so beautiful now—why? Because we do not *see* it now. What we see now is her absence: but her Death is not her absence, but her Presence somewhere else. That is what we *knew* was beautiful, as long as we could see it. Do not be frightened, dearest, by the slow inevitable laws of human nature, we shall climb back into the mountain of vision: we shall be able to use the word, with the accent of Whitman. "Disembodied, triumphant, dead."

In the *Notebook* he was writing:

> There is a heart within a distant town
> Who loves me more than treasure or renown
> Think you it strange and wear it as a crown.
>
> Is not the marvel here; that since the kiss
> And dizzy glories of that blinding bliss
> One grief has ever touched me after this.

We see Gilbert in the next two letters more concerned about a grand dinner of the J.D.C. than about his future fame and fortune. In the second he mentions almost casually that he is leaving Fisher Unwin. From now on he was to live by his pen.

11 Warwick Gardens,
W.
Tuesday Night. 3rd Oct. 1899.

. . . Nothing very astonishing has happened yet, though many astonishing things will happen soon. The Final Perfection of Humanity I expect shortly. The Speaker for this week—the first of the New Speaker, is coming out soon, and may contain something of mine though I cannot be quite sure. A rush of the Boers on Natal, strategically quite possibly successful, is anticipated by politicians. The rising of the sun tomorrow morning is predicted by astronomers. My father again is engaged in the crucial correspondence with Fisher Unwin, at least it has begun by T.F.U. stating his proposed terms—a rise of 5/—from October, another rise possible but undefined in January, 10 per cent royalty for the Paris book and expenses for a fortnight in Paris. These, as I got my father to heartily agree, are vitiated to the bone as terms by the absence of any assurance that I shall not have to write "Paris," for which I am really paid nothing, *outside* the hours of work for which I am paid 25/—. In short, the net result would be that instead of gaining more liberty to rise in the literary world, I should be selling the small liberty of rising that I have now for five more shillings. This my father is declining and asking for a better settlement. The diplomacy is worrying, yet I enjoy it: I feel like Mr. Chamberlain on the eve of war. I would stop with T.F.U. for £100 a year—but not for less. Which means, I think, that I shall not stop at all.

But all these revolutions, literary, financial and political fade into insignificance compared with the one really tremendous event of this week. It will take place on Saturday next. The sun will stand still upon Leicester Square and the Moon on the Valley of Wardour St. For then will assemble the Grand Commemorative Meeting of the Junior Debating Club. The Secretary, Mr. L.R.F. Oldershaw, will select a restaurant, make arrangements and issue the proclamations, or, to use the venerable old Club phrase "the writs." When this gorgeous function is over, you must expect a colossal letter. Everyone of the old Brotherhood, scattered over many cities and callings, has hailed the invitation, and is coming, with the exception of Bentley, who will send a sensational telegram from Paris. The fun is expected to be fast and furious, the undercurrent of emotion (twelve * years old) is not likely to be much disguised. As I say, I

* See footnote, p. 279.

will write you a sumptuous description of it; it is somewhat your due, for the thing is, and always will be, one of the main strands of my life. . . .

None can say what will occur. It is one of those occasions when Englishmen are not much like the pictures of them in Continental satires . . . there is more in this old affair of ours than possibly meets the eye. It is a thing that has left its roots deep in the hearts of twelve strangely different men. . . . And now that seven of us have found the New Life that can only be found in Woman, it would be mean indeed not to turn back and thank the old. . . .

11, Warwick Gardens, W.

. . . This is the colossal letter. I trust you will excuse me if the paper is conceived on a similar scale of Babylonian immensity. I cannot make out exactly whether I did or did not post a letter I wrote to you on Saturday. If I did not, I apologise for missing the day. If I did, you will know by this time one or two facts that may interest you, the chief of which is that I am certainly leaving Fisher Unwin, with much mutual courtesy and goodwill.

This fact may interest you, I repeat: at this moment I am not sure whether it interests me. For my head, to say nothing of another organ, is filled with the thundering cheers and songs of the dinner on Saturday night. It was, I may say without hesitation, a breathless success. Cholmeley, who must be experienced being both a school-master, a diner out and a clever man, told me he had never in his life heard eleven better speeches. I quite agree with him, merely adding his own. Everyone was amusing and what is much better, singularly characteristic. Will you forgive me, dearest, if I reel off to the only soul that can be trusted to enjoy my enjoyment, a kind of report of the meeting? It will revivify my own memories. And one thing at least that I said in my speech I thoroughly believed in —"if there is any prayer I should be inclined to make it is that I should forget nothing in my life."

The proceedings opened with dinner. The illustrated menus were wildly appreciated: every person got all the rest to sign on the menu and then took it away as a memento. Then the telegrams from Kruger, Chamberlain, Dreyfus and George Meredith were read. Then I proposed the toast of the Queen. I merely said that nothing could ever be alleged against the Queen, except the fact that she is not a member of the J.D.C. and that I thought it spoke well for the chivalry of Englishmen that with this fact she had never been publicly taunted. I said I knew that the virtues of Queen Victoria had become somewhat platitudinous, but I thought it was a fortunate country in which the virtues of its powerful ones are platitudes. The toast was then drunk. . . .

After a pause and a little conversation, I called upon Lawrence Solomon to propose the toast of "The School." He was very amusing indeed. Most of his speech would not be very comprehensible to an outsider for it largely consisted of an ingenious dove-tailing of the sentences in the Latin and Greek Arnold. I shall never forget the lucid and precise enunciation with which he delivered the idiotic sentences in those works, more especially where he said, "Such a course would be more agreeable to Mr. Cholmeley and I would rather gratify such a man as he than see the King of the Persians."

Cholmeley, amid roars of welcome, rose to respond. I think I must have told you in a former letter that Cholmeley is a former class-master of ours, a former house-master of Bentley's, and one of the nicest men at St. Paul's. We invited him as the only visitor. He said a great deal that was very amusing, mostly a commentary on Solomon's remarks about the Latin Arnold. One remark he made was that he possessed one particular Latin Arnold, formerly the property of the President, which he had withdrawn from him "with every expression of contumely"—because it was drawn all over with devils. He made some very sound remarks about the Club as an answer to the common charge against St. Paul's School that it was aridly scholastic, without spontaneous growth in culture or sentiment.

Then Fordham proposed "The Ladies." He was killing. Fordham is a personality whom I think you do not know. He is one of the most profoundly humourous men I ever knew, but his humour is more thickly coated on him, so to speak, than Bentley or Oldershaw, i.e., it is much more difficult to make him serious. He is one of the most fascinating "typical Englishmen" I ever knew: strong, generous, flippant on principle, rowdy by physical inspiration, successful, popular, married—a man to discharge all the normal functions of life well. But his most entertaining gift which he displayed truly sumptuously on this occasion is a wonderful gift of burlesque and stereotyped rhetoric. With melodramatic gestures he drew attention to the torrents of the President's blood pouring "from the wound of the tiny god." Amid sympathetic demonstration he protested against the pathos of the toast, "the conquered on the field of battle toasting the conquerors." As the only married member of the Club he ventured to give us some advice on (A) Food, (B) Education, (C) Intercourse. He sat down in a pure whirlwind of folly, without saying a word about the feelings that were in all hearts, including his own, just then. But I was delighted to find that marriage had not taken away an inch of his incurable silliness.

Nothing could be a greater contrast than the few graceful and dignified but very restrained words in which Bertram responded to the toast. He is not a man who cares to make fun of women, however genially.

Then came Langdon-Davies, whom I called upon to propose "The Club." His was perhaps the most interesting case of all. When I knew Langdon-Davies in the Junior Debating Club, he was one of the most frivolous young men I ever knew. . . . But knowing that he was a good speaker in a light style, and had been President of the Cambridge Union, I put him down to propose the Club, thinking that we should have enough serious speaking and would be well to err on the side of entertainment.

Langdon-Davies got up and proceeded to deliver a speech that made me jump. It was, I thought, the best speech of the evening: but I am sure it was the most serious, the most sympathetic and a long way the most frankly emotional.

He said that the Club was not now a club in the strict sense. It was two things preeminently and everlastingly—a memory and an influence. He spoke with a singular sort of subdued vividness of the influence the Club had had on him in boyhood. He then turned to the history of the Club. And here, my dearest lady, I am pained to have to report that he launched suddenly and dramatically into a most extraordinary, and apparently quite sincere eulogium upon myself and the influence I had on my schoolfellows. I will not repeat his words—I did not believe them, but they took me by surprise and shook me somewhat. Mr. B. N. Langdon-Davies, I may remark, and yourself, are the only persons who have ever employed the word "genius" in connection with me. I trust it will not occur again.

I replied. My speech was a medley, but it appeared very successful. I discussed largely the absence of any successor to the J.D.C. I described how I watched the boys leaving school today—a solitary figure, clad in the latest fashion, moodily pacing the Hammersmith Road—and asked myself "where among these is the girlish gush of a Bentley—the passionate volubility of a Vernède, the half-ethereal shyness of a Fordham?!!" I admitted that we had had misfortunes, one of us had a serious illness, another had had a very good story in the Strand Magazine: but I thought that a debating club of 12 members that had given three presidents to the University Unions, had not done badly. The rest was sentimental. Then began a most extraordinary game of battledore and shuttlecock. Vernède proposed the Secretary, Mr. Oldershaw. Mr. Oldershaw, instead of replying properly, proposed Mr. Bentley and the absent members. Waldo responded for these or rather instead of responding proposed Mr. Maurice Solomon. Mr. Maurice Solomon instead of responding proposed Mr. Salter. The latter was the only one who had not spoken and on rising he explained his reasons for refusing. He had not been in the same room with Mr. Cholmeley, he said, since he had sat five years ago in the Lower Fourth * and Mr. Cholmeley had told him that he talked too much. He had no desire on his first reappearance to create in Mr. Cholmeley's mind the idea that he had been at it ever since.

After this we passed on to singing and nearly brought down the roof of Pinoli's restaurant. Cholmeley, the awful being of whose classic taste in Greek iambics I once stood in awe, sang with great feeling a fragment of lyric literature of which the following was, as far as I remember, the refrain:

> "Singing Chooral-i-chooral-i-tiddity
> Also—Chooral-i-chooral-i-tay
> And chanting Chooral-i-chooral-i-dititty
> Not forgetting—chooral-i-chooral-i-day—"

Vernède sang a Sussex pothouse chorus in an indolent and refined way which was exquisitely incongruous: Waldo and Langdon-Davies also sang. I recited an Ode which I had written for the occasion and Lucian recited one of Bentley's poems that came out in an Oxford magazine. Then we sang the Anthem † of the J.D.C., of which the words are, "I am a Member—I'm a Member—Member of the J.D.C. I belong to it forever—don't you wish that you were me."

Then we paid the bill. Then we borrowed each other's arms and legs in an inextricable tangle and sang "Auld Lang Syne." Then we broke up.

* See footnote, p. 279. At no time did dates mean anything to Gilbert.
† It was sung to the tune of "Clementine."

There now. Five mortal pages of writing and nothing about you in it. How relieved you must be, wearied out with allusions to your hair and your soul and your clothes and your eyes. And yet it has been every word of it about you really. I like to make my past vivid to you, especially this past, not only because it was on the whole, a fine, healthy, foolish, manly, enthusiastic, idiotic past, with the very soul of youth in it. Not only because I am a victim of the prejudice, common I trust to all mankind, that no one ever had such friends as I had. . . .

Readers of the *Autobiography* will remember that many many years later, at the celebration of Hilaire Belloc's sixtieth birthday, the guests threw the ball to one another in just this same fashion. Chesterton had by then so far forgotten this earlier occasion that he spoke of the Belloc birthday party as the only dinner in his life at which every diner made a speech.

Two more extracts from his letters must be given, showing the efforts made by Frances to look after Gilbert, and his reactions. One of his friends remarked that Gilbert's life was unique in that, never having left home for a boarding school or University, he passed from the care of his mother to the care of his wife. I think too that the degree of his physical helplessness affected all who came near him with the feeling that while he might lead them where he would intellectually, it was their task to look after a body that would otherwise be wholly neglected.

The old religionists used to talk about a man being "a fool for Christ's sake"—Certainly I have been a blithering fool for your sake. I went to see the doctor, as you requested. He asked me what he could do for me. I told him I hadn't the least idea, but people thought my cold had been going on long enough. He said, "I've no doubt it has." He then, to afford some relief to the idiotic futility of the situation, wrote me a prescription, which I read on my way up to business, weeping over the pathetic parts and laughing heartily at the funny ones. I have since had some of it. It tastes pretty aimless.

I cannot remember for certain whether I mentioned in my letter that I had had an invitation including yourself, from my Aunt Kate for this Friday. As you do not refer to it, I expect I didn't—so I wrote to her giving both our thanks and explaining the state of affairs. "All is over," I said, "between that lady and myself. Do not name her to me, lest the hideous word 'Woman' should blind me to the seraphic word 'Aunt.' My life is a howling waste—but what matter? Ha! Ha! Ha!" I cannot remember my exact words, of course. . . .

. . . I am a revolting object. My hair is a matted chaos spread all over the floor, my beard is like a hard broom. My necktie is on the wrong way up: my bootlaces trail half-way down Fleet St. Why not? When one's attempts at reformation are "not much believed in" what other course is open but a contemptuous relapse into liberty?

Your last letter makes me much happier. I put great faith in the healing power of the great winds and the sun. "Nature," as Walt Whitman says, "and her primal sanities." Mrs. S . . . , also, is a primal sanity. It is not, I believe, considered complimentary, in a common way, to approach an attractive lady and say pleasantly, "You are thousands of years old." Or, "You seem to me as old as the mountains." Therefore I do not say it. But I always feel that anyone beautiful and strong is really *old*—for the really old things are not decrepit: decrepit things are dying early. The Roman Empire was decrepit. A sunrise cloud is old.

So I think there are some people, who even in their youth, seem to have existed always: they bear the mark of the elemental things: the things that recur; they are as old as springtime, as old as daybreak— as old as Youth.

CHAPTER X

Who is G.K.C.?

THE BOER WAR—and the whole country enthusiastically behind it. The Liberal Party as a whole went with the Conservatives. The leading Fabians—Bernard Shaw, Mr. and Mrs. Sidney Webb, Hubert Bland, Cecil Chesterton and the "semidetached Fabian" H. G. Wells—were likewise for the war. Only a tiny minority remained in opposition, most of whom were pacifists or cranks of one kind or another. To the sane minority of this minority Gilbert found himself belonging. It is something of a tribute to the national feeling at such a moment of tension that (as an American has noted) "Chesterton was the one British writer, utterly unknown before, who built up a great reputation, and it was gained, not through nationalistic support, but through determined and persistent opposition to British policy." *

In his *Daily News* column a correspondent later asked him to define his position. Chesterton replied, "The unreasonable patriot is one who sees the faults of his fatherland with an eye which is clearer and more merciless than any eye of hatred, the eye of an irrational and irrevocable love." His attitude sprang, he claimed, not from defect but from excess of patriotism.

It is hard to imagine anything that would clarify better the ideas of a strong mind than finding itself in opposition. This opposition began at home, in argument with Cecil. Later the two brothers would agree about most main issues, but now Cecil was a Tory democrat, Gilbert a pro-Boer, and what was known

* *Chesterton,* by Cyril Clemens, p. 20.

as a little Englander. The tie between the two brothers was very close. As the "Innocent Child" developed into the combative companion, there is no doubt that he proportionately affected Gilbert. All their friends talk of the endless amicable arguments through which both grew. Conrad Noel remembers parties at Warwick Gardens during the Boer War at which the two brothers "would walk up and down like the two pistons of an engine" to the disorganisation of the company and the dismay of their parents. It was at this time that Frances, engaged to a deeply devoted Gilbert, found even that devotion insufficient to pry him and Cecil apart when an argument had got well under way.

"I must go home, Gilbert. I shall miss my train."

Usually he would have sprung to accompany her, but now she must miss many trains before the brothers could be separated.

Frances told me that when they were at the seaside the landlady would sometimes clear away breakfast, leaving the brothers arguing, come to set lunch and later set dinner while still they argued. They had come to the seaside but they never saw the sea.

Once Frances was staying with them at a house they had taken by the sea. Her room was next to Cecil's and she could not sleep for the noise of the discussion that went on hour after hour. About one in the morning she rapped on the wall and said, "O Cecil, do send Gilbert to bed." A brief silence followed, and then the remark, in a rather abashed voice, "There's no one here." Cecil had been arguing with himself. Gilbert too argued with himself for the stand he was taking was a hard one. Mr. Belloc has told me that he felt Gilbert suffered at any word against England, that his patriotism was passionate. And now he had himself to say that he believed his country to be in the wrong. To admit it to himself, to state it to others.

This autumn of 1899 G.K. began to write for the *Speaker*. The weekly of this title had long been in a languishing condition when it was taken over by a group of young Liberals of very marked views. Hammond became editor and Philip Comyns Carr sub-editor. Sir John Simon was among the group for a short while, but he soon told one of them that he feared close association with the *Speaker* might injure his career. F. Y. Eccles was in charge of the review department. He is able to date the start of what was known as the "new" *Speaker* with great exactitude, for when the first number was going to press the ultimatum had been sent to Kruger and the editors hesitated as to whether they should take the risk of announcing that it was war in South Africa. They decided against, but before their second number appeared war had been declared.

My difficulty in getting a picture of the first meeting of Belloc and Chesterton illustrates the problem of human testimony and the limits of that problem. For I imagine a scripture critic, old style, would end by concluding that the men never met at all.

F. Y. Eccles, E. C. Bentley and Lucian Oldershaw all claim to have made the momentous introduction, Mr. Eccles adding that it took place at the office of the *Speaker*, while Gilbert himself has described the meeting twice: once in the street, once in a restaurant. Belloc remembers the introduction as made in the year 1900 by Lucian Oldershaw, who was living at the time with Hammond. Mr. Oldershaw usually has the accuracy of the hero-worshipper and upon this matter he adds several amusing details. For some time he had been trying to get the group on the *Speaker* to read Chesterton and had in vain taken several articles to the office. Mr. Eccles declared the handwriting was that of a Jew and he prejudiced Belloc, says Oldershaw, against reading "anything written by my Jew friend."

But when at last they did meet, Belloc "opened the conversation by saying in his most pontifical manner, 'Chesterton, you wr-r-ite very well.'" Chesterton was then 26, Belloc four years older. It was at the Mont Blanc, a restaurant in Gerrard St., Soho, and the meeting was celebrated with a bottle of Moulin au Vent.

The first description given by Gilbert himself is at once earlier and more vivid than the better known one in the *Autobiography*.

When I first met Belloc he remarked to the friend who introduced us that he was in low spirits. His low spirits were and are much more uproarious and enlivening than anybody else's high spirits. He talked into the night, and left behind in it a glowing track of good things. When I have said that I mean things that are good, and certainly not merely *bons mots,* I have said all that can be said in the most serious aspect about the man who has made the greatest fight for good things of all the men of my time.

We met between a little Soho paper shop and a little Soho restaurant; his arms and pockets were stuffed with French Nationalist and French Atheist newspapers. He wore a straw hat shading his eyes, which are like a sailor's, and emphasizing his Napoleonic chin. . . .

The little restaurant to which we went had already become a haunt for three or four of us who held strong but unfashionable views about the South African War, which was then in its earliest prestige. Most of us were writing on the *Speaker.* . . .

. . . What he brought into our dream was this Roman appetite for reality and for reason in action, and when he came into the door there entered with him the smell of danger.*

"It was from that dingy little Soho café," Chesterton writes in the *Autobiography,* "that there emerged the quadruped, the twiformed monster Mr. Shaw has nicknamed the Chesterbelloc."

Listening to Belloc is intoxicating. I have heard many brilliant talkers, but none to whom that word can so justly be applied. He goes to your head, he takes you off your feet, he leaves you breathless, he can convince you of anything. My mother and brother both counted it as one of the great experiences of their lives to have dined with Belloc in a small Paris Restaurant (Aux Vendanges de Bourgogne) and then to have walked with him the streets of that glorious city while he discoursed of its past. Imagination staggers before the picture of a Belloc in his full

---

* Introduction to: *Hilaire Belloc: The Man and His Work* by C. C. Mandell and E. Shanks, 1916.

youth and vigour in a group fitted to strike from him his brightest fire at a moment big with issues for the world's future.

In Chesterton's *Autobiography* a chapter is devoted to the "Portrait of A Friend," while Belloc in turn has said something of Chesterton in obituary notices and also in a brief study of his position in English literature. None of these documents give much notion of the intellectual flame struck out by one mind against the other. It has often been asked how much Belloc influenced Chesterton.

The best test of an influence in a writer's life is to compare what he wrote before with what he wrote after he was first subjected to it. It is easy to apply this test to Belloc's influence on G.K.C. because of the mass we still have of his boyhood writings. In pure literature, in philosophy and theology he remains untouched by the faintest change. Pages from the Notebook could be woven into *Orthodoxy*, essays from *The Debater* introduced into *The Victorian Age in Literature*, and it would look simply like buds and flowers on the same bush. Belloc has characterized himself as ignorant of English literature and says he learnt from Chesterton most of what he knows of it, while there is no doubt Chesterton was by far the greater philosopher.

With politics, sociology, and history (and the relation of religion to all three) it is different. Belloc himself told me he thought the chief thing he had done for Chesterton when they first met was to open his eyes to reality—Chesterton had been unusually young for his twenty-six years and unusually simple in regard to the political scene. He was in fact the young man he himself was later to describe as knowing all about politics and nothing about politicians. The four years between the two men seemed greater than it was, partly because of Belloc's more varied experience of life—French military training, life at Oxford, wide travel and an early marriage.

Belloc, then, could teach Chesterton a certain realism about politics—which meant a certain cynicism about politicians. Far more valuable, however, was what Belloc had to give him in sociology. We have seen that G.K. was already dissatisfied with Socialism before he met Belloc: it may be that by his consideration of the nature of man he would later have reached the positions so individually set out in *What's Wrong with the World*—but this can only remain a theoretical question. For Belloc did actually at this date answer the sociological question that Chesterton at this date was putting: answered it brilliantly and answered it truly. Every test that G.K. could later apply—of profound human reality, of truth divinely revealed—convinced him that the answer was true.

He had, he has told us, been a Socialist because it was so horrible not to be one, but he now learned of the historical Christian alternative—equally opposed to Socialism and to Capitalism—well-distributed property. This had worked in the past, was still working in many European countries, could be made to work again in England. The present trend appeared to Belloc to be towards the Servile State, and in the book with this title and a second book *The Restoration of Property* he later developed his sociology. After this first meeting, two powerful and very different minds would reciprocally influence one another. An admirer of both told me that he thought Chesterton got the idea of small property from Belloc but gave Belloc a fuller realization of the position of the family. One difference between them is that Belloc writes sociology as a textbook while Chesterton writes it as a human document. All the wealth of imagination that Belloc pours into *The Path to Rome* or *The Four Men* he sternly excludes from *The Servile State*. The poet, traveller, essayist is one man, the sociologist another.

The third field of influence was history. Here Belloc did Chesterton two great services—he restored the proportion of English history, and he put England back into its context. Since the Reformation, English history had been written with all the stress on the Protestant period. Lingard had written earlier but had not been popularized and certainly would not be used at St. Paul's School. And even Lingard had laid little stress on the social effects of the Reformation. Mr. Hammond's contemporary work on English social history fitted into Belloc's more vivid if less documented vision—none of this could be disregarded by later writers.

Belloc, too, restored that earlier England to the Christendom to which it belonged. The England of Macaulay or of Green had, like Mr. Mantalini's dowager, either no outline or a "demned outline" for it was cut out of a larger map. And Chesterton was always seeking an outline of history.

To get England back into the context of Christendom is a great thing: just how great must depend upon how rightly Christendom is conceived. One cannot always escape the feeling that Belloc conceives it too narrowly. His famous phrase "The Faith is Europe and Europe is the Faith" omits too much—the East out of which Christianity came; the new worlds into which Europe has flowed. Belloc of course knows these things and has often said them. It is rather a question of emphasis, of how things loom in the mind when judgments have to be made. In that sense he does tend to narrow the Faith to Europe: in exactly the same sense he does tend to narrow Europe to France. Born in France of a French father, educated in England, Belloc chose his mother's nationality, chose to be English; but his Creator had chosen differently, and there is not much a man can do in competition with his Creator. I do not for a moment suggest that Belloc, having chosen to be English, is conscious of anything but loyalty to the country of his adoption. The thing lies far below the mind's conscious movements. Belloc thinks of himself as an Englishman with a patriotic duty to criticise his country, but his *feelings* are not really those of an Englishman. Once at least he recognised this when he wrote the verse:

England to me that never have malingered,
Nor spoken falsely, nor your flattery used,
Nor even in my rightful garden lingered—:*
What have you not refused?

And just as France was Belloc's rightful garden so England was Chesterton's. When first they talked of the Church he told Belloc that he wanted the example of "someone entirely English who should none the less have come in." When criticising his country his voice has the note of pain that only love can give. Belloc saw him as intensely national "English of the English . . . a mirror of England . . . he writes with an English accent."

It is of some interest that after meeting Belloc Gilbert added notes to two early poems, each note reflecting a judgment of Belloc's—on the Dreyfus case which Belloc saw as all French Catholics saw it: on Anglo-American relations which Belloc saw as most Latin Europeans would see it.

(1) The first was the poem entitled "To a Certain Nation"— addressed to France in commentary on the Dreyfus case of 1899 which must be briefly explained for those who are too young to remember the excitement it caused. Captain Dreyfus, a Jewish officer in the French army, had been found guilty of treachery and sent to Devil's Island. All France was divided into two camps on the question of his guilt or innocence. In general, Catholics and what we should call the Right were all for his guilt; atheists, anti-clericals and believers in the Republic were for his innocence. Passions were roused to fury on both sides. English opinion was almost entirely for his innocence. I was a small girl at the time and I remember that my brother and I amused ourselves by crying *Vive Dreyfus,* on all possible and impossible occasions, for the annoyance of our pious French governess. I remember also that our parents were startled by the

_____
* Italics mine.

vehemence of the French Catholic paper *La Croix* from which our governess imbibed her views. Ultimately the case was re-opened, and Dreyfus, after years of horror on Devil's Island, found not guilty and restored to his rank in the army. But there are, I know, Catholic Frenchmen alive today who refuse to be-lieve in his innocence and hold that the whole thing was a Jew-ish-Masonic plot that hampered the French espionage service and nearly lost us the war of 1914.

In the first edition of *The Wild Knight*, written before the meeting with Belloc, Gilbert, like any other English Liberal, had assumed Dreyfus' innocence and in the poem "To a Certain Nation" had reproached the France of the Revolution, the France he had loved, as unworthy of herself.

> . . . and we
> Who knew thee once, we have a right to weep.

The Note in the second edition shows him as now undecided about Dreyfus' guilt and concludes: "There may have been a fog of injustice in the French courts; I know that there was a fog of injustice in the English newspapers."

(2) In "An Alliance" Chesterton had gloried in "the blood of Hengist" and hymned an Anglo-American alliance with the en-thusiasm of a young Republican who took for granted the links of language and of origin that might draw together two great coun-tries into something significant:

> In change, eclipse, and peril
> Under the whole world's scorn,
> By blood and death and darkness
> The Saxon peace is sworn;
> That all our fruit be gathered
> And all our race take hands,
> And the sea be a Saxon river
> That runs through Saxon lands.

But in the Note to the second edition, he says:

In the matter of the "Anglo-American Alliance" I have come to see that our hopes of brotherhood with America are the same in kind as our hopes of brotherhood with any other of the great independent nations of Christendom. And a very small study of history was sufficient to show me that the American Nation, which is a hundred years old, is at least fifty years older than the Anglo-Saxon race.*

The poem was of course only a boyish expression of a boyish dream; like all dreams, like all boyhood dreams especially, it omitted too much; yet it contained a thought that might well have borne rich fruit in Gilbert's Catholic life.

My mother told me once that when after three years' study of Queen Elizabeth's character she came to a different conclusion from Belloc, she found it almost impossible to resist his power and hold on to her own view. It must be realised that Chesterton actually preferred the attitude of a disciple. A mutual friend has told me that Chesterton listened to Belloc all the time and said very little himself. In matters historical where he felt his own ignorance, Gilbert's tendency was simply to make an act of faith in Belloc.

On nothing were the two men more healthily in accord than on the Boer War. In an interesting study of Belloc, prefixed to a French translation of *Contemporary England*, F. Y. Eccles explains how he and most of the *Speaker* group differed from the pacifist pro-Boers, who hated the South African war because they hated all wars. The young Liberals on the *Speaker* were not pacifists. They hated the war because they thought it would harm England—harm her morally—to be fighting for an unjust cause, and even materially to be shedding the blood of her sons and pouring out her wealth at the bidding of a handful of alien financiers. Thus far Gilbert was among one group with whom he was in fullest sympathy. But I think he went further. Mr. Eccles told me that most of the *Speaker* group had no sym-

* Collected Poems, p. 318.

pathy with the Boers. Gilbert had. He thought of them as human beings who might well have been farmers of Sussex or of Kent, something of an older civilization, resisting money power and imperialism and perishing thereby.

Few, indeed, of the Liberal Party held Chesterton's ideal—an England territorially small, spiritually great. The *Speaker* was struggling against odds: it was the voice of a tiny group. To Gilbert it seemed that this mattered nothing so long as that little group held to their great ideas, so long as the paper represented not merely a group or a party but the Liberal Idea. In an unfinished letter to Hammond is to be found this Idea as he saw it and his dawning disappointment even with the paper that most nearly stood for it:

I am just about to commit a serious impertinence. I believe however that you will excuse it because it is about the paper and I know there is not another paper dead or alive for which I would take the trouble or run the risk of offence.

I am hearing on all sides the *Speaker* complained of by the very people who should be and would be (if they could) its enthusiastic supporters and I cannot altogether deny the truth of their objections, though I am glad to notice both in them and in myself the fact that those objections are tacitly based on the assumption of the *Speaker* having an aim and standard higher than other papers. If the *Speaker* were a mere party rag like "Judy" or "The Times," it would be only remarkable for moderation, but to us who have built hopes on it as the pioneer of a younger and larger political spirit it is difficult to be silent when we find it, as it seems to us, poisoned with that spirit of ferocious triviality which is the spirit of Birmingham eloquence, and with that evil instinct which has disintegrated the Irish party, the instinct for hating the man who differs from you slightly, more than the man who differs from you altogether.

Of two successive numbers during the stress of the fight (a fight in which we had first to unite our army and then to use it) a considerable portion was devoted, first to sneering at "The Daily News" and then to sneering at "The Westminster Gazette." . . .

There is a sentence in the Book of Proverbs which expresses the whole of my politics. "For the liberal man deviseth liberal things and by his liberality he shall stand." Now what I object to is sneering at "The Westminster" as a supporter of Chamberlain when everyone knows that it hardly lets a day pass without an ugly caricature of him. What I object to in this is that it is talking Brummagem—it is not "devising liberal things" but spiteful, superficial, illiberal things. It is claptrap and temporary deception of the "Patriotism before Politics" order. . . .

To all this you will say there is an obvious answer. The *Speaker* is a party paper and does not profess to be otherwise. But here I am sure we are mistaking our mission. What the *Speaker* is (I hope and believe) destined to do, is to renovate Liberalism, and though Liberalism (like every other party) is often conducted by claptrap, it has never been renovated by claptrap, but by great command of temper and the persistent exposition of persuasive and unanswerable truths. It is while we are in the desert that we have the vision: we being a minority, must be all philosophers: we must think for both parties in the State. It is no good our devoting ourselves to the flowers of mob oratory with no mob to address them to. We must, like the Free Traders, for instance, have discoveries, definite truths and endless patience in explaining them. We must be more than a political party or we shall cease to be one. Time and again in history victory has come to a little party with big ideas: but can anyone conceive anything with the mark of death more on its brow than a little party with little ideas? *

Such Liberalism was not perhaps of this world. It certainly was not of the Liberal Party!

Gilbert argued much with himself during these years. He had come out of his time of trial with firm faith in God and in man. But his philosophy was still in the making, and he made it largely out of the material supplied by ordinary London suburban society and by the rather less usual society of cranks and enthusiasts so plentiful at the end of the nineteenth century. He has written in the *Autobiography* of the artistic and dilettante groups where everyone discussed religion and no one

* Undated, handwritten letter in a notebook.

practised it, of the Christian Socialists and other societies into which he and Cecil found their way, and of some of the friendships they formed. Among these one of the closest was with Conrad Noel who wrote in answer to my request for his recollections:

We met G.K.C. for the first time at the Stapleys' in Bloomsbury Square, at a series of meetings of the Christo-Theosophic Society. He was like a very big fish out of water; he was comparatively thin, however, in those days, nearly forty years ago. We had been much intrigued by the weekly contribution of an unknown writer to "The Speaker" and "The Nation"—brilliant work, and my wife and I, independently, came to the conclusion when we heard this young man speak that it must be he. The style was unmistakable.

I thought of writing to him to congratulate him on his speech, but before I could do so, I got a letter from him, saying that he was coming to hear me in the same series in a week or so; it was thus we first became acquainted, and the acquaintance ripened into a warm friendship with us both. He and his brother Cecil were in and out of our flat in Paddington Green, where I was assistant curate. He was genial, bubbling over with jokes, at which he roared with laughter.

The question was becoming insistent: when would there be enough money for Frances and Gilbert to get married?

In one letter Frances asks him what he thinks of Omar Khayyam. He replies at great length, and concludes:

You see the result of asking me for an opinion. I have written it very hurriedly: if I had paused I might make an essay of it. (Commercial Pig!) Never mind, sweetheart, that Essay might be a saucepan some day—or at any rate a cheap toast-rack.

Of his belief in God, in man, in goodness, as against the pessimist outlook of the day, Gilbert, as we have seen, felt profound certitude. That his outlook was one that held him back from many fields of opportunity he was already partly conscious. A fragment of a letter to Frances expresses this feeling.

. . . I find I cannot possibly come tonight as my Canadian uncle keeps his last night in England in a sort of family party. And I abide by my father's house—said our Lady of the Snows.

I have just had a note from Rex, asking me, with characteristic precision, if I can produce a play in the style of Maeterlinck by 6.30 this afternoon, or words to that effect. The idea is full of humour. He remarks, as a matter of fact, that there is just a remote chance of his getting the Stage Society to act my play of The Wild Knight. This opens to me a vista of quite new ambition. Why only at the Stage Society?—I see a visionary programme.

The Wild Knight............	Mr. Charles Hawtree
Captain Redfeather..........	Mr. Penley
Olive	Miss Katie Seymour
Priest	Sir Henry Irving
Lord Orm..................	Mr. Arthur Roberts

I am working and must get on with my work. I do not feel any despondency about it because I know it is good and worth doing. It is extraordinary how much more moral one is than one imagines. At school I never minded getting into a row if it were *really* not my fault. Similarly, I have never cared a rap for rejections or criticisms, since I had got a point of view to express which I was certain held water. Some people think it holds water—on the brain. But I don't mind. Bless them.

I am afraid, darling, that this doctrine of patience is hard on you. But really it's a grand thing to think oneself right. It's what this whole age is starving for. Something to suffer for and go mad and miserable over—that is the only luxury of the mind. I wish I were a convinced Pro-Boer and could stare down a howling mob. But I *am* right about the Cosmos, and Schopenhauer and Co. are wrong. . . .

Two interesting points in this letter are the remark about wishing to be a convinced Pro-Boer—which he certainly became —and the suggestion of a possible performance of *The Wild Knight*. Perhaps the letter was written before he had finally taken his stand (it has no dating postmark), or perhaps it merely means that his convictions on the cosmos are more absolute than on the war. As to *The Wild Knight*: it was never acted and its publication was made possible only by the generosity of Gilbert's father. For a volume of comic verse, *Greybeards at Play*, which appeared earlier in the same year (1900), he could find a publisher, but serious poetry has never been easy to launch.

The letter that follows has a more immediate bearing on their own future:

> 11, Warwick Gardens,
> Good Friday. 1900.

. . . As you have tabulated your questions with such alarming precision I must really endeavour to answer them categorically.

(1) How am I? I am in excellent health. I have an opaque cold in my head, cough tempestuously and am very deaf. But these things I count as mere specks showing up the general blaze of salubrity. I am getting steadily better and I don't mind how slowly. As for my spirits a cold never affects them: for I have plenty to do and think about indoors. One or two little literary schemes—trifles doubtless—claim my attention.

(2) Am I going away at Easter? The sarcastic might think it a characteristic answer, but I can only reply that I had banished the matter from my mind, a vague problem of the remote future until you asked it: but since this is Easter and we are not gone away I suppose we are not going away.

(3) I will meet you at Euston on Tuesday evening though hell itself should gape and bid me stop at home.

(4) I am not sure whether a review on Crivelli's art is out this week: I am going to look.

(5) Alas! I have not been to Nutt. There are good excuses, but they are not the real ones. I will write to him now. Yes: Now.

(6) Does my hair want cutting? My hair seems pretty happy. You are the only person who seems to have any fixed theory on this. For all I know it may be at that fugitive perfection which has moved you to enthusiasm. Three minutes after this perfection, I understand, a horrible degeneration sets in: the hair becomes too long, the figure disreputable and profligate: and the individual is unrecognised by all his friends. It is he that wants cutting then, not his hair.

(7) As to shirt-links, studs and laces, I glitter from head to foot with them.

(8) I have had a few skirmishes with Knollys but not the general engagement. When this comes off, you shall have news from our correspondent. [Knollys was Frances's brother.]

(9) I have got a really important job in reviewing—the Life of Ruskin for the Speaker. As I have precisely 73 theories about Ruskin it will be brilliant and condensed. I am also reviewing the Life of the Kendals, a book on the Renascence and one on Correggio for "The Bookman."

(10) How far is it to Babylon? Babylon I am firmly convinced is just round the corner: if one could be only certain which corner. This conviction is the salt of my life.

(11) Really and truly I see no reason why we should not be married in April if not before. I have been making some money calculations with the kind assistance of Rex, and as far as I can see we could live in the country on quite a small amount of regular literary work. . . .

P.S. Forgot the last question.

(12) Oddly enough, I was writing a poem. Will send it to you.

Gilbert's engagement had given him the impetus to earn more but he was always entirely unpractical. His salary at Fisher Unwin's had been negligible and he was not making much yet by the journalism which was now his only source of income. The repeated promise to "write to Nutt" is very characteristic. For Nutt was the manager of the solitary publisher who was at the moment prepared to put a book of Gilbert's on the market at his own risk!

Although they did not manage to get married this year, by the end of it he was becoming well known. The articles, in the *Speaker* especially, were attracting attention and *Greybeards at Play* had a considerable success. This, the first of Gilbert's books to be published, is a curiosity. It is made up of three incredibly witty satirical poems—"The Oneness of the Philosopher with Nature," "The Dangers Attending Altruism on the High Seas" and "The Disastrous Spread of Aestheticism in All Classes." The illustrations drawn by himself are as witty as the verses. By the beginning of 1901 his work was being sought for by other Liberal periodicals and he was writing regularly for the *Daily News*. The following letter to Frances bears the postmark Feb. 8, 1901.

Somewhere in the Arabian Nights or some such place there is a story of a man who was Emperor of the Indies for one day. I am rather in the position of that person: for I am Editor of the *Speaker* for one day. Hammond is unwell and Hirst has gone to dine with John Morley, so the latter asked me to see the paper through for this number. Hence this notepaper and the great hurry and brevity which I fear must characterise this letter.

There are a few minor amusing things, however, that I have a moment to mention.

(1) The "Daily News" have sent me a huge mass of books to review, which block up the front hall. A study of Swinburne—a book on Kipling—the last Richard Le Gallienne—all very interesting. See if I don't do some whacking articles, all about the stars and the moon and the creation of Adam and that sort of thing. I really think I could work a revolution in daily paper-writing by the introduction of poetical prose.

(2) Among other books that I have to review came, all unsolicited, a book by your old friend Schofield. Ha! Ha! Ha! It's about the Formation of Character, or some of those low and beastly amusements. I think of introducing parts of my Comic Opera of the P.N.E.U. into the articles.

(3) Another rather funny thing is the way in which my name is being spread about. Belloc declares that everyone says to him "Who discovered Chesterton?" and that he always replies "The genius Oldershaw." This may be a trifle Gallic, but Hammond has shown me more than one letter from Cambridge dons and such people demanding the identity of G.K.C. in a quite violent tone. They excuse themselves by offensive phrases in which the word "brilliant" occurs, but I shouldn't wonder if there was a thick stick somewhere at the back of it.

Belloc, by the way, has revealed another side of his extraordinary mind. He seems to have taken our marriage much to heart, for he talks to me, no longer about French Jacobins and Mediaeval Saints, but entirely about the cheapest flats and furniture, on which, as on the others, he is a mine of information, assuring me paternally that "it's the carpet that does you." I should think this fatherly tone would amuse you.

Now I must leave off: for the pages have come up to be seen through the press. . . .

Greybeards at Play its author never took very seriously. It was not included in his Collected Poems and he does not even mention it in his *Autobiography*. He attached a great deal more importance to *The Wild Knight and Other Poems*. It was a volume of some fifty poems, many of which had already appeared in *The Outlook* and *The Speaker*. It was published late in 1900 and produced a crop of enthusiastic reviews and more and more people began to ask one another, "Who is G. K. Chesterton?" One reviewer wrote: "If it were not for the haunting fear of losing a humourist we should welcome the author of *The Wild Knight* to a high place among the poets." Another spoke of the "curious intensity" of the volume. Among those who were less pleased was John Davidson, on whom the book had been fathered by one reviewer, and who denied responsibility for such "frantic rubbish," and also a "reverent" reviewer who complained, "It is scattered all over with the name of God."

To Frances, Gilbert wrote:

I have been taken to see Mrs. Meynell, poet and essayist, who is enthusiastic about the Wild Knight and is lending it to all her friends.

Last night I went to Mrs. Cox's Book Party. My costume was a great success, everyone wrestled with it, only one person guessed it, and the rest admitted that it was quite fair and simple. It consisted of wearing on the lapel of my dress coat the following letters. U.U.N.S.I.J. Perhaps you would like to work this out all by yourself—But no, I will have mercy and not sacrifice. The book I represented was "The Letters of Junius."

Mrs. Meynell never came to know Gilbert well and her daughter says in the biography that her mother realised his "critical approval" (admiration would be a better word) of her own work only by reading his essays. But he once wrote an introduction for a book of hers and her admiration of him would break out frequently in amusing exclamations: "I hope the papers are nice to my Chesterton. He is mine much more, really, than Belloc's." * "If I had been a man, and large, I should have been Chesterton." †

Brimley Johnson, who was to have been Gilbert's brother-in-law, sent *The Wild Knight* to Rudyard Kipling. His reply is amusing and also touching, for Mr. Johnson was clearly pouring out, in interest in Gilbert's career and in forwarding his marriage with Frances, the affections that might merely have been frozen by Gertrude's death.

The Elms, Rottingdean,
Nov. 28th.

DEAR MR. JOHNSON,

Many thanks for the *Wild Knight*. Of course I knew some of the poems before, notably *The Donkey* which stuck in my mind at the time I read it.

I agree with you that there is any amount of promise in the work —and I think marriage will teach him a good deal too. It will be curious to see how he'll develop in a few years. We all begin with arrainging (sic) and elaborating all the Heavens and Hells and stars and tragedies we can lay our poetic hands on—Later we see folk— just common people under the heavens—

Meantime I wish him all the happiness that there can be and for yourself such comfort as men say time brings after loss. It's apt to be a weary while coming but one goes the right way to get it if one interests oneself in the happiness of other folk. Even though the sight of this happiness is like a knife turning in a wound.

Yours sincerely,

RUDYARD KIPLING.

P.S. Merely as a matter of loathsome detail, Chesterton has a bad attack of "aureoles." They are spotted all over the book. I think every one is bound in each book to employ unconsciously some pet word but that was Rossetti's.

Likewise I notice "wan waste" and many "wans" and things that "catch and cling." He is too good not to be jolted out of that. What

* *Alice Meynell,* p. 259.
† *Ibid,* p. 260.

do you say to a severe course of Walt Whitman—or will marriage make him see people?

Gilbert had already taken both prescriptions—Walt Whitman and "folk, just common people under the heavens." (Many years later James Agate wrote in *Thursdays and Fridays:* "Unlike some other serious thinkers, Chesterton understood his fellow men; the woes of a jockey were as familiar to him as the worries of a judge.") Perhaps some slight echoes of Swinburne did remain in this collection. Many earlier poems exist in the Swinburne manner, not of thought but of expression: Gilbert left an absolute command that these should never be published.

All Englishmen were stricken by the death of Queen Victoria. Mr. Somers Cocks, who had come to know Gilbert through his intimacy with Belloc, remembers that he wept when he heard of it. The tears may almost be heard in a letter to Frances.

Today the Queen was buried. I did not see the procession, first because I had an appointment with Hammond (of which more anon) and secondly because I think I felt the matter too genuinely. I like a crowd when I am triumphant or excited: for a crowd is the only thing that can *cheer,* as much as a cock is the only thing that can crow. Can anything be more absurd than the idea of a man cheering alone in his back bedroom? But I think that reverence is better expressed by one man than a million. There is something unnatural and impossible, even grotesque, in the idea of a vast crowd of human beings all assuming an air of delicacy. All the same, my dear, this is a great and serious hour and it is felt so completely by all England that I cannot deny the enduring wish I have, quite apart from certain more private sentiments, that the noblest Englishwoman I have ever known was here with me to renew, as I do, private vows of a very real character to do my best for this country of mine which I love with a love passing the love of Jingoes. It is sometimes easy to give one's country blood and easier to give her money. Sometimes the hardest thing of all is to give her truth.

I am writing an article on the good friend who is dead: I hope particularly that you will like it. The one I really like so far is Belloc's in the "Speaker." I had, as I said, many things to say, but owing to the hour and a certain fatigue and idiocy in myself, I have only space for the most important.

Hammond sent for me today and asked me seriously if I would help him in writing a book on Fox, sharing work, fame and profits. I told him that I had no special talent for research: he replied that he had no talent for literary form. I then said that I would be delighted to give him such assistance as I honestly thought valuable enough for him to split his profits for, that I thought I could give him such assistance in the matter of picturesqueness and plan of idea, more especially as Fox was a great hero of mine and the philosophy of his life involves the whole philosophy of the Revolution and of the love of mankind. We arranged that we would make a preliminary examination of the Fox record and then decide. . . .*

Three more letters, two to Frances, one to his mother, complete the outline of this eventful period. He was now determined to get married quickly. For the first time and entirely without rancour, he realised the inevitable competition in the world of journalism. The struggle for success meant men fighting one another. Other journalists were fighting him; but truly enough, though with a rare dispassionateness, he realised that this meant a need for daily bread in others similar to his own.

> 11, Warwick Gardens, W.
> (postmark: Feb. 19, 1901)

. . . I hope that in your own beautiful kindness you will be indulgent just at this time if I only write rough letters or postcards. I am for the first time in my life, thoroughly *worried,* and I find it a rather exciting and not entirely unpleasant sensation. But everything depends just now, not only on my sticking hard to work and doing a lot of my very best, but on my thinking about it, keeping wide awake to the turn of the market, being ready to do things not in half a week, but in half an hour; getting the feelings and tendencies of other men and generally living in work. I am going to see Lehmann tomorrow and many things may come of it. I cannot express to you what it is to feel the grip of the great wheel of real life on you for the first time. For the first time I know what is meant by the word "enemies"—men who deliberately dislike you and oppose

* This book was never written nor even, I think, begun.

your career—and the funny thing is that I don't dislike them at all myself. Poor devils—very likely they want to be married in June too.

I am a Socialist, but I love this fierce old world and am beginning to find a beauty in making money (in moderation) as in making statues. Always through my head one tune and words of Kipling set to it.

> "They passed one resolution, your sub-committee believe
> You can lighten the curse of Adam when you've light-
> ened the curse of Eve.
> And till we are built like angels, with hammer and
> chisel and pen
> We'll work for ourselves and a woman, for ever and
> ever—Amen."

11, Warwick Gardens, W.
(postmark: March 4, 1901)

. . . I have delayed this letter in a scandalous manner because I hoped I might have the arrangements with the Daily News to tell you; as that is again put off, I must tell you later. The following, however, are grounds on which I believe everything will turn out right this year. It is arithmetic. "The Speaker" has hitherto paid me £70 a year, that is £6 a month. It has now raised it to £10 a month, which makes £120 a year. Moreover they encourage me to write as much as I like in the paper, so that assuming that I do something extra (poem, note, leader) twice a month or every other number, which I can easily do, that brings us to nearly £150 a year. So much for "The Speaker." Now for the "Daily News," both certainties and probabilities. Hammond (to whom you will favour me by being eternally grateful) pushed me so strongly with Lehmann for the post of manager of the literary page that it is most probable that I shall get it. . . . If I do, Hammond thinks they couldn't give me less than £200 a year. So that if this turns out right, we have £350, say, without any aid from "Bookman," books, magazine articles or stories.

Let us however, put this chance entirely on one side and suppose that they can give me nothing but regular work on the "Daily News." I have just started a set of popular fighting articles on literature in the "Daily News" called "The Wars of Literature." They will appear at least twice a week, often three times. For each of these I am paid about a guinea and a half. This makes about £3 a week which is £144 a year. Thus with only the present certainties of "Speaker" and "Daily News" we have £264 a year, or very likely (with extra "Speaker" items) £288, close on £300. This again may be reinforced by all sorts of miscellaneous work which I shall get now my name is getting known, magazine articles, helping editors or publishers, reading Mss. and so on. In all these calculations I have kept deliberately under the figures, not over them: so that I don't think I have failed altogether to bring my promise within reasonable distance of fact already. Belloc suggested that I should write for the "Pilot" and as he is on it, he will probably get me some work. Hammond has become leader-writer on the "Echo" and will probably get me some reviewing on that. And between ourselves, to turn with intense relief, from all this egotism, Hammond and I have a little scheme on hand for getting Oldershaw a kind of editorial place on the "Echo" where they want a brisk but cultivated man of the world. I think we can bring it off: it is a good place for an ambitious young man. It would give me more happiness than I can say, while I am building my own house of peace, to do something for the man who did so much in giving me my reason for it.

> For well Thou knowest, O God most wise
> How good on earth was his gift to me
> Shall this be a little thing in thine eyes
> That is greater in mine than the whole great sea?

I am afraid . . . that this is a very dull letter. But you know what I am. I can be practical, but only deliberately, by fixing my mind on a thing. In this letter, I sum up my last month's thinking about money resources. I haven't given a thought yet to the application and distribution of them in rent, furniture, etc. When I have done thinking about that you will get another dull letter. I can keep ten poems and twenty theories in my head at once. But I can only think of one practical thing at a time. The only conclusion of this letter is that on any calculation whatever, we ought to have £300 a year, and be on the road to four in a little while. With this before you I daresay you (who are more practical than I) could speculate and suggest a little as to the form of living and expenditure. . . .

Gilbert's mother perhaps needed more convincing. The letter to her has no postmark but the £300 a year has grown to almost £500 and a careful economy is promised.

Mrs. Barnes
The Orchards
Burley. Hants.

My dearest Mother,

Thank you very much for your two letters. If you get back to Kensington before me (I shall return on Thursday night: I find I work here very well) would you mind sending on any letters. You might send on the cheque: though that is not necessary.

There is a subject we have touched on once or twice that I want to talk to you about, for I am very much worried in my mind as to whether you will disapprove of a decision I have been coming to with a very earnest belief that I am seeking to do the right thing. I have just had information that my screw from "The Speaker" will be yet further increased from £120 a year to £150, or, if I do the full amount I can, £190 a year. I have also had a request from the "Daily News" to do two columns a week regularly, which [is] rather over £100 a year, besides other book reviews. My other sources of income which should bring the amount up to nearly £150 more, at any rate, I will speak of in a moment.

There is something, as I say, that is distressing me a great deal. I believe I said about a year ago that I hoped to get married in a year, if I had money enough. I fancy you took it rather as a joke: I was not so certain about it myself then. I have however been coming very seriously to the conclusion that if I pull off one more affair —a favourable arrangement with Reynolds' Newspaper, whose editor wants to see me at the end of this week, I shall, unless you disapprove, make a dash for it this year. When I mentioned the matter a short time ago, you said (if I remember right) that you did not think I ought to marry under £400 or £500 a year. I was moved to go into the matter thoroughly then and there, but as it happened I knew I had one or two bargains just coming off which would bring me nearer to the standard you named, so I thought I would let it stand over till I could actually quote them. Believe me, my dearest mother, I am not considering this affair wildly or ignorantly: I have been doing nothing but sums in my head for the last months. This is how matters stand. The Speaker editor says they will take as much as I like to write. If I write my maximum I get £192 a year from them. From the Daily News, even if I do not get the post on the staff which was half promised me, I shall get at least £100 a year with a good deal over for reviews outside "The

Wars of Literature." That makes nearly £300. With the Manchester Sunday Chronicle I have just made a bargain by which I shall get £72 a year. This makes £370 a year altogether. The matter now, I think, largely depends on Reynolds' Newspaper. If I do, as is contemplated, weekly articles and thumbnail sketches, they cannot give me less than £100 a year. This would bring the whole to £470 a year, or within £30 of your standard. Of course I know quite well that this is not like talking of an income from a business or a certain investment. But we should live a long way within this income, if we took a very cheap flat, even a workman's flat if necessary, had a woman in to do the laborious daily work and for the rest waited on ourselves, as many people I know do in cheap flats. Moreover, journalism has its ups as well as downs, and I, I can fairly say, am on the upward wave. Without vanity and in a purely businesslike spirit I may say that my work is talked about a great deal. It is at least a remarkable fact that every one of the papers I write for (as detailed above) came to me and asked me to do work for them: from the Daily News down to the Manchester Sunday Chronicle. I have, as I say, what seems to me a sufficient income for a start. That I shall have as good and better I am as certain as that I sit here. I know the clockwork of these papers and among one set of them I might almost say that I am becoming the fashion.

Do not, please, think that I am entertaining this idea without realising that I shall have to start in a very serious and economical spirit. I have worked it out and I am sure we could live well within the above calculations and leave a good margin.

I make all these prosaic statements because I want you to understand that I know the risks I think of running. But it is not any practical question that is distressing me: on that I think I see my way. But I am terribly worried for fear you should be angry or sorry about all this. I am only kept in hope by the remembrance that I had the same fear when I told you of my engagement and that you dispelled it with a directness and generosity that I shall not forget. I think, my dear Mother, that we have always understood each other really. We are neither of us very demonstrative: we come of some queer stock that can always say least when it means most. But I do think you can trust me when I say that I think a thing really right, and equally honestly admit that I can hardly explain why. To explain why I know it is right would be to communicate the incommunicable, and speak of delicate and sacred things in bald words. The most I can say is that I know Frances like the back of my hand and can tell without a word from her that she has never recovered from a wound * and that there is only one kind of peace that will heal it.

I have tried to explain myself in this letter: I can do it better in a letter, somehow, but I do not think I have done it very successfully. However, with you it does not matter and it never will matter, how my thoughts come tumbling out. You at least have always understood what I meant.

Always your loving son,

GILBERT.

* Gertrude's death.

CHAPTER XI

Married Life in London

The suburbs are commonly referred to as prosaic. That is a matter of taste. Personally I find them intoxicating.
Introduction to *Literary London.*

THE WEDDING DAY drew near and the presents were pouring in.

"I feel like the young man in the Gospel," said Gilbert to Annie Firmin, "sorrowful, because I have great possessions."

Conrad Noel married Gilbert and Frances at Kensington Parish Church on June 28, 1901. As Gilbert knelt down the price ticket on the sole of one of his new shoes became plainly visible. Annie caught Mrs. Chesterton's eye and they began to laugh helplessly. Annie thinks, too, that for once in their lives Gilbert and Cecil did not argue at the Reception.

Lucian Oldershaw drove ahead to the station with the heavy luggage, put it on the train and waited feverishly. That train went off (with the luggage), then another, and at last the happy couple appeared. Gilbert had felt it necessary to stop on the way "in order to drink a glass of milk in one shop and to buy a revolver with cartridges in another." The milk he drank because in childhood his mother used to give him a glass in that shop. The revolver was for the defense of his bride against possible dangers. They followed the luggage by a slow train.

This love of weapons, his revolver, his favourite sword-stick, remained with him all his life. It suggested the adventures that he always bestowed on the heroes of his stories and would himself have loved to experience. He noted in *Twelve Types* Scott's love of armour and of weapons for their own sakes—the texture, the power, the beauty of a sword-hilt or a jewelled dagger. As a child would play with these things Gilbert played with them, but they stood also in his mind for freedom, adventure, personal responsibility, and much else that the modern world had lost.

The honeymoon was spent on the Norfolk Broads. On the way they stopped at Ipswich "and it was like meeting a friend in a fairy-tale to find myself under the sign of the White Horse on the first day of my honeymoon." Annie Firmin was staying in Warwick Gardens for the wedding and afterwards. Gilbert's first letter, from the Norfolk Broads, began "I have a wife, a piece of string, a pencil and a knife: what more can any man want on a honeymoon."

Asked on his return what wallpapers he would prefer in the house they had chosen, he asked for brown paper so that he could draw pictures everywhere. He had by no means abandoned this old habit, and Annie remembers an illness during which he asked for a long enough pencil to draw on the ceiling. Their quaint little house in Edwardes Square, Kensington, lent to them by Mr. Boore, an old friend of Frances, was close to Warwick Gardens. "I remember the house well," wrote E. C. Bentley later, "with its garden of old trees and its general air of Georgian peace. I remember too the splendid flaming frescoes, done in vivid crayons, of knights and heroes and divinities with which G.K.C. embellished the outside wall at the back, beneath a sheltering portico. I have often wondered whether the landlord charged for them as dilapidations at the end of the tenancy."

They were only in Edwardes Square for a few months and then moved to Overstrand Mansions, Battersea, where the rest of their London life was spent. It was here I came to know them a few years later. As soon as they could afford it they threw drawing-room and dining-room together to make one big room. At one end hung an Engagement board with what Father

O'Connor has described as a *"loud* inscription"—LEST WE FOR-
GET. Beside the engagements was pinned a poem by Hilaire
Belloc:

> Frances and Gilbert have a little flat
> At eighty pounds a year and cheap at that
> Where Frances who is Gilbert's only wife
> Leads an unhappy and complaining life:
> While Gilbert who is Frances' only man
> Puts up with it as gamely as he can.

The Bellocs chose life in the country much earlier than the
Chestertons, and an undated letter to Battersea threatens due
reprisals in an exclusion from their country home, if the Chestertons are not prepared to receive him in town at a late hour.

Kings Land, Shipley, Horsham

It will annoy you a good deal to hear that I am in town tomorrow
Wednesday evening and that I shall appear at your Apartment at
10.45 or 10.30 at earliest. P.M.! You are only just returned. You are
hardly settled down. It is an intolerable nuisance. You heartily wish
I had not mentioned it.

Well, you see that [arrow pointing to "Telegrams, Coolham, Sussex"], if you wire there before *One* you can put me off, but if you
do I shall melt your keys, both the exterior one which forms the
body or form of the matter and the interior one which is the mystical
content thereof.

Also if you put me off I shall not have you down here ever to see
the *Oak Room,* the *Tapestry Room,* the *Green Room* etc.

Yrs,

H.B.

Early in his Battersea life Gilbert received a note from Max
Beerbohm, the great humourist, introducing himself and suggesting a luncheon together.

I am quite different from my writings (and so, I daresay, are you
from yours)—so that we should not necessarily fail to hit it off.

I, in the flesh, am modest, full of commonsense, very genial, and
rather dull.

What you are remains to be seen—or not to be seen—by me, according to your decision.

Gilbert's decision was for the meeting and an instant liking grew into a warm friendship. As in J.D.C. days Gilbert had written verse about his friends, so now did he try to sum up an impression, perhaps after some special talk:

> And Max's queer crystalline sense
> Lit, like a sea beneath a sea,
> Shines through a shameless impudence
> As shameless a humility.
> Or Belloc somewhat rudely roared
> But all above him when he spoke
> The immortal battle trumpets broke
> And Europe was a single sword.*

Somewhere about this time must have occurred the incident mentioned by George Bernard Shaw in a note which appeared in the *Mark Twain Quarterly* (Spring, 1937):

I cannot remember when I first met Chesterton. I was so much struck by a review of Scott's *Ivanhoe* which he wrote for the *Daily News* in the course of his earliest notable job as feuilletonist to that paper that I wrote to him asking who he was and where he came from, as he was evidently a new star in literature. He was either too shy or too lazy to answer. The next thing I remember is his lunching with us on quite intimate terms, accompanied by Belloc.

The actual first meeting, forgotten by Shaw, is remembered by Gilbert's brother-in-law, Lucian Oldershaw. He and Gilbert had gone together to Paris where they visited Rodin, then making a bust of Bernard Shaw. Mr. Oldershaw introduced Gilbert to G.B.S., who, Rodin's secretary told them, had been endeavouring to explain at some length the nature of the Salvation Army, leading up (one imagines) to an account of *Major Barbara*. At the end of the explanation, Rodin's secretary remarked—to a

* Unpublished fragment.

rather apologetic Shaw—"The Master says you have not much French but you impose yourself."

"Shaw talked Gilbert down," Mr. Oldershaw complained. That the famous man should talk more than the beginner is hardly surprising, but all through Gilbert's life the complaint recurs on the lips of his admirers, just as a similar complaint is made by Lockhart about Sir Walter Scott. Chesterton, like Scott, abounded in cordial admiration of other men and women and had a simple enjoyment in meeting them. And Chesterton was one of the few great conversationalists—perhaps the only one— who would really rather listen than talk.

In 1901 appeared his first book of collected essays, *The De-fendant*. The essays in it had already appeared in *The Speaker*. Like all his later work it had the mixed reception of enthusiasts who saw what he meant, and puzzled reviewers who took refuge in that blessed word "paradox." "Paradox ought to be used," said one of these, "like onions to season the salad. Mr. Chesterton's salad is all onions. Paradox has been defined as 'truth standing on her head to attract attention'. Mr. Chesterton makes truth cut her throat to attract attention."

Without denying that his love of a joke led him into inde-fensible puns and suchlike fooleries (though Mgr. Ronald Knox tells me he is prepared to defend all of G.K.'s puns), I think nearly all his paradoxes were either the startling expression of an entirely neglected truth, or the startling re-emphasis of the neglected side of a truth. Once, he said: "It is a paradox, but it is God, and not I, who should have the credit of it." He proved his case a few years later in the chapter of *Orthodoxy* called "The Paradoxes of Christianity." What it amounted to was roughly this: paradox must be of the nature of things because of God's infinity and the limitations of the world and of man's mind. To us limited beings God can express His idea only in fragments. We can bring together apparent contradic-tions in those fragments whereby a greater truth is suggested.

If we do this in a sudden or incongruous manner we startle the unprepared and arouse the cry of paradox. But if we will not do it we shall miss a great deal of truth.

Chesterton also saw many proverbs and old sayings as containing a truth which the people who constantly repeated them had forgotten. The world was asleep and must be awakened. The world had gone placidly mad and must be violently restored to sanity. That the methods he used annoyed some is undeniable, but he did force people to think, even if they raged at him as the unaccustomed muscles came into play.

"I believe," he said in a speech at this date, "in getting into hot water. I think it keeps you clean." And he believed intensely in keeping out of a narrow stream of merely literary life. To those who exalted the poet above the journalist he gave this answer:

The poet writing his name upon a score of little pages in the silence of his study, may or may not have an intellectual right to despise the journalist: but I greatly doubt whether he would not morally be the better if he saw the great lights burning on through darkness into dawn, and heard the roar of the printing wheels weaving the destinies of another day. Here at least is a school of labour and of some rough humility, the largest work ever published anonymously since the great Christian cathedrals.*

He plunged then into the life of Fleet Street and held it his proudest boast to be a journalist. But he had his own way of being a journalist:

On the whole, I think I owe my success (as the millionaires say) to having listened respectfully and rather bashfully to the very best advice, given by all the best journalists who had achieved the best sort of success in journalism; and then going away and doing the exact opposite. For what they all told me was that the secret of success in journalism was to study the particular journal and write

* "A Word for the Mere Journalist." *Darlington North Star*: February 3, 1902.

what was suitable to it. And, partly by accident and ignorance and partly through the real rabid certainties of youth, I cannot remember that I ever wrote any article that was at all suitable to any paper. . . . I wrote on a Nonconformist organ like the old *Daily News* and told them all about French cafés and Catholic cathedrals; and they loved it, because they had never heard of them before. I wrote on a robust Labour organ like the old *Clarion* and defended mediaeval theology and all the things their readers had never heard of; and their readers did not mind me a bit.*

Mr. Titterton, who worked also on the *Daily News* and came at this time to know G.K. in the Pharos Club, says that at first he was rather shy of the other men on the staff but after a dinner at which he was asked to speak he came to know and like them and to be at home in Fleet Street. He liked to work amid human contact and would write his articles in a public-house or in the club or even in the street, resting the paper against a wall.

Frank Swinnerton records † a description given him by Charles Masterman of

how Chesterton used to sit writing his articles in a Fleet St. café, sampling and mixing a terrible conjunction of drinks, while many waiters hovered about him, partly in awe, and partly in case he should leave the restaurant without paying for what he had had. One day . . . the headwaiter approached Masterman. "Your friend," he whispered, admiringly, "he very clever man. He sit and laugh. And then he write. And then he laugh at what he write."

He loved Fleet Street and did a good deal of drinking there. But not only there. When (in the *Autobiography*) he writes of wine and song it is not Fleet Street and its taverns that come back to his mind but "the moonstruck banquets given by Mr. Maurice Baring," the garden in Westminster where he fenced with real swords against one more intoxicated than himself,

* *Autobiography*, pp. 185–6.
† *Georgian Scene*, p. 94.

songs shouted in Auberon Herbert's rooms near Buckingham Palace.

After marriage Frances seems to have given up the struggle, so ardently pursued during their engagement, to make him tidy. By a stroke of genius she decided instead to make him picturesque. The conventional frock-coat worn so unconventionally, the silk hat crowning a mat of hair, disappeared, and a wide-brimmed slouch hat and flowing cloak more appropriately garbed him. This was especially good as he got fatter. He was a tall man, six foot two. As a boy he had been thin, but now he was rapidly putting on weight. Neither he nor Cecil played games (the tennis did not last!) but they used to go for long walks, sometimes going off together for a couple of days at a time. Gilbert still liked to do this with Frances, but the sedentary daily life and the consumption of a good deal of beer did not help towards a graceful figure. By 1903 G.K. was called a fat humourist and he was fast getting ready to be Dr. Johnson in various pageants. By 1906—he was then thirty-two—he had become famous enough to be one of the celebrities painted or photographed for exhibitions; and Bernard Shaw described a photo of him by Coburn:

Chesterton is "our Quinbus Flestrin," the young Man Mountain, a large abounding gigantically cherubic person who is not only large in body and mind beyond all decency, but seems to be growing larger as you look at him—"swellin' wisibly," as Tony Weller puts it. Mr. Coburn has represented him as flowing off the plate in the very act of being photographed and blurring his own outlines in the process. Also he has caught the Chestertonian resemblance to Balzac and unconsciously handled his subject as Rodin handled Balzac. You may call the placing of the head on the plate wrong, the focussing wrong, the exposure wrong if you like, but Chesterton is right and a right impression of Chesterton is what Mr. Coburn was driving at.

The change in his appearance G.K. celebrated in a stanza of his "Ballade of the Grotesque":

I was light as a penny to spend,
   I was thin as an arrow to cleave,
I could stand on a fishing-rod's end
      With composure, though on the *qui vive*;
      But from Time, all a-flying to thieve,
   The suns and the moons of the year,
      A different shape I receive;
   The shape is decidedly queer.

"London," said a recently arrived American, "is the most marvellously fulfilling experience. I went to see Fleet Street this morning, and met G. K. Chesterton face to face. Wrapped in a cloak and standing in the doorway of a pie-shop, he was composing a poem reciting it aloud as he wrote. The most striking thing about the incident was that no one took the slightest notice."

I doubt if any writer, except Dickens, has so quickly become an institution as Chesterton. Nor, of course, would his picturesqueness in Fleet Street or his swift success as a journalist have accomplished this but for the vast output of books on every conceivable subject.

But before I come to the books written during those years at Battersea, a word must be said of another element besides his journalistic contacts that was linking G.K. with a wider world than the solely literary. We have seen that even when his religion was at its lowest point, in the difficult Art School days, he never lost it entirely—"I hung on to religion by one thin thread of thanks." In the years of the Notebook, he advanced very far in his pondering on and acceptance of the great religious truths. But this did not as yet mean attachment to a Church. Then he met Frances. "She actually practised a religion. This was something utterly unaccountable both to me and to the whole fussy culture in which she lived." Now that they were married, Frances, as a convinced Anglo-Catholic, was bringing more clergy and other Anglican friends into Gilbert's circle. Moreover, he was lecturing all over England, and this brought him into contact with all sorts of strange religious beliefs. "Amid all this scattered thinking . . . I began to piece together fragments of the old religious scheme; mainly by the various gaps that denoted its disappearance. And the more I saw of real human nature, the more I came to suspect that it was really rather bad for all these people that it had disappeared." *

In 1903-04 he had a tremendous battle (the detail of which will be treated in the next chapter) in the *Clarion* with Robert Blatchford. In it he adumbrated many of the ideas that were later developed in *Orthodoxy*. Of the arguments used by Blatchford and his atheist friends, G.K. wrote that the effect on his own mind was: "Almost thou persuadest me to be a Christian." In a diary kept by Frances spasmodically during the years 1904-05, she notes that Gilbert has been asked to preach as the first of a series of lay preachers in a city church. She writes:

March 16th. One of the proudest days of my life. Gilbert preached at St. Paul's, Covent Garden for the C.S.U. [Christian Social Union] *Vox populi vox Dei.* A crammed church—he was very eloquent and restrained. Sermons will be published afterwards.

Published they were: under the title, *Preachers from the Pew.*

March 30th. The second sermon: "The Citizen, tne Gentleman and the Savage." Even better than last week. "Where there is no vision the people perisheth."

When it is remembered that the *Browning,* the *Watts, Twelve Types* and *The Napoleon of Notting Hill* had all been published and received with acclaim, it is touching that Frances should speak thus of the "proudest day" of her life. That Gilbert should himself have vision and show it to others remained her strongest aspiration. Not thus felt all his admirers. The Blatchford controversy on matters religious became more than many of them could bear.

* *Autobiography,* p. 177.

A plaintive correspondent [says the *Daily News*], who seems to have had enough of the eternal verities and the eternal other things, sends us the following "lines written on reading Mr. G. K. Chesterton's forty-seventh reply to a secularist opponent":

What ails our wondrous "G.K.C."
　Who late, on youth's glad wings,
Flew fairylike, and gossip'd free
　Of translunary things,

That thus, in dull didactic mood,
　He quits the realms of dream,
And like some pulpit-preacher rude,
　Drones on one dreary theme?

Stern Blatchford, *thou* hast dashed the glee
　Of our Omniscient Babe;
Thy name alone now murmurs he,
　Or that of dark McCabe.

All vain his cloudy fancies swell,
　His paradox all vain,
Obsessed by that malignant spell
　Of Blatchford on the brain.

　　　　　　　　　　　　　　　　H.S.S.*

Mr. Noel has a livelier memory of Gilbert's religious and social activities. On one occasion he went to the Battersea flat for a meeting at which he was to speak and Gilbert take the chair, to establish a local branch of the Christian Social Union. The two men got into talk over their wine in the dining-room (then still a separate room) and Frances came in much agitated. "Gilbert you must dress. The people will be arriving any moment."

"Yes, yes, I'll go."

The argument was resumed and went on with animation. Frances came back. "Gilbert, the drawing-room is half full and people are still arriving." At last in despair she brought Gil-

* *Daily News*, 12 January, 1904.

bert's dress-clothes into the dining-room and made him change there, still arguing. Next he had to be urged into the drawing-room. Established at a small table he began to draw comic bishops, quite oblivious of the fact that he was to take the chair at the now assembled meeting. Finally Frances managed to attract his attention, he leaped up overthrowing the small table and scattering the comic bishops.

"Surely this story," said a friend to whom I told it, "proves what some people said about Chesterton's affectation. He must have been posing."

I do not think so, and those who knew Gilbert best believed him incapable of posing. But he was perfectly capable of wilfulness and of sulking like a schoolboy. It amused him to argue with Mr. Noel, it did not amuse him at all to take the chair at a meeting. So, as he was not allowed to go on arguing, he drew comic bishops.

There was, too, more than a touch of this wilfulness in the second shock he administered to respectable Battersea later in the evening. An earnest young lady asked the company for counsel as to the best way of arranging her solitary maid's evening out. "I'm so afraid," ended the appeal, "of her going to the Red Lion."

"Best place she could go," said Gilbert. And occasionally he would add example to precept, for society and Fleet Street were not the only places for human intercourse. "At present," commented a journalist, "he is cultivating the local politics of Battersea; in secluded ale houses he drinks with the frequenters and learns their opinions on municipal milk and on Mr. John Burns."

"Good friends and very gay companions," Gilbert calls the Christian Social Union group of whom, beside Conrad Noel, were Charles Masterman, Bishop Gore, Percy Dearmer, and above all Canon Scott Holland. Known as "Scotty" and adored by many generations of young men, he was "a man with a natural surge of laughter within him, so that his broad mouth seemed always to be shut down on it in a grimace of restraint." * Like Gilbert, he suffered from the effect of urging his most serious views with apparent flippancy and fantastic illustrations. In the course of a speech to a respectable Nottingham audience he remarked, "I dare say several of you here have never been in prison."

"A ghastly stare," says Gilbert, describing this speech, "was fixed on all the faces of the audience; and I have ever since seen it in my own dreams; for it has constituted a considerable part of my own problem."

Gilbert's verses, summarizing the meeting as it must have sounded to a worthy Nottingham tradesman, are quoted in the *Autobiography* and completed in *Father Brown on Chesterton.* I have put them together here for they show how merrily these men were working to change the world.

> The Christian Social Union here
> Was very much annoyed;
> It seems there is some duty
> Which we never should avoid,
> And so they sang a lot of hymns
> To help the Unemployed.
>
> Upon a platform at the end
> The speakers were displayed
> And Bishop Hoskins stood in front
> And hit a bell and said
> That Mr. Carter was to pray,
> And Mr. Carter prayed.
>
> Then Bishop Gore of Birmingham
> He stood upon one leg
> And said he would be happier
> If beggars didn't beg,
> And that if they pinched his palace
> It would take him down a peg.

* *Autobiography*, p. 169.

He said that Unemployment
Was a horror and a blight,
He said that charities produced
Servility and spite,
And stood upon the other leg
And said it wasn't right.

And then a man named Chesterton
Got up and played with water,
He seemed to say that principles
Were nice and led to slaughter
And how we always compromised
And how we didn't orter.

Then Canon Holland fired ahead
Like fifty cannons firing,
We tried to find out what he meant
With infinite enquiring,
But the way he made the windows jump
We couldn't help admiring.

I understood him to remark
(It seemed a little odd.)
That half a dozen of his friends
Had never been in quod.
He said he was a Socialist himself,
And so was God.

He said the human soul should be
Ashamed of every sham,
He said a man should constantly
Ejaculate "I am"
When he had done, I went outside
And got into a tram.

Partly perhaps to console himself for the loss of his son's daily
company, chiefly, I imagine, out of sheer pride and joy in his
success, Edward Chesterton started after the publication of *The
Wild Knight* pasting all Gilbert's press-cuttings into volumes.
Later I learnt that it had long been Gilbert's weekly penance

to read these cuttings on Sunday afternoon at his father's house. Traces of his passage are visible wherever a space admits of a caricature, and occasionally, where it does not, the caricature is superimposed on the text.

His growing fame may be seen by the growing size of these volumes and the increased space given to each of his books. *Twelve Types* in 1902 had a good press for a young man's work and was taken seriously in some important papers, but its success was as nothing compared with that of the *Browning* a year later. The bulk of *Twelve Types,* as of *The Defendant,* had appeared in periodicals, but never in his life did Gilbert prepare a volume of his essays for the press without improving, changing and unifying. It was never merely a collection, always a book.

Still, the *Browning* was another matter. It was a compliment for a comparatively new author to be given the commission for the English Men of Letters Series. Stephen Gwynn describes the experience of the publishers:

On my advice the Macmillans had asked him to do Browning in the "English Men of Letters," when he was still not quite arrived. Old Mr. Craik, the Senior Partner, sent for me and I found him in white fury, with Chesterton's proofs corrected in pencil; or rather not corrected; there were still thirteen errors uncorrected on one page; mostly in quotations from Browning. A selection from a Scotch ballad had been quoted from memory and three of the four lines were wrong. I wrote to Chesterton saying that the firm thought the book was going to "disgrace" them. His reply was like the trumpeting of a crushed elephant. But the book was a huge success.*

In fact, it created a sensation and established G.K. in the front rank. Not all the reviewers liked it, and one angry writer in the *Athenaeum* pointed out that, not content with innumerable inaccuracies about Browning's descent and the events of his life, G.K. had even invented a line in "Mr. Sludge the Medium." But every important paper had not only a review but

* Quoted in *Chesterton,* by Cyril Clemens, p. 14.

a long review, and the vast majority were enthusiastic. Chesterton claimed Browning as a poet not for experts but for every
man. His treatment of the Browning love affair, of the poet's
obscurity, of "The Ring and the Book," all receive this same
praise of an originality which casts a true and revealing light
for his readers. As with all his literary criticism, the most famous
critics admitted that he had opened fresh windows on the subject for themselves.

This attack on his inaccuracy and admiration for his insight
constantly recurs with Chesterton's literary work. Readers noted
that in the *Ballad of the White Horse* he made Alfred's left wing
face Guthrum's left wing. He was amused when it was pointed
out, but never bothered to alter it. His memory was prodigious.
All his friends testify to his knowing by heart pages of his
favourite authors (and these were not few). Ten years after his
time with Fisher Unwin, Frances told Father O'Connor that
he remembered all the plots and most of the characters of the
"thousands" of novels he had read for the firm. But he trusted
his memory too much and never verified. Indeed, when it was
a question merely of verbal quotation he said it was pedantic
to bother, and when latterly Dorothy Collins looked up his
references he barely tolerated it.

Again while he constantly declared that he was no scholar,
he said things illuminating even to scholars. Thus, much later,
when Chesterton's *St. Thomas Aquinas* appeared, the Master-
General of the Dominican Order, Père Gillet, O.P., lectured on
and from it to large meetings of Dominicans. Mr. Eccles told
me that talking of Virgil, G.K. said things immensely illuminating for experts on Latin poetry. In a very different field, Mr.
Oldershaw noted after their trip to Paris that though he could
set Gilbert right on many a detail yet his generalisations were
marvellous. He had, said Mr. Eccles, an intuitive mind. He had,
too, read more than was realised, partly because his carelessness
and contempt for scholarship misled. Where the pedant would

have referred and quoted and cross-referred, he went dashing on, throwing out ideas from his abundance and caring little if among his wealth were a few faults of fact or interpretation. "Abundance" was a word much used of his work just now, and in the field of literary criticism he was placed high, and had an enthusiastic following. We may assume that the *Browning* had something to do with Sir Oliver Lodge's asking him in the next year (1904) to become a candidate for the Chair of Literature at Birmingham University. But he had no desire to be a professor.

Frances, in her diary, notes some of their widening contacts and engagements. The mixture of shrewdness and simplicity in her comments will be familiar to those who knew her intimately. Meeting her for the first time I think the main impression was that of the "single eye." She abounded in Gilbert's sense, as my mother commented after an early meeting, and ministered to his genius. Yet she never lost an individual, markedly feminine point of view, which helped him greatly, as anyone can see who will read all he wrote on marriage. He shows an insight almost uncanny in the section called, "The Mistake About Women" in *What's Wrong with the World.* "Some people," he said in a speech of 1905, "when married gain each other. Some only lose themselves." The Chestertons gained each other. And by the sort of paradox he loved, Frances did so by throwing the stream of her own life unreservedly into the greater river of her husband's. She writes in her Diary, for 1904:

Gilbert and I meet all sorts of queer, well-known, attractive, unattractive people and I expect this book will be mostly about them. . . .

Feb. 17th. We went together to Mr. and Mrs. Sidney Colvin's "At home." It was rather jolly but too many clever people there to be really nice. The clever people were Mr. Joseph Conrad, Mr. Henry James, Mr. Laurence Binyon, Mr. Maurice Hewlett, and a great many more. Mr. and Mrs. Colvin looked so happy.

Feb. 23rd. Gilbert went as Mr. Lane's guest to a dinner of the

"Odd Volumes" at the Imperial Restaurant. The other guest was Baden Powell. He and Gilbert made speeches. . . .

March 8th. Gilbert was to speak on "Education" at a C.S.U. meeting at Sion College, but a debate on the Chinese Labour in South Africa was introduced instead and went excitingly. There is to be a big meeting of the C.S.U. to protest. Though I suppose it's all no good now. When the meeting was over we adjourned to a tea-shop and had immense fun. Gilbert, Percy Dearmer and Conrad Noel walked together down Fleet Street, and never was there a funnier sight. Gilbert's costume consisted of a frock coat, huge felt hat and walking stick brandished in the face of the passers-by, to their exceeding great danger. Conrad was dressed in an old lounge suit of sober grey with a clerical hat jauntily stuck on the back of his head (which led someone to remark, "Are you here in the capacity of a private gentleman, poor curate, or low-class actor?"). Mr. Dearmer was clad in wonderful clerical garments of which he alone possesses the pattern, which made him look like a Chaucer Canterbury Pilgrim or a figure out of a Noah's ark. They swaggered down the roadway talking energetically. At tea we talked of many things, the future of the "Commonwealth" chiefly . . .

March 22nd. Meeting of Christian Theosophical Society at which Gilbert lectured on "How Theosophy appears to a Christian." He was very good. Herbert Burrows vigorously attacked him in debate afterwards . . . *Napoleon of Notting Hill* was published.

April 27th. The Bellocs and the Noels came here to dinner. Hilaire in great form recited his own poetry with great enthusiasm the whole evening . . .

May 9th. The Literary Fund Dinner. About the greatest treat I ever had in my life. J. M. Barrie presided. He was so splendid and so complimentary. Mrs. J. M. Barrie is very pretty, but the most beautiful woman there was Mrs. Anthony Hope—copper coloured hair, masses, with a wreath of gardenias—green eyes—and a long neck, very beautiful figure. The speakers were Barrie, Lord Tennyson, Comyns Carr, A. E. W. Mason, Mrs. Craigie (who acquitted herself wonderfully) and Mrs. Flora Annie Steel. After the formal dinner was a reception at which everyone was very friendly. It is wonderful the way in which they all accept Gilbert, and one well-known man told me he was the biggest man present. Anyhow there was the feeling of brotherhood and fellowship in the wielding of "the lovely and loathely pen" (J. M. Barrie's speech).

May 12th. Went to see Max Beerbohm's caricature of Gilbert at the Carfax Gallery. "G.K.C.—Humanist—Kissing the World." It's more like Thackeray, very funny though.

June 9th. A political "at home" at Mrs. Sidney Webb's—Saw Winston Churchill and Lloyd George. Politics and nothing but politics is dull work though, and an intriguer's life must be a pretty poor affair. Mrs. Sidney Webb looked very handsome and moved among her guests as one to the manner born. I like Mrs. Leonard Courtenay who is always kind to me. Charlie Masterman and I had a long talk on the iniquities of the "Daily News" and goodness knows they are serious enough.

June 22nd. An "at home" at Mrs. ——'s proved rather a dull affair save for a nice little conversation with Watts Dunton. His walrusy appearance which makes the bottom of his face look fierce, is counteracted by the kindness of his little eyes. He told us the inner story of Whistler's "Peacock Room" which scarcely redounds to Whistler's credit. The Duchess of Sutherland was there and many notabilities. Between ourselves Mr. —— is a good-hearted snob. His wife nice, intelligent, but affected (I suppose unconsciously). I don't really like the "precious people." They worry me.

June 30th. Graham Robertson's "at home" was exceedingly select. I felt rather too uncultivated to talk much. Mr. Lane tucked his arm into mine and requested to know the news which means, "tell me all your husband is doing, or going to do, how much is he getting, who will publish for him, has he sold his American rights, etc." Cobden's three daughters looked out of place, so solid and sincere are they. It was all too grand. No man ought to have so much wealth.

July 5th. Gilbert went today to see Swinburne—I think he found it rather hard to reconcile the idea with the man, but he was interested, though I could not gather much about the visit. He was amused at the compliments which Watts Dunton and Swinburne pay to each other unceasingly.

December 8th. George Alexander has an idea that he wants Gilbert to write a play for him, and sent for him to come and see him. He was apparently taken with the notion of a play on the Crusades, and although there is at present no love incident in Gilbert's mind, Alexander introduced and acted the supposed love scene with great spirit. It may come off some day perhaps.

December 31st. H. Belloc's been very ill but is better, thank God.

1905

Feb. 1st. Gilbert, a guest at the "Eighty Club" dinner. Rhoda and I went to after dinner speeches. G. W. E. Russell (Chair). Augustine Birrell guest and Sir Henry Fowler. It amused me hugely. Russell so imprudent and reckless, Birrell so prudent and incapable of giving himself away, Sir Henry Fowler so commonplace and trite. He looked so wicked. I thought of Mr. Haldane's story of Fowler's fur coat and his single remark on examining it: "skunk."

Feb. 11th. Rather an interesting lunch at Mrs. J. R. Green's. Jack Yeats and Mrs. Thursby were there. The atmosphere is too political and I imagine Mrs. Green to be a bit of a wire-puller, though I believe a nice woman.

Feb. 24th. Mr. Halliwell Sutcliffe came over. He is amusing and nice. Very puzzled at Gilbert's conduct, which on this particular occasion was peculiarly eccentric.

March 9th. I had an amusing lunch at the Hotel Cecil with Miss Bisland (representative of McClure). Evidently thinks a lot of Gilbert and wants his work for McClure. O ye gods and little fishes! The diplomatic service ought to be all conducted by women. I offered her Margaret's poems in exchange for a short interview with Meredith which she wishes Gilbert to undertake.

March 14th. Gilbert dined at the Buxtons, met Asquith.

March 19th. Lienie is in town and we have been with her to call on the Duchess of Sutherland. When I had got used to the splendour it was jolly enough. Her Grace is a pretty, sweet woman who was very nervous, but got better under the fire of Gilbert's chaff. She made him write in her album which he did, a most ridiculous poem of which he should be ashamed. It must be truly awful to live in the sort of way the Duchess does and endeavour to keep sane.

May 20th. Words fail me when I try to recall the sensation aroused by a J.D.C. dinner. It seems so odd to think of these men as boys, to realize what their school life was and what a powerful element the J.D.C. was in the lives of all. And there were husbands and wives, and the tie so strong, and the long, long thoughts of schoolboys and schoolgirls fell on us, as if the battle were still to come instead of raging round us.

May 24th. We went together to see George Meredith. I suppose many people have seen him in his little Surrey Cottage; Flint Cottage, Boxhill. He has a wonderful face and a frail old body. He talks without stopping except to drink ginger-beer. He told us many stories, mostly about society scandals of some time back. I remember he asked Gilbert, "Do you like babies?" and when Gilbert said, "Yes," he said "So do I, especially in the comet stage."

June 5th. Granville Barker came to see Gilbert, touching the possibility of a play.

June 29th. A garden party at the Bishop's House, Kennington. The Bishop told me that A. J. Balfour was very impressed with "Heretics." Guild of St. Matthew Service and rowdy supper. Gilbert made an excellent speech.

July 5th. Gilbert dined at the Asquiths; met Rosebery. I think he hated it.

July 16th. Gilbert went to see Mrs. Grenfell at Taplow. He met Balfour, Austen Chamberlain and George Wyndham. Had an amusing time, no doubt. Says Balfour is most interesting to talk to but appears bored. George Wyndham is delightful.

One felt always with both Frances and Gilbert that this society life stayed on the surface—amusing, distracting, sometimes welcome, sometimes boring—but never infringing the deeper reality of their relationships with old friends, with their own families, with each other. Frances wrote endless business and other letters for them both: in just a handful, mainly to Father O'Connor, does she show her deeper life of thought and feeling. Gilbert had little time now for writing anything but books and articles. Never a very good correspondent he had become an exceedingly bad one. Annie Firmin's engagement to Robert Kidd produced one of the few letters that exist. It is handwritten and undated.

A Restaurant somewhere.

MY DEAR ANNIE,

I have thought of you, I am quite certain, more often than I have of any human being for a long time past—except my wife who recalls herself continually to me by virtues, splendours, agreeable memories, screams, pokers, brickbats and other things. And yet, though whenever my mind was for an instant emptied of theology and journalism and patriotism and such rot, it has been immediately filled with you, I have never written you a line.

I am not going to explain this and for a good reason. It is a part of the Mystery of the Male, and you will soon, even if you do not already, get the hang of it, by the society of an individual who while being unmistakably a much better man than I am, is nevertheless male. I can only say that when men want a thing they act quite differently to women. We put off everything we want to do, in the ordinary way. If the Archangel Michael wrote me a complimentary letter tomorrow (as perhaps he may) I should put it in my pocket, saying, "How admirable a reply shall I write to that in a week or a month or so." I put off writing to you because I wanted to write something that had in it all that you have been, to me, to all of us. And now instead I am scrawling this nonsense in a tavern after lunch.

My very dear old friend, I am of a sex that very seldom takes real trouble, that forgets the little necessities of time, that is by nature lazy. I never wanted really but one thing in my life and that I got. Any person inspecting 60 Overstrand Mansions may see that somewhat excitable thing—free of charge. In another person, whom with maddening jealousy I suspect of being some inches taller than I am, I believe I notice the same tendency towards monomania. He also, being as I have so keenly pointed out, male, he also—I think has only wanted one thing seriously in his life. He also has got it: another male weakness which I recognize with sympathy.

All my reviewers call me frivolous. Do you think all this kind of thing frivolous? Damn it all (excuse me) what can one be but frivolous about serious things? Without frivolity they are simply too tremendous. That you, who, with your hair down your back, played at bricks with me in a house of which I have no memory except you and the bricks, that you should be taken by someone of my miserable sex—as you ought to be—what is one to say? I am not going to wish you happiness, because I am quite placidly certain that your happiness is inevitable. I know it because my wife is happy with me and the wild, weird, extravagant, singular origin of this is a certain enduring fact in my psychology which you will find paralleled elsewhere.

God bless you, my dear girl.

Yours ever,

GILBERT CHESTERTON.

Married in 1903, Annie and her husband took another flat in Overstrand Mansions.

"Gilbert never cared what he wore," she writes. "I remember one night when my husband and I were living in the same block of flats he came in to ask me to go and sit with Frances who wasn't very well, while he went down to the House to dine with Hugh Law—Gilbert was very correctly dressed except for the fact that he had on one boot and one slipper! I pointed it out to him, and he said: 'Do you think it matters?' I told him I was sure Frances would not like him to go out like that—the only argument to affect him! When he was staying with me here in Vancouver, Dorothy Collins had to give him the once-over before he went lecturing—they had left Frances in Palos Verdes as she wasn't well."

In 1904, were published a monograph on Watts, *The Napoleon of Notting Hill* and an important chapter in a composite book, *England a Nation*.

The *Watts* is among the results of Gilbert's art studies. Its reviewers admired it somewhat in the degree of their admiration for the painter. But for a young man at that date to have seen the principles of art he lays down meant rare vision. The portrait-painter, he says, is trying to express the reality of the man himself but "he is not above taking hints from the book of life with its quaint old woodcuts." G.K. makes us see all the painter could have thought or imagined as he sets us before "Mammon" or "Jonah" or "Hope," and bids us read their legend and note the texture and lines of the painting. His distinction between the Irish mysticism of Yeats and the English mysticism of Watts is especially valuable, and the book, perhaps even more than the *Browning* or the *Dickens,* manifests Gilbert's insight into the mind of the last generation. The depths and limitations of the Victorian outlook may be read in *G. F. Watts.*

The story of the writing of *The Napoleon* was told me in

part by Frances, while part appeared in an interview * given by Gilbert, in which he called it his first important book:

I was "broke"—only ten shillings in my pocket. Leaving my worried wife, I went down Fleet Street, got a shave, and then ordered for myself, at the Cheshire Cheese, an enormous luncheon of my favourite dishes and a bottle of wine. It took my all, but I could then go to my publishers fortified. I told them I wanted to write a book and outlined the story of "Napoleon of Notting Hill." But I must have twenty pounds, I said, before I begin.

"We will send it to you on Monday."

"If you want the book," I replied, "you will have to give it to me today as I am disappearing to write it." They gave it.

Frances meanwhile sat at home thinking, as she told me, hard thoughts of his disappearance with their only remaining coin. And then dramatically he appeared with twenty golden sovereigns and poured them into her lap. Referring to this incident later, Gilbert said, "What a fool a man is, when he comes to the last ditch, not to spend the last farthing to satisfy the inner man before he goes out to fight a battle with wits." But it was his way to let the money shortage become acute and then deal with it abruptly. Frank Swinnerton relates that when, as a small boy, he was working for J. M. Dent, Gilbert appeared after office hours with a Dickens preface but refused to leave it because Swinnerton, the only soul left in the place, could not give him the agreed remuneration.

The *Napoleon* is the story of a war between the London suburbs, and grew largely from his meditations on the Boer War. Besides being the best of his fantastic stories, it contains the most picturesque account of Chesterton's social philosophy that he ever gave. But it certainly puzzled some of the critics. One American reviewer feels that he might have understood the book if he "had an intimate knowledge of the history of the various boroughs of London and of their present-day character-

---

* Quoted in *Chesterton*, by Cyril Clemens, pp. 16–17.

istics." Others treat the story as a mere joke, and many feel that
it is a bad descent after the *Browning*. "Too infernally clever for
anything," says one.

Auberon Quin, King of England, chosen by lot (as are all
kings and all other officials by the date of this story, which is a
romance of the future), is one of the two heroes of this book.
He is simply a sense of humour incarnate. His little elfish face
and figure was recognised by old Paulines as suggested by a
form master of their youth; but by the entire reviewing world
as Max Beerbohm. The illustrations by Graham Robertson were
held to be unmistakably Max. Frances notes in her diary:

A delightful dinner party at the Lanes. . . . The talk was mostly
about *Napoleon*. Max took me in to dinner and was really nice. He
is a good fellow. His costume was extraordinary. Why should an
evening waistcoat have four large white pearl buttons and why
should he look that peculiar shape? He seems only pleased at the
way he has been identified with King Auberon. "All right, my dear
chap," he said to G., who was trying to apologize. "Mr. Lane and I
settled it all at a lunch." I think he was a little put out at finding
no red carpet put down for his royal feet and we had quite a discussion as to whether he ought to precede me into the dining room.
Graham Robertson was on my left. He was jolly too, kept on producing wonderful rings and stones out of his pockets. He said he
wished he could go about covered in the pieces of a chandelier.
The other guests were Lady Seton, Mrs. W. K. Clifford, Mr. W. W.
Howells and his daughter (too Burne-Jonesy to be really attractive),
Mr. Taylor (police magistrate), and Mrs. Eichholz (Mrs. Lane's
mother) who is more beautiful than anything except a wee baby.
In fact, she looks exactly like one, so dainty and small. She can
never at any time have been as pretty as she is now.

Gilbert and Max and I drove to his house (Max's), where he
basely enticed us in. He gave me fearful preserved fruits which
ruined my dress—but he made himself very entertaining. Home 1.30.

Caring for nothing in the world but a joke, King Auberon
decrees that the dull and respectable London boroughs shall
be given city guards in resplendent armour, each borough to

have its own coat of arms, its city walls, tocsin, and the like. The idea is taken seriously by the second hero, Adam Wayne of Notting Hill, an enthusiast utterly lacking any sense of humour who goes to war with the other boroughs of London to protect a small street which they have designed to pull down in the interests of commercial development. Pimlico, Kensington and the rest attack Notting Hill. Men bleed and die in the contest and by the magic of the sword the old ideas of local patriotism and beauty in civic life return to England. The conventional politician, Barker, who begins the story in a frock-coat and irreproachable silk hat, ends it clad in purple and gold.

When Notting Hill, become imperial minded, goes down to destruction in a sea of blood, Auberon Quin confesses to Wayne that this whole story, so full of human tragedy and hopes and fears, had been merely the outcome of a joke. To him all life was a joke, to Wayne an epic; and this antagonism between the humorist and the fanatic has created the whole wild story. Wayne has the last word:

"I know of something that will alter that antagonism, something that is outside us, something that you and I have all our lives perhaps taken too little account of. The equal and eternal human being will alter that antagonism, for the human being sees no real antagonism between laughter and respect, the human being, the common man, whom mere geniuses like you and me can only worship like a god. When dark and dreary days come, you and I are necessary, the pure fanatic, the pure satirist. We have between us remedied a great wrong. We have lifted the modern cities into that poetry which every one who knows mankind knows to be immeasurably more common than the commonplace. But in healthy people there is no war between us. We are but the two lobes of the brain of a ploughman. Laughter and love are everywhere. The cathedrals, built in the ages that loved God, are full of blasphemous grotesques. The mother laughs continually at the child, the lover laughs continually at the lover, the wife at the husband, the friend at the friend. Auberon Quin, we have been too long separated; let us go out together. You have a halberd and I a sword, let us start our wanderings over the world. For we are its two essentials. Come, it is already day."

In the blank white light Auberon hesitated a moment. Then he made the formal salute with his halberd, and they went away together into the unknown world.*

This is very important to the understanding of Chesterton. With him, profound gravity and exuberant fooling were always intermingled and some of his deepest thoughts are conveyed by a pun. He always claimed to be intensely serious while hating to be solemn and it was a mixture apt to be misunderstood. If gravity and humour are the two lobes of the average man's brain, the average man does not bring them into play simultaneously to anything like the extent that Chesterton did.

Auberon Quin and Adam Wayne are the most living individuals in any of his novels—just because they are the two lobes of his brain individualised. All his stories abound in adventure, are admirable in their vivid descriptions of London or the countryside of France or England seen in fantastic visions. They are living in the portrayal of ideas by the road of argument. But the characters are chiefly energies through whose lips Gilbert argues with Gilbert until some conclusion shall be reached.

In 1905 came *The Club of Queer Trades*—least good of the fantasia—and even admirers have begun to wonder if too many fields are being tried; in 1906, *Dickens* and *Heretics*.

It will remain a moot point whether the *Browning* or the *Dickens* is Chesterton's best work of literary criticism. The *Dickens* is the more popular, largely because Dickens is the more popular author. Most Dickens idolators read anything about their idol if only for the pleasure of the quotations. And no Dickens idolator could fail to realise that here was one even more rapt in worship than himself. After the publication of *Charles Dickens,* Chesterton undertook a series of prefaces to the novels. In one of them he took the trouble to answer one only of the

* Pp. 300–301.

criticisms the book had produced: the comment that he was reading into the work of Dickens something that Dickens did not mean.

Criticism does not exist to say about authors the things that they knew themselves. It exists to say the things about them which they did not know themselves. If a critic says that the *Iliad* has a pagan rather than a Christian pity, or that it is full of pictures made by one epithet, of course he does not mean that Homer could have said that. If Homer could have said that the critic would leave Homer to say it. The function of criticism, if it has a legitimate function at all, can only be one function—that of dealing with the subconscious part of the author's mind which only the critic can express, and not with the conscious part of the author's mind, which the author himself can express. Either criticism is no good at all (a very defensible position) or else criticism means saying about an author the very things that would have made him jump out of his boots.*

He attended not at all to the crop of comments on his inaccuracies. One reviewer pointed out that Chesterton had said that every postcard Dickens wrote was a work of art; but Dickens died on June 9th, 1870 and the first British postcard was issued on October 1st, 1870. "A wonderful instance of Dickens's never-varying propensity to keep ahead of his age." After all, what did such things matter? Bernard Shaw, however, felt that they did. He wrote a letter from which I think Gilbert got an important hint, utilized later in his introduction to *David Copperfield*:

6th September, 1906.

Dear G.K.C.

As I am a supersaturated Dickensite, I pounced on your book and read it, as Wegg read Gibbon and other authors, right slap through.

In view of a second edition, let me hastily note for you one or two matters. First and chiefly, a fantastic and colossal howler in the best manner of Mrs. Nickleby and Flora Finching.

There is an association in your mind (well founded) between the

* Introduction to "Old Curiosity Shop." Reprinted in *Criticisms and Appreciations of the Works of Charles Dickens,* 1933 ed. pp. 51-2.

quarrel over Dickens's determination to explain his matrimonial difficulty to the public, and the firm of Bradbury and Evans. There is also an association (equally well founded) between B. & E. and Punch. They were the publishers of Punch. But to gravely tell the XX century that Dickens wanted to publish his explanation in Punch is gas and gaiters carried to an incredible pitch of absurdity. The facts are: B. & E. were the publishers of Household Words. They objected to Dickens explaining in H.W. He insisted. They said that in that case they must take H.W. out of his hands. Dickens, like a lion threatened with ostracism by a louse in his tail, published his explanation, which stands to this day, and informed his readers that they were to ask in future, not for Household Words, but for All the Year Round. Household Words, left Dickensless, gasped for a few weeks and died. All the Year Round, in exactly the same format, flourished and entered largely into the diet of my youth.

. . .

There is a curious contrast between Dickens's sentimental indiscretions concerning his marriage and his sorrows and quarrels, and his impenetrable reserve about himself as displayed in his published correspondence. He writes to his family about waiters, about hotels, about screeching tumblers of hot brandy and water, and about the seasick man in the next berth, but never one really intimate word, never a real confession of his soul. David Copperfield is a failure as an autobiography because when he comes to deal with the grown-up David, you find that he has not the slightest intention of telling you the truth—or indeed anything—about himself. Even the child David is more remarkable for the reserves than for the revelations: he falls back on fiction at every turn. Clennam and Pip are the real autobiographies.

I find that Dickens is at his greatest after the social awakening which produced Hard Times. Little Dorrit is an enormous work. The change is partly the disillusion produced by the unveiling of capitalist civilization, but partly also Dickens's discovery of the gulf between himself as a man of genius and the public. That he did not realize this early is shown by the fact that he found out his wife *before he married her* as much too small for the job, and yet plumbed the difference so inadequately that he married her thinking he could go through with it. When the situation became intolerable, he must have faced the fact that there was something more than "incompatibilities" between him and the average man and woman. Little Dorrit is written, like all the later books, frankly and somewhat sadly, *de haut en bas*. In them Dickens recognizes that quite everyday men are as grotesque as Bunsby. Sparkler, one of the most extravagant of all his gargoyles, is an untouched photograph almost. Wegg and Riderhood are sinister and terrifying because they are simply real, which Squeers and Sikes are not. And please remark that whilst Squeers and Sikes have their speeches written with anxious verisimilitude (comparatively) Wegg says, "Man shrouds and grapple, Mr. Venus, or she dies," and Riderhood describes Lightwood's sherry (when retracting his confession) as, "I will not say a hocussed wine, but a wine as was far from 'elthy for the mind." Dickens doesn't care what he makes Wegg or Riderhood or Sparkler or Mr. F's aunt say, because he knows them and has got them, and knows what matters and what doesn't. Fledgeby, Lammle, Jerry Cruncher, Trabbs's boy, Wopsle, etc. etc. are human beings as seen by a master. Swiveller and Mantalini are human beings as seen by Trabbs's boy. Sometimes Trabbs's boy has the happier touch. When I am told that young John Chivery (whose epitaphs you ignore whilst quoting Mrs. Sapsea's) would have gone barefoot through the prison against rules for Little Dorrit had it been paved with red hot ploughshares, I am not so affected by his chivalry as by Swiveller's exclamation when he gets the legacy—"For she (the Marchioness) shall walk in silk attire and siller hae to spare." Edwin Drood is no good, in spite of the stone throwing boy, Buzzard and Honeythunder. Dickens was a dead man before he began it. Collins corrupted him with plots. And oh! the Philistinism; the utter detachment from the great human heritage of art and philosophy! Why not a sermon on that?

G.B.S.

Note in the Introduction to *David Copperfield* what G.K. says as to the break between the two halves of the book. He calls it an instance of weariness in Dickens—a solitary instance. Is not Shaw's explanation at once fascinating and probable?

Kate Perugini, the daughter of Dickens, wrote two letters of immense enthusiasm about the book saying it was the best thing written about her father since Forster's biography. But she shatters the theory put forth by Chesterton that Dickens thrown into intimacy with a large family of girls fell in love with them all and happened unluckily to marry the wrong sister. At the time of the marriage her mother, the eldest of the sisters, was only eighteen, Mary between fourteen and fifteen "very young and childish in appearance," Georgina eight and Helen three! Nothing could better illustrate the clash between enthusiasm and despair that fills a Chestertonian while reading any of his literary biographies. For so much is built on this theory which the slightest investigation would have shown to be baseless.

Heretics aroused animosity in many minds. Dealing with Browning or Dickens a man may encounter literary prejudices or enthusiasms, but there is not the intensity of feeling that he finds when he gets into the field with his own contemporaries. Reviewers who had been extending a friendly welcome to a beginner found that beginner attacking landmarks in the world of letters, venturing to detest Ibsen and to ask William Archer whether he hung up his stocking on Ibsen's birthday, accusing Kipling of lack of patriotism. It is, said one angrily, "unbecoming to spend most of his time criticising his contemporaries." "His sense of mental perspective is an extremely deficient one." "The manufacture of paradoxes is really one of the simplest processes conceivable." "Mr. Chesterton's sententious wisdom."

In fact it was like the scene in *The Napoleon of Notting Hill* when most people present were purple with anger but an intellectual few were purple with laughter. And even now most of the reviewers seemed not to understand where G.K. stood or what was his philosophy. "Bernard Shaw," says one, "whom *as a disciple* * he naturally exalts." This, after a series of books in which G.K. had exposed, with perfect lucidity and a wealth of examples, a view of life differing from Shaw's in almost every particular. One reviewer clearly discerned the influence of Shaw in *The Napoleon of Notting Hill*, "but without a trace of Shaw's wonderful humour and perspicacity."

* Italics mine.

Belloc's approval was hearty. He wrote:

I am delighted with what I have read in the Daily Mail. Hit them
again. Hurt them. Continue to binge and accept my blessing. Give
them hell. It is the only book of yours I have read right through.
Which shows that I don't read anything. Which is true enough. This
letter is written in the style of Herbert Paul. Continue to bang
them about.

You did wrong not to come to the South coast. Margate is a
fraud. What looks like sea in front of it is really a bank with hardly
any water over it. I stuck on it once in the year 1904 so I know all
about it. Moreover the harbour at Margate is not a real harbour.
Ramsgate round the corner has a real harbour on the true sea. In
both towns are citizens not averse to bribes. Do not fail to go out
in a boat on the last of the ebb as far as the Long Nose. There you
will see the astonishing phenomenon of the tide racing down the
North Foreland three hours before it has turned in the estuary of
the Thames, which you at Margate foolishly believe to be the sea.
Item no one in Margate can cook.

Gilbert was not really concerned in this book to bang his
contemporaries about so much as to study their mistakes and so
discover what was wrong with modern thought. Shaw, George
Moore, Ibsen, Wells, The Mildness of the Yellow Press, Omar
and the Sacred Vine, Rudyard Kipling, Smart Novelists and
the Smart Set, Joseph McCabe and a Divine Frivolity—the collection was a heterogeneous one. And in the introduction the
author tells us he is not concerned with any of these men as a
brilliant artist or a vivid personality, but "as a Heretic—that is
to say a man whose view of things has the hardihood to differ
from mine . . . as a man whose philosophy is quite solid, quite
coherent and quite wrong. I revert to the doctrinal methods of
the thirteenth century, inspired by the general hope of getting
something done."

In *England a Nation* and even more in the study of Kipling
in this book there is one touch of inconsistency which we shall
meet with again in his later work. He hated Imperialism yet he

glorified Napoleon; himself ardently patriotic he accused Kipling of lack of patriotism on the ground that a man could not at once love England and love the Empire. For there was a curious note in the anti-Imperialism of the Chesterbelloc that has not always been recognised. The ordinary anti-Imperialist holds that England has no right to govern an Empire and that her leadership is bad for the other dominions. But the Chesterbelloc view was that the Dominions were inferior and unworthy of a European England. The phrase "suburbs of England" (quoted in a later chapter) was typical. But Kipling was thrilled by those suburbs and Chesterton, who had as a boy admired Kipling, attacks him in *Heretics* for lack of patriotism. *Puck of Pook's Hill* was not yet written, but like Kipling's poem on Sussex it expressed a patriotism much akin to Gilbert's own. Remember the man who returned from the South African veldt to be the Squire's gardener—"Me that have done what I've done, Me that have seen what I've seen"—that man, with eyes opened to a sense of his own tragedy, was speaking for Chesterton's people of England who "have not spoken yet." Yes, they have spoken through the mouth of English genius: as Langland's Piers Plowman, as Dickens's Sam Weller, but not least as Kipling's Tommy Atkins. It was a pity Chesterton was deaf to this last voice. With a better understanding of Kipling he might in turn have made Kipling understand what was needed to make England "Merrie England" once again, have given him the philosophy that should make his genius fruitful.

For the huge distinction between Chesterton and most of his contemporaries lay not in the wish to get something done but in the conviction that the right philosophy alone could produce fruitful action. A parable in the Introduction shows the point at which his thinking had arrived.

Suppose that a great commotion arises in the street about something, let us say a lamp-post, which many influential persons desire to pull down. A grey-clad monk, who is the spirit of the Middle Ages, is approached upon the matter, and begins to say, in the arid manner of the Schoolmen, "Let us first of all consider, my brethren, the value of Light. If Light be in itself good—" At this point he is somewhat excusably knocked down. All the people make a rush for the lamp-post, the lamp-post is down in ten minutes, and they go about congratulating each other on their unmediaeval practicality. But as things go on they do not work out so easily. Some people have pulled the lamp-post down because they wanted the electric light; some because they wanted old iron; some because they wanted darkness, because their deeds were evil. Some thought it not enough of a lamp-post, some too much; some acted because they wanted to smash municipal machinery; some because they wanted to smash something. And there is war in the night, no man knowing whom he strikes. So, gradually and inevitably, today, tomorrow, or the next day, there comes back the conviction that the monk was right after all, that all depends on what is the philosophy of Light. Only what we might have discussed under the gas-lamp, we now must discuss in the dark.*

Every year during this time at Battersea, the press books reveal an increasing flood of engagements. Gilbert lectures for the New Reform Club on "Political Watchwords," for the Midland Institute on "Modern Journalism," for the Men's Meeting of the South London Central Mission on "Brass Bands," for the London Association of Correctors of the Press at the Trocadero, for the C.S.U. at Church Kirk, Accrington, at the Men's Service in the Colchester Moot Hall. He debates at the St. German's Literary Society, maintaining "that the most justifiable wars are the religious wars"; opens the Anti-Puritan League at the Shaftesbury Club, speaks for the Richmond and Kew branch of the P.N.E.U. on "The Romantic Element in Morality," for the Ilkley P.S.A., on "Christianity and Materialism," and so on without end. All these are on a few pages of his father's collection, interspersed with clippings recording articles in reviews innumerable, introductions to books, interviews and controversies.

* *Heretics*, pp. 22-3.

There was almost no element of choice in these engagements. G.K. was intensely good-natured and hated saying No. He was the lion of the moment and they all wanted him to roar for them. In spite of the large heading, "Lest we forget," that met his eye daily in the drawing-room, he did forget a great deal—in fact, friends say he forgot any engagement made when Frances was not present to write it down directly it was made. She had to do memory and all the practical side of life for him. There might have been one slight chance of making Gilbert responsible in these matters—that chance was given to his parents and by them thrown away. How far it is even possible to groom and train a genius is doubtful: anyhow no attempt was made. Waited on hand and foot by his mother, never made to wash or brush himself as a child, personally conducted to the tailor as he grew older, given by his parents no money for which to feel responsible, not made to keep hours—how could Frances take a man of twenty-seven, and make him over again?

But there is, of course, a most genuine difficulty in all this, which Gilbert once touched on when he denied the accusation of absence of mind. It was, he claimed, presence of mind—on his thoughts—that made him unaware of much else. And indeed no man can be using his mind furiously in every direction at once. Anyone who has done even a little creative work, any-one even who has lived with people who do creative work, knows the sense of bewilderment with which the mind comes out of the world of remoter but greater reality and tries to adjust with that daily world in which meals are to be ordered, letters answered, and engagements kept. What must this pain of adjustment not have been to a mind almost continuously creative? For I have never known anyone work such long hours with a mind at such tension as Gilbert's.

There was no particular reason why he should have written his article for the *Daily News* as the reporter writes his—at top speed at a late hour—but he usually did. The writing of it was left till the last minute and, if at home, he would need Frances to get it off for him before the deadline was reached. But he often wrote by preference in Fleet Street—at the Cheshire Cheese or some little pub where journalists gathered—and then he would hire a cab to take the article a hundred yards or so to the *Daily News* office.

The cab in those days was the hansom with its two huge wheels over which one perilously ascended, while the driver sat above, only to be communicated with by opening a sort of trap door in the roof. Gilbert once said that the imaginative Englishman in Paris would spend his days in a café, the imaginative Frenchman in London would spend his driving in a hansom. In the *Napoleon,* the thought of the cab moves him to write:

> Poet whose cunning carved this amorous cell
> Where twain may dwell.

E. V. Lucas, his daughter tells us, used to say that if one were invited to drive with Gilbert in a hansom cab it would have to be two cabs: but this is not strictly true. For in those days I drove with Gilbert and Frances too in a hansom—he and I side by side, she on his knee. We must have given to the populace the impression he says any hansom would give on first view to an ancient Roman or a simple barbarian—that the driver riding on high and flourishing his whip was a conqueror carrying off his helpless victims.

Like the "buffers" at the Veneering election, he spent much of his time "taking cabs and getting about"—or not even getting about in them, but leaving them standing at the door for hours on end. Calling on one publisher he placed in his hands a letter that gave excellent reasons why he could not keep the engagement! The memory so admirable in literary quotations was not merely unreliable for engagements but even for such matters as street numbers and addresses. Edward Macdonald, who worked with him later, on *G.K.'s Weekly*, relates how some months after the paper had changed its address he failed one day to turn up at a board meeting.

Finally he appeared with an explanation. On calling a taxi at Marylebone he realized that he could not give the address, so he told the driver to take him to Fleet Street. There as his memory still refused to help, he stopped the taxi outside a tea-shop, left it there while he was inside, and ordering a cup of tea began to turn out all his pockets in the hope of finding a letter or a proof bearing the address. Then as no clue could be found, he told the driver to take him to a bookstall that stocked the paper. At the first and second he drew blanks but at the third bought a copy of his own paper and thus discovered the address.

I am not sure at what date he began to hate writing anything by hand. My mother treasured two handwritten letters. I have none after a friendship of close on thirty years. But I remember on his first visit to my parents' home in Surrey his calling Frances that he might dictate an article to her. His writing was pictorial and rather elaborate. "He drew his signature rather than writing it," says Edward Macdonald, who remembers him saying as he signed a cheque: 'With many a curve my banks I fret.' I wonder if Tennyson fretted his." At one of our earliest meetings I asked him to write in my Autograph Book. It was at least five years before the *Ballad of the White Horse* appeared, but the lines may be found almost unchanged in the Ballad:

VERSES MADE UP IN A DREAM
(which you won't believe)
People, if you have any prayers
  Say prayers for me.
And bury me underneath a stone
  In the stones of Battersea.
Bury me underneath a stone,
  With the sword that was my own;
To wait till the holy horn is blown
  And all poor men are free.

The dream went on, he said, for pages and pages. And I think Frances was anxious, for the mind must find rest in sleep.

The little flat at Battersea was a vortex of requests and engagements, broken promises and promises fulfilled, author's ink and printer's ink, speeches in prospect and speeches in memory, meetings and social occasions. A sincere admirer wrote during this period of his fears of too great a strain on his hero— and from 1904 to 1908 the only change was an increase of pressure:

I see that Chesterton has just issued a volume on the art of G. F. Watts. His novel was published yesterday. Soon his monograph on Kingsley should be ready. I believe he has a book on some modern aspects of religious belief in the press. He is part-editor of the illustrated booklets on great authors issued by the Bookman. He is contributing prefaces and introductions to odd volumes in several series of reprints. He is a constant contributor to the Daily News and the Speaker; he is conducting a public controversy with Blatchford of the Clarion on atheism and free-thinking; he is constantly lecturing and debating and dining out; it is almost impossible to open a paper that does not contain either an article or review or poem or drawing of his, and his name is better known now to compositors than Bernard Shaw.

Now, both physically and mentally Chesterton is a Hercules, and from what I hear of his methods of work he is capable of a great output without much physical strain; nevertheless, it is clear, I think, to anyone that at his present rate of production he must either wear or tear. No man born can keep so many irons in the fire and not himself come between the hammer and the anvil. It is a pitiable thing to have a good man spend himself so recklessly; and I repeat once more that if he and his friends have not the will or power to restrain him, then there should be a conspiracy of editors and publishers in his favour. Not often is a man like Chesterton born. He should have his full chance. And that can only come by study and meditation, and by slow, steady accumulation of knowledge and wisdom.*

* Shan F. Bullock in the *Chicago Evening Post*. 9th April, 1906.

In a volume made up of Introductions written at this time to individual novels of Dickens, we find a passage that might well be Gilbert's summary of his own life:

The calls upon him at this time were insistent and overwhelming; this necessarily happens at a certain stage of a successful writer's career. He was just successful enough to invite offers and not successful enough to reject them . . . there was almost too much work for his imagination, and yet not quite enough work for his housekeeping. . . . And it is a curious tribute to the quite curious greatness of Dickens that in this period of youthful strain we do not feel the strain but feel only the youth. His own amazing wish to write equalled or outstripped even his readers' amazing wish to read. Working too hard did not cure him of his abstract love of work. Unreasonable publishers asked him to write ten novels at once; but he wanted to write twenty novels at once.

Thus too with Gilbert. The first eight years of his married life saw in swift succession the publication of ten books comprising literary and art criticism and biography, poetry, fiction (or rather fantasy), light essays and religious philosophy. All these were so full at once of the profound seriousness of youth, and of the bubbling wine of its high spirits, as to recall another thing Gilbert said: that Dickens was "accused of superficiality by those who cannot grasp that there is foam upon deep seas."

That was the matter in dispute about himself, and very furiously disputed it was during these years. Was G.K. serious or merely posing, was he a great man or a mountebank, was he clear or obscure, was he a genius or a charlatan? "Audacious reconciliation," he pleaded—or rather asserted, for his tone could seldom be called a plea, "is a mark not of frivolity but of extreme seriousness."

A man who deals in harmonies, who only matches stars with angels, or lambs with spring flowers, he indeed may be frivolous; for he is taking one mood at a time, and perhaps forgetting each mood as it passes. But a man who ventures to combine an angel and an octopus must have some serious view of the universe. The man who should write a dialogue between two early Christians might be a mere writer of dialogues. But a man who should write a dialogue between an early Christian and the Missing Link would have to be a philosopher. The more widely different the types talked of, the more serious and universal must be the philosophy which talks of them. The mark of the light and thoughtless writer is the harmony of his subject matter; the mark of the thoughtful writer is its apparent diversity. The most flippant lyric poet might write a pretty poem about lambs; but it requires something bolder and graver than a poet, it requires an ecstatic prophet, to talk about the lion lying down with the lamb.*

A man starting to write a thesis on Chesterton's sociology once complained bitterly that almost none of his books were indexed, so he had to submit to the disgusting necessity of reading them all through, for some striking view on sociology might well be embedded in a volume of art criticism or be the very centre of a fantastic romance. Chesterton's was a philosophy universal and unified and it was at this time growing fast and finding exceedingly varied techniques of expression. But the whole of it was in a sense in each of them—in each book, almost in each poem. As he himself says of the universe of Charles Dickens, "there was something in it—there is in all great creative writers—like the account in Genesis of the light being created before the sun, moon and stars, the idea before the machinery that made it manifest. Pickwick is in Dickens's career the mere mass of light before the creation of sun or moon. It is the splendid, shapeless substance of which all his stars are ultimately made." And again, "He said what he had to say and yet not all he had to say. Wild pictures, possible stories, tantalising and attractive trains of thought, perspectives of adventure, crowded so continually upon his mind that at the end there was a vast mass of them left over, ideas that he literally had not the opportunity to develop, tales that he literally had not the time to tell."

* G. K. Chesterton. *Criticisms and Appreciations of the Works of Charles Dickens*. Dent. 1933 pp. 68–9.

CHAPTER XII

Clearing the Ground for Orthodoxy

G. K. CHESTERTON: A CRITICISM (published anonymously in 1908) was a challenge thrown to the world of letters, for it demanded the recognition of Chesterton as a force to be reckoned with in the modern world. As its title implied, the book was by no means a tribute of sheer admiration and agreement. Gilbert was rebuked for that love of a pun or an effective phrase that sometimes led him into indefensible positions. It was hotly asked of him that he should abandon his unjust attitude toward Ibsen. He was accused of calling himself a Liberal and being in fact a Tory. But even in differing from him the book showed him as of real importance, not least in the sketch given of his life and of the influences that had contributed to the formation of his mind. It did too another thing: it clarified his philosophical position for the world at large. For some time now many had been demanding such a clarification. When G.K. attacked the Utopia of Wells and of Shaw, both Wells and Shaw had been urgent in their demands that he should play fair by setting forth his own Utopia. When he attacked the fundamental philosophy of G. S. Street, Mr. Street retorted that it would be time for him to worry about his philosophy when G.K.'s had been unfolded. (G.K.'s retort to this was *Orthodoxy!*)

G. K. Chesterton: a Criticism—far the best book that has ever been written about Chesterton—showed at last a mind that had really grasped his philosophy and could even have outlined his

Utopia. Perhaps this was the less surprising as it ultimately turned out to have been written by his brother Cecil.

I do not know at what stage Cecil revealed his authorship, but I remember that at first Frances told me only that they suspected Cecil because it was from the angle of his opinions that the book criticised many of Gilbert's. However, I was at that date only an acquaintance and the truth may still have been a family secret. At any rate Cecil it was, and it is small wonder if after all those years of arguing he understood something of the man with whom he had been measuring forces. But he did better than that—for he explained him to others without ever having resort to these arguments, which after all were more or less private property. He explained G.K.'s general philosophy from the *Napoleon,* his ideas of cosmic good from *The Wild Knight* and *The Man Who Was Thursday,* which had just been published that same year, 1908

In this last fantastic story the group of anarchists (distinguished by being called after the days of the week) turn out, through a series of incredible adventures to be, all save one, detectives in disguise. The gigantic figure of Sunday before whom they all tremble turns from the chief of the anarchists, chief of the destructive forces, into—what? The sub-title, "A Nightmare," is needed, for Sunday would seem to be some wild vision, seen in dreams, not merely of forces of good, of sanity, of creation, but even of God Himself.

When, almost twenty years later, *The Man Who Was Thursday* was adapted for the stage,* Chesterton said in an interview:

In an ordinary detective tale the investigator discovers that some amiable-looking fellow who subscribes to all the charities, and is fond of animals, has murdered his grandmother, or is a trigamist. I thought it would be fun to make the tearing away of menacing masks reveal benevolence.

Associated with that merely fantastic notion was the one that there is actually a lot of good to be discovered in unlikely places, and that

* By Ralph Neale and Mrs. Cecil Chesterton.

we who are fighting each other may be all fighting on the right side. I think it is quite true that it is just as well we do not, while the fight is on, know all about each other; the soul must be solitary; or there would be no place for courage.

A rather amusing thing was said by Father Knox on this point. He said that he should have regarded the book as entirely pantheist and as preaching that there was good in everything if it had not been for the introduction of the one real anarchist and pessimist. But he was prepared to wager that if the book survives for a hundred years —which it won't—they will say that the real anarchist was put in afterwards by the priests.

But, though I was more foggy about ethical and theological matters than I am now, I was quite clear on that issue; that there was a final adversary, and that you might find a man resolutely turned away from goodness.

People have asked me whom I mean by Sunday. Well, I think, on the whole, and allowing for the fact that he is a person in a tale —I think you can take him to stand for Nature as distinguished from God. Huge, boisterous, full of vitality, dancing with a hundred legs, bright with the glare of the sun, and at first sight, somewhat regardless of us and our desires.

There is a phrase used at the end, spoken by Sunday: "Can ye drink from the cup that I drink of?" which seems to mean that Sunday is God. That is the only serious note in the book, the face of Sunday changes, you tear off the mask of Nature and you find God.

Monsignor Knox * has called *The Man Who Was Thursday* "an extraordinary book, written as if the publisher had commissioned him to write something rather like the Pilgrim's Progress in the style of the Pickwick Papers"—which explains perhaps why some reviewers called it irreverent. The very wildness of it conveys a sense of thoughts seething and straining in an effort to express the inexpressible. Later in his more definitely philosophical books G.K. could say calmly much that here he splashes "on a ten leagued canvas with brushes of comet's hair"—with all the violent directness of a vision.

* In the panegyric preached at Westminster Cathedral, June 27, 1936.

Of that vision his brother began the interpretation in his challenging book. Reactions were interesting, for even those who wanted most ardently to say that Cecil's book should not have been written found that it was necessary to say it loudly and to say it at great length. Their very violence showed their sense of Chesterton as a peril even when they abused anyone who felt him to be a portent. It was not the kind of contempt that is really bestowed on the contemptible.

The *Academy* expended more than two columns saying:

We propose to deal with the quack and leave his sycophants and lickspittles to themselves . . .

One skips him in his numerous corners of third and fourth rate journals [e.g. *The Illustrated London News, The Bookman, Daily News!*] and one avoids his books because they are always and inevitably a bore.

Lancelot Bathurst had also dared to write of G.K. in his daily life as a journalist, so the article goes on:

Let us kneel with the Hon. Lancelot at his greasy burgundy-stained shrine, what time the jingling hansom waits us with its rolling occupant and his sword-stick and his revolver and his pockets stacked with penny dreadfuls. . . .

The fact is we have in Mr. Chesterton the true product of the deboshed hapenny press. . . . If the hapenny papers ceased to notice him forthwith it seems to us more than probable that he would cease at once to be of the highest importance in literary circles and the Bishops and Members of Parliament who have honoured him with their kind notice would be compelled to drop him. . . .

Most of the reviews were very different from this one, which is certainly great fun (although some few other reviewers suggested that Gilbert himself wrote the *Criticism*). I have wondered whether the *Academy* notices of his own books, all much like this, were written by a personal enemy or merely by one of the "jolly people" as he often called them who were maddened by his views.

For some years now Gilbert had been gathering in his mind the material for *Orthodoxy*. Some of the ideas we have seen faintly traced in the Notebook and *The Coloured Lands*, but they all grew to maturity in the atmosphere of constant controversy. In a controversy with the Rev. R. J. Campbell we see, for instance, his convictions about the reality of sin shaping under our eyes. Discussing Modernism in the *Nation*, he analyses the difference between the true development of an idea and the mere changing from one idea to another. Modernism claiming to be a development was actually an abandonment of the Christian idea.

For the Catholic, this is among the most interesting of his controversies. In the course of it he refers to "the earlier works of Newman and the literature of the Oxford Movement" to support his view of the Anglican position. I have already said that Chesterton read far more than was usually supposed, because he read so quickly and with so little parade of learning, and it has been too lightly assumed that the statement in *Orthodoxy* that he avoided works of Christian Apologetic meant that he had not read any of the great Christian writers of the past. True, he was not then or at any time reading books of Apologetic. He must, however, have been reading something more life-giving, as we learn from a single hint. Asked to draw up a Scheme of Reading for 1908 in *T.P.'s Weekly*, he suggests Butler's *Analogy*, Coleridge's *Confessions of an Enquiring Spirit*, Newman's *Apologia*, St. Augustine's *Confessions* and the *Summa* of St. Thomas Aquinas.

It was absurd, he said in this article, to suppose that the ancients did not see our modern problems. The truth was that the great ancients not only saw them, but saw through them. Butler had sketched the "real line along which Christianity must ultimately be defended." These great writers all remained modern, while the "New Theology" takes one back to the time of crinolines. "I almost expect to see Mr. R. J. Campbell in pegtop trousers, with very long side-whiskers."

In this controversy, although not yet a Catholic, he showed the gulf between the Modernist theory of development and the Newman doctrine, with a clarity greater than any Catholic writer of the time.

A man who is always going back and picking to pieces his own first principles may be having an amusing time but he is not developing as Newman understood development. Newman meant that if you wanted a tree to grow you must plant it finally in some definite spot. It may be (I do not know and I do not care) that Catholic Christianity is just now passing through one of its numberless periods of undue repression and silence. But I do know this, that when the great flowers break forth again, the new epics and the new arts, they will break out on the ancient and living tree. They cannot break out upon the little shrubs that you are always pulling up by the roots to see if they are growing.

Against R. J. Campbell he showed in a lecture on "Christianity and Social Reform" how belief in sin as well as in goodness was more favourable to social reform than was the rather woolly optimism that refused to recognize evil. "The nigger-driver will be delighted to hear that God is immanent in him. . . . The sweater that . . . he has not in any way become divided from the supreme perfection of the universe." If the New Theology would not lead to social reform, the social Utopia to which the philosophy of Wells and of Shaw was pointing seemed to Chesterton not a heaven on earth to be desired, but a kind of final hell to be avoided, since it banished all freedom and human responsibility. Arguing with them was again highly fruitful, and two subjects he chose for speeches are suggestive—"The Terror of Tendencies" and "Shall We Abolish the Inevitable?"

In the *New Age* Shaw wrote about Belloc and Chesterton and

so did Wells, while Chesterton wrote about Wells and Shaw, till the Philistines grew angry, called it self-advertisement and log-rolling and urged that a Bill for the abolition of Shaw and Chesterton should be introduced into Parliament. But G.K. had no need for advertisement of himself or his ideas just then: he had a platform, he had an eager audience. Every week he wrote in the *Illustrated London News*, beginning in 1905 to do "Our Notebook" (this continued till his death in 1936). He was still writing every Saturday in the *Daily News*. Publishers were disputing for each of his books. Yet he rushed into every religious controversy that was going on, because thereby he could clarify and develop his ideas.

The most important of all these was the controversy with Blatchford, Editor of the *Clarion*, who had written a rationalist Credo, entitled *God and My Neighbour*. In 1903–4, he had the generosity and the wisdom to throw open the *Clarion* to the freest possible discussion of his views. The Christian attack was made by a group of which Chesterton was the outstanding figure, and was afterwards gathered into a paper volume called *The Doubts of Democracy*.

One essay in this volume, written in 1903, is of primary importance in any study of the sources of *Orthodoxy*, for it gives a brilliant outline of one of the main contentions of the book and shows even better than *Orthodoxy* itself what he meant by saying that he had first learnt Christianity from its opponents. It is clear that by now he believed in the Divinity of Christ. The pamphlet itself has fallen into oblivion and Chesterton's share of it was only three short essays. I think it well to quote a good deal from the first of these, because in it he has put in concentrated form and with different illustrations what he developed five years later. There is nothing more packed with thought in the whole of his writings than these essays.

The first of all the difficulties that I have in controverting Mr. Blatchford is simply this, that I shall be very largely going over his

own ground. My favourite text-book of theology is *God and My
Neighbour*, but I cannot repeat it in detail. If I gave each of my
reasons for being a Christian, a vast number of them would be
Mr. Blatchford's reasons for not being one.

For instance, Mr. Blatchford and his school point out that there
are many myths parallel to the Christian story; that there were
Pagan Christs, and Red Indian Incarnations, and Patagonian Cruci-
fixions, for all I know or care. But does not Mr. Blatchford see the
other side of the fact? If the Christian God really made the human
race, would not the human race tend to rumours and perversions
of the Christian God? If the centre of our life is a certain fact, would
not people far from the centre have a muddled version of that fact?
If we are so made that a Son of God must deliver us, is it odd that
Patagonians should dream of a Son of God?

The Blatchfordian position really amounts to this—that because
a certain thing has impressed millions of different people as likely
or necessary, therefore it cannot be true. And then this bashful
being, veiling his own talents, convicts the wretched G.K.C. of
paradox . . .

The story of a Christ is very common in legend and literature.
So is the story of two lovers parted by Fate. So is the story of two
friends killing each other for a woman. But will it seriously be
maintained that, because these two stories are common as legends,
therefore no two friends were ever separated by love or no two
lovers by circumstances? It is tolerably plain, surely, that these two
stories are common because the situation is an intensely probable
and human one, because our nature is so built as to make them
almost inevitable . . .

Thus, in this first instance, when learned sceptics come to me and
say, "Are you aware that the Kaffirs have a sort of Incarnation?" I
should reply: "Speaking as an unlearned person, I don't know. But
speaking as a Christian, I should be very much astonished if they
hadn't."

Take a second instance. The Secularist says that Christianity has
been a gloomy and ascetic thing, and points to the procession of
austere or ferocious saints who have given up home and happiness
and macerated health and sex. But it never seems to occur to him
that the very oddity and completeness of these men's surrender make
it look very much as if there were really something actual and solid
in the thing for which they sold themselves. They gave up all

pleasures for one pleasure of spiritual ecstasy. They may have been mad; but it looks as if there really were such a pleasure. They gave up all human experiences for the sake of one superhuman experience. They may have been wicked, but it looks as if there were such an experience.

It is perfectly tenable that this experience is as dangerous and selfish a thing as drink. A man who goes ragged and homeless in order to see visions may be as repellant and immoral as a man who goes ragged and homeless in order to drink brandy. That is a quite reasonable position. But what is manifestly not a reasonable position, what would be, in fact, not far from being an insane position, would be to say that the raggedness of the man, and the stupefied degradation of the man, proved that there was no such thing as brandy.

That is precisely what the Secularist tries to say. He tries to prove that there is no such thing as supernatural experience by pointing at the people who have given up everything for it. He tries to prove that there is no such thing by proving that there are people who live on nothing else.

Again I may submissively ask: "Whose is the Paradox?" . . .

Take a third instance. The Secularist says that Christianity produced tumult and cruelty. He seems to suppose that this proves it to be bad. But it might prove it to be very good. For men commit crimes not only for bad things, far more often for good things. For no bad things can be desired quite so passionately and persistently as good things can be desired, and only very exceptional men desire very bad and unnatural things.

Most crime is committed because, owing to some peculiar complication, very beautiful or necessary things are in some danger . . .

. . . And when something is set before mankind that is not only enormously valuable, but also quite new, the sudden vision, the chance of winning it, the chance of losing it, drive them mad. It has the same effect in the moral world that the finding of gold has in the economic world. It upsets values, and creates a kind of cruel rush.

We need not go far for instances quite apart from the instances of religion. When the modern doctrines of brotherhood and liberality were preached in France in the eighteenth century the time was ripe for them, the educated classes everywhere had been growing towards them, the world to a very considerable extent welcomed them. And yet all that preparation and openness were unable to prevent the burst of anger and agony which greets anything good. And if the slow and polite preaching of rational fraternity in a rational age ended in the massacres of September, what an *a fortiori* is here! What would be likely to be the effect of the sudden dropping into a dreadfully evil century of a dreadfully perfect truth? What would happen if a world baser than the world of Sade were confronted with a gospel purer than the gospel of Rousseau?

The mere flinging of the polished pebble of Republican Idealism into the artificial lake of eighteenth century Europe produced a splash that seemed to splash the heavens, and a storm that drowned ten thousand men. What would happen if a star from heaven really fell into the slimy and bloody pool of a hopeless and decaying humanity? Men swept a city with the guillotine, a continent with a sabre, because Liberty, Equality, and Fraternity were too precious to be lost. How if Christianity was yet more maddening because it was yet more precious?

But why should we labour the point when One who knew human nature as it can really be learnt, from fishermen and women and natural people, saw from his quiet village the track of this truth across history, and, in saying that He came to bring not peace but a sword, set up eternally His colossal realism against the eternal sentimentality of the Secularist?

Thus, then, in the third instance, when the learned sceptic says: "Christianity produced wars and persecutions," we shall reply: "Naturally."

And, lastly, let me take an example which leads me on directly to the general matter I wish to discuss for the remaining space of the articles at my command. The Secularist constantly points out that the Hebrew and Christian religions began as local things; that their god was a tribal god; that they gave him material form, and attached him to particular places.

This is an excellent example of one of the things that if I were conducting a detailed campaign I should use as an argument for the validity of Biblical experience. For if there really are some other and higher beings than ourselves, and if they in some strange way, at some emotional crisis, really revealed themselves to rude poets or dreamers in very simple times, that these rude people should regard the revelation as local, and connect it with the particular hill or river where it happened, seems to me exactly what any reasonable human being would expect. It has a far more credible look than if they had talked cosmic philosophy from the beginning. If they had, I should have suspected "priestcraft" and forgeries and third-century Gnosticism.

If there be such a being as God, and He can speak to a child, and if God spoke to a child in the garden, the child would, of course, say that God lived in the garden. I should not think it any less likely to be true for that. If the child said: "God is everywhere; an impalpable essence pervading and supporting all constituents of the Cosmos alike"—if, I say, the infant addressed me in the above terms, I should think he was much more likely to have been with the governess than with God.

So if Moses had said God was an Infinite Energy, I should be certain he had seen nothing extraordinary. As he said He was a Burning Bush, I think it very likely that he did see something extraordinary. For whatever be the Divine Secret, and whether or no it has (as all people have believed) sometimes broken bounds and surged into our world, at least it lies on the side furthest away from pedants and their definitions, and nearest to the silver souls of quiet people, to the beauty of bushes, and the love of one's native place.

Thus, then, in our last instance (out of hundreds that might be taken), we conclude in the same way. When the learned sceptic says: "The visions of the Old Testament were local, and rustic, and grotesque," we shall answer: "Of course. They were genuine."

Thus, as I said at the beginning, I find myself, to start with, face to face with the difficulty that to mention the reasons that I have for believing in Christianity is, in very many cases, simply to repeat those arguments which Mr. Blatchford, in some strange way, seems to regard as arguments against it. His book is really rich and powerful. He has undoubtedly set up these four great guns of which I have spoken. I have nothing to say against the size and ammunition of the guns. I only say that by some strange accident of arrangement he has set up those four pieces of artillery pointing at himself. If I were not so humane, I should say: "Gentlemen of the Secularist Guard, fire first."

He goes on in the next essay to talk of the positive arguments for Christianity, of "this religious philosophy which was, and will be again, the study of the highest intellects and the foundation of the strongest nations, but which our little civilisation has for a while forgotten." Very briefly he then deals with Determinism and Freewill, the need for the Supernatural and the question of the Fall. Dealing with the Fall he uses one of his most brilliant illustrations. We speak, he says, of a manly man, but not of a whaley whale. "If you wanted to dissuade a man from drinking his tenth whisky, you would slap him on the back and say, 'Be a man.' No one who wished to dissuade a crocodile from eating his tenth explorer would slap it on the back and say, 'Be a crocodile.' For we have no notion of a perfect crocodile; no allegory of a whale expelled from his Whaley Eden."

Continuing the swift sketch of some elements of Christian theology, Chesterton next deals with Miracles. While the development in *Orthodoxy* makes this section look very slight, there are passages that make one realize the mental wealth of a man who could afford to leave them behind and rush on. Blatchford had said that no English judge would accept the evidence for the resurrection and G.K. answers that possibly Christians have not all got "such an extravagant reverence for English judges as is felt by Mr. Blatchford himself. The experiences of the Founder of Christianity have perhaps left us in a vague doubt of the infallibility of Courts of Law."

In reference to the many rationalists whose refusal to accept any miracle is based on the fact that "Experience is against it," he says: "There was a great Irish Rationalist of this school who when he was told that a witness had seen him commit a murder said that he could bring a hundred witnesses who had not seen him commit it."

The final essay on "The Eternal Heroism of the Slums" has two main points. It begins with an acknowledgment of the crimes of Christians, only pointing out that while Mr. Blatchford outlaws the Church for this reason, he is prepared to invoke the State whose crimes are far worse. But the most vigorous part of the essay is a furious attack on determinism. Blatchford apparently held that bad surroundings inevitably produced bad men. Chesterton had seen the heroism of the poor in the most evil surroundings and was furious at "this association of vice with poverty, the vilest and the oldest and the dirtiest of all the stories that insolence has ever flung against the poor." Men can and do lead heroic lives in the worst of circumstances because there is in humanity a power of responsibility, there is freewill. Blatchford, in the name of humanity, is attacking the greatest of human attributes.

More numerous than can be counted, in all the wars and persecutions of the world, men have looked out of their little grated windows and said, "at least my thoughts are free." "No, No," says the face of Mr. Blatchford, suddenly appearing at the window, "your thoughts are the inevitable result of heredity and environment. Your thoughts are as material as your dungeons. Your thoughts are as mechanical as the guillotine." So pants this strange comforter, from cell to cell.

I suppose Mr. Blatchford would say that in his Utopia nobody would be in prison. What do I care whether I am in prison or no, if I have to drag chains everywhere. A man in his Utopia may have, for all I know, free food, free meadows, his own estate, his own palace. What does it matter? he may not have his own soul.

An architect once discoursed to me on the need of humility in face of the material: the stone and marble of his building. Thus Chesterton was humble before the reality he was seeking to interpret. Pride, he once defined as "the falsification of fact by the introduction of self." To learn, a man must "subtract *himself* from the study of any solid and objective thing." This humility he had in a high degree and also that rarer humility which saw his friends and his opponents alike as his intellectual equals. "Almost anybody," Monsignor Knox once said, "was an ordinary person compared with him." But this was an idea that certainly never occurred to him.

The philosophy shaping into *Orthodoxy* was stimulated by newspaper controversy, and also by the talk in which Gilbert always delighted. As I have noted he loved to listen and he was a little slow in getting off the mark with his own contribution. Many years later an American interviewer described him, when he did get going, as answering questions in brief essays. Frank Swinnerton has admirably described the manner of speech so well remembered by his friends:

His speech is prefaced and accompanied by a curious sort of humming, such as one may hear when glee singers give each other the note before starting to sing. He pronounces the word "I" (without egotism) as if it were "Ayee," and drawls, not in the highly gentlemanly manner which Americans believe to be the English accent, and which many English call the Oxford accent, but in a manner peculiar to himself, either attractive or the reverse according to one's taste (to me attractive).*

Even more attractive to most of us was his fashion of making us feel that we had contributed something very worthwhile. He would take something one had said and develop it till it shone and glowed, not from its own worth but from what he had made of it. Almost anything could thus become a starting point for a train of his best thought. And the style disliked by some in his writings was so completely the man himself that it was the same in conversation as in his books. He would approach a topic from every side throwing light on those contradictory elements that made a paradox. He himself had what he attributes to St. Thomas—"that instantaneous presence of mind which alone really deserves the name of wit." Asked once the traditional question what single book he would choose if cast on a desert island, he replied Thomas's *Guide to Practical Shipbuilding*.

In talk, as in his books, G.K. loved to play upon words, and sometimes of course this was merely a matter of words and the puns were bad ones. Once, for instance, after translating the

* *Georgian Scene*, p. 94.

French phrase for playing truant as "he goes to the bushy school —or the school among the bushes," he adds "not lightly to be confounded with the Art School at Bushey." This is indefensible, but rare. Christopher Morley has noted how "his play upon words often led to a genuine play upon thoughts. . . . One of Chesterton's best pleasantries was his remark on the so-called Emancipation of Women. 'Twenty million young women rose to their feet with the cry *We will not be dictated to*: and proceeded to become stenographers.'" He complained in a review of a novel "Every modern man is an atlas carrying the world; and we are introduced to a new cosmos with every new character. . . . Each man has to be introduced accompanied by his cosmos, like a jealous wife or on the principle of 'love me love my dogma.'"

Each of Chesterton's readers can think of a hundred instances of this inspired fooling: many have been given in this book and many will yet be given. But the thing went far deeper than fooling: it has been compared by Mr. Belloc to the gospel parables as a method of teaching and of illumination. "He made men see what they had not seen before. He made them *know*. He was an architect of certitude, whenever he practiced the art in which he excelled."

Belloc's analysis of this special element in Chesterton's style, alike written and spoken, is of first rate importance to an understanding of the man whose mind at this date was still rapidly developing while his method of expression had become what it remained to the end of his life.

His unique, his capital, genius for illustration by parallel, by example, is his peculiar mark. The word "peculiar" is here the operative word. . . . No one whatsoever that I can recall in the whole course of English letters had his amazing—I would almost say superhuman—capacity for parallelism.

Now parallelism is a gift or method of vast effect in the conveyance of truth.

Parallelism consists in the illustration of some unperceived truth by its exact consonance with the reflection of a truth already known and perceived . . .

Whenever Chesterton begins a sentence with, "It is as though" (in exploding a false bit of reasoning), you may expect a stroke of parallelism as vivid as a lightning flash.

. . . Always, in whatever manner he launched the parallelism, he produced the shock of illumination. He *taught*.

Parallelism was so native to his mind; it was so naturally a fruit of his mental character that he had difficulty in understanding why others did not use it with the same lavish facility as himself.

I can speak here with experience, for in these conversations with him or listening to his conversation with others I was always astonished at an ability in illustration which I not only have never seen equalled, but cannot remember to have seen attempted. He never sought such things; they poured out from him as easily as though they were not the hard forged products of intense vision, but spontaneous remarks.*

To return to the Blatchford controversy: a final point of interest is a psychological one. G.K. admits his difficulty in using in his arguments the reverent solemnity of the Agnostic. He realizes that he is thought flippant because he is amusing on a subject where he is more certain than "of the existence of the moon. . . . Christianity is itself so jolly a thing that it fills the possessor of it with a certain silly exuberance, which sad and high-minded Rationalists might reasonably mistake for mere buffoonery." But if this is his own psychology he faces too the special difficulty of theirs—the main and towering barrier that he wished but hardly hoped to surmount. He was the first person, I think, to see that Free Thought was no longer a young movement, but old and even fossilized. It had formed minds which were now too set to be altered. It had its own dogmas and its own most rigid orthodoxy. "You are armed to the teeth," he told the readers of the *Clarion*, "and buttoned up to the chin with the great agnostic Orthodoxy, perhaps the most placid and perfect of all the ortho-

* *On the Place of Gilbert Chesterton in English Letters*, pp. 36–41.

doxies of men. . . . I approach you with the reverence and the courage due to a bench of bishops."

The *Clarion* controversy was, as we have seen, in 1903 and 1904, when Chesterton was approaching thirty. Others of those I have mentioned came later. But I don't think any or even all of them fully explain the depth and richness of *Orthodoxy*.

CHAPTER XIII

Orthodoxy

Philosophy is either eternal or it is not philosophy. . . . A cosmic philosophy is not constructed to fit a man; a cosmic philosophy is constructed to fit a cosmos. A man can no more possess a private religion than he can possess a private sun and moon.

Introduction to the Book of Job.

BECAUSE *Orthodoxy* is supremely Chesterton's own history of his mind more must be said of it than of his other published works. For "This book is the life of a man. And a man is his mind." The Notebook shows him thinking and feeling in his youth exactly on the lines that he recalls—but they were only lines—in fact an outline. The richness of life was needed, the richness of thought, to turn the outline into the masterpiece. No man, not even Chesterton, could have written *Orthodoxy* at the age of twenty. It was sufficiently remarkable that he should have written it at thirty-five: but only a man who had been thinking along those lines at twenty and much earlier could have written it at all. For the book is as he says "a sort of slovenly autobiography." It is not so much an argument for Orthodoxy as the story of how one man discovered Orthodoxy as the only answer to the riddle of the universe.

In an interview, given shortly after its publication, Gilbert told of a temptation that had once been his and which he had overcome almost before he realized he had been tempted. That temptation was to become a prophet like all the men in *Heretics*, by emphasizing one aspect of truth and ignoring the others. To do this would, he knew, bring him a great crowd of disciples. He had a vision—which constantly grew wider and deeper—of the many-sided unity of Truth, but he saw that all the prophets of the age, from Walt Whitman and Schopenhauer to Wells and Shaw, had become so by taking one side of truth and making it all of truth. It is so much easier to see and magnify a part than laboriously to strive to embrace the whole:

> . . . a sage feels too small for life,
> And a fool too large for it.

Not that he condemned as fools the able men of his generation. For Wells he had a great esteem, for Shaw a greater. Whitman he had in his youth almost idolized. But increasingly he recognized even Whitman as representing an idea that was too narrow because it was only an aspect. There was not room in Whitman's philosophy for some of the facts he had already discovered and he felt he had not yet completed his journey. He must not, for the sake of being a prophet and of having a following, sacrifice— I will not say a truth already found, but a truth that might still be lurking somewhere. He could not be the architect of his own intellectual universe any more than he had been the creator of sun, moon and earth. "God and humanity made it," he said of the philosophy he discovered, "and it made me."

He had begun in boyhood, as we have seen, by realizing that the world as depicted in fairy tales was saner and more sensible than the world as seen by the intellectuals of his own day. These men had lost the sense of life's value. They spoke of the world as a vast place governed by iron laws of necessity. Chesterton felt in it the presence of will, while the mere thought of vastness was to him about as cheerful a conception as that of a jail that should with its cold empty passages cover half the county. "These expanders of the universe had nothing to show us except more and more infinite corridors of space lit by ghastly suns and empty of all that was divine."

These people professed that the universe was one coherent thing; but they were not fond of the universe. But I was frightfully fond of the universe and wanted to address it by a diminutive. I often did so; and it never seemed to mind. Actually and in truth I did feel that these dim dogmas of vitality were better expressed by calling the world small than by calling it large. For about infinity there was a sort of carelessness which was the reverse of the fierce and pious care which I felt touching the pricelessness and the peril of life. They showed only a dreary waste; but I felt a sort of sacred thrift. For economy is far more romantic than extravagance. To them stars were an unending income of halfpence; but I felt about the golden sun and the silver moon as a schoolboy feels if he has one sovereign and one shilling.

These subconscious convictions are best hit off by the colour and tone of certain tales. Thus I have said that stories of magic alone can express my sense that life is not only a pleasure but a kind of eccentric privilege. I may express this other feeling of cosmic cosiness by allusion to another book always read in boyhood, "Robinson Crusoe," which I read about this time, and which owes its eternal vivacity to the fact that it celebrates the poetry of limits, nay, even the wild romance of prudence. Crusoe is a man on a small rock with a few comforts just snatched from the sea: the best thing in the book is simply the list of things saved from the wreck. The greatest of poems is an inventory. . .

I really felt (the fancy may seem foolish) as if all the order and number of things were the romantic remnant of Crusoe's ship. That there are two sexes and one sun, was like the fact that there were two guns and one axe. It was poignantly urgent that none should be lost; but somehow, it was rather fun that none could be added. The trees and the planets seemed like things saved from the wreck: and when I saw the Matterhorn I was glad that it had not been overlooked in the confusion. I felt economical about the stars as if they were sapphires (they are called so in Milton's Eden): I hoarded the hills. For the universe is a single jewel, and while it is a natural cant to talk of a jewel as peerless and priceless, of this jewel it is literally true. This cosmos is indeed without peer and without price: for there cannot be another one." *

* *Orthodoxy*, Chapter IV, pp. 112-5.

A fragment of an essay on Hans Anderson that cannot be later than the age of seventeen shows Gilbert trying to shape part of what he calls here, "The Ethics of Elfland," but a large part was, as he says, "subconscious." In this chapter he sums up the results of musings about the universe begun so long ago—small wonder that he had seemed to sleep over his lessons while he was seeing these visions and dreaming these dreams which after every effort to tell them he still knows remains half untold:

. . . the attempt to utter the unutterable things. These are my ultimate attitudes towards life; the soils for the seeds of doctrine. These in some dark way I thought before I could write, and felt before I could think; that we may proceed more easily afterwards, I will roughly recapitulate them now. I felt in my bones; first, that this world does not explain itself. It may be a miracle with a supernatural explanation; it may be a conjuring trick, with a natural explanation. But the explanation of the conjuring trick, if it is to satisfy me, will have to be better than the natural explanations I have heard. The thing is magic, true or false. Second, I came to feel as if magic must have a meaning, and meaning must have some one to mean it. There was something personal in the world, as in a work of art; whatever it meant it meant violently. Third, I thought this purpose beautiful in its old design, in spite of its defects, such as dragons. Fourth, that the proper form of thanks to it is some form of humility and restraint: we should thank God for beer and Burgundy by not drinking too much of them. We owed, also, an obedience to whatever made us. And last, and strangest, there had come into my mind a vague and vast impression that in some way all good was a remnant to be stored and held sacred out of some primordial ruin. Man had saved his good as Crusoe saved his goods; he had saved them from a wreck. All this I felt and the age gave me no encouragement to feel it. And all the time I had not even thought of Christian theology.*

This theology came with the answers to all the tremendous questions asked by life. Here the convert has one great advan-

* *Ibid,* pp. 155-6.

tage over the Catholic brought up in the Faith. Most of us hear
the answers before we have asked the questions: hence intellectually we lack what G.K. calls "the soils for the seeds of doctrine."
It is nearly impossible to understand an answer to a question
you have not formulated. And without the sense of urgency that
an insistent question brings, many people do not even try. All
the years of his boyhood and early manhood Chesterton was
facing the fundamental questions and hammering out his
answers. At first he had no thought of Christianity as even a
possible answer. Growing up in a world called Christian, he
fancied it a philosophy that had been tried and found wanting.
It was only as he realized that the answers he was finding for
himself always fitted into, were always confirmed by, the Christian view of things that he began to turn towards it. He sees a
good deal of humour in the way he strained his voice in a painfully juvenile attempt to utter his new truths, only to find that
they were not his and were not new, but were part of an eternal
philosophy.

In the chapter called "The Flag of the World" he tells of the
moment when he discovered the confirmation and reinforcing
of his own speculations by the Christian theology. The point at
which this came concerned his feelings about the men of his
youth who labelled themselves Optimist and Pessimist. Both,
he felt, were wrong. It must be possible at once to love and to
hate the world, to love it more than enough to get on with it,
to hate it enough to get it on. And the Church solved this difficulty by her doctrine of creation and of Original Sin. "God had
written not so much a poem, but rather a play; a play he had
planned as perfect, but which had necessarily been left to human
actors and stage-managers who had since made a great mess
of it."

As to that mess the Christian could be as pessimist as he
liked, as to the original design he must be optimist, for it was
his work to restore it. "St. George could still fight the dragon

. . . if he were as big as the world he could yet be killed in the name of the world."

And then followed an experience impossible to describe. It was as if I had been blundering about since my birth with two huge and unmanageable machines, of different shapes and without apparent connection—the world and the Christian tradition. I had found this hole in the world: the fact that one must somehow find a way of loving the world without trusting it; somehow one must love the world without being worldly. I found this projecting feature of Christian theology, like a sort of hard spike, the dogmatic insistence that God was personal, and had made a world separate from Himself. The spike of dogma fitted exactly into the hole in the world—it had evidently been meant to go there—and then the strange thing began to happen. When once these two parts of the two machines had come together, one after another, all the other parts fitted and fell in with an eerie exactitude. I could hear bolt after bolt over all the machinery falling into its place with a kind of click of relief. Having got one part right, all the other parts were repeating that rectitude, as clock after clock strikes noon. Instinct after instinct was answered by doctrine after doctrine. Or, to vary the metaphor, I was like one who had advanced into a hostile country to take one high fortress. And when that fort had fallen the whole country surrendered and turned solid behind me. The whole land was lit up, as it were, back to the first fields of my childhood. All those blind fancies of boyhood which in the fourth chapter I have tried in vain to trace on the darkness, became suddenly transparent and sane. I was right when I felt that I would almost rather say that grass was the wrong colour than say that it must by necessity have been that colour: it might verily have been any other. My sense that happiness hung on the crazy thread of a condition did mean something when all was said: it meant the whole doctrine of the Fall. Even those dim and shapeless monsters of notions which I have not been able to describe, much less defend, stepped quietly into their places like colossal caryatides of the creed. The fancy that the cosmos was not vast and void, but small and cosy, had a fulfilled significance now, for anything that is a work of art must be small in the sight of the artist; to God the stars might be only small and dear, like diamonds. And my haunting instinct that somehow good was not merely a tool to be used, but a relic to be guarded, like the goods from Crusoe's ship—even that had been the wild whisper of something originally wise, for, according to Christianity, we were indeed the survivors of a wreck, the crew of a golden ship that had gone down before the beginning of the world.*

In a chapter called "The Paradoxes of Christianity," the richness of his mind is most manifest; and in that chapter can best be seen what Mr. Belloc meant when he told me Chesterton's style reminded him of St. Augustine's. Talking over with an old schoolfellow of his the list of books he had, as we have seen, drawn up for *T.P.'s Weekly,* I discovered deep doubt as to whether Gilbert would really have read these books, as most of us understand reading, combined with a conviction that he would have got out of them at a glance more than most of us by prolonged study. I have certainly never known anyone his equal at what the schoolboy calls "degutting" a book. He did not seem to study an author, yet he certainly knew him.

But it remained that his own mind, reflecting and experiencing, made of his own life his greatest storehouse, so that in all this book there was, as my father pointed out in the *Dublin Review* at the time, an intensely original new light cast on the eternal philosophy about which so much had already been written. The discovery specially needed, perhaps, for his own age was that Christianity represented a new balance that constituted a liberation. The ancient Greek or Roman had aimed at equilibrium by enforcing moderation and getting rid of extremes. Christianity "made moderation out of the still crash of two impetuous emotions." It "got over the difficulty of combining furious opposites by keeping them both, and keeping them both furious." "The more I considered Christianity, the more I felt that while it had established a rule and order, the chief aim of that order was to give room for good things to run wild." Thus inside Christianity the pacifist could become a monk, and the

* *Orthodoxy,* Chapter V, pp. 142–4.

warrior a Crusader, St. Francis could praise good more loudly
than Walt Whitman, and St. Jerome denounce evil more darkly
than Schopenhauer—but both emotions must be kept in their
place. I remember how George Wyndham laughed as he recited
to us the paragraph where this idea reached its climax.

And sometimes this pure gentleness and this pure fierceness met
and justified their juncture; the paradox of all the prophets was
fulfilled, and, in the soul of St. Louis, the lion lay down with the
lamb. But remember that this text is too lightly interpreted. It is
constantly assumed, especially in our Tolstoyan tendencies, that
when the lion lies down with the lamb the lion becomes lamb-like.
But that is brutal annexation and imperialism on the part of the
lamb. That is simply the lamb absorbing the lion instead of the lion
eating the lamb. The real problem is—Can the lion lie down with
the lamb and still retain his royal ferocity? *That* is the problem the
Church attempted; *that* is the miracle she achieved.*

All this applied not only to the release of the emotions, the
development of all the elements that go to make up humanity,
but even more to the truths of Revelation. A heresy always means
lopping off a part of the truth and, therefore, ultimately a loss
of liberty. Orthodoxy, in keeping the whole truth, safeguarded
freedom and prevented any one of the great and devouring ideas
she was teaching from swallowing any other truth. This was the
justification of councils, of definitions, even of persecutions and
wars of religion: that they had stood for the defence of reason
as well as of faith. They had stood to prevent the suicide of
thought which must result if the exciting but difficult balance
were lost that had replaced the classical moderation.

The Church could not afford to swerve a hair's breadth on some
things if she was to continue her great and daring experiment of the
irregular equilibrium. Once let one idea become less powerful and
some other idea would become too powerful. It was no flock of
sheep the Christian shepherd was leading, but a herd of bulls and

* *Orthodoxy*, Chapter VI, pp. 178-9.

tigers, of terrible ideals and devouring doctrines, each one of them strong enough to turn to a false religion and lay waste the world. Remember that the Church went in specifically for dangerous ideas; she was a lion tamer. The idea of birth through a Holy Spirit, of the death of a divine being, of the forgiveness of sins, or the fulfilment of prophecies, are ideas which, any one can see, need but a touch to turn them into something blasphemous or ferocious. . . . A sentence phrased wrong about the nature of symbolism would have broken all the best statues in Europe. A slip in the definitions might stop all the dances; might wither all the Christmas trees or break all the Easter eggs. Doctrines had to be defined within strict limits, even in order that man might enjoy general human liberties. The Church had to be careful, if only that the world might be careless.

This is the thrilling romance of Orthodoxy. People have fallen into a foolish habit of speaking of orthodoxy as something heavy, humdrum, and safe. There never was anything so perilous or so exciting as orthodoxy. It was sanity: and to be sane is more dramatic than to be mad. It was the equilibrium of a man behind madly rushing horses, seeming to stoop this way and to sway that, yet in every attitude having the grace of statuary and the accuracy of arithmetic. The Church in its early days went fierce and fast with any warhorse; yet it is utterly unhistoric to say that she merely went mad along one idea, like a vulgar fanaticism. She swerved to left and right, so as exactly to avoid enormous obstacles. She left on one hand the huge bulk of Arianism, buttressed by all the worldly powers to make Christianity too worldly. The next instant she was swerving to avoid an orientalism, which would have made it too unworldly. The orthodox Church never took the tame course or accepted the conventions; the orthodox Church was never respectable. It would have been easier to have accepted the earthly power of the Arians. It would have been easy, in the Calvinistic seventeenth century, to fall into the bottomless pit of predestination. It is easy to be a madman: it is easy to be a heretic. It is always easy to let the age have its head; the difficult thing is to keep one's own. It is always easy to be a modernist; as it is easy to be a snob. To have fallen into any of those open traps of error and exaggeration which fashion after fashion and sect after sect set along the historic path of Christendom—that would indeed have been simple. It is always simple to fall; there are an infinity of angles at which one falls, only one at which one stands. To have fallen into any one of the fads from Gnosticism to Christian Science would indeed have been obvious and tame. But to have avoided them all has been one whirling adventure; and in my vision the heavenly chariot flies thundering through the ages, the dull heresies sprawling and prostrate, the wild truth reeling but erect.*

No quotation can adequately convey the wealth of thought in the book. Yet amazingly, the *Times* reviewer rebuked G.K. for substituting emotion for intellect, partly on the strength of a sentence in the chapter called "The Maniac." "The madman is the man who has lost everything except his reason." The reviews, when one reads them as a whole, exactly confirm what Wilfrid Ward said in the *Dublin Review*: that whereas he had regarded *Orthodoxy* as a triumphant vindication of his own view that G.K. was a really profound thinker, he found to his amazement that those who had thought him superficial, hailed it as a proof of theirs.

Obviously with a man so much concerned with ultimates the place accorded him in letters will depend upon whether one agrees or disagrees with his conclusions. In a country that is not Catholic this consideration must affect the standing of any Catholic thinker. Thus Newman was considered by Carlyle to have "the brain of a moderate sized rabbit," yet by others his is counted the greatest mind of the century. Similarly Arnold Bennett could credit Chesterton with only a second-class intellectual apparatus—because he was a dogmatist. To this Chesterton replied (in *Fancies versus Fads*): "In truth there are only two kinds of people, those who accept dogmas and know it and those who accept dogmas and don't know it. My only advantage over the gifted novelist lies in my belonging to the former class." If one grasps the Catholic view of dogma the answer is satisfying; if not the objector is left with his original objection—as against Chesterton, as against Newman. And Chesterton had the

* *Orthodoxy*, Chapter VI, pp. 182–5.

extra disadvantage of being a journalist famous for his jokes now moving in Newman's unquestioned field of philosophy and theology. It was in part the difficulty of convincing a man against his will. These critics, as Wilfrid Ward pointed out, read superficially and looked only at the fooling, the fantastic puns and comparisons, ignoring the underlying deep seriousness and lines of thought that made him, as it then seemed boldly, rank Chesterton with such writers as Butler, Coleridge and Newman. Taking as his text the saying, "Truth can understand error, but error cannot understand truth," Wilfrid Ward called his article, "Mr. Chesterton among the Prophets."

He showed especially the curious confusion made in such comments as the one I have quoted from the *Times,* and made clearer what Chesterton was really saying by a comparison with the "illative sense" of Cardinal Newman. It is the usual difficulty of trying to express a partly new idea. Newman had coined an expression, but it did not express all he meant, still less all that Chesterton meant. Yet it was difficult to use the word "reason" in this particular discussion, without giving to it two different meanings. For in two chapters, "The Maniac" and "The Suicide of Thought," Chesterton was concerned to show that Authority was needed for the defence of reason (in the larger sense) against its own power of self-destruction. Yet the maniac commits this suicide by an excessive use of reason (in the narrower sense). "He is not hampered by a sense of humour or by charity, or by the dumb certainties of experience. He is the more logical for losing certain sane affections. . . . He is in the clean and well-lit prison of one idea: he is sharpened to one painful point."

To Chesterton it seemed that most of the modern religions and philosophies were like the argument by which a madman suffering from persecution mania proves that he is in a world of enemies: it is complete, it is unanswerable, yet it is false. The madman's mind "moves in a perfect but narrow circle. . . . The insane explanation is quite as complete as the sane one, only it is not so large. . . . There is such a thing as a narrow universality; there is such a thing as a small and cramped eternity; you may see it in many modern religions." Philosophies such as Materialism, Idealism, Monism, all have in their explanations of the universe this quality of the madman's argument of "covering everything and leaving everything out." The Materialist, like the Madman is "unconscious of the alien energies and the large indifference of the earth; he is not thinking of the real things of the earth, of fighting peoples or proud mothers or first love or fear upon the sea. The earth is so very large and the cosmos is so very small."

People sometimes say, "life is larger than logic," when they want to dismiss logic, but that was not Chesterton's way. He wanted logic, he needed logic, as part of the abundance of the mind's life, as part of a much larger whole. What was the word— we are looking for it still—for a use of the mind that included all these things; logic and imagination, mysticism and ecstasy and poetry and joy; a use of the mind that could embrace the universe and reach upwards to God without losing its balance. The mind must work in time, yet it can reach out into Eternity: it is conditioned by space but it can glimpse infinity. The modern world had imprisoned the mind. Far more than the body it needed great open spaces. And Chesterton, breaking violently out of prison, looked around and saw how the Church had given health to the mind by giving it space to move in and great ideas to move among. Chesterton, the poet, saw too that man is a poet and must therefore, "get his head into the heavens." He needs mysticism and among Her great ideas, the Church gives him mysteries.

Chapter XIV

Bernard Shaw

This chapter was read by G.B.S. His remarks are printed in foot-notes. The one page altered substantially by him is reproduced.

WHEN ANYONE IN the early years of the century made a list of the English writers most in the public eye, such a list always included the names of Bernard Shaw and G. K. Chesterton. But a good many people in writing down these names did so with unconcealed irritation and I think it is important at this stage to see why.

These men were constantly arguing with each other; but the literary public felt all the same that they represented something in common, and the literary public was by no means sure that it liked that something. It could not quite resist Bernard Shaw's plays; it loved Chesterton whenever it could rebuke him affectionately for paradox and levity. What that public succumbed to in these men was their art: it was by no means so certain that it liked their meaning. And so the literary public elected to say that Shaw and Chesterton were having a cheap success by standing on their heads and declaring that black was white. The audience watched a Shaw v. Chesterton debate as a sham fight or a display of fireworks, as indeed it always partly was; for each of them would have died rather than really hurt the other. But Shaw and Chesterton were operating on their minds all the time. They were allowed to sit in the stalls and applaud. But they were themselves being challenged; and that spoilt their comfort.

Chesterton in his *Autobiography* complains of the falsity of

most of the pictures of England during the Victorian era. The
languishing, fainting females, who were in fact far stronger-
minded than their grand-daughters today, the tyrannical pious
fathers, the dull conventional lives: it all rings false to anyone
who grew up in an average Victorian middle-class home and
was happy enough there. There was, however, one thing fundamentally wrong in such homes; and it was on this fundamental
sin that he agreed with Shaw in waging a relentless war.

The middle classes of England were thoroughly and smugly
satisfied with social conditions that were intolerable for the great
mass of their fellow countrymen. They had erected between the
classes artificial barriers and now did not even look over the top
of them. I remember how when my mother started a settlement
in South London the head worker told us she often saw women
groping in the dirt under the fish barrows for the heads and tails
of fishes to boil for their children. The settlement began to give
the children dinners of dumplings or rice pudding and treacle,
and many well-to-do friends would give my mother a pound or
so to help this work. But the suggestion that government should
intervene was Socialism: the idea that here was a symptom of a
widespread evil, was scouted utterly. People might have learnt
much from their own servants of how the rest of humanity were
living, but while, said Chesterton, they laughed at the idea of the
mediaeval baron whose vassals ate below the salt, their own vassals ate and lived below the floor. At no time in the Christian past
had there been such a deep and wide cleavage in humanity.

The first thing that G.K.C. and G.B.S., Wells too, and Belloc,
were all agreed upon was that the upper and middle classes of
England must be reminded, if need were by a series of earth-
quakes, that they were living in an unreal world. They had forgotten the human race to which they belonged. They, a tiny
section, spoke of the mass of mankind as "the poor" or "the lower
orders" almost as they might speak of the beasts of the forest,
as beings of a different race. Chesterton had a profound and

noble respect for the poor: Shaw declared that they were "useless, dangerous, and ought to be abolished." But for both men, the handful of quarrelsome cliques called the literary world was far too small, because it was so tiny a section of the human race.

Shaw and Chesterton had, in fact, discovered the social problem. Today, whether people intend to *do* anything about it or not, it is impossible to avoid knowing something about it. But at that date the idea was general that all was as well as could be expected in an imperfect world. The trades unionists were telling a different story, but they could not hope to reach intellectually the classes they were attacking. Here were men who could not be ignored, and I cannot but think that it was sometimes the mere utterance of unwelcome truth in brilliant speech that aroused the cry of "paradox."

I hear many people [wrote Chesterton], complain that Bernard Shaw deliberately mystifies them. I cannot imagine what they mean; it seems to me that he deliberately insults them. His language, especially on moral questions, is generally as straight and solid as that of a bargee and far less ornate and symbolic than that of a hansom-cabman. The prosperous English Philistine complains that Mr. Shaw is making a fool of him. Whereas Mr. Shaw is not in the least making a fool of him; Mr. Shaw is, with laborious lucidity, calling him a fool. G.B.S. calls a landlord a thief; and the landlord, instead of denying or resenting it, says, "Ah, that fellow hides his meaning so cleverly that one can never make out what he means, it is all so fine-spun and fantastical." G.B.S. calls a statesman a liar to his face, and the statesman cries in a kind of ecstasy, "Ah, what quaint, intricate and half-tangled trains of thought! Ah, what elusive and many-coloured mysteries of half-meaning!" I think it is always quite plain what Mr. Shaw means, even when he is joking, and it generally means that the people he is talking to ought to howl aloud for their sins. But the average representative of them undoubtedly treats the Shavian meaning as tricky and complex, when it is really direct and offensive. He always accuses Shaw of pulling his leg, at the exact moment when Shaw is pulling his nose.*

* *George Bernard Shaw,* pp. 82-3.

Chesterton was, however, in agreement with the ordinary citizen and in disagreement with Shaw as to much of Shaw's essential teaching. And here we touch a matter so involved that even today it is hard to disentangle it completely. I suppose it will always be possible for two observers to look at human beings acting, to hear them talking, and to arrive at two entirely different interpretations of what they mean. This is certainly the case with any very recent period, and perhaps especially with our own recent history. We have within living memory ended a period and begun an exceedingly different period, and we tend to judge the former by the light—or the darkness—of the latter. The Victorian age, even in its extreme old age, was still tacitly assuming and legally enforcing as axioms the Christian moral system, especially in regard to marriage and all sex questions, and the sacred nature of property. To read many disquisitions on that period today one would suppose that no one living really believed in these things: that humbug explained the first and greed the second.

This is surely a false perspective. The age was an enormously conventional one: these fundamental ideas had become fossilized and meaningless for an increasing number of younger people. But when Bernard Shaw called himself an atheist out of a kind of insane generosity towards Bradlaugh (see his letter to G.K. later in this chapter) or described all property as theft, it was a real moral indignation that was roused in many minds. Real, but exceedingly confused. It testified to the need of the ordinary man to live by a creed that he need not question. Shaw and Chesterton were philosophers, and philosophers love asking questions as well as answering them. But the average man wants to live by his creed, not question it, and the elder Victorians had still some kind of creed.

There were many who believed in God. There were others who believed that the Christian moral system must remain, because it had commended itself to man's nature as the highest and best and was the true fruit of evolutionary progress. There were certainly some who were angry because they thought chaos must follow any tampering with the existing social order. But if you take the mass of those who tried to laugh Bernard Shaw aside and grew angry when they could not do so, you find at the root of the anger an intense dislike of having any part of a system questioned which was to them unquestionable, which they had erected into a creed. They thought Shaw's ideas dangerous and wanted to keep them from the young. They did not want anyone to ask how a civilisation had laid its principles open to this brilliant and effective siege. They hated Shaw's questions before they began to hate his answers. And that is probably why so many linked Chesterton with Shaw—he gave different answers, but he was asking many of the same questions. He questioned everything as Shaw did—only he pushed his questions further: they were deeper and more searching. Shaw would not accept the old Scriptural orthodoxy; G.K. refused to accept the new Agnostic orthodoxy; neither man would accept the orthodoxy of the scientists; both were prepared to attack what Butler had called "the science ridden, art ridden, culture ridden, afternoon-tea ridden cliffs of old England."

They attacked first by the mere process of asking questions; and the world thus questioned grew uneasy and seemed to care curiously little for the fact that the two questioners were answering their own questions in an opposite fashion. Where Shaw said: "Give up pretending you believe in God, for you don't," Chesterton said: "Rediscover the reasons for believing or else our race is lost." Where Shaw said: "Abolish private property which has produced this ghastly poverty," Chesterton said: "Abolish ghastly poverty by restoring property."

And the audience said: "these two men in strange paradoxes seem to us to be saying the same thing, if indeed they are saying anything at all." Chesterton wrote later of a young man

When anyone in the early years of the century made
a list of the English writers most in the public eye, such a list
always included the names of ~~George~~ Bernard Shaw and G. K. Chesterton.
But a good many people in writing down these names did so with
unconcealed irritation and I think it is important at this stage
to see why.

These men were constantly arguing with one another;
but the literary public felt all the same that they represented
something in common, and the literary public was, by no means sure
that it liked that something. It ~~liked~~ could not quite resist Bernard Shaw's plays; ~~even to idolatry~~;
it loved Chesterton whenever it could rebuke
him affectionately for paradox and levity. What that public ~~liked~~ unconcerned
~~about these~~ in these men was their art: it was by no means so certain that
it liked their meaning. And so the literary public elected to
say that Shaw and Chesterton ~~did not really mean what they said, did not really mean anything at all.~~ were having a cheap success by standing on their heads and
declaring that black was white.

The audience ~~would gladly have~~ watched a Shaw v.
Chesterton ~~combat~~ debate as a sham fight or a display of fireworks, as indeed it
always partly was; for each of them would have died rather than really hurt the other. ~~But~~
they knew at bottom that ~~that was not what~~ Shaw and Chesterton were
~~offering them~~ operating on their minds all the time. They were ~~not to be~~ allowed to sit in the stalls
and applaud. ~~They~~ But they were themselves being challenged; and that ~~they did not like~~ spoilt their comfort.

Chesterton in his Autobiography complains of the
falsity of most of the pictures of England during the Victorian
era. The languishing, fainting females who were in fact far
stronger-minded than their grand-daughters today, the tyrannical

PAGE OF MS. ALTERED BY BERNARD SHAW

whose aunt "had disinherited him for socialism because of a lecture he had delivered against that economic theory"; and I well remember how often after my own energetic attempts to explain why a Distributist was not a Socialist, I was met with a weary, "Well, it's just the same." It was just the same question; it was an entirely different answer, but the audience, annoyed by the question, never seemed to listen to the answer. One man was saying: "Sweep away the old beliefs of humanity and start fresh"; the other was saying: "Rediscover your reasons for these profound beliefs, make them once more effective, for they are of the very nature of man."

Shaw and Chesterton were themselves deeply concerned about the answers. Both sincere, both dealing with realities, they were prepared to accept each other's sincerity and to fight the matter out, if need were, endlessly. Being writers they conducted their discussions in writing: being journalists they did so mainly in the newspapers, to the delight or fury of other journalists. A jealous few were enraged at what they called publicity hunting, but most realised that it was not a private fight. Anyone might join in and a good many did.

Belloc was in the fight as early as Chesterton, and of course, on the same side. G.B.S. who had invented "The Chesterbelloc" declared that Chesterton felt obliged to embrace the dogmas of Catholicism lest Belloc's soul should be damned. H. G. Wells agreed in the main with Shaw: both were Fabians and both were ready with a Fabian Utopia for humanity, which Belloc and Chesterton felt would be little better than a prison. Cecil Chesterton, coming in at an angle of his own, wrote some effective articles. He was a Fabian—actually an official Fabian—but his outlook already embraced many of the Chesterbelloc human and genial ideals, although he still ridiculed their Utopia of the peasant state, small ownership and all that came later to be called Distributism. Like the *Clarion,* the *New Age* (itself a socialist paper) saw the wisdom of giving a platform to both sides, and in this paper appeared the best articles that the controversy produced.

Meanwhile the private friendship between G.B.S. and G.K.C. was growing apace. Very early on, Shaw had begun to urge G.K. to write a play. G.K. was, perhaps, beginning to feel that newspaper controversy did not give him space to say all he wanted about Shaw (or perhaps it was merely that Messrs. Lane had persuaded him to promise them a book on Shaw for a series they were producing!). Anyhow, in a letter of 1908, Shaw again urges the play and gives interesting information for the book.

Ayot St. Lawrence, Welwyn, Herts.
1st March 1908.

My dear G.K.C.

What about that play? It is no use trying to answer me in The New Age: the real answer to my article is the play. I have tried fair means: The New Age article was the inauguration of an assault below the belt. I shall deliberately destroy your credit as an essayist, as a journalist, as a critic, as a Liberal, as everything that offers your laziness a refuge, until starvation and shame drive you to serious dramatic parturition. I shall repeat my public challenge to you; vaunt my superiority; insult your corpulence; torture Belloc; if necessary, call on you and steal your wife's affections by intellectual and athletic displays, until you contribute something to the British drama. You are played out as an essayist: your ardor is soddened, your intellectual substance crumbled, by the attempt to keep up the work of your twenties in your thirties. Another five years of this; and you will be the apologist of every infamy that wears a Liberal or Catholic mask. You, too, will speak of the portraits of Vecelli and the Assumption of Allegri, and declare that Democracy refuses to lackey-label these honest citizens as Titian and Correggio. Even that colossal fragment of your ruined honesty that still stupendously dismisses Beethoven as "some rubbish about a piano" will give way to remarks about "a graceful second subject in the relative minor." Nothing can save you now except a rebirth as a dramatist. I have done my turn; and I now call on you to take yours and do a man's work.

It is my solemn belief that it was my Quintessence of Ibsenism
that rescued you and all your ungrateful generation from Materialism and Rationalism.* You were all tired young atheists turning to
Kipling and Ruskinian Anglicanism whilst I, with the angel's wings
beating in my ears from Beethoven's 9th symphony (oh blasphemous
walker in deafness), gave you in 1880 and 1881 two novels in which
you had your Rationalist-Secularist hero immediately followed by
my Beethovenian hero. True, nobody read them; but was that my
fault? They are read now, it seems, mostly in pirated reprints, in
spite of their appalling puerility and classical perfection of style
(you are right as to my being a born pedant, like all great artists);
and are at least useful as documentary evidence that I was no more
a materialist when I wrote *Love Among the Artists* at 24 than when
I wrote *Candida* at 39.

My appearances on the platform of the Hall of Science were
three in number. Once for a few minutes in a discussion, in opposition to Bradlaugh, who was defending property against Socialism.
Bradlaugh died after that, though I do not claim to have killed him.
The Socialist League challenged him to debate with me at St.
James's Hall; but we could not or would not agree as to the proposition to be debated, he insisting on my being bound by all the
publications of the Democratic Federation (to which I did not
belong) and I refusing to be bound by anything on earth or in
heaven except the proposition that Socialism would benefit the
English people. And so the debate never came off.

Now in those days they were throwing Bradlaugh out of the
House of Commons with bodily violence; and all one could do was
to call oneself an atheist all over the place, which I accordingly did.
At the first public meeting of the Shelley Society at University
College, addressed by Stopford Brooke, I made my then famous
(among 100 people) declaration "I am a Socialist, an Atheist and
a Vegetarian" (ergo, a true Shelleyan) whereupon two ladies who
had been palpitating with enthusiasm for Shelley under the impression that he was a devout Anglican, resigned on the spot.

My second Hall of Science appearance was after the last of the
Bradlaugh-Hyndman debates at St. James's Hall, where the two
champions never touched the ostensible subject of their difference—
the Eight Hours Day—at all, but simply talked Socialism or Anti-
Socialism with a hearty dislike and contempt for one another.

* Cecil avowed this as far as he was concerned. G.B.S.

G. V. Foote was then in his prime as the successor of Bradlaugh; and as neither the Secularists nor the Socialists were satisfied with the result of the debate, it was renewed for two nights at the Hall of Science between me and Foote. A verbatim report was published for sixpence and is now a treasure of collectors. Having the last word on the second night, I had to make a handsome wind-up; and the Secularists were much pleased by my declaring that I was altogether on Foote's side in his struggle with the established religion of the country.

When Bradlaugh died, the Secularists wanted a new leader, because B.'s enormous and magnetic personality left a void that nobody was big enough to fill—it was really like the death of Napoleon in that world. There was J. M. Robertson, Foote, and Charles Watts. But Bradlaugh liked Foote as little as most autocrats like their successors; and when he, before his death surrendered the gavel (the hammer for thumping the table to secure order at a meeting) which was the presidential sceptre of the National Secular Society, he did so with an ill will which he did not attempt to conceal; and so though Foote was the nearest size to Bradlaugh's shoes then available, he succeeded him at the disadvantage of inheriting the distrust of the old chief. J. M. Robertson you know: he was not a mob orator. Watts was not sufficient: he had neither Foote's weight (being old) nor Robertson's scholarship.

So whilst the survivors of Bradlaugh were trying to keep up the Hall of Science and to establish a memorial library, etc. there, they cast round for new blood. What more natural than that they should think of me as a man not afraid to call himself an atheist and able to hold his own on the platform? Accordingly, they invited me to address them; and one memorable night I held forth on Progress in Freethought. I was received with affectionate hope; and when the chairman announced that I was giving my share of the gate to the memorial library (I have never taken money for lecturing) the enthusiasm was quite touching. The anti-climax was super-Shavian. I proceeded to smash materialism, rationalism, and all the philosophy of Tyndall, Helmholtz, Darwin and the rest of the 1860 people into smithereens. I ridiculed and exposed every inference of science, and justified every dogma of religion, especially showing that the Trinity and the Immaculate Conception were the merest common sense. That finished me up as a possible leader of the N.S.S. Robertson came on the platform, white with honest Scotch Rationalist rage, and denounced me with a fury of conviction that startled his own followers. Never did I grace that platform again. I repeated the address once to a branch of the N.S.S. on the south side of the Thames—Kensington, I think—and was interrupted by yells of rage from the veterans of the society. The Leicester Secularists, a pious folk, rich and independent of the N.S.S., were kinder to me; but they were no more real atheists than the congregation of St. Paul's is made wholly of real Christians.

Foote is still bewildered about me, imagining that I am a pervert. But anybody who reads my stuff from the beginning (a Shelleyan beginning, as far as it could be labelled at all) will find implicit, and sometimes explicit, the views which, in their more matured form, will appear in that remarkable forthcoming masterpiece, "Shavianism: a Religion."

By the way, I have omitted one more appearance at the Hall of Science. At a four nights' debate on Socialism between Foote and Mrs. Besant, I took the chair on one of the nights.

I take advantage of a snowy Sunday afternoon to scribble all this down for you because you are in the same difficulty that beset me formerly: namely, the absolute blank in the history of the immediate past that confronts every man when he first takes to public life. Written history stops several decades back; and the bridge of personal recollection on which older men stand does not exist for the recruit. Nothing is more natural than that you should reconstruct me as the last of the Rationalists (his real name is Blatchford); and nothing could be more erroneous. It would be much nearer the truth to call me, in that world, the first of the mystics.

If you can imagine the result of trying to write your spiritual history in complete ignorance of painting, you will get a notion of trying to write mine in ignorance of music. Bradlaugh was a tremendous platform heavyweight; but he had never in his life, as far as I could make out, seen anything, heard anything or read anything in the artistic sense. He was almost beyond belief incapable of intercourse in private conversation. He could tell you his adventures provided you didn't interrupt him (which you were mostly afraid to do, as the man was a mesmeric terror); but as to exchanging ideas, or expressing the universal part of his soul, you might as well have been reading the letters of Charles Dickens to his family—those tragic monuments of dumbness of soul and noisiness of pen. Lord help you if you ever lose your gift of speech, G.K.C.! Don't forget that the race is only struggling out of its dumbness, and that it is only in moments of inspiration that we get out a sentence. All the rest is padding.

Yours ever

G. BERNARD SHAW.

In the book on Shaw which appeared in August 1909, G.K. did as he had done with his other literary studies: gave (inaccurately) only as much biography as seemed absolutely necessary, and mainly discussed ideas. He saw Shaw as an Irishman, yet lacking the roots of nationality since he belonged to a mainly alien governing class. He saw him as a Puritan yet without the religious basis of Puritanism. And thirdly, he saw him as so swift a progressive as to be ahead of his own thought and ready to slay it in the name of progress.

All these elements in Shaw made for strength but also created limitations, "Shaw is like the Venus of Milo; all that there is of him is admirable." Where he fails is in being unable to see and embrace the full complexity of life. "His only paradox is to pull out one thread or cord of truth longer and longer into waste and fantastic places. He does not allow for that deeper sort of paradox by which two opposite cords of truth become entangled in an inextricable knot. Still less can he be made to realise that it is often this knot which ties safely together the whole bundle of human life . . . here lies the limitation of that lucid and compelling mind; he cannot quite understand life, because he will not accept its contradictions." Humanity is built of these contradictions, therefore Shaw pities humanity more than he loves it. "It was his glory that he pitied animals like men; it was his defect that he pitied men almost too much like animals. Foulon said of the democracy, 'Let them eat grass.' Shaw said, 'Let them eat greens.' He had more benevolence but almost as much disdain."

As a vegetarian and a water drinker Shaw himself lacked, in Chesterton's eyes, something of complete humanity. And in discussing social problems he was more economist than man. "Shaw (one might almost say) dislikes murder, not so much because it wastes the life of the corpse as because it wastes the time of the murderer." This lack of the full human touch is felt, even in the plays, because Shaw cannot be irrational where humanity always is irrational. In *Candida* "It is completely and disastrously false to the whole nature of falling in love to make the young Eugene complain of the cruelty which makes Candida defile her fair hands with domestic duties. No boy in love with a beautiful woman would ever feel disgusted when she peeled potatoes or trimmed lamps. He would like her to be domestic. He would simply feel that the potatoes had become poetical and the lamps gained an extra light. This may be irrational; but we are not talking of rationality, but of the psychology of first love.* It may be very unfair to women that the toil and triviality of potato-peeling should be seen through a glamour of romance; but the glamour is quite as certain a fact as the potatoes. It may be a bad thing in sociology that men should deify domesticity in girls as something dainty and magical; but all men do. Personally I do not think it a bad thing at all; but that is another argument." †

Yet Shaw's limitations are those of a great man and a genius. In an age of narrow specialism he has "stood up for the fact that philosophy is not the concern of those who pass through Divinity and Greats, but of those who pass through birth and death." In an age that has almost chosen death, "Shaw follows the banner of life; but austerely, not joyously." Nowhere, in dealing with Shaw's philosophy, does Chesterton note his debt to Butler. Shaw has himself mentioned it, and no reader of Butler could miss it, especially in this matter of the Life Force. It is the special paradox of our age, Chesterton notes, that the

---

* No two love affairs are the same. This sentence assumed that they are all the same. To Eugene, the poet living in a world of imagination and abhorring reality, Candida was what Dulcinea was to Don Quixote. G.B.S.

† *George Bernard Shaw*, pp. 120-1.

life force should thus need assertion and can thus be followed without joy.

> To every man and woman, bird, beast, and flower, life is a love-call to be eagerly followed. To Bernard Shaw it is merely a military bugle to be obeyed. In short, he fails to feel that the command of Nature (if one must use the anthropomorphic fable of Nature instead of the philosophic term God) can be enjoyed as well as obeyed. He paints life at its darkest and then tells the babe unborn to take the leap in the dark. That is heroic; and to my instinct at least Schopenhauer looks like a pigmy beside his pupil. But it is the heroism of a morbid and almost asphyxiated age. It is awful to think that this world which so many poets have praised has even for a time been depicted as a man-trap into which we may just have the manhood to jump. Think of all those ages through which men have talked of having the courage to die. And then remember that we have actually fallen to talking of having the courage to live.*

Here comes the great parting of the two men's thought. G.K. believed in God and in joy. But he saw that Shaw had much of value for this strange diseased world. His primary value was not merely (as some said) that he woke it up. The literary world might not be awake to the social evil, but it was painfully awake to the ills, real or imaginary, inherent in human life.

> We do not need waking up; rather we suffer from insomnia, with all its results of fear and exaggeration and frightful waking dreams. The modern mind is not a donkey which wants kicking to make it go on. The modern mind is more like a motor-car on a lonely road which two amateur motorists have been just clever enough to take to pieces but are not quite clever enough to put together again.†

Shaw had not merely asked questions of the age: that would have been worse than useless. What he had done was at moments to rise above his own thoughts and give, through his characters, inspired answers: G.K. instances *Candida*, with its

* *George Bernard Shaw.* Week-End Library, p. 190.
† *Ibid*, pp. 245–6.

revelation of the meaning of marriage when the woman stays with the strong man because he is so weak and needs her. And Shaw had brought back philosophy into drama—that is, he had recreated the atmosphere, lost since Shakespeare,* in which men were thinking, and might, therefore, find the answers that the age needed. And here again we come back to the world which these men were shaking and to the respective philosophies with which they looked at it. It was a world of conventions and these conventions had become empty of meaning. Throw them away, said Shaw and Wells; no, said Chesterton; keep them and look for their meaning; Revolution does not mean destruction: it means restoration.

The same sort of discussion buzzed around this book as around the controversies of which it might be called a prolongation. Shaw himself reviewed it in an article in the *Nation,* in which he called it, "the best work of literary art I have yet provoked. . . . Everything about me which Mr. Chesterton had to divine he has divined miraculously. But everything that he could have ascertained easily by reading my own plain directions on the bottle, as it were, remains for him a muddled and painful problem." From an interchange of private letters it would seem that the move to Beaconsfield took place later in this year than I had supposed. Bernard Shaw's letter is probably not written many days after an undated one to him from G.K.:

48, Overstrand Mansions,
Battersea Park. S.W.

DEAR BERNARD SHAW,

I trust our recent tournaments have not rendered it contrary to the laws of romantic chivalry (which you reverence so much) for me to introduce to you my friend Mr. Pepler, who is a very nice man indeed though a social idealist, and who has, I believe, something of a practical sort to ask of you. Please excuse abruptness in

---

* Hard on Goethe and Ibsen, to say nothing of Mozart's Magic Flute and Beethoven's 9th symphony. G.B.S.

Of course, I meant English drama. M.W.

this letter of introduction; we are moving into the country and every piece of furniture I begin to write at is taken away and put into a van.

Always yours sincerely,

G. K. CHESTERTON.

10, Adelphi Terrace, W.C.
30th October 1909.

CHESTERTON.
SHAW SPEAKS.
ATTENTION!

I saw your man and consoled him spiritually; but that is not the subject of this letter. I still think that you could write a useful sort of play if you were started. When I was in Kerry last month I had occasionally a few moments to spare; and it seemed to me quite unendurable that you should be wasting your time writing books about me. I liked the book very much, especially as it was so completely free from my own influence, being evidently founded on a very hazy recollection of a five-year-old perusal of Man and Superman; but a lot of it was fearful nonsense. There was one good thing about the scientific superstition which you came a little too late for. It taught a man to respect facts. You have no conscience in this respect; and your punishment is that you substitute such dull inferences as my "narrow puritan home" for delightful and fantastic realities which you might very easily have ascertained if you had taken greater advantage of what is really the only thing to be said in favour of Battersea; namely, that it is within easy reach of Adelphi Terrace. However, I have no doubt that when Wilkins Micawber junior grew up and became eminent in Australia, references were made to *his* narrow puritan home; so I do not complain. If you had told the truth, nobody would have believed it.

Now to business. When one breathes Irish air, one becomes a practical man. In England I used to say what a pity it was you did not write a play. In Ireland I sat down and began writing a scenario for you. But before I could finish it I had come back to London; and now it is all up with the scenario: in England I can do nothing but talk. I therefore now send you the thing as far as I scribbled it; and I leave you to invent what escapades you please for the hero, and to devise some sensational means of getting him back to heaven again, unless you prefer to end with the millennium in full swing.*

But experience has made me very doubtful of the efficacy of help as the means of getting work out of the right sort of man. When I was young I struck out one invaluable rule for myself, which was, Whenever you meet an important man, contradict him. If possible, insult him. But such a rule is one of the privileges of youth. I no longer live by rules. Yet there is one way in which you may possibly be insultable. It can be plausibly held that you are a venal ruffian, pouring forth great quantities of immediately saleable stuff, but altogether declining to lay up for yourself treasures in heaven. It may be that you cannot afford to do otherwise. Therefore I am quite ready to make a deal with you.

A full length play should contain about 18,000 words (mine frequently contain two or three times that number). I do not know what your price per thousand is. I used to be considered grossly extortionate by Massingham and others for insisting on £3. 18,000 words at £3 per thousand is £54. I need make no extra allowance for the republication in book form, because even if the play aborted as far as the theatre is concerned, you could make a book of it all the same. Let us assume that your work is worth twice as much as mine: this would make £108. I have had two shockingly bad years of it pecuniarily speaking, and am therefore in that phase of extravagance which straitened means have always produced in me. Knock off 8% as a sort of agent's commission to me for starting you on the job and finding you a theme. This leaves £100. I will pay you £100 down on your contracting to supply me within three months with a mechanically possible, i.e., stageable drama dealing with the experiences of St. Augustine after re-visiting England. The literary copyright to be yours, except that you are not to prevent me making as many copies as I may require for stage use. The stage right to be mine; but you are to have the right to buy it back from me for £250 whenever you like.† The play, if performed, to be announced as your work and not as a collaboration. All rights which I may have in the scenario to go with the stage right and literary copyright as prescribed as far as you may make use of it. What do you say?? There is a lot of spending in £100.

* The scenario dealt with the return of St. Augustine to the England he remembered converting.

† I could not very well offer him £100 as a present. G.B.S.

One condition more. If it should prove impossible to achieve a performance otherwise than through the Stage Society (which does not pay anything), a resort to that body is not to be deemed a breach of the spirit of our agreement.

Do you think it would be possible to make Belloc write a comedy? If he could only be induced to believe in some sort of God instead of in that wretched little conspiracy against religion which the pious Romans have locked up in the Vatican, one could get some drive into him. As it is, he is wasting prodigious gifts in the service of King Leopold and the Pope and other ghastly scarecrows. If he must have a Pope, there is quite a possible one at Adelphi Terrace.

For the next few days I shall be at my country quarters, Ayot St. Lawrence, Welwyn, Herts. I have a motor car which could carry me on sufficient provocation as far as Beaconsfield; but I do not know how much time you spend there and how much in Fleet Street. Are you only a week-ender; or has your wise wife taken you properly in hand and committed you to a pastoral life.

Yours ever,

G. Bernard Shaw.

P.S. Remember that the play is to be practical (in the common managerial sense) only in respect of its being mechanically possible as a stage representation. It is to be neither a likely-to-be-successful play nor a literary lark: it is to be written for the good of all souls.

Among the reviewers of the book, our old friend, the *Academy*, surprised me by hating Shaw so much more than Chesterton that the latter came off quite lightly. There was a good deal of the usual misunderstanding and lists were made of self-contradictions on the author's part. Still in the main the press was sympathetic and even enthusiastic. But when Shaw reviewed Chesterton on Shaw, more than one paper waxed sarcastic on the point of royalties and remuneration gained by these means. The funniest of the more critical comments on the way these men wrote of one another was a suggestion made in the *Bystander* that Shaw and Chesterton were really the same person:

. . . Shaw, it is said, tired of Socialism, weary of wearing Jaegers, and broken down by teetotalism and vegetarianism, sought, some years ago, an escape from them. His adoption, however, of these attitudes had a decided commercial value, which he did not think it advisable to prejudice by wholesale surrender. Therefore he, in order to taste the forbidden joys of individualistic philosophy, meat, food and strong drink, created "Chesterton." This mammoth myth, he decided, should enjoy all the forms of fame which Shaw had to deny himself. Outwardly, he should be Shaw's antithesis. He should be beardless, large in girth, smiling of countenance, and he should be licensed to sell paradoxes only in essay and novel form, all stage and platform rights being reserved by Shaw.

To enable the imposition to be safely carried out, Shaw hit on the idea of residence close to the tunnel which connects Adelphi with the Strand. Emerging from his house plain, Jaeger-clad, bearded and saturnine Shaw, he entered the tunnel, in a cleft in which was a cellar. Here he donned the Chesterton properties, the immense padding of chest, and so on, the Chesterton sombrero hat and cloak and pince-nez, and there he left the Shaw beard and the Shaw clothes, the Shaw expression of countenance, and all the Shaw theories. He emerged into the Strand "G.K.C.," in whose identity he visited all the cafés, ate all the meats, rode in all the cabs, and smiled on all the sinners. The day's work done, the Chesterton manuscripts delivered, the proofs read, the bargains driven, the giant figure returned to the tunnel, and once again was back in Adelphi, the Shaw he was when he left it—back to the Jaegers, the beard, the Socialism, the statistics, and the sardonic letters to the *Times*.*

Bernard Shaw is a man of unusual generosity, but I think from his letters he must also be quite a good man of business. G.K. was so greatly the opposite that G.B.S. urged him again and again to do the most ordinary things to protect the literary rights of himself and others. Thus, in the only undated letter in the whole packet, he begs Gilbert to back up the Authors' Society:

My dear G.K.C.,

I am one of the unhappy slaves who, on the two big committees of your Trade Union (the Society of Authors) drudge at the heart-

* From *The Bystander*. 1 September, 1909.

breaking work of defending our miserable profession against being devoured, body and soul, by the publishers—themselves a pitiful gang of literature-struck impostors who are crumpled up by the booksellers, who, though small folk, are at least in contact with reality in the shape of the book buyer. It is a ghastly and infuriating business, because the authors *will* go to lunch with their publishers and sell them anything for £20 over the cigarettes, but it has to be done; and I, with half a dozen others, have to do it.

Now I missed the last committee meeting (electioneering: I am here doing two colossal meetings of miners every night for Keir Hardie); but the harassed secretary writes that it was decided to take proceedings in the case of a book of yours which you (oh Esau, Esau!) sold to John——(John is a—well—no matter: when you take your turn on the committee you will find him out) and that though the German lawyer has had £7 and is going ahead (£7 worth of law in Germany takes you to the House of Lords) everything is hung up because you will not answer Thring's* letters. Thring, in desperation, appeals to me, concluding with characteristic simplicity that we must be friends because you have written a book about me. As the conclusion is accidentally and improbably true, I now urge you to give him whatever satisfaction he requires. I have no notion what it is, or what the case is about; but at least answer his letters, however infuriating they may be. Remember: you pay Thring only £500, for which you get integrity, incorruptibility, implacability, and a disposition greatly to find quarrel in a straw on your behalf (even with yourself) and don't complain if you don't get £20,000 worth of tact into the bargain. And your obligations to us wretched committee men are simply incalculable. We get nothing but abuse and denigration: authors weep with indignation when we put our foot on some blood-sucking, widow-cheating, orphan starving scoundrel and ruthlessly force him to keep to his mite of obligation under an agreement which would have revolted Shylock: unless the best men, the Good Professionals, help us, we are lost. We get nothing and spend our time like water for you.

All we ask you to do is to answer Thring and let us get along with your work.

---

* Herbert Thring was the barrister employed by the Society of Authors.

Look here: *will* you write to Thring.
Please write to Thring.
I say: have you written to Thring yet?

G.B.S.

I doubt whether he had. Those chance sums he poured from time to time into Frances' lap were usually not what they should have been, an advance on a royalty. *Orthodoxy* he sold outright for £100. No man ever worked so hard to earn so little.

When later Gilbert employed Messrs. A. P. Watt as his literary agents a letter to them (undated, of course, and written on the old notepaper of his first Battersea flat) shows a mingling of gratitude to his agents with entire absence of resentment towards his publishers, which might be called essence of Chesterton:

The prices you have got me for books, compared with what I used weakly to demand, seem to me to come out of fairyland. It seems to me that there is a genuine business problem which creates a permanent need for a literary agent. It consists in this—that our work, even when it has become entirely a duty and a worry, still remains in some vague way a pleasure. And how can we put a fair price on what is at once a worry and a pleasure? Suppose someone comes to me and says, "I offer you sixpence for your *History of the Gnostic Heresy*." Why, after all, should I charge more than sixpence for a work it was so exuberant to write? You, on the other hand, seeing it from the outside, would say that it was worth—so and so. And you would get it.

Shaw continued his attempts to stimulate the reluctant playwright. Two years after drafting the scenario, he writes:

10 Adelphi Terrace, W.C.
5th April 1912.

DEAR MRS. CHESTERTON,

I have promised to drive somebody to Beaconsfield on Sunday morning; and I shall be in that district more or less for the rest of the day. If you are spending Easter at Overroads, and have no visitors who couldn't stand us, we should like to call on you at any time that would be convenient.

The convenience of time depends on a design of my own which I wish to impart to you first. I want to read a play to Gilbert. It began by way of being a music-hall sketch; so it is not 3½ hours long as usual: I can get through it in an hour and a half. I want to insult and taunt and stimulate Gilbert with it. It is the sort of thing he could write and ought to write: a religious harlequinade.* In fact, he could do it better if a sufficient number of pins were stuck into him. My proposal is that I read the play to him on Sunday (or at the next convenient date), and that you fall into transports of admiration of it; declare that you can never love a man who cannot write things like that; and definitely announce that if Gilbert has not finished a worthy successor to it before the end of the third week next ensuing, you will go out like the lady in A Doll's House, and live your own life—whatever that dark threat may mean.

If you are at home, I count on your ready complicity; but the difficulty is that you may have visitors; and if they are pious Gilbert will be under a tacit obligation not to blaspheme, or let me blaspheme, whilst they are beneath his roof (my play is about Christian Martyrs, and perfectly awful in parts); and if they are journalists, it will be necessary to administer an oath of secrecy. I don't object to the oath; and nothing would please Gilbert more than to make them drink blood from a skull: the difficulty is, they wouldn't keep it. In short, they must be the right sort of people, of whom the more the merrier.

Forgive this long rigmarole: it is only to put you in possession of what *may* happen if you approve, and your invitations and domestic circumstances are propitious.

Yours sincerely,

G. Bernard Shaw.

Chesterton at last did write *Magic*—but that belongs to another chapter.

Like the demand for a play, the theme of finance recurs with great frequency in Shaw's letters, and after *Magic* appeared he wrote to Frances telling her that "in Sweden, where the marriage laws are comparatively enlightened, I believe you could obtain

* Androcles and The Lion evidently. G.B.S.

a divorce on the ground that your husband threw away an important part of the provision for your old age for twenty pieces of silver. . . . In future, the moment he has finished a play and the question of disposing of it arises, lock him up and bring the agreement to me. Explanations would be thrown away on him."

CHAPTER XV

From Battersea to Beaconsfield
(1909-1911)

IN 1909, WITH *Orthodoxy* well behind him, and *George Bernard Shaw* just published, Gilbert and his wife left London for the small country town that was to be their home for the rest of their lives. It was an odd coincidence that they should leave Overstrand Mansions, Battersea, and come to Overroads, Beaconsfield, for they did not name their new home but found it ready christened.

It will be remembered that in one of the letters during the engagement Gilbert had suggested a country home. The reason for the choice of Beaconsfield he gives in the *Autobiography*:

After we were married, my wife and I lived for about a year in Kensington, the place of my childhood; but I think we both knew that it was not to be the real place for our abode. I remember that we strolled out one day, for a sort of second honeymoon, and went upon a journey into the void, a voyage deliberately objectless. I saw a passing omnibus labelled "Hanwell" and, feeling this to be an appropriate omen,* we boarded it and left it somewhere at a stray station, which I entered and asked the man in the ticket-office where the next train went to. He uttered the pedantic reply, "Where do you want to go to?" And I uttered the profound and philosophical rejoinder, "Wherever the next train goes to." It seemed that it went to Slough; which may seem to be singular taste, even in a train. However, we went to Slough, and from there set out walking with even less notion of where we were going. And in that fashion we passed through the large and quiet cross-roads of a sort of village,

* At Hanwell is London's most famous lunatic asylum.

and stayed at an inn called The White Hart. We asked the name of the place and were told that it was called Beaconsfield (I mean of course that it was called Beconsfield and not Beaconsfield), and we said to each other, "This is the sort of place where some day we will make our home." *

They both wanted a home. They both deeply desired a family. The wish is normal to both man and woman, normal in a happy marriage, and theirs was unusually happy; it was almost abnormally keen in both Frances and Gilbert. Few men have so greatly loved children. As a schoolboy his letters are full of it—making friends with Scottish children on the sands, with French children by the medium of pictures. Later he was writing "In Defence of Baby Worship" and welcoming with enthusiasm the arrival of his friends' children into the world.

In the Notebook he had written:

> Sunlight in a child's hair.
> It is like the kiss of Christ upon all children.
> I blessed the child: and hoped the blessing
>   would go with him
>   And never leave him;
> And turn first into a toy, and then into a game
>   And then into a friend,
> And as he grew up, into friends
>   And then into a woman.

GRASS AND CHILDREN

Grass and children
There seems no end to them.
But if there were but one blade of grass
Men would see that it is fairer than lilies,
And if we saw the first child
We should worship it as the God come on earth.

ROUNDS

> I find that most round things are nice,
> Particularly Eternity and a baby.

* *Autobiography*, p. 219.

Frances cared no less deeply both for Eternity and for babies and for many years went on hoping for the family that would complete their lives. At last it was decided to have an operation to enable her to have children. Her doctor writes:

I well remember an incident which occurred during her convalescence from that operation. I received a telephone call from the matron of the Nursing Home in which Mrs. Chesterton was staying, suggesting that I should come round and remonstrate with Mr. Chesterton. On my arrival I found him sitting on the stairs, where he had been for two hours, greatly incommoding passers up and down and deaf to all requests to move on. It appeared that he had written a sonnet to his wife on her recovery from the operation and was bringing it to give her. He was not however satisfied with the last line, but was determined to perfect it before entering her room to take tea with her.

By the time they left London she must, I think, have given up the hope she had so long cherished. Still if there could not be children there might be perhaps something of a home. In the conditions of their life, there was danger that any house of bricks and mortar should be rather a headquarters than a home, and it was lucky that he was able to feel she took home with her wherever they went—

> Your face that is a wandering home
> A flying home for me.

The years before them were to be filled with the vast activities that not only took Gilbert to London and all over England incessantly, but were to take him increasingly over Europe and America. Beaconsfield gave a degree of quiet that made it possible, when they *were* able to be at home, not to be swamped by engagements and to lead a life of their own. Gilbert could go to London when he liked, but he need not always be on tap, so to say, for all the world. Frances could have a garden and indulge her hungry appetite for all that was fruitful. G.K., later, under the title "The Homelessness of Jones" * showed his love for a house rather than a flat, and they gave even to their first little house "Overroads" the stamp of a real home.

For a man and his wife to leave London for the country might seem to be their own affair. Not so, however, with the Chestertons. After a lapse of over thirty years I find the matter still a subject of furious controversy and indeed passion. Frances, says one school of opinion, committed a crime against the public good by removing Gilbert from Fleet Street. No, says the other school, she had to move him or he would have died of working too hard and drinking too much. The suggestion, which I believe to be a fact, that Gilbert himself wanted to move, is seldom entertained.

There is in all this the legitimate feeling of distress among any group at losing its chief figure, its pride and joy. "I lost Gilbert," Lucian Oldershaw once said, "first when I introduced him to Belloc, next when he married Frances, and finally when he joined the Catholic Church. . . . I rejoiced, though perhaps with a maternal sadness, at all these fulfillments."

Cecil wanted his brother always on hand. Belloc was already in the country—a far more remote country—but even he, coming up to London, mourned to my mother, "She has taken my Chesterton from me." Talking it over however after the lapse of years, he agreed that in all probability the move was a wise one. What may be called the smaller fry of Fleet Street are less reasonable. One cannot avoid the feeling that in all this masculine life so sure of its manhood, there lingered something of the "schwärmerei" of the Junior Debating Club furiously desiring each to be first with Gilbert. And in his love of Fleet Street he so identified himself with them all that they felt he was one of them and did not recognise the horizons wider than theirs that were opening before him.

My husband and I are experts in changing residences and

* A chapter in *What's Wrong with the World.*

we listened with the amusement of experts to the talk of theorists. For it was so constantly assumed that on one side of a choice is disaster, on the other perfection. Actually perfection does not belong to this earthly state: if you go to Rome, as Gilbert himself once said, you sacrifice a rich suggestive life at Wimbledon. Newman writing of a far greater and more irrevocable choice called his story *Loss and Gain*—but he had no doubt that the gain outweighed the loss. There were in Gilbert's adult life three other big decisions—decisions of the scale that altered its course. The first was his marriage. The second was his reception into the Church. The third was his continued dedication to the paper that his brother and Belloc had founded. In deciding to marry Frances he was acting against his mother's wishes, to which he was extremely sensitive. His decision to become a Catholic had to be made alone: he had the sympathy of his wife but not her companionship. In the decision to edit the paper he had not even fully her sympathy: she always felt his creative work to be so much more important and to be imperilled by the overwork the paper brought. Gilbert was a man slow in action but it would be exceedingly difficult to find instances of his doing anything that he did not want to do. The theorists about marriage are like the theorists about moving house, if they do not know that decisions made by one party alone are rare indeed and stick out like spikes in the life of a normal and happy couple. Of the vast majority of decisions it is hard to say who makes them. They make themselves: after endless talk: on the tops of omnibuses going to Hanwell or elsewhere: out walking: breakfasting—especially breakfasting in bed. They make themselves—above all in the matter of a move—in fine weather: during a holiday: on a hot London Sunday: when a flat is stuffy: when the telephone rings all day: when a book is on the stocks.

Other writers have left London that they might create at leisure and choose their own times for social intercourse. Why does no one say their wives dragged them away? Simply, I

FIGURES FROM THE TOY THEATRE

think, that being less kind and considerate than Gilbert, they do not mind telling their friends that they are not always wanted. This Gilbert could not do. If people said how they would miss him, how they hated his going, he would murmur vague and friendly sounds, from which they deduced all they wanted to deduce. Was it more weakness or strength, that tenderness of heart that could never faintly suggest to his friends that they would miss him more than he would miss them? "I never wanted but one thing in my life," he had written to Annie Firmin. And that "one thing" he was taking with him.

Anyhow, the move accomplished, he enjoyed defending it in every detail, and did so especially in his *Daily News* articles. The rush to the country was not uncommon in the literary world of the moment, and his journalist friends had urged the point that Beaconsfield was not true country, was suburban, was being built over. His friends, G.K. replied, were suffering from a weak-minded swing from one extreme to the other. Men who had praised London as the only place to live in were now vying with one another to live furthest from a station, to have no chimneys visible on the most distant horizon, to depend on tradesmen who only called once a week from cities so distant that fresh-baked loaves grew stale before delivery. "Rival ruralists would quarrel about which had the most completely inconvenient postal service; and there were many jealous heartburnings if one friend found out any uncomfortable situation which the other friend had thoughtlessly overlooked."

Gilbert, on the contrary, noted soon after his arrival that Beaconsfield was beginning to be built over and he noted it with satisfaction. "Within a stone's throw of my house they are building another house. I am glad they are building it and I am glad it is within a stone's throw." He did not want a desert, he did not want a large landed estate, he wanted what he had got—a house and a garden. He adventurously explored that garden, finding a kitchen-garden that had "somehow got attached" to the premises, and wondering why he liked it; speaking to the gardener, "an enterprise of no little valour," and asking him the name "of a strange dark red rose, at once theatrical and sulky," which turned out to be called Victor Hugo; "watching (with regret) a lot of little black pigs being turned out of my garden."

Watching the neighbouring house grow up from its foundation he noted in an article called, "The Wings of Stone," what was the reality of a staircase. We pad them with carpets and rail them with banisters, yet every "staircase is truly only an awful and naked ladder running up into the infinite to a deadly height." (A correspondent pointed out in a letter to the *Daily News* that here he had touched a reality keenly felt by primitive peoples. When Cetewayo, King of Zululand, visited London, he would go upstairs only on hands and knees and that with manifest terror.) The paddings of civilisation may be useful, yet Gilbert held more valuable a realisation of the realities of things. Vision is not fancy, but the sight of truth.

In the Notebook he had written

> There are three things that make me think;
>   things beyond all poetry:
> A yellow space or rift in evening sky:
> A chimney or pinnacle high in the air;
> And a path over a hill.

Chesterton had always the power of conveying in words a painter's vision of some unforgettable scene with the poet's words for what the artist not only sees but imagines. Such flashes became more frequent as he looked through the doorway of his little house. Go through *The Ball and the Cross* with this in mind and you will see what I mean. "The crimson seas of the sunset seemed to him like a bursting out of some sacred blood, as if the heart of the world had broken." "There is nothing more beautiful than thus to look as it were through the archway of a house; as if the open sky were an interior chamber,

and the sun a secret lamp of the place." Best of all to illustrate
this special quality is a longer passage from the *Poet and the
Lunatics*.

For the most part he was contented to see the green semicircles
of lawn repeat themselves like a pattern of green moons; for he
was not one to whom repetition was merely monotony. Only in
looking over a particular gate at a particular lawn, he became pleasantly conscious, or half conscious, of a new note of colour in the
greenness; a much bluer green, which seemed to change to vivid
blue, as the object at which he was gazing moved sharply, turning
a small head on a long neck. It was a peacock. But he had thought
of a thousand things before he thought of the obvious thing. The
burning blue of the plumage on the neck had reminded him of blue
fire, and blue fire had reminded him of some dark fantasy about
blue devils, before he had fully realised even that it was a peacock
he was staring at. And the tail, that trailing tapestry of eyes, had
led his wandering wits away to those dark but divine monsters of
the Apocalypse whose eyes were multiplied like their wings, before
he had remembered that a peacock, even in a more practical sense,
was an odd thing to see in so ordinary a setting.

Yet always to Chesterton the beauty of nature was enhanced
by the work of men, and if in London men had swarmed too
closely, it was not to get away from them but to appreciate them
more individually that he chose the country. Yes, his literary
friends would say: in the real country that is true: the farmer,
the labourer, even the village barber and the village tradesmen
are worth knowing, but not suburban neighbours. Against such
discrimination the whole democracy of Chesterton stood in
revolt. All men were valuable, all men were interesting, the
doctor as much as the barber, the clergyman as much as the
farmer. All men were children of God and citizens of the world.
If he had a choice in the matter it was discrimination against
the literary world itself with all the fads that tended to smother
its essential humanity. Nothing would have induced him to
discriminate against the suburban. In the last year of his life

he wrote in the *Autobiography*: "I have lived in Beaconsfield from the time when it was almost a village, to the time when, as the enemy profanely says, it is a suburb."

For the author of *The Napoleon of Notting Hill* this would hardly be a conclusive argument against any place. We should, he once said, "regard the important suburbs as ancient cities embedded in a sort of boiling lava spouted up by that volcano, the speculative builder." That "lava" itself he found interesting, but beneath or beside it a little town like Beaconsfield had its share in the great sweep of English history. Something of the "seven sunken Englands" could be found in the Old Town which custom marked off pretty sharply from the "New Town." Burke had lived in Beaconsfield and was buried there; and Gilbert once suggested to Mr. Garvin that they should appear at a local festival, respectively as Fox ("a part for which I have no claim except in circumference") and Burke ("I admire Burke in many things while disagreeing with him in nearly everything. But Mr. Garvin strikes me as being rather like Burke").

At the barber's he was often seen sitting at the end of a line patiently awaiting his turn, for he could never shave himself and it was only years later that Dorothy Collins conceived and put into execution the bold project of bringing the barber to the house. Probably an article would be shaping while he waited and the barber's conversation might put the finishing touches to it. There were in fact two barbers, one of the old town, one of the new. "I once planned," he says, "a massive and exhaustive sociological work, in several volumes, which was to be called 'The Two Barbers of Beaconsfield' and based entirely upon the talk of the two excellent citizens to whom I went to get shaved. For those two shops do indeed belong to two different civilisations."

Despite his love for London, Gilbert had always felt that life in a country town held one point of special superiority—in it you discovered the Community. In London you chose your friends—which meant that you narrowed your life to people of one kind. He had noted in the family itself a valuable widening:

The supreme adventure is being born. There we do walk suddenly into a splendid and startling trap. There we do see something of which we have not dreamed before. Our father and mother do lie in wait for us and leap out on us, like brigands from a bush. Our uncle is a surprise. Our aunt is, in the beautiful common expression, a bolt from the blue. When we step into the family, by the act of being born, we do step into a world which is incalculable, into a world which has its own strange laws, into a world which could do without us, into a world that we have not made.*

Here in Beaconsfield the Chestertons grew into the community: the clergyman, the doctor, the inn-keeper, the barber, the gardener. And like the relatives who spring upon you at birth these worthy citizens seemed to Gilbert potentials of vast excitement and varied interest. Discussing an event of much later date—a meeting to decide whether a crucifix might be erected as a local war memorial—he thus describes the immense forces he found in that small place:

Those who debated the matter were a little group of the inhabitants of a little country town; the rector and the doctor and the bank manager and the respectable tradesmen of the place, with a few hangers-on like myself, of the more disreputable professions of journalism or the arts. But the powers that were present there in the spirit came out of all the ages and all the battlefields of history; Mahomet was there and the Iconoclasts, who came riding out of the East to ruin the statues of Italy, and Calvin and Rousseau and the Russian anarchs and all the older England that is buried under Puritanism; and Henry the Third ordering the little images for Westminster and Henry the Fifth, after Agincourt, on his knees before the shrines of Paris. If one could really write that little story of that little place, it would be the greatest of historical monographs.†

A keen observer often added to the Beaconsfield community in those days was Father (now Monsignor) John O'Connor,

---

Heretics, pp. 191–2.   † *Autobiography*, p. 244.

close friend of both Gilbert and Frances and inspirer of "Father Brown" of detective fame. They had first become friends in 1904 when they met at the house of a friend in Keighley, Yorkshire, and walked back over the moors together to visit Francis Steinthal at Ilkley. This Jew, of Frankfort descent, was a great friend of the Chestertons and on their many visits to him the friendship with Father O'Connor ripened. With both Frances and Gilbert it was among the closest of their lives. Their letters to him show it: the long talks, and companionable walks over the moors, have an atmosphere of intimacy that is all the more convincing because so little stressed in his book. Father O'Connor has a pardonable pride in the idea that their talks suggested ideas to Gilbert, he takes pleasure in his character of "Father Brown," but he reveals the atmosphere of unique confidence and intimacy by the very absence of all parade of it.

Both he and Gilbert have told the story of how the idea of the detective priest first dawned. On their second meeting Father O'Connor had startled, indeed almost shattered Gilbert, with certain rather lurid knowledge of human depravity which he had acquired in the course of his priestly experience. At the house to which they were going, two Cambridge undergraduates spoke disparagingly of the "cloistered" habits of the Catholic clergy, saying that to them it seemed that to know and meet evil was a far better thing than the innocence of such ignorance. To Gilbert, still under the shock of a knowledge compared with which "these two Cambridge gentlemen knew about as much of real evil as two babies in the same perambulator," the exquisite irony of this remark suggested a thought. Why not a whole comedy of cross purposes based on the notion of a priest with a knowledge of evil deeper than that of the criminal he is converting? He carried out this idea in the story of "The Blue Cross," the first Father Brown detective story. Father O'Connor's account adds the details that he had himself once boasted of buying five sapphires for five shillings, and that he always carried a large umbrella and many brown paper parcels. At the Stein-thal dining table, an artist friend of the family made a sketch of Father O'Connor which later appeared on the wrapper of *The Innocence of Father Brown.*

Beyond one or two touches of this sort the idea had been a suggestion for a character, not a portrait, and in the *Autobiography* and in the *Dickens* Gilbert has a good deal to say of interest to the novelist about how such suggestions come and are used. He never believed that Dickens drew a portrait, as it were, in the round. Nature just gives hints to the creative artist. And it used to amuse "Father Brown" to find that such touches of observation as noting where an ash-tray had got hidden behind a book seemed to Gilbert quasi miraculous. Left to himself he merely dropped ashes on the floor from his cigar. "He did not smoke a pipe and cigarettes were prone to set him on fire in one place or another."

A frequent visitor, Father O'Connor noted his fashion of work and reading, and the abstracted way he often moved and spoke. "Call it mooning, but he never mooned. He was always working out something in his mind, and when he drifted from his study to the garden and was seen making deadly passes with his sword-stick at the dahlias, we knew that he had got to a dead end in his composition and was getting his thoughts into order."

He played often, too, with a huge knife which he had for twenty-four years. He took it abroad with him, took it to bed: Frances had to retrieve it often from under his pillow in some hotel. Once at a lecture in Dublin he drew it absent-mindedly to sharpen a pencil: as it was seven and a half inches long shut, and fourteen open, the amusement of the audience may be imagined. In origin it was, Father O'Connor relates, a Texan or Mexican general utility implement. It was with this knife that he won my daughter's heart many years later when she, aged three, had not seen him for some time and had grown shy of him. A little scared of his enormousness she stood far off. He did not look in her direction but began to open and shut the vast blade. Next she was on his knee. A little later we heard her remark, "Uncle Gilbert, you make jokes just like my Daddy." And from him came, "I do my best."

The prototype of Father Brown tells of the easy job in detection when Gilbert had been reading a book:

He had just been reading a shilling pamphlet by Dr. Horton on the Roman Menace or some such fearful wild fowl. I knew he had read it, because no one else could when he had done. Most of his books, as and when read, had gone through every indignity a book may suffer and live. He turned it inside out, dog-eared it, pencilled it, sat on it, took it to bed and rolled on it, and got up again and spilled tea on it—if he were sufficiently interested. So Dr. Horton's pamphlet had a refuted look when I saw it."

Father O'Connor was not the only friend who was added to the Beaconsfield group with some frequency. It was easy enough to run down from London or over from Welwyn (home of G.B.S.) or from Oxford or Cambridge. It was most conveniently central. Gilbert's brethren of the pen were especially apt to appear at all seasons and always found friendly welcome. For he continued to call himself neither poet nor philosopher but journalist. Father O'Connor had tried to persuade him, as he neatly puts it, to "begin to print on handmade paper with gilt edges." But Frances begged him to drop the idea: "You will not change Gilbert, you will only fidget him. He is bent on being a jolly journalist, to paint the town red, and he does not need style to do that. All he wants is buckets and buckets of red paint."

Journalists coming down from London describe the "jolly" welcome, beer poured, the sword-stick flourished, conversation flowing as freely as the beer. It meant a pleasant afternoon and it meant good copy. They visited him in the country, they observed him in town. One interviewer returned with a photo which showed Chesterton "in a somewhat négligé condition," the result as he admitted of reading W. W. Jacobs "rolling about on the floor waving his legs in the air."

He was seen working a swan boat at the White City: "he collapsed it and the placid lake became a raging sea." He was seen thinking and even reading under the strangest weather conditions: one man saw him under a gas lamp in the street in pouring rain with an open book in his hand. Reading in Fleet Street one day Gilbert discovered suddenly that the Lord Mayor's Show was passing. He began to reflect on the Show so deeply that he forgot to look at it.

Overroads I remember as a little triangular house, much too small for the sort of fun the Chestertons enjoyed. Frances bought a field opposite to it and there built a studio. The night the studio was opened Father O'Connor remembers a large party at which charades were acted. He himself as Canon Cross-Keys gave away the word so that "Belfry" was loudly shouted by the opposition group. The rival company acting Torture got away with it successfully, especially, complains our Yorkshire priest "as 'ure' was pronounced 'yaw' in the best southern manner."

On that night, returning to the house, Father O'Connor offered his arm to Gilbert who "refused it with a finality foreign to our friendship." Father O'Connor went on ahead and Gilbert following in the dark stumbled over a flowerpot and broke his arm. Perhaps because his size made him self-consciously aware of awkwardness Gilbert hated being helped. Father Ignatius Rice, another close friend, says the only time he ever saw Gilbert annoyed was when he offered him an arm going upstairs.

Gilbert and Frances would both visit Father O'Connor in his Yorkshire Parish of Heckmondwike. One year they took rooms at Ilkley and he remembers Gilbert adorning with huge frescoes the walls of the attic and Frances sitting in the window singing,

"O swallow, swallow flying south" while Gilbert "did a blazon of some fantastic coat of arms."

The closeness of the intimacy is seen in a letter quoted by Father O'Connor * in which Gilbert explained why Frances and he were unable to come to Heckmondwike for a promised visit.

(July 3rd, 1909)

I would not write this to anyone else, but you combine so unusually in your own single personality the characters of (1) priest, (2) human being, (3) man of the world, (4) man of the other world, (5) man of science, (6) old friend, (7) new friend, not to mention Irishman and picture dealer, that I don't mind suggesting the truth to you. Frances has just come out of what looked bad enough to be an illness, and is just going to plunge into one of her recurrent problems of pain and depression. The two may be just a bit too much for her and I want to be with her every night for a few days—there's an Irish Bull for you!

One of the mysteries of Marriage (which must be a Sacrament and an extraordinary one too) is that a man evidently useless like me can yet become at certain instants indispensable. And the further oddity (which I invite you to explain on mystical grounds) is that he never feels so small as when he knows that he is necessary.

But sometimes she would send him off whether she was well or ill, and on Father O'Connor would rest the heavy responsibility of getting him on to his next destination or safe back home. He tells of one such experience.

He was most dutiful and obedient to orders, but they had to be written ones and backed by the spoken word. He brought his dress-suit, oh! with what loving care, to Bradford on Sunday for Sheffield for Monday, but a careful host found it under the bed in Bradford just as his train left for Sheffield. Sent at once it was to Beaconsfield, where it landed at 5 P.M. on Thursday, just allowing him ten minutes to change and entrain for London.

Scene at Beaconsfield:

"What on earth have you done with your dress-suit, Gilbert?"

* *Father Brown on Chesterton*, p. 123.

"I must have left it behind, darling, but I brought back the ties, didn't I?" *

Another time he came back without his pyjamas. They had been lost early in the journey. "Why didn't you buy some more?" his wife asked. "I didn't know pyjamas were things you could buy," he said, surprised. Probably if one were Gilbert one couldn't! Father O'Connor arriving at Overroads without baggage found that Gilbert's pyjamas went around him exactly twice.

Lecturing engagements had of course not come to an end with the move although they had (mercifully) somewhat lessened. What increased with the distance from London was the problem—never fully solved—of getting Gilbert to the right place at the right time and in clothes not too wildly wrong. When he lectured in Lancashire they stayed at Crosby with Francis Blundell (my brother-in-law), and my sister remembers Frances as incessantly looking through her bag for letters and sending telegrams to confirm engagements that had come unstuck or to refuse others that were in debate. The celebrated and now almost legendary telegram from Gilbert to Frances told as from a hundred different cities was really sent: "Am in Market Harborough. Where ought I to be?"

Desperate, she wired, "Home," because, as she told me later, it was easier to get him home and start him off again. That day's engagement was lost past recall.

Charles Rowley of the Ancoats Brotherhood received a wire, reply paid, from Snow Hill Station, Birmingham: "Am I coming to you tonight or what?" Reply: "Not this Tuesday but next Wednesday."

So home he came again to Overroads.

The Chestertons made a host of friends in Beaconsfield but the children always held pride of place. The doctor's little boy, running along the top of the wall, looked down at Gilbert and

* *Ibid*, p. 43.

remarked to his delight, "I think you're an ogre." But when the nurse was heard threatening punishment if he did not get down "that minute," the child was told by the ogre, "This wall is meant for little boys to run along." One child, asked after a party if Mr. Chesterton had been very clever, said, "You should see him catch buns in his mouf."

What was unusual both with Gilbert and Frances was the fact that they never allowed their disappointment in the matter of children to make them sour or jealous of others who had the joy that they had not. All through their lives they played with other people's children: they chose on a train a compartment full of children: they planned amusements, they gave presents to the children of their friends. Over my son's bed hangs a silver crucifix chosen with loving care by Frances after Gilbert had stood godfather to him. And he was one of very many.

Gilbert was however a complete realist as to the ways and manners of the species he so loved.

Playing with children [he wrote at this time] is a glorious thing: but the journalist in question has never understood why it was considered a soothing or idyllic one. It reminds him, not of watering little budding flowers, but of wrestling for hours with gigantic angels and devils. Moral problems of the most monstrous complexity besiege him incessantly. He has to decide before the awful eyes of innocence, whether, when a sister has knocked down a brother's bricks, in revenge for the brother having taken two sweets out of his turn, it is endurable that the brother should retaliate by scribbling on the sister's picture-book, and whether such conduct does not justify the sister in blowing out the brother's unlawfully lit match.

Just as he is solving this problem upon principles of the highest morality, it occurs to him suddenly that he has not written his Saturday article; and that there is only about an hour to do it in. He wildly calls to somebody (probably the gardener) to telephone to somewhere for a messenger; he barricades himself in another room and tears his hair, wondering what on earth he shall write about. A drumming of fists on the door outside and a cheerful bellowing encourage and clarify his thoughts. . . . He sits down desperately;

the messenger rings at the bell; the children drum on the door; the servants run up from time to time to say the messenger is getting bored; and the pencil staggers along, making the world a present of fifteen hundred unimportant words, and making Shakespeare a present of a portion of Gray's *Elegy*; putting "fantastic roots wreathed high" instead of "antique roots peep out." * Then the journalist sends off his copy and turns his attention to the enigma of whether a brother should commandeer a sister's necklace because the sister pinched him at Littlehampton.

In the Notebook he had written:

NORTH BERWICK

On the sands I romped with children
Do you blame me that I did not improve myself
By bottling anemones?
But I say that these children will be men and women
And I say that the anemones will not be men and women
    (Not just yet, at least, let us say).
And I say that the greatest men of the world might
    romp with children
And that I should like to see Shakespeare romping
    with children
And Browning and Darwin romping with children
And Mr. Gladstone romping with children
And Professor Huxley romping with children
And all the Bishops romping with children;
And I say that if a man had climbed to the stars
And found the secrets of the angels,
The best thing and the most useful thing he could do
Would be to come back and romp with children.

M. V.

An almost elvish little girl with loose brown hair, doing
    needlework. I have spoken to her once or twice.
I think I must get another book of the same size as this
    to make notes about her.

---

* Chesterton had actually made this slip, and the present quotation is from the article he wrote in apology.

From the Christmas party at Overroads all adults were excluded—no nurses, no parents. The children would hang on Gilbert's neck in an ecstasy of affection and he and Frances schemed out endless games for them. Gilbert had started a toy theatre before he left London, cutting out and painting figures and scenery, and devising plots for plays. Two of the favourites were "St. George and the Dragon" and "The Seven Champions of Christendom."

The atmosphere of Overroads is perhaps best conveyed through Gilbert's theories concerning his toy theatre and the other theatricals such as Charades sometimes played there. When it came to the toy theatre set up to amuse the children, he frankly felt that he was himself child No. 1 and got the most amusement out of it. He felt too that the whole thing was good enough to be worth analysing in its rules and its effects. And so he drew up a paper of rules and suggestions for its use.

I will not say positively that a toy-theatre is the best of theatres; though I have had more fun out of it than out of any other. But I will say positively that the toy-theatre is the best of all toys. It sometimes fails; but generally because people are mistaken in the matter of what it is meant to do, and what it can or cannot be expected to do; as if people should use a toy balloon as a football or a skipping rope as a hammock. . . .

Now the first rule may seem rather contradictory; but it is quite true and really quite simple. In a small theatre, because it is a small theatre, you cannot deal with small things. Because it is a small theatre it must only deal with large things. You can introduce a dragon; but you cannot really introduce an earwig; it is too small for a small theatre. And this is true not only of small creatures, but of small actions, small gestures and small details of any kind. . . . All your effects must be made to depend on things like scenery and background. The sky and the clouds and the castles and the mountains and so on must be the exciting things; along with other things that move all of a piece, such as regiments and processions; great and glorious things can be done with processions. . . . In a real comedy the whole excitement may consist in the nervous curate dropping his tea-cup; though I do not recommend this incident for the drama of the drawing-room. But if he were nervous, let us say, about a thunder-storm, the toy-theatre could hardly represent the nervousness but it might manage the thunder-storm. It might be quite sensational and yet entirely simple; for it would largely consist of darkening the stage and making horrible noises behind the scenes. . . .

The second and smaller rule, that really follows from this, is that everything dramatic should depend not on a character's action, but simply on his appearance. Shakespeare said of actors that they have their exits and their entrances; but these actors ought really to have nothing else except exits and entrances. The trick is to so arrange the tale that the mere appearance of a person tells the important truth about him. Thus, supposing the drama to be about St. George let us say, the mere abrupt appearance of the dragon's head (if of a proper ferocity) will be enough to explain that he intends to eat people; and it will not be necessary for the dragon to explain at length, with animated gestures and playful conversation, that his nature is carnivorous and that he has not merely dropped in to tea.

There is some further discussion on colour effects ("I like very gay and glaring colours, and I like to give them a good chance to glare"). The paper concludes on a more serious note:

It is an old story, and for some a sad one, that in a sense these childish toys are more to us than they can ever be to children. We never know how much of our after imaginations began with such a peep-show into paradise. I sometimes think that houses are interesting because they are so like doll houses and I am sure the best thing that can be said for many large theatres is that they may remind us of little theatres. . . .

I do not look back, I look forward to this kind of puppet play; I look forward to the day when I shall have time to play with it. Some day when I am too lazy to write anything, or even to read anything, I shall retire into this box of marvels; and I shall be found still striving hopefully to get inside a toy-theatre.

Adults as well as children enjoyed this toy and it was often described by interviewers. Like the sword-stick, the great cloak and flapping hat, it was felt by some to be Gilbert's way of attracting attention. But it was just one of Gilbert's ways of amusing himself. A small nephew of Frances was living with them at the time and it was funny to watch him fencing with his huge uncle who was obviously enjoying himself rather the more of the two. On my first visit to Overroads, I noticed how as we talked my host's pencil never ceased. One evening I collected and kept an imposing red Indian and a caricature of Chesterton himself in a wheelbarrow being carried off to the bonfire. I came in too for one of the grown-up parties in which guessing games were a feature. Lines from the poets were illustrated and we had to guess them. At another party, Dr. Pocock told me, G.K. did the Inns of Beaconsfield, of which the most successful drawing was that of a sadly dilapidated dragon being turned away from the inn door: "Dragon discovers with disgust that he cannot put up at the George."

Sometimes these drawings were the prize of whoever guessed the line of verse they illustrated, sometimes they were sold for a local charity. The Babies' Convalescent Home was a favourite object and one admirable picture (reproduced in *The Coloured Lands*) shows the "Despair of King Herod at discovering children convalescing from the Massacre."

The two closest friendships of early Beaconsfield life were with the rector, Mr. Comerline and his wife, who are now dead, and Dr. and Mrs. Pocock. Dr. Pocock was the Chestertons' doctor as well as their friend, and he tells me that his great difficulty in treating Gilbert lay in his detachment from his own physical circumstances. If there was anything wrong with him he usually didn't notice it. "He was the most uncomplaining person. You had to hunt him all over" to find out if anything was wrong.

This detachment from circumstances still extended to his

FIGURES FROM THE TOY THEATRE

appearance and Frances one day begged Dr. Pocock to take him to a good tailor. It was a huge success: he had never looked so well as he did now—for a few weeks. And then the tailor said to Dr. Pocock, "Mr. Chesterton has broken my heart. It took twice the material and twice the time to make for him, but I *was* proud of it." His tailor like his doctor was apt to become a friend. Mrs. Pocock recalls how he would go to a dinner of the tradesmen of Beaconsfield and come back intensely interested and wanting to tell her all about it.

"You always went away," Dr. Pocock said, "chuckling over something," and he summed up the years of their friendship, saying, "You never saw him without getting delight from his presence."

Sometimes he would grow abstracted in the train of his own thought, and Father Ignatius Rice remembers an occasion when he was one of a group discussing really bad lines of poetry. Gilbert broke into something Frances was saying with the words, "That irritating person Milton"—then, realising he had interrupted her, he broke off and apologised profusely. When she had finished he went on "That irritating person Milton—I can't find a single bad line in him."

Frances one day came in rather suddenly when Dr. Pocock was there, and Gilbert exclaimed, "Oh you've broken it." She looked round thinking she must have knocked something over. "No," he said, "it was an idea." "It will come back," said Frances. "No," he said, "it got broken." More usually he was indifferent to interruptions: sometimes he welcomed them as grist for his mind's mill. Daily life went on around him and often in his articles one can find traces of Frances's daily activities as well as his own.

Attending him for his broken arm, Dr. Pocock told him at a certain stage to write something—anything—to see if he could use a pen again. After an instant's thought, Gilbert headed his paper with the name of a prominent Jew and wrote:

> I am fond of Jews
> Jews are fond of money
> Never mind of whose
> I am fond of Jews
> Oh, but when they lose
> Damn it all, it's funny.

The name at the head (which wild horses would not drag from me) is the key to this impromptu. It was really true that Gilbert was fond of very many Jews. In his original group of J.D.C. friends, four Jews had been included and with three of these his friendship continued through life. Lawrence Solomon and his wife were among the Beaconsfield neighbours and he saw them often. There was another kind of Jew he very heartily disliked but he was at great pains to draw this distinction himself.

Speaking at the Jewish West End Literary Society in 1911 he put the question of what the real Jewish problem was: The Jews, he said, were a race, born civilised. You never met a Jewish clod or yokel. They represented one of the highest of civilised types. But while all other races had local attachments, the Jews were universal and scattered. They could not be expected to have patriotism for the countries in which they made their homes: their patriotism could be only for their race. In principle, he believed in the solution of Zionism. And then the reporter in large letters made a headline: "Mr. Chesterton said that speaking generally, as with most other communities, THE POOR JEWS WERE NICE AND THE RICH WERE NASTY."

Many years later in Palestine he was to be driven around the country, as he has described in *The New Jerusalem,* by one of these less wealthy Jews who had sacrificed his career in England to his national idealism. And later yet, after G.K.'s death, Rabbi Wise, a leader of American Jewry, paid him tribute (in a letter to Cyril Clements dated September 8, 1937):

Indeed I was a warm admirer of Gilbert Chesterton. Apart from his delightful art and his genius in many directions, he was, as you know, a great religionist. He as Catholic, I as Jew, could not have seen eye to eye with each other, and he might have added "particularly seeing that you are cross-eyed"; but I deeply respected him. When Hitlerism came, he was one of the first to speak out with all the directness and frankness of a great and unabashed spirit. Blessing to his memory!

CHAPTER XVI

A Circle of Friends

IN THE LAST chapter, this chapter and to a considerable extent those that follow, down to the break made by Gilbert's illness and the war of 1914, it is unavoidable that the same years should be retraced to cover a variety of aspects. For their home was for both Gilbert and Frances the centre of a widening circle. Although I visited Overroads, it seems to me, looking back, I saw them just then much more frequently in London and elsewhere. Several times they stayed at Lotus, our Surrey home. The first time it was a weekend of blazing summer weather. Lady Blennerhassett was there—formerly Countess Leyden and a favourite disciple of Döllinger. I remember she delighted Gilbert by her comment on Modernism. "I must," she said, "have the same religion as my washerwoman, and Father Tyrrell's is not the religion for my washerwoman." We sat on the terrace in the sunshine and Lady Blennerhassett asked suddenly whether the soles of our boots were, like hers, without hole or blemish. We all looked very odd as we stuck our feet out and tried to see the soles. Gilbert, offered a wicker chair, preferred the grass because, he said, there was grave danger he might unduly "modify" the chair.

After a meeting of the Westminster Dining Society (the predecessor of the Wiseman), he wrote my mother an unnecessary apology:

DEAR MRS. WILFRID WARD—

I have wanted for some days past to write to you, but could not make up my mind whether I was making my position worse or better. But I do want to apologise to you for the way in which I threw out your delightful Catholic Dining Society affair the other day. I behaved badly, dined badly, debated badly and left badly; yet the explanation is really simple. I was horribly worried, and I do not worry well; when I am worried I am like a baby. My wife was that night just ill enough to make a man nervous, a stupid man, and I had sworn to her that I would fulfill some affairs that night on which she was keen. As she is better now and only wants rest, I feel normal and realise what a rotter I must have looked that night. As Belloc wrote in a beautiful epitaph—

> "He frequently would flush with fear when other
>   people paled,
> He Tried to Do his Duty . . . but how damnably
>   he failed."

This is the epitaph of yours sincerely,

G. K. CHESTERTON.

My father and mother were hardly less excited than I at the discovery of the greatest man of the age, for so we all felt him to be. Gilbert later described my father as "strongly co-operative" with another's mind, and this was perhaps his own chief characteristic in conversation. The two men did not agree on politics, but on religion their agreement was deep and constantly grew deeper as they co-operated in exploring it. Our headquarters were in Surrey but when we came up to London every spring my parents wanted to bring the Chestertons into touch with all their friends. They tended to think of their luncheon table as Chesterton "supported" by those most worthy of the honour. One of the first was of course George Wyndham, already a friend and admirer of Gilbert's. At this luncheon they discussed the modern press, 18th Century lampoons, the ingredients of a good English style, the lawfulness of Revolution, the causes of Napoleon, Scripture criticism, Joan of Arc, public executions, how to bring about reforms. It was absurd, G.K. said, to think that gaining half a reform led to the other half. Supposing it was agreed that every man ought to have a cow, but you say, "We can't manage that just yet: give him half a cow." He doesn't care for it and he leaves it about, and he never asks for the other half.

Talking of the Eastern and Western races Gilbert said it was curious that while the Easterns were so logical and clear in their religion, they were so unpractical in every-day life; the religion of the Westerns is mystical and full of paradoxes. Yet they are far more practical. "The Eastern says fate governs everything and he sits and looks pretty; we believe in Free-will and Predestination and we invent Babbage's Calculating Machine."

As the group grew into one another's thought the talk intensified and we got from considering East and West to considering our own countrymen. What makes a man essentially English? Dickens had it. Johnson had it. "You couldn't," said G.K., "imagine a Scotch Johnson, or an Irish Johnson, or a French or German Johnson."

George Wyndham told us, as we got on to the topic of patriotism, that he had a fear he hardly liked to utter. As we urged him he said he feared a big war might come and we might be defeated. Gilbert agreed that he too had felt that fear. "But," he said, "if you were to say that in the House or I to write it in a paper we should be denounced as unpatriotic."

Small wonder the talk had time to range, for these scrappy notes are all that remain of a meeting beginning about one o'clock and lasting until five. At that hour two little old sisters, the Miss Blounts, known in our family as "the little B's," happened to call on my mother. I shall never forget their faces as they looked at the huge man in the armchair, and the other guests all absorbed and animated, and realised that they were interrupting a luncheon party. A swift glance at the little old ladies, another at the clock, and the party broke up, to remain my most cherished memory for months: until my next visit to their home, when Gilbert and I arrived at the use of each other's

Christian names, an agreement that he insisted on calling The Pact of Beaconsfield.

How deep he saw when in his "Defence of Hermits" he analysed a chief joy of human intercourse:

. . . The best things that happen to us are those we get out of what has already happened. If men were honest with themselves, they would agree that actual social engagements, even with those they love, often seem strangely brief, breathless, thwarted or inconclusive. Mere society is a way of turning friends into acquaintances. The real profit is not in meeting our friends, but in having met them. Now when people merely plunge from crush to crush, and from crowd to crowd, they never discover the positive joy of life. They are like men always hungry, because their food never digests; also, like those men, they are cross.*

There was time in the country for the food of social intercourse to digest. I notice too that in the list of Gilbert's friends quiet-voiced men stood high: Max Beerbohm, Jack Phillimore, Monsignor O'Connor, Monsignor Knox, his own father, Maurice Baring: all these represent a certain spaciousness and leisureliness which was what he asked of friendship. Even if they were in a hurry, they never seemed so.

Jack Phillimore both he and we saw on and off at this time but had often to enjoy in anticipation or in retrospect. Professor, at one time of Greek at another of Latin, at Glasgow University, he was the kind of man Gilbert specially appreciated: he wrote of Phillimore after his death something curiously like what he wrote of his own father—"he was a supreme example of unadvertised greatness, and the thing which is larger inside than outside." At Oxford Phillimore had been known as "one of Belloc's lambs." He was very much one of the group who were to run the *Eye-Witness* and *New Witness* but though he always adored Belloc, no one who knew him in the fulness of his powers could think of him as anyone's lamb. He was a quiet,

* *The Well and the Shallows,* pp. 104–5.

humorous, deeply intelligent man: a scholar of European repute, whose knowledge of Mediaeval Latin verse equalled his Classical scholarship.

Gilbert's keen observation of his friends is never shown better than in what he wrote of Phillimore:

Like a needle pricking a drum, his quietude seemed to kill all the noise of our loud plutocracy and publicity. In all this he was supremely the scholar, with not a little of the satirist.

And yet there was never any man alive who was so unlike a don. His religion purged him of intellectual pride, and certainly of that intellectual vanity which so often makes a sort of seething fuss underneath the acid sociability of academic centres. He had none of the tired omniscience which comes of intellectual breeding in and in. He seemed to be not so much a professor as a practiser of learning. He practised it quietly but heartily and humorously, exactly as if it had been any other business. If he had been a sailor, like his father the Admiral, he would have minded his own business with exactly the same smile and imperceptible gesture. Indeed, he looked much more like a sailor than a professor; his dark square face and clear eyes and compact figure were of a type often seen among sailors; and in whatever academic enclave he stood, he always seemed to have walked in from outside, bringing with him some of the winds of the world and some light from the ends of the earth.*

To return to my own notes. It is horribly characteristic that I wrote them in an undated notebook, but I think that luncheon which lasted so long must have been in 1911. The same year my father persuaded both the Synthetic Society to elect Chesterton and Chesterton to attend the Synthetic. Of his first meeting my father wrote to George Wyndham:

Had you been at the Synthetic last night you would have witnessed a memorable scene.

Place: Westminster Palace Hotel. Time: 9.40.

A. J. B. [Arthur Balfour, leader of the Conservative Party] is speaking persuasively and in carefully modulated tones to an atten-

* *G.K.'s Weekly,* Nov. 27, 1926.

tive audience. Suddenly a crash as though the door were blown open.
A. J. B. brought to a halt. The whole company look round and in
rushes a figure exactly like the pictures of Mr. Wind when he blows
open the door and forces an entrance in the German child's story
"Mr. Wind and Madame Rain"—a figure enormous and distended, a
kind of walking mountain but with large rounded corners. It was
G. K. C. who, enveloped in a huge Inverness cape of light colour,
thus made his debut at the Synthetic. He rushed (not walked) to a
chair, and was dragged chair and all by Waggett and me as near as
might be to the table, where with a fresh crash he deposited his
stick, and then his hat. And there he sat, eager and attentive, forgetting all about his stick and hat and coat, filling up the whole
space at the bottom of the table, drawing caricatures of the company on a sheet of foolscap, a memorable figure, very welcome to
me, but arousing the fury of the conventional and the "dreary and
well-informed" well represented by Bailey Saunders who has been
at me here half the morning trying to convince me that he will ruin
the society and ought never to have been elected.

Some of the reactions of this new recruit have been touched
on in his *Autobiography*:

There I met old Haldane, yawning with all his Hegelian abysses,
who appeared to me as I must have appeared to a neighbour in a
local debating club when he dismissed metaphysical depths and
pointed at me saying: "There is that Leviathan whom Thou hast
made to take his sport therein.". . .
There also I met Balfour, obviously preferring any philosophers
with any philosophies to his loyal followers of the Tory Party. Perhaps religion is not the opium of the people, but philosophy is the
opium of the politicians.

My father belonged to another group besides the Synthetic
Society for which it seemed to him that Gilbert was even more
ideally fitted. *The* Club was founded by Dr. Johnson, the home
of the best talk in the land, where Garrick and Goldsmith were
at times shouted down by the great Lexicographer—a sign, said
Chesterton, of his modesty and his essential democracy: Johnson
was too democratic to reign as king of his company: he pre-

ferred to contend with them as an equal. The old formula still
in use had informed my father "you have had the honour to
be elected," but Wilfrid Ward felt that the election of the
modern Dr. Johnson would be an honour to The Club. To his
intense disgust he found that only George Wyndham could be
relied upon for whole-hearted support. What may be called the
"social" element in The Club had become too strong to welcome a man who boasted in all directions of belonging to the
Middle Classes and whose friends merely urged the claim that
he was one of the few today who could talk as well as Johnson.

Gilbert met many politicians in other ways but only with one
of them did he feel a really close harmony. Of George Wyndham's opinions he said in the *Autobiography* that they were "of
the same general colour as my own," and he went on to stress
the word "colour" as significant of the whole man. To depict
him in political cartoons as "St. George" had not in it the sort
of absurdity of the pictures of the more frigid and philosophic
Balfour as "Prince Arthur." George really did suggest the ages
of chivalry. "He had huge sympathy with gypsies and tramps."
There was about him "an inward generosity that gave a gusto
or relish to all he did."

The Chestertons' appreciation of George Wyndham was deepened for them both by an affection, indeed almost a reverence,
for "the deep mysticism of his wife; a woman not to be forgotten by anyone who ever knew her, and still less to be merely
praised by anyone who adequately appreciated her." For a
period at any rate Gilbert and Frances were much in contact
with the extreme Anglo-Catholic group in the Church of England. In the best of that group—and many of them are very
very good—there is a sense of taking part in a crusade to restore Catholicism to the whole country. Canon Scott Holland
led a campaign for social justice and many of the same group
mixed this with devotion to Our Lady, belief in the Real
Presence, and a profound love of the Catholic past of England.

George Wyndham's wife, Lady Grosvenor, was one of this group and also her friend Father Philip Waggett of the Cowley Fathers. Father Waggett, a member of the Synthetic Society and intimate with my parents, became also intimate with the Chestertons.

Ralph Adams Cram described his own meeting with Chesterton, arranged by Father Waggett.

Father Waggett asked my wife and myself once when we were staying in London, whom we would like best to meet—"anyone from the King downward." We chose Chesterton who was a very particular friend of Father Waggett. At that time we put on a dinner at the Buckingham Palace Hotel (in those days the haunt of all the County families) and in defiance of fate, had this dinner in the public dining room. We had as guests Father Waggett, G. K. C. and Mrs. Chesterton. The entrance into the dining room of the short processional created something of a sensation amongst the aforesaid County families there assembled. Father Waggett, thin, cropheaded monk in cassock and rope; G. K. C., vast and practically globular; little Mrs. Chesterton, very South Kensington in moss green velvet; my wife and myself.

The dinner was a riot. I have the clearest recollection of G. K. C. seated ponderously at the table, drinking champagne by magnums, continually feeding his face with food which, as he was constantly employed in the most dazzling and epigrammatic conversation, was apt to fall from his fork and rebound from his corporosity, until the fragments disappeared under the table.

He and Father Waggett egged each other on to the most preposterous amusements. Each would write a triolet for the other to illustrate. They were both as clever with the pencil as with the pen, and they covered the backs of menus with most astonishing literary and artistic productions. I particularly remember G. K. C. suddenly looking out of the dining room window towards Buckingham Palace and announcing that he was now prepared "to write a disloyal triolet!" This was during the reign of King Edward VII, and the result was convincing. I have somewhere the whole collection of these literary productions with their illustrations, but where they are I do not know.*

* *Chesterton* by Cyril Clemens, pp. 36–37.

On a second visit of the Chestertons to Lotus, George Wyndham was there. He had told us of his habit of "shouting the Ballad of the White Horse to submissive listeners" and we had hoped for the same treat. But Gilbert got the book and kicked it under his chair defying us to recover it. We had at that time a vast German cook—of a girth almost equal to his own and possessed of unbounded curiosity in the matter of our guests. Gilbert declared that as he sat peacefully in the drawing room she approached him holding out a paper which he supposed to be a laundry list, and then started back exclaiming that she had thought him to be Mrs. Ward

It was on this visit that he remarked to a lady who happened to be the granddaughter of a Duke: "You and I who belong to the jolly old upper Middle Classes." Had he been told about her ancestry he would, I imagine, have felt that he had paid her an implied compliment by not being aware of it. For into the world of the aristocracy he and Frances had been received in London, and he viewed it with the same calm humour and potential friendliness as he had for all the rest of mankind. When Frances in her Diary pitied the Duchess of Sutherland and felt that a single day of such a life as the Duchess lived would drive her crazy, she was expressing Gilbert's taste as well as her own for a certain simplicity of life. Social position neither excited nor irritated him. He liked or disliked an aristocrat exactly as he liked or disliked a postman. Gilbert and Cecil Chesterton really were, as Conrad Noel said, personally unconcerned about class. They had, however, a principle against the position of the English aristocracy which will be better understood in the light of their general social and historical outlook. What might be called the social side of it was often expressed by G.K. when lecturing on Dickens. Thus, speaking at Manchester for the Dickens centenary, he was reported as saying:

The objection to aristocracy was quite simple. It was not that aristocrats were all blackguards. It was that in an aristocratic state, people sat in a huge darkened theatre and only the stage was lighted. They saw five or six people walking about and they said, "That man looks very heroic striding about with a sword." Plenty of people outside in the street looked more heroic striding about with an umbrella; but they did not see these things, all the lights being turned out. That was the really philosophic objection to an aristocratic society. It was not that the lord was a fool. He was about as clever as one's own brother or cousin. It was because one's attention was confined to a few people that one judged them as one judged actors on the stage, forgetting everybody else.

Chesterton thought everybody should be remembered whether suburban, proletarian, aristocrat or pauper. Shortly after the removal to Beaconsfield he was summoned to give evidence before a Parliamentary Commission on the question of censorship of the theatre. Keep it, he said, to the surprise of many of his friends, but change the manner of its exercise. Let it be no longer censorship by an expert but by a jury—by twelve ordinary men. These will be the best judges of what really makes for morality and sound sense. He had come to give evidence, he said, not as a writer but as the representative of the gallery, and he was concerned only with "the good and happiness of the English people."

One bewildered Commissioner was understood to murmur that their terms of reference were not quite so wide as that.

The chapter in the *Autobiography* called "Friendships and Foolery" ends suddenly with a reference to the war but, like the whole book, it leaps wildly about. One point in it is interesting and links up with the introduction to Titterton's *Drinking Songs* that Gilbert later wrote. To shout a chorus is natural to mankind and G.K. claims that he had done it long before he heard of Community Singing. He sang when out driving, or walking over the moors with Father O'Connor; he sang in Fleet

Street with Titterton and his journalist friends; he sang the *Red Flag* on Trade Union platforms and *England Awake* in Revolutionary groups. There was, he claims, a legend that in Auberon Herbert's rooms not far from Buckingham Palace "we sang Drake's Drum with such passionate patriotism that King Edward the Seventh sent in a request for the noise to stop."

Yet it was all but impossible to teach Gilbert a tune, and Bernard Shaw felt this (as we have seen) a real drawback to his friend's understanding of his own life and career. Music was to Shaw what line and color were to Chesterton; but to Chesterton singing was just making a noise to show he felt happy. Once he wrote a poem called "Music"—but only as one more flower in the wreath he was always weaving for Frances—who was, says Monsignor Knox, the heroine of all his novels.*

> Sounding brass and tinkling cymbal,
> He that made me sealed my ears,
> And the pomp of gorgeous noises,
> Waves of triumph, waves of tears,
>
> Thundered empty round and past me,
> Shattered, lost for evermore,
> Ancient gold of pride and passion,
> Wrecked like treasure on a shore.
>
> But I saw her cheek and forehead
> Change, as at a spoken word,
> And I saw her head uplifted
> Like a lily to the Lord.
>
> Nought is lost, but all transmuted,
> Ears are sealed, yet eyes have seen;
> Saw her smiles (O soul be worthy!),
> Saw her tears (O heart be clean!)†

Against the background of all these activities the books went on pouring out as fast from Overroads as they had from Over-

---

* *The Listener,* June 19, 1941.   † *Collected Poems,* p. 129.

strand. A town full of friends forty minutes' journey from London was not exactly the desert into which admirers had advised Gilbert to flee, but he would never have been happy in a desert: he needed human company. He also needed to produce. "Artistic paternity," he once said, "is as wholesome as physical paternity." And certainly he never ceased to bring forth the children of his mind. Within two years of the move seven books were published:

The Ball and the Cross, February 1910,
What's Wrong with the World, June 1910,
Alarms and Discursions, November 1910,
Blake, November 1910,
Criticisms and Appreciations of Dickens, January 1911,
Innocence of Father Brown, August 1911,
Ballad of the White Horse, August 1911.

Of these books, *Alarms and Discursions* and the Dickens criticisms are collections and arrangements of already published essays. Meanwhile other essays were being written to become in turn other books at a later date.

The *Blake* is a brilliant short study of art and mysticism. After reading it you feel you understand Blake in quite a new way. And then you wonder—is this illumination light on Blake or simply light on Chesterton? It must never be forgotten that the writer was himself a "spoilt" artist—which means a man with almost enough art in him to have been in the ranks of men consecrated for life to art's service.

"Father Brown" had first made his appearance in magazines and these detective stories became the most purely popular of Gilbert's books. It was a new genre: detection in which the mind of a man means more than his footprints or cigar ash, even to the detective. The one reproduced in most anthologies—"The Invisible Man"—depends for its solution on the fact that certain people are *morally* invisible. To the question "Has anyone been here" the answer "No" does not include the milkman or the postman: thus the postman is the morally invisible man who has committed the crime. A thread of this sort runs through all the stories, but they are, like all his romances, full too of escape and peril and wild adventure.

Life on several occasions imitated Gilbert's fancies. Thus the Azeff revelations followed his fantastic idea in *The Man Who Was Thursday* of the anarchists who turn out to be detectives in disguise. The technique of Father Brown himself was imitated by a man in Detroit who recovered a stolen car by putting himself imaginatively in the thief's place and driving an exactly similar car around likely corners till he came suddenly upon his own, left in a lonely road. He wrote to tell Gilbert of this adventure.

From Chicago came an even odder example. "It is extremely difficult," wrote the *Tribune*, "to determine the proper relationship of the Chiesa-Prudente-Di Cossato duels to Mr. Gilbert K. Chesterton's book, *The Ball and the Cross*" . . .

The flight in search of a duelling ground; the pursuit by the police; the friendly intervention of the anarchist wineshop-keeper, Volpi; the offer of his backyard for fighting purposes; the unfriendly intervention of the police; the friendly intervention of the reporters; the renewed and insistently unfriendly intervention of the police commissioner; the disgust of the duellists; the extreme disgust of the anarchist; the renewed flight of the fighters, seconds, physicians, reporters, and the anarchist over the back fences—all these and other incidents are essentially Chestertonian.

The Di Cossato affair was carried off with fully as much spirit and dash; with fully as many automobiles, seconds, physicians, reporters and police, all scampering over the country roads until the artistic deputy and the aged veteran of the war of 1859, outdistancing their pursuers, could find opportunity in comparative peace to cut the glorious gashes of satisfied honour in each other's faces.*

Two months after this an interviewer from the *Daily News* visited Beaconsfield and splashed headlines in the paper to the

* *Chicago Tribune,* 12 March 1910.

effect that the spirit of Chesterton was inspiring a fight between the leaseholders in Edwardes Square and a firm which had bought up their garden to erect a super-garage. Barricades were erected by day and destroyed in the night: a wild-eyed beadle held the fort with a garden roller, and said G.K. "the creatures of my Napoleon [of Notting Hill] have entered into the bodies of the staid burghers of Kensington."

In none of these cases was there any likelihood, as the *Chicago Tribune* noted, of the actors in life having read the books they were spiritedly staging. "Ideas have a life of their own," the *Daily News* interviewer tentatively ventured, but he may have been puzzled as G.K. "agreed heartily" in the words, "I am no dirty nominalist."

Chesterton kept the reviewers busy as well as the interviewers and in all his stories they noted one curiosity: "If time and space—or any circumstances—interfere with the cutting of his Gordian knots, he commands time and space to make themselves scarce, and circumstances to be no more heard of."

About time and space this is true in a unique degree. For him time seems to have had no existence, or perhaps rather to have been like a telescope elongating and shortening at will. As a young man, it may be remembered, he gave in the course of one letter two quite irreconcilable statements of the length of time since events in his school days. He had indeed the same difficulty about time as about money—he mentions in the *Autobiography* that after his watch was stolen during a pro-Boer demonstration he never bothered to possess another. In his stories this oddity became more marked. In *The Ball and the Cross* he relates adventures performed in leaping on and off an omnibus in such fashion that the bus must have covered several miles of ground: and then we are suddenly told it had gone the few score yards from the bottom of Ludgate Hill to the top. Still stranger are the records in *The Man Who Was Thursday* and *Manalive* of the

happenings of a single day, while in *The Return of Don Quixote*
a new organisation of society is described as though many years
old and then suddenly announced as having been on foot some
weeks.

But to return for one moment to the more serious aspects of
the work of these years. While *What's Wrong With the World*
(discussed in some detail in the next chapter) is the first sketch
of his social views—a kind of blueprint for a sane and human
sort of world—the other books with all their foolery hold a serious purpose. They should be read as illustrations of the philosophy of *Orthodoxy*—both the book he had written and the thing
of which he had said "God and humanity made it and it made
me."

"This row of shapeless and ungainly monsters which I now
set before the reader," he says of his essays (in the "Introduction on Gargoyles" in *Alarms and Discursions*), "does not consist of separate idols cut out capriciously in lonely valleys or
various islands. These monsters are meant for the gargoyles of
a definite cathedral. I have to carve the gargoyles, because I can
carve nothing else; I leave to others the angels and the arches
and the spires. But I am very sure of the style of the architecture
and of the consecration of the church."

The story of *The Ball and the Cross*, already indicated to the
reader by the American-Italian duel which seemed like a parody
of it, has the double interest of its bearing on the world of
Chesterton's day and its glimpses at a stranger world to come.
A young Highlander, coming to London, sees in an atheist book-
shop an insult to Our Lady. He smashes the window and challenges the owner to a duel. Turnbull, the atheist, is more than
ready to fight; but the world, caring nothing for religious opinions, regards anyone ready to fight for them as a madman and
is mainly concerned with keeping the peace. Pursued by all the
resources of modern civilisation, the two men spend the rest of

the book starting to fight, being interrupted and arrested by the police, escaping, arguing and fighting again. They end up in an asylum with a garden where again they talk endlessly and where the power of Lucifer the prince of this world has enclosed everyone who has been concerned in their wild flight, so that no memory of it may live on the earth.

The two sides of Chesterton's brain are engaged in the duel of minds in this book, and some of his best writing is in it, both in the description of the wild rush across sea and land and in the discussions between the two men. G.K.'s affection for the sincere atheist is noteworthy and his hatred is reserved for the shuffler and the compromiser. It was grand to have such a man as Turnbull to convert—"one of those men in whom a continuous appetite and industry of the intellect leave the emotions very simple and steady. His heart was in the right place but he was quite content to leave it there. His head was his hobby." This might be Chesterton himself—in fact, it is Chesterton himself—and the climax belongs to a later world than that of 1911. For pointing to the Ball bereft of the Cross, the Highlander calls out: "It staggers, Turnbull. It cannot stand by itself; you know it cannot. It has been the sorrow of your life. Turnbull, this garden is not a dream, but an apocalyptic fulfillment. This garden is the world gone mad."

About the time this book appeared Gilbert was asked by an Anglican Society to lecture at Coventry. He said "What shall I lecture on?" They answered "Anything from an elephant to an umbrella." "Very well," he said, "I will lecture on an umbrella." He treated the umbrella as a symbol of increasing artificiality. We wear hair to protect the head, a hat to protect the hair, an umbrella to protect the hat. Gilbert said once he was willing to start anywhere and develop from anything the whole of his philosophy. In the Notebook he had written:

BOOTLACES

Once I looked down at my bootlaces
 Who gave me my bootlaces?
The bootmaker? Bah!
Who gave the bootmaker himself?
What did I ever do that I should be
 given bootlaces?

After the lecture on the umbrella two priests saw him at the railway bookstall and asked him if the rumour was true that he was thinking of joining the Church. He answered, "It's a matter that is giving me a great deal of agony of mind, and I'd be very grateful if you would pray for me."

The following year he broached the subject to Father O'Connor when they were alone in a railway carriage. He said he had made up his mind, but he wanted to wait for Frances "as she had led him into the Anglican Church out of Unitarianism." Frances told Father O'Connor when he came to Overroads later, at the beginning of Gilbert's illness, that she "could not make head or tail" of some of her husband's remarks, especially one about being buried at Kensal Green. When Father O'Connor told her what had been on Gilbert's mind she was half amused at the hints he had been dropping: she recognised his reluctance to move without her, but I think she probably realised too that even to himself his conviction seemed in those years at times more absolute, at times less. We shall see in a later chapter his own analysis of his very slow progress. Meanwhile in his books he was at once deepening and widening his vision of the faith.

Fragments of verse used in *The Ballad of the White Horse* had come to Gilbert in his sleep; a great white horse had been the romance of his childhood; the beginning of his honeymoon under the sign of the White Horse at Ipswich had been "a trip to fairyland." But it is hard to say when the motif of the White

Horse, the verses ringing in his head, and the ideas that make the poem, came together into what many think the greatest work of his life.

In *Father Brown on Chesterton* we are told of the long time the poem took in the making. They talked of it on the Yorkshire moors in 1906 and Father O'Connor noted how Frances "cherished it. . . . I could see she was more in love with it than with anything else he had in hand." Father O'Connor also gives some interesting illustrations of the way talk ministers to a work of genius. He had begun one day "by saying lightly that none of us could become great men without leaning on the little ones: could not well begin our day but for those who started theirs first for our sake, lighting the fire and cooking the breakfast." This was said just before the dressing bell rang and between the bell and dinner Gilbert had written about nine verses beginning with King Alfred's meditation:

> And well may God with the serving folk
> Cast in His dreadful lot
> Is not He too a servant
> And is not He forgot?

In 1907, Gilbert published in the *Albany Review* a "Fragment from a Ballad Epic of Alfred" which evoked the comment "Mr. Chesterton certainly has in each eye a special Röntgen ray attachment."

He wrote *The White Horse* guided by his favourite theory that to realise history we should not delve into the details of research but try only to see the big things—for it is those that we generally overlook.

People talk about features of interest; but the features never make up a face. . . . They will toil wearily off to the tiniest inscription or darkest picture that is mentioned in a guide book as having some reference to Alfred the Great or William the Conqueror; but they care nothing for the sky that Alfred saw or the hills on which William hunted.

In the King Alfred country especially can be found "the far-
flung Titanic figure of the Giant Albion whom Blake saw in
visions, spreading to our encircling seas." *

Gilbert wrote a sketch for the *Daily News* about this time,
telling how an old woman in a donkey cart whom they had
left far behind on the road went driving triumphantly past when
the car they were in broke down. For this expedition, as so often
later, he made full use of the modern invention he derided. In
an open touring car hired for the occasion, Gilbert in Inverness
cape and shapeless hat, Frances beside him snugly wrapped up,
they

> Saw the smoke-hued hamlets quaint
> With Westland King and Westland Saint,
> And watched the western glory faint
> Along the road to Frome.

The note struck in the dedication and recurring throughout
the poem is that of the Christian idea which had made England
great and which he had learnt from Frances:

> Wherefore I bring these rhymes to you
> Who brought the cross to me,
> Since on you flaming without flaw
> I saw the sign that Guthrum saw
> When he let break his ships of awe
> And laid peace on the sea.

In the poem Christian men, whether they be Saxon or Roman
or Briton or Celt, are banded together to fight the heathen
Danes in defence of the sacred things of faith, in defence of
the human things of daily life, in defence even of the old traditions of pagan England

> . . . because it is only Christian men
> guard even heathen things.

Gilbert constantly disclaimed the idea that he took trouble
over anything: "taking trouble has never been a weakness of

* *G.K.'s Weekly,* Apr. 16, 1927.

mine": but in what might be termed a large and loose way he really did take immense trouble over what interested him. King Alfred is not an almost mythical figure like King Arthur and an outline of his story with legendary fringes can be traced in the Wessex country and confirmed by literature. Gilbert wanted this general story: he did not want antiquarian exactness of detail.

Into the mouths of Guthrum and of King Alfred, he put the expression of the pagan and the Christian outlook. Nor did he hesitate to let King Alfred prophesy at large concerning the days of G. K. Chesterton. The poem is a ballad in the sense of the old ballads that were stirring stories: it is also an expression of the threefold love of Gilbert's life: his wife, his country and his Faith. And as in all great poetry, there is a quality of eternity in this poem that has made it serve as an expression of the eternal Spirit of man.

During the first world war many soldiers had it with them in the trenches: "I want to tell you," the widow of a sailor wrote, "that a copy of the Ballad of the White Horse went down into the Humber with the R.38. My husband loved it as his own soul—never went anywhere without it."

Almost thirty years have passed and today the poem still speaks. Greeting Jacques Maritain on the occasion of his six-tieth birthday, Dorothy Thompson quoted King Alfred's asser-tion of Christian freedom against "the pagan nazi conquerors of his day." After Crete the *Times* had the shortest first leader in its history. Under the heading *Sursum Corda* was a brief statement of the disaster, followed by the words of Our Lady to King Alfred:

> I tell you naught for your comfort,
> Yea, naught for your desire,
> Save that the sky grows darker yet
> And the sea rises higher.

Night shall be thrice night over you,
And heaven an iron cope.
Do you have joy without a cause,
Yea, faith without a hope?

The unbreakable strength of that apparently faint and tenuous thread of faith appeared in the sequel. Many had the Ballad in hand in those dark days; many others wrote to the *Times* asking the source of the quotation. Months later when Winston Churchill spoke of "the end of the beginning," the *Times* returned to *The White Horse* and gave the opening of Alfred's speech at Ethandune:

"The high tide!" King Alfred cried.
"The high tide and the turn!"

CHAPTER XVII

The Disillusioned Liberal

The English were not wrong in loving liberty. They were only wrong in losing it.

G.K.'s Weekly, June 1, 1933.

ONE MAIN DIFFICULTY in writing biography lies in the various strands that run through every human life. It is as I have already said impossible to keep a perfect chronological order with anyone whose occupations and interests were so multifarious. In the present chapter and the two that follow we shall consider the movement of Chesterton's mind upon politics and sociology. This will involve going back to the general Election of 1906 and forward to the Marconi Trial of 1913. For those who are interested in his poetry or his humour or his philosophy or his theology but not at all in his sociological and political outlook, I fear that these three chapters may loom a little uninvitingly. If they are tempted to skip them altogether, I shall not blame them; yet they will miss a great deal that is vital to the understanding of his whole mind and the course his life was to take. These are not the most entertaining chapters in the book, but if we are really to know Chesterton the events they cover must be considered most carefully.

As a boy Gilbert Chesterton spoke of politics as absorbing "for every ardent intellect"; and during these years he was himself deeply concerned with the politics of England. The ideal Liberalism sketched in his letter to Hammond during the Boer War * had appeared to him, if not perfectly realised, at least capa-

* See above, pp. 135–6.

287

ble of realisation, in the existing Liberal Party. The Tory Party
was in power and all its acts, to say nothing of its general inepti-
tude, appeared to Liberals as positive arguments for their own
party. At this date so convinced a Tory as Lord Hugh Cecil
could describe his own party as "to mix metaphors, an eviscerated
ruin." * Several letters and postcards from Mr. Belloc announcing his own election as Liberal member for South Salford show
the high hope with which young Liberalism was viewing the
world in 1906:

(undated)
I have, as you will have seen, pulled it off by 852. It is huge fun.
I am now out against all Vermin: Notably South African Jews.
The Devil is let loose: let all men beware. H. B.

(Written across top of letter)
Tomorrow Monday Meet the Manchester train arriving Euston
6.10 and oblige your little friend HB   *St. Hilary's Day.*

Don't fail to meet that train. Stamps are cheap! HB

I beg you. I implore you. *Meet that 6.10 train.*

HB
Stamps are a drug in the market.

852
Meet that train!
Stamps are *given away* now in *Salford.*

From 1902, when the general election left the Conservatives
still in power, until 1906 the Liberal party had been, as Chesterton described it, "in the desert." And the younger members of
the party were deeply concerned with hammering out a positive
philosophy which might inspire a true programme for their own
party. A group of them wrote a book called *England A Nation*
with the sub-title *Papers of A Patriot's Club.* The Patriot's Club
had no real existence, but I imagine that Lucian Oldershaw
who edited the book believed that its publication might create

* In a letter to Wilfrid Ward.

the club. Belloc was not one of the contributors, but Hugh Law wrote ably on Ireland, J. L. Hammond on South Africa, and Conrad Noel, Henry Nevinson and C. F. G. Masterman on other aspects of the political scene.

The whole book is on a fairly high level but Chesterton's essay was the only one much noticed by reviewers. It was the introductory chapter, far longer than any of the others, and gave the key to the whole book. Entitled "The Idea of Patriotism" it was, like *The Napoleon of Notting Hill*, which it does much to illumine, a plea for patriotism that was really for England and not for the British Empire. Such a patriotism recognizes the limitations proper to nationality and admits, nay admires, other patriotisms for other nations. Thus, in Chesterton's eyes a true English patriot should also be an ardent home ruler for Ireland since Ireland too was a nation.

He stressed the danger that the nationhood of England should be absorbed and lost in the Imperial idea. The claim that in an empire the various races could learn much from one another he considered a bit of special pleading on the part of Imperialists. England had learned much from France and Germany but, although Ireland had much to teach, we had not learned from Ireland. The real patriotism of the Englishman had been dimmed both by the emphasis on the Imperial idea and by the absence of roots in his own land. The governing classes had destroyed those roots and had almost forgotten the existence of the people. From the dregs and off-scourings of the population a vast empire had been created, but the people of England were not allowed to colonize England.

The Education Bill of 1902, brought in by the Conservatives and giving financial support to Church schools, saw Gilbert in general agreement with the Liberal attacks. He did not yet appreciate the Catholic idea that education must be of one piece and he did not think it fair that the country should support specifically Catholic schools. Parents could give at home the religious instruction they wanted their children to have. But with that fairness of mind which made it so hard for him to be a party man he saw why the Liberal "Compromise" of simple Bible teaching for all in the State schools could not be expected to satisfy Catholics. He wrote to the *Daily News:*

The Bible compromise is certainly in favour of the Protestant view of the Bible. The thing, properly stated, is as plain as the nose on your face. Protestant Christianity believes that there is a Divine record in a book; that everyone ought to have free access to that book; that everyone who gets hold of it can save his soul by it, whether he finds it in a library or picks it off a dustcart. Catholic Christianity believes that there is a Divine army or league upon earth called the Church; that all men should be induced to join it; that any man who joins it can save his soul by it without ever opening any of the old books of the Church at all. The Bible is only one of the institutions of Catholicism, like its rites or its priesthood; it thinks the Bible only efficient when taken as part of the Church. . . . This being so, a child could see that if you have the Bible taught alone, anyhow, by anybody, you do definitely decide in favour of the first view of the Bible and against the second.

Discussing a few years later whether it was possible or satisfactory to teach the Bible simply as Literature he put his finger on the Catholic objection. "I should not mind," he said, "children being told about Mohammed because I am not a Mohammedan. If I were a Mohammedan I should very much want to know what they were told about him."

While as for the unfortunate teacher: in case a child should ask if the things in the Bible happened, "Either the teacher must answer him insincerely and that is immorality, or he must answer him sincerely, and that is sectarian education, or he must refuse to answer him at all, and that is first of all bad manners and a sort of timid tyranny . . ."

Chesterton's Liberalism received a further shock from the fact that Liberals, in attacking the Bill, were attacking also the Catholic faith and raising the cry of No Popery. In a correspondence with Dr. Clifford he reminded him of how they had stood together against popular fanaticism during the Boer War.

There are two cries always capable of raising the English in their madness—one that the Union Jack is being pulled down, and one that the Pope is being set up. And upon the man who raises one of them responsibility will lie heavy till the last day. For when they are raised, the best are mixed with the worst, every rational compromise is dashed to pieces, every opponent is given credit for the worst that the worst of his allies has by his worst enemy been said to have said. That horror of darkness swept across us when the war began. . . .

Beyond all question this is true—that if we choose to fight on the "No Popery" cry, we may win. But I can imagine something of which I should be prouder than of any victory—the memory that we had shown our difference from Mr. Chamberlain simply and finally in this—that to our hand had lain (as it once laid to his) an old, an effectual, an infallible, and a filthy weapon, and that we let it lie.*

Yet it was fairly easy to be a Liberal in opposition. At the elections of 1902 (which the Liberals lost) and 1906 (which they won) Chesterton canvassed for the Liberal party. Charles Masterman used to tell a story of canvassing a street in his company. Both started at the same end on opposite sides of the road. Masterman completed his side and came back on the other to find Chesterton still earnestly arguing at the first house. For he was passionately serious in his belief that the Liberal Party stood for a real renewal, even revolution, in the life of England. "At the present moment of victory," says the report of a speech by Gilbert following the great swing of the Liberal party into power in 1906, he called for "that magnanimity towards the defeated that characterized all great conquerors. It was important that all should develop—even the Tory." It needed the experience of seeing the Liberal party in power to shake his faith.

In the new House of Commons the Conservatives were in

* Letter to the *Daily News,* October 1902.

a minority: against them were the two old parties—the Liberals and the Irish members who were in general allied to them, and a small group forming a new party known as Labour. The Labour Members who got into Parliament in 1906 and 1909 were regarded by Conservatives as being a kind of left-wing extension of the Liberal Party. Such a Liberal as Chesterton saw them there with delight, and, although he would still have called himself a Liberal, he at first hoped in the Labour men as something more truly expressive of the people's wishes.

In an introduction to *From Workhouse to Westminster,* a life of Will Crooks, Gilbert expressed a good deal of his own political philosophy. As a democrat he believed in the ideal of direct government by the people. But obviously this was only possible in a world that was also his ideal—a world consisting of small and even of very small states. The democrat's usual alternative, representative government, was, Gilbert said, symbolic in character. Just as religious symbolism "may for a time represent a real emotion and then for a time cease to represent anything, so representative government may for a time represent the people, and for a time cease to represent anything."

Further, the very idea of representation itself involved two perfectly distinct notions: a man throws a shadow or he throws a stone. "In the first sense, it is supposed that the representative is like the thing he represents. In the second case, it is only supposed that the representative is useful to the thing he represents." Workmen, like Conservatives, sent men to Parliament not to show what they themselves were like, but to attack the other party in their name. "The Labour Members as a class are not representatives but missiles. . . . Working men are not at all like Mr. Keir Hardie. If it comes to likeness, working men are more like the Duke of Devonshire. But they throw Mr. Keir Hardie at the Duke of Devonshire, knowing that he is so curiously shaped as to hurt anything at which he is thrown."* In

* Introduction to *From Workhouse to Westminster,* p. XV.

the same way Mr. Balfour was entirely unlike the Tory squires who used him as a weapon. To this rule, that men do not choose to be represented by their like, Chesterton took Will Crooks as the one exception:

You have not yet seen the English people in politics. It has not yet entered politics. Liberals do not represent it; Tories do not represent it; Labour Members, on the whole, represent it rather less than Tories or Liberals. When it enters politics it will bring with it a trail of all the things that politicians detest; prejudices (as against hospitals), superstitions (as about funerals), a thirst for respectability passing that of the middle classes, a faith in the family which will knock to pieces half the Socialism of Europe. If ever that people enters politics it will sweep away most of our revolutionists as mere pedants. It will be able to point only to one figure, powerful, pathetic, humorous and very humble, who bore in any way upon his face the sign and star of its authority.*

It was sad enough after this to see Will Crooks fathering one of those very Bills for the interference with family life which Chesterton most hated. But, indeed, the years that followed the 1906 election are a story of a steadily growing disillusionment with the realities of representative government in England.

Chesterton wrote regularly for the *Daily News* and was regarded as one of their most valuable contributors. But when, following an attack in the House of Commons on the Liberal leader Campbell-Bannerman over the sale of peerages, he sent in an article on the subject, the Editor A. G. Gardiner wrote (July 12, 1907):

I have left your article out tonight not because I do not entirely agree with its point of view but because just at this moment it would look like backing Lea's unmannerly attack on C. B. I am keeping the article in type for a later occasion when the general question is not complicated with a particularly offensive incident.

* *Ibid.*, p. XX.

It was a test case, and it seemed to Chesterton not a question of good manners, but of something far more fundamental. The assertion had been made in the House of Commons that peerages were being sold, and that the price of such sales was the chief support of the secret party funds. But the *Daily News* was a Liberal paper and this was an attack on the Liberal party. Chesterton replied (July 14, 1907):

I am sure you know by this time that I never resent the exclusion of my articles as such. I should always trust your literary judgment, if it were a matter of literature only: and I daresay you have often saved me from an indiscretion and your readers from a bore. Unfortunately this matter of the party funds is not one of that sort. My conscience does not often bother you, but just now the animal is awake and roaring. Your paper has always championed the rights of conscience, so mine naturally goes to you. If you disagreed with me, it would be another matter. But since you agree with me (as I was sure you would) it becomes simply a question of which is the more important, politeness or political morality. I agree that Lea did go to the point of being unmannerly. So did Plimsoll, so did Bradlaugh: so did the Irish members. But surely it would be a very terrible thing if anyone could say "The Daily News suppressed all demand for the Plimsoll line," or "The Daily News did not join in asking for Bradlaugh's political rights." I am sure that this is not your idea. You think that this matter can be better raised later on. I am convinced of its urgency. I am so passionately convinced of its urgency that if you will not help me to raise it now, I must try some other channel. They are going on Monday to raise a "breach of privilege" (which is simply an aristocratic censorship of the Press) in order to crush this question through the man who raised it: and to crush it forever. I have said that I think Lea's questions violent and needless. But they are not attacking his questions. They are attacking his letter, which contains nothing that I do not think, probably nothing that you do not think. Lea is to be humiliated and broken because he said that titles are bought; as they are: because he said that poor members are reminded of their dependence on the party funds; as they are: because he said that all this was hypocrisy of public life; as it is. . . .

One thing is quite certain. Unless some Liberal journalists speak on

Monday or Tuesday, the secret funds and the secret powers are safe. These Parliamentary votes mark eras: they are meant to. And that vote will not mark a defence of C. B. The letter had nothing to do with C. B. It will mark the final decision that any repetition of what Lea said in his letter is an insult to the House. That is, any protest against bought titles will be an insult to the House. Any protest against secret funds will be an insult to the House.

I would willingly burn my article if I were only sure you would publish one yourself tomorrow on the same lines. But if not, here is at least one thing you can do. An article, even signed, may perhaps commit the paper too much. But your paper cannot be committed by publishing a letter from me stating my opinions. It might publish a letter from Joe Chamberlain, stating his opinions. I therefore send you a short letter, pointing out the evil, and disassociating it as far as possible from the indiscretions of Lea. I am sure you will publish this, for it is the mere statement of a private opinion and as I am not an M. P. I can say what I like about Parliament. You will not mind my confessing to you my conviction and determination in this matter. I do not think we could quarrel, even if we had to separate.

The letter was published, and was quoted in the House of Commons by Lord Robert Cecil amid general applause. But it was twenty years before a Bill was passed that forbade this particular unpleasantness.

While political corruption stirred Chesterton deeply, I think his outlook was even more affected by the progressive Socialism of Liberal legislation. He had honestly believed that the Liberal Party stood, on the whole, for liberty. He found that it stood increasingly for daily and hourly interference with the lives of the people. He found too that the Liberal papers, which he held should have been foremost in criticism of these measures, were as determined to uphold measures brought in by a Liberal Government as they had been to attack anything that the Tories brought forward.

It has been well said by Mr. Belloc that Chesterton could never write as a party man. But to the ordinary party newspaper such an attitude was utterly incomprehensible. I think that we can also see at this point how alien his fundamental outlook was from that even of the best members of his own Party. A great admirer said to me the other day that it had taken her a long time to appreciate Chesterton's sociology. "You see, I was brought up to think that it was quite right for the poor to have their teeth brushed by officials." This is undoubtedly the normal Socialistic outlook and the outlook most abhorrent to Chesterton. "The philanthropist," he once said, "is not a brother; he is a supercilious aunt."

The five years of Liberal Government had been disillusioning to many others besides Belloc and the Chesterton brothers. Probably many men in newspaper offices and elsewhere continued vaguely to support the party to which their own paper belonged. But there were others who were in those days going through a struggle between principles and Party which became increasingly acute. Gilbert has described his own feelings in a review of Galsworthy's play *Loyalties*, written several years later during the first World War.

. . . The author of *Loyalty* suffers one simple and amazing delusion. He imagines that in those pre-war politics Liberalism was on the side of Labour. On this point at least I can correct him from the most concrete experience. In the newspaper office where his hero lingered, wondering how much longer he could stand its Pacificism, I was lingering and wondering how much longer I could stand its complete and fundamental Capitalism, its invariable alliance with the employer, its invariable hostility to the striker. No such scene as that in which the Liberal editor paced the room raving about his hopes of a revolution ever occurred in the Liberal newspaper office that I knew; the least hint of a revolution would have caused quite as much horror there as in the offices of the *Morning Post*. On nothing was the Pacifist more pacifist than upon that point. No workman so genuine as the workman who figures in *Loyalty* ever figured among such Liberals. The fact is that such Liberalism was in no way whatever on the side of Labour; on the contrary, it was on the side of the Labour Party. . . .

Both Chesterton and Belloc had begun to point out that a Free Press had almost disappeared from England. The revenue of most of the newspapers depended not on subscriptions but on advertisement. Therefore nothing could be said in them which was displeasing to their wealthy advertisers. Nor was this the worst of it. Very rich men were often owners of half a dozen papers or more and dictated their policy. An outstanding example was Alfred Harmsworth—Lord Northcliffe—whose newspapers ranged from the *Times* through the *Daily Mail* to *Answers*. Thus to every section of the English people, Harmsworth was able to convey day by day such news as he thought best together with his own outlook and philosophy of life such as it was. Still worse, the *Times* had not lost in the eyes of Europe, to say nothing of America, that reputation it had held so long of being *the* official expression of English opinion. It was still the *Jupiter* of Trollope's day, the maker of ministries or their undoing. In the days of a Free Press a paper held such a position in virtue of the talents of its staff. Editors were then powerful individuals and would brook little interference. But today the editor was commonly only the mouthpiece of the owner.

It is surprising that Gilbert and the official Liberal Press so long tolerated one another. The *Daily News* and other papers owned by Mr. Cadbury (of Cadbury's Cocoa) were often referred to as "the Cocoa Press" and it happened that it was not in the end political disagreement alone that brought the Chesterton-Cadbury alliance to an end. In one of Gilbert's poems in praise of wine are the lines:

> Cocoa is a cad and coward,
> Cocoa is a vulgar beast.

In the *Autobiography* he tells us that after he had published the poem he felt he could write no longer for the *Daily News*. He went from the *Daily News* to the *Daily Herald*, to the Editor of which he wrote that the *News* "had come to stand for almost everything I disagree with; and I thought I had better resign before the next great measure of social reform made it illegal to go on strike." G.K. was a considerable asset to any paper and had recently been referred to by Shaw (in a debate with Belloc) as "a flourishing property of Mr. Cadbury's."

Politically the break was bound to come, for even when *Dickens* was published Gilbert Chesterton had reached the stage of saying "as much as ever I did, more than ever I did, I believe in Liberalism. But there was a rosy time of innocence when I believed in Liberals." At this time too he infuriated an orthodox Liberal journalist by saying of the party leaders "Some of them are very nice old gentlemen, some of them are very nasty old gentlemen, and some of them are old without being gentlemen at all." An orthodox church journalist in a periodical charmingly entitled *Church Bells* got angrier yet. "A certain Mr. G. K. Chesterton," he wrote, had, when speaking for the C.S.U. in St. Paul's Chapter House, remarked "the best of his Majesty's Ministers are agnostics, and the worst devil worshippers." *Church Bells* cries out: "We only mention this vulgar falsehood because we regret that an association, with which the names of many of our respected ecclesiastics are connected, should have allowed the bad taste and want of all gentlemanly feeling displayed by the words quoted, to have passed unchallenged." "Vulgar falsehood" is surely charming.

But perhaps even deeper than his disillusionment with any Party was his growing sense of the unreality of the political scene. He has described it in the *Autobiography*:

I was finding it difficult to believe in politics; because the reality seemed almost unreal, as compared with the reputation or the report. I could give twenty instances to indicate what I mean, but they would be no more than indications, because the doubt itself was doubtful. I remember going to a great Liberal club, and walking about in a large crowded room, somewhere at the end of which a bald gentleman with a beard was reading something from a manuscript in a low voice. It was hardly unreasonable that we did not listen to him, because we could not in any case have heard; but I think a very large number of us did not even see him . . . it is possible, though not certain, that one or other of us asked carelessly what was supposed to be happening in the other corner of the large hall. . . . Next morning I saw across the front of my Liberal paper in gigantic headlines the phrase: "Lord Spencer Unfurls the Banner." Under this were other remarks, also in large letters, about how he had blown the trumpet for Free Trade and how the blast would ring through England and rally all the Free-Traders. It did appear, on careful examination, that the inaudible remarks which the old gentleman had read from the manuscript were concerned with economic arguments for Free Trade; and very excellent arguments too, for all I know. But the contrast between what that orator was to the people who heard him, and what he was to the thousands of newspaper-readers who did not hear him, was so huge a hiatus and disproportion that I do not think I ever quite got over it. I knew henceforward what was meant, or what might be meant, by a Scene in the House, or a Challenge from the Platform, or any of those sensational events which take place in the newspapers and nowhere else.*

As in *Orthodoxy* Chesterton had formulated his religious beliefs, so in *What's Wrong With the World* he laid the foundations of his sociology. It will be remembered that, giving evidence before the Commission on the Censorship, Chesterton declared himself to be concerned only with the good and happiness of the English people. Where he differed from nearly every other social reformer was that he believed that they should themselves decide what was for their own good and happiness.

"The body of ideas," says Monsignor Knox of Gilbert's sociology, "which he labelled, rather carelessly, 'distributism' is a body of ideas which still lasts, and I think will last, but it is not exactly a doctrine, or a philosophy; it is simply Chesterton's reaction to life." †

* Pp. 201-2. † *The Listener*, June 19, 1941.

It may be said that a man's philosophy is in the main a formulation of his reaction to life. Anyhow *life* seems to be the operative word—for it is the word that best conveys the richness of this first book of Chesterton's sociology. All the wealth of life's joys, life's experiences, is poured into his view of man and man's destiny. Already developing manhood to its fullest potential he found in this book a new form of expression. To quote Monsignor Knox again, "I call that man intellectually great who is an artist in thought . . . I call that man intellectually great who can work equally well in any medium." The poet-philosopher worked surprisingly well in the medium of sociology.

He had intended to call the book, "What's Wrong?" and it begins on this note of interrogation. The chapter called "The Medical Mistake" is a brilliant attack on the idea that we must begin social reform by diagnosing the disease. "It is the whole definition and dignity of man that in social matters we must actually find the cure before we find the disease." The thing that is most terribly wrong with our modern civilisation is that it has lost not only health but the clear picture of health. The doctor called in to diagnose a bodily illness does not say: we have had too much scarlet fever, let us try a little measles for a change. But the sociological doctor does offer to the dispossessed proletarian a cure which, says Chesterton, is only another kind of disease. We cannot work towards a social ideal until we are certain what that ideal should be. We must, therefore, begin with principles and we are to find those principles in the nature of man, largely through a study of his history. Man has had historically—and man needs for his fulfilment—the family, the home and the possession of property. The notion of property has, for the modern age, been defiled by the corruptions of capitalism; but modern capitalism is really a negation of property because it is a denial of its limitations. He summarises this idea with one of his most brilliant illustrations: "It is the negation of property that the Duke of Sutherland should have all the farms in one estate; just as it would be the negation of marriage if he had all our wives in one harem."

But property in its real meaning is almost the condition for the survival of the family. It is its protection, it is the opportunity of its development. God has the joy of unlimited creation —He can make something out of nothing; but He has given to Man the joy of limited creation—Man can make something out of anything. "Fruitful strife with limitations," self-expression "with limits that are strict and even small,"—all this belongs to the artist, but also to the average man. "Property is merely the art of the democracy."

The family, protected by the possession of some degree of property, will grow by its own laws. What are these laws? Clearly there are two sets of problems, one concerned with life within the family, the other with the relation of the family to the state. These two sets of problems provide the subject-matter of the book. On both Chesterton felt that there had been insufficient thinking. Thus he says of the first: "There is no brain-work in the thing at all; no root query of what sex is, of whether it alters this or that." And of the second: "It is quite unfair to say that Socialists believe in the State but do not believe in the Family. But it is true to say that Socialists are especially engaged in strengthening and renewing the State; and they are not especially engaged in strengthening and renewing the Family. They are not doing anything to define the functions of father, mother and child, as such—they have no firm instinctive sense of one thing being in its nature private and another public."

It is precisely this kind of root-thinking that the book does. In the free family there will be a division of the two sides of life, between the man and the woman. The man must be, to a certain extent, a specialist; he must do one thing well enough to earn the daily bread. The woman is the universalist; she must do a hundred things for the safeguarding and development of the home. The modern fad of talking of the narrowness of domesticity especially provoked Chesterton. "I cannot," he said

with the utmost energy of imagination conceive what they mean. When domesticity, for instance, is called drudgery, all the difficulty arises from a double meaning in the word. If drudgery only means dreadfully hard work, I admit the woman drudges in the home, as a man might drudge at the Cathedral of Amiens or drudge behind a gun at Trafalgar. But if it means that the hard work is more heavy because it is trifling, colourless and of small import to the soul, then as I say, I give it up; I do not know what the words mean. To be Queen Elizabeth within a definite area, deciding sales, banquets, labours and holidays; to be Whiteley within a certain area, providing toys, boots, sheets, cakes and books; to be Aristotle within a certain area, teaching morals, manners, theology, and hygiene; I can understand how this might exhaust the mind, but I cannot imagine how it could narrow it. How can it be a large career to tell other people's children about the Rule of Three, and a small career to tell one's own children about the universe? How can it be broad to be the same thing to everyone, and narrow to be everything to someone? No; a woman's function is laborious, but because it is gigantic, not because it is minute. I will pity Mrs. Jones for the hugeness of her task; I will never pity her for its smallness.*

While he was writing these pages and after their appearance in print, G.K. was constantly asked to debate the question of Women's Suffrage. He was an anti-suffragist, partly because he was a democrat. The suffrage agitation in England was conducted by a handful of women, mainly of the upper classes; and it gave Cecil Chesterton immense pleasure to head articles on the movement with the words, "Votes for Ladies." G.K. too felt that the suffrage agitation was really doing harm by dragging a red herring across the path of necessary social reform. If the vast majority of women did not want votes it was undemocratic to force votes upon them. Also, if rich men had

* *What's Wrong With the World*, chapter 3, "The Emancipation of Domesticity."

oppressed poor men all through the course of history, it was exceedingly probable that rich women would also oppress poor women. Both in *What's Wrong With the World* and in debating on the subject, Chesterton brushed aside as absurd and irrelevant the suggestion that women were inferior to men and what was called the physical force argument. But he did maintain that if the vote meant anything at all (which it probably did not in the England he was living in), it meant that side of life which belongs to masculinity and which the normal woman dislikes and rather despises.

All we men had grown used to our wives and mothers, and grandmothers, and great aunts all pouring a chorus of contempt upon our hobbies of sport, drink and party politics. And now comes Miss Pankhurst with tears in her eyes, owning that all the women were wrong and all the men were right. . . . We told our wives that Parliament had sat late on most essential business; but it never crossed our minds that our wives would believe it. We said that everyone must have a vote in the country; similarly our wives said that no one must have a pipe in the drawing-room. In both cases the idea was the same. "It does not matter much, but if you let those things slide there is chaos." We said that Lord Huggins or Mr. Buggins was absolutely necessary to the country. We knew quite well that nothing is necessary to the country except that the men should be men and the women women. We knew this; we thought the women knew it even more clearly; and we thought the women would say it. Suddenly, without warning, the women have begun to say all the nonsense that we ourselves hardly believed when we said it. . . .*

All the agitated reformers who were running about and offering their various nostrums were prepared to confess that something had gone very wrong with modern civilisation. But they suggested that what was wrong with the present generation of adults could be set right for the coming generation by means of education. In the last part of the book, "Education or the Mistake about the Child," he put the unanswerable question: How

* From chapter VII, *The Modern Surrender.*

are we to give what we have not got? "To hear people talk one would think [education] was some sort of magic chemistry, by which, out of a laborious hotch-potch of hygienic meals, baths, breathing-exercises, fresh-air and freehand drawing, we can produce something splendid by accident; we can create what we cannot conceive." The social reformers who were talking about education seem not to have seen very clearly what they meant by the word. They argued about whether it meant putting ideas into the child or drawing ideas out of the child. In any case, as Chesterton pointed out, you must choose which kind of ideas you are going to put in or even which kind you are going to draw out. "There is indeed in each living creature a collection of forces and functions; but education means producing these in particular shapes and training them for particular purposes, or it means nothing at all."

But to decide what they were trying to produce was altogether too much for the men who were directing education in our Board Schools. The Public Schools * of England were often the target of Chesterton's attacks; but they had, he declared, one immense superiority over the Board Schools. The men who directed them knew exactly what they wanted and were on the whole successful in producing it. Those responsible for the Board Schools seemed to have no idea excepting that of feebly imitating the Public Schools. One disadvantage of this was that, at its worst and at its best, the Public School idea could only be applicable to a small governing class. The other disadvantage was that whereas in the Public Schools the masters were working with the parents and trying to give the boys the same general shape as their homes would give them, the Board Schools were doing nothing of the kind. The schoolmaster of the poor never worked with the parents; often he ignored them; sometimes he positively worked against them. Such education was, Chesterton held, the very reverse of that which would prevail in

* See footnote, p. 20.

a true democracy. "We have had enough education for the people; we want education by the people."

Chesterton felt keenly that while the faddists were perfectly prepared to take the children out of the hands of any parents who happened to be poor, they had not really the courage of their own convictions. They would expatiate upon methods; they could not define their aims; they would take refuge in such meaningless terms as progress or efficiency or success. They were not prepared to say what they wanted to succeed in producing, towards what goal they were progressing or what was the test of efficiency. And part of this inability arose from their curious fear of the past. Most movements of reform have looked to the past for great part of their inspiration. To reform means to shape anew, and he pointed out that every revolution involves the idea of a return. On this point, G.K. attacked two popular sayings. One was "You can't put the clock back"; but, he said, you can and you do constantly. The clock is a piece of mechanism which can be adjusted by the human finger. "There is another proverb: 'As you have made your bed, so you must lie on it'; which again is simply a lie. If I have made my bed uncomfortable, please God, I will make it again."

It is easy to understand that this sort of philosophy should be out of tune with the Socialist who looked with contempt on the wisdom of his forefathers. It is less easy to understand why it was unacceptable also to most of the Tories. One reviewer asked whether Mr. Chesterton was the hoariest of Conservatives or the wildest of Radicals. And with none of his books are the reviews so bewildered as they are with this one. "The universe is ill-regulated," said the *Liverpool Daily Post,* "according to the fancy of Mr. Chesterton; but we are inclined to think that if the deity were to talk over matters with him, he would soon come to see that a Chestertonian cosmos would be no improvement on things as they are." On the other hand, the *Toronto*

Globe remarks, "His boisterous optimism will not admit that there is anything to sorrow over in this best of all possible worlds." The *Observer* suggested that Chesterton would find no disciples because "his converts would never know from one week to another what they had been converted to"; while the *Yorkshire Post* felt that the chief disadvantage of the book was that "a shrewd reader can pretty accurately anticipate Mr. Chesterton's point of view on any subject whatsoever."

It seems almost incredible that so definite a line of thought, so abundantly illustrated, should not have been clear to all his readers. Some reviewers, one supposes, had not read the book; but surely the *Daily Telegraph* was deliberately refusing to face a challenge when it wrote: "His whole book is an absurdity, but to be absurd for three hundred pages on end is itself a work of genius." That particular reviewer was shirking a serious issue. He was the official Tory. But those whom I might call the unofficial Tories, such men for instance as my own father, received much of this book with delight and yet declined to take Chesterton's sociology seriously. And I think it is worth trying to see why this was the case.

In a letter to the *Clarion*, G.K. outlines his own position: "If you want praise or blame for Socialists I have enormous quantities of both. Roughly speaking (1) I praise them to infinity because they want to smash modern society. (2) I blame them to infinity because of what they want to put in its place. As the smashing must, I suppose, come first, my practical sympathies are mainly with them." *

Such a confession of faith seemed shocking to the honest old-fashioned Tory. And because it shocked him, he made the mistake of calling it irresponsible. Chesterton frequently urged revolution as the only possible means of changing an intolerable state of things. But the word "revolution" suggested streets running with blood. And, on the other hand, they had not the very

* Letter to the *Clarion*, February 8, 1910.

faintest conception of how intolerable the state of things was against which Chesterton proposed to revolt. I think it must be said too that he was a little hazy as to the exact nature of the revolution he proposed. He certainly hoped to avoid the guillotine! And even when urging the restoration of the common lands to the people of England, he appended a note in which he talked of a land purchase scheme similar to that which George Wyndham had introduced in Ireland. But besides this tinge of vagueness in what he proposed, there was another weakness in his presentment of his sociology which I think was his chief weakness as a writer.

It would be hard to find anyone who got so much out of words, proverbs, popular sayings. He wrung every ounce of meaning out of them; he stood them on their heads; he turned them inside out. And everything he said he illustrated with an extraordinary wealth of fancy; but when you come to illustration by way of concrete facts there is a curious change. In his sociology, he did the same thing that his best critics blamed in his literary biographies. He would take some one fact and appear to build upon it an enormous superstructure and then, very often, it would turn out that the fact itself was inaccurately set down; and the average reader, discovering the inaccuracy, felt that the entire superstructure was on a rotten foundation and had fallen with it to the ground. Yet the ordinary reader was wrong. The "fact" had not been the foundation of his thought, but only the thing that had started him thinking. If the "fact" had not been there at all, his thinking would have been neither more nor less valid. But most readers could not see the distinction.

It is a little difficult to make the point clear; but anyone who has read the *Browning* and the *Dickens* and then read the reviews of them will recognise what I mean. It was universally acknowledged that Chesterton might commit a hundred inaccuracies and yet get at the heart of his subject in a way that the most painstaking biographer and critic could not emulate. The more deeply cne reads Dickens or Browning, the more even one studies their lives, the more one is confirmed as to the profound truth of the Chesterton estimate and the genius of his insight. A superficial glance sees only the errors; a deeper gaze discovers the truth. It is exactly the same with his sociology. But here we are in a field where there is far more prejudice. When Chesterton talked of State interference and used again and again the same illustration—that of children whose hair was forcibly cut short in a Board School—two questions were asked by Socialists: Was this a solitary incident? Was it accurately reported? When a pained doctor wrote to the papers saying the incident had been merely one of a request to parents who had gladly complied for fear their children should catch things from other and dirtier children, it appeared as though G.K. had built far too much on this one point. It was not the case. He was not building on the incident, he was illustrating by the incident. But it must be admitted that he was incredibly careless in investigating such incidents; and quite indifferent as to his own accuracy. And this was foolish, for he could have found in Police Court records, in the pages of *John Bull* and later of the *Eye Witness* itself, abundance of well verified illustrations of his thesis.

In the same way, when he talked of the robbery of the people of England by the great landlords, he did not take the slightest trouble to prove his case to the many who knew nothing of the matter. It must be remembered that the sociological side of English history was only just beginning to be explored to any serious extent. In the *Village Labourer,* Mr. and Mrs. Hammond point out to what an extent they had had to depend on the Home Office papers and contemporary documents for the mass of facts which this book and the *Town Labourer* brought for the first time to the knowledge of the general public. Chesterton had worked with Hammond on the *Speaker* for some years. Just as with his book about Shaw so too with the background of his sociology he could have gone round the corner and got the required information. He knew the thing in general terms; he would not be bothered to make that knowledge convincing to his readers. If to his genius for expounding ideas had been added an awareness of the necessity of marshalling and presenting facts, he must surely have convinced all men of goodwill.

For in this matter the facts were there to marshal. It was less than a hundred years since the last struggle of the English yeomen against a wholesale robbery and confiscation that catastrophically altered the whole shape of our country. And it seems to have left no trace in the memory of the English poor. In *Northanger Abbey,* Jane Austen describes Catherine Morland finding the traces of an imaginary crime. But Chesterton comments that the crime she failed to discover was the very real one that the owner of Northanger Abbey was not an Abbot. The ordinary Englishman, however, thinks little of a crime that consisted in robbing "a lot of lazy monks." That they had possessed so much of the land of England merely seemed to make the act a more desirable one: yet it was a confiscation, not so much of monks' land as of the people's land administered by the monasteries.

What is even less realised is how much of the structure of the mediaeval village remained after the Reformation and how widespread was small ownership nearly to the end of the eighteenth century, when Enclosures began estimated by the Hammonds at five million acres. This land ceased in effect to be the common property of the poor and became the private property of the rich. This business of the Enclosures must be treated at some little length because it had the same key position in Chesterton's sociological thinking as the Marconi Case (shortly to be discussed) had in his political.

In every village of England had been small freeholders, copyholders and cottagers, all of whom had varying degrees of possession in the common lands which were administered by a manorial court of the village. These common lands were not mere stretches of heath and gorse but consisted partly of arable cultivated in strips with strict rules of rotation, partly of grazing land and partly of wood and heath. Most people in the village had a right to a strip of arable, to cut firing of brushwood and turf, and rushes for thatch, and to pasture one or more cows, their pigs and their geese. A village cowherd looked after all the animals and brought them back at night. Cobbett in his *Cottage Economy* (to a new edition of which Chesterton wrote a preface) reckoned that a cottager with a quarter-acre of garden could well keep a cow on his own cabbages plus common-land grazing, could fatten his own pig and have to buy very little food for his family except grain and hops for home-baking and brewing. He puts a cottager's earnings, working part-time for a farmer, at about 10 sh. a week. This figure would vary, but the possession of property in stock and common rights would tide over bad times. A man with fire and food could be quasi-independent; and indeed some of the larger farmers, witnessing before Enclosure Enquiry Committees, complained of this very spirit of independence as producing idleness and "sauciness."

The case for the Enclosures was that improved agricultural methods could not be used in the open fields: more food was grown for increasing town populations: much waste land ploughed: livestock immeasurably improved. Only later was the cost counted when cheap imported food for these same towns had slain English agriculture. The "compensation" in small plots or sums of money could not for the smaller commoners replace what they had lost—even when they succeeded in getting it. Claims had to be made in writing—and few cottagers could write. How difficult too to reduce to its money value a claim for cutting turf or pasturing pigs and geese. A commissioner, who had administered twenty Enclosure Acts, lamented to Arthur Young that he had been the means of ruining two thousand poor people. But the gulf was so great between rich and poor that all that the commons had meant to the poor was not glimpsed by the rich. Arthur Young had thought the benefits of common "perfectly contemptible," but by 1801 he was deeply repentant and trying in vain to arrest the movement he had helped to start.

Before enclosure, the English cottager had had milk, butter and cheese in plenty, home-grown pork and bacon, home-brewed beer and home-baked bread, his own vegetables (although Cobbett scorned green rubbish for human food and advised it to be fed to cattle only), his own eggs and poultry. After enclosure, he could get no milk, for the farmers would not sell it; no meat, for his wages could not buy it; and he no longer had a pig to provide the fat bacon commended by Cobbett. Working long hours he lived on bread, potatoes and tea, and insufficient even of these. Lord Winchelsea, one of the very few landowners who resisted the trend of the time, mentioned in the House of Lords the discovery of four labourers, starved to death under a hedge, and said this was a typical occurrence.

At the beginning of the Enclosure period the Industrial Revolution was barely in its infancy. A large part of the spinning, weaving and other manufactures was carried on in the cottages of men who had gardens they could dig in and cows and pigs of their own. The invention of power machines, the discovery of coal wherewith those machines could be worked, led to the concentration of factories in the huge cities. But it was the drift from the villages of dispossessed men, together with the cheap child labour provided by Poor Law Guardians, that made possible the starvation wages and the tyranny of the factory system. And here the tyrants were largely of a different class. There were some landowners who also had factories, and more who possessed coal-mines, but many of the manufacturers had themselves come from the class of the dispossessed.

Successful manufacturers made money—a great deal of money. Many of the men's appeals gave the figures at which the goods were sold in contrast with their rate of wages, and the contrast is startling. So, as the towns grew, the masters left the smoke they were creating and bought country places and became country gentlemen, preserved their own game and judged their own tenants. And thus disappeared yet another section of the ancient country folk. For the large landowners would seldom sell and the land bought by the new men was mostly the land of small farmers and yeomen. This was the age of new country houses with a hundred rooms and vast offices that housed an army of servants. "Labour was cheap," the descendants of those who built just then will tell you, as they gaze disconsolate at their unwieldy heritage. Old and new families alike built or rebuilt, added and improved.

Cobbett rode rurally and angrily through the ruins of a better England (described a century earlier by another horseman, Daniel Defoe). Goldsmith mourned an early example in his "Deserted Village," but they are the only voices in an abundant literature. Jane Austen is, indeed, the perfect example of what Chesterton always realised—the ignorance that was almost innocence with which the wealthy had done their work of destruction. He did not account them as evil as they would seem by a mere summary of events. And what he saw at the root of those events was in his eyes still present: England was still possessed and still governed by a minority. The Conservatives were "a minority that was rich," the liberals "a minority that was mad." And those two minorities tended to join together and rob and oppress the ordinary man, in the name of some theory of progress and perfection.

Thus the Protestant Reformation had closed the monasteries, which were the poor man's inns, in the name of a purer religion; the economists had taken away his land and driven him into the factories with a promise of future wealth and prosperity. These had been the experts of their day. Now the new experts were telling him with equal eagerness that hygienic flats and communal kitchens would bring about for him the new Jerusalem. But never did the expert think of asking Jones, the ordinary man, what he himself wanted. Jones just wanted the "divinely ordinary things"—a house of his own and a family life. And that was still denied him as is related in the chapter called "The Homelessness of Jones."

In a debate in the Oxford Union, G.K. maintained that the House of Lords was a menace to the State, because it failed precisely in what was supposed to be its main function, that of conservation. It had not saved, it had destroyed the Church lands and the common lands; it was ready to pass any Bill that affected only the lower classes. "We are all Socialists now," Sir William Harcourt had lately said, and Chesterton saw that Socialism would mean merely further restriction of liberty and continued coercion of the poor by the experts and the rich. So, looking at the past, Chesterton desired a restoration which he often called a Revolution. There were two forms of government that might succeed—a real Monarchy, in which one ordinary man governed many ordinary men—or a real democracy, in which many ordinary men governed themselves. Aristocracy may have begun well in England when it was an army protecting England: when the Duke was a Dux. Now it was merely plutocracy and it had become "an army without an enemy billeted on the people."

All this and more formed the background of Chesterton's mind. But what he wrote was a comment on the scene, not a picture of it. He wrote of the terrible irony whereby "the Commons were enclosing the commons." He spoke of the English revolution of the eighteenth century, "a revolution of the rich against the poor." He mourned with Goldsmith the destruction of England's peasantry. He cried aloud like Cobbett, for he too had discovered the murder of England his mother. But his cry was unintelligible and his hopes of a resurrection unmeaning to those who knew not what had been done to death.

CHAPTER XVIII

The Eye Witness

THE PUBLICATION OF *What's Wrong With the World* brings us to 1910. Gilbert had, as we have seen, originally intended to call the book *What's Wrong?* laying some emphasis on the note of interrogation. It amused him to perplex the casual visitor by going off to his study with the muttered remark: "I must get on with What's Wrong." The change of name and the omission of the note of interrogation (both changes the act of his publishers) represented a certain loss, for indeed Gilbert was still asking himself what was wrong when he was writing this book, although he was very certain what was right— his ideals were really a clear picture of health. His doubts about the achievement of those ideals in the present world and with his present political allegiance were, as he suggests in the *Autobiography*, vague but becoming more definite.

Did this mean that he ever looked hopefully towards the other big division of the English political scene—the Tory or Conservative party to which his brother had once declared he belonged without knowing it? That would be a simpler story than what really happened in his mind—and I confess that I am myself sufficiently vague and doubtful about part of what the Chesterbelloc believed they were discovering, to find it a little difficult to describe it clearly. Cecil Chesterton and Belloc set down their views in a book called *The Party System*. Gilbert made his clear in letters to the Liberal Press.

The English party system had often enough been attacked

for its obvious defects and indeed the *New Witness's* even livelier contemporary *John Bull* was shouting for its abolition. But Belloc and Cecil Chesterton had their own line. Their general thesis was that not only did the people of England not govern, Parliament did not govern either. The Cabinet governed and it was chosen by the real rulers of the party. For each party was run by an oligarchy, and run roughly on the same lines. Lists were given of families whose brothers-in-law and cousins (though not yet their sisters and their aunts) found place in the Ministry of one or other political party. Moreover, the governing families on both sides were in many cases connected by birth or marriage and all belonged to the same social set. But money too was useful: men could buy their way in. Each party had a fund, and those who could contribute largely had of necessity an influence on party policy. The existent Liberal Government had brought to a totally new peak the art of swelling its fund by the sale of titles: which in many instances meant the sale of hereditary governing powers, since those higher titles which carry with them a seat in the House of Lords were sold like the others, at a higher rate naturally. For the rank and file member, a political career no longer meant the chance for talents and courage to win recognition in an open field. A man who believed that his first duty was to represent his constituents stood no chance of advancement. Certainly a private member could not introduce a bill as his own and get it debated on its merits.

None of this was new, though the book did it rather exceptionally well. What was new was the theory that the two party oligarchies were secretly one, that the fights between the parties were little more than sham fights. The ordinary party member was unaware of this secret conspiracy between the leaders and would obey the call of the party Whip and accept a sort of military discipline with the genuine belief that the defeat of his party would mean disaster to his country.

Belloc had discovered for himself the impotence of the private member. He had, as we have seen, been elected to Parliament by South Salford in 1906 as a Liberal. In Parliament he proposed a measure for the publication of the names of subscribers to the Party Funds. Naturally enough the proposal got nowhere. Also naturally enough the Party Funds were not forthcoming to support him at the next election. He fought and won the seat as an Independent. At the second election of 1910 he declined to stand, having lucidly explained to the House of Commons in a final speech that a seat there was of no value under the existing system.

Thus Belloc's own experience, and a thousand other things, went to prove the stranglehold the rulers of the party had on the party. But did it prove, or did the book establish, the theory of a behind-scenes conspiracy between the small groups who controlled each of the great historical parties, which was the theme not only of *The Party System* but also of Belloc's brilliant political novels—notably *Mr. Clutterbuck's Election* and *Pongo and the Bull?*

Of the stranglehold there was no doubt and Gilbert soon found it too much for his own allegiance to the Liberal Party or any other. At the election of 1910, he addressed a Liberal meeting at Beaconsfield and dealt vigorously with constant Tory questions and interjections from the back of the hall. He obviously enjoyed the fight and a little later he spoke for the "League of Young Liberals" and was photographed standing at the back of their van. But although he went to London to vote for John Burns in Battersea and would probably have continued to vote Liberal or Labour, he showed at a Women's Suffrage meeting in 1911 a growing scepticism about the value of the vote. He was reported as saying, "If I voted for John Burns now, I should not be voting for anything at all (laughter)."

It must have been irritating that this interpolation "laughter" was liable to occur when Chesterton was most serious; he did not change quickly but in the alteration of his outlook towards his party, his growing doubt whether it stood for any real values, he was very serious. In the years that followed the coming into power of Liberalism there were a multitude of Acts described as of little importance and passed into law after little or no discussion. At the same time, private members complained that they could get no attention for really urgent matters of social reform. The *Nation,* as a party paper, defended the state of things and talked of official business and of want of time. Their attitude was vigorously attacked by Gilbert, whose first letter (Jan. 17, 1911) ended with this paragraph:

Who ever dreamed of getting "perfect freedom and fulness of discussion" except in heaven? The case urged against Cabinets is that we have no freedom and no discussion, except that laid down despotically by a few men on front benches. Your assurance that Parliament is very busy is utterly vain. It is busy on things the dictators direct. That small men and small questions get squeezed out among big ones, that is a normal disaster. With us, on the contrary, it is the big questions that get squeezed out. The Party was not allowed really to attack the South African War, for fear it should alienate Mr. Asquith. It was not allowed to object to Mr. Herbert Gladstone (or is it Lord Gladstone? This blaze of democracy blinds one) when he sought to abolish the Habeas Corpus Act, and leave the poorer sort of pickpockets permanently at the caprice of their jailers. Parliament is busy on the aristocratic fads; and mankind must mark time with a million stamping feet, while Mr. Herbert Samuel searches a gutter-boy for cigarettes. That is what you call the congestion of Parliament.

The Editor of the *Nation* was so rash as to append to this letter the words, "We must be stupid for we have no idea what Mr. Chesterton means." This was too good an opening to be lost. G.K. returned to the charge and I feel that this correspondence is so important in various ways that the next two letters should be given in full.

SIR,

In a note to my last week's letter you remark, "We must be stupid; but we have no idea what Mr. Chesterton means." As an old friend I can assure you that you are by no means stupid; some other explanation of this unnatural darkness must be found; and I find it in the effect of that official party phraseology which I attack, and which I am by no means alone in attacking. If I had talked about "true Imperialism," or "our loyalty to our gallant leader," you might have thought you knew what I meant; because I meant nothing. But I do mean something; and I do want you to understand what I mean. I will, therefore, state it with total dullness, in separate paragraphs; and I will number them.

(1) I say a democracy means a State where the citizens first desire something and then get it. That is surely simple.

(2) I say that where this is deflected by the disadvantage of representation, it means that the citizens desire a thing and tell the representatives to get it. I trust I make myself clear.

(3) The representatives, in order to get it at all, must have some control over detail; but the design must come from popular desire. Have we got that down?

(4) You, I understand, hold that English M. P.s today do thus obey the public in design, varying only in detail. That is a quite clear contention.

(5) I say they don't. Tell me if I am getting too abstruse.

(6) I say our representatives accept designs and desires almost entirely from the Cabinet class above them; and practically not at all from the constituents below them. I say the people does not wield a Parliament which wields a Cabinet. I say the Cabinet bullies a timid Parliament which bullies a bewildered people. Is that plain?

(7) If you ask why the people endure and play this game, I say they play it as they would play the official games of any despotism or aristocracy. The average Englishman puts his cross on a ballot-paper as he takes off his hat to the King—and would take it off if there were no ballot-papers. There is no democracy in the business. Is that definite?

(8) If you ask why we have thus lost democracy, I say from two causes; (a) The omnipotence of an unelected body, the Cabinet; (b) the party system, which turns all politics into a game like the Boat Race. Is that all right?

(9) If you want examples I could give you scores. I say the people

did not cry out that all children whose parents lunch on cheese and beer in an inn should be left out in the rain. I say the people did not demand that a man's sentence should be settled by his jailers instead of by his judges. I say these things came from a rich group, not only without any evidence, but really without any pretence, that they were popular. I say the people hardly heard of them at the polls. But here I do not need to give examples, but merely to say what I mean. Surely I have said it now.

Yours,

G. K. CHESTERTON.

January 26th, 1911.
Editor's Note.

Mr. Chesterton is precise enough now, but he is precisely wrong. There are grains of truth in his premises, a bushel of exaggeration in his conclusions. We have not "lost democracy"; the two instances which he alleges, both of which we dislike, are too small to prove so large a case.

To this G. K. replied:

SIR,

I want to thank you for printing my letters, and especially for your last important comment, in which you say that the Crimes and Children's Acts were bad, but are "too small" to support a charge of undemocracy. And I want to ask you one last question, which is *the* question.

Why do you think of these things as small? They are really enormous. One alters the daily habits of millions of people; the other destroys the public law of thousands of years. What can be more fundamental than food, drink, and children? What can be more catastrophic than putting us back in the primal anarchy, in which a man was flung into a dungeon and left there "till he listened to reason?" There has been no such overturn in European ethics since Constantine proclaimed the cross.

Why do you think of these things as small? I will tell you. Unconsciously, no doubt, but simply and solely because the Front Benches did not announce them as big. They were not "first-class measures"; they were not "full-dress debates." The governing class shot them through in the quick, quiet, secondary way in which they pass things that the people positively detests; not in the pompous, lengthy, oratorical way in which they present measures that the people merely bets on, as it might on a new horse. A "first-class measure" means, for instance, tinkering for months at some tottery compromise about a Religious Education that doesn't exist. The reason is simple. "Sound Church Teaching" and "Dogmatic Christianity" both happen to be hobbies in the class from which Cabinets come. But going to public-houses and going to prison are both habits with which that class is, unfortunately, quite unfamiliar. It is ready, therefore, at a stroke of the pen, to bring all folly into the taverns and all injustice into the jails.

Yours,
G. K. CHESTERTON.

February 2nd, 1911.

It was not only in the *Nation* that such letters as these appeared. "We can't write in every paper at once," runs a letter in the *New Age*. "We do our best." ("We" meant Gilbert, Cecil and Hilaire Belloc.) And G.K. goes on to answer four questions which have been put by a correspondent signing himself, "Political Journalist."

First, in whose eyes but ours has the Party System lost credit? I say in nearly everybody's. If this were a free country, I could mention offhand a score of men within a stone's throw; an innkeeper, a doctor, a shopkeeper, a lawyer, a civil servant. As it is, I may put it this way. In a large debating society I proposed to attack the Party System, and for a long time I could not get an opposer. At last, I got one. He defended the Party System on the ground that people must be bamboozled more or less.

Second, he asks if the Party System does not govern the country to the content of most citizens. I answer that Englishmen are happy under the Party System solely and exactly as Romans were happy under Nero. That is, not because government was good, but because Life is good, even without good government. Nero's slaves enjoyed Italy, not Nero. Modern Englishmen enjoy England but certainly not the British Constitution. The legislation is detested, wherever it is even felt. The other day a Cambridge don complained that, when out bicycling with his boys, he had to leave them in the rain while he drank a glass of cider. Count the whole series of human souls between a costermonger and a Cambridge don, and you will see a nation in mutiny.

Third, "What substitute, etc., etc." Here again, the answer is simple and indeed traditional. I suggest we should do what was always suggested in the riddles and revolutions of the recent centuries. In the seventeenth century phrase, I suggest that we should "call a free Parliament!"

Fourth, "Is Democracy compatible with Parliamentary Government?" God forbid. Is God compatible with Church Government? Why should He be? It is the other things that have to be compatible with God. A church can only be a humble effort to utter God. A Parliament can only be a humble effort to express Man. But for all that, there is a deal of commonsense left in the world, and people do know when priests or politicians are honestly trying to express a mystery—and when they are only taking advantage of an ambiguity.

G. K. CHESTERTON.

Encouraged by the excitement that had attended the publication of *The Party System* its authors decided to attempt a newspaper of their own. This paper is still in existence but it has in the course of its history appeared under four different titles. To avoid later confusion I had better set these down at the outset.

The Eye Witness, June 1911–October 1912
The New Witness, November 1912–May 1923
G. K.'s Weekly, 1925–1936
The Weekly Review, 1936 till today

During the first year of its existence *The Eye Witness* was edited by Belloc. Cecil Chesterton took over the editorship after a short interregnum during which he was assistant editor. Charles Granville had financed it. When he went bankrupt the title was altered to *The New Witness*. When Cecil joined the Army in 1916, G.K. became Editor. In 1923 the paper died, but two years later rose again under the title, *G.K.'s Weekly*. After Gilbert's own death Belloc took it back. Today, as *The Weekly Review*, it is edited by Reginald Jebb, Belloc's son-in-law. With all these changes of name, the continuity of the paper is unmistakable. Its main aim may be roughly defined under two headings. 1. To fight for the liberty of Englishmen against increasing enslavement to a Plutocracy. 2. To expose and combat corruption in public life.

The fight for Liberty appears in the letters quoted above in the form of an attack on certain bills: Belloc unified and defined it with real genius in the articles which became two of his most important books: *The Servile State* and *The Restoration of Property*. If these two books be set beside Chesterton's *What's Wrong With the World* and *The Outline of Sanity* the Chester-belloc sociology stands complete.

In his *Cobbett*, G.K. was later to emphasise tne genius with which Cobbett saw the England of today a hundred years before it was there to be seen. Belloc in the same way saw both what was coming and the way in which it was coming. Especially far-sighted was his attitude to Lloyd George's Compulsory Health Insurance Act. It was the first act of the kind in England and the scheme in outline was: every week every employed person must have a stamp stuck on a card by his employer, of which he paid slightly less and the employer slightly more than half the cost. The money thus saved gave the insured person free medical treatment and a certain weekly sum during the period of illness. Agricultural labourers were omitted from the act and a ferment raged on the question of domestic servants, who were eventually included in its operation. It was practically acknowledged that this was done to make the Act more workable financially. For domestic servants were an especially healthy class and, moreover, in most upper and middle-class households they were already attended by the family doctor without cost to themselves.

The company in which the *Eye Witness* found itself in opposing this Act was indeed a case of "strange bedfellows." For the opposition was led by the Conservatives (on the ground that the Act was Socialism). Many a mistress and many a maid did I hear in those days in good Conservative homes declaring they would rather go to prison than "lick Lloyd George's stamps."

Most Liberals, on the other hand, regarded the Act as an example of enlightened legislation for the benefit of the poor. The *Eye Witness* saw in it the arrival of the Servile State. Their main objections cut deep. As with compulsory education, but in much more far-reaching fashion, this Act took away the liberty and the personal responsibilities of the poor—and in doing so put them into a category—forever ticketed and labelled, separated from the other part of the nation. As people for whom everything had to be done, they were increasingly at the mercy of their employers, of Government Inspectors, of philanthropic societies, increasingly slaves.

What was meant by the Servile State? It was, said Belloc, an "arrangement of society in which so considerable a number of the families and individuals are constrained by positive law to labour for the advantage of other families and individuals as to stamp the whole community with the mark of such labour." It was, quite simply, the return of slavery as the condition of the poor: and the Chesterbelloc did not think, then or ever, that any increase of comfort or security was a sufficient good to be bought at the price of liberty.

In a section of the paper called "Lex versus the Poor," the editor made a point of collecting instances of oppression. A series of articles attacked the Mentally Deficient Bill whereby poor parents could have their children taken from them—those children who most needed them and whom they often loved and clung to above the others, and a Jewish contributor to the paper, Dr. Eder, pointed out in admirable letters how divided was the medical profession itself on what constituted mental deficiency and whether family life was not far more likely to develop the mind than segregation with other deficients in an Institution.

To the official harriers of the poor were added further inspectors sent by such societies as the National Society for the Prevention of Cruelty to Children. Cruelty to children, as Gilbert often pointed out, is a horrible thing, but very seldom proved of parents against their own children. The word was stretched to cover anything that these inspectors called neglect. Lately we have read of a case, and many like it were reported in the *New Witness*, where failure to wash children adequately was called cruelty. And what was the remedy? To take away the father, the breadwinner, to prison. For insufficient food and clothes to substitute destitution, for insufficient care to remove the only one the children had to care for them at all: always to break up the family.

Worst of all was the question of school attendance: While a child of three was dying of starvation, the mother was at the Police Court where she was fined for not sending an older child to school. As she could not pay the fine her husband was sent to prison for a week. A child died of consumption. The parents said at the inquest they had not dared to keep her at home when she got sick, for fear of the school inspector.

As he had in *What's Wrong With the World* been fired by the thought of the landless poor of England, so now these stories stirred Gilbert deeply. He saw the philanthropists like the Pharisees, unheeding the wisdom learned by the Wise Men at Bethlehem: saw them with their busy pencils peering at the Mother's omissions while the vast crimes of the State went unchallenged. He wrote a poem called "The Neglected Child" and "dedicated in a glow of Christian Charity to a philanthropic Society."

> The Teachers in the Temple
> They did not lift their eyes
> For the blazing star on Bethlehem
> Or the Wise Men grown wise.
>
> They heeded jot and tittle,
> They heeded not a jot
> The rending voice in Ramah
> And the children that were not.

Or how the panic of the poor
Choked all the fields with flight,
Or how the red sword of the rich
Ran ravening through the night.

They made their notes; while naked
And monstrous and obscene
A tyrant bathed in all the blood
Of men that might have been.

But they did chide Our Lady
And tax her for this thing,
That she had lost Him for a time
And sought Him sorrowing.

To most of the *Eye Witness* group the fight for freedom was so bound up with the fight against corruption that all was but one fight. I think that when they looked back they were too much inclined to see the shadow of Lloyd George behind them as well as around them: that in fact the Liberal Party of those years had brought with it a new descent in political decency—a descent which would have startled both Gladstone and the more cynical Disraeli. Of this more when we come to Marconi. Meanwhile there was certainly a whole lot to fight about and the group responsible for the *Witness,* not content with the pen, formed a Society entitled "The League for Clean Government," with Mr. John Scurr as Secretary. This League specialised in promoting the candidature of independent Members of Parliament for such vacancies as occurred between general elections, and in attacking Party "Place men." Doubtless other elements were present at some of these by-Elections but the League boasted its success on several occasions, notably in the three defeats sustained by C. F. G. Masterman.

Charles Masterman had been with Gilbert and Cecil Chesterton a member of the group of young Christian Socialists that drew its inspiration in great part from Canon Scott-Holland. He had gone further than most of them in his practical sympathy and understanding for the destitute. With a friend he had taken a workman's flat in the slums and he had written a somewhat florid but very moving book recording conditions experienced as well as observed. He was one of the Young Liberals who entered Parliament full of ardour to fight the battles of the poor. The sequel as they saw it may best be told by Belloc and Cecil Chesterton themselves. In *The Party System* they wrote:

. . . Mr. Masterman entered Parliament as a Liberal of independent views. During his first two years in the House he distinguished himself as a critic of the Liberal Ministry. He criticised their Education Bill. He criticised with especial force the policy of Mr. John Burns at the Local Government Board. His conduct attracted the notice of the leaders of the party. He was offered office, accepted it, and since then has been silent, except for an occasional rhetorical exercise in defence of the Government. One fact will be sufficient to emphasise the change. On March 13th, 1908, Mr. Masterman voted for the Right to Work Bill of the Labour Party. In May of the same year he accepted a place with a salary of £1200 a year—it has since risen to £1500. On April 20th, 1909, he voted, at the bidding of the Party Whips, against the same Bill which he had voted for in the previous year. Yet this remarkable example of the "peril of change" * does not apparently create any indignation or even astonishment in the political world which Mr. Masterman adorns. On the contrary, he seems to be generally regarded as a politician of exceptionally high ideals. No better instance need be recorded of the peculiar atmosphere it is the business of these pages to describe.

At the succeeding General Election, Masterman was not re-elected. And he failed again in a couple of by-elections. In all these elections, the League for Clean Government campaigned fiercely against him. There was certainly in the feeling of Belloc and Cecil Chesterton towards Masterman a great deal of the bitterness that moved Browning to write, "Just for a handful of silver he left us," and I do not think there is anything in the

* The title of one of Masterman's books was *In Peril of Change*.

history of the paper that created so strong a feeling against it in certain minds. There seemed something peculiarly ungenerous in the continued attacks after a series of defeats, in the insistence with which Masterman's name was dragged in, always accompanied by sneers. Replying to a remonstrance to this effect, Cecil Chesterton, then Editor of the *New Witness*, stated that in his considered opinion it was a duty to make a successful career impossible to any man convicted of selling his principles for success.

I dwell on this matter of Masterman for two reasons. The first is that it was one of the rare occasions on which Gilbert Chesterton disagreed with his brother and Belloc. Gilbert was a very faithful friend: it would be hard to find a broken friendship in his life. He had moreover much of the power that aroused his enthusiasm in Browning of going into the depths of a character and discovering the virtue concealed there. And as with Browning his explanation took account of elements that really existed but could find no place in a more narrowly adverse view.

"Many of my own best friends," he wrote of Masterman, "entirely misunderstood and underrated him. It is true that as he rose higher in politics, the veil of the politician began to descend a little on him also; but he became a politician from the noblest bitterness on behalf of the poor; and what was blamed in him was the fault of much more ignoble men. . . . But he was also an organiser and liked governing; only his pessimism made him think that government had always been bad, and was now no worse than usual. Therefore, to men on fire for reform, he came to seem an obstacle and an official apologist." After G.K. became Editor of the *New Witness* the attacks on Masterman ceased, but he did not differ from the two earlier Editors in his views on the ethics of political action or the principles of social reform.

The second reason for which the Masterman matter must

be dwelt on is because it affords the best illustration of one curious fact in connection with the *Eye* and *New Witness* campaign. When the *Life of Masterman* recently appeared I seized it eagerly that I might read an authoritative defence of his position. I searched the Index under *Eye Witness, New Witness, Cecil Chesterton* and *League for Clean Government*. No one of them was mentioned. At last I discovered under *Belloc* and *Scurr* a faint allusion to their activities at a by-election in which Belloc was coupled with the Protestant Alliance leader Kensit as part of a contemptible opposition, and the unnamed League for Clean Government described as "those working with Mr. Scurr"! Clearly where it is possible to use against something powerful the weapon of ignoring it as though it were something obscure, that weapon is itself a powerful one. Against the *New Witness* it was used perpetually.

A paper which included among its contributors Hilaire Belloc, G. K. Chesterton, J. S. Phillimore, E. C. Bentley, Wells, Shaw, Katharine Tynan, Desmond McCarthy, F. Y. Eccles, G. S. Street—to name only those who come first to mind—obviously stood high. Cecil Chesterton's own editorials, Hugh O'Donnell's picturesque series *Twenty Years After,* the high level of the reviewing and (oddly enough, considering the paper's outlook) the financial articles of Raymond Radclyffe, were all outstanding. The sales (at sixpence) were never enormous but the readers were on a high cultural level. The correspondence pages are always interesting.

The *Eye Witness* group, besides courage, had high spirits and they had wit. "Capulet's" rhymes; the series of Ballades written by Baring, Bentley, Phillimore, Belloc and G.K.C.; "Mrs. Markham's History" written by Belloc: there was little of this quality in the other weeklies. Side by side with the serious attacks was a line of satire and of sheer fooling. The silver deal in India was being attacked in the editorials, while Mrs. Markham explained to Tommy how good, kind Lord Swaythling, really a Samuel, had lent money to his brother Mr. Montague (another Samuel) for the benefit of the poor people of India. The next week Tommy and Rachel grew enthusiastic about the kindness of Lord Swaythling in *borrowing* money that the Indian Government could not use. Mrs. Markham too made Rachel take a pencil and write out a list of Samuels including the Postmaster-General, now so busy over the Marconi Case. The next lesson was about titles. Then came one about policemen, and finally about company promoters and investments. How a promoter guesses there is oil somewhere, how money is lent to dig for it ("But, Mamma! how can money dig?"), how the Company promoter may find no oil, how if they think he has cheated them the rich men who lent their money can have him tried by twelve good men and true—(*Tommy:* "How do they know the men are good and true, Mamma?" *Mrs. M.:* "They do this by taking them in alphabetical order out of a list.").

Perhaps the combination of irony thinly veiling intensity of purpose, with humour sometimes degenerating into wild fooling, damned them in the eyes of many. But there was a more serious obstacle to the real effectiveness they might otherwise have had. When it was unavoidable to name the *New Witness* its opponents referred to it as though to a "rag." Why was this possible? Principally I think because of the violence of its language. Most Parliamentary matters to which it made reference were spoken of as instances of "foul" corruption or "dirty" business. Transactions by Ministers were said to "stink," while the Ministers themselves were described as carrying off or distributing "swag" and "boodle." In Vol. II of the *Eye Witness*, for instance, we find the "game of boodle," "dirty trick," "Keep your eye on the Railway Bill: you are going to be fleeced," and "stunt" and "ramp" *passim*. Mr. Lloyd George and Sir Rufus Isaacs are always called "George" and "Isaacs." The General of the Salvation Army is invariably "Old Booth," while in the headlines the word "Scandal" constantly recurs. Even admirers were at times like Fox's followers who

> Groaned "What a passion he was in tonight!
> Men in a passion must be in the wrong
> And heavens how dangerous when they're built so strong."
> Thus the great Whig amid immense applause
> Scared off his clients and bawled down his cause,
> Undid reform by lauding Revolution
> Till cobblers cried "God save the Constitution."

CHAPTER XIX

Marconi

IN HIS *Autobiography* Gilbert Chesterton has set down his belief that the Marconi Scandal will be seen by historians as a landmark in English history. To him personally the revelations produced by it were a great shock and gave the death-blow to all that still lingered of his belief in the Liberal Party. For the rest of his life it may almost be called an obsession with him. In his eyes it was so great a landmark that as others spoke of events as pre- or post-war, he divided the political history of England into pre- and post-Marconi. It meant as much for his political outlook as the Enclosures for his social. It is necessary to know what happened in the Marconi Case if we are to understand a most important element in Chesterton's mental history.

The difficulty is to know what did happen. The main lines of a very complicated bit of history have never, so far as I know, been disentangled by anyone whose only interest was to disentangle them: and the partisans have naturally tangled them more. I wrote a draft chapter after reading the two thousand page report of the Parliamentary Committee, the six hundred page report of Cecil Chesterton's Trial, and masses of contemporary journalism. Then, in the circumstances I have related in the Introduction, I called in my husband's aid. The rest of this chapter is mainly his.

I. WHAT THE MINISTERS DID

The Imperial Conference of 1911 had approved the plan of a chain of state-owned wireless stations to be erected throughout the British Empire. The Post Office—Mr. Herbert Samuel being the Postmaster-General—was instructed to put the matter in hand. After consideration of competing systems, the Marconi was chosen. The Marconi Wireless Telegraph Co. of London— of which Mr. Godfrey Isaacs was Managing Director—was asked to tender for the work. Its tender was accepted on March 7, 1912. The main terms of the tender were as follows:

The Company was to erect stations in various parts of the Empire at a cost to the Government of £60,000 per station; these were then to be operated by the Governments of the United Kingdom and the Dominions and Colonies concerned; and the Marconi Company was to receive 10% of the gross receipts. The Agreement was for 28 years, though the Postmaster-General might terminate it at the end of eighteen years. But there was one further clause (Clause 10) allowing for termination *at any time* if the Government should find it advantageous to use a different system.

The acceptance of this tender was only the first stage. A contract had to be drawn up, and nothing would be finalised till this contract had been accepted by Parliament. In fact the contract was not completed till July 19. On that day it was placed on the table of the House of Commons.

For the understanding of the Marconi Case, the vital period is the four months of 1912 between March 7, when the tender was accepted, and July 19 when the contract was tabled. Let us concentrate upon that four-month period. The Postmaster-General issued no statement whatever on the matter but on March 8 the Company sent out a circular to its shareholders telling them the good news—but making the news look even better than it was by omitting all reference to Clause 10, which entitled the Government to substitute some rival system at any time it pleased. The Postmaster-General issued no correction because, as he said later, he had not been aware of the omission.

Immediately after, Godfrey Isaacs left for America to con-

sider the affairs of the American Marconi Company, capitalised
at $1,600,000, of which he was a Director. More than half its
shares were owned by the English Company. On behalf of
the English Company he bought up the rights of the American
Company's principal rival, and then sold these rights (at a profit
not stated but apparently very considerable) to the American
Company for $1,400,000. To handle all this and allow for vast
developments hoped for from this purchase and from a very
favourable agreement Godfrey Isaacs had negotiated with Western Union, the American Company was to be re-organized as a
$10,000,000 Company—two million shares at $5 each. The
American Company—whose own repute in America was too low
for any hope of raising money on that scale from the American
public—seems to have agreed to the Godfrey Isaacs plan only
on condition that the English Company should guarantee the
subscription; and Godfrey Isaacs made himself personally responsible for placing 500,000 shares. (It should be remembered
that the pound was then worth just under five dollars: a $5
share was worth £1.1.3, or £1$\frac{1}{16}$ in English money.)

Godfrey Isaacs returned to England. On April 9 he lunched
with his brothers Harry and Rufus—Rufus being Attorney-
General in the British Government. He told them of the arrangements he had made—arrangements which were not yet made
known to the public—and of the new stock about to be issued,
and offered them 100,000 shares, out of the 500,000 for which
he had made himself responsible, at the face value of £1.1.3.
Rufus refused—one reason for his refusal being that the shares
were not a good "buy," as the prospects of the Company did not
warrant so large a new issue of capital. Harry took 50,000.

We now come to the transactions which the public was later
to lump together rather crudely as "Ministers Gambling in
Marconis."

A. On April 17—roughly a week after the luncheon—Rufus
Isaacs bought 10,000 of Harry's shares at £2. He made the point

later that buying from Godfrey would have been improper as Godfrey was director of a company with which the Government was negotiating, but that it was all right to buy from Harry who had bought from Godfrey. (Harry having paid only £1.1.3 was willing to let Rufus have them for the same price. But Rufus thought it only fair to pay the higher price. This is all the more remarkable because only a week earlier he had thought these same shares bad value at roughly half the price he was now prepared to pay.) Of his 10,000 shares, Rufus immediately sold 1000 to the Chancellor of the Exchequer, David Lloyd George, and 1000 to the Master of Elibank, who was chief Whip of the Liberal Party then in office. It is to be noted that no money passed at this time in any of those transactions: Rufus did not pay Harry, Lloyd George and Elibank did not pay Rufus.

Nor did the shares pass. Indeed the shares did not as yet exist, as it was not till the next day, April 18, that the American Marconi Company authorised the issue of the new capital. On the day after that, April 19, the shares were put on the market at £3.5.0. That same day they rose to £4. In the course of the day Rufus Isaacs sold 700 shares at an average price of £3.6.6, which on the face of it looks like clearing £3000 more than he had paid for all his shares and still having 3000 shares left. But he explained later that there had been pooling arrangements between himself and his brother, and himself and his two friends: so that the upshot of his day's transactions was that he had sold 2856 of his own shares, and 357 each for Lloyd George and Elibank.* The triumvirate therefore still had 6430 shares of which 1286 belonged to Lloyd George and Elibank.

*Rufus' explanation boils down to this: he and Harry had arranged that whatever either sold in the course of the day should be totalled and divided in the proportion of their holdings. Rufus sold 7000 shares, Harry 10,850: a total of 17,850. Rufus had taken 1/5 of Harry's 50,000 shares, so one-fifth of the shares sold were allotted as his—i.e. 3570. Lloyd George and Elibank had each taken 1/10 of Rufus', therefore each was considered to have sold 357.

On April 20 these two sold a further 1000 of their 1286 shares at £3.5/32.

B. On May 22 Lloyd George and Elibank bought 3000 more shares at £2.5/32. As they were not due to deliver the shares previously sold by them at £3.6.6 and £3.5/32 till June 20, this new purchase had something of the look of a "bear" transaction.

C. In April and May the Master of Elibank bought 3000 shares for the account of the Liberal Party, of whose funds he had ·charge.

These three transactions are all that the three politicians ever admitted, and nothing more was ever proved against them. As we have seen there was no documentary evidence of the principal transaction (the one I have called A), except that Rufus sold 7000 shares on April 19. In his acquiring of the shares, no broker was employed. Rufus did not pay Harry for the shares until January 6, 1913, some nine months later, when the enquiry was already on. There was no evidence other than his own word that 10,000 was the number he had agreed to take or £2 the price that he had agreed to pay, or that he had bought from Harry and not from Godfrey, or that of the 7000 shares he had certainly sold at a huge profit on April 19 half were sold for Harry. There was, indeed, no evidence that the shares were not a gift.

Even on what they admitted, they had obviously acted improperly. The contract with the English Marconi Company was not yet completed, Parliament had not been informed of its terms, Parliament therefore had yet to decide whether it would accept or reject it. Three members of Parliament had committed two grave improprieties:

(1) They had purchased shares—directly or at one remove— from the Managing Director of a Company seeking a contract from Parliament, in circumstances that were practically equivalent to receiving a gift of money from him. They received

shares which the general public could not have bought till two days later and then only at over 50% more than the politicians paid.* (On this count, the fact that the shares were American Marconis made no difference: the point is that they were valuable shares sold to ministers at a special low price. This need not have been bribery, but it *is* a fact that one way of bribing a man is to buy something from him at more than it is worth, or sell something to him at less than it is worth.)

(2) They—and through the Chief Whip's action the whole Liberal Party, though it did not know it—were financially interested in the *acceptance* by Parliament of the contract. For though they had not bought shares in the English Company (with which the contract was being made) but with the American Company (which had no direct interest in the contract), none the less it would have lowered the value of the American shares if the British Parliament had rejected the Marconi System and chosen some other in preference. I may say at once that I feel no certainty that the transaction was a sinister effort to bribe ministers. But had it been, exactly the right ministers were chosen. They were the Chancellor of the Exchequer, who has charge of the nation's purse; the Attorney-General, who advises upon the legality of actions proposed; the Chief Whip, who takes the Party forces into the voting lobby. It was this same Chief Whip, the Master of Elibank, that had carried the sale of honours to a new height in his devotion to the increase of his Party's funds.

II. THE PARLIAMENTARY ENQUIRY

On July 19, 1912, the contract was put on the table of the House of Commons. In the ordinary course it would have come up for a vote some time before the end of the Parliamentary

* H. T. Campbell of Bullett, Campbell & Grenfell, the English Marconi Company's official brokers, gave evidence before the Parliamentary Committee that it would have been impossible for the general public to buy the shares before April 19. And as we have seen, they opened on that day at £3.5.0.

Session. But criticism of the contract was growing on the ground that it was too favourable to the Marconi Company. And rumours were flying that members of the Government had been gambling in Marconi shares (which, as we have seen, they had, though not in English Marconis).

Even before the tabling of the contract, members of Parliament, notably Major Archer-Shee, a Conservative, had been harrying Mr. Herbert Samuel, the Postmaster-General. On July 20, and in weekly articles following, it was attacked as a thoroughly bad contract by a writer in the *Outlook*, Mr. W. R. Lawson. On August 1, a Labour Member asked a question in the House about the rising price of Marconis. The feeling that enquiry was needed was so strong that on August 6, the last day but one of the session, the Prime Minister (who knew something of his colleagues' purchase of Marconis but never mentioned it) promised the House that the Marconi Agreement would not be rushed through without full discussion. In spite of this Herbert Samuel * and Elibank both tried hard to get the contract approved that day or the next. When it was quite clear that Parliament would not allow this, Herbert Samuel insisted on making a general statement on the contract. He too knew of the Ministers' dealings in American Marconis, but did not mention them. There was no debate or division. The question of ratification or rejection was postponed till the House should meet again in October.

On August 8, Cecil Chesterton's paper the *New Witness* launched its first attack on the whole deal (though without reference to Ministerial gambling in Marconis) under the headline "The Marconi Scandal":

Isaacs' brother is Chairman of the Marconi Company It has therefore been secretly arranged between Isaacs and Samuel that the British people shall give the Marconi Company a very large sum

* The argument he put to Major Archer-Shee, M.P. was that the stations were urgently needed for Imperial defence.

of money through the agency of the said Samuel, and for the benefit of the said Isaacs. Incidentally, the monopoly that is about to be granted to Isaacs No. 2, through the ardent charity of Isaacs No. 1 and his colleague the Postmaster-General, is a monopoly involving antiquated methods, the refusal of competing tenders far cheaper and far more efficient, and the saddling of this country with corruptly purchased goods, which happen to be inferior goods.

The article went on to say that these "swindles" were apt to occur in any country, but that England alone lacked the will to punish them: "it is the lack of even a minimum standard of honour urging even honest men to protest against such villainy that has brought us where we are."

In September L. J. Maxse's *National Review* had a criticism of the contract by Major Archer-Shee, M.P., with editorial comment as well. In the same month the *Morning Post* and the *Spectator* pressed for further enquiry. The October number of the *National Review* contained a searching criticism of the whole business and called special attention to the Stock Exchange gamble in American Marconis.

A few days later—on October 11—the re-assembled House of Commons held the promised debate. In the light of what we know, it is fascinating to read how nobody told a lie exactly and the truth was concealed all the same. Here is Sir Rufus Isaacs. He begins by formulating the rumours against Mr. Herbert Samuel and Mr. Lloyd George and himself. But he is careful to formulate them in such a way that he can truthfully deny them. The rumours, he says, were that the Ministers had dealt in the shares of a Company with which the Government was negotiating a contract: "Never from the beginning . . . have I had one single transaction with the shares of that Company."

Literally true, as you see. The contract was with the English Company, the shares he had bought were in the American Company. He made no allusion to that purchase.

Mr. Herbert Samuel—who is not accused of having purchased shares himself but who knew of what his colleagues had done— treads the same careful line: "I say that these stories that members of the Cabinet, knowing the contract was in contemplation, and feeling that possibly the price of shares might rise, themselves, directly or indirectly bought any of those shares, or took any interest in this Company through any other party whatever, have not one syllable of truth in them. Neither I myself nor any of my colleagues have at any time held one shilling's worth of shares in this Company, directly or indirectly, or have derived one penny profit from the fluctuations in their prices." However, he promised a Parliamentary Committee to enquire into the whole affair.

Isaacs had denied any transactions with "that Company," Samuel with "this Company." Neither had ventured to say "the English Company"—for that would instantly have raised the question of the American Company. It is an odd truth that has to be phrased so delicately. Lloyd George, the first of the ministers to speak, managed better. He flew into a rage with an interjector: "The hon. member said something about the Government, and he has talked about 'rumours.' I want to know what these rumours are. If the hon. gentleman has any charge to make against the Government as a whole, or against individual members of it, I think it ought to be stated openly. The reason why the Government wanted *a frank discussion before going to Committee** was because we wanted to bring here these rumours, these sinister rumours, that have been passing from one foul lip to another behind the backs of the House." He sat down, still in a white heat, without having denied anything.

The Master of Elibank did not deny anything either. He was not there. He was, indeed, no longer in the House of Commons. He had inherited the title of Lord Murray of Elibank. He

* Italics mine.

had left England in August and did not return till the enquiry was over: nor did he send any communication of any sort.

As we have seen, no literal lie was told. But Parliament and the country assumed that the Ministers had denied any gambling in Marconis of any sort. And the Ministers must have known that this was what their denials had been taken to mean.*

On October 29 the names were announced of the members appointed to the promised Committee of Enquiry. As usual they represented the various parties in proportion to their numbers in the House. The Liberals were in office, supported by Irish Nationalists and Labour Members: 9 members of the Committee (including the Chairman) were from these parties; 6 were Conservatives. One might have expected that the careful evasions in the House would have meant only a brief respite for the Ministers who had been so economical of the truth. They would appear before the Committee and then the whole thing would emerge. But though the Committee was appointed at the end of October and met three times most weeks thereafter, five months went by and no Minister was called. The plain fact is that Mr. Samuel's department, the Post Office, slanted the enquiry in a different direction right at the start by putting in evidence a confidential Blue Book and suggesting that Sir Alexander King, secretary to the Post Office, be heard first.

On the question of the goodness or badness of the contract itself, the Committee uncovered much that was interesting. It emerged that the Poulsen System had offered to erect stations at a cost of about £36,000 less per station than the Marconi, and that the Admiralty itself had estimated a cost, if they were undertaking the work, about the same as the Poulsen offer. But, by a

* Rufus Isaacs' son mentions a theory held by some (though he thinks there are strong arguments against it) that Rufus' silence was due to instructions from the Prime Minister, Mr. Asquith, who was not anxious to have the connection of Lloyd George with the matter disclosed, "fearing that his personal unpopularity would lead to such an exacerbation of the attacks that the prestige of the whole Government might be seriously impaired." (*Rufus Isaacs, First Marquess of Reading*, pp. 248-9.)

confusion as to whether their figure did or did not include freight charges, the Admiralty estimate had been put down at £10,000 higher than it was! Nor was this the only confusion. When Sir Alexander King spoke of "concessions" made to the Government by the Marconi Company, he admitted under cross-questioning that there was no written record of these concessions. He spoke of various vitally important conversations and was not able to produce a Minute. Letters referred to were found to have been lost from the Post Office files.

Further, it appeared that while most rigid tests were to be required of the other systems, the Marconi people had been constantly taken almost on their own word alone. "Mr. Isaacs and Mr. Marconi both told us," said Sir Alexander King at one point, when asked whether he had had technical advice on a point of working.

"You will excuse me," said Mr. Harold Smith, "if for the moment I ignore the opinion of Mr. Marconi and Mr. Isaacs. I ask you who was the expert who gave you this information."

Then too as to the terms. The Government had proposed 3% on the gross takings. Godfrey Isaacs had held out for 10%, and got it. Moreover, the royalty was to be paid as long as a single Marconi patent was in use at the stations. Considering that by the Patents Act the Government had the legal right to take over *any* invention while paying reasonable compensation, the provision which gave so high a royalty to the Marconi Company was severely criticised. Again the right was given to the Marconi Company to advise on any fresh invention that should be offered to the Post Office—which meant that any invention made by their rivals was entirely at their mercy.

Naturally enough the question was pressed home whether the Post Office had really sought the advice of its own technical experts. It transpired that a technical sub-committee had been called once, and had recommended a further investigation of the Poulsen System. The report of this sub-committee had been

shelved, and the members never summoned for a second meeting.

Early in January 1913, the Parliamentary Committee (against
the advice of Herbert Samuel) asked for a special sub-committee
of experts to go into the merits of the various wireless systems
and report within three months at latest. It is not surprising
that the *New Witness* commented on this as "a surrender of the
most decided type, for it proposes to do what Samuel himself
clearly ought to have done before he entered into the contract."

The report of this technical sub-committee showed that there
had been a good deal of exaggeration in the first attack by the
New Witness on the worth of the Marconi System. If one single
system was to be used, it was the only one capable of carrying
out the Government's requirements. But the sub-committee held
that as wireless was in a state of rapid development, it would be
better not to be tied to any one system. And they added that
while the nature of the contract itself was not within their terms
of reference, they must not be held to approve it.

From its examination of the contract, the Committee passed
on to examine journalists and others as to the rumours against
Ministers. And still the Ministers were not called.

On February 12, 1913, L. J. Maxse, Editor of *The National
Review*, was being examined by the Committee. Suddenly he
put his finger on the precise spot. Having expressed surprise at
the non-appearance of Ministers, he went on: "One might have
conceived that they would have appeared at its first sitting
clamoring to state in the most categorical and emphatic manner
that neither directly nor indirectly, in their own names or in
other people's names, have they had any transactions whatsoever, either in London, Dublin, New York, Brussels, Amster-
dam, Paris, or any other financial centre, in any shares in any
Marconi Company throughout the negotiations with the Government. . . ."

"Any shares in any Marconi Company": the direct question was at last put.

On February 14, just two days later, something very curious happened. *Le Matin*, a Paris daily paper, published a story to the effect that Mr. Maxse had charged that Samuel, Rufus Isaacs and Godfrey Isaacs had bought shares in the English Marconi Company at 50 francs (about £2 in those days) before the negotiations with the Government were started and had resold them at 200 francs (about £8) when the public learnt that the contract was going through. It was an extraordinary piece of clumsiness for any paper to have printed such a story: certainly Mr. Maxse had made no such charge. It was an extraordinary stroke of luck, if the Ministers wanted to tell their story in Court, that they should have this kind of clumsy libel to deny. And it is at least a coincidence that Rufus Isaacs happened, as his son tells us, to be in Paris when *Le Matin* printed the story. Samuel and Rufus Isaacs announced that they would prosecute and that Sir Edward Carson and F. E. Smith were their counsel. This decision to prosecute a not very important French newspaper, while taking no such step against papers in their own country, caused Gilbert Chesterton to write a "Song of Cosmopolitan Courage": *

> I am so swift to seize affronts,
>   My spirit is so high,
> Whoever has insulted me
>   Some foreigner must die.
>
> I brought a libel action,
>   For the *Times* had called me "thief,"
> Against a paper in Bordeaux,
>   A paper called *Le Juif*.
>
> *The Nation* called me "cannibal"
>   I could not let it pass—
> I got a retractation
>   From a journal in Alsace.

* *New Witness*, Vol. I, p. 655.

And when *The Morning Post* raked up
    Some murders I'd devised,
A Polish organ of finance
    At once apologised.

I know the charges varied much;
    At times, I am afraid
The Frankfurt Frank withdrew a charge
    The *Outlook* had not made.

And what the true injustice
    Of the *Standard's* words had been,
Was not correctly altered
    In the *Young Turk's Magazine.*

I know it sounds confusing—
    But as Mr. Lammle said,
The anger of a gentleman
    Is boiling in my head.

The hearing of the case against *Le Matin* came on March 19. As that paper had withdrawn and apologised only three days after printing the story, there was no actual necessity for statements by Rufus Isaacs and Samuel. But they had decided to answer Maxse's question, to admit the dealings in American Marconis which they had not mentioned to the House of Commons: or rather to get their lawyer to tell the story and then answer his questions on the matter in a Court case where there could be no cross-examination because the Defendants were not contesting the case. Sir Edward Carson mentioned the American purchase at the end of a long speech and almost as an afterthought—"really the matter is so removed from the charges made in the libel that I only go into it at all . . . because of the position of the Attorney-General and because he wishes in the fullest way to state this deal, so that it may not be said that he keeps anything whatsoever back." As *The Times* remarked (9 June, 1913): "The fact was stated casually, as though it had been a matter at once trifling and irrelevant.

Only persons of the most scrupulous honour, who desired that nothing whatsoever should remain hid would, it was suggested, have thought necessary to mention it at all."

The statement was not really as full as Carson's phrasing would seem to suggest. The court was told that Rufus Isaacs had bought 10,000 shares—but not from whom he had bought them: that he had paid market price, but not what the price was, nor that the shares were not on the market: that he had sold 1000 shares each to Lloyd George and Elibank, and had sold some on their behalf, but not that these two had had further buyings and sellings on their own. It was stated for Sir Rufus and reiterated by him that he had lost money on the deal—the reason being that while he had gained on the shares sold, the shares he still held had slumped. (It is difficult to see why Rufus Isaacs and later Lloyd George made such a point of the loss on their Marconi transactions. They can hardly have bought the shares in order to lose money on them, and their initial sellings showed a very large profit. Indeed Rufus Isaacs' loss depended on his having paid his brother £2 for the shares, and again upon the 7000 shares he sold on the opening day being only partly on his own behalf, and there is only his own word for these two statements. If Rufus lost, he lost to his brother, who had been willing to sell at cost price, with whom he had a pooling arrangement, and who made an enormous profit. If Rufus lost, the loss remained in the family.)

A week after the hearing of the *Matin* case, Rufus Isaacs appeared for the first time before the Parliamentary Committee, almost five months after its formation. His problem was not so much to explain his dealings in American Marconis, as to account for his silence in the House of Commons. His one desire that day in Parliament, it seems, had been to answer the "foul lies" being uttered against him, which he was "quite unable to find any foundation for, quite unable to trace the source of, quite unable to understand how they were started":

obviously his dealings in American Marconis could have no possible bearing on these rumours, so he did not mention them: "I confined my speech entirely . . . to dealing with the four specific charges *which I formulated.*" *

The Chairman, Sir Albert Spicer, suggested that one way to scotch the rumours would have been to mention his investment in American Marconis, "because both being Marconis you could easily understand one might get confused with the other." This question always drove Rufus Isaacs into a rage and indeed he met all difficult questions with rages which to this day, across the gulf of thirty years, seem simulated, and not convincingly.

Why had he not earlier asked the Committee to hear the story of the American shares? "I took the view . . . that I had no right to claim any preferential position . . . and it seemed to me that it might almost savour of presumption if I had asked the Committee to take my evidence or any Minister's evidence, out of the ordinary turn in which the Committee desired it." All the same he had once written a letter to the Committee asking to be heard but "on consideration did not send it."

During his examination the element of strain between the two parties on the Committee, which had been evident throughout the enquiry, was very much intensified—Lord Robert Cecil and the Conservatives courteously but tenaciously trying to get at the truth, the Ministerialists determined to shield their man. There is a most unpleasing contrast between the earlier bullying of the journalists (who after all were not on trial) and the deference the majority now showed to Ministers (who were).

Rufus Isaacs twisted and turned incredibly. But he did admit to Lord Robert Cecil that he had obtained the shares before they were available to the general public and at a price lower than that at which they were afterwards introduced to them. He tried later to modify this admission by saying that he had been

* Italics mine.

told of dealings by others before April 17, but he could give no details: and the evidence of the Marconi Company's broker (quoted above, page 336 footnote) is decisive.

Two points of special interest emerged from his evidence. The first was that he had not told the whole story in the *Matin* case. He now mentioned that Lloyd George and Elibank had sold a further 1000 of the shares he held for them on the second day, July 20; and went on to tell of the purchase of 3000 shares by the same pair, the so-called "bear" transaction of May 22. The second was more unpleasing still. He admitted that he had told the story of the American Marconis privately to two friends *on the Committee*—Messrs. Falconer and Booth—who had kept the matter to themselves and had—or at least appeared to have—continually steered the Committee away from this dangerous ground. Rufus Isaacs' son actually says that his father "had informed Mr. Falconer and Mr. Handel Booth privately of these transactions, in order that they might be forearmed when the journalists came to give evidence." *

On March 28 Lloyd George appeared before the Committee. Mrs. Charles Masterman gives an account of Rufus Isaacs grooming Lloyd George for the event:

There was a really very comic, though somewhat alarming, scene between Rufus and George on the following Sunday. George had to give evidence on the Monday—the following day—and Rufus discovered that George was still in a perfect fog as to what his transaction really had been, and began talking about "buying a bear." I have never seen Rufus so nearly lose his temper, and George got extremely sulky, while Rufus patiently reminded him what he had paid, what he still owed, when he had paid it, who to, and what for. It was on that occasion also that Charlie and Rufus tried to impress upon him with all the force in their power to avoid technical terms and to stick as closely as possible to the plainest and most ordinary language. *As is well known, George made a great success of his evidence.*† (Italics mine.)

* *Rufus Isaacs, First Marquess of Reading,* p. 256.
† *C. F. G. Masterman,* p. 255.

I cannot imagine why she thought so. Hugh O'Donnell's description in the *New Witness* of Isaacs and Lloyd George as they appeared before the Committee accords perfectly with the impression produced by a reading of the evidence:

. . . While the simile of a panther at bay, anxious to escape, but ready with tooth and claw, might be applied to Sir Rufus Isaacs, something more like "a rat in a corner" might be suggested by the restless, snapping, furious little figure which succeeded. Let us compromise by saying that Mr. Lloyd George was singularly like a spitting, angry cat, which had got, perhaps, out of serious danger from her pursuers, but which caterwauled and spat and swore with vigour and venomousness quite surprising in that diminutive bulk. "Dastardly," "dishonourable," "disgraceful," "disreputable," "skulking," "cowardly!"

Asked why he had not mentioned his Marconi purchases in the House of Commons, Lloyd George gave two answers: (1) "There was no time on a Friday afternoon" (2) "I could not get up and take time when two Ministers had already spoken." Why had he not asked to be heard sooner by the Committee? He understood that Sir Rufus had expressed the willingness of all the accused Ministers to be heard. Like Sir Rufus, Lloyd George mentioned that he had lost money on his Marconi transactions.

The obstruction within the Committee continued to the end. The question had arisen whether Godfrey had had the right to sell the shares at his own price or for his own profit. He had sold a considerable number of shares to relations and friends at £1.1.3, whereas shares were sold to the general public at £3.5.0. Others of his shares he sold on the Stock Exchange at varying prices, all high. But were the shares his? Or did they belong to the English Company? If they were his he was entitled to sacrifice vast profits on some by selling at cost to his relations, and to take solid profits on others by selling at what he could get in the open market. But if he was simply selling as an agent of the

Company, he had no right to make so fantastic a present of one lot of shares and was bound to hand over to the Company profits made on the others.

He told the Committee that the 500,000 shares had been sold to him outright but that he had passed on £46,000 of profits to the Company. He said that a record of this sale of 500,000 shares to him would be found in the minutes of the English Company. The books of the Company were inspected and it was found that no such minute existed. Lord Robert Cecil naturally wished to recall Godfrey Isaacs to explain the discrepancy between his statements and the records. The usual 8 to 6 majority decided that there was no need to recall Godfrey. It looked rather as if the shares Godfrey had sold to Harry and Harry to Rufus at such favourable prices belonged to—and should have been sold for the profit of—the Company.

On May 7 the Committee concluded its hearings and its members were marshalling their ideas for the Report. But there was one fact for them and the public still to learn. Early in June they were re-called to hear about it. A London stockbroker had absconded: a trustee was appointed to handle his affairs and it was discovered that the fleeing stockbroker had acted for the still absent Elibank, had indeed bought American Marconis for him—a total of 3000: and as it later appeared, these had been bought for the funds of the Liberal Party. The comment of *The Times* (June 9, 1913) on "the totally unnecessary difficulty which has been placed in the way of getting at the truth" seems moderate enough.

III. The Trial of Cecil Chesterton

Meanwhile the *New Witness* had not been neglecting its self-appointed task of striking at every point that looked vulnerable. On January 9, 1913, an article appeared attacking the city record of Mr. Godfrey Isaacs and listing the bankrupt companies—there were some twenty of them—of which he had been promoter or director. Some more ardent spirit in the *New Witness* office sent sandwichmen to parade up and down in front of Godfrey Isaacs' own office bearing a placard announcing his "Ghastly Failures." Cecil Chesterton said later that he had not ordered this to be done, but he refused to disclaim responsibility.

The placard was the last straw. Godfrey's solicitors wrote to Cecil saying that Godfrey would prosecute unless Cecil promised to make no further statement reflecting on his honour till both had given evidence before the Parliamentary Committee. Cecil replied: "I am pleased to hear that your client, Mr. Godfrey Isaacs, proposes to bring an action against me." And in the *New Witness* (February 27, 1913) he wrote: "We are up against a very big thing. . . . You cannot have the honour (and the fun) of attacking wealthy and powerfully entrenched interests without the cost. We have counted the cost; we counted it long ago. We think it good enough—much more than good enough."

The case came on at the Old Bailey on May 27. It is worth recalling the exact position at this time. The Parliamentary Committee had concluded its hearings three weeks earlier and was now preparing its report. (Cecil Chesterton had not given evidence before it, for though he had frequently demanded to be summoned, when at last the summons came he excused himself on the plea of ill-health and the further plea that he wished to reserve his evidence for his own trial.) The *Matin* case had been heard a couple of months earlier. Everything that was ever to be known about ministerial dealings in Marconis was by now known, except for Elibank's separate purchase on behalf of the Party Funds, which was made public just at the end of the trial.

Sir Edward Carson and F. E. Smith were again teamed, as in the *Matin* case. The charge was criminal libel. Cecil insisted on facing the charge alone. His various contributors had joined in the attack but Cecil would not give the names of the authors of unsigned articles and took full responsibility as Editor.

Carson's opening speech for the Prosecution divided the six alleged libels under two main heads: One set, said Carson, charged Godfrey Isaacs with being a corrupt man who induced his corrupt brother to use his influence with the corrupt Samuel to get a corrupt contract entered into. The opening attack under this head has already been quoted.* Later attacks did not diminish in violence: "the swindle or rather theft—impudent and barefaced as it is": "when Samuel was caught with his hand in the till (or Isaacs if you prefer to put it that way)."

The second set charged that Godfrey Isaacs had had transactions with various companies which, had the Attorney-General not been his brother, would have got him prosecuted. There is the same violence here: "This is not the first time in the Marconi affair that we find these two gentlemen [Godfrey and Rufus] swindling": and again: "The files at Somerset House of the Isaacs companies cry out for vengeance on the man who created them, who manipulated them, who filled them with his own creatures, who worked them solely for his own ends, and who sought to get rid of some of them when they had served his purpose by casting the expense of burial on to the public purse."

There is no need to describe the case in detail. On the charges concerned with the contract and ministerial corruption, the same witnesses (with the notable exception of Lloyd George) gave much the same evidence as before the Parliamentary Committee. Very little that was new emerged. The contract looked worse than ever after Cecil Chesterton's Counsel, Ernest Wild, had examined witnesses, but Mr. Justice Phillimore insisted that it had nothing to do with the case "whether the contract was badly drawn or improvident."

But indeed all this discussion of the contract was given an air of unreality by the extraordinary line the Chesterton Defence took. It distinguished between the two sets of charges, offering to justify the second (concerning Godfrey Isaacs' business

* See *supra*, pp. 337–8.

record) but claiming that the first set brought accusation of corruption not against Godfrey but against Rufus and Herbert Samuel—who were not the prosecutors. It was an impossible position to say that Ministers were fraudulently giving a fraudulent contract to Godfrey Isaacs but that this did not mean that he was in the fraud. Cecil showed up unhappily under cross-examination on this matter, but from the point of view of his whole campaign worse was to follow: for Cecil withdrew the charges of corruption he had levelled at the Ministers!

Here are extracts from the relevant sections of the cross-examination by Sir Edward Carson:

Carson: And do you now accuse him [Godfrey Isaacs] of any abominable business—I mean in relation to obtaining the contract?

Cecil Chesterton: Yes, certainly; I now accuse Mr. Isaacs of very abominable conduct between March 7 and July 19.

Carson: Do you accuse the Postmaster General of dishonesty or corruption?

C. Chesterton: What I accused the Postmaster General of was of having given a contract which was a byword for laxity and thereby laying himself open reasonably to the suspicion that he was conferring a favour on Mr. Godfrey Isaacs because he was the Attorney-General's brother.

Carson: I must repeat my question, do you accuse the Postmaster-General of anything dishonest or dishonourable?

C. Chesterton: After the Postmaster-General's denials on oath I must leave the question; I will not accuse him of perjury.

Carson: And therefore you do not accuse him of anything dishonest or dishonourable?

After Some Further Questioning

Judge: That is evasion. Do you or do you not accuse him?
C. Chesterton: I have said "No."

Later

C. Chesterton: My idea at that time was that Sir Rufus Isaacs had influenced Mr. Samuel to benefit Godfrey Isaacs.

Carson: You have not that opinion now?

C. Chesterton: Sir Rufus has denied it on oath and I accepted his denial.

Cecil still insisted that though the Ministers had not been corrupted, what had come to light about Godfrey's offer of American Marconi shares to his brother showed that Godfrey had tried to corrupt them. Godfrey could not have enjoyed the case very much. There was much emphasis on his concealment of Clause 10 (allowing the Government to terminate at any time): and Sir Alexander King, secretary to the Post Office, admitted that Godfrey Isaacs had asked that it be kept quiet: but this was not among the accusations Cecil had levelled at him. In his summing up, Mr. Justice Phillimore indicated the possibility that the shares Godfrey had so gaily sold belonged not to himself but to the English Marconi Company—merely adding that this question was not relevant to the present case. Further the record of his company failures *was* rather ghastly.

Here is a section of his cross-examination as to the companies he had been connected with before the Marconi Company—remember that there were twenty of them!

Wild: I am trying to discover a success.

Judge: It is not an imputation against a man that he has been a failure.

Wild: Here are cases after cases of failure.

Isaacs: That is my misfortune.

Judge: You might as well cross-examine any speculative widow.

Wild: A speculative widow would not be concerned in the management.

* * *

Wild: Can you point to one success except Marconi in the whole of your career?

Isaacs: In companies?

Wild: Yes.

Isaacs: A complete success, no; I should not call any one of them a complete success, but I may say that each of them was an endeavour to develop something new.

But Carson had made the point in his opening speech that though Godfrey Isaacs had been connected with so many failures, he had not been accused by the shareholders of anything dishonourable: in his closing speech he pointed out that "not one single City man had been brought forward to say that he had been deceived to the extent of one sixpence by the representations of Mr. Isaacs." And indeed the evidence called by the Defence in this present case, however suspicious it may have made some of his actions appear, did not establish beyond doubt any actual illegality.

The trial ended on June 9. The Judge summed up heavily against Cecil Chesterton. The jury was out only forty minutes. The verdict was "Guilty." Cecil Chesterton, says the *Times,* "smiled and waved his hand to friends and relations who sat beside the dock." The Judge preached him a solemn little homily and then imposed a fine of £100 and costs. The Chestertons and all who stood with them held that so mild a fine instead of a prison sentence for one who had been found guilty of criminal libel on so large a scale was in itself a moral victory. "It is a great relief to us," ran the first Editorial in the *New Witness* after the conclusion of the trial, "to have our hands free. We have long desired to re-state our whole case about the Marconi disgrace, in view of the facts that are now before us and the English people. . . . When we began our attack . . . we were striking at something very powerful and very dangerous . . . we were striking at it in the dark. The politicians saw to that. Our defence is that if we had not ventured to strike in the dark, we and the people of England should be in the dark still."

There can be no question of Cecil Chesterton's courage. But he may have exaggerated a little in saying that if the *New*

Witness had not struck in the dark the nation would still be in the dark: Parliament had already refused to approve the contract without proper discussion and the *Outlook* was attacking vigorously, *before* the first *New Witness* attack. And there are grave drawbacks to the making of charges in the dark which later have to be withdrawn. Cecil's withdrawal of his charges against the Ministers and his failure to substantiate his charges against Godfrey's company record may have done more to hinder than help the cause of clean government. But his courage remains: and, if one has to choose, one prefers the immoderate man who said more than he knew to the careful men who said so much less. Gilbert giving evidence at the trial had said that he envied his brother the dignity of his present position. And with the Isaacs brothers in mind, one sees the point.

IV. After Thoughts

Four days after the verdict against Cecil Chesterton, the Parliamentary Committee produced its report. There had been a draft report somewhat critical of the Marconi-buying Ministers by the Chairman, Sir Albert Spicer; and another considerably more critical by Lord Robert Cecil. Lord Robert's report said that Rufus Isaacs had committed "grave impropriety in making an advantageous purchase of shares . . . upon advice and information not yet fully available to the public. . . . By doing so he placed himself, however unwittingly, in a position in which his private interests or sense of obligation might easily have been in conflict with his public duty. . . ." Of his silence in the House, Lord Robert said: "We regard that reticence as a grave error of judgment and as wanting in frankness and in respect for the House of Commons."

Upon this Rufus Isaacs' son comments: "The vehemence of this language was not calculated to commend the draft to the majority of the Committee." Vehemence seems hardly the word;

but at any rate the Committee did not adopt either Lord Robert's report or Sir Albert Spicer's.

By the usual party vote of 8 to 6, it adopted a report prepared by Mr. Falconer (one of the two whom Rufus Isaacs had approached privately) which simply took the line that the Ministers had acted in good faith and refrained from criticising them.

Parliament debated the matter a few days later on a Conservative motion: "That this House regrets the transactions of certain of its Ministers in the shares of the Marconi Company of America, and the want of frankness displayed by Ministers in their communications on the subject to the House." Rufus Isaacs' son speaks of the certain ruin of his father's career if "by some unpredictable misadventure" the motion had been carried. It would indeed have had to be an "unpredictable misadventure" for the voting was on the strictest party lines: which means that the House did not express its real opinion at all: the motion was defeated by 346 to 268. Lloyd George and Rufus Isaacs expressed regret for any indiscretion there might have been in their actions: Rufus explained that he would not have bought the shares—"if I had thought that men could be so suspicious of any action of mine." In the debate the Leader of the Opposition, Arthur Balfour, somewhat disdainfully refused to make political capital out of the business. Lloyd George and Isaacs were loudly cheered by their own Party—though whether they were cheered for having bought American Marconis or for having concealed the purchase from the House there is now no means of discovering. At any rate their careers were not damaged: the one went on to become Lord Chief Justice of England and later Viceroy of India: the other became Prime Minister during the war of 1914–1918.

One question arising from the episode is whether it meant what Cecil Chesterton and Belloc thought it meant in the world of party politics, or something entirely different. They seem throughout to have assumed that their thesis of collusion between the Party Leaders was proved by this scandal: it seems to me quite as easy to make the case that it was *disproved*.

A Conservative first raises the matter by inconvenient questions in the House. A group of young Conservatives pay the costs of Cecil Chesterton's defence. When a Parliamentary Committee is appointed to enquire into the alleged corruption, the story of every session becomes one of a Conservative minority trying hard to ferret out the truth and a ministerial majority determined to prevent their succeeding. Finally the leading Conservative Commissioner, Lord Robert Cecil, issues a restrained but most damning report which is, as a matter of course, rejected by the Liberal majority.

A Conservative M.P. told me he thought the great mistake made was that it had all been made "too much of a party question." Unless you already disbelieved quite violently in the existence of the two parties this would certainly be the effect upon you of reading the report of the Commission Sessions, and all that can be set against it is the fact that Mr. Balfour did, in the House of Commons, utter a conventional form of words which, as has been said, really amounted to a refusal to make political capital out of the affair.

I do not say, for I do not pretend to know, if this is the correct interpretation: it is certainly the obvious one.

Douglas Jerrold in a brilliant article on Belloc,* treats his theory of the Party System as a false one, and maintains that he mistook for collusion that degree of co-operation that alone could enable a country to be governed at all under a party system. A certain continuity must be preserved if, in the old phrase, "The King's Government is to be carried on"—but such continuity did not spell a corrupt collusion. If at this distance of

* "Hilaire Belloc and the Counter Revolution" in *For Hilaire Belloc.*

time such a view can be held by a man of Mr. Jerrold's ability it could certainly be held at the time by the majority—and it may be that the continual assumption of an unproved fact got in the way in the fight against more obvious evil.

For bound up with this question is another: *The Eye Witness* seemed so near success and yet never quite succeeded. Might it have done so had it been founded with a single eye to creative opportunity—to the attack on the Servile State and the building of some small beginning of an alternative? *G.K.'s Weekly* was a slight improvement from that point of view—for it did create the Distributist League; but both papers, I think, had from their inception a divided purpose that made failure almost inevitable.

The fight against corruption which had been placed equal with the fight for property and liberty at the start of the *Eye Witness* is a noble aim. But, like the other, it is a life work. To do it a man must have time to spend verifying rumours or exploding them, following up clues, patiently waiting on events. I began to read the files with an assumption of the accuracy of the claims of the *Eye* and *New Witness* as to its own achievement in all this, but when the dates and facts in the Marconi case had been tabulated for me chronologically I began to wonder. Again and again the editor stated that *The New Witness* had been first to unearth the Marconi matter. But it hadn't. As we have seen, questions in the House and attacks in other papers had *preceded* their first mention of the subject.

So too the statement that the Marconi affair had proved how little Englishmen cared about corruption seemed almost absurd when one read not only the Conservative but also the Liberal comment of the time. "Political corruption is the Achilles heel of Liberalism," said an outstanding Liberal Editor; while Hugh O'Donnell in the *New Witness* paraphrased the wail of the "Cadbury" papers:

'Tis the voice of the Cocoa
I hear it exclaim
O Geordie, dear Geordie
Don't do it again.

Just how scandalous *was* the Marconi scandal? At this distance of time it is difficult to arrive at any clear view. There are two main problems—the contract and the purchase of American Marconis.

The contract seems very definitely to have been unduly favourable to the Company; clauses were so badly drawn that they had to be supplemented by letters which had no legal effect; documents were lost, other tenders misinterpreted, other systems perhaps not fully examined, the report of a sub-committee shelved, Godfrey Isaacs allowed to issue a misleading report without correction from the Post Office. It all may spell corruption: but it need not. No one familiar with the workings of a Government department is likely to be surprised at any amount of muddle and incompetence. Matters are forgotten and then in the effort to make up for lost time important steps are simply omitted. Officials are pig-headed and unreasonable. And as to lost documents—

What of the ministers' dealings in shares? Godfrey *may* have been using Rufus to purchase ministerial favour. If so, he could hardly have done so on the comparatively small scale of the dealings known to us. The few thousand involved could not have meant an enormous amount to Rufus. He had, it is true, begun his career on the Stock Exchange, found himself insolvent and been "hammered." But he had gone on to make large sums at the Bar—up to thirty thousand pounds a year; and his salary as Attorney-General was twenty thousand a year.

There may, of course, have been far heavier purchases than we know about: the piece-by-piece emergence of what we do know gives us no confidence that all the pieces ever emerged.

We have only the word of the two brothers for most of the story and one comes to feel that their word has no great meaning. But, allowing for all that, it is possible that Godfrey may have wanted Rufus to have the American shares out of family affection: of the shares Godfrey personally disposed of, a very large number went to relations and close friends—mother, sisters, his wife's relations—who certainly could not help to get his contract through Parliament. If this, the most charitable interpretation, is also the true one, Rufus and his political friends acted with considerable impropriety in snatching at this opportunity of quick and easy money. The rest of the story is of their efforts to prevent this impropriety being discovered. Had they mentioned it openly in Parliament on October 11, the matter might have ended there. But they lacked the nerve: the occasion passed: and nothing remained, especially for Rufus, but evasion, shiftiness, half-truth passing as whole truth, the farce of indignant virtue—a performance which left him not a shred of dignity and ought to have made it unthinkable that he should ever again be given public office. The perfect word on the whole episode was uttered, not by either Gilbert or Cecil Chesterton or by any of their friends, but by Rudyard Kipling. The case had meant a great deal to him. On June 15, a Conservative neighbour of Kipling wrote to Gilbert:

I cannot let the days pass without writing to congratulate you and your brother on the result of the Isaacs Trial. . . . I do feel, as many thousands of English people must feel, that the *New Witness* is fighting on the side of English Nationalism and that is our common battle. My neighbour, Rudyard Kipling, has followed every phase of the fight with interest of such a kind that it almost precluded his thinking of anything else at all and when he gets hold of the *New Witness* (my copy) I never can get it back again. You see, however much we have all disagreed—do disagree—we are all in the same boat about a lot of things of the first rank. . . . We can't afford to differ just now if we *do* agree—it's all too serious.

When Isaacs was appointed Viceroy of India, Kipling wrote the poem:

GEHAZI

Whence comest thou, Gehazi
    So reverend to behold
In scarlet and in ermine
    And chain of England's gold?
From following after Naaman
    To tell him all is well,
Whereby my zeal has made me
    A judge in Israel.

Well done, well done, Gehazi,
    Stretch forth thy ready hand,
Thou barely 'scaped from Judgment,
    Take oath to judge the land.
Unswayed by gift of money
    Or privy bribe more base,
Or knowledge which is profit
    In any market place.

Search out and probe, Gehazi,
    As thou of all canst try
The truthful, well-weighed answer
    That tells the blacker lie:
The loud, uneasy virtue,
    The anger feigned at will,
To overbear a witness
    And make the court keep still.

Take order now, Gehazi,
    That no man talk aside
In secret with the judges
    The while his case is tried,
Lest he should show them reason,
    To keep the matter hid,
And subtly lead the questions
    Away from what he did.

> Thou mirror of uprightness,
>   What ails thee at thy vows,
> What means the risen whiteness
>   Of skin between thy brows?
> The boils that shine and burrow,
>   The sores that slough and bleed—
> The leprosy of Naaman
>   On thee and all thy seed?
>
> Stand up, stand up, Gehazi,
>   Draw close thy robe and go
> Gehazi, judge in Israel.
>   A leper white as snow!

As the *Times* leading article of June 19, 1913, put it: "A man is not blamed for being splashed with mud. He is commiserated. But if he has stepped into a puddle which he might easily have avoided, we say that it is his own fault. If he protests that he did not know it was a puddle, we say that he ought to know better; but if he says that it was after all quite a clean puddle, then we judge him deficient in the sense of cleanliness. And the British public like their public men to have a very nice sense of cleanliness."

That, fundamentally, was what troubled Gilbert Chesterton then and for the rest of his life. He was not himself an investigator of political scandals—in that field he trusted his brother and Belloc, and on this particular matter Cecil had certainly said more than he knew and possibly more than was true. But it did not take an expert to know that some of the men involved in the Marconi Case had no very nice sense of cleanliness: and these men were going to be dominant in the councils of England, and to represent England in the face of the world, for a long time to come.

CHAPTER XX

The Eve of the War (1911-1915)

DURING THE EARLIER YEARS of the *New Witness* Gilbert had nothing to do with the editing, and his contributions to it were only part of the continuing volume of his weekly journalism. It would be almost impossible to trace all the articles in papers and magazines that were never republished: the volumes of essays appearing year by year probably contained the best among them. He was still in 1911 writing for the *Daily News* and every week until his death he continued to do "Our Notebook" for the *Illustrated London News*. I have found an unpublished Ballade he wrote on the subject:

BALLADE OF A PERIODICAL

In icy circles by the Behring Strait,
In moony jungles where the tigers roar,
In tropic isles where civil servants wait,
And wonder what the deuce they're waiting for,
In lonely lighthouses beyond the Nore,
In English country houses crammed with Jews,
Men still will study, spell, perpend and pore
And read the Illustrated London News.

Our fathers read it at the earlier date
And twirled the funny whiskers that they wore
Ere little Levy got his first estate
Or Madame Patti got her first encore.
While yet the cannon of the Christian tore
The lords of Delhi in their golden shoes
Men asked for all the news from Singapore
And read the Illustrated London News.

But I, whose copy is extremely late
And ought to have been sent an hour before
I still sit here and trifle with my fate
And idly write another ballad more.
I know it is too late; and all is o'er,
And all my writings they will now refuse
I shall be sacked next Monday. So be sure
And read the Illustrated London News.

ENVOY

Prince, if in church the sermon seems a bore
Put up your feet upon the other pews,
Light a Fabrica de Tabagos Flor
And read the Illustrated London News.

Debating and lecturing went on, and an amusing letter from Bernard Shaw shows the preparations for a Three Star Show— Shaw against Chesterton with Belloc in the chair—in 1911. An exactly similar debate years later was published in a slender volume entitled *Do We Agree?* On both occasions the crowd was enormous and many had to be turned away. All three men were immensely popular figures and all three were at their best debating in a hall of moderate size where swift repartee could be followed by the whole audience.

Gilbert always shone on these occasions. The challenge of a debate brought forth all his powers of wit and humour. His opponent furnished material on which he could work. And how he enjoyed himself! Frank Swinnerton once heard him laugh so much that he gave himself hiccups for the rest of the evening. I heard him against Miss Cicely Hamilton and against Mr. Selfridge and felt the only drawback to be that the fight was so very unequal. The Selfridge debate in particular was sheer cruelty, so utterly unaware was the business man that he was being intellectually massacred by a man who regarded all that Selfridge's stores stood for as the ruin of England. Occasionally Mr. Selfridge looked bewildered when the audience rocked with laughter at some phrase that clearly conveyed no meaning to him at all. But so complete was his failure to understand what it was all about that when the meeting was over he asked if Chesterton would not write his name with a diamond on a window of his store already graced with many great names. For once Chesterton was at a loss for words. "Oh, how jolly!" he murmured feebly.

Very different was it when he debated with Bernard Shaw with Belloc as third performer.

> Ayot St. Lawrence, Welwyn, Herts.
> 27th Oct. 1911.
> Don't be dismayed: this doesn't need a reply.

MY DEAR G.K.C.

With reference to this silly debate of ours, what you have to bear in mind is this.

I am prepared to accept any conditions. If they seem unfair to me from the front of the house, all the better for me; therefore do not give me that advantage unless you wish to, or are—as you probably are—as indifferent to the rules as I am.

The old Hyndman-Bradlaugh & Shaw-Foote debates (S-F. was a two-nighter) were arranged thus. Each debater made 3 speeches: 1 of 30 minutes, 1 of 15 and 1 of 10. Strict time was kept (the audiences were intensely jealous of the least departure from the rules); and the chairman simply explained the conditions and called Time without touching the subject of debate.

The advantages of this were, (a) that the opponent or the opener could introduce fresh matter up to the end of his second speech, and was tied up in that respect for the last 10 minutes only, and (b) that the debate was one against one, and not one against two (and with less time allowed for him at that), as it must have been had the chairman dealt with the subject.

The disadvantages for us are that we both want Belloc to let himself go (I simply thirst for the blood of his Servile State—I'll servile him); and nobody wants to tie you down to matter previously introduced when you make your final reply. We shall all three talk all over the shop—possibly never reaching the Socialism department—and Belloc will not trouble himself about the rules of public meeting and debate, even if there were any reason to suppose that he is acquainted with them. (Do you recollect how Parnell and Biggar floored the House in the palmy days of obstruction by meanly getting up the subject of public order, which no one else suspected the existence of?)

I therefore conclude that we had better make it to some extent a clowns' cricket match, and go ahead as in the debates with Sanders & Macdonald & Cicely Hamilton, which were all wrong technically. In a really hostile debate it is better to be as strict as possible; but as this is going to be a performance in which three Macs who are on the friendliest terms in private will belabor each other recklessly on wooden scalps and pillowed waistcoats and trouser seats, we need not be particular.

Still, you had better know exactly what you are doing: hence this wildly hurried scrawl.

Did you see my letter in Tuesday's *Times*? Magnificent!

My love to Mrs. Chesterton, and my most distinguished consideration to Winkle.* To hell with the Pope!

Ever

G.B.S.

P.S. I told Sanders to explain to you that you would be entitled to half the gate (or a third if Belloc shares) and that you were likely to overlook this if you were not warned. I take it that you have settled this somehow.

At the second of these debates Belloc opened the proceedings by announcing to the audience "You are about to listen, I am about to sneer." His only contribution to the debate was to recite a poem:

> Our civilisation
> Is built upon coal
> Let us chant in rotation
> Our civilisation
> That lump of damnation
> Without any soul
> Our civilisation
> Is built upon coal.

* The Chestertons' dog who preceded Quoodle of the poem.

Bernard Shaw was on the friendliest terms with the others and admired their genius but thought it ill directed. Belloc, he had told Chesterton, was "wasting prodigious gifts" in the service of the Pope.

"I have not met G.K.C.: Shaw always calls him a man of colossal genius" writes Lawrence of Arabia to a friend.

As a lecturer Chesterton's success was less certain than as a debater. Many of his greatest admirers say they have heard him give very poor lectures. He was often nervous and worried beforehand. "As a lecture," wrote the *Yorkshire Weekly Post* after a performance in this year (1911), "it was a fiasco, but as an exhibition of Chesterton it was pleasing." Although his writing appeared almost effortless he did in fact take far more pains about it than he did in preparing for a lecture. He seemed quite incapable of remembering the time or place of appointment, or of getting there on time, if at all. Stories are told of his non-appearance on various platforms. My husband remembers a meeting in a London theatre at which Chesterton had been billed as one of the speakers. The meeting, arranged by the Knights of the Blessed Sacrament, was well under way before he arrived, panting but unperturbed. His apology ran something like this: "As knights you will understand my not being here at the beginning, for the whole point of knighthood was that the knight should arrive late but not too late. Had St. George not been late there would have been no story. Had he been too late, there would have been no princess."

Even more annoying was his habit of beginning his lecture by saying he had not prepared it. Such a remark is not likely to please any audience, least of all an audience that has paid for admission and knows that the lecturer is receiving a large fee. But money, whether he was receiving it or giving it away, meant nothing to him. He had not a strong voice, and I have seen him, when a microphone was provided, holding a paper of notes between himself and it. An ardent admirer of his writing told me he made far too many jokes about his size. Yet how pleasing they sometimes were: when his Chairman for instance, after a long wait, said he had feared a traffic accident: "Had I met a tram-car," Chesterton replied, "it would have been a great, and if I may say so, an equal encounter."

He thought badly of his own lecturing and began once by saying: "I might call myself a lecturer; but then again I fear some of you may have attended my lectures."

Actually, in spite of the jokes, his thoughts were centred entirely on his subject, not on himself. An anonymous Society Diarist quoted by Cosmo Hamilton writes of an occasion when: "he was given, rather foolishly, a little gold period chair and as he made his points it slowly collapsed under him. He rose just in time and sinking into another chair that someone put behind him began at the word he had last spoken. No acting could have secured such an effect of complete indifference. It was evident that he had barely noticed the incident."

Ellis Roberts completes the picture. He knew Gilbert already as a brilliant talker and came to hear him from a platform:

"I remember the manner of his lecture. It seemed to be written on a hundred pieces of variously shaped paper, written in ink and pencil (of all colours) and in chalk. All the pages were in a splendid and startling disorder and I remember being at first a little disappointed. Then the papers were abandoned and G.K.C. talked." *

At this time Bernard Shaw scored a victory over his friend. For beside lecturing, journalism and the publication of three considerable and two minor books, Chesterton between 1911 and the War wrote the play that Shaw had been so insistently demanding. The books were: *Manalive* 1911, *A Miscellany of Men* (Essays) 1912, *The Victorian Age in Literature* February 1913, *The Wisdom of Father Brown* 1914, *The Flying Inn*

* *Reading for Pleasure*, p. 96.

1914. The play was *Magic* produced at the Little Theatre in October 1913. One who admired it was George Moore. He wrote to Forster Bovill (November 24, 1913):

I followed the comedy of *Magic* from the first line to the last with interest and appreciation, and I am not exaggerating when I say that I think of all modern plays I like it the best. Mr. Chesterton wished to express an idea and his construction and his dialogue are the best that he could have chosen for the expression of that idea: therefore, I look upon the play as practically perfect. The Prologue seems unnecessary, likewise the magician's love for the young lady. That she should love the magician is well enough, but it materialises him a little too much if he returns that love. I would have preferred her to love him more and he to love her less. But this spot, if it be a spot, is a very small one on a spotless surface of excellence.

I hope I can rely upon you to tell Mr. Chesterton how much I appreciated his Play as I should like him to know my artistic sympathies.

"Artistic sympathies" is not ungenerous considering how Chesterton had written of George Moore in *Heretics*.

It is rather comic that all the reviews hailing from Germany where the play was very soon produced compare Chesterton with Shaw and many of them say that he is the better playwright. "He means more to it," a Munich paper was translated as saying, "than the good old Shaw." Chesterton's superiority can hardly be entertained in the matter of technique. Actually what the critic meant was that he preferred the ideas of Chesterton to the ideas of Shaw. Both men were chiefly concerned with ideas. But while Shaw excelled chiefly in presenting them through brilliant dialogue, G.K.'s deeper thoughts were conveyed in another fashion. The Duke might almost, it is true, have been a Shaw character, but the fun the audience got out of him was the least thing they received. Chesterton once said that he suspected Shaw of being the only man who had never written any poetry. Many of us suspect that Chesterton never wrote anything else. This play is a poem and the greatest character in it is atmosphere. Chesterton believed in the love of God and man, he believed in the devil: love conquers diabolical evil and the atmosphere of this struggle is felt even in the written page and was felt more vividly in the theatre. After a passage of many years those who saw it remember the moment when the red lamp turned blue as a felt experience.

But as to popularity, in England at least, it would be absurd to compare G.K. with G.B.S. The play's run was a brief one and it was years before he attempted another.

Chesterton was fighting corruption, fighting the Servile State. Above all things he was fighting sterility, fighting it in the name of life—life with its richness, its variety, its sins and its virtues, with its positively outrageous sanity. "Thank you for being alive," wrote an admirer to him.

Manalive is above all things a hymn to life. It is the acid test of a Chestertonian. Reviewers became wildly enthusiastic or bitterly scornful. Borrowing from his own phrase about Pickwick I am inclined to say that men not in love with life will not appreciate *Manalive*—nor, I should imagine, heaven. The ideas that make up the book had been long in his head. The story of White Wynd written while he was at the Slade School tells one half of the story, an unpublished fragment of the same period entitled "The Burden of Balham" the other half. The Great Wind that blows Innocent Smith to Beacon House is the wind of life and it blows through the whole story. Before an improvised Court of Law Smith is tried on three charges: housebreaking—but it was his own house that he broke into to renew the vividness of ownership; bigamy—but it was his own wife with whom he repeatedly eloped to renew the ecstasy of first love; murder with a large and terrifying revolver—but he dealt life not death from its barrel. For he used it only to threaten those who said they were tired of life or that life was not worth living, and he forced them through fear of death to hymn the praises of life.

The explanation given by Smith to Dr. Eames, the Master of Brakespeare College, of his ideas and his purpose gives the note of fooling and profundity filling the whole book.

"I want both my gifts to come virgin and violent, the death and the life after death. I am going to hold a pistol to the head of the Modern Man. But I shall not use it to kill him—only to bring him to life. I begin to see a new meaning in being the skeleton at the feast."

"You can scarcely be called a skeleton," said Dr. Eames smiling.

"That comes of being so much at the feast," answered the massive youth. "No skeleton can keep his figure if he is always dining out. But that is not quite what I meant: what I mean is that I caught a kind of glimpse of the meaning of death and all that—the skull and the crossbones, the *Memento Mori*. It isn't only meant to remind us of a future life, but to remind us of a present life too. With our weak spirits we should grow old in Eternity if we were not kept young by death. Providence has to cut immortality into lengths for us, as nurses cut the bread and butter into fingers."

Manalive appeared in 1911. Next year came what is perhaps his best-known single piece of writing, *The Ballad of Lepanto*. In the spring of 1912 he had taken part in a debate at Leeds, affirming that all wars were religious wars. Father O'Connor supported him with a magnificent description of the battle of Lepanto. Obviously it seized Gilbert's mind powerfully, for while he was still staying with Father O'Connor, he had begun to jot down lines and by October of that year the poem was published. One might fill a book with the tributes it has received from that day to this. Perhaps none pleased him more than a note from John Buchan (June 21, 1915): "The other day in the trenches we shouted your Lepanto."

The Victorian Age in Literature made many of his admirers again express the wish that he would stay in the field of pure literature. His characterisations of some of the Victorian writers were sheer delight.

Ruskin had a strong right hand that wrote of the great mediaeval Minsters in tall harmonies and traceries as splendid as their own; and also, so to speak, a weak and feverish left hand that was always fidgeting and trying to take the pen away—and write an evangelical tract about the immorality of foreigners . . . it is not quite unfair to say of him that he seemed to want all parts of the Cathedral except the altar.

Tennyson was a provincial Virgil . . . he tried to have the universal balance of all the ideas at which the great Roman had aimed: but he hadn't got hold of all the ideas to balance. Hence his work was not a balance of truths, like the universe. It was a balance of whims; like the British Constitution . . . he could not think up to the height of his own towering style.

. . . While Emily Bronte was as unsociable as a storm at midnight and while Charlotte Bronte was at best like that warmer and more domestic thing a house on fire—they do connect themselves with the calm of George Eliot, as the forerunners of many later developments of the feminine advance. Many forerunners (if it comes to that) would have felt rather ill if they had seen the things they foreran.

The best and most profound part of the book was however the working out of certain generalisations—the effect on the literature of the period of the Victorian compromise between religion and rationalism ("Macaulay, it is said, never talked about his religion: but Huxley was always talking about the religion he hadn't got"): the break-up of the compromise when Victorian Protestantism and Victorian rationalism simultaneously destroyed one another; the uniqueness of the nonsense-writing of the later Victorian period.

In one illuminating passage Chesterton defends what seems at first sight merely his own habit of getting dates and events in their wrong order.

The mind moves by instincts, associations, premonitions and not by fixed dates, or completed processes. Action and reaction will occur simultaneously: or the cause actually be found after the effect. Errors will be resisted before they have been properly promulgated: notions will be first defined long after they are dead . . . thus Wordsworth shrank back into Toryism, as it were, from a Shelleyan extreme of pantheism as yet disembodied. Thus Newman took down the iron sword of dogma to parry a blow not yet delivered, that was coming from the club of Darwin. For this reason no one can understand tradition or even history who has not some tenderness for anachronism.

This was not merely special pleading: it contains a profound truth. Wilfrid Ward proved it of Newman in the biography that G.K. had probably just been reading. Chesterton noted it himself in his book on Cobbett who, as he said, saw what was not yet there. It is almost the definition of genius. Already at this date Chesterton and Belloc were fighting much that to the rest of us only became fully apparent long afterwards.

"I think you would make a very good God," wrote E. V. Lucas to Chesterton. There is indeed something divine in an almost ceaseless outpouring of creative energy. But only God can create tirelessly and Chesterton was at this time beginning to be tired. You can see it in *The Flying Inn*. The book is still full of vitality and the lyrics in it, later published separately under the title *Wine, Water and Song*, are as good in that kind as any that he ever wrote. But with all its vigour the book is a less joyful one than *Manalive* and it is a much more angry one. *Manalive* was a paean of joy to life. *The Flying Inn* is fighting for something necessary to its fulness—freedom.

It must have been just while he was writing it that there were threatenings of a case against him by Lever Brothers on account of a lecture given at the City Temple on "The Snob as Socialist." In answering a question he spoke of Port Sunlight as "corresponding to a Slave Compound." Others besides Lever Brothers were shocked and some clarification was certainly called for.

Belloc and Chesterton meant by Slavery not that the poor were being bullied or ill treated but that they had lost their liberty. Gilbert went so far as to point out how much there was to be said in defence of a Slave state. Under Slavery the poor were usually fed, clothed and housed adequately. Slaves had often been much more comfortable in the past than were free men in the world of today. A model employer might by his regulations greatly increase the comfort of his workers and yet enslave them.

A letter from Bernard Shaw advising him to get up certain details asks the question of whether the workman at Port Sunlight would forfeit his benefits and savings should he leave. "If this is so," wrote Shaw, "then, though Lever may treat him as well as Pickwick would no doubt have treated old Weller, if he had consented to take charge of *his* savings, Lever is master of his employee's fate, and captain of his employee's soul, which is slavery." He went on to offer financial help in fighting the case. The "Christian Commonweal" had reported Chesterton's speech and was also threatened with the law. To the editor G. K. wrote:

Only a hasty line to elongate the telephone. I am sorry about this business for one reason only; and that is that you should be even indirectly mixed up in it. Lever can sue me till he bursts: I'm not afraid of him. But it does seem a shame when I've often attacked you (always in good faith and what was meant for good humour), and when you've heaped coals of fire by printing my most provocative words, that your chivalry should get you even bothered about it. I am truly sorry and ask pardon—of you, but not of old Sun and Soapsuds, I can tell you.

Another very hasty line about the way I shall, if necessary, answer; about which I feel pretty confident. I should say it is absurd to have libel actions about Controversies, instead of about quarrels. It would mean every Capitalist being prosecuted for saying that Socialism is robbery and every Socialist for saying property is theft. By great luck, the example lies at the threshold of the passage quoted. The worst I said of Port Sunlight was that it was a slave-compound. Why, that was the very phrase about which half the

governing class argued with the other half a few years ago! Are all
who called the Chinese slaves to be sued by all who didn't? Am I
prosecuted for a Terminology . . . enough, you know the rest. Go
on with the passage and you will see the luck continues. Abrupt,
brief, and perhaps abbreviated as my platform answer was, it really
does contain all the safeguards against imputing cruelty or human
crime to poor Lever. It defines slavery as the imposition of the
master's private morality; as in the matter of the pubs. It expressly
suggests it does not imply cruelty: for it goes out of its way to say
that such slaves may be better off under such slavery. So they were,
physically, both in Athens and Carolina. It then says that a merely
mystical thing, which I think is Christianity, makes me think this
slavery damnable, even if it is comfortable. I would defend all this,
as a lawful sociological comment, in any Court in civilisation.

I tell you my line of defence, to use discreetly and at your discretion. If the other side are bent on fighting, I should reserve the
defence. If they seem open to reason, I should point out that it is
on our side.

His old schoolfellow Salter was also his solicitor and a letter
to Wells shows in part the advice Salter gave.

DEAR WELLS,

I am asked to make a suggestion to you that looks like, and
indeed is, infernal impudence: but which a further examination will
rob of most of its terrors. Let not these terrors be redoubled when
I say that the request comes from my solicitor. It is a great lark; I
am writing for him when he ought to be writing for me.

In the forthcoming case of Lever v. Chesterton & Another, the
Defendant Chesterton will conduct his own case; as his heart is not,
like that of the lady in the song, Another's. He wants to fight it
purely as a point of the liberty of letters and public speech; and to
show that the phrase "slavery" (wherein I am brought in question)
is current in the educated controversy about the tendency of Capitalism today. The solicitor, rather to my surprise, approves this general sociological line of defence; and says that I may be allowed one
or two witnesses of weight and sociological standing—not (of course)
to say my words are defensible, still less that my view is right—but
simply to say that the Servile State, and servile terms in connection
with it, are known to them as parts of a current and quite unmali-

cious controversy. He has suggested your name: and when I have written this I have done my duty to him. You could not, by the laws of evidence, be asked to mix yourself up with my remarks on Lever: you could only be asked, if at all, whether there was or was not a disinterested school of sociology holding that Capitalism is close to Slavery—quite apart from anybody. Do you care to come and see the fun?

Yours always,

G. K. CHESTERTON.

The suggested line was so successful that Wells's testimony was not called for. The case was withdrawn. No apology was even asked from Gilbert, whose solicitor tells me that Messrs. Lever "behaved very reasonably when once it was made clear to them that Gilbert was not a scurrilous person making a vulgar and slanderous attack upon their business."

With H. G. Wells as with Shaw, Gilbert's relations were exceedingly cordial, but with a cordiality occasionally threatened by explosions from Wells. Gilbert's soft answer however invariably turned away wrath and all was well again. "No one," Wells said to me, "ever had enmity for him except some literary men who did not know him." They met first, Wells thinks, at the Hubert Blands, and then Gilbert stayed with Wells at Easton. There they played at the non-existent game of Gype and invented elaborate rules for it. Cecil came too and they played the War game Wells had invented. "Cecil," says Wells, comparing him with Gilbert, "seemed condensed: not quite big enough for a real Chesterton."

They built too a toy theatre at Easton and among other things dramatized the minority report of the Poor Law Commission. The play began by the Commissioners taking to pieces Bumble the Beadle, putting him into a huge cauldron and stewing him. Then out from the cauldron leaped a renewed rejuvenated Bumble several sizes larger than when he went in.

In the early days of their acquaintance Wells remembers meeting the whole Chesterton family in the street of a French

town and inviting them to lunch. His own youngest son, a
small boy, had left the room for a moment when Wells exclaimed: "Where's Frank? Good God, Gilbert, you're sitting
on him."

The anxious way in which Gilbert got up and turned apolo-
getically towards his own chair was unforgettable. An absent-
minded man who in a gesture of politeness once gave his seat
to three ladies in a bus might well be alarmed over the fate of a
small boy found under him.

In his memoirs Wells relates another pleasing story of a
Chestertonian encounter:

I once saw [Henry] James quarrelling with his brother William
James, the psychologist. He had lost his calm; he was terribly un-
nerved. He appealed to me, to me of all people, to adjudicate on
what was and what was not permissible in England. William was
arguing about it in an indisputably American accent, with an indecently naked reasonableness. I had come to Rye with a car to
fetch William James and his daughter to my home at Sandgate.
William had none of Henry's passionate regard for the polish upon
the surface of life and he was immensely excited by the fact that
in the little Rye inn, which had its garden just over the high brick
wall of the garden of Lamb House, G. K. Chesterton was staying.
William James had corresponded with our vast contemporary and
he sorely wanted to see him. So with a scandalous directness he had
put the gardener's ladder against that ripe red wall and clambered
up and peeped over!

Henry had caught him at it. It was the sort of thing that isn't
done. It was most emphatically the sort of thing that isn't done.
. . . Henry instructed the gardener to put away that ladder and
William was looking thoroughly naughty about it.

To Henry's manifest relief, I carried William off and in the road
just outside the town we ran against the Chestertons who had been
for a drive in Romney Marsh; Chesterton was heated and I think
rather swollen by the sunshine; he seemed to overhang his one-
horse fly; he descended slowly but firmly; he was moist and steamy
but cordial; we chatted in the road and William got his coveted
impression.

The two must have suited each other a good deal better than Chesterton and the more conventional brother. Of Henry's reactions there was a comment from the other side of the Atlantic.

The *Louisville Post* reported that Henry James, being asked on a visit to his native country, "What do you think of Chesterton in England?" replied "In England we do not think of Chesterton." The *Post* commented rather neatly "This 'we' of our compatriot must be considered as either mythical or editorial—unless indeed it refers to that small and exquisite circle which immediately surrounds and envelopes him." In his *Autobiography* Gilbert is appreciative but amusing, describing Henry James's reactions to the arrival of Belloc from a walking tour unbrushed, unwashed and unshaven. After reading *Dickens*, William wrote from Cambridge, Mass.:

O, Chesterton, but you're a darling! I've just read your Dickens— it's as good as Rabelais. Thanks!

Wells, asked to debate with Gilbert, wrote to Frances:

Spade House, Sandgate.
(undated)

DEAR MRS. CHESTERTON

God forbid that I should seem a pig [here a small pig is drawn] and indeed I am not and of all the joys in life nothing would delight me more than a controversy with G.K.C., whom indeed I adore. [Here is drawn a tiny Wells adoring a vast Chesterton.]

But—I have been recklessly promising all and everyone who asks me to lecture or debate; "If ever I do so again it will be for you," and if once I break the vow I took last year—

Also we are really quite in agreement. It's a mere difference in fundamental theory which doesn't really matter a rap—except for after dinner purposes.

Yours ever,

H. G. WELLS.

Frances thought Wells was good for Gilbert, he tells me, because he took him out walking, but when the two men were alone Gilbert would say supplicatingly "We won't go for a walk today, will we?" "He thought it terrifying," said Wells, "the way my wife tidied up." Frances, too, tidied up, but cautiously. "She prevented G.K.," says Wells, "from becoming too physically gross. He ought not to have been allowed to use the word 'jolly' more than forty times a day."

He could not, Wells thought, have gone on living in a London which was that of ordinary social life, whether Mayfair or Bloomsbury. "Either the country or Dr. Johnson's London." And of the relation seen by Chesterton between liberty and conviviality he said, "Every time he lifted a glass of wine he lifted it against Cadbury."

In spite of growing restrictions as to sales and hours the Inn still remained for Chesterton a symbol of freedom in a world increasingly enslaved. It was pointed out to him how great a peril lay in drink, how homes were broken up and families destroyed through drunkenness. After the war began, a letter from one of his readers stressed a real danger:

Now I do beg you, Mr. Chesterton, much as you love writing in praise of drink, to give it a rest during the war. . . . You may have the degradation of any number of silly boys to your account without knowing it. . . .

I have written with a freedom—you will say perhaps rudeness—which a casual meeting with you, and a great admiration for your work by no means justifies, but which other things perhaps do. I beg you to forgive me.

It seems to me that this charge he never quite answered. To claim liberty is one thing, to hymn the glories of wine is quite another. And when he was attacked for the latter he always defended the former, saying that he did not deny the peril but that all freedom meant peril—peril must be preferred to slavery. There were things in which a man must be free to choose even if his choice be evil. This was a part of Chesterton's whole philosophy about drink—a subject on which he wrote constantly.

It is interesting to note the stages of its development in his mind.

The Chesterton family had not a Puritan tradition in the sense of being teetotal. But Lucian Oldershaw tells me that in their boyhood 'he always felt G.K. himself to be a bit of a Puritan and I have come upon a boyish poem that seems to confirm this in the matter of wine.

THE TEA POT

Raised high on tripod, flashing bright, the Holy Silver Urn
Within whose inmost cavern dark, the secret waters burn
Before the temple's gateway the subject tea-cups bow
And pass it steaming with thy gift, thy brown autumnal glow.
Within thy silver fortress, the tea-leaf treasure piled
O'er which the fiery fountain pours its waters undefiled
Till the witch-water steals away the essence they enfold
And dashes from the yawning spout a torrent-arch of gold.
Then fill an honest cup my lads and quaff the draught amain
And lay the earthen goblet down, and fill it yet again
Nor heed the curses on the cup that rise from Folly's school
The sneering of the drunkard and the warning of the fool.

*   *   *

Leave to the Stuart's cavalier the revel's blood-red wine
To hiccup out a tyrant's health and swear his Right Divine
Mine, Cromwell's * cup to stir within, the spirit cool and sure
To face another Star Chamber, a second Marston Moor.
Leave to the genius-scorner, the sot's soul-slaying urns
That stained the fame of Addison, and wrecked the life of Burns
For Etty's hand his private Pot, that for no waiter waits †
For Cowper's lips his "Cup that cheers but not inebriates."

Goal of Infantine Hope, Unknown, mystic Felicity
Sangrael of childish quest much sought, aethereal "Real Tea"
Thy faintest tint of yellow on the milk and water pale
Like Midas' stain on Pactolus, gives joy that cannot fail.

* Cromwell's teapot was among the first used in England.
† Etty, the artist made his own tea in all hotels in a private pot.

Childhood's "May I have *real* tea" had grown into the tea-table of the Junior Debating Club, and Lucian Oldershaw remembers Gilbert as a young man still lunching at tea shops. I found recently two versions of a fragment of a story called "The Human Club," written when he was at the Slade School. The second version opens:

A meal was spread on the table, for the members of the Human Club were, as their name implies, human, however glorified and transformed: the meal, however, consisted principally of tea and coffee, for the Humans were total abstainers, not with the virulent assertion of a negative formula, but as an enlightened ratification of a profound social effort (hear, hear), not as the meaningless idolatry (cheers) of an isolated nostrum (renewed cheers), but as a chivalrous sacrifice for the triumph of a civic morality (prolonged cheers and uproar).

The aims of the Human Club were many but among the more practical and immediate was the entire perfection of everything.

"Perfection is impossible," said the host, Eric Peterson, bowing his colossal proportions over the coffee-pot. He was in the habit of showing these abrupt rifts of his train of thought, like gigantic fragments of a frieze. But he said then quite simply, with no change in his bleak blue eyes, "Perfection is impossible, thank God. The impossible is the eternal."

We are a long way from tea the "Oriental," cocoa the "vulgar beast," and wine the true festivity of man that we find in *Wine, Water and Song*. Chesterton had meanwhile discovered the wine-drinking peasants of France and Italy: he had discovered what were left of the old-fashioned inns of England where cider or beer are drunk by the sort of Englishmen he had come to love best—the poor. In his revolt against that dreary and pretentious element that he most hated in the middle classes he had come to feel that the life of the poor, as they themselves had shaped it when they were free men, was the ideal. And that ideal included moderate drinking, drinking to express joy in life and to increase it.

Already in *Heretics* (1904) he had in the essay called "Omar and the Sacred Vine" attacked the evil of pessimistic drinking. A man should never drink because he is miserable, he will be wise to avoid drink as a medicine for, health being a normal thing, he will tend in search of it to drink too much. But no man expects pleasure all the time, so if he drinks for pleasure the danger of excess is less.

The sound rule in the matter would appear to be like many other rules—a paradox. Drink because you are happy, but never because you are miserable. Never drink when you are wretched without it, or you will be like the grey-faced gin-drinker in the slum; but drink when you would be happy without it, and you will be like the laughing peasants of Italy. Never drink because you need it, for this is rational drinking, and the way to death and hell. But drink because you do not need it, for this is irrational drinking, and the ancient health of the world.*

But the human will must be brought into action and the gifts of God must be taken with the thanksgiving that is restraint. "We must thank God for beer and burgundy by not drinking too much of them." The topic seemed to fascinate him: he returned to it again and again. In one essay he described himself opening all the windows in a private bar to get rid of the air of secrecy that he hated. Wine should be taken, not secretly but

> Frankly and in fellowship
> As men in inns do dine.

Cocktails he abominated—and in fact strong spirits were almost as evil as wine and beer were good. In an essay "The Cowardice of Cocktails" † he is especially scathing in his comment on those who urge "that they give a man an appetite for his meals."

This is unworthy of a generation that is always claiming to be candid and courageous. In the second aspect, it is utterly unworthy

---

* *Heretics.* John Lane, chapter VII, p. 103.
† From *Sidelights on New London & Newer York*, p. 45.

of a generation that claims to keep itself fit by tennis and golf and all sorts of athletics. What are these athletes worth if, after all their athletics, they cannot scratch up such a thing as a natural appetite? Most of my own work is, I will not venture to say, literary, but at least sedentary. I never do anything except walk about and throw clubs and javelins in the garden. But I never require anything to give me an appetite for a meal. I never yet needed a tot of rum to help me to go over the top and face the mortal perils of luncheon.

Quite rationally considered, there has been a decline and degradation in these things. First came the old drinking days which are always described as much more healthy. In those days men worked or played, hunted or herded or ploughed or fished, or even, in their rude way, wrote or spoke, if only expressing the simple minds of Socrates or Shakespeare, and *then* got reasonably drunk in the evening when their work was done. We find the first step of the degradation, when men do not drink when their work is done, but drink in order to do their work. Workmen used to wait in queues outside the factories of forty years ago, to drink nips of neat whisky to enable them to face life in the progressive and scientific factory. But at least it may be admitted that life in the factory was something that it took some courage to face. These men felt they had to take an anaesthetic before they could face pain. What are we to say of those who have to take an anaesthetic before they can face pleasure? What of those, who when faced with the terrors of mayonnaise eggs or sardines, can only utter a faint cry for brandy? What of those who have to be drugged, maddened, inspired and intoxicated to the point of partaking of meals, like the Assassins to the point of committing murders? If, as they say, the use of the drug means the increase of the dose, where will it stop, and at what precise point of frenzy and delusion will a healthy grown-up man be ready to rush headlong upon a cutlet or make a dash for death or glory at a ham-sandwich? This is obviously the most abject stage of all; worse than that of the man who drinks for the sake of work, and much worse than that of the man who drinks for the sake of play.

Wine, Chesterton maintained, should not be drunk as an aid to creative production, yet one may find that increased power of creation sometimes follows in its wake. And here of course was a danger to a man who worked as hard as Chesterton. He sometimes spoke of himself as "idle," but I think it would be hard to match either his output or his hours of creative work. I remember one visit that I paid to Beaconsfield when he was writing one of his major books. He was in his study by 10 in the morning, emerged for lunch at 1 and went back from about 2:30 to 4:30. After tea he worked again until a 7:30 dinner. His wife and I went to bed about 10:30 leaving him preparing his material for the next day. Towards 1 A.M. a ponderous tread as he passed my door on his way to bed woke me to a general impression of an earthquake.

In a passage in *Magic* G.K. makes his hero say, "I happen to have what is called a strong head and I have never been really drunk." It was true of himself, but in these years just before the Great War, before his own severe illness, intimate friends have told me that they had seen him unlike himself, that they felt he had come to depend, "almost absent-mindedly" one said, on the stimulus of wine for the sheer physical power to pour forth so much.

Besides overwork G.K. was in these years mentally oppressed by the strain of the Marconi Case, and then almost overwhelmed by the horror of the World War. A man very tender of heart, sensitive and intensely imaginative, he could not react as calmly as Cecil himself did to what both believed the probability of the latter's imprisonment. And when that strain was removed there remained the stain on national honour, the opening gulf into which he saw his country falling. To him the Marconi Case was a heavier burden than the war. For, as he saw it, in the Marconi Case the nation was wrong in enduring corruption and in the war the nation was magnificently right in resisting tyranny.

So Chesterton felt, yet the outbreak of the war with all its human suffering to mind and body weighed heavily upon him too. He wrote *The Barbarism of Berlin* of which I will say something in the next chapter—for it belongs to those writings of the war period the series of which is so consistent that in his *Autobiography* he was able to claim that he had no sympathy "with the rather weak-minded reaction that is going on round us. At the first outbreak of the War I attended the conference of all the English men of letters, called together to compose a reply to the manifesto of the German professors. I at least among all those writers can say, 'What I have written I have written.'"

Then his illness came upon him. Dr. Pocock, coming for a first visit, found the bed partly broken under the weight of the patient who was lying in a grotesquely awkward position, his hips higher than his head.

"You must be horribly uncomfortable," he said.

"Why, now you mention it," said G.K., like a man receiving a new idea, "I suppose I am."

The doctor ordered a water-bed, and almost the last words he heard before the patient sank into coma were, "I wonder if this bally ship will ever get to shore."

The illness lasted several months. We can follow its progress (and his) in extracts from letters * written to Father O'Connor by Frances:

Nov. 25th, 1914. You must pray for him. He is seriously ill and I have two nurses. It is mostly heart-trouble, but there are complications. He is quite his normal self, as to head and brain, and he even dictates and reads a great deal.

Dec. 29th, 1914. Gilbert had a bad relapse on Christmas Eve, and now is being desperately ill. He is not often conscious, and is so weak—I feel he might ask for you—if so I shall wire. Dr. is still hopeful, but I feel in despair.

Jan. 3rd, 1915. If you came he would not know you, and this condition may last some time. The brain is dormant, and must be kept so. If he is sufficiently conscious at any moment to understand, I will ask him to let you come—or will send on my own responsibility. Pray for his soul and mine.

* They are printed in *Father Brown on Chesterton*, pp. 98 ff.

Jan. 7th, 1915. Gilbert seemed decidedly clearer yesterday, and though not quite so well today the doctor says he has reason to hope the mental trouble is working off. His heart is stronger, and he is able to take plenty of nourishment. Under the circumstances therefore I am hoping and praying he may soon be sufficiently himself to tell us what he wants done. I am dreadfully unhappy at not knowing how he would wish me to act. His parents would never forgive me if I acted only on my own authority. I do pray to God He will restore him to himself that we may know. I feel in His mercy He will, even if death is the end of it—or the beginning shall I say?

Jan. 12th, 1915. He is really better I believe and by the mercy of God I dare hope he is to be restored to us. Physically he is stronger, and the brain is beginning to work normally, and soon I trust we shall be able to ask him his wishes with regard to the Church. I am so thankful to think that *we* can get at his desire.

In January 1915 Frances wrote to my mother: "Gilbert remains much the same in a semi-conscious condition—sleeping a great deal. I feel absolutely hopeless; it seems impossible it can go on like this. The impossibility of reaching him is too terrible an experience and I don't know how to go through with it. I pray for strength and you must pray for me."

"Dearest Josephine," she wrote in a later undated letter, "Gilbert is today a little better, after being practically at a standstill for the past week. He *asked* for me today, which is a great advance, and hugged me. I feel like Elijah (wasn't it?) and shall go in the strength of that hug forty days. The recovery will be very slow, the doctors tell me, and we have to prevent his using his brain at all."

In this letter she begged to see my mother, and I remember when they met she told her that one day she had tried to test whether Gilbert was conscious by asking him, "Who is looking after you?" "He answered very gravely, 'God' and I felt so small," she said. Presently Frances told my mother that Gilbert had talked to her about coming into the Catholic Church. It was just at this time that she wrote to tell Father O'Connor

that Gilbert said to her "Did you think I was going to die?" and
followed this with the question, "Does Father O'Connor know?"
After her conversation with my mother Frances wrote to her:

March 21

I think I would rather you did not tell anyone just yet of what
I told you regarding my husband and the Catholic Church. Not
that I doubt for a moment that he meant it and knew what he was
saying and was relieved at saying it, but I don't want the world at
large to be able to say that he came to this decision when he was
weak and unlike himself. He will ratify it no doubt when his complete manhood is restored. I know it was not weakness that made
him say it, but you will understand my scruples. I know in God's
good time he will make his confession of faith—and if death comes
near him again I shall know how to act.

Thanks for all your sympathy. I *did* enjoy seeing you.

On Easter Eve Frances wrote two letters, one to Father
O'Connor, one to my mother. To Father O'Connor she said:

All goes well here, though still very very slowly—G's mind is
gradually clearing, but it is still difficult to him to distinguish
between the real and the unreal. I am quite sure he will soon be
able to think and act for himself, but I dare not hurry matters at
all. I have told him I am writing to you often and he said, "That is
right—I'll see him soon. I want to talk to him." He wanders at times,
but the clear intervals are longer. He repeated the Creed last night,
this time in English.

To my mother:

I feel the enormous significance of the resurrection of the body
when I think of my dear husband, just consciously laying hold of
life again. Indeed, I will pray that your dear ones may be kept in
safety. God bless you for all your sympathy. I am so glad that Gilbert's decision (for I am sure it was a decision) has made you so
happy. I dare not hurry anything, the least little excitement upsets
him—last night he said the Creed and asked me to read parts of
Myers' "St. Paul." He still wanders a good deal when tired but is
certainly a little stronger. Love and Easter blessings to you all.

We ourselves were passing then through the shadow of death. Almost as Gilbert rose again to this life my father passed into life eternal. One of the very few letters I possess in Gilbert's own handwriting was also one of the first he wrote on recovery. It was to my mother:

I fear I have delayed writing to you, and partly with a vague feeling that I might so find some way of saying what I feel on your behalf and others'; and of course it has not come. Somewhat of what the world and a wider circle of friends have lost I shall try to say in the *Dublin Review,* by the kindness of Monsignor Barnes, who has invited me to contribute to it; but of all I feel, and Frances feels, and of the happy times we have had in your house, I despair of saying anything at all.

I can only hope you and yours will be able to read between the lines of what I write either here or there; and understand that the simultaneous losses of a good friend and a fine intellect have a way of stunning rather than helping the expression of either. I would say I am glad he lived to see what I feel to be a rebirth of England, if his mere presence in an older generation did not prove to me that England never died.

This sense of the rebirth of England gave to Gilbert's restored life a special quality of triumph that abode down to the end of the war.

CHAPTER XXI

The War Years

G ILBERT WAS TAKING up life again and with it the old friendships and the old debates, in the new atmosphere created by the war.

To Bernard Shaw he wrote:

June 12th, 1915

MY DEAR BERNARD SHAW,

I ought to have written to you a long time ago, to thank you for your kind letter which I received when I had recovered and still more for many other kindnesses that seem to have come from you during the time before the recovery. I am not a vegetarian; and I am only in a very comparative sense a skeleton. Indeed I am afraid you must reconcile yourself to the dismal prospect of my being more or less like what I was before; and any resumption of my ordinary habits must necessarily include the habit of disagreeing with you. What and where and when is "Uncommon Sense about the War?" How can I get hold of it? I do not merely ask as one hungry for hostilities, but also as one unusually hungry for good literature. "Il me faut des géants," as Cyrano says; so I naturally wish to hear the last about you. You probably know that I do not agree with you about the War; I do not think it is going on of its own momentum; I think it is going on in accordance with that logical paradox whereby the thing that is most difficult to do is also the thing that must be done. If it were an easy war to end it would have been a wicked war to begin. If a cat has nine lives one must kill it nine times, saving your humanitarian feelings, and always supposing it is a witch's cat and really draws its powers from Hell. I have always thought that there was in Prussia an evil will; I would not have made it a ground for going to war, but I was quite sure of it long before there was any war at all. But I suppose we shall some day have an opportunity of arguing about all that. Meanwhile my thanks and good wishes are as sincere as my opinions; and I do not think those are insincere.

Yours always sincerely,

G. K. Chesterton.

Bernard Shaw replied:

22nd June 1915

My dear Chesterton

I am delighted to learn under your own hand that you have recovered all your health and powers with an unimpaired figure. You have also the gratification of knowing that you have carried out a theory of mine that every man of genius has a critical illness at 40, Nature's object being to make him go to bed for several months. Sometimes Nature overdoes it: Schiller and Mozart died. Goethe survived, though he very nearly followed Schiller into the shades. I did the thing myself quite handsomely by spending eighteen months on crutches, having two surgical operations, and breaking my arm. I distinctly noticed that instead of my recuperation beginning when my breakdown ended, it began before that. The ascending curve cut through the tail of the descending one; and I was consummating my collapse and rising for my next flight simultaneously.

It is perfectly useless for you to try to differ with me about the war. Nobody can differ with me about the war: you might as well differ from the Almighty about the orbit of the sun. I have got the war right; and to that complexion, you too must come at last, your nature not being a fundamentally erroneous one.

At the same time, it is a great pity you were not born in Ireland. You would have had the advantage of hearing the burning patriotism of your native land expressing itself by saying exactly the same things about England that English patriotism now says about Prussia, and of recognizing that though they were entirely true, they were also a very great nuisance, as they prevented people from building the future by conscientious thought. Also, Cecil would have seen what the Catholic Church is really like when the apostolic succession falls to the farmer's son who is cleverer with school books than with agricultural implements. In fact you would have learned a devil of a lot of things for lack of which you often drive me to exclaim "Gilbert, Gilbert, why persecutest thou me."

As to the evil will, of course there is an evil will in Prussia. Prussia isn't Paradise. I have been fighting that evil will, in myself and others, all my life. It is the will of the brave Barabbas, and of the militant Nationalists who admired him and crucified the pro-Gentile. But the Prussians must save their own souls. They also have their Shaws and Chestertons and a divine spark in them for these to work on. . . . What we have to do is to make ridiculous the cry of "Vengeance is mine, saith Podsnap," and, whenever any-one tells an Englishman a lie, to explain to the poor devil that it *is* a lie, and that he must stop cheering it as a splendid speech. For an Englishman never compares speeches either with facts or with previous speeches: to him a speech is art for art's sake, the disciples of our favoured politicians being really, if they only knew it, dis-ciples of Whistler. Also, and equally important, we have to bear in mind that the English genius does not, like the German, lie in disciplined idealism. The Englishman is an Anarchist and a grum-bler: he has no such word as Fatherland, and the idea which he supposes corresponds to it is nothing but the swing of a roaring chorus to a patriotic song. Also he is a muddler and a slacker, because tense and continuous work means thought; and he is lazy and fat in the head. But as long as he is himself, and grumbles, it does not matter. Given a furious Opposition screaming for the dis-grace of tyrannical and corrupt ministers, and a press on the very verge of inviting Napoleon to enter London in triumph and deliver a groaning land from the intolerable burden of its native rulers' incapacity and rapacity and obsolescence, and the departments will work as well as the enemy's departments (perhaps better), and the government will have to keep its wits at full pressure. But once let England try what she is trying now: that is, to combine the devoted silence and obedience of the German system with the slack and muddle of Coodle and Doodle, and we are lost. Unless you keep up as hot a fire from your ink-bottle on the Government as the soldier keeps up from the trenches you are betraying that soldier. Of course they will call you a pro-German. What of that? They call ME a pro-German. We also must stand fire. As Peer Gynt said of hell, if the torture is only moral, it cannot be so very bad.

I grieve to say that some fool has stolen my title, and issued a two page pamphlet called Uncommon Sense about the War. So I shall have to call mine More Common Sense About the War. It is not yet in type: I haven't yet quite settled its destination.

Any chance of seeing you both if we drive over from Ayot to Beaconsfield some Sunday or other afternoon.

Yours ever,

G.B.S.

Wells too was rejoicing over his recovery—

DEAR OLD G.K.C.,

I'm so delighted to get a letter from you again. As soon as I can I will come to Beaconsfield and see you. I'm absurdly busy in bringing together the Rulers of the country and the scientific people of whom they are totally ignorant. Lloyd George has never heard of Ramsey—and so on, and the hash and muddle and quackery on our technical side is appalling. It all means boys' lives in Flanders and horrible waste and suffering. Well, anyhow if we've got only obscure and cramped and underpaid scientific men we have a bench of fine fat bishops and no end of tremendous lawyers. One of the best ideas for the Ypres position came from Robert Mond but the execution was too difficult for our officers to attempt. So we've got a row of wounded and mangled men that would reach from Beaconsfield to Great Marlow—just to show we don't take stock in these damned scientific people.

Yours ever,

H.G.

No one however mad could have called Gilbert a pro-German: it was perhaps the only accusation the *New Witness* escaped. But while he largely agreed with Shaw's analysis of the Englishman as a natural Anarchist and grumbler, while he believed in the voluntary principle and disliked conscription, his general outlook was as different from Shaw's as were the pamphlets they both wrote.

In a book addressed to a German professor G.K. frankly confessed the real *Crimes of England*, for which she was now making reparation.

To any Englishman living in the native atmosphere the suggestion that England had been preparing an aggression against

Germany seemed more than faintly ludicrous. We were not engaged in plotting in Europe—on the contrary we were far too careless of Europe. And the funds of the Liberal Party (which was in power) actually depended chiefly on Quaker Millionaires who were noted pacifists and at whose bidding national honour was jeopardised by our delay in declaring our support of France. We were not prepared for war and probably only the shock of the invasion of Belgium made *certain* our stand with France.

. . . It may seem an idle contradiction to say that our strength in this war came from not being prepared. But there is a truth that cannot be otherwise expressed. The strongest thing in sane anger is surprise. If we had time to think we might have thought better—that is worse. Everything that could be instinctive managed to be strong; the instant fury of contempt with which the better spirit in our rulers flung back the Prussian bribe; the instant solidarity of all parties; above all, the brilliant instinct by which the Irish leader cast into the scale of a free Europe the ancient sword of Ireland.*

Our crimes were in the past, not the present. The first had been when we gave aid to Prussia against Austria, Austria which was "not a nation" but "a kind of Empire, a Holy Roman Empire that never came," which "still retained something of the old Catholic comfort for the soul." We had helped to put Prussia instead of Austria at the head of the Germanies—Prussia which in the person of Frederick the Great "hated everything German and everything good." Francophile as Chesterton was, he yet had a certain tenderness for those old Germanies which "preserved the good things that go with small interests and strict boundaries, music, etiquette, a dreamy philosophy and so on."

Our next crimes had been in calling Prussia to our aid against Napoleon and in failing to assist Denmark against her. And by far our worst had been the using of Prussian mercenaries with their ghastly tradition of cruelty in Ireland in the '98.

There is in this little book one drawback from the historian's

* *The Uses of Diversity.*

point of view: its view of the past is so oddly selective. Doubtless it is lawful to examine your own nation's conscience as you do your own—and not your neighbour's. Yet history should be rather an examination of facts than an examination of conscience. And historically Richelieu's policies had had quite something to say in the creation of Prussia; the conscript armies of the French Revolution had first made Europe into an armed camp. It was an undue simplification to insist exclusively on The Crimes of England.

But even while he did so Chesterton rejoiced that now at long last England was on the right side, on the side of Europe and of sanity. The *New Witness* group had always seen the issue as their countrymen were now suddenly beginning to see it. They had no sympathy with the "liberal" thinking, made in Germany, that had in the name of biblical and historical criticism been undermining the bases of Christianity. Their love of logic and of clarity had made German philosophy intolerable to them —it was wind, and it was fog. Finally their love of France had always made them conceive of Europe as centering in that country. For them there was one profound satisfaction even amid the horrors of war: that the issues were so clear.

But were they as clear to the whole world? If not they must be made so.

There were two main problems to be overcome in this matter, one of which was less pronounced at the time than it became later—the economic interpretation of history. Started by Karl Marx the idea that all history can be interpreted solely by economic causes has come since to have an extraordinary popularity even among those whose own philosophy and sociology are most widely removed from Marx. It is a view which Chesterton would always have dismissed with the contempt it deserves. Both he and Belloc saw as the determining factor in history, because it is the determining factor in human life, the free will of man. This does not mean that they would deny that the economic factor has often been powerful in conquering man's liberty, or a motive in its exercise. But Chesterton regarded the present age as a diseased one precisely because the money motive held so disproportionate a place in it. He looked back to the past and saw the world of today as almost unique in that respect. He looked forward to the future and hoped for a release from it.

And as he looked back into the past he saw something in the history of mankind far stronger than the economic motive—whether that mean the strife for wealth or the mere struggle for subsistence. He saw the all-pervading power of religion, which in bygone ages had presided over man's activities and turned the exercise of that most noble faculty free-will to the building of a civilization today undreamed of.

But in 1914 it was easier to get away from the economic interpretation of history than it was to overcome another difficulty in the minds of those who had not the Chesterton vision of Europe, and to whom it seemed that in a war between nations it was extremely likely that all parties were more or less equally to blame. "History," said Chesterton, "tends to be a façade of faded picturesqueness for most of those who have not specially studied it: a more or less monochrome background for the drama of their own day." But the nature of that background and the vision of today's drama will vary with the varying angle of historic vision.

There were two possible meanings for the statement that all nations were to blame for the world war. All nations had gone away from God. Motives of personal and national greed had ousted the old ideal of Christendom. It might roughly be said that no nation was seriously trying to seek the Kingdom of God and His Justice. International Finance had become a shadow resting on all the earth, and it could not have got this power if Governments had been governing solely for the good of their peoples. "Bow down your heads before God," is the invocation constantly used in the Missal during the penitential season of

Lent and the government of every nation needed this call to repentance.

With this interpretation Chesterton would have agreed. All nations were to blame for the predisposing causes that made a world-war possible. But when we come to the question of actual responsibility for making this particular war, the statement means something very different and something with which Chesterton was prepared to join issue. Against him those who disliked France or England, and saw the history of those two countries as a history of Imperialism, were saying: if Germany had not attacked France, France would have attacked Germany; or: England would have been equally treacherous if it had paid her—look at the Treaty of Limerick.

Chesterton kept imploring people simply to look at the facts. Germany had in fact broken her word to France and attacked her. France had not attacked Germany. Germany had invaded Belgium. England had not invaded Holland "to seize a naval and commercial advantage; and whether they say that we wished to do it in our greed or feared to do it in our cowardice, the fact remains that we did not do it. Unless this common-sense principle be kept in view, I cannot conceive how any quarrel can possibly be judged. A contract may be made between two persons solely for material advantage on each side: but the moral advantage is still generally supposed to lie with the person who keeps the contract." *

The promise and the vow were fundamental to Chesterton's view of human life. Discussing divorce he claims as essential to manhood the right to bind oneself and to be taken at one's word. The marriage vow was almost the only vow that remained out of the whole mediaeval conception of chivalry and he could not endure to see it set at nought. But even in the modern world there still remained some notion of the sacredness of a solemn promise.

* *The Barbarism of Berlin*, 15–16.

"It is plain that the promise, or extension of responsibility through time, is what chiefly distinguishes us, I will not say from savages, but from brutes and reptiles. This was noted by the shrewdness of the Old Testament, when it summed up the dark, irresponsible enormity of Leviathan in the words, 'Will he make a pact with thee?'. . . The vow is to the man what the song is to the bird, or the bark to the dog; his voice whereby he is known." * There were two chief marks whereby it seemed to Chesterton that the Prussian invasion of Belgium was fundamentally an attack on civilization. Contempt for a promise was the first. He called it the war on the word.

The other mark of barbarism he called the refusal of reciprocity. "The Prussians," he wrote, "had been told by their literary men that everything depends upon Mood: and by their politicians that all arrangements dissolve before 'necessity.'" † This was not merely a contempt for the word but also an assumption that German necessity was like no other necessity because the German "cannot get outside the idea that he, because he is he and not you, is free to break the law; and also to appeal to the law." Thus the Kaiser at once violated the Hague Convention openly himself and wrote to the President of the United States to complain that the Allies were violating it. "For this principle of a quite unproved racial supremacy is the last and worst of the refusals of reciprocity." ‡

If these two ideas were allowed to prevail they must destroy civilization and so to Chesterton the war was a crusade and, to his profound joy, was understood as such by the people of England. The democratic spirit of our country "is rather unusually sluggish and far below the surface. And the most genuine and purely popular movement that we have had since the Chartists has been the enlistment for this war." Chesterton loved the heroic humour of the trenches: the cry of "Early Doors" from the boys rushing on death; the term Blighty for

* *Ibid*, 32–33.   † *Ibid*, 37.   ‡ *Ibid*, p. 60.

England and congratulations on a severe wound as a "good Blighty one"; the song under showers of bullets, "When It's Raining Keep Your Umbrella Up." The English, he once said, had no religion left except their sense of humour but I think he meant that they hung out humour somewhat defiantly as a smoke-screen for other things.

Anyhow he doubted neither that the war was worth winning nor that it could be won by our soldiers and sailors. And with the soldiers and sailors stood the munition workers and the Trades Unions which had sacrificed their cherished rights for the war period. If the only danger to England was on the Home Front it was not, in his eyes, to be found in the mass of the nation. Nor was he at first too apprehensive of the actions of the Government. Asquith and Sir Edward Grey might have been slow in declaring war but both were patriotic Englishmen and with them stood with equal patriotism the mass of the governing classes. If as has later been said the war had really been brought about by English political and financial interests, it is strange that Lord Desborough, head of the London house of J. P. Morgan and a leading financier of England, should have lost his two elder sons and the Prime Minister his eldest.

But the *New Witness* did see two dangers at home which might jeopardise the success of our armies in the field and bring about a premature and dishonourable peace. These were international finance, and the Press magnates.

Nothing so reminds me of how we were all feeling about the daily papers just then as finding this letter to E. C. Bentley (dated July 20, 1915):

I was delighted to hear from you though very sorry to hear you have been bad. I mean physically bad; morally and intellectually you have evidently been very good. Seriously, I think you have done something to save this country; for the *Telegraph* continues to be almost the only paper that the crisis has sobered and not tipsified. I take it in myself and know many others who do so. Part of the fun about 'Armsworth is that quite a lot of old ladies of both sexes go about distinguishing elaborately between the *Daily Mail* and the *Times*.* It is a stagnant state of mind created in people who have never been forced by revolution or other public peril to distinguish between the things they are used to and the thoughts for which the things are supposed to stand. If you printed the whole of Ally Sloper's Half Holiday and called it the Athenaeum, they would read it with unmoved faces. So long as St. Paul's Cathedral stood in the usual place they would not mind if there was a Crescent on top of it instead of a Cross. By the way, I see the Germans have actually done what I described as a wild fancy in the Flying Inn; combined the Cross and the Crescent in one ornamental symbol. . . .

I am inclined to think that the attack upon Harmsworth which the *New Witness* developed attributed too much to purposed malice and did not allow enough for the journalistic craving for news and for "scoops." Probably some of the posters and articles to which they objected were not the work of Lord Northcliffe but of some young journalist anxious to sell his paper. Nevertheless the *New Witness* attack was not only largely justified but was also remarkably courageous. The staff of the *New Witness* were themselves journalists and men of letters. In both capacities as powerful a newspaper owner as Lord Northcliffe could damage them severely—and did. Never henceforward would any of them be able to write in one of his numerous papers, never would one of their books receive a favourable review. For Belloc did not hesitate to call Lord Northcliffe a traitor for the way in which he had attacked Kitchener, while Cecil amused himself by reviewing and pointing out the illiteracy of that strange peer's own writing. Later too when the Harmsworth papers were in full cry for the fall of Asquith and the substitution of Lloyd George, the *New Witness* took a strong stand. They pointed out too the way in

* Both these papers were then owned by the same man—Alfred Harmsworth, who had become Lord Northcliffe.

which censorship was exercised against the smaller newspapers while the Northcliffe press seemed immune. Here was the fundamental danger. Whatever the motive, some of the attacks and articles printed were undoubtedly calculated, in military language, to cause alarm and despondency. It was appalling that in time of war this should be permitted; and, as they saw it, permitted because the Harmsworth millions had been used to secure a hold on certain politicians. To the *New Witness* "George" was simply Harmsworth's man.

Meanwhile at Easter, 1916, came the awful tragedy of the Irish rising. Chesterton had fallen into the sleep of his long illness soon after the splendid gesture in which Redmond had offered the sword of Ireland to the allied cause. And there seems little doubt that in making this offer Redmond had with him, for the last time, the people of Ireland. Recruiting began well but that awful fate of stupidity that seems to overtake every Englishman dealing with Ireland even now was overwhelming the two countries. Sir Francis Vane, an Irish officer in the British Army, described in a series of articles in the *New Witness* the blunders made in the recruiting campaign: such things as prominent Protestant Unionists being brought to the fore, national sentiment discouraged, waving of Union Jacks, appeals to patriotism not for Ireland but for England.

Vane himself found his attempt at recruiting on national lines unpopular with authority and in the midst of his successful effort was recalled to England. Still, though recruiting slackened, the cause of the Allies remained in Ireland the popular cause and the Easter Rising was the work only of a handful of men. Its immediate cause was the fact that although the Home Rule Bill had been passed and was on the Statute Book its operation was again deferred. All Irishmen saw this as a breach of faith yet the majority were not at that time behind the rising. The severity of its repression turned it almost overnight into a national cause and erected yet another barrier against friendship between England and Ireland.

For this friendship Chesterton longed ardently and worked passionately, nor did he believe the barriers insurmountable. He even held that there was between the people of the two countries a natural affinity. "There is something common to all the Britons, which even Acts of Union have not torn asunder. The nearest name for it is insecurity, something fitting in men walking on cliffs and the verge of things. Adventure, a lonely taste in liberty, a humour without wit, perplex their critics and perplex themselves. Their souls are fretted like their coasts." * The Irish and the English had suffered oppression at the same hands—those of the rulers of England. If Prussian soldiers had been used against Irish peasants, so too had they been used against English Chartists. A typical Englishman, William Cobbett, had suffered fine and long imprisonment because of his protest against the flogging of an English soldier by a German mercenary.

"Telling the truth about Ireland," wrote Chesterton, "is not very pleasant to a patriotic Englishman; but it is very patriotic." † For the lack of the essential patriotism of admitting past sin the rulers of England were perpetuating an evil that many of them sincerely desired to end. For this was a case where the right road could only be found by retracing the steps of a long road of wrong.

Before the end of the war G.K. visited Ireland and in the book that he wrote after this visit may be found his best analysis of all this matter. Ireland, he believed, was making a mistake in not throwing herself into the cause of the defeat of Germany, not because she owed anything to England but because of what Prussia was and of what Europe meant. Ireland had been the friend of France and the enemy of Prussia

* *A Short History of England,* p. 7.
† *The Crimes of England,* p. 57.

long before England had been either; she would do well to
hold to her ancient allegiance.

It was true that Ireland had been betrayed by the Liberal
promise of Home Rule—but the men who betrayed her were
the Marconi men! Redmond had made the great mistake of his
career when from motives of patriotism for Ireland he had
helped the party hacks of the Government Committee to whitewash these men, who had gone on to betray Ireland as they
were then betraying England. England too needed Home Rule.
England too needed deliverance from her "degenerate and
unworthy governing class."

There are a few pages in *Irish Impressions*—now out of
print—which find their place here in illustration of what he
meant by his championship of nationality:

A brilliant writer . . . once propounded to me his highly personal
and even perverse type of internationalism by saying, as a sort of unanswerable challenge, "Wouldn't you rather be ruled by Goethe than
by Walter Long?" I replied that words could not express the wild love
and loyalty I should feel for Mr. Walter Long, if the only alternative
were Goethe. I could not have put my own national case in a clearer
or more compact form. I might occasionally feel inclined to kill Mr.
Long; but under the approaching shadow of Goethe, I should feel
more inclined to kill myself. That is the deathly element in dena-
tionalisation; that it poisons life itself, the most real of all realities. . . .

Some people felt it an affectation that the Irish should put
up their street signs in Gaelic but G.K. defended it. "It is well
to remember that these things, which we also walk past every
day, are exactly the sort of things that always have, in the
nameless fashion, the national note."

It is this sensation of stemming a stream, of ten thousand things
all pouring one way, labels, titles, monuments, metaphors, modes
of address, assumptions in controversy, that make an Englishman
in Ireland know that he is in a strange land. Nor is he merely

bewildered, as among a medley of strange things. On the contrary, if he has any sense, he soon finds them unified and simplified to a single impression, as if he were talking to a strange person. He cannot define it, because nobody can define a person, and nobody can define a nation. He can only see it, smell it, hear it, handle it, bump into it, fall over it, kill it, be killed for it, or be damned for doing it wrong. He must be content with these mere hints of its existence; but he cannot define it, because it is like a person, and no book of logic will undertake to define Aunt Jane or Uncle William. We can only say, with more or less mournful conviction, that if Aunt Jane is not a person, there is no such thing as a person. And I say with equal conviction that if Ireland is not a nation, there is no such thing as a nation. . . .

* * * *

In September 1916 Cecil Chesterton bade farewell to the *New Witness*. He was in the army as a private in the East Surreys, and G.K. took over the editorship.

I like Chesterton's paper, the *New Witness* [wrote an American journalist in the *New York Tribune* (no, *not* yet Herald-Tribune)], since G.K.C. has taken it over. . . . Gilbert Chesterton seems to me the best thing England has produced since Dickens. . . . I like the things he believes in, and I hate sociological experts and prohibitionists and Uhlan officers, which are the things he hates. I feel in him that a very honest man is speaking. . . . I like his impudence to Northcliffe. . . . As a journalist Chesterton gets only about a quarter of himself into action. But even a quarter of Chesterton is good measure. . . . He works very hard at his journalism. That is why he doesn't do it as well as his careless things, which give him fun. But for all that there is no other editorial page in England or the United States written with the snap, wit and honest humanity of his paragraphs. I hope he won't blunt himself by overwork. It would be an international loss if that sane, jolly mind is bent to routine. England has need of him.

The overwork and the high quality of it were alike undeniable, but after the long repose of his illness G.K. seemed like a giant refreshed and ready to run his course. Each week's

New Witness had an Editorial, besides the paragraphs of which the *New York Tribune* speaks (not all of these however written by himself), and a signed article under the suggestive general heading "At the Sign of the World's End." The difference between articles and a real book, and the degree of work needed to turn the one into the other, may be seen if the essays on Marriage in the paper be compared with *The Superstition of Divorce* for which they furnished material, and those on Ireland with *Irish Impressions*. There were besides very many articles in other papers English and American and he was also writing his *History of England*.

If all Englishmen had kept the same unwavering gaze at reality as Chesterton much of what he called "the rather feeble-minded reaction" that followed the war might have been avoided and with it the advent of Hitler. Particularly he opposed the tendency to call "Kaiserism" what is now called "Hitlerism" and should always be called Prussianism. While agreeing that care should be taken not to write of German atrocities that could not be substantiated he insisted that there was no ground for forgetting or ignoring the findings of the American enquiry in Belgium which had established more than enough. These horrors, the bombing of civilians, shelling of open towns and sinking of passenger ships culminating with the *Lusitania*, were in the main what brought America into the war. Here, as with England, Chesterton did not admit as primary what has since been so exclusively stressed—the economic motive. Here as with England he took the volunteer army as one great proof of the will of a Nation. And those of us who remember can testify that in America as in England the will of the people was ahead of the decision of the politicians.

On one point Chesterton's articles have a special interest: the question of reprisals. When the Germans broke yet another of the promises of the Hague Convention and initiated the use of poison gas there was much discussion as to the ethics of reprisals and G.K. used against reprisals two arguments one of which was a rare example of a fallacy in his arguments. If a wasp stings you, he said, you do not sting back. No, we might reply, but you squash it—you have as a man an advantage over a wasp and so do not need to use its own weapons to defeat it.

His other argument is far more powerful—is indeed overwhelming. If you use, even as reprisals, unlawful weapons, it is harder to prove you did not initiate them. And I remember well another feeling at the time expressed by G.K. which was I believe that of the majority of English people—if we use these things, if we accept the Prussian gospel of "frightfulness" then spiritually we have lost the war. Spiritually Prussia has conquered: as she has engulfed the old Germanies and, first imposing her rule, then gained acceptance of her ideas, so it may be with us. Ideas are everything and the barbarians destroy more with ideas even than by material weapons, horrible as these may be.

Inclined at first to hope for the fruits of democracy from the Russian revolution Chesterton was soon being reproached by H. G. Wells for "dirty" suspiciousness about the Bolshevik leaders and their motives. But the collapse of Russia and the defeat of Rumania alike only strengthened the necessity of the fight to a finish with Prussia that became as the months passed the absorbing aim of the *New Witness*. In the treaties respectively of Brest-Litovsk and Bukarest Germany imposed upon these two countries incredibly harsh terms.

Thus wrote the *New Witness* after the Treaty of Bukarest:

We should like to ask the Pacifists and Semi-Pacifists, who are fond of official documents, if they have read the White Paper dealing with the plain facts about the peace with Roumania. If they have a single word to say on the subject, we should be much interested to hear what it is. It makes absolutely plain two facts, both of which have a sort of frightful humour after all the humanitarian talk about no annexations and no indemnities. The first is that the conquerors have annexed in a direct and personal sense beyond what is commonly meant by annexation; the second is that they have indemnified themselves by an immediate coercion and extortion, which is generally veiled by the forms of a recognised indemnity. In annexing some nine thousand square miles, they have been particular to attach whole forests to the hunting-grounds of Hungarian nobles and the timber of Hungarian wood merchants; not merely annexing as a conqueror annexes, but rather stealing as an individual steals. Further, the fun growing fast and furious, they have taken country containing a hundred and thirty thousand Roumanians, merely because it is uninhabited land. For the second point, we often speak figuratively of tyrants enslaving a country; but Teutons do literally enslave. All the males of the occupied land, which happens to be two-thirds of Roumania, are driven to work on pain of death or prison. All this is clear and satisfactory enough; but the White Paper keeps the best to the last. It is this sentence we would commend to our peaceful friends: "The German delegates informed the Roumanian delegates, who were appalled at being required to accept such conditions, that they would appreciate their moderation when they knew those which would be imposed on the Western Powers after the victory of the Central Empires."

The reminder was needed. Far less than most people was Chesterton subject to that weakness of the human spirit that brings weariness in sustained effort and premature relaxation. Prussia had not, he said, shown any evidence of repentance—merely of regret for lack of success. The Kaiser said he had not wanted this war. No, said Chesterton, he wanted a very different war. Chesterton might and did say later that he himself had wanted a very different peace—the destruction of Prussia, the reconstruction of the old German states—but at present he wanted only to fight on until this became possible.

I do not think he ever hated anybody—but he did hate Prussianism as the "wickedness that hindered loving," and he had no liking for "the patronizing pacifism of the gentleman [it was Romain Rolland] who took a holiday in the Alps and said he was above the struggle; as if there were any Alp from which the soul can look down on Calvary. There is, indeed, one mountain among them that might be very appropriate to so detached an observer—the mountain named after Pilate, the man who washed his hands." *

His keen imagination could visualize the sufferings caused by war. Vicariously he knew something of the life of the trenches, for Cecil like many another C. Man † had managed to get to France. A delightful article on Comradeship shows, what letters from soldiers confirm, how perfectly at home was Private Chesterton among his fellows and how much loved by them.

I can understand a pagan, but not a Christian, who simply dismisses the suffering of our soldiers as useless. He is like Dr. Hyde scorning Father Damien or like those who cried at the foot of the Cross: He saved others, Himself He cannot save. They saved others these men, their suffering was that of the human race whose head is Christ. With Him they bore, even if they knew it not, that mysterious burden of humanity that makes some men question God's existence but draws others into conscious membership of His mystical body. Many were so drawn in those days and there seemed a new lifting up of the Cross. The *New Witness* does, I think, lack one note a little. They were too busy hating Prussianism to give thought to the Christian command to love Prussians, whose sufferings too were those of humanity.

Into the opposite error there was no risk that they would fall. Never for them would heroism be belittled in the name of the very horrors it was encountering. In one article Belloc touched on this strange perversion and reminded his readers that the power to ravage and destroy was not really a new result of modern machinery. Attila and his Huns had inflicted even greater devastation and had left a desert behind them. Bar-

---

* *Uses of Diversity*, p. 40 (Fountain Library)
† English soldiers are classed A. B. or C., according to their degree of physical fitness, and Cecil was in Class C.

barism in its nature was destructive and we were encountering barbarism. In so doing we were acting the part of Christian men.

But the old fights still had to be waged on the home front: against the money power and against what the *New Witness* called Prussianism at home. Unceasingly they battled for fair treatment for soldiers' wives and children, for freedom from unmeaning and unnecessary regulations, against the profiteering by big firms and the consequent crushing of small. About two thousand small butchers' shops for instance had to close at the very beginning of the war owing to a cornering of supplies by the large firms. Against this and all the ramifications of the meat "scandal" the *New Witness* struggled, publishing, they claimed, facts unpublished elsewhere and inspiring questions in the House of Commons. Belloc's irony, Chesterton's wit, point these articles and make them worth reading as literature; and there is some of the old fooling. A further series on the Servile State is attacked by Shaw who thinks that Belloc, since he is not a socialist, must be a follower of Herbert Spencer! G.K. accounts for this by saying that Shaw had not read Belloc. "How do you know," retorts Shaw, "it is not Herbert Spencer I have not read? Suppose you had your choice of not reading a book by Belloc and not reading one by Spencer which would you choose? Hang it all, be reasonable.".

The economic front was never abandoned and the paper continued to attack all forms of Socialism including the re-creation of Bumble by Mrs. Sidney Webb, with all the regimentation of the poor "for their own good" that Bumble represented. The inner secrets of the Fabian Office are unfolded by Shaw in a letter to Gilbert (dated Aug. 6, 1917).

MY DEAR G.K.C.

If you want to expose a scandalous orgy in the *New Witness*, you may depend on the following as being a correct account by an eye witness.

You know that there is a body called The Fabian Research Department, of which I have the hollow honour to be Perpetual Grand, the real moving spirit being Mrs. Sidney Webb. A large number of innocent young men and women are attracted to this body by promises of employment by the said Mrs. S.W. in works of unlimited and inspiring uplift, such as are unceasingly denounced, along with Marconi and other matters, in your well-written organ.

Well, Mrs. Sidney Webb summoned all these young things to an uplifting At Home at the Fabian Office lately. They came in crowds and sat at her feet whilst she prophesied unto them, with occasional comic relief from the unfortunate Perpetual Grand. At the decent hour of ten o'clock, she bade them good night and withdrew to her own residence and to bed. For some accidental reason or other I lingered until, as I thought, all the young things had gone home. I should explain that I was in the two pair back. At last I started to go home myself. As I descended the stairs I was stunned by the most infernal din I have ever heard, even at the front, coming from the Fabian Hall, which would otherwise be the back yard. On rushing to this temple I found the young enthusiasts sprawling over tables, over radiators, over everything except chairs, in a state of scandalous abandonment, roaring at the tops of their voices and in a quite unintelligible manner a string of presumably obscene songs, accompanied on the piano with frantic gestures and astonishing musical skill by a man whom I had always regarded as a respectable Fabian Researcher, but who now turned out to be a Demon Pianist out-Heroding (my secretary put in two rs, and explains that she was thinking of Harrods) Svengali. A horribly sacrilegious character was given to the proceedings by the fact that the tune they were singing when I entered was Luther's hymn *Eine Feste Burg ist Unser Gott.* As they went on (for I regret to say that my presence exercised no restraint whatever) they sang their extraordinary and incomprehensible litany to every tune, however august its associations, which happened to fit it. These, if you please, are the solemn and sour neophytes whose puritanical influence has kept you in dread for so many years.

But I have not told you the worst. Before I fled from the building I did at last discover what words it was they were singing. When it first flashed on me, I really could not believe it. But at the end of the next verse no doubt or error was possible. The young maenad nearest me was concluding every strophe by shrieking that she didn't care where the water went if it didn't get into the wine.* Now you know.

I have since ascertained that a breviary of this Black Mass can be obtained at the Fabian Office, with notes of the numbers of the hymns Ancient and Modern, and all the airs sacred and profane, to which your poems have been set.

This letter needs no answer—indeed, admits of none. I leave you to your reflections.

Ever

G.B.S.

"The Shaw Worm Turns on Wells" was a headline in the *New Witness* over a vigorous and light-hearted attack. The others were apt to score off Wells in these exchanges because he lost light-heartedness and became irritable. Even with Gilbert he sometimes broke out, although in a calmer moment he told Shaw that to get angry with Chesterton was an impossibility. With Cecil Chesterton it was only too easy to get angry—at any rate as he appeared in the *New Witness*. But I think when he heard Cecil was in France Wells must have regretted one of the letters he wrote to Gilbert, just before the change of editorship.

It was curious, the contrast between the genial personality so loved by his friends and the waspishness so often shown by Cecil and his staff in the columns of the paper. "His extraordinary personality," writes E. S. P. Haynes, "wonderfully penetrated the eccentricity of his appearance. His features were slightly fantastic and his voice was as loudly discordant as his laughter; but the real charm and generosity of his character were so transparent that one never seemed to be conscious of the physical medium."

Yet with all my sympathy for many of the *New Witness* ideas my nerves jangle when I read the volumes of Cecil's editorship, and I think jangled nerves explain if they do not excuse this outburst by Wells:

* The refrain of a poem in *The Flying Inn.*

My dear G.K.C.

Haven't I on the whole behaved decently to you? Haven't I always shown a reasonable civility to you and your brother and Belloc? Haven't I betrayed at times a certain affection for you? Very well, then you will understand that I don't start out to pick a needless quarrel with the *New Witness* crowd. But this business of the Hueffer book in the *New Witness* makes me sick. Some disgusting little greaser named —— has been allowed to insult old F.M.H. in a series of letters that make me ashamed of my species. Hueffer has many faults no doubt but firstly he's poor, secondly he's notoriously unhappy and in a most miserable position, thirdly he's a better writer than any of your little crowd and fourthly, instead of pleading his age and his fat and taking refuge from service in a greasy obesity as your brother has done, he is serving his country. His book is a great book and —— just lies about it—I guess he's a dirty minded priest or some such unclean thing—when he says it is the story of a stallion and so forth. The whole outbreak is so envious, so base, so cat-in-the-gutter-spitting-at-the-passer-by, that I will never let the *New Witness* into the house again.

Regretfully yours,

H. G. Wells.

Gilbert replied:

11 Warwick Gardens, Kensington W.

My dear Wells,

As you will see by the above address I have been away from home; and must apologise for delay; I am returning almost at once, however. Most certainly you have always been a good friend to me, and I have always tried to express my pride in the fact. I know enough of your good qualities in other ways to put down everything in your last letter to an emotion of loyalty to another friend. Any quarrel between us will not come from me; and I confess I am puzzled as to why it should come from you, merely because somebody else who is not I dislikes a book by somebody else who is not you, and says so in an article for which neither of us is even remotely responsible. I very often disagree with the criticisms of ——; I do not know anything about the book or the circumstances of Hueffer. I cannot help being entertained by your vision of ——, who is not a priest, but a poor journalist, and I believe a Free-Thinker.

But whoever he may be (and I hardly think the problem worth a row between you and me) he has a right to justice: and you must surely see that even if it were my paper, I could not either tell a man to find a book good when he found it bad, or sack him for a point of taste which has nothing in the world to do with the principles of the paper. For the rest, Haynes represents the *New Witness* much more than a reviewer does, being both on the board and the staff; and he has put your view in the paper—I cannot help thinking with a more convincing logic. Don't you sometimes find it convenient, even in my case, that your friends are less touchy than you are?

By all means drop any paper you dislike, though if you do it for every book review you think unfair, I fear your admirable range of modern knowledge will be narrowed. Of the paper in question I will merely say this. My brother and in some degree the few who have worked with him have undertaken a task of public criticism for the sake of which they stand in permanent danger of imprisonment and personal ruin. We are incessantly reminded of this danger; and no one has ever dared to suggest that we have any motive but the best. If you should ever think it right to undertake such a venture, you will find that the number of those who will commit their journalistic fortunes to it is singularly small: and includes some who have more courage and honesty than acquaintance with the hierarchy of art. It is even likely that you will come to think the latter less important.

Yours, sans rancune,

G. K. CHESTERTON.

P.S. On re-reading your letter in order to be as fair as I am trying to be, I observe you specially mention ——'s letters. You will see, of course, that this does not make any difference; to stop letters would be to stop Haynes' letter and others on your side; and these could not be printed without permitting a rejoinder. I post this from Beaconsfield, where anything further will find me.

It ended as all quarrels did that anyone started with Gilbert:

DEAR G.K.C.

Also I can't quarrel with you. But the Hueffer business aroused my long dormant moral indignation and I let fly at the most sensitive part of the *New Witness* constellation, the only part about whose soul I care. I hate these attacks on rather miserable exceptional people like Hueffer and Masterman. I know these aren't perfect men but their defects make quite sufficient hells for them without these public peltings. I suppose I ought to have written to C.C. instead of to you. One of these days I will go and have a heart to heart talk to him. Only I always get so amiable when I meet a man. He, C.C., needs it—I mean the talking to.

Yours ever

H.G.

Through the war's progress Wells appeared to Chesterton to be expressing with a powerful and individual genius not his own considered views but the reactions of public opinion. As Mr. Britling he saw the war through, and even called it "a war to end war." As Mr. Clissold he asked of what use it had all been. Chesterton speaks of him as a "rather unstable genius," and the genius and instability alike can be seen in his meteor appearances in the *New Witness* and in his books. Several of these he sent to Gilbert, who wrote (Sept. 12, 1917):

I have been trying for a long time, though perpetually baulked with business and journalism, to write and thank you for sending me, in so generous a manner, your ever interesting and delightful books; especially as divisions touching the things we care most about, drive me, every time I review them, to deal more in controversy and less in compliment than I intend. The truth and the trouble, is that both of us are only too conscious that there is a Great War going on all the time on the purely mental plane; and I cannot help thinking your view is often a heresy; and I know only too well that when you lead it, it is likely to be a large heresy. I fear that being didactic means being disproportionate; and that the temptation to attack something I think I can correct leads to missing (in my writing, not in my reading) a thousand fine things that I could never imitate. It is lucky for me that you are not very often a book-reviewer, when I bring out my own shapeless and amateurish books.

In the *Autobiography* G.K. calls Wells a sportive but spiritual child of Huxley. He delighted in his wit and swiftness of mind, but he summarized in the same book the quality which runs through all his work.

I have always thought that he re-acted too swiftly to everything; possibly as a part of the swiftness of his natural genius. I have never ceased to admire and sympathise; but I think he has always been too much in a state of reaction. To use the name which would probably annoy him most, I think he is a permanent reactionary. Whenever I met him, he seemed to be coming from somewhere, rather than going anywhere. . . . And he was so often nearly right, that his movements irritated me like the sight of somebody's hat being perpetually washed up by the sea and never touching the shore. But I think he thought that the object of opening the mind is simply opening the mind. Whereas I am incurably convinced that the object of opening the mind, as of opening the mouth, is to shut it again on something solid.

No change of mood in the public meant any change in the *New Witness* group. In a powerful article in reply to an old friend who asked for peace because the war was destroying freedom, Belloc told him that freedom had gone long since for the mass of Englishmen. "How many," wrote G.K., "pacifists or semi-pacifists . . . resisted the detailed destruction of all liberty for the populace *before the war*? It is a bitter choice between freedom and patriotism, but how many fought for freedom before it gave them the chance of fighting against patriotism?" *

Again and again they touched the spot on the question of trading with the enemy. In this as in all their attacks they made one point of enormous importance. Do not, they said, look for traitors and spies among waiters and small traders—look up, not down. You will find them in high places if you will dare to look. They dared.

And here came in once more what was commonly regarded as a strange crank peculiar to the Chesterbelloc—their outlook

* *New Witness*, May 31, 1917.

towards Jews. Usually those who referred to it spoke of a religious prejudice. Again and again the *New Witness*, not always patiently but with unvarying clarity, explained. They had no religious prejudice against Jews, they had not even a racial prejudice against Jews (though this I think was true only of some of the staff). Their only prejudice was against the pretence that a Jew was an Englishman.

It was undeniable that there were (for example) Rothschilds in Paris, London and Berlin, all related and conducting an international family banking business. There were d'Erlangers in London and Paris (pronounced in the French style) whose cousins were Erlangers (pronounced in the German style) in Berlin. How, the *New Witness* asked, could members of such families feel the same about the war as an Englishman? They could not, to put it at its lowest, have the same primary loyalty to England or to Germany either. Their primary loyalty must be, indeed it ought to be, to their own race and kindred.

Yet this was surely an excessive simplification. We have only to remember that lately a son of the d'Erlanger house died gallantly as an English airman: we have only to remember the thousands of Jews who fought in our ranks in this war and the last. Very many Jews *are* patriotic for England and for America: many were patriotic for Germany. This, no doubt, makes the problem more acute, but any discussion is nonsense that omits this certain fact. There are Jews patriotic first for the country they live in, the country that gave them home and citizenship, of which often their wives and mothers are descended; there are others who feel that Jewry is their *patria*.

This was the fact the *New Witness* could never forget. A Jew might not be specially pro-German in feeling, yet his actions might help Germany by being pro-Jewish. International Jewish trading *was* trading with the enemy and was to a very large extent continuing in spite of assurances to the contrary. Moreover international finance was getting nervous over the continuance of the war as a menace to its own future: it wanted peace, a peace that should still leave it in possession in this country—and in Germany. Gilbert Chesterton was passionately determined to cast it out.

He was a Zionist. He wished for the Jewish people the peaceful possession of a country of their own, but he demanded urgently that they should no longer be allowed to govern his country. Marconi still obsessed him, and the surrender of English politics to the money power seemed to him to represent as great a danger for the future as Prussianism. For a moment the two dangers were the one danger, and against them was set the people of England.

It was at this moment that Chesterton published his epic of the English people which he called a History. Frank Swinnerton has told * how this book came to be written. Chatto & Windus (for whom Swinnerton worked) had asked G.K. to write a history of England: he refused "on the ground that he was no historian." Later he signed a contract with the same publishers for a book of essays, then discovered that he was already under contract to give this book to another firm. He asked Chatto & Windus to cancel their contract and offered to write something else for them. Swinnerton's account continues:

The publishers, concealing jubilation, sternly recalled their original proposal for a short history of England. Shrieks and groans were distinctly heard all the way from Beaconsfield, but the promise was kept. The *Short History of England* was what Chesterton must have called a wild and awful success. It probably has been the most generally read of all his books. But while the credit for it is his, he must not be blamed for impudence in essaying history, when the inspiration arose in another's head (not mine) and when in fact no man ever went to the writing of a literary work with less confidence.

You can find no dates in this History and a minimum of facts, but you can find vision. The history professors at London Uni-

* *Georgian Scene*, p. 93.

versity said to Lawrence Solomon that it was full of inaccuracies, yet "He's got something we hadn't got." G.K. might well have borrowed from Newman and called it an Essay in Aid of a History of England. He showed "something of the great moral change which turned the Roman Empire into Christendom, by which each great thing, to which it afterwards gave birth, was baptised into a promise or at least into a hope of permanence. It may be that each of its ideas was, as it were, mixed with immortality."

The English people had been free and happy as a part of this great thing, cultivating their own land, establishing by their Guilds a social scheme based upon "pity and a craving for equality," building cathedrals and worshipping God, with the "Holy Land much nearer to a plain man's house than Westminster, and immeasurably nearer than Runnymede." All life was made lovely by "this prodigious presence of a religious transfiguration in common life" and only began to darken with the successful "Rebellion of the Rich" under Henry VIII.

Probably too big a proportion is given by Chesterton to the great crime that overshadowed for him the rest of English history. Yet he does justice in brilliant phrasing to the Eighteenth Century Whigs: still more to Chatham and Burke and to Dr. Johnson whom he so loved and to whom he was often compared. But supremely he loved Nelson "who dies with his stars on his bosom and his heart upon his sleeve." For Nelson was the type and chief exemplar of the ordinary Englishman.

. . . The very hour of his death, the very name of his ship, are touched with that epic completeness which critics call the long arm of coincidence and prophets the hand of God. His very faults and failures were heroic, not in a loose but in a classic sense; in that he fell only like the legendary heroes, weakened by a woman, not foiled by any foe among men. And he remains the incarnation of a spirit in the English that is purely poetic; so poetic that it fancies itself a thousand things, and sometimes even fancies itself prosaic. At a recent date, in an age of reason, in a country already calling itself dull and business-like, with top-hats and factory chimneys already beginning to rise like towers of funereal efficiency, this country clergyman's son moved to the last in a luminous cloud, and acted a fairy tale. He shall remain as a lesson to those who do not understand England, and a mystery to those who think they do. In outward action he led his ships to victory and died upon a foreign sea; but symbolically he established something indescribable and intimate, something that sounds like a native proverb; he was the man who burnt his ships, and who for ever set the Thames on fire.

The *Ballad of the White Horse* had been a poem about English legends and origins. The *History* too was called a poem by the reviewers. And it was. It was a poem about Falstaff and Sam Weller and even the Artful Dodger who in so many British colonies had turned into Robinson Crusoe. His rulers had tried to educate him, they had tried to Germanize him and to teach him "to embrace a Saxon because he was the other half of an Anglo-Saxon." All English culture had been based for a century and more on ardent admiration for German *Kultur*. And then—

. . . the day came, and the ignorant fellow found he had other things to learn. And he was quicker than his educated countrymen, for he had nothing to unlearn.

He in whose honour all had been said and sung, stirred, and stepped across the border of Belgium. Then were spread out before men's eyes all the beauties of his culture and all the benefits of his organization; then we beheld under a lifting daybreak what light we had followed and after what image we had laboured to refashion ourselves. Nor in any story of mankind has the irony of God chosen the foolish things so catastrophically to confound the wise. For the common crowd of poor and ignorant Englishmen, because they only knew that they were Englishmen, burst through the filthy cobwebs of four hundred years and stood where their fathers stood when they knew that they were Christian men. The English poor, broken in every revolt, bullied by every fashion, long despoiled of property, and now being despoiled of liberty, entered history with a noise of trumpets, and turned themselves in two years into one of the iron armies of the world. And when the critic of politics and literature, feeling that this war is after all heroic, looks around him to find the hero, he can point to nothing but a mob.

Chapter XXII

After the Armistice

T HE MONTHS THAT followed the signing of the Armistice were the darkest in Gilbert Chesterton's life. Nothing but the immense natural high spirits of the *New Witness* group could have carried them through the many years in which they cried their unheeded warnings to England. But now as the war drew to an end a new note of optimism had become audible. The Prussian menace was almost conquered. Our soldiers would return and would bring with them the courage and confidence of victors. They might overthrow the governing plutocracy and build again an England of freedom and sanity. But one soldier did not return—the one to whom this group looked for comradeship and inspiration. On December 6, 1918, Cecil Chesterton died in hospital in France.

"His courage was heroic, native, positive and equal," wrote Belloc, "always at the highest potentiality of courage. . . ."

Gilbert wrote:

He lived long enough to march to the victory which was for him a supreme vision of liberty and the light. The work which he put first he did before he died. The work which he put second, but very near to the other, he left for us to do. There are many of us who will abandon many other things, and recognize no greater duty than to do it.

This second work was the fight at home against corruption and for freedom for the English people. It is impossible to remember Gilbert Chesterton vividly and to write the word bitter-

ness. It was rather with a profound and burning indignation
that he thought of his fellow Englishmen who had fought and
died—and then looked up and saw "Marconi George" and
"Marconi Isaacs," still rulers of the fate of his country. Thus
meditating he wrote an "Elegy in a Country Churchyard."

> The men that worked for England
> They have their graves at home:
> And bees and birds of England
> About the cross can roam.
>
> But they that fought for England,
> Following a falling star,
> Alas, alas for England
> They have their graves afar.
>
> And they that rule in England,
> In stately conclave met,
> Alas, alas for England
> They have no graves as yet.*

Strange irony of Cecil Chesterton's last weeks: his old enemy
Godfrey Isaacs brought an action for perjury against Sir Charles
Hobhouse. Both men's Counsel agreed and the judge stressed
that perjury lay on one side or the other. The case was given
against Isaacs. He appealed and his appeal was dismissed.
Perjury had lain on one side or the other!

Meanwhile news came that Rufus Isaacs, now Lord Reading,
had gone with Lloyd George to Paris to attend the Peace Conference. All that this might mean: the peril to Poland: the
danger of a Prussia kept at the head of the Germanies for the
sake of international finance: an abasement of England before
those countries that had not forgotten Marconi: all this was
vivid to Gilbert Chesterton. In the same number of the *New
Witness* in which he mourned his brother (Dec. 13, 1918), he
wrote under "The Sign of the World's End" an Open Letter to
Lord Reading:

* *Collected Poems*, p. 65.

My Lord—I address to you a public letter as it is upon a public question: it is unlikely that I should ever trouble you with any private letter on any private question; and least of all on the private question that now fills my mind. It would be impossible altogether to ignore the irony that has in the last few days brought to an end the great Marconi duel in which you and I in some sense played the part of seconds; that personal part of the matter ended when Cecil Chesterton found death in the trenches to which he had freely gone; and Godfrey Isaacs found dismissal in those very Courts to which he once successfully appealed. But believe me I do not write on any personal matter; nor do I write, strangely enough perhaps, with any personal acrimony. On the contrary, there is something in these tragedies that almost unnaturally clarifies and enlarges the mind; and I think I write partly because I may never feel so magnanimous again. It would be irrational to ask you for sympathy; but I am sincerely moved to offer it. You are far more unhappy; for your brother is still alive.

If I turn my mind to you and your type of politics it is not wholly and solely through that trick of abstraction by which in moments of sorrow a man finds himself staring at a blot on the tablecloth or an insect on the ground. I do, of course, realise, with that sort of dull clarity, that you are in practise a blot on the English landscape, and that the political men who made you are the creeping things of the earth. But I am, in all sincerity, less in a mood to mock at the sham virtues they parade than to try to imagine the more real virtues which they successfully conceal. In your own case there is the less difficulty, at least in one matter. I am very willing to believe that it was the mutual dependence of the members of your family that has necessitated the sacrifice of the dignity and independence of my country; and that if it be decreed that the English nation is to lose its public honour, it will be partly because certain men of the tribe of Isaacs kept their own strange private loyalty. I am willing to count this to you for a virtue as your own code may interpret virtue; but the fact would alone be enough to make me protest against any man professing your code and administering our law. And it is upon this point of your public position, and not upon any private feelings, that I address you today.

Not only is there no question of disliking any race, but there is not here even a question of disliking any individual. It does not raise the question of hating you; rather it would raise, in some strange fashion, the question of loving you. Has it ever occurred to you how much a good citizen would have to love you in order to tolerate you? Have you ever considered how warm, indeed how wild, must be our affection for the particular stray stock-broker who has somehow turned into a Lord Chief Justice, to be strong enough to make us accept him as Lord Chief Justice? It is not a question of how much we dislike you, but of how much we like you; of whether we like you more than England, more than Europe, more than Poland the pillar of Europe, more than honour, more than freedom, more than facts. It is not, in short, a question of how much we dislike you, but of how far we can be expected to adore you, to die for you, to decay and degenerate for you; for your sake to be despised, for your sake to be despicable. Have you ever considered, in a moment of meditation, how curiously valuable you would really have to be, that Englishmen should in comparison be careless of all the things you have corrupted, and indifferent to all the things that you may yet destroy? Are we to lose the War which we have already won? That and nothing else is involved in losing the full satisfaction of the national claim of Poland. Is there any man who doubts that the Jewish International is unsympathetic with that full national demand? And is there any man who doubts that you will be sympathetic with the Jewish International? No man who knows anything of the interior facts of modern Europe has the faintest doubt on either point. No man doubts when he knows, whether or no he cares. Do you seriously imagine that those who know, that those who care, are so idolatrously infatuated with Rufus Daniel Isaacs as to tolerate such risk, let alone such ruin? Are we to set up as the standing representative of England a man who is a standing joke against England? That and nothing else is involved in setting up the chief Marconi Minister as our chief Foreign Minister. It is precisely in those foreign countries with which such a minister would have to deal, that his name would be, and has been, a sort of pantomime proverb like Panama or the South Sea Bubble. Foreigners were not threatened with fine and imprisonment for calling a spade a spade and a speculation a speculation; foreigners were not punished with a perfectly lawless law of libel for saying about public men what those very men had afterwards to admit in public. Foreigners were lookers-on who were really allowed to see most of the game, when our public saw nothing of the game; and they made not a little game of it. Are they henceforth to make game of everything that is said and done in the name of England in the affairs of Europe? Have you the serious impudence to call us Anti-Semites because we are not so extravagantly fond of one particular Jew as to endure this for him alone? No, my lord; the beauties of your character shall not so blind us to all elements of reason and self-preservation; we can still control our affections; if we are fond of you, we are not quite so fond of you as that. If we are anything but Anti-Semite, we are not Pro-Semite in that peculiar and personal fashion; if we are lovers, we will not kill ourselves for love. After weighing and valuing all your virtues, the qualities of our own country take their due and proportional part in our esteem. Because of you she shall not die.

We cannot tell in what fashion you yourself feel your strange position, and how much you know it is a false position. I have sometimes thought I saw in the faces of such men as you that you felt the whole experience as unreal, a mere masquerade; as I myself might feel it if, by some fantastic luck in the old fantastic civilisation of China, I were raised from the Yellow Button to the Coral Button, or from the Coral Button to the Peacock's Feather. Precisely because these things would be grotesque, I might hardly feel them as incongruous. Precisely because they meant nothing to me I might be satisfied with them, I might enjoy them without any shame at my own impudence as an alien adventurer. Precisely because I could not feel them as dignified, I should not know what I had degraded. My fancy may be quite wrong; it is but one of many attempts I have made to imagine and allow for an alien psychology in this matter; and if you, and Jews far worthier than you, are wise they will not dismiss as Anti-Semitism what may well prove the last serious attempt to sympathise with Semitism. I allow for your position more than most men allow for it; more, most assuredly, than most men *will* allow for it in the darker days that yet may come. It is utterly false to suggest that either I or a better man than I, whose work I now inherit, desired this disaster for you and yours, I wish you no such ghastly retribution. Daniel son of Isaac. Go in peace; but go.

Yours,

G. K. CHESTERTON.

In those last sentences the spirit of prophecy was upon Chesterton after a truly dark and deep fashion. Yet even he did not guess that the retribution he feared would fall, not upon that "tribe of Isaacs" thus established in English government, but upon the unfortunate Jewish people as a whole, from the German nation that Isaacs had gone to Paris to protect. For there was no doubt in Chesterton's mind that it was his work at the Peace Conference to strive for the survival of Prussia, no matter how Europe and the rest of the Germanies suffered. The *New Witness* hated the Treaty of Versailles in its eventual form as much as Hitler hates it, but for a very different reason.

All human judgments are limited and no doubt there was a mixture of truth and error in Chesterton's view of the years that followed. But in the universal reaction from the war-spirit to Pacifism the truths he was urging received scant attention, his really amazing prophecies fell on deaf ears. "He will almost certainly," Monsignor Knox has said,* "be remembered as a prophet, in an age of false prophets." And it is not insignificant that today it has become the fashion to say, as he said twenty-five years ago and steadily reiterated, that the peace of 1918 was only an armistice.

Just before leaving England for the Front, Cecil had married Miss Ada Jones, who had long worked with him on the paper, and who continued to write both for it and later for *G.K.'s Weekly*, doing especially the dramatic criticism under the pen-name of J. K. Prothero. Later on she was to become famous for her exploit in spending a fortnight investigating in the guise of a tramp the London of down-and-out women. She wrote *In Darkest London* and founded the Cecil Houses to improve the very bad conditions she had discovered and in memory of her husband. At this date Mrs. Cecil Chesterton visited Poland and wrote a series of articles describing the Polish struggle for life and freedom. Several Poles also contributed articles to the paper. There was not I imagine on the staff one single writer with the

* In the panegyric preached in Westminster Cathedral, June 27, 1936.

kind of ignorance that enabled Lloyd George to confess in Paris that he did not know where Teschen was.

Here was the first tragedy of Versailles. The representatives of both America and England were ignorant of the reality of Europe: Wilson was (as Chesterton often said) a much better man than Lloyd George, but he knew as little of the world which he had come to reconstruct. He was, too, a political doctrinaire preferring "what was not there" in the shape of a League of Nations to the real nations of Poland or Italy. And with the American as with the Welshman international finance stood beside the politicians and whispered in their ears. An interesting article appeared in the *New Witness* by an American who said that no leading journal in his own country would print it any more than any English one. He described the opposition of masses of ordinary Americans to the League of Nations and how a Chicago banker, who however had no international interests, had heartily agreed with this opposition. But the same banker had written to him next day eating his own words. In the interim he had met the other bankers. This American correspondent held with the *New Witness* that the League of Nations was mainly a device of international finance so framed as to enlist also the support of pacifist idealists who really believed it would make for peace.

Only one thing, said the *New Witness*, would make for a stable peace: remove Prussia from her position at the head of Germany: make her regaining of it impossible. Make a strong Poland, and a strong Italy, as well as a strong France. Later on they said they had disapproved of the weakening of Austria, but though I do not doubt that this is true in principle I cannot find much mention of Austria in the paper: Poland, Italy and Ireland fill their columns—and the freeing of England.

They claimed that theirs was in the main the policy of Clemenceau—but both Chesterton and Belloc admitted that Clemenceau, even if he desired a strong Poland as a barrier between Germany and Russia, shared with his colleagues an equal responsibility in the destruction of Austria which proved so fatal. He was too much a freemason to desire many Catholic states. The interests of France were not those of Italy, which certainly went to the wall and was turned thereby from friend and ally into enemy. And the *New Witness* summed up the fate of Ireland in the suggestion that Lloyd George had said to Wilson: "If you won't look at Ireland, I won't look at Mexico." Both Lloyd George and Wilson were too anti-Catholic to do other than dislike (in Lloyd George's case *hate* is the word) Catholic Poland. It is certain that Lloyd George in particular worked savagely against the Poland that should have been. A commission appointed by the Peace Conference reported in favour of Poland owning the port of Danzig and territory approximating to her age-long historic boundaries and in particular including East Prussia in which there was still a majority of Poles: Lloyd George sent back the report for revision: they made it again on the same lines.

It was a strange anomaly that this man should have sat at the Council Table representing a great country. In the past men had sat there who not only knew much of Europe themselves but who had as their advisers the Foreign office with all its experience and tradition. Belloc pointed out in an article on Versailles that the English tradition had been to hold a balance between conflicting extremes and thus to bring about a peace that at least ensured stability for a long period. But here was a man too ignorant to realize the dangers of his own ignorance and therefore seek help from experience. This peace would be, Belloc foretold, the parent of many wars. The Czechs got much of what they wanted just as d'Annunzio got Fiume for Italy—by seizing it. Poland waited for Versailles and trusted her allies, yet while the Peace Conference was actually in session Germans were persecuting Poles in East Prussia so that many thousands of them fled into Poland proper and thus diminished the Polish population of East Prussia before any plebiscite could be taken there.

Lloyd George and Churchill sent a British expeditionary force to Archangel to assist the "White" Russians but when the Bolsheviks invaded Poland she was not supported. Nor did the Allies send her the raw material they had promised, to rebuild her commercial life. Again and again our papers reported pogroms in Poland. Yet close investigation by writers for the *New Witness* failed to discover any pogroms in the cities in which they were reported as occurring.

Powerful are the words in which, in April 1919, Chesterton foretells the future that will result if power and her historic port are refused to Poland.

. . . We know that a flood threatens the West from the meeting of two streams, the revenge of Germany and the anarchy of Russia; and we know that the West has only one possible dyke against such a flood, which is not the mere existence, but the might and majesty of Poland. We know that without some such Christian and chivalric shield on that side, we shall have half Europe and perhaps half Asia on our backs.

We know exactly what the Germans think about our nationalities in the West, and exactly what the Bolshevists think about any nationalities anywhere. We know that if the Poles have a port and a powerful line of communication with the West, they will be eager to help the West. We know that if they have no port they will have no reason to help the West and no power to help anybody. We know that if they lose their port it will not be by any act of English public opinion or any public opinion, but by the most secret of all secret diplomacy; that it will not even be given up by the English to the Germans, but by German Jews to other German Jews. We know that such international adventurers would still find themselves floating on the top of any tide that drowned the nations, and that they do not care what nations they drown. We know that out of the whole world the Polish port is the one place that should have been held, and the one place that is being surrendered.

In short, we know what everybody knows and scarcely anybody says.

There is one word to be added for those detached persons who see no particular objection to England ceasing to be English, who do not care about the national names of the West, which have been the greatest words in the poetry of the world. So far as we know there is only one ideal they do care about, and they will not get it. Whatever else this betrayal means it does not mean peace. The Poles have raised revolution after revolution, when three colossal Empires prevented them from being a nation at all. It is not in the realm of sanity to suppose that, if we make them half a nation, they will not some day attempt to be a whole nation. But we shall come back to the place where we started, after another cycle of terror and torment and abominable butchery—and to a place where we might, in peace and perfect safety, stand firm today.

"Not by any act of English public opinion" would Poland be weakened, not by any act of English opinion Prussia strengthened or Ireland oppressed. It was the horror of the situation that no act of English public opinion seemed possible, for the organs of action were stultified. When they *could* act by fighting and by dying Englishmen had done it grandly. Not all that they had done had, Chesterton believed, been lost. Because of them the Cross once more had replaced the crescent over the Holy City of Jerusalem, because of them Alsace and Lorraine were French once more and Poland lived again. But their sufferings and their death had not availed yet to save England.

And what is theirs, though banners blow on Warsaw risen again,
Or ancient laughter walks in gold through the vineyards of Lorraine,
Their dead are marked on English stones, their loves on English
  trees,
How little is the prize they win, how mean a coin for these—
How small a shrivelled laurel-leaf lies crumpled here and curled:
They died to save their country and they only saved the world.*

In the *New Witness* he wrote (July 25, 1919):

On Peace Day I set up outside my house two torches, and twined them with laurel; because I thought at least there was nothing

* *Collected Poems*, pp. 79–80, "The English Graves."

pacifist about laurel. But that night, after the bonfire and the fireworks had faded, a wind grew and blew with gathering violence,
blowing away the rain. And in the morning I found one of the
laurelled posts torn off and lying at random on the rainy ground;
while the other still stood erect, green and glittering in the sun.
I thought that the pagans would certainly have called it an omen;
and it was one that strangely fitted my own sense of some great
work half fulfilled and half frustrated. And I thought vaguely of
that man in Virgil, who prayed that he might slay his foe and
return to his country; and the gods heard half the prayer, and the
other half was scattered to the winds. For I knew we were right to
rejoice; since the tyrant was indeed slain and his tyranny fallen for
ever; but I know not when we shall find our way back to our own
land.

English soldiers in Ireland felt, as we all remember, a strong
sympathy with the Irish people: most of them, said the *New
Witness*, became Sinn Feiners. This was an exaggeration, but
certainly their opposition to acting as terrorists led to the employment in their stead of the jail-birds known as Black and
Tans.

And in England itself the feeling was stirring that grew
stronger as the years passed. The soldiers, who were the nation,
had won the victory, the politicians had thrown it away. A
rushed election before most of the men were demobilized had
brought back the same old politicians by turning, so G.K. put it,
"collusion" into "coalition." A Coalition Government had been
in war-time "comprehensible and defensible; precisely because
it is not concerned with construction or reconstruction but only
with the warding off of destruction." A peace-time coalition
could do nothing but show up the absurdity of the old party
labels. For if these meant anything they meant that their wearers
wanted an entirely different kind of construction, at which
therefore they could not collaborate. How could a real Tory
co-operate in construction with a genuine Radical? It was the
culmination of unreality.

The idea that it succeeded (for the moment) because the country really believed that Lloyd George had won the war seemed to Chesterton the crowning absurdity. It succeeded because the party machines combined to finance their candidates and offered them to a rather dazed country whose men were still in great numbers under arms. "There is naturally no dissentient when hardly anybody seems to be sentient. Indifference is called unanimity."

How then could this indifference be thrown off: How could the returning manhood of the nation be given a true democracy: was there still hope? If there was, never had the *New Witness* been more needed than now. It had told the truth about political corruption, today it had to fight it: "We are not divided now into those who know and those who do not know. We are divided now into those who care and those who do not care." Thus wrote Chesterton in an article about his own continued editorship of the paper.

Politics would never have been my province, either in the highest or the lowest sense. . . . I have hitherto known myself to be merely a stop-gap; but my action, or rather inaction, as a stop-gap, has come terribly to an end. That gap will never be filled now, till God restores all the noble ruin that we name the world; and the wisest know best that the gap will yawn as hopelessly in the history of England as in the story of our private lives. I must now either accept this duty entirely or abandon it entirely. I will not abandon it; for every instinct and nerve of intelligence I have tells me that this is a time when it must not be abandoned. I must accept a comparison that must be a contrast, and a crushing contrast; but though I can never be so good as my brother, I will see if I can be better than myself.

The same attacks on financiers and others constantly reiterated might well have put Gilbert in the dock where his brother had stood. But I think the upshot of the case against Cecil had not been entirely encouraging to the winners. Then too, G.K.'s immense popularity made such an attack a still more doubtful move. Cecil had been less well-known than Gilbert: but far better-known than a Mr. Fraser and a Mr. Beamish, a pair of cranks against whom Sir Alfred Mond brought a libel action in 1919 for having—in a placard shown in a window in a back street—called him a traitor and accused him of having traded with the enemy.

In this case Sir Alfred Mond (of the Mond Nickel Company) giving evidence: "said that he always disregarded charges made by irresponsible persons. Charges had been made against him in the *New Witness*, which was edited by Mr. Gilbert Chesterton. All the world regarded Mr. Chesterton as 'irresponsible,' but he was certainly amusing, and he (the witness) had read most of his books. He had once procured with some difficulty a copy of the *New Witness*." His Lordship—Did Mr. Chesterton charge the witness with being a traitor? Mr. Smith (Counsel for the defence)—Yes, in the *New Witness*.*

"Irresponsible" was not quite the *mot juste*. The unfortunate Fraser and Beamish were not of the metal to win that or any case in that or any court. There was a kind of solemn buffoonery in choosing these two as responsible opponents in preference to the irresponsible G.K. Chesterton. At any rate damages of £5000 were given against them—which gives some measure of the risk G.K. took in making exactly the same attacks.

Gilbert had not so much natural buoyancy as Cecil: he got far less fun out of making these attacks. Still less had he the recklessness that made Cecil indifferent even to the charge of inaccuracy. That charge was in fact the only one that Gilbert feared. Writing to a contributor whose article he had held back in order to verify an accusation made in it, Gilbert remarked that he had no fear of a lawsuit when he was certain of his facts: he did not fear fine or imprisonment:—he had one fear only, "I am afraid of being answered."

There was another thing he feared: hurting or distressing his

* *Times* report of *Mond v. Fraser and Another*, Dec. 3rd, 1919.

friends. This was especially a danger for one, so many of whose
friends were also his opponents in politics or religion: and who
was now editing a paper of so controversial a character. With
H. G. Wells he had a real bond of affection, and an interesting
correspondence with and about him illustrates all Gilbert's qualities: consideration for his subordinates: for his friendships; concern for the integrity of his paper: sense of responsibility to
Cecil's memory.

During an editorial absence the assistant editor, Mr. Titterton,
had accepted a series of articles called "Big Little H. G. Wells"
from Edwin Pugh, which seemed to be turning into an attack on
Wells instead of an appreciation. Chesterton wrote to Mr.
Titterton and simultaneously to Wells himself—

DEAR WELLS,

The sudden demands of other duties, which I really could not
see how to avoid, has prevented my attending to the *New Witness*
lately: and I have only just heard, on the telephone, that you have
written a letter to the paper touching an unfortunate difference
between you and Edwin Pugh. I don't yet know the contents of
your letter but of course I have told my *locum tenens* that it is to
be printed whatever it is, this week or next. I am really exceedingly
distressed to have been out of the business at the time; but if you
knew the circumstances I think you would see the difficulty; and my
editorial absence has not been a holiday. As it is, I agreed to the
general idea of a study of your work by Pugh; and I confess it never
even crossed my mind that anybody would write such a thing except
as a tribute to your genius and the intellectual interest of the subject;
nor can I believe it now. It may strike you as so ironical as to be
incredible; but it is really one of those ironies that are also facts,
that I rather welcomed the idea of a criticism in the paper (which
so often differs from you) from a modernist and collectivist standpoint more like your own. I should imagine Pugh would agree with
you more than I do, and not less. I will not prejudge the quarrel
till I understand more of it; but I now write at once to tell you that
I would not dream of tolerating anything meant to be a mere personal attack on you, even if I resigned my post on the point; and
I had already written to the office to say so. But I do not believe for

a moment that Pugh means any such thing; I regarded him as a strong Wellsian and even more of an admirer than myself; though he might be so modern as to use a familiar and mixed method of portraiture, which is too modern for my tastes, but which many use besides he. For the moment I suggest a possible misunderstanding, which he may well correct by a further explanation. I had said something myself in my weekly article, demurring to a possible undervaluing of you, long before I heard of your own letter. Even when I am in closer touch with things, of course, many things appear in the paper with which I wholly disagree; but the notion of a mere campaign against you would always have seemed to me as abominable and absurd as it does now; I do not believe any one can entertain it; and certainly I do not. I am perfectly willing to do you anything that can fairly be shown to be justice, whether it were explanation or apology or anything else. This is all I can say without your letter and Pugh's side of the case; but I feel I should say this at once.

Yours sincerely,

G. K. CHESTERTON.

P.S. I have arranged for your letter to appear in next week's number; but I may have more light on Pugh's attitude by then.

To Titterton he wrote:

. . . I do hope this work will not turn into anything that looks like a mere attack on Wells, especially in the rather realistic and personal modern manner, which I am perhaps too Victorian myself to care very much about. I do not merely feel this because I have managed to keep Wells as a friend on the whole. I feel it much more (and I know you are a man to understand such sentiments) because I have a sort of sense of honour about him as an enemy, or at least a potential enemy. We are so certain to collide in controversial warfare, that I have a horror of his thinking I would attack him with anything but fair controversial weapons. My feeling is so entirely consistent with a faith in Pugh's motives, as well as an admiration of his talents, that I honestly believe I could explain this to him without offence. . . .

I am honestly in a very difficult position on the *New Witness*, because it is physically impossible for me really to edit it, and also do enough outside work to be able to edit it unpaid, as well as having a little over to give it from time to time. What we should have done without the loyalty and capacity of you and a few others I can't imagine. I cannot oversee everything that goes into the paper; . . . I cannot resign, without dropping as you truly said, the work of a great man who is gone; and who, I feel, would wish me to continue it. It is like what Stevenson said about marriage and its duties: "There is no refuge for you; not even suicide." But I should have to consider even resignation, if I felt that the acceptance of Pugh's generosity really gave him the right to print something that I really felt bound to disapprove. It may be that I am needlessly alarmed over a slip or two of the pen, in vivid descriptions of a very odd character, and that Pugh really admires his Big Little H. G. as much as I thought he did at the beginning of the business. . . . If the general impression on the reader's mind is of the Big Wells and not the Little Wells, I think the doubt I mean would really be met.

Somehow the letter to Titterton got into the hands of a Mr. Hennessy who, after Gilbert's death, sent it to Wells.

Wells wrote, "Thank you very much for that letter of G.K.C.'s. It is exactly like him. From first to last he and I were very close friends and never for a moment did I consider him responsible for Pugh's pathetic and silly little outbreak. I never knew anyone so steadily true to form as G.K.C."

Besides the cleansing of public life two other things were seen as vital by the *New Witness*, the restoration of well-distributed property and the restoration of liberty. Under the heading "Reconstruction of Property" Belloc set out a series of proposals, highly practical and very far from what is usually called revolutionary: that savings for instance made on a small scale should be helped by a very high rate of interest; that the purchase by small men of small parcels of land or businesses or houses should be freed from legal charges while these should be made heavier for those who purchased on a large scale thus encouraging small property and checking huge accumulation. He pointed out how vast sums could be found for such subsidies out of the money spent today on an education which the poor detested for their children and which most of the wealthy admitted to be an abject failure. Most of those, he noted, who oppose Distributism do so on the ground that the proposals are unpractical or revolutionary, which generally means that they have not examined the proposals. His own were certainly practical and would by many be called reactionary. But he admitted one doubt—besides the overwhelming difficulty of turning the current of modern socialism—the doubt whether Englishmen from long disuse had not lost the appetite for property.

Chesterton's own line of approach to the double problem was also twofold. In a volume of Essays published near the end of the war and called *The Utopia of Usurers* he remarked: "That anarchic future which the more timid Tories professed to fear has already fallen upon us. We are ruled by ignorant people."

The old aristocracy of England, in his view, had made many mistakes but certain things they had understood very well. The modern governing class "cannot face a fact, or follow an argument, or feel a tradition; but least of all can they, upon any persuasion read through a plain impartial book, English or foreign, that is not specially written to soothe their panic or to please their pride." There had been reality in the claim of the old aristocracy to understand matters not known to the people. They had read history: they were familiar with other languages and other lands. They had a great tradition of foreign diplomacy. Even the study of philosophy and theology, today confined to a handful of experts, was not alien to them. On all this had rested what right they had to govern. But today "They rule them by the smiling terror of an ancient secret. They smile and smile but they have forgotten the secret."

On the other hand the ordinary workman had the advantage over his probably millionaire master by the necessity of knowing something. He must be able to use his tools, he must know "enough arithmetic to know when prices have risen." The hard business of living taught him something. Give him a chance of more through property and liberty and see what he will build on that foundation. The war had already shown not only the

courage of our men but their contrivance: their trench newspapers, songs and jests: their initiative as sailors and as airmen:
at home the same thing was happening. Allotments had sprung
up everywhere and solved the problem of potato shortage. Men
were doing for themselves a rough kind of building. The in-
clination to get away from the machine and do things oneself
was on the increase.

Armistice and the men's return were heralded by outdoor
tea-parties with ropes stretched across the streets for safety. The
outburst of pageants was spontaneous and national. "It is time,"
said Chesterton, "for an army of amateurs; for England is perishing of the professionals." Vitality seemed to be flowing back
into national life, but Bureaucracy does not love vitality. Agitated Town Councils met and stopped the tea-parties; fought
against street markets through which allotment holders could
sell their produce cheaply; put heavy rates on land reclaimed
and buildings erected by hard work. Town families living in
single rooms had secured plots on building estates and run up
shacks for themselves and their families. They were forbidden
to live in these dwellings—only intended as temporary, but far
more healthy than living eight people to a room in a slum. The
New Witness suspected that the real objection in the eyes of
Councillors was a lowering of the value of neighbouring plots
for wealthier purchasers.

Worst of all, the allotments were taken: fields sold for speculative building, land dug in public parks taken away in the name
of "amenities." The little spark that could have been fanned
into a flame was crushed out.

An episode of a few years later best illustrates the spirit
Chesterton was fighting. In 1926 a threat arose to the traffic
monopoly from soldiers who put their war gratuities into the
purchase of omnibuses which they drove themselves. The London General Omnibus Company decided to crush them and
with the aid of a Government Commission succeeded. Chester-

ton's paper followed the struggle with passionate interest. Just as he believed that the small shop actually served the public better than the large, so too he believed that these owner-drivers would serve it better than the Combine. But if it could have been proved that the Combine was more efficient Gilbert would still have championed the Independents. It was better for the Community that men should take responsibility and initiative for themselves even if the work could be done more efficiently by wage slaves. To his dismay he found that the Trade Unions did not dream of applying this test and that they were aligned against the Pirates—as the independent owners were usually called.

He had always been an ardent supporter of the Trade Unions. To him it had seemed they were trying to do the work of the ancient Guilds under far more difficult conditions. But after the war for the first time a little note of doubt creeps into his voice when he is speaking of them. They were still vocal for the rights of labour, but they had begun to lay stress exclusively on the less important of those rights.

Writing of the loss of the allotments he suggested in one article that the Trades Unions might well use some part of their funds in purchasing land to be held in perpetuity by their members. But I doubt if he much expected that they would do so. Many Trade Unionists were working for the Bus Company and were more concerned about their conditions of work than about the handful of drivers who were their own masters. But the Unions had begun to stress almost solely the question of hours and of wages: to fight for good conditions but no longer for control or ownership: to demand security but to agree to abandon many of their rights in return.

It was a chill fear and for long he resisted it, but in these terrible years it had begun to shake him. Were the people of England losing the appetite for freedom and for property? Were the Trades Unions, from lack of leadership and confusion of thought, beginning to accept the Servile State?

Chapter XXIII

Rome via Jerusalem

SHORTLY AFTER THE war Gilbert and Frances set out on their travels, going in 1919 to Palestine, home through Italy early in 1920, and starting out again the following year for a lecture tour in the United States.

To his friendship with Maurice Baring Gilbert owed their being able to make the first of these journeys as well as much else. The picture entitled "Conversation Piece" of Chesterton, Belloc and Baring is well known. Was it Chesterton himself who christened it "Baring, Overbearing and Past Bearing?" Many elements united the three in a close friendship: love of literature, love of Europe, a common view of the philosophy of history and of life. Frances Chesterton often said that of all her husband's friends she thought there was none he loved better than Maurice Baring. They often wrote Ballades together—a French form which they, with Phillimore and others, had re-popularised in English. A telegram from Gilbert refusing a celebration runs like a refrain:

> Prince, Yorkshire holds me now
> By Yorkshire hams I'm fed
> I can't assist your row
> I send ballades instead.

These "Ballades Urbane" were a feature in the *New Witness* —but many of those the three friends composed were strictly not for publication but recited to friends behind closed doors. Gilbert's memory was useful: he knew all his own and the others:

Once Belloc forgot the Envoi to one of his own ballades and Gilbert finished it for him. Even to Maurice Baring, G.K. wrote less often than he intended and one apologetic Ballade carries the refrain:

I write no letters to the men I love.

I have always fancied that Maurice Baring gave Gilbert the idea for his story *The Man Who Knew Too Much*. First in the diplomatic service, then doing splendidly as an airman in the war, a member of the great banking family, related to most of the aristocracy and intimate with most of the rest, he is like the hero of the book in a sort of detachment, a slight irony about a world that he has not cared to conquer. Impossible for a mere acquaintance to say whether he views that world with all the disillusionment of Chesterton's hero—but anyhow such a suggestion from life is never more than a hint for creative art. Another side is seen in the *Autobiography*—in the stories of Maurice Baring plunging into the sea in evening dress on the occasion of his fiftieth birthday, and of the smashing by Gilbert of a wine-glass that became in retrospect a priceless goblet (which had "stood by Charlemagne's great chair and served St. Peter at High Mass") and now inspired the refrain:

I like the sound of breaking glass.

A good deal of glass was broken by the stones of this group of men whose own house was made of tolerably strong materials.

There is quite a bundle of Mr. Baring's letters to Gilbert, and, in spite of the apologetic ballade, a fair number of answers. Two of these last are written early in 1919, the second of which opens the question of the Jerusalem visit:

May 23, 1919

MY DEAR MAURICE,

I am the Prince of unremembered towers destroyed before the birth of Babylon; I am also the [writer] of unremembered letters, and to a much greater extent the designer and imaginer of unwritten letters: and I cannot remember whether I ever acknowledged properly your communications about Claudel, especially your interesting remarks about the comparative coolness of Henri de Regnier about him. It struck me because I think it is part of something I have noticed myself; a curious and almost premature conservatism in the older generation of revolutionaries, particularly when they were pagan revolutionaries. Not that I suppose de Regnier is particularly old or in the stock sense a revolutionist; but I think you will know the break between the generations to which I refer. I remember having exactly the same experience the only time I ever talked to Swinburne. I had regarded (and resisted) him in my boyhood as a sort of Antichrist in purple, like Nero holding his lyre, and I found him more like a very well-read Victorian old maid, almost entirely a *laudator temporis acti* disposed to say that none of the young men would ever come up to Tennyson—which may be quite true for all I know. I fancy it has something to do with the very fact that their revolt was pagan, and being temporal was also temporary. When that particular fashion in caps of liberty has gone out, they have nothing to fall back on but the feeling which Swinburne himself puts into the mouth of the pagan on the day when Constantine issued the proclamation.

"But to me their new device is barren, the days are bare
  Things long gone over suffice, and men forgotten that were."

I only tell you all this because you might find it amusing to keep an eye on the *New Statesman* as well as the *New Witness,* where there is a small repetition of the same thing. Bernard Shaw has written an article which is supposed to be about his view of me and Socialism; but which may be said more truly to be about his blindness to Hilary and his Servile State. It is quite startling to me to find how wholly he misses Hilary's point; and how wildly he falls back on a sort of elderly impatience with our juvenile paradox and fantasticality. I shall answer him as abusively as my great personal liking for him will allow and I think Hilary is going to do the same; so if you ever see such papers, you might enjoy the fun.

Yours always,
G. K. CHESTERTON.

Dear Maurice,

Thank you ever so much for your interesting letter. I think you
are right every time about Gosse and Claudel; or rather about
Claudel and Gosse. For though I think Gosse a very valuable old
Victorian in his way, I do not think he is on the same scale as the
things that have lately been happening in the world; and Claudel
is one of them. He has happened like a great gun going off; and I
think I saw a line of his on the subject of such a discharge of
artillery in the war. It ran, "And that which goes forth is France;
terrible as the Holy Ghost." I doubt if Gosse has ever seen that
France even in a flash and a bang; I don't see how he could. Remember the religion in which he grew up, by his own very graphic
account of it; a man is not entirely emancipated from such very positive Puritanism by anything so negative as Agnosticism. Nothing
but a religion can cast out a religion. Being so sensitive on behalf
of Renan is simply not understanding the great historical passions
about a heresiarch. It means that famous intellectuals must not
hate each other; because they all belong to the Savile Club. Please
do not think I mean merely that Gosse is a snob; I think he is a
jolly old gentleman and a good critic of French poetry; but not of
Gesta Dei Per Francos. Your points against him are quite logical;
I suppose the controversy will not be conducted in public, or I
should feel inclined to join in it. Anyhow, I wish it could be continued between us as a conversation in private, for I have long
wanted to talk to you about serious things.

Meanwhile, as not wholly unconnected with the serious things,
could you possibly do me a great favour? It is very far from being
the first great favour you have done me; and I should fear that
anyone less magnanimous would fancy I only wrote to you about
such things. But the situation is this. An excellent offer has been
made to me to write a book about Jerusalem, not political but
romantic and religious, so to speak; I conceive it as mostly about
pilgrimages and crusades, in poetical prose, and working up to
Allenby's great entrance. The offer includes money to go to Jerusalem but cannot include all the political or military permissions
necessary to go there. I have another motive for wanting to go
there, which is much stronger than the desire to write the book;
though I do think I could do it in the right way and, what matters
more, on the right side. Frances is to come with me, and all the
doctors in creation tell her she can only get rid of her neuritis if

she goes to some such place and misses part of an English winter.
I would do anything to bring it off, for that reason alone. You are
a man who knows everybody; do you know anybody on Allenby's
staff; or know anybody who knows anybody on Allenby's staff;
or know anybody who would know anybody who would know
anything about it? I am told that it cannot be done as yet in the
ordinary way by Cook's; and that the oracle must be worked in
some such fashion. If you should be so kind as to refer to any worried soldier or official, I should like it understood that I am not
nosing about touching any diplomatic or military matter; France
in Syria, or any copy for the *New Witness*. I only want to write
semi-historical rhetoric on the spot. If you could possibly help in
this matter, I really think you would be helping things you yourself care about; and one person, not myself, who deserves it. I will
not say it would be killing two birds with one stone, which might
seem a tragic metaphor; but bringing one bird at least to life; and
allowing the other bird, who is a goose, to go on a wild goose-
chase.

Yours always,
G. K. CHESTERTON.

It was much needed change and refreshment for both Gilbert
and Frances. Her Diary shows a vivid enjoyment of all the
scenes and happenings: going into the Church of the Nativity
with a door "so low you can hardly get in—this done to prevent
the cattle from straying in"; seeing camels on the roof of a convent; standing godmother to an Armenian carpenter's baby:

The officiator in a cape of white silk embroidered in gold and a
wonderful crown supposed to represent the temple. The godfather
(a young man) was in a red velvet gown. After a good many
prayers and much chanting the babe, beautifully dressed, was
taken to the font (which was in the side of the wall) and there
were more prayers and chanting. Then cushions were laid on the
floor and the child undressed, all of us assisting. At this point I
was asked to stand Godmother and gladly consented. The baby,
by this time quite naked, was handed to the priest who immersed
him completely under the water three times—giving him the name
of Pedros (Peter). Before being re-clothed he was anointed with

oil—the forehead, eyes, nose, mouth, ears, heart, hands and feet all being signed with the Cross. The child was by this time crying lustily and it was some business to get him dressed, especially as he was swaddled in bands very completely. When ready he was handed to me and he lay stiff in my arms whilst I held two large lighted candles. I followed the priest from the font to the little altar, where a chain and a little gold cross were bound round his head (signifying that he was now a Christian). Then the priest touched his lips with the sacramental wafer, and touched his nose with myrrh. After the Blessing, we left the church in a procession, the godfather carrying the baby. At the threshold of the house the priest took it and delivered it to the mother who sat waiting for it, also holding the two candles. Again the priests muttered a few prayers and blessed mother, child and godparents. The father is an Armenian carpenter by trade—very nice people. Mother very pretty. The parents insisted that we should stay for refreshments and we were handed a very nice liquor in lovely little glasses and a very beautiful sort of pastry. Afterwards cups of weak tea and cakes.

The various rites and ceremonies in Jerusalem interested Frances deeply but the Diary shows no awareness of the differences that separated the various kinds of Christians. The Diary ends with the return through Rome where she and I met, to the surprise of both of us, in the street, while a friend travelling with them met my mother. "Both meetings were miraculous," Frances comments. Since the letters to my mother during Gilbert's illness in 1915 we had heard no more about his spiritual pilgrimage. There was much eager talk at this meeting but no opportunity occurred and certainly none was sought for any confidences. As we waved goodbye after their departing train my mother said thoughtfully: "Frances did rather play off Jerusalem against Rome, didn't she?"

In fact, as we learned later, this visit to Jerusalem had been a determining factor in Gilbert's conversion. Many people both in and outside the Church had been wondering what had so long delayed him. The mental progress from the vague Liberalism of the *Wild Knight* to the splendid edifice of *Orthodoxy* had been a swift one. For the book was written in 1908 and already several years earlier in *Heretics* and in his newspaper contests with Blatchford, Gilbert Chesterton had shown his firm belief in the Godhead of Our Lord, in Sacraments, in Priesthood and in the Authority of the Church. But it was not yet the Catholic and Roman Church. There is a revealing passage in the *Autobiography*: "And then I happened to meet Lord Hugh Cecil. I met him at the house of Wilfrid Ward, that great clearing house of philosophies and theologies. . . . I listened to Lord Hugh's very lucid statements of his position. . . . The strongest impression I received was that he was a Protestant. I was myself still a thousand miles from being a Catholic; but I think it was the perfect and solid Protestantism of Lord Hugh that fully revealed to me that I was no longer a Protestant."

The time that thousand miles took is a real problem—the years before the illness during which he talked of joining the Church, the seven further years before he joined it. Cecil Chesterton had been received before the war—just at the beginning of the Marconi Case, in fact—and the entire outlook of both brothers had seemed to make this inevitable, not only theologically but sociologically and historically. Alike in their outlook on Europe today or on the great ages of the past, it was a Catholic civilisation based on Catholic theology that seemed to them the only true one for a full and rich human development.

I think in this matter a special quality and its defect could be seen in Gilbert. For most people intensity of thought is much more difficult than action. With him it was the opposite. He used his mind unceasingly, his body as little as possible. I remember one day going to see them when he had a sprained ankle and learning from Frances how happy it made him because nobody could bother him to take exercise. The whole of practical life he left to her. But joining the Church was not only something to be thought about, it was something really practical that had to be done, and here Frances could not help him.

"He will need Frances," said Father O'Connor to my mother, "to take him to church, to find his place in his prayer-book, to examine his conscience for him when he goes to Confession. He will never take all those hurdles unaided." Frances never lifted a finger to prevent Gilbert from joining the Catholic Church. But obviously before she was convinced herself she could not help him. The absence of help was in this case a very positive hindrance.

I remember one day on a picnic Gilbert coming up to me with a very disconsolate expression and asking where Frances was. I said, "I don't know but I can easily find her. Do you want her?" He answered, "I don't want her now but I may want her at any minute." Many men depend upon their wives but very few men admit it so frankly. And if he was unpractical to a point almost inconceivable, Frances herself could be called practical only in comparison with him. The confused mass of papers through which she had to hunt to find some important document lingers in the memory.

Another element that made action lag behind conviction with Chesterton was his perpetual state of overwork. Physically inactive, his mind was never barren but issued in an immense output: several books every year besides editing and articles: there were even two years in which no fewer than six books were published. To focus his attention on the deepest matters, it was vital to escape from the net of work and worry.

Returning from Jerusalem, Gilbert wrote from Alexandria to Maurice Baring:

My dear Maurice,

To quote a poet we agree in thinking ridiculously underrated by recent fashions, my boat is on the shore and my bark is on the sea; but before I go, Tom Moore (if I may so by a flight of fancy describe you), I feel impelled to send you this hurried line to thank you, so far as this atrocious hotel pen will allow me, for the wonderful time I have had in Palestine, which is so largely owing to you. There is also something even more important I want very much to discuss with you; because of certain things that have been touched on between us in former times. I will only say here that my train of thought, which really was one of thought and not fugitive emotion, came to an explosion in the Church of the Ecce Homo in Jerusalem; a church which the guidebooks call new and the newspapers call Latin. I fear it may be at least a month before we meet; for the journey takes a fortnight and may be prolonged by a friend ill in Paris; and I must work the moment I return to keep a contract. But if we could meet by about then I could thank you better for many things.

Yours illegibly,
G. K. CHESTERTON.

The contract that had to be kept was in all probability the writing of *The New Jerusalem*. It is a glorious book. Until I read them more carefully I had always accepted G.K.'s own view that books of travel were a weak spot in his multifarious output. He said of himself that he always tended to see such enormous significance in every detail that he might just as well describe railway signals near Beaconsfield as the light of sunset over the Golden Horn. But *The New Jerusalem* is no mere book of description. It is the book of a man seeing a vision.

To understand how this vision broke upon him we have first to try to understand something jealously hidden by Gilbert Chesterton—his own suffering. Even as a boy—in the days of the toothache and still more torturing earache—he had written

> Though pain be stark and bitter
> And days in darkness creep
> Not to that depth I sink me
> That asks the world to weep.

So much did he acclaim himself enrolled under the banner of joy that I think most people miss the companion picture to the

favourite one of the Happy Warrior. No warrior can fight un-
tiringly through a long lifetime without wounds, without
temptations to abandon the struggle and seek a less glorious
peace. If in what are commonly called practical matters Chesterton was weak, he was in this almost superhumanly strong. His
fame did not rest upon success in the field of sociology and
politics. He could have increased it by neglecting the good of
England for which he fought, and living in literature, poetry
and fantasy. Here all acclaimed him great, whereas most tolerated or despised as a hobby or a weakness the work he was
pouring into the fight for England. In this time after the Armistice it was by a naked effort of the will that he held his ground.
The loss of Cecil with his light-hearted courage, his energy and
buoyancy, was immeasurable. And I know—for we talked of it
together—that Frances had not the complete sympathy with
Gilbert over the paper that she had over his other work. It
seemed to her too great a drain on his time and energy: it made
the writing of his important books more difficult. She would not,
she told me, try to stop it as she knew how much he cared, but
she would have rejoiced if he had chosen to let it go.

And the fight that he had almost enjoyed in Cecil's company
had become a harder one, not merely because he was alone but
because the nature of the foe had changed. He was fighting now
not individual abuses but the mood of pessimism that had over-
taken our civilisation. In an Article entitled *Is It Too Late?* he
defined this pessimism as "a paralysis of the mind; an impotence
intrinsically unworthy of a free man." He stated powerfully the
case of those who held that our civilisation was dying and that
it was too late to make any further efforts:

The future belongs to those who can find a real answer to that
real case. . . . The omens and the auguries are against us. There
is no answer but one; that omens and auguries are heathen things;
and that we are not heathens. . . . We are not lost unless we lose

MR. AND MRS. CHESTERTON—1922
From a photograph by Alice Boughton

ourselves. . . . Great Alfred, in the darkness of the Ninth Century, when the Danes were beating at the door, wrote down on his copy of Boethius his denial of the doctrine of fate. We, who have been brought up to see all the signs of the times pointing to improvement, may live to see all the signs in heaven and earth pointing the other way. If we go on it must be in another name than that of the Goddess of Fortune.

It was that other Name, in which he had so long believed, that he realised with the freshness of novelty on this journey to Jerusalem. He made in the Holy City and in the fields of Palestine a new discovery of Christ and of the Christian Thing. As he looked over the Dead Sea and almost physically realised what evil meant, he heard the voice of the divine Deliverer saying to the demons: "Go forth and trouble him not any more." In the cave at Bethlehem he realised the "little local infancy" whereby the creator of the world had chosen to redeem the world. All through the book there are glimpses of what he tells more fully in *The Everlasting Man*. Between the two books all that he had seen and thought in Palestine lay in his mind, and grew there, and fructified for our understanding. But he had seen it all in that first vision.

Jerusalem first impressed Chesterton as a mediaeval city and from its turrets he could readily picture Godfrey de Bouillon, Richard the Lion-Hearted and Saint Louis of France. Through the Crusades he views what was meant by Christendom and sets over against it at once the greatness and the barrenness of Islam:

The Moslem had one thought, and that a most vital one; the greatness of God which levels all men. But the Moslem had not one thought to rub against another, because he really had not another. It is the friction of two spiritual things, of tradition and invention, or of substance and symbol, from which the mind takes fire. The Creeds condemned as complex have something like the secret of sex; they can breed thoughts.

Today we of Christendom have fallen below ourselves but yet we have something left of the power to create whether it be a theology or a civilisation. Talking to an old Arab in the desert, Chesterton heard him say that in all these years of Turkish rule the Turks had never given to the people a cup of cold water. And as the old man spoke he heard the clank of pipes and he knew that it was the English soldiers who were bringing water through the desert to Jerusalem.

A chapter on Zionism discusses with sympathy to both parties the difficulties of the Jewish settlement in Palestine. In Palestine he found his Jewish friend and co-worker on the *New Witness,* Dr. Eder, who had gone there ardent in the cause of Zionism; and Chesterton himself remained convinced that some system akin to Zionism was the only possible solution of this enormous problem—possibly a system of Jewish cantons in various countries. But he was equally convinced that the English government was destroying the chances of success for Zionism by sending Jews as governors in England's name to that or any other Eastern country.

Even in this book there is struck at times a note of the doom he feared was overhanging us. He heard "Islam crying from the turret and Israel wailing from the wall," and yet he seemed too to hear a voice from all the peoples of Jerusalem "bidding us weep not for them, who have faith and clarity and a purpose, but weep for ourselves and for our children." In his fighting articles he had asserted the supremacy of the human will over fate: in this book he sees how that will must be renewed, purified and made once more mighty by the same power that built the ancient civilisation of Christendom.

Jerusalem gave to Chesterton the fuller realisation of two great facts. First he saw that the supernatural was needed not only to conquer the powers of evil but even to restore the good things that should be natural to man. As he put it in the later book, "Nature may not have the name of Isis; Isis may not be really looking for Osiris. But it is true that Nature is really looking for something. Nature is always looking for the supernatural." Yet man, even strengthened by the supernatural, cannot suffice for the fight, without a leader who is more than man. In the land of Christ's childhood, His teaching and His suffering, there came to Gilbert Chesterton "a vision more vivid than a man walking unveiled upon the mountains, seen of men and seeing; a visible God."

All visions must fade into the light of common day, and the return home meant the resumption of hard labour.

"For the moment," wrote Gilbert to Maurice Baring, "as Balzac said, I am labouring like a miner in a landslide. Normally I would let it slide. But if I did in this case I should break two or three really important contracts, which I find I have returned from Jerusalem just in time to save."

(A few years later when Sheed and Ward started, Gilbert wanted to write a number of books for us to publish. His secretary found that he had then thirty books contracted for with a variety of publishers!)

He had got home in April 1920: and a lecture tour was planned for the United States at the beginning of the following year. The eight months between saw the completion and publication of *The Uses of Diversity* (collected essays), *The New Jerusalem* and *The Superstition of Divorce*. And still went on the *New Witness*, the *Illustrated London News*, articles, introductions, lectures, conferences. Two letters to Maurice Baring clearly belong to these months:

MY DEAR MAURICE,

I am so awfully distressed to hear you are unwell again; I do not know whether I ought even to bother you with my sentiments; beyond my sympathy; but if it is not too late, or too early,

I will call on you early next week; probably Monday, but I will let you know for certain before then. I would have called on you long ago, let alone written, but for this load of belated work which really seems to bury me day after day. I never realised before that business can really block out much bigger things. As you may possibly guess, I want to consider my position about the biggest thing of all, whether I am to be inside it or outside it. I used to think one could be an Anglo-Catholic and really inside it; but if that was (to use an excellent phrase of your own) only a Porch, I do not think I want a Porch, and certainly not a Porch standing some way from the building. A Porch looks so silly, standing all by itself in a field. Since then, unfortunately, there have sprung up round it real ties and complications and difficulties; difficulties that seemed almost duties. But I will not bother you with all that now; and I particularly do not want you to bother yourself, especially to answer this unless you want to. I know I have your sympathy; and please God, I shall get things straight. Sometimes one suspects the real obstacles have been the weaknesses one knows to be wrong, and not the doubts that might be relatively right, or at least rational. I suppose all this is a common story; and I hope so; for wanting to be uncommon is really not one of my weaknesses. They are worse, probably, but they are not that. There are other and in the ordinary sense more cheerful things I would like to talk of; things I think we could both do for causes we certainly agree about. Meanwhile, thank you for everything; and be sure I think of you very much.

Yours always,
G. K. Chesterton.

My dear Maurice,

This is the shortest, hastiest and worst written letter in the world. It only tells you three things: (1) that I thank you a thousand times for the book; (2) that I have to leave for America for a month or two, earlier than I expected; but I am glad, for I shall see something of Frances, without walls of work between us; and (3) that I have pretty well made up my mind about the thing we talked about. Fortunately, the thing we talked about can be found all over the world.

Yours always,
G. K. Chesterton.

I will not write here of the American scene but will talk of it in a later chapter along with the second tour Gilbert made in the States. It seems best to complete now the story of his journey of the mind. A reserved man tells more of himself indirectly than directly. Readers of the *Autobiography* complain that it is concerned with everything in the world except G. K. Chesterton. You can certainly search its pages in vain for any account of the process of his conversion: for that you must look elsewhere: in the poems to Our Lady, in *The Catholic Church and Conversion,* in *The Well and the Shallows,* and in the letters here to be quoted.

In *The Catholic Church and Conversion* he sketches the three phases through which most converts pass, all of which he had himself experienced. He sums them up as "patronizing the Church, discovering the Church, and running away from the Church." In the first phase a man is taking trouble ("and taking trouble has certainly never been a particular weakness of mine") to find out the fallacy in most anti-Catholic ideas. In the second stage he is gradually discovering the great ideas enshrined in the Church and hitherto hidden from him. "It is these numberless glimpses of great ideas, that have been hidden from the convert by the prejudices of his provincial culture, that constitute the adventurous and varied second stage of the conversion. It is, broadly speaking, the stage in which the man is unconsciously trying to be converted. And the third stage is perhaps the truest and most terrible. It is that in which the man is trying not to be converted. He has come too near to the truth, and has forgotten that truth is a magnet, with the powers of attraction and repulsion." *

To a certain extent it is a fear which attaches to all sharp and irrevocable decisions; it is suggested in all the old jokes about the shakiness of the bridegroom at the wedding or the recruit who takes the shilling and gets drunk partly to celebrate, but partly

* *The Catholic Church and Conversion,* p. 61.

also to forget it. But it is the fear of a fuller sacrament and a mightier army. . . .*

The man has exactly the same sense of having committed or compromised himself; or having been in a sense entrapped, even if he is glad to be entrapped. But for a considerable time he is not so much glad as simply terrified. It may be that this real psychological experience has been misunderstood by stupider people and is responsible for all that remains of the legend that Rome is a mere trap. But that legend misses the whole point of the psychology. It is not the Pope who has set the trap or the priests who have baited it. The whole point of the position is that the trap is simply the truth. The whole point is that the man himself has made his way towards the trap of truth, and not the trap that has run after the man. All steps except the last step he has taken eagerly on his own account, out of interest in the truth; and even the last step, or the last stage, only alarms him because it is so very true. If I may refer once more to a personal experience, I may say that I for one was never less troubled by doubts than in the last phase, when I was troubled by fears. Before that final delay I had been detached and ready to regard all sorts of doctrines with an open mind. Since that delay has ended in decision, I have had all sorts of changes in mere mood; and I think I sympathise with doubts and difficulties more than I did before. But I had no doubts or difficulties just before. I had only fears; fears of something that had the finality and simplicity of suicide. But the more I thrust the thing into the back of my mind, the more certain I grew of what Thing it was. And by a paradox that does not frighten me now in the least, it may be that I shall never again have such absolute assurance that the thing is true as I had when I made my last effort to deny it.†

The whole of Catholic theology can be justified, says Gilbert, if you are allowed to start with those two ideas that the Church is popularly supposed to oppose: Reason and Liberty. "To become a Catholic is not to leave off thinking, but to learn how to think. It is so in exactly the same sense in which to recover from palsy is not to leave off moving but to learn how to move." The convert has learnt long before his conversion that the

* *Ibid*, p. 65.   † *Ibid*, pp. 62–3.

Church will not force him to abandon his will. "But he is not unreasonably dismayed at the extent to which he may have to use his will." This was the crux for Gilbert. "There is in the last second of time or hairbreadth of space, before the iron leaps to the magnet, an abyss full of all the unfathomable forces of the universe. The space between doing and not doing such a thing is so tiny and so vast."

Father Maturin said after his conversion that for at least ten years before it the question had never been out of his mind for ten waking minutes. It was about ten years since Gilbert had first talked to Father O'Connor of his intention to join the Church, but in his case thought on the subject could not have been so continuous. Still he had time for patronising, discovery, and running away, all in leisurely fashion. External efforts to help him had been worse than useless: as he indicates in *The Catholic Church and Conversion,* they had always put him back.

"Gilbert could not be hustled," says Maurice Baring of his whole habit of mind and body.

"You could fluster Gilbert but not hustle him," says Father O'Connor.

They were both too wise to try.

In two letters Gilbert said that the two people who helped him most at this time were Maurice Baring and Father Ronald Knox, who had both gone through the same experience themselves.

Besides the positive mental processes of recognition, repulsion and attraction exercised by the Church, Gilbert was affected to some extent both by affection for the Church of England and disappointment with it. The profound joy of his early conversion to Christianity was linked with Anglicanism and so too were many friendships and the continued attachment to it of Frances. But what he said to Maurice Baring about a Porch is representative. Like Father Maturin he felt he owed so much to his Anglican friends: he hated to stress overmuch the revulsion from Anglicanism in the process of conversion. But it did at this date contribute to the converging arguments.

He wrote to Maurice Baring:

So many thanks for the sermons, which I will certainly return as you suggest. I had the other day a trying experience, and I think a hard case of casuistry; I am not sure that I was right; but also not by any means sure I was wrong. Long ago, before my present crisis, I had promised somebody to take part in what I took to be a small debate on labour. Too late, by my own carelessness, I found to my horror it had swelled into a huge Anglo-Catholic Congress at the Albert Hall. I tried to get out of it, but I was held to my promise. Then I reflected that I could only write (as I was already writing) to my Anglo-Catholic friends on the basis that I was one of them now in doubt about continuing such; and that their conference in some sense served the same purpose as their letters. What affected me most, however, was that by my own fault I had put them into a hole. Otherwise, I would not just now speak from or for their platform, just as I could not (as yet at any rate) speak from or for yours. So I spoke very briefly, saying something of what I think about social ethics. Whether or not my decision was right, my experience was curious and suggestive, though tragic; for I felt it like a farewell. There was no doubt about the enthusiasm of those thousands of Anglo-Catholics. But there was also no doubt, unless I am much mistaken, that many of them besides myself would be Roman Catholics rather than accept things they are quite likely to be asked to accept—for instance, by the Lambeth Conference. For though my own distress, as in most cases I suppose, has much deeper grounds than clerical decisions, yet if I cannot stay where I am, it will be a sort of useful symbol that the English Church has done something decisively Protestant or Pagan. I mean that to those to whom I cannot give my spiritual biography, I can say that the insecurity I felt in Anglicanism was typified in the Lambeth Conference. I am at least sure that much turns on that Conference, if not for me, for large numbers of those people at the Albert Hall. A young Anglo-Catholic curate has just told me that the crowd there cheered all references to the Pope, and laughed at every mention of the Archbishop of Canterbury. It's a queer state of things. I am concerned most, however, about somebody I value more than the Archbishop of Canterbury; Frances, to whom I owe much of my own faith, and to whom therefore (as far as I can see my way) I also owe every decent chance for the controversial defence of her faith. If her side can convince me, they have a right to do so; if not, I shall go hot and strong to convince her. I put it clumsily, but there is a point in my mind. Logically, therefore, I must await answers from Waggett and Gore as well as Knox and McNabb; and talk the whole thing over with her, and then act as I believe.

This is a dusty political sort of letter, with nothing in it but what I think, and nothing of what I feel. For that side of it, I can only express myself by asking for your prayers.

The accident of his having to speak at this Congress, where he was received with enormous enthusiasm, probably led to a fuller analysis of this element in his thought. I put here a letter he wrote to Maurice Baring soon after his conversion, because it sums up the Anglican question as he finally saw it:

Feb. 14th, 1923

Please forgive me for the delay; but I have been caught in a cataract of letters and work in connection with the new paper we are trying to start; and am now dictating this under conditions that make it impossible for it to resemble anything so personal and intimate as the great unwritten epistle to which you refer. But I will note down here very hurriedly and in a more impersonal way, some of the matters that have affected me in relation to the great problem.

To begin with, I am shy of giving one of my deepest reasons because it is hard to put it without offence, and I am sure it is the wrong method to offend the wavering Anglo-Catholic. But I believe one of my strongest motives was mixed up with the idea of honour. I feel there is something mean about not making complete confession and restitution after a historic error and slander. It is not the same thing to withdraw the charges against Rome one by one, or restore the traditions to Canterbury one by one. Suppose a young prig refuses to live with his father or his friend or his wife, because wine is drunk in the house or there are Greek statues in the hall. Suppose he goes off on his own and develops broader ideas. On the day he drinks his first glass of wine, I think it is essential to his honour that he should go back to his father or his friend and say, "You are right and I was wrong, and we will drink wine together." It is not consonant with his honour that he should set up a house of his own with wine and statues and every parallel particular, and still treat the other as if he were in the wrong. That is mean because it is making the best of both; it is combining the advantages of being right with the advantages of having been wrong. Any analogy is imperfect; but I think you see what I mean.

The larger version of this is that England has really got into so wrong a state, with its plutocracy and neglected populace and materialistic and servile morality, that it must take a sharp turn that will be a sensational turn. No *evolution* into Catholicism will have that moral effect. Christianity is the religion of repentance; it stands against modern fatalism and pessimistic futurism mainly in saying that a man can go back. If we do decidedly go back it will show that religion is alive. For the rest, I do not say much about the details of continuity and succession, because the truth is they did not much affect me. What I see is that we cannot complain of England suffering from being Protestant and at the same time claim that she has always been Catholic. That there has always been a High Church Party is true; that there has always been an Anglo-Catholic Party may be true, but I am not so sure of it. But there is one matter arising from that which I do think important. Even the High Church Party, even the Anglo-Catholic Party only confronts a particular heresy called Protestantism upon particular points. It defends ritual rightly or even sacramentalism rightly, because these are the things the Puritans attacked. If it is not the heresy of an age, at least it is only the anti-heresy of an age. But since I have been a Catholic, I have become conscious of being in a much vaster arsenal, full of arms against countless other potential enemies. The Church, as the Church and not merely as ordinary opinion, has something to say to philosophies which the merely High Church has never had occasion to think about. If the next movement is the very reverse of Protestantism, the Church will have something to say about it; or rather has already something to say about it. You might unite all High Churchmen on the

High Church quarrel, but what authority is to unite them when the devil declares his next war on the world?

Another quality that impresses me is the power of being decisive first and being proved right afterwards. This is exactly the quality a supernatural power would have; and I know nothing else in modern religion that has it. For instance, there was a time when I should have thought psychical enquiry the most reasonable thing in the world, and rather favourable to religion. I was afterwards convinced, by experience and not merely faith, that Spiritualism is a practical poison. Don't people see that *when* that is found in experience, a prodigious prestige accrues to the authority which, long before the experiment, did not pretend to enquire but simply said, "Drop it." We feel that the authority did not discover; it knew. There are a hundred other things of which that story is true, in my own experience. But the High Churchman has a perfect right to be a Spiritualistic enquirer; only he has not a right to claim that his authority knew beforehand the truth about spiritualistic enquiry.

Of course there are a hundred things more to say; indeed the greatest argument for Catholicism is exactly what makes it so hard to argue for it. It is the scale and multiplicity of the forms of truth and help that it has to offer. And perhaps, after all, the only thing that you and I can really say with profit is exactly what you yourself suggested; that we are men who have talked to a good many men about a good many things, and seen something of the world and the philosophies of the world and that we have not the shadow of a doubt about what was the wisest act of our lives.

This letter, as we have seen, was written afterwards. Meanwhile the story of the last slow but by no means uncertain steps is best told in a series of undated letters to Father Ronald Knox:

Dear Father Knox,

It is hard not to have a silly feeling that demons, in the form of circumstances, get in the way of what concerns one most, and I have been distracted with details for which I have to be responsible, in connection with the *New Witness*, which is in a crisis about which shareholders etc. have to be consulted. I can't let my brother's paper, that stands for all he believed in, go without doing all I can; and I am trying to get it started again, with Belloc to run it if possible. But the matter of our meeting has got into every chink of my thoughts, even the pauses of talk on practical things. I could not explain myself at that meeting; and I want to try again now.

I could not explain what I mean about my wife without saying much more. I see in principle it is not on the same level as the true Church; for nothing can be on the same level as God. But it is on quite a different level from social sentiments about friends and family. I have been a rottenly irresponsible person till I began to wear the iron ring of Catholic responsibilities. But I really have felt a responsibility about her, more serious than affection, let alone passion. First, because she gave me my first respect for sacramental Christianity; second, because she is one of the good who mysteriously suffer. . . .

I have, however, a more practical reason for returning to this point. So far as my own feelings go, I think I might rightly make application to be instructed as soon as possible; but I should not like to take so serious a step without reopening the matter with her, which I could do by the end of a week. I have had no opportunity before, because she has only just recovered from an illness, and is going away for a few days. But at about the end of next week, say, everything ought to be ready. Meanwhile I will write to you again, as I ought to have done before, but this tangle of business ties me up terribly just now. Perhaps you could tell me how I could arrange matters with some priest or religious in London, whose convenience it would suit if I came up once or twice a week, or whatever is required; or give me the address of someone to write to, if that is the correct way. There are priests at High Wycombe which is nearer; but I imagine they are very busy parochial clergy.

I had meant to write to you about the convictions involved in a more abstract way, but I fear I have filled my letter with one personal point. But, as I say, I will write to you again about the other matters; and as they are more intellectual and less emotional, I hope I may be a little more coherent.

Yours very sincerely,

G. K. CHESTERTON.

P.S. This has been delayed even longer than I thought, for business bothers of my own and the paper's, plus finishing a book and all my journalism, are bewildering me terribly.

DEAR FATHER KNOX,

Please excuse this journalistic paper, but the letter-block seems undiscoverable at this time of night. I ought to have written before; but we have been in some family trouble; my father is very ill, and as he is an old man, my feelings are with him and my mother in a way more serious than anything except the matter of our correspondence. Essentially, of course, it does not so much turn the current of my thoughts as deepen it; to see a man so many million times better than I am, in every way, and one to whom I owe everything, under such a shadow makes me feel, on top of all my particular feelings, the shadow that lies on us all. I can't tell you what I feel of course; but I hope I may ask for your prayers for my people and for me. My father is the very best man I ever knew of that generation that never understood the new need of a spiritual authority; and lives almost perfectly by the sort of religion men had when rationalism was rational. I think he was always subconsciously prepared for the next generation having less theology than he has; and is rather puzzled at its having more. But I think he understood my brother's conversion better than my mother did; she is more difficult, and of course I cannot bother her just now. However, my trouble has a practical side, for which I originally mentioned it. As this may bring me to London more than I thought, it seems possible I might go there after all, instead of Wycombe, if I knew to whom to go. Also I find I stupidly destroyed your letter with the names of the priests at Wycombe to whom you referred me. Would it bother you very much to send me the names again, and any alternative London ones that occur to you; and I will let you know my course of action then. Please forgive the disorder of my writing—and feeling.

> Yours sincerely,
> G. K. CHESTERTON.

DEAR FATHER KNOX,

I was just settling down three days ago to write a full reply to your last very kind letter, which I should have answered long before, when I received the wire that called me instantly to town. My father died on Monday; and since then I have been doing the little I can for my mother; but even that little involves a great deal of business—the least valuable sort of help. I will not attempt to

tell you now all that this involves in connection with my deeper
feelings and intentions; for I only send you this interim scribble
as an excuse for delaying the letter I had already begun; and which
nothing less than this catastrophe would have prevented me finishing. I hope to finish it in a few days. I am not sure whether I
shall then be back in Beaconsfield; but if so it will be at a new
address:

Top Meadow
Beaconsfield.
Yours in haste,
G. K. Chesterton.

Dear Father Knox,

I feel horribly guilty in not having written before, and I do most
earnestly hope you have not allowed my delay to interfere with
any of your own arrangements. I have had a serious and very
moving talk with my wife; and she is only too delighted at the
idea of your visit in itself; in fact she really wants to know you
very much. Unfortunately, it does not seem very workable at the
time to which I suppose you referred. I imagine it more or less
corresponds to next week; and we have only one spare bedroom
yet, which is occupied by a nurse who is giving my wife a treatment that seems to be doing her good and which I don't want to
stop if I can help it. I am sure you will believe that my regret
about this difficulty is really not the conventional apology; though
heaven knows all sorts of apologies are due to you. Touching the
other idea of Lady Lovat's most generous invitation I am not so
sure, as that again depends at the moment on the treatment; but
of course I shall let Lady Lovat know very soon in any case; and
make other arrangements, as you suggested. In our conversation
my wife was all that I hope you will some day know her to be;
she is incapable of wanting me to do anything but what I think
right; and admits the same possibility for herself: but it is much
more of a wrench for her, for she has been able to practise her
religion in complete good faith; which my own doubts have prevented me from doing.

I will write again very soon.

Yours sincerely,
G. K. Chesterton.

P.S. I am ashamed to say this has been finished fully forty-eight hours after I meant it to go, owing to executor business. Nobody so unbusinesslike as I am ought to be busy.

DEAR FATHER KNOX,

This is only a wild and hasty line to show I have not forgotten, and to ask you if it would be too late if I let you know in a day or two, touching your generous suggestion about your vacation. I shall know for certain, I think, at latest by the end of the week; but just at the moment it depends on things still uncertain, about a nurse who is staying here giving my wife a treatment of radiant heat—one would hardly think needed in this weather; but it seems to be doing her good, I am thankful to say.

If this is pushing your great patience too far, please do not hesitate to make other arrangements if you wish to; and I shall no doubt be able to do the same. But I should love to accept your suggestion if possible.

Yours sincerely,
G. K. CHESTERTON.

DEAR FATHER KNOX,

Just as I am emerging from the hurricane of business I mentioned to you, I find myself under a promise a year old to go and lecture for a week in Holland; and I write this almost stepping on to the boat. I don't in the least want to go; but I suppose the great question is there as elsewhere. Indeed, I hear it is something of a reconquered territory; some say a third of this heroic Calvinist state is now Catholic. I have no time to write properly; but the truth is that even before so small a journey I have a queer and perhaps superstitious feeling that I should like to repeat to you my intention of following the example of the worthy Calvinists, please God; so that you could even cite it if there were ever need in a good cause. I will write to you again and more fully about the business of instruction when I return, which should be in about ten days.

Yours always sincerely,
G. K. CHESTERTON.

DEAR FATHER KNOX,

I ought to have written long ago to tell you what I have done about the most practical of business matters. I have again been torn in pieces by the wars of the *New Witness*; but I have managed to have another talk with my wife, after which I have written to our old friend Father O'Connor and asked him to come here, as he probably can, from what I hear. I doubt whether I can possibly put in words why I feel sure this is the right thing, not so much for my sake as for hers. We talk about misunderstandings; but I think it is possible to understand too well for comfort; certainly too well for my powers of psychological description. Frances is just at the point where Rome acts both as the positive and the negative magnet; a touch would turn her either way; almost (against her will) to hatred, but with the right touch to a faith far beyond my reach. I know Father O'Connor's would be the touch that does not startle, because she knows him and is fond of him; and the only thing she asked of me was to send for him. If he cannot come, of course I shall take other action and let you know. I doubt if most people could make head or tail of this hasty scrawl: but I think you will understand.

Yours sincerely,

G. K. CHESTERTON.

Father Knox wrote on July 17, 1922, "I'm awfully glad to hear that you've sent for Father O'Connor and that you think he's likely to be available. I must say that, in the story, Father Brown's powers of neglecting his parish always seemed to me even more admirable than Dr. Watson's powers of neglecting his practice; so I hope this trait was drawn from the life."

Father O'Connor has described the two days before the reception: "On Thursday morning, on one of our trips to the village, I told Mrs. Chesterton: 'There is only one thing troubling Gilbert about the great step—the effect it is going to have on you.' 'Oh! I shall be infinitely relieved. You cannot imagine how it fidgets Gilbert to have anything on his mind. The last three months have been exceptionally trying. I should be only too glad to come with him, if God in His mercy would show the way clear, but up to now He has not made it clear enough to me to justify such a step.' So I was able to reassure Gilbert that afternoon. We discussed at large such special points as he wished, and then I told him to read through the Penny Catechism to make sure there were no snags to a prosperous passage. It was a sight for men and angels all the Friday to see him wandering in and out of the house with his fingers in the leaves of the little book, resting it on his forearm whilst he pondered with his head on one side."

The ceremony took place in a kind of shed with corrugated iron roof and wooden walls—a part of the Railway Hotel, for at this time Beaconsfield had no Catholic Church. Father Ignatius Rice, O.S.B., another old and dear friend, came over from the Abbey at Douai, to join Father O'Connor at breakfast at the Inn and they afterwards walked up together to Top Meadow. What follows is from notes made by my husband of a conversation with Father Rice. They found Gilbert in an armchair reading the catechism "pulling faces and making noises as he used to do when reading."

He got up and stuffed the catechism in his pocket. At lunch he drank water and poured wine for everyone else. About three they set out for the Church. Suddenly Father O'Connor asked G.K. if he had brought the Ritual. G.K. plunged his hand in his pocket, pulled out a threepenny shocker with complete absence of embarrassment, and went on searching till at last he found the prayer book.

While G.K. was making his confession to Father O'Connor, Frances and Father Rice went out of the chapel and sat on the yokels' bench in the bar of the inn. She was weeping.

After the baptism the two priests came out and left Gilbert and Frances inside. Father Rice went back for something he had forgotten and he saw them coming down the aisle. She was still weeping, and Gilbert had his arm round her comforting her. . . .

He wrote the sonnet on his conversion that day. He was in brilliant form for the rest of the day, quoting poetry and jesting in the highest spirits. . . .

He joined the Church "to restore his innocence." Sin was almost the greatest reality to him. He became a Catholic because of the Church's practical power of dealing with sin.

Immediately, he wrote to his mother and to Maurice Baring, who had anxiously feared he had perhaps offended Gilbert, so long was it since he had heard from him.

My dearest Mother,

I write this (with the worst pen in South Bucks) to tell you something before I write about it to anyone else; something about which we shall probably be in the position of the two bosom friends at Oxford, who "never differed except in opinion." You have always been so wise in not judging people by their opinions, but rather the opinions by the people. It is in one sense a long story by this time; but I have come to the same conclusion that Cecil did about needs of the modern world in religion and right dealing, and I am now a Catholic in the same sense as he, having long claimed the name in its Anglo-Catholic sense. I am not going to make a foolish fuss of reassuring you about things I am sure you never doubted; these things do not hurt any relations between people as fond of each other as we are; any more than they ever made any difference to the love between Cecil and ourselves. But there are two things I should like to tell you, in case you do not realise them through some other impression. I have thought about you, and all that I owe to you and my father, not only in the way of affection, but of the ideals of honour and freedom and charity and all other good things you always taught me: and I am not conscious of the smallest break or difference in those ideals; but only of a new and necessary way of fighting for them. I think, as Cecil did, that the fight for the family and the free citizen and everything decent must now be waged by [the] one fighting form of Christianity. The other is that I have thought this out for myself and not in a hurry of feeling. It is months since I saw my Catholic friends and years since I talked to them about it. I believe it is the truth. I must end now, you know with how much love; for the post is going.

Always your loving son,
GILBERT.

Dear Maurice,

My abominable delay deserves every penalty conceivable, hanging, burning and boiling in oil; but really not so inconceivable an idea as that I should be offended with you at any time (let alone

after all you have done in this matter) however thoroughly you
might be justified in being offended with me. Really and truly my
delay, indefensible as it is, was due to a desire and hope of writing
you a letter quite different from all those I have had to write to
other people; a very long and intimate letter, trying to tell you all
about this wonderful business, in which you have helped me so
much more than anyone else. The only other person I meant to
write to in the same style is Father Knox; and his has been delayed
in the same topsy-turvy way. I am drowning in whirlpools of work
and worry over the *New Witness* which nearly went bankrupt for
good this week. But worry does not worry so much as it did
before . . . Unless it is adding insult to injury, I shall send the
long letter after all. This I send off instantly on receipt of yours.
Please forgive me; you see I humiliate myself by using your
stamped envelope.

Yours always,

G. K. CHESTERTON.

This sense that the Church was needed to fight for the world
was very strong in Gilbert when he hailed it to his mother as
the "one fighting form of Christianity." In the *New Witness* he
answered near this time a newspaper suggestion that the Church
ought to "move with the times."

The Cities of the Plain might have remarked that the heavens
above them did not altogether fit in with their own high civilisation and social habits. They would be right. Oddly enough, however, when symmetry was eventually restored, it was not the
heavens that had been obliged to adapt themselves. . . .

The Church cannot move with the times; simply because the
times are not moving. The Church can only stick in the mud with
the times, and rot and stink with the times. In the economic and
social world, as such, there is no activity except that sort of automatic activity that is called decay; the withering of the high flowers
of freedom and their decomposition into the aboriginal soil of
slavery. In that way the world stands much at the same stage as it
did at the beginning of the Dark Ages. And the Church has the
same task as it had at the beginning of the Dark Ages; to save all
the light and liberty that can be saved, to resist the downward drag

of the world, and to wait for better days. So much a real Church would certainly do; but a real Church might be able to do more. It might make its Dark Ages something more than a seed-time; it might make them the very reverse of dark. It might present its more human ideal in such abrupt and attractive a contrast to the inhuman trend of the time, as to inspire men suddenly for one of the moral revolutions of history; so that men now living shall not taste of death until they have seen justice return.

We do not want, as the newspapers say, a Church that will move with the world. We want a Church that will move the world. We want one that will move it away from many of the things towards which it is now moving; for instance, the Servile State. It is by that test that history will really judge, of any Church, whether it is the real Church or no.

Chapter XXIV

Completion

THERE IS ONE part of this story that has not been told with the rest: Our Lady's share in Gilbert's conversion. The Chesterton family had been quite without the strange Protestant prejudice that in the minds of many Englishmen sets the Mother of God against God the Son. Our Lady was respected though of course not invoked. In a boyhood poem Gilbert took the blasphemous lines of Swinburne's "Hymn to Proserpine" and wrote a kind of parody in reverse turning the poem into a hymn to Mary. He would, too, recite Swinburne's own lines "deliberately directing them away from Swinburne's intention and supposing them addressed to the new Christian Queen of life, rather than to the fallen Pagan queen of death."

> But I turn to her still; having seen she shall surely
>   abide in the end
> Goddess and maiden and queen be near me now
>   and befriend.

Nor was it only admiration for art that made him write—also in early youth:

THE NATIVITY OF BOTTICELLI

> Do you blame me that I sit hours before this picture?
> But if I walked all over the world in this time
> I should hardly see anything worth seeing that is not
>   in this picture.

Father O'Connor sees in *The Catholic Church and Conversion* a hint that Mr. Belloc had been of those who tried to hustle

Gilbert in his younger days. But on this profound reality of Mary's help they could meet many years before Gilbert had finished the slow rumination of mind and the painful effort of will that had held him so long. Here is an early letter Belloc wrote to his friend:

Reform Club, Manchester.
11 Dec. 1907.

MY DEAR GILBERT,

I am a man afraid of impulse in boats, horses and all action though driven to it. I have never written a letter such as I am writing now, though I have desired to write some six or seven since I became a grown man. In the matter we discussed at Oxford I have a word to say which is easier to say on paper than by word of mouth, or rather, more valuable. All intellectual process is doubtful, all inconclusive, save pure deduction, which is a game if one's first certitudes are hypothetical and immensely valuable if one's first certitude is fixed, yet remains wholly dependent on that.

Now if we differed in all main points I would not write thus, but there are one or two on which we agree. One is "Vere passus, immolatus in cruce pro homine." Another is in a looking up to our Dear Lady, the blessed Mother of God.

I recommend to you this, that you suggest to her a comprehension for yourself, of what indeed *is* the permanent home of the soul. If it is here you will see it, if it is there you will see it. She never fails us. She has never failed me in any demand.

I have never written thus—as I say—and I beg you to see nothing in it but what I say. There is no connection the reason can seize—but so it is. If you say "I want *this*" as in your case to know one way or the other—She will give it you: as She will give health or necessary money or success in a pure love. She is our Blessed Mother.

I have not used my judgment in this letter. I am inclined to destroy it, but I shall send it. Don't answer it.

Yours ever

H. BELLOC.

At top of letter: "My point is If it is right She knows. If it is not right She knows."

Gilbert believed it, and he knew that as he came to the Church he was coming to Our Lady.

Now I can scarcely remember a time when the image of Our Lady did not stand up in my mind quite definitely, at the mention or the thought of all these things. I was quite distant from these things, and then doubtful about these things; and then disputing with the world for them, and with myself against them; for that is the condition before conversion. But whether the figure was distant, or was dark and mysterious, or was a scandal to my contemporaries, or was a challenge to myself—I never doubted that this figure was the figure of the Faith; that she embodied, as a complete human being still only human, all that this Thing had to say to humanity. The instant I remembered the Catholic Church, I remembered her; when I tried to forget the Catholic Church, I tried to forget her! When I finally saw what was nobler than my fate, the freest and the hardest of all my acts of freedom, it was in front of a gilded and very gaudy little image of her in the port of Brindisi, that I promised the thing that I would do, if I returned to my own land.*

In his *Chaucer*, G.K. quoted with considerable amusement a learned critic who said it was "possible" that the poet had "passed through a period of intense devotion, more especially towards the Virgin Mary." "It is," he comments. "It does occur from time to time. I do not quite understand why Chaucer must have 'passed through' this fit of devotion; as if he had Mariolatry like the measles. Even an amateur who has encountered this malady may be allowed to testify that it does not usually visit its victim for a brief 'period'; it is generally chronic and (in some sad cases I have known) quite incurable." †

The Queen of Seven Swords is the great expression of Gilbert's "chronic" love of Our Lady:

> And men looked up at the woman made for the
> morning
> When the stars were young,
> For whom more rude than a beggar's rhyme in
> the gutter
> These songs were sung.

* *The Well and the Shallows*, pp. 176–7.
† *Chaucer*, p. 121.

"The Return of Eve" exemplified a favourite thought of his: when the journalist keeps repeating that the life of religion does not lie in dusty dogmas we should stop him with a great shout, for he is wrong at the very start. It is from the seed of dogma and from that seed alone that all the flowers of art and poetry and devotion spring. In the days of his boyhood, when he thought of Our Lady with a vague and confused respect as "*The* Madonna" he could not have written "The Return of Eve." That flower came from the seed of the doctrine of the Immaculate Conception.

Our Lady is the Mother of God and our Mother: this doctrine blossomed as he wrote:

> I found One hidden in every home
> A voice that sings about the house.
> A nurse that scares the nightmares off
> A mother nearer than a spouse
>
> Whose picture once I saw; and there
> Wild as of old and weird and sweet
> In sevenfold splendour blazed the moon
> Not on her brow; beneath her feet.

This poem, "The White Witch" has in it a mingling of the old classical stories of his boyhood and the new light of Christian reality. In *The Everlasting Man* he saw the myths as hunger and the Faith as bread. Men's hearts today were withered because they had forgotten to eat their bread. The hunger of the pagans was a healthier thing than the jaded sterility of the modern world. Our Lady was ready to give that world the Bread of Life once more. And as he meditated on the mystery of the Virgin Birth he saw God making purity creative. She alone who overcame all heresies could overcome the hideous heresy of birth prevention.

> That Christ from this creative purity
> Came forth your sterile appetites to scorn.
> So: in her house Life without Lust was born,
> So in your house Lust without Life shall die.

"Gaude, Virgo Maria, cunctas haereses sola interemisti." Was this phrase from Our Lady's office ringing in Gilbert's mind as he sang of the Seven Champions of Christendom disarmed and worsted in the fight, going back to Our Lady to find that she had hidden their swords where the gospels tell us she hid and pondered all things—in her heart? From her wounded heart, Mary takes the seven swords to rearm the saints who have to reconquer the earth.

Certainly he must often have thought of the Litany. So many verses are based on it. Our Lord as a baby climbs the Ivory Tower of His Mother's body and kisses the Mystic Rose of her lips:

> A woman was His walking home
> Foederis Arca Ora pro nobis.

And he thinks of the sun, moon and stars as trinkets for her to play with:

> With the great heart a woman has
> And the love of little things.

For she is a woman: Regina Angelorum, Queen of Powers and Archangels, she yet belongs to the human race.

> Our Lady went into a strange country,
>   Our Lady, for she was ours
> And had run on the little hills behind the houses
>   And pulled small flowers;
> But she rose up and went into a strange country
>   With strange thrones and powers.

From a welter of comment and correspondence that followed his conversion—challenging, scorning, rejoicing, welcoming, I select two letters from the two closest of Gilbert's Catholic friends—Hilaire Belloc and Maurice Baring.

i.VIII.22.

My dear Gilbert,

I write to you, from these strange surroundings, the first line upon the news you gave me. I must write to you again when I have col-

lected myself: for my reactions are abominably slow. I have, however, something to say immediately: and that is why I write this very
evening, just after seeing Eleanor off at the Station. The thing I
have to say is this (I could not have said it before your step: I can
say so now. Before it would have been like a selected pleading.) The
Catholic Church is the exponent of *Reality*. It is true. Its doctrines
in matters large and small are statements of what is. This it is which
the ultimate act of the intelligence accepts. This it is which the will
deliberately confirms. And that is why Faith though an act of the
Will is Moral. If the Ordnance Map tells us that it is 11 miles to
[a place] then, my mood of lassitude as I walk through the rain at
night making it *feel* like 30, I use the Will and say "No. My intelligence has been convinced and I compel myself to use it against
my mood. It is 11 and though I feel in the depths of my being
to have gone 20 miles and more, I *know* it is not yet 11 I have
gone."

I am by all my nature of mind sceptical. . . . And as to the doubt
of the soul I discover it to be false: a mood: not a conclusion. My
conclusion—and that of all men who have ever once *seen* it—is the
Faith: Corporate, organised, a personality, teaching. A thing, not a
theory. It.

To you, who have the blessing of profound religious emotion, this
statement may seem too desiccate. It is indeed not enthusiastic. It
lacks meat.

It is my misfortune. In youth I had it: even till lately. Grief has
drawn the juices from it. I am alone and unfed, the more do I affirm
the Sanctity, the Unity, the Infallibility of the Catholic Church. By
my very isolation do I the more affirm it, as a man in a desert knows
that water is right for man: or as a wounded dog, not able to walk,
yet knows the way home.

The Catholic Church is the natural home of the human spirit.
The odd perspective picture of life which looks like a meaningless
puzzle at first, seen from that *one* standpoint takes a complete order
and meaning, like the skull in the picture of the Ambassadors.

So much for my jejune contribution: not without value; because
I know you regard my intelligence—a perilous tool God gave me for
his own purposes; one bringing nothing to me.

But beyond this there will come in time, if I save my soul, the
flesh of these bones—which bones alone I can describe and teach.

I know—without feeling (an odd thing in such a connection) the reality of Beatitude: which is the goal of Catholic Living.

> In hac urbe lux solennis
> Ver aeternum pax perennis
> Et aeterna gaudia.

Yours,

H. B.

Maurice Baring wrote:

August 25: 1922.

MY DEAR GILBERT,

When I wrote to you the other day I was still cramped by the possibility of the news not being true although I *knew* it was true. I *felt* it was true at once. Curiously enough I felt it had happened before I saw the news in the newspaper at all. I felt that your ship had arrived at its port. But the more I felt this, the more unwilling I was to say anything before I heard the news from a source other than the newspapers. I gave way to an excess, a foolish excess perhaps of scruple. But you will, I think, understand this. In writing to you the other day I expressed not a tenth part of what I felt and feel and that baldly and inadequately. Nothing for years has given me so much joy. I have hardly ever entered a church without putting up a candle to Our Lady or to St. Joseph or St. Anthony for you. And both this year and last year in Lent I made a Novena for you. I know of many other people, better people far than I, who did the same. Many Masses were said for you and prayers all over England and Scotland in centres of Holiness. I will show you some day a letter from some Nuns on the subject. A great friend of mine one of the greatest saints I have known, Sister Mary Annunciation of the Convent Orphanage, Upper Norwood, used always to pray for you. She, alas, died last year.

Did I ever quote you a sentence of Bernard Holland on the subject of Kenelm Henry Digby when the latter was received?

"Father Scott . . . who, at last, guided him through the narrow door where one must bend one's head, into the internal space and freedom of the eternal and universal Catholic Church." *Space* and *freedom*: that was what I experienced on being received; that is what I have been most conscious of ever since. It is the exact opposite of what the ordinary Protestant conceives to be the case. To him and not only to him but to the ordinary English agnostic the convert to Catholicism is abandoning his will and his independence, sometimes they think even his nationality; at the best they think he is sheltering himself in a walled garden; at the worst they think he has closed on himself an iron door: and shackled himself with foolish chains and sold his birthright for a crown of tinsel.

And yet their own experience, the testimony of their eyes if they would only use them, ought to suggest to them that they might perhaps be mistaken.

It would be difficult for anyone to make out a case for the UnEnglishness of Manning or indeed of any prominent English Catholic whether a born Catholic or a convert.

It would be difficult for them to prove that Belloc was a writer wanting in independence. It would be difficult for them to convince any one that Father Vaughan and Lord Fitzalan were wearing foolscaps.

And anybody who has thought about history or looked on at politics must have reflected that freedom resides where there is order and not where there is license: or no-order.

It is true in politics; it is true in art. It is the basis of our whole social life in England. Russia has just given us the most startling of object lessons. The English with their passion for Committees, their Club-rules and their well organised traffic are daily realising the fact, however little they may recognise the theory. Only the law can give us freedom, said Goethe talking of art. "Und das Gesetz kann nur die Freiheit geben."

Well all I have to say, Gilbert, is what I think I have already said to you, and what I have said not long ago in a printed book. That I was received into the Church on the Eve of Candlemass 1909, and it is perhaps the *only act* in my life, which I am quite certain I have never regretted. Every day I live, the Church seems to me more and more wonderful; the Sacraments more and more solemn and sustaining; the voice of the Church, her liturgy, her rules, her discipline, her ritual, her decisions in matters of Faith and Morals more and more excellent and profoundly wise and true and right, and her children stamped with something that those outside Her are without. There I have found Truth and reality and everything outside Her is to me compared with Her as dust and shadow. Once more

God bless you and Frances. Please give her my love. In my prayers for you I have always added her name.

Yours,

MAURICE.

It was a bit of great good fortune, although at the time he did not feel it so, that the death of the *New Witness* in 1922 for lack of funds, left Gilbert some months for uninterrupted creative thought before *G.K.'s Weekly* took its place. Lawrence Solomon, friend of his boyhood and at this time a near neighbour, has told me not only how happy his conversion had made Gilbert but also how it had seemed to bring him increased strength of character. Worry, he had told Maurice Baring, did not worry so much as of old because of a fundamental peace. In this atmosphere were written two of his most important books: *St. Francis of Assisi* published 1923, *The Everlasting Man* published 1925.

In a poem he has expressed his sense of conversion as a new light that had transfigured life: indeed of a new life given to him:

> After one moment when I bowed my head
> And the whole world turned over and came upright,
> And I came out where the old road shone white,
> I walked the ways and heard what all men said.
>
> .   .   .   .
>
> They rattle reason out through many a sieve
> That stores the sand and lets the gold go free:
> And all these things are less than dust to me
> Because my name is Lazarus and I live.*

Both books shine with that light on the white road of man's endeavour, thrill with that life. Gilbert felt now the clue to history in his fingers and he used it increasingly. *The Everlasting Man* is the *Orthodoxy* of his later life and one difficulty in deal-

* *Collected Poems*, p. 387, "The Convert."

ing with it adequately was expressed in a letter from William Lyon Phelps thanking the author for "a magnificent work of genius and never more needed than now. I took out my pencil to mark the most important passages, but I quickly put my pencil in my pocket for I found I had to mark every sentence." Reading the book for perhaps the seventh time I can only say (I hope without irreverence) what G.K. himself says happens to those who can read the words of the Gospels "simply enough." They "will feel as if rocks had been rolled upon them. Criticism is only words about words; and of what use are words about such words as these."

"Rocks rolled upon them." Did he not feel crushed, overwhelmed at times by his own thought on these immensities, or can the philosopher carry his thoughts as lightly as Gilbert so often seemed to carry his? I think not always. He must have needed superhuman strength to conceive and give birth to this mighty book. The thoughts sketched in *The New Jerusalem* had grown to their full fruition in an atmosphere of meditation. It would be much easier to give an outline of *The Everlasting Man* than of *Orthodoxy*, much harder to give an idea of it. For *Orthodoxy* consists of a hundred brilliant arguments while *The Everlasting Man* really is a vision of history supported by a historical outline. Comparing his own effort with that of H. G. Wells, Chesterton says, "I do not believe that the best way to produce an outline of history is to rub out the lines." He is like Wells however in not being a specialist but claiming "the right of the amateur to do his best with the facts the specialists provide"—only their specialists are different specialists and their facts therefore largely different facts.

Chesterton, unlike most converts, wrote concerning his own conversion the least interesting of his later books: but in *The Everlasting Man* he is not at all concerned with his own spiritual wayfaring, he merely wants to make everyone else look at what he has come to see at the end of the way. The book is an attempt

to get outside Man and thus see him as the strange being he
really is: to get outside Christianity and see for the first time its
uniqueness among the religions of the world. Why are not all
men aware of the uniqueness of Man among the animals and
the uniqueness of the Church among religions? Because they do
not really look at either. Familiarity has dulled the edge of awareness. Men must be made to see them as though for the first time;
and it is the towering achievement of this book that reading it
we do so see them. "I desire to help the reader to see Christendom from the outside in the sense of seeing it as a whole against
the background of other historic things; just as I desire him to
see humanity as a whole against the background of natural
things. And I say that in both cases when seen thus, they stand
out from their background like supernatural things." This being
his desire, he divides the book into two parts—"the first being
the main adventure of the human race in so far as it remained
heathen; and the second a summary of the real difference that
was made by it becoming Christian."

Notable as the first part is, it is only a preparation for the second, which shows the Church not as one religion among many
but as the *only* religion, for it is the only Thing that binds into
one both Philosophy (or Thought) and Mythology (or Poetry),
giving us a Logos Who is also the Hero of the strangest story in
the world. He asks the man who *talks* of reading the Gospels
really to read them as he might read his daily paper and to feel
the terrific shock of the words of Christ to the Pharisees or the
behaviour of Christ to the money-changers: to look at the
uniqueness of the Church that has died so often but like Her
Founder risen again from the dead.

Two untrue things, he felt, were constantly reiterated about
the gospel—one that the Church had overlaid and made difficult
a plain and simple story: the other that the hero of this story was
merely human and taught a morality suitable to his own age,
inapplicable in our more complicated society. To anyone who

really read the gospels the instant impression would be rather that they were full of dark riddles which only historic Christianity has clarified. The Eunuchs of the heavenly Kingdom would be an idea dark and terrible but for the historic beauty of Catholic virginity. The ideal of man and woman "in one flesh" inseparable and sanctified by a sacrament became clear in the lives of the great married saints of Christendom. The apparent idealisation of idleness above service in the story of Mary and Martha was lit up by the sight of Catherine and Clare and Teresa shining above the little home at Bethany. The meek inheriting the earth became the basis of a new Social Order when the mystical monks reclaimed the lands that the practical kings had lost.

Thus if the gospel was a riddle the Church was the answer to the riddle because both were created by One Who Knew: Who saw the ages in which His own creation was to find completion: Whose morality was not one of another age but of another world.

Chesterton gathered history in his mind and saw together before the Christmas Crib the shepherds who had found their shepherd, the philosopher kings who "would stand for the same human ideal if their names had really been Confucius or Pythagoras or Plato. They were those who sought not tales but the truth of things; and since their thirst for truth was itself a thirst for God, they also have had their reward. But even in order to understand that reward, we must understand that for philosophy as much as mythology, that reward was the completion of the incomplete." *

G.K. too had needed the completion of incomplete human thought: he too had followed the star from a far country. It had been a fancy of his boyhood, caught from a fairytale, that evil lurked somewhere in a hidden room of the human house and the human heart. He saw in the history of the ancients a con-

* *The Everlasting Man*, p. 211.

sciousness of the Fall, in the sadness of their songs a sense of "the Presence of the Absence of God." But at Bethlehem he saw the transformation that had come upon the whole race of man with that little local infancy concealing the mighty power of God who had put Himself under the feet of the world.

It is rather as if a man had found an inner room in the very heart of his own house, which he had never suspected; and seen a light from within. It is as if he found something at the back of his own heart that betrayed him into good. It is not made of what the world would call strong materials; or rather it is made of materials whose strength is in that winged levity with which they brush us and pass. It is all that is in us but a brief tenderness, that is there made eternal; all that means no more than a momentary softening that is in some strange fashion become a strengthening and a repose; it is the broken speech and the lost word that are made positive and suspended unbroken; as the strange kings fade into a far country and the mountains resound no more with the feet of the shepherds; and only the night and the cavern lie in fold upon fold over something more human than humanity.*

It seems to me profoundly significant that Gilbert studied first in the Little Poor Man of Assisi what Christ could do in one man before he came on to the study of what He had done in mankind as a whole, of Who He was who had done it. For the man thus chosen embodied the ideals that Gilbert had seen dimly in his boyhood—ideals that most of us accept a little reluctantly from the Church, but which had actually attracted him towards the Church. St. Francis "had found the secret of life in being the servant and the secondary figure". . . "he seems to have liked everybody, but especially those whom everybody disliked him for liking." "By nature he was the sort of man who has that vanity which is the opposite of pride, that vanity which is very near to humility. He never despised his fellow creatures and therefore he never despised the opinion of

* *Ibid*, p. 223.

his fellow creatures, including the admiration of his fellow creatures." "He was above all things a great giver; and he cared chiefly for the best kind of giving which is called thanksgiving. If another great man wrote a grammar of assent, he may well be said to have written a grammar of acceptance; a grammar of gratitude. He understood down to its very depths the theory of thanks; and its depths are a bottomless abyss."

Here, in St. Francis, Gilbert saw the apotheosis of his old boyish thought—that thanksgiving is a duty and a joy, that we should love not "humanity" but each human. Things shadowed in the Notebook are in *St. Francis,* for

the transition from the good man to the saint is a sort of revolution; by which one for whom all things illustrate and illuminate God becomes one for whom God illustrates and illuminates all things. It is rather like the reversal whereby a lover might say at first sight that a lady looked like a flower, and say afterwards that all flowers reminded him of his lady. A saint and a poet standing by the same flower might seem to say the same thing; but indeed though they would both be telling the truth, they would be telling different truths. For one the joy of life is a cause of faith, for the other rather a result of faith.*

The Everlasting Man and the *St. Francis* seem to me the highest expression of Gilbert's mysticism. I have hesitated to use the word for it is not one to be used lightly but I can find no other. Like most Catholics I have been wont to believe that to be a mystic a man must first be an ascetic and Gilbert was not an ascetic in the ordinary sense. But is there not for the thinker an asceticism of the mind, very searching, very purifying? In his youth he had told Bentley that creative writing was the hardest of hard labour. That sense of the pressure of thought that made Newman call creative writing "getting rid of pain by pain"; the profound depression that often follows; the exhaustion that seems like a bottomless pit. St. Theresa said the hardest

* *St. Francis of Assisi,* p. 111.

penance was easier than mental prayer: was not much of Gilbert's thought a contemplation?

Faith, thanksgiving, love, surely these far above bodily asceticism can so clear a man's eyesight that he may fittingly be called a mystic since he sees God everywhere. "The less a man thinks of himself, the more he thinks of his good luck and of all the gifts of God." Only a poet who was more than a poet could see so clearly of what like St. Francis was.

When we say that a poet praises the whole creation, we commonly mean only that he praises the whole cosmos. But this sort of poet does really praise creation, in the sense of the act of creation. He praises the passage or transition from nonentity to entity; there falls here also the shadow of that archetypal image of the bridge, which has given to the priest his archaic and mysterious name. The mystic who passes through the moment when there is nothing but God does in some sense behold the beginningless beginnings in which there was really nothing else. He not only appreciates everything but the nothing of which everything was made. In a fashion he endures and answers even the earthquake irony of the Book of Job; in some sense he is there when the foundations of the world are laid, with the mornings stars singing together and the sons of God shouting for joy.*

But there was in all those years another element besides the giving of thanks and the joy of creation: an abiding grief for the sorrows of the sons of men and especially those of his own land. In this mood the *Cobbett* was written.

Nine years separate the publication of *William Cobbett* from that of the *History of England*. Written at the time when Englishmen were fighting so magnificently, that book had radiated G.K.'s own mood of hope, but to read *Rural Rides*, to meditate on Cobbett's England, and then turn to the England of the hour was not cheerful. For Cobbett "did not draw precise diagrams of things as they were. He only had frantic and fantastic nightmares of things as they are." † And these nightmares haunted Cobbett's biographer.

* *St. Francis of Assisi*, pp. 112–13.
† *Cobbett*, p. 22.

What he saw was not an Eden that cannot exist, but rather an Inferno that can exist, and even that does exist. What he saw was the perishing of the whole English power of self-support, the growth of cities that drain and dry up the countryside, the growth of dense dependent populations incapable of finding their own food, the toppling triumph of machines over men, the sprawling omnipotence of financiers over patriots, the herding of humanity in nomadic masses whose very homes are homeless, the terrible necessity of peace and the terrible probability of war, all the loading up of our little island like a sinking ship; the wealth that may mean famine and the culture that may mean despair; the bread of Midas and the sword of Damocles. In a word, he saw what we see, but he saw it when it was not there. And some cannot see it—even when it is there.*

Two men had written of the Reformation as the ultimate origin of these evils at a time when it was still the fashion to treat it as the dawn of all good. Lingard, himself a Catholic, had written cautiously, with careful documentation and moderate tone. Cobbett, a Protestant, had written hastily and furiously, but both men had drawn in essentials the same picture. Chesterton suspected that Cobbett was treated with contempt, Lingard with respect, largely because of the difference in the tone of the two men. Lingard spoke restrainedly but Cobbett's voice was raised in a loud cry:

He was simply a man who had discovered a crime: ancient like many crimes; concealed like all crimes. He was as one who had found in a dark wood the bones of his mother, and suddenly knew she had been murdered. He knew now that England had been secretly slain. Some, he would say, might think it a matter of mild regret to be expressed in murmurs. But when he found a corpse he gave a shout; and if fools laughed at anyone shouting, he would shout the more, till the world should be shaken with that terrible cry in the night.

It is that ringing and arresting cry of "Murder!" wrung from him as he stumbled over those bones of the dead England, that distinguishes him from all his contemporaries.†

* *Ibid,* pp. 14, 15.   † *Ibid,* pp. 176–77.

Yet, for the Christian, hope remains: no murder can be the end. "Christianity has died many times and risen again; for it had a God who knew the way out of the grave." This quotation is from the chapter called "Five Deaths of the Faith" in *The Everlasting Man*. Several times in the book Chesterton puts aside tempting lines of thought with the remark that he intends to develop them later—in one of the unwritten books that he always felt were so much better than those he actually wrote. Would any human life have been long enough to develop them all? Anyhow, even the whole of this life was not available.

As I turn to the story of the weekly paper rising again from its ashes I ask myself the question I have often asked: was it worth while? I cannot answer the question. Something of his manhood seemed to Gilbert bound up with this struggle, and it may be he would have been a lesser man had he abandoned it. And yet at moments imagining the poetry, the philosophy that might have been ours—another *White Horse,* another *Everlasting Man*—I am tempted to wish that these years had not thus been sacrificed to the paper which enshrined his brother's memory.

Chapter XXV

The Reluctant Editor (1925-1930)

I tell you naught for your comfort
Yea naught for your desire
Save that the sky grows darker yet
And the sea rises higher.
                    Ballad of the White Horse

COULD GILBERT HAVE divided his life between literary work, his home at Top Meadow, and those other elements called in the Autobiography "Friendship and Foolery," that life might well have been as he himself called it "indefensibly fortunate and happy." But he could not. Part of his philosophy of joy was that thanks must be given—for sunsets, for dandelions, for beech trees, for home and friends. And this thanks could only be the taking of his part in the fight. He would never, he once said, have turned of his own accord to politics: it is arguable that it would have been better if he never had. But his brother had plunged into the fray with that very political paper the *New Witness* and his brother's death had left it in Gilbert's hands. He felt the task to be a sacred legacy, and when the paper died for lack of funds his one thought was how to start it again.

For many months he kept the office in being and paid salaries to a skeleton staff, consisting of Mr. Gander, the deaf old manager, Miss Dunham (now Mrs. Phillips) and an office boy. Mr. Titterton would stroll in and play cricket with the office boy with a paper ball and a walking-stick. Endless discussions were held as to how to re-start the paper and whether under the old name or a new one. Bernard Shaw had his own view. He wrote:

11 Feb.: 1923

My dear Chesterton

Not presume to dictate (I have all Jingle's delicacy); but if everybody else is advising you, why should not I?

T.P.'s Weekly always had a weakly sound. But it established itself sufficiently to make that form of title the trade mark of a certain sort of paper. Hence *Jack O'London's Weekly*. It also set the trade sheep running that way.

You have the precedents of Defoe and Cobbett for using your own name; but D.D.'s Weekly is unthinkable, and W.C.'s Weekly indecent. Your initials are not euphonious: they recall that brainy song of my boyhood, U-pi-dee.

> Jee Kay see, kay see, kay see,
> Jee Kay see, Jee Kay see.
> Jee Kay see, Kay see, Kay see,
> Jee Kay see Kay see.

Chesterton is a noble name; but Chesterton is Weakly spoils it. Call it simply

CHESTERTON'S

That is how it will be asked for at the bookstalls. You may be obliged to call later ventures Chesterton's Daily or Chesterton's Annual, but this one needs no impertinently superfluous definition: Chesterton's Perennial is amusing enough to be excusable; but a joke repeated every week is no joke. A picture cover like that of Punch might stand even that test if it were good enough; but where are you to find your Doyle?

Week is a detestable snivelling word: nothing can redeem it, not even the Sermon on the Mount. Seven Days is better, but reminds one of the police court as well as of the creation. Every Seven Days would sound well. But *Chesterton's* leaves no room for anything else. I am more than usually sure that I am right.

Frances quite agrees with me. How would you like it if she were to publish a magazine and call it Fanny's First Paper?

Ever

G.B.S.

If Gilbert answered this letter his answer has disappeared. He seems to have asked permission to publish it—probably with a view to collecting further opinions.

10 Adelphi Terrace, London, W.C.2.
February 16th 1923.

MY DEAR G.K.C.

Of course you may publish any letter of mine that you care to, at your discretion.

. . . But not only will the publication of a letter from me not add one to your circulation (nothing but a permanent feature will do that), but it may lead you to disregard the advice I give to all the people who start Labour papers (about two a week or so), which always is, "Don't open with an article to say that your paper supplies a want; don't blight your columns with 'messages'; don't bewilder your readers with the family jokes of your clique; else there will be no second number." Ponder this: it is sound.

Your main difficulty is that the class whose champion you have made yourself reads either Lloyd's or nothing. To the rural proprietor, no longer a peasant, art, including *belles lettres,* is immorality, and people who idealize peasants, unpractical fools. Also the Roman Catholic Church, embarrassed by recruits of your type and born scoffers like Belloc, who cling to the Church because its desecration would take all the salt out of blasphemy, will quietly put you on the unofficial index. The Irish will not support an English journal because it occasionally waves a green flag far better than they can wave it themselves. And the number of Jews who will buy you just to see what you say about them is not large enough to keep you going. Thus there is absolutely no public for your policy; and though there is a select one for yourself one and indivisible, it is largely composed of people to whom your oddly assorted antipathies and pseudo-racial feuds are uncongenial. Besides, on these fancies of yours you have by this time said all you have to say so many thousand times over, that your most faithful admirers finally (and always suddenly) discover they are fed up with the *New Witness* and cannot go on with it. This last danger becomes greater as you become older, because when we are young we can tell ourselves a new story every night between our prayers and our sleep; but later on we find ourselves repeating the same story with intensifications and improvements night after night until we are tired of it; and in the end (which you have not yet reached) a story revived from the old repertory has to last for months, and is more and more shaky as a protection against thinking of business, or lying there a prey to unwelcome reminiscences. And what happens to the story of the imaginative child happens also to the sermon or the feuilleton of the adult. It is inevitably happening to you.

That is the case against the success of CHESTERTON's.

Your only chance finally is either to broaden your basis, or to have no basis at all, like Dickens in "Household Words" and "All The Year Round," and say, "Give me something with imagination in it, and I can do without politics or theoretic sociology of any kind." This is perhaps the only true catholicism in literature; but it will hardly serve your turn; because all the articles and stories that Dickens got are now mopped up by the popular press, which in his day stuck to politics and news and nothing else. So I am afraid you will have to stand for a policy, or at least a recognisable attitude, unless you are prepared to write a detective story every week and make Belloc write a satirical story as well.

You could broaden your basis if you had money enough to try the experiment of giving ten poor but honest men in Beaconsfield and ten more in London capital enough to start for themselves as independent farmers and shopkeepers. The result would be to ruin 18 out of the twenty, and possibly to ruin the lot. You would then learn from your feelings what you would never learn from me, that what men need is not property but honorable service. Confronted either with 20 men ruined by your act, or 18 ruined and one Fascination Fledgby owning half a street in London, and the other half a parish in Bucks, you would—well, perhaps join the Fabian Society.

The pseudo race feuds you should drop, simply because you cannot compete with the *Morning Post,* which gives the real thing in its succulent savagery whilst you can give only a "wouldn't hurt a fly" affectation of it. In religion too you are up against the fact that an editor, like an emperor, must not belong to a sect. Wells is on the right tack: my tack. See my prefaces to Androcles and Methuselah. We want the real Catholic Church above the manufactured one. The manufactured one is useful as the Salvation Army is useful, or the formulas of the Church of Christ Scientist; but they do not strike on the knowledge box of the modern intellectual; and it is on the modern intellectual that you are depending. I am an Irishman, and know how far the official Catholic Church can go. Your ideal Church does not exist and never can exist within the official organization, in which Father Dempsey will always be efficient and Father Keegan futile if not actually silenced; and I know that an officially Catholic Chesterton is an impossibility.

However, you must find out all this for yourself as I found it out for myself. Mere controversy is waste of time; and faith is a curious thing. I believe that you would not have become a professed official Catholic if you did not believe that you believe in transubstantiation; but I find it quite impossible to believe that you believe in transubstantiation any more than, say, Dr. Saleeby does. You will have to go to Confession next Easter; and I find the spectacle—the box, your portly kneeling figure, the poor devil inside wishing you had become a Fireworshipper instead of coming there to shake his soul with a sense of his ridiculousness and yours—all incredible, monstrous, comic, though of course I can put a perfect literary complexion on it in a brace of shakes.

Now, however, I am becoming personal (how else can I be sincere?). Besides I am going on too long and the lunch bell is ringing. So forgive me, and don't bother to answer unless you cannot help it.

Ever,
G. Bernard Shaw.

Meanwhile, Shaw as usual responded cordially to Gilbert's wish to make him an early attraction in the paper—but also as usual urged him towards the theatre:

10th Dec. 1924.

By all means send me a screed about Joan [of Arc] for the cockpit. But I protest I have no views about her. I am only the first man modest enough to know his place *auprès d'elle* as a simple reporter and old stage hand.

You should write plays instead of editing papers. Why not do George Fox, who was released from the prisons in which Protestant England was doing its best to murder him, by the Catholic Charles II? George and Joan were as like as two peas in pluck and obstinacy.

G.B.S.

The specimen advance number was published before the end of 1924. In the leading article G.K. gave his reasons for agreeing finally to use his own name—although in the form attacked by Shaw. He had first viewed the proposal with a "horror which has since softened into loathing." He had looked for a title that should indicate the paper's policy. But while that policy was in fact a support of human normality: well-distributed property, freedom and the family—yet the surrounding atmosphere was so abnormal that "any title defining our doctrine makes it look doctrinaire." A name like *The Distributive Review* would suggest that a Distributist was like a Socialist, a crank or a pedant with a new theory of human nature. "It is so old that it has become new. At the same time I want a title that does suggest that the paper is controversial and that this is the general trend of its controversy. I want something that will be recognised as a flag, however fantastic and ridiculous, that will be in some sense a challenge, even if the challenge be received only with genial derision. I do not want a colourless name; and the nearest I can get to something like a symbol is merely to fly my own colours."

Although the paper was never exclusively Catholic, that flag was for G.K. as it had been for Cecil of a very definite pattern and very clear colours: religiously the paper stood for Catholic Christianity, socially for the theory of small ownership, personal responsibility and property. It was in strong opposition especially to Socialism and even more to Communism. Bernard Shaw, Gilbert once said, wanted to distribute money among the poor—"we want to distribute power."

During the last part of Cecil's editorship his wife had been Assistant Editor of the *New Witness* and she had so continued when Gilbert first became Editor. But she was neither a Catholic nor a Distributist. Religion seems not to have interested her, and her political outlook was entirely different from Gilbert's. In *The Chestertons* she dismissed Distributism as "quite without first principles" and "a pious hope and no more." * Obviously it was impossible for Gilbert to start his new paper with an Assistant

* I have learnt, as this book goes to press, that Mrs. Cecil became a Catholic in 1941.

Editor in entire disagreement with his views. I have sometimes wondered whether his intense dislike of having to tell Mrs. Cecil this was not almost as strong a factor in the delay as the money problem.

There was no break in their relations: she went on writing for the paper, doing chiefly the dramatic criticism. But it is clear from her own account of the incident that she wholly misconstrued Gilbert's attitude and did not realise how far she herself had drifted from Cecil's views as well as from Gilbert's.

Shaw wrote again:

> Reid's Palace Hotel
> Funchal, Madeira.
> 16th January, 1925.

My dear G.K.C.

The sample number has followed me out here. What a collector's treasure!

Considering that I had Cecil's own assurance that my Quintessence of Ibsenism rescued him from Rationalism, and that it was written in 1889 (I abandoned Rationalism consciously and explicitly in 1881) I consider John Prothero's introduction of me to your readers as a recently converted Materialist Rationalist to be a most unnatural act; and it would serve her right if I never spoke to her again.

Rationalism is the bane of the Church. A Roman priest always wants to argue with you. A Church of England parson flies in terror from an argument, a fundamentally sensible course. George Fox simply knocked arguers out with his "I have experimental knowledge of God." St. Thomas Aquinas was like me: he knew the worthlessness of ratiocination because he could do it so well, and yet despaired of the Inspirationists in practical life because they did it so badly.

J.K.P. doesn't know her way about in this controversy; and I cannot take up her challenge.

What makes me uneasy about the prospectus is that you drag in anti-Prohibition. You might as well have declared for Brighter London at once, or said that the paper would be printed at the office of the *Morning Advertiser*. You run the risk of the money coming from The Trade. However, *non olet*. Only, remember the fate of all the editors—Gardiner, Donald, Massingham, etc., etc.—who have written without regard to their proprietors. The strength of your position is that they can hardly carry on with your name in the title without you. But they can kill the paper by stopping supplies if it does not pay; and the chances are that it will not. I have never had a farthing of interest on my shares in the New Statesman, and don't expect I ever shall. Therefore keep your list of shareholders as various and as uncommercial as you can: get Catholic money rather than beer money.

As I am the real patentee of the Distributive State, and the D.S. is Socialism; and as, furthermore, the Church must remain at least neutral on Prohibition, as in the United States, where a Catholic priest has just set a praiseworthy example of neutrality by bringing about a record cop of bootleggers, and as the success of Prohibition is so overwhelming that it is bound to become a commonplace of civilization, you must regard it as at least possible that you will some day make the paper Socialist and Dry (with a capital). Therefore do not undertake to oppose anything: stand for what you propose to advocate, whether as to property or drink or anything else, but don't state your solutions as antitheses.

By the way, don't propose equal distribution of land. It is like equal distribution of metal, rough on those who get the lead and rather too jolly for those who get the gold. Your equal distribution must come to equal distribution of the national income in terms of money.

The £500 a year is absurd. Do you realize that it is £250 at pre-war rates, and subject to heavy taxation: net £375—pre-war 182-10-0? You have sold yourself into slavery for ten years for £3-10-2 a week. Are you quite mad? Make it at least £1500, plus payment for copy.

Ever

G.B.S.

Of course it was not merely a question of inadequate payment for his work: as time went on, a large part of the financial burden of the paper had to be carried by him. Lord Howard de Walden helped generously and so did Mr. Chivers. Other donations came in but mostly very small ones. No proper accounts were kept: no watch on how the money went. And from time to time Gilbert would pay off a printing bill of £500 or so and go ahead hoping for better times. The money aspect did not worry him, I think, at first. There was always more to be made by a little extra effort: though a time was to come when every extra effort wearied him cruelly. But there was one thing he could not bear—quarrels on the Board or on the staff and above all the suggestion that he should adjudicate.

"He was a bad judge of men," one of his staff told me. "He never shirked an intellectual issue, but in a practical crisis he was inclined to slide out."

"He could never," said another, "stand up to accusations from one man against another."

The first start was made with the existing staff of three. Miss Dunham was sub-editor and was usually left to see the paper through the press. G.K. would come up once or twice a week and dictate his own articles.

"You never knew when he was coming," she says, "but you always knew when he was there by the smell of his cigar." He was practically a chain smoker and he always used the same brand. He left drawings on the blotter and everything else. He had no idea of time and when he said, "I think I'll go out now," he might stay out an hour or so, or he might not return at all. Lighting a cigar or cigarette he would make a sign in the air with the match. He never omitted this ritual, and Miss Dunham thinks it became like tapping the railings was to Dr. Johnson.

"He used to come in and swing about on his little feet," she said. And it is true that his feet like his voice seemed too small to belong to the rest of him. Her great difficulty was that she could not get him to read and select among the contributions: too often this was left to her and she felt painfully inadequate to the task.

For the first year all the Notes of the Week were written by G.K. Then he got Mr. Titterton as Assistant Editor: and after that, said the Assistant Editor with simplicity, "You couldn't always tell good Titterton from bad Chesterton." Everyone who worked at the office adored G.K.: especially the "little" people, typists, secretaries, office boys.

"He was so kind," Miss Dunham said. "He never got angry. He never minded being interrupted. If his papers blew away he never got impatient. His patience hurt one." She had never seen him angry.

That the paper was ever got out seems wonderful as the staff recall those days. Yet I think that all the stories about Gilbert's inefficiency as Editor have contributed towards an impression that I shared myself until quite lately—that *G.K.'s Weekly* was immeasurably inferior to the *New Witness*. Going more carefully through the files I have begun to question that impression.

The paper was produced under certain obvious disadvantages. Even spending some days a week in London and telephoning freely it is not easy to edit a paper from the country. Gilbert thought of himself as a bad editor, and was not in fact a very good one. The contributions he accepted were uneven in quality: both Leaders and Notes of the Week when not written by him tended to be weak imitations of either himself or Belloc—tinged at times with an air of omniscience tolerable in Belloc but quite intolerable in his imitators. Just occasionally the equally unedited Notes and Leader were in contradiction of each other. Yet the paper remains an exceedingly interesting one. Analysing my earlier and late impressions I concluded that my earlier feeling of boredom sprang from the inevitable effect of the *New Witness* coming first and therefore having been read first. It is a disadvantage of consistency that, as Bernard Shaw remarked, you have said the same thing, you have told the same story, so often as the years go by.

Taking a rest of a year and returning fresh to *G.K.'s Weekly* I was surprised at finding how much I enjoyed reading it and also at finding that it had been of more practical use than I remembered to the cause it served. The trend of the whole world is to make the State powerful and the family powerless. It was something that in these years *G.K.'s Weekly* should have helped to smash two bills of this nature—the Mental Deficiency and the Canal Children's Bills. Both these aimed at taking children from their parents, the first in the cause of health, the second of education. Against both Gilbert wrote brilliantly and successfully.

G.K.'s Weekly has much more G.K. in it and quite as much Belloc as in the earlier years of the *New Witness*. Eric Gill, too, long a friend of the Chestertons, became the chief contributor on art. In 1925 he spent a night at Top Meadow to discuss the policy of the paper, especially with reference to industrialism and art. A little later the Gills moved from Wales much nearer to Beaconsfield and the two men met fairly often. Gill's letters are interesting. They are mostly before the visit to Beaconsfield and probably led to it. He begins by attacking Gilbert for "(1) supporting Orpenism as against Byzantinism and (2) thinking that the art of painting *began* with Giotto, whereas Giotto was really much more the end."

In June 1925, G.K. was asking him to write about Epstein. Gill agreed to do so but insisted that Chesterton and Belloc must not disagree with him but "accept my doctrine as the doctrine of *G.K.'s Weekly* in matters of art—just as I accept yours in other matters." "I don't intend to write for you as an outsider (have I not put almost my last quid into your blooming Company?—7% or not). . . . God forbid that you should have an art critic who'll go round the picture shows for you and write bilge about this painter and that—this 'art movement' and that."

In the first state of effervescence the labour he delighted in quite deadened the pain of the Editor's chair. Gilbert was prepared if necessary to write the whole paper and to treat it as a variant on the Toy Theatre or the Sword Stick:

It was said that the Chicago pork machine used every part of a pig except the squeal. It might be said that the Fleet Street press machine uses only the squeal. . . .

In short, nobody reading the newspapers could form the faintest notion of how intelligent we newspaper people are. The whole machine is made to chop up each mind into meaningless fragments and waste the vast mass even of those. Such a thing as one complete human being appearing in the press is almost unknown; and when an attempt is made at it, it necessarily has a certain air of eccentric egotism. That is a risk which I am obliged to run everywhere in this paper and especially on this page. As I have said, the whole business of actually putting a paper together is a new game for me to play, to amuse my second childhood; and it combines some of the characters of a jigsaw and a crossword puzzle. But at least I am called upon to do a great many different sorts of things; and am not tied down to that trivial specialism of the proletarian press.*

And again

This paper exists to insist on the rights of man; on possessions that are of much more political importance than the principle of one man one vote. I am in favour of one man one house, one man one field; nay I have even advanced the paradox of one man one wife. But I am almost tempted to add the more ideal fancy of one man one magazine . . . to say that every citizen ought to have a weekly paper of this sort to splash about in . . . this kind of scrap book to keep him quiet.†

G.K. goes on to talk of an old idea of his: that a young journalist should write one article for the *Church Times* and another for the *Pink 'Un* and then put them into the wrong envelopes.

It is that sort of contrast and that sort of combination that I am going to aim at in this paper . . . I cannot see why convictions should look dull or why jokes should be insincere. I should like a man to pick up this paper for amusement and find himself involved in an argument. I should like him to pursue it purely for the sake of argument and find himself pulled up short by a joke . . . I never can see why a thing should not be both popular and serious; that is, in the sense of being both popular and sincere.

* March 28, 1925.   † April 4, 1925.

For the paper had a most serious purpose. He acknowledged its defects of bad printing (which the printers indignantly denied), bad proof-reading, bad editing, and claimed "to raise against the banner of advertisement the noble banner of apology." Because a creative revolution was what he wanted, words and forms were hard to find. It was easy to dress up stale ideas in a new dress but the terminology for something outside the old hack party programmes had to be fresh minted.

He proposed various changes after a few months' running and introduced them thus:

We should be only too glad if for this week only our readers would have the tact to retire and leave us alone. We are in a Hegelian condition, a condition not so much of Being as of Becoming. And no generous person should spy on an unfortunate fellow creature who is going through the horrible and degrading experience of being a Hegelian. It is even more embarrassing than being caught in the very act of evolution, which every clear headed person would desire to avoid.*

In this number he began *The Return of Don Quixote* and also a sort of scrapbook. He invited contributions dealing with every sort of approach to Distributism and promised "more than one series of constructive proposals and definite schemes of legislation. We do not promise that all these schemes will exactly agree with each other or that we shall agree with all of them. Some will be more conservative, some more drastic than our own view." This article ends on an ambitious note. Very varying schemes will be admitted, but the idea of the paper will thereby be strengthened not destroyed—

For what we desire is not a paltry party programme but a Renaissance.

It was not the first time he had demanded a revolution but, as the depression hit our country and Big Business seemed less

* December 12, 1925.

and less capable of coping with it, the demand became more understandable and the fight against Monopoly more urgent.

A thinking man should always attack the strongest thing in his own time. For the strongest thing of the time is always too strong. . . . The great outstanding fact and feature of our time is Monopoly.*

I have already referred to a debate on Monopoly between Chesterton and Mr. Gordon Selfridge, in which Selfridge, with the familiar unreality of the millionaire, maintained that there was no such thing. Anyone was free to open a store in rivalry of Selfridge's or to start a paper that should eclipse the *Daily Mail!* The only real monopoly, he added gracefully, was that of a genius like Chesterton whose work the ordinary man could not emulate. The graceful compliment Chesterton answered by offering to share his last epigram with Mr. Selfridge: but as to the main contention, what could he say? It was at once too easy and absolutely impossible to answer such a speech—or more truly such a speaker: only in a Country of the Blind could he have won a hearing. But Chesterton persevered. Even in 1924 the shadow of large scale unemployment had begun. And at this singularly inappropriate time came the Empire Exhibition at Wembley. In the failure of its appeal Chesterton saw hope: for he believed that from a frank facing of truth his country might yet conquer the coming perils.

That was the real weakness of Wembley; that it so completely mistook the English temperament as to appeal to a stale mood. It appealed to a stale mood of success; when we need to appeal to a new and more noble mood of failure, or at least of peril. The English . . . no longer care to be told of an Empire on which the sun never sets. Tell them the sun is setting, and they will fight though the battle go against them to the going down of the sun: if they do not stay it, like Joshua. . . .

We seriously propose that England should take her stand among

* April 25, 1925.

the unhappy nations; it is too dismal a fate to go on being one of the happy ones. We must be as proud as Spain and Poland and Serbia; nations made more dear to their lovers by their disasters. Our disasters have begun; but they do not seem to have endeared us to anybody in particular. Our sorrow has come; but we gain no extra loyalty by it. The time has come to claim our crown of thorns; or at least not to cover it any longer with such exceedingly faded flowers.*

Always Chesterton was haunted by the present war. He had seen the Prussian peril conquered: he saw it rising again. Even before the advent of Hitler he knew that the tribe which had stolen from Austria and Denmark, had invaded France and crushed Poland was without repentance, and he feared that again the stupidity (or the greed) behind English and American policy was giving it another opportunity— "Those sturdy Teutons," he wrote ironically, "from whom we were descended up to the outbreak of the Great War, and from whom we are now showing signs of being descended again."

The misfortune was that Englishmen had ceased to try to get free from "a secret government; conducted by we know not whom, and achieving we know not what. The real national life of our country is unconscious of its own national policy. The right hand of the Englishman, that holds the plough or the sword, knows not what his left hand doth with the pen and the cheque-book. Man is man; and Mond is master of his fate." For our government he apologised to France. He saw it as one and the same fight—against a heathenish money power and heathen Prussia. And the beating of the dark wings of enemy aeroplanes sounded in his dreams. As early as 1925 he wrote a Christmas play of St. George and the Dragon in which the Turkish Knight embodied his vision of Prussia and St. George spoke prophetically for England.

* March 21, 1925.

SAINT GEORGE: I know that this is sure
    Whatever man can do, man can endure,
    Though you shall loose all laws of fight, and fashion
    A torture chamber from a tilting yard,
    Though iron hard as doom grow hot as passion,
    Man shall be hotter, man shall be more hard,
    And when an army in your hell fire faints,
    You shall find martyrs who were never saints.

(They wound each other and the doctor comes to the help of the Turkish knight.)

PRINCESS: Why should we patch this pirate up again?
    Why should you always win and win in vain?
    Bid him not cut the leg but cut the loss.

SAINT GEORGE: I will not fire upon my own red cross.

PRINCESS: If you lay there, would he let *you* escape?

SAINT GEORGE: I am his conqueror and not his ape.

DOCTOR: Be not so sure of conquering. He shall rise
    On lighter feet, on feet that vault the skies.
    Science shall make a mighty foot and new,
    Light as the feather feet of Perseus flew,
    Long as the seven leagued boots in tales gone by,
    This shall bestride the sea and ride the sky.
    Thus shall he fly, and beat above your nation
    The clashing pinions of Apocalypse,
    Ye shall be deep sea fish in pale prostration
    Under the sky foam of his flying ships.

    When terror above your cities, dropping doom,
    Shall shut all England in a lampless tomb,
    Your widows and your orphans now forlorn
    Shall be no safer than the dead they mourn.
    When all their lights grow dark, their lives grow gray,
    What will those widows and those orphans say?

SAINT GEORGE: Saint George for Merrie England.

He saw the aeroplanes in vision and he saw courage and patriotism. I think he must rejoice today that betrayal of the allied cause has not been at the hands of an Englishman. He had said many hard things about the English aristocracy and gentry: but these two virtues he had always granted were theirs. And in his vision he saw hope:

England may soon be poor enough to be praised with an undivided heart. We are not sure that the ruins of Wembley may not be the restoration of Westminster. It is when a nation has recovered from the illusion of owning everything that it discovers that it does stand for something; and for that something it will fight with a lucid and just tenacity which no mere megalomania can comprehend. We are not so perverse as to wish to see England ruined that she may be respected. But we do think she will be happy in having the sort of respect that could remain even if she were ruined. Patriotic as the English have always been, the patriotism of their educated class has seldom had this peculiar sort of extra energy that is given by a conscience completely at rest. If that were added, they might well make such a stand as would astound the world. All their other virtues, their humour and sporting spirit and freedom from the morbidities and cruelties of fatigue, might enter into their full heritage when joined to the integrity and intellectual dignity that belong to self defence and self respect. We are far from sure that the world has not yet to see our nation in its finest phase.

What may be in the womb of night we know not, nor what are those dim outlines that show on the horizon.

"In truth" he wrote, "no man knows how near we are to death or to dawn. I am not sure whether I am making this speech from a scaffolding or a scaffold."

It is easy for the young to undertake hard things: they never know how hard they are. And they are certain of success. The "lessons of experience" signify to the young that other men have failed: their own experience shall teach others the meaning of success. But to begin again at fifty, with the special spring of youth gone and with the sad lessons of one's own experience in the mind: this calls indeed for a rare courage. Gilbert knew

all the cost in time, energy, money and reputation that he would
have to pay—that he did pay. And he stood increasingly alone.
Cecil's had been the irreparable loss, but others of the old circle
were dropping out and their places were not filled.

Jack Phillimore's death in 1926 was a heavy blow. To his
memory Gilbert dedicated *The Queen of Seven Swords,* published the year of his death.

> You go before me on all roads
> On bridges broad enough to spread
> Between the learned and the dunce
> Between the living and the dead.

The gulf between the Socialist group and the Distributist
had become far more obvious than of yore: Shaw and Wells
would still write for G.K. but only because he was their friend.
If F. Y. Eccles, if Desmond McCarthy today contributed, it
would too be chiefly from affection for Gilbert. One article by
Mr. McCarthy described the old days when the original *Eye
Witness* was in being and he, Cecil and Belloc sat around the
table editing it and sticking triolets thrown off in hot haste into
those nasty little spaces left by articles that did not quite fit, or
supplying three or four articles and a Ballade Urbane while the
printers waited.

> We have to print a triolet
>   When space is clamouring for matter
> We try to put it off and yet
> We have to print a triolet
> It is with infinite regret
>   That we admit the silly patter
> We have to print a triolet
>   When space is clamouring for matter.

Such joyous scrambles are proper to youth, and now none of
them were young.

All authors worthy of the name have found their own platform and made permanent engagements by middle life: professional men are absorbed by work and life: they simply had not time to give as of yore to build up this new-old venture.

The names of Shaw and Wells continue to appear among the contributors, often enough in religious debate. Reading the files and visiting the two men to talk of Gilbert, I made one discovery that is curious from whichever side you look at it. Two able and indeed brilliant men betrayed not only an amazing degree of ignorance concerning the tenets of Catholicism but also a bland conviction that they knew them well. Wells in conversation based his claim on the fact that he had long been intimately acquainted with an ex-nun. Shaw I fancy felt he must know all about something that had surrounded him in infancy—for, as the reader must have noticed, he is much preoccupied by the thought of his Irish descent and education.

But what seems to me even stranger about the situation is the absence on the Catholic side of any effort to explain to these men the doctrines they misconstrued. When Wells, for instance, gave a crude and inaccurate statement of the doctrine of the Fall, Belloc laughed at him, Chesterton and Father McNabb both wrote long and picturesque articles, illuminating to a believer but, as instruction to an unbeliever, quite useless. A correspondence that seemed likely to drag on forever ended abruptly with Wells asking about the Fall, "Tell me, did it really happen?" to which Chesterton briefly replied, "Yes."

I imagine he thought he and the other writers had said this several times already, but in fact they had not. Perhaps they did not realise where the beginning must be made in instructing otherwise instructed men on the subject of Catholicism. It is all very interesting and curious. But it largely explains why Bernard Shaw found it hard to believe that Gilbert believed in Transubstantiation. Has any Catholic ever explained the philosophic meaning of Transubstantiation to the Great Old Irish Man of English Letters? Even Gilbert was perhaps too much inclined simply to play the fool in high-spirited fashion with those who attacked the Faith in his paper or other papers. But then how well he played it!

Here are some imaginary interviews on

. . . the recently discovered traces of an actual historical Flood: a discovery which has shaken the Christian world to its foundations by its apparent agreement with the Book of Genesis. . . .

The Dean of St. Paul's remarked: "I do not see that there is any cause for alarm. Protestantism is still founded on an impregnable rock: on that deep and strong foundation of disbelief in the Bible which supports the spiritual and intellectual life of all true Christians today. Even if dark doubts should arise, and it should seem for the moment as if certain passages in the Scripture story were true, we must not lose heart; the cloud will pass: and we have still the priceless possession of the Open Bible, with all its inexhaustible supply of errors and inconsistencies: a continual source of interest to scholars and a permanent bulwark against Rome. . . .

Mr. H. G. Wells exclaimed: "I am interested in the Flood of the future: not in any of these little local floods that may have taken place in the past. I want a broader, larger, more complete and co-ordinated sort of Flood: a Flood that will really cover the whole ground. I want to get people to understand that in the future we shall not divide water, in this petty way, into potty little ponds and lakes and rivers: it will be one big satisfying thing, the same everywhere. *Après moi le Déluge.* Belloc in his boorish boozy way may question my knowledge of French: but I fancy that quotation will settle him.*

On the favourite topic of modern advertisement, having read an essay which said that good salesmanship made "everything in the garden beautiful," Gilbert again thought of Genesis:

There was only one actor in that ancient drama who seems to have had any real talent for salesmanship. He seems to have undertaken to deliver the goods with exactly the right preliminaries of promises and praise. He knew all about advertisement: we may say he knew all about publicity, though not at the moment addressing a

* March 30, 1929.

very large public. He not only took up the slogan of Eat More Fruit, but he distinctly declared that any customers purchasing his particular brand of fruit would instantly become as gods. And as this is exactly what is promised to the purchasers of every patent medicine, popular tonic, saline draught or medicinal wine at the present day, there can be no question that he was in advance of his age. It is extraordinary that humanity, which began with the apple and ended with the patent medicine, has not even yet become exactly like gods. It is still more extraordinary (and probably the result of a malicious interpolation by priests at a later date) that the record ends with some extraordinary remarks to the effect that one thus pursuing the bright career of Salesmanship is condemned to crawl on his stomach and eat a great deal of dirt.*

The relation between Belloc and the paper, as between Belloc and Gilbert himself, was a unique one. Not indeed its "onlie begetter," he was equally with Cecil begetter of the original paper and its first editor. He was Gilbert's chief guide to the historical and political scene of Europe. Both men shared, had fought all their lives for, their ideas of Freedom, the Family, Restoration of Property and all that is involved in Catholic Christianity. And Belloc said repeatedly that he had no platform for the continuous expression of these ideas. Such books as his *Cruise of the Nona* found still as wide a public as had *The Path to Rome* a quarter century earlier, and in those books his philosophy may be read. But he had, too, urgent commentaries on Foreign Affairs and Current Politics—and for these *G.K.'s Weekly* became his platform as completely as the *New Witness* had been in the past. To Gilbert this appeared one chief value of his paper: in an article from which I quote in the next chapter he gives it as one of the two reasons for which he toiled to keep *G.K.'s Weekly* in existence.

Week by week Belloc on Current or Foreign Affairs wrote of what was happening and what would presently come of it. And who can say reading those articles today that it would not

* March 23, 1929.

have changed the defeats of this war into victory at a far earlier date had our statemen read and heeded—the analysis for instance of the peril of the aeroplane, of the threat to the Empire from Japan, the importance of keeping Italy's friendship in the Mediterranean, the growing strength of Germany and the awful risk we took in allowing her to rearm, in failing to arm against her?

Whether he was right or, as many held, wildly wrong about what underlay our failures of judgment, his views must be briefly traced because of their effect on Gilbert and others. In the financial world he saw England in the first years after the war dominated by the International Banking Power, which made us as it were a local branch of Wall Street. In his view it was the bankers both of America and England who first insisted that Germany could not pay her reparations and later made England repudiate her own war debts to America (though she had, he showed, already paid in interest and principal more than half of what had been lent). The banks did this because they had lent commercially both to Germany and England sums whose safety meant more to them than moneys merely owing to the nations—which would not benefit the banks! England thus became subservient to the United States and had to follow American financial policies. It was these policies that led to the abandonment of the unwritten alliance with France and especially to allowing Germany to rearm (helped by loans from these same banks), to reoccupy the Rhineland and remilitarise the Ruhr.

Next, in Belloc's view, came a worse stage yet in which the banks had given place to Big Business which was increasingly controlling Parliament. The plutocracy that had bit by bit eaten into our aristocracy and gained ascendancy in the Government was not, like our ancient aristocracy, trained for the business and was utterly uninformed especially in foreign affairs. The one remaining hope, the permanent officials, especially of the Foreign

Office, were less and less listened to; latterly he held too that even the Foreign Office had lost its old sure touch. Hence a constant vacillation in our policies which weakened England's position and made certain some terrible disaster.

This fear is ever present in Belloc's articles and ever brooded on by the Editor. He rallied his forces to urge, week after week, the possible alternative to disaster—the recovery by the People of England of power and freedom, the restoration of England to its place in a restored Europe, freed from the German menace. Despite the natural high spirits a certain gloom and more than a touch of fierceness mark the work of these years. Summing up "the twenties" of the century, Chesterton saw them as singularly bankrupt spiritually and intellectually, and he foresaw from their sowing a miserable harvest.

CHAPTER XXVI

The Distributist League and Distributism

*To say we must have Socialism or Capitalism is like saying
we must choose between all men going into monasteries and a
few men having harems. If I denied such a sexual alternative
I should not need to call myself a monogamist; I should be
content to call myself a man.*

Advance number of *G.K.'s Weekly*, Nov. 1924

FROM *G.K.'s Weekly* grew THE DISTRIBUTIST LEAGUE. Its
start in 1926 was marked by intense enthusiasm, and its
progress was recorded week by week in the paper. The inaugural
meeting took place in Essex Hall, Essex Street, Strand, on
September 17, 1926. G.K. summed up their aim in the words:
"Their simple idea was to restore possession." He added that
Francis Bacon had long ago said: "Property is like muck, it is
good only if it be spread." The following week the first committee meeting took place. Chesterton was elected President;
Captain Went, Secretary, and Maurice Reckitt, Treasurer.
It was planned to form a branch in Birmingham. Alternative
names were discussed: The Cobbett Club, the Luddite League,
the League of Small Property:

The Cow and Acres, however suitable as the name of a public
house at which we could assemble, is too limited as an economic
statement. . . .

The League of the Little People (President, Mr. G. K. Chesterton) may seem at first too suggestive of the fairies; but it has been
strongly supported among us:

And again: Suppose we call our movement, "The Lost Property

League" . . . the idea of the restoration of lost property is far more essential to our whole conception than even the idea of liberty, as now commonly understood. The Liberty and Property Defense League implies that property is there to be defended. "The Lost Property League" describes the exact state of the case.*

In October another meeting of the central branch was held in Essex Hall to debate "Have We Lost Liberty?" The Croydon and Birmingham branches were arranging meetings, G.K. conferred with the members of the Manchester branch, and Glasgow announced that it was only awaiting the christening to form a branch. Bath held its first public meeting, with the Mayor in the chair, and the meeting had to overflow into a very large hall.

It was decided to reduce the price of the paper to twopence—Twopenny Trash † was the title of the leading article—in order to give the League an opportunity of extending the paper's radius of action as an organ of the League's principles. . . . *"Every reader who has been buying one copy at sixpence, must take three copies at twopence* until his two surplus copies have secured two new readers. . . . The League would have to make itself responsible for the success of this experiment and save the paper which gave it birth, or die of inanition, for it is certainly not yet strong enough to leave its mother." ‡

It is clear that Gilbert's hopes at this stage ran high. He had not dreamed that the initial success of the League would be so great. Recording a sensational increase in the sale of the paper, he wrote on November 13, 1926: "It was when we faced defeat that we were surprised by victory; and we are quite serious in believing that this is part of a practical philosophy that may yet outlast the philosophy of bluff."

Recording a meeting of the League: he wrote:

We find it difficult to express the effect the meeting had upon us. We were astonished, we were overwhelmed. Had we anything to do

* From an article called, "Name This Child" and another later article.
† This was the name given to Cobbett's *Weekly Register* by his enemies.
‡ *G.K.'s Weekly*, November 6, 1926.

with the making of this ardent, eager, indefatigable creature? The answer is, of course, that though we had something to do with the shaping of the body, we had nothing to do with the birth of the soul. That was a miracle, a miracle we had hoped for, and which yet, when it happened, overwhelmed us. We have the happy feeling that we have helped to shape something which will go far above and beyond us. . . . There were well over 100 members present, many of them spoke, and nearly all the others would have spoken if there had been time to hear them. It was a great night.*

Father Vincent McNabb has said truly that there are no words for the real things. Thus Distributism is not only a rather ugly word but also a word holding less than half the content of the idea they were aiming at. Belloc covered more of it in the title of his book: *The Restoration of Property*, while perhaps a better name still was *The Outline of Sanity*. This Chesterton had chosen for a series of articles that became a book. He was asking for a return to the sanity of field and workshop, of craftsman and peasant, from the insanity of trusts and machinery, of unemployment, over-production and starvation. "We are destroying food because we do not need it. We are starving men because we do not need them."

After the first meeting of the League, the notes of the week recorded that the printing order for the paper based on actual demand had risen in two weeks from 4,650 to 7,000. "Of course we owe everything to the League which in Manchester, Liverpool, Glasgow, Croydon, Chatham, Worthing, Chorley, Cambridge, Oxford, Bath and London has made the newsagents aware of the paper." By November 27, the sales had risen to over 8,000. Then was held the first formal meeting of the central branch of the League, at which it was agreed: "that members should make a habit of dealing at small shops." They should avoid even small shops which sweat their employees, each branch should prepare a list of small shops for the use of its members.

* November 13, 1926.

And that is only a beginning. We hope to enlist the support of the small farmer and the small master craftsman. We hope, little by little, to put the small producer in touch with the small retailer. We hope in the end to establish within the state a community, almost self-supporting, of men and women pledged to Distributism, and to a large extent practising it. Less and less, then, will the juggling of finance have power over us; for it does not matter what they call the counters when you are exchanging hams for handkerchiefs, or pigs for pianos.

The Cockpit is worth reading during the months that follow, for here were voiced any criticisms that the readers had to make of the paper and of the League—any criticism that the League had to make of itself. There was plenty. Many leaguers and readers felt for instance that the spirit of criticism of others was too fully developed in the paper, so that when attempts were made to act on distributive principles by people not in league with the League they were given short shrift instead of meeting even modified encouragement. The League was begged to spend more time clarifying its principles, less time in criticism. But much more fundamental was the constantly recurrent question: When is the League going to begin to do something? To this the answer, given often by G.K. himself was that, while the League hoped in time to create that community of which he had written, its own work was only that of Propaganda—of a wider and wider dissemination of the principles of Distributism. Their work, they said, was to talk.

Outdoor propaganda started in Glasgow and came thence to London. In October 1931 the Secretary said they must "convince men there is a *practical* alternative to Capitalism and Socialism, *by showing them how to set about achieving it.*" And in November he subscribed to opinions voiced in the Cockpit for the last two years by saying that the London Branch acted in the spirit of "a pleasant Friday evening debating society, which regarded discussion as an end in itself." One would imagine that all this meant a call to action, but the action was merely the establishment of a Research Department and the start of a new paper *The Distributist* for the discussion of the League's domestic business. The Research Secretary will explain his plans, enroll volunteers and allot tasks, thus "equipping the League with the information for lack of which it is as yet unable to agree on practical measures." The effectiveness of its Propaganda would, members were told, depend on its research.

"The pious appointment of investigators," wrote a Leader in *G.K.'s Weekly* in reference to a Government commission, "to report what is already common knowledge is nothing less than a face-saving, time-marking, shifty expedient." I don't think this article was one of Gilbert's, but I do wonder whether as time went on he did not recall his own old comparison between the early Christian and the modern Socialist. For Distributists far more than Socialists should have been vowed to action. There was a grave danger both of making their propaganda ineffective by lack of example and of weakening themselves as Distributists.

Yet there were many difficulties in their path, some of which may best be seen if we go back a little and recall the way in which the Encyclical *Rerum Novarum* was received by Catholics at the end of the last century. Written in Europe where the remains of the mediaeval social structure still lingered on far more than in industrial England or America, it was taken by the more conservative Catholics as a general confirmation of the established order. I well remember people like my own father and Father Bernard Vaughan quoting it in this sense. And if they tended to advert to only one half of it, the more radical Catholics readily obliged by appearing conscious solely of the other half and thus enabling themselves to be dismissed as one-sided.

Unfortunately they were worse than one-sided: they were curiously blind, with rare exceptions, to those true implications of the document which spelt Distributism—for which the word had not then been coined—or the Restoration of Property. "*The law, therefore, should favour ownership and its policy should be to induce as many people as possible to become owners.* Many excellent results will follow from this; and first of all, property will certainly become more equitably divided. For the effect of social change and revolution has been to divide society into two widely different castes. . . . *If workpeople can be encouraged to look forward to obtaining a share in the land, the result will be that the gulf between vast wealth and deep poverty will be bridged over, and the two orders will be brought nearer together.*"* Yet the Pope's words were treated almost as an acceptance of the existing conditions of property by the more conservative, while the more radical simply tried to evade them. The question of my youth undoubtedly was: how far can a Catholic go on the road to Socialism?

Distributism would seem today to have cut like a sword the knot of this mental confusion, but it did not do so for many people. I suppose the leading Distributist among the clergy was Father Vincent McNabb and I have heard him called a Socialist a hundred times. And even among those who had accepted the Distributist ideal and had now had fifteen years of the *New Witness* and *G.K.'s Weekly* to meditate upon—to say nothing of the Belloc and Chesterton books—there was still a good deal of confusion of mind to be cleared up. The Chesterbelloc had begun a mental revolution, but even the mind cannot be turned upside down in a moment of time: and then there is the will to be considered.

Gilbert often claimed that the Society he advocated was the norm, that the modern world was abnormal, was insane. But to achieve the norm in an abnormal world calls for high courage and a high degree of energy. It is much easier to sit and drink beer while planning the world that one wishes was there—the

* *Rerum Novarum* (translation in Husslein's *The Christian Social Manifesto*). Italics mine.

world of simplicity, hard work and independence. And about the details of this new world there was room for a variety of opinion. The Distributists soon began to argue and even to quarrel—about the admission of machinery into the Distributist state, about the nature of one another's Distributism and what was necessary to constitute a Distributist. The effect on Gilbert is interesting, for it showed his belief in the importance of the League. He hoped, he said, that the quarrel would not "turn into a dispute"—that it would remain a personal quarrel. "For impersonal quarrel is schism." He urged again and again that the dogmas of their creed should be defined.

Heaven forbid that we should ever be True Distributists: as a substitute for being Distributists. It would be a dismal thing to join the long and wavering procession of True Christians, True Socialists, True Imperialists; who are now progressing drearily into a featureless future; ready to change anything whatever except their names. These people escape endlessly by refusing definition which they call dogma. . . .

Practical politics are necessary, but they are in a sense narrow; and by themselves they do tend to split the world up into small sects. Only dogma is sufficiently universal to include us all.

Of the world surrounding him which refused definitions he said, "Because there is no image there is nothing except imaginaries." * But I think there must have been some blushes on Distributists' cheeks as they read his apology for some slight absence of mind. He explained his own "ghastly ignorance" of the details of the dispute, "which is bound up with the economic facts of the position," with the fact especially of

my own highly inadequate rendering of the part of the Financier. I am the thin and shadowy approximation to a Capitalist. . . . I could only manage until very lately to keep this paper in existence at all, by earning the money in the open market; and more especially in that busy and happy market where corpses are sold in batches; I mean the mart of Murder and Mystery, the booth of the Detective

* October 12, 1929.

Story. Many a squire has died in a dank, garden arbour, transfixed by a mysterious dagger, many a millionaire has perished silently though surrounded by a ring of private secretaries, in order that Mr. Belloc may have a paper in which he is allowed to point out that a great Empire does not default because it is growing richer. Many a shot has rung out in the silent night, many a constable has hurled himself through a crashing door, from under which there crawled a crimson stain, in order that there might be a page somewhere for Mr. Kenrick's virile and logical exposition of the principles of Distributism. Many an imperial jewel has vanished from its golden setting, many a detective crawled about on the carpet for clues, before some of those little printers' bills could be settled which enabled the most distinguished and intelligent of Distributists to denounce each other as Capitalists and Communists, in the columns of the *Cockpit* and elsewhere. This being my humble and even highly irrelevant contribution to the common team-work, it is obvious that it could not be done at the same time as a close following of the varying shades of thought in the Distributist debates. And, this ignorance of mine, though naturally very irritating to people better informed, has at least the advantage of giving some genuineness to my impartiality. I have never belonged distinctively to any of the different Distributist groups. I have never had time.

As time went on however and the disputes continued, he wrote a series of articles* which have in them that note so special to him, so embarrassing to some of his admirers, of deep and genuine respect for every person and every opinion. The small numbers of the Distributists, the greatness of the work to be done by them, would make any split in their ranks "a tremendous tragedy." The difficulty in keeping any movement in being was that of holding together the ardent pioneers and the rank and file.

Men who really have common convictions tend to break up. It is only those who have no convictions who always hang together. . . . Roughly the position is that there is a moderate body which regards extremists as visionary; a more extreme body which regards moderates as ineffective; and lastly a catastrophic simplification in the

* September 10, 17, 24, October 1, 1932.

social scene, which makes the simple enthusiast seem more fitted to the simple disaster.

There were two approaches that should be made to these differences. The first was to state the fundamental principles of Distributism. The crux of the quarrel was the question of machinery. But even those who held that machinery should be abolished in the Distributist State held it, he claimed, not as a first principle, but as a deduction from their first principles. Chesterton himself felt that machinery should be limited but not abolished: the order of things had been historically that men had been deprived of property and enslaved on the land *before* the machine-slavery of industrialism had become possible. The whole history of the machine might have been reversed in a state of free men. If a machine were used on a farm employing fifty men that would do the work of forty, it means forty men become unemployed, "but it is only because they were employed that they are unemployed. Now you and I, I hope to heaven, are not trying to increase employment. It is almost the only thing that is as bad as unemployment." In other words, he did not want men to be employees. Men working for themselves, men their own employers, their own employees—that was the objective of Distributism. A wide distribution of property was its primary aim. And he did not want the League to consist entirely of extremists lest it should be thought to consist entirely of cranks, especially at a moment when "intelligent people are beginning to like Distributism *because* Distributism is normal."

The other approach was heralded in the final article of the series (October 1, 1932) by a reference to the excitement over the Buckfast Benedictines who had just built their Abbey Church with their own hands—an adventure

to which, if I understand it as completely as I share it, the English blood will never be entirely cold. But about these new heroes of architecture there is one note that is not new; that comes from a very ancient tradition of psychology and morals. And that is that the adventurer has a right to his adventure; and the amateur has a right to his hobby; or rather to his love. But neither has any right to a general judgment of coldness or contempt for those whose hobby is human living; and whose chief adventures are at home. You will never hear the builders of Buckfast shouting aloud, "Down with Downside; for it was designed by a careful Gothic architect!" You will never hear them say, "How contemptible are these Catholics who pray in common churches; tawdry with waxwork imagery and Repository Art." Of the great adventurers who advance out of the Christian past,. in search of Christian. future, you could never say that the pioneers despise the army.

What seemed to Chesterton the oddest feature in the opposition to his idea of sanity was the apparent assumption that he was offering an impossible ideal to a world that was already working quite well. With bland disregard of the breakdown of their own system, the orthodox economists were challenging him to establish the flawlessness of his. They laughed at the Distributist desire if not to abolish at least to limit machinery. They adjured him to be more practical. Chesterton had replied in an earlier article:

There may be, and we ourselves believe there are, a certain number of things that had better be always done by machinery. . . . Machinery is now being used to produce numberless things that nobody needs. Machinery is being used to produce more machinery, to be used merely for the production of things that nobody needs. Machinery is being used to produce very badly things that everybody wants produced very well.

Machinery is being used for enormously expensive transport of things that might just as well be used where they are. Machinery is being used to take things thousands of miles in order to sell them and bring them back again because they are not sold. Machinery is being used to produce ornament that nobody ever looks at and architecture that nobody wants to look at. Machinery is taking suicides to Monte Carlo and coals to Newcastle, and all normal human purpose and intelligence to Bedlam; and our critics gaze at

it reverently and ask us how we expect ever to be so practical as
that.*

This desperate situation must be met by strengthening the
home, re-establishing the small workshop, re-creating the English peasantry. But first the ground might have to be cleared.

One phrase used in his articles—the "catastrophic simplification of the social scene"—reminds us once more how keenly
aware Gilbert was of something that had not yet happened, the
present war with its break-up of the social order. In the article,
from which I have been quoting, he compares the urgency of
the hour to the period of the French Revolution; in his *Outline
of Sanity* seven years earlier he had stressed the Distributist
ideal as the last chance to

do deliberately and well what nemesis will do wastefully and without pity; whether we cannot build a bridge from these slippery
downward slopes to freer and firmer land beyond, without consent-
ing yet that our most noble nation must descend into that valley of
humiliation in which nations disappear from history.†

In this book which he had tried in vain, he tells us, to make
"a grammar of Distributism," he touches on the enormous
changes that had made such a grammar of far greater urgency.
When *Rerum Novarum* was issued, or even eighteen years later
when G.K. wrote *What's Wrong with the World,* individualist
competition had not yet given place to the Trust, Combine or
Merger. "The American Trust is not private enterprise. It would
be truer to call the Spanish Inquisition private judgment." The
decline of trade had hardly begun at the turn of the Century,
liberty was still fairly widespread. But today we had lost liberty
as well as property and were living under the worst features of a
Socialist State. "I am one of those who believe that the cure for
centralisation is decentralisation."

Both in the book and in the paper he urged constantly a

---

* June 13, 1925.   † *Outline of Sanity,* p. 34.

double line of escape towards the restoration of freedom, initiative, property and the free family: the one line was the comparatively negative one of winning such concessions from the State as would make action possible, the other was personal action to be taken without any State aid or even encouragement. The germ of recovery lay in human nature. If you get poison out of a man's system "the time will come when he himself will think he would like a little ordinary food. If things even *begin* to be released they will begin to recover." To the question did Chesterton believe Distributism would save England, he answered, "No, I think Englishmen will save England, if they begin to have half a chance. I am therefore in this sense hopeful. I believe that the breakdown has been a breakdown of machinery and not of men."

A most difficult question to answer is the degree of the League's success. Its stated aim was propaganda, the spreading of ideas. "There is a danger that the tendency to regard talking as negligible may invade our little movement . . . our main business is to talk." One sees the point, of course; yet I cannot help feeling that it would have been better if the majority of Leaguers had done some bit of constructive work towards a Distributist world and sweated out of their system the irritability that found vent in some of their quarrels. After all the fight for freedom as far as it concerned attacking government was carried on week by week by the small group running the paper. The main body of Distributists would have learnt their own principles better by trying to act them, and been far more effective in conveying them to others.

Some members saw the need of individual action. Father Vincent set out in one number of the paper Fifteen Things that men could do for themselves as a step to the practice of a Distributist philosophy. Father Vincent, indeed, must be put beside Chesterton and Belloc as a really great Distributist writer. Useful books were written too by Mr. Heseltine and Mr. Blyton, who both also set to work to grow their own food. Mr. Blyton is still writing and still growing food. A workshop was started at Glasgow (probably the most active of the Branches), Father Vincent came to a League meeting clad in home-spun and home-woven garments, Mr. Blyton urged the example of what had been done by the Society of Friends in creating real wealth in the hands of the poor by their allotment schemes. (A weakness was visible; I think, in the very different and contemptuous treatment of Ford's effort to promote part-time farming among his workers during the depression because it was made by Ford, who was certainly no Distributist.)

But the most inspiring article in the paper in many a year was written by a man who, having tried in vain to get his writings printed, decided to start practising Distributism. He had pondered long, he says, on how the Rank and File of the Movement who were neither writers nor speakers should help, and the answer came to him "Do it yourself." After a fascinating description of how he built "the nucleus of a dwelling house against the time that a small plot of land could be secured" he ends:

By responsible work a man can best realise the dignity of his human personality. But most of us are caught in the net of industry and the best way out would seem to be to create, that is to employ one's leisure in conscious creative effort. This usually means the use of hand as well as head, and the concentration on some familiar craft. The aim also should be to acquire ownership in a small way; that is to acquire the means of production. If we are not at all events partly independent, how is it possible to urge on others the principles of small ownership.

In saying this he spoke from experience, for he had found that before he began his experiment his friends were exasperated by references to the principles of Distributism, while the sight of the building in progress began to convert them.

I have found many letters striking the note of gratitude to Gilbert for his goodness and the inspiration he has given. One of these, written by a sailor from H.M.S. *Hood*, is pure Distributism: "Your articles are so interesting tho' so hard to understand. . . . Why not come down a bit and educate the working class who are always in trouble because they don't know what they want. You see, sir, your use of words and phrases are so complicated, personally that's why I'm so fascinated when I read them, but really us average Council School educated people can't learn from you as we should . . . but what I do understand helps me to live. . . ."

The sailor goes on to tell the story of his life: a workhouse child, a farm boy: a seaman on a submarine who spent his "danger money" on a bit of land in Cornwall, married now and with two boys. "What a thrill of pleasure we have when we gaze over our land. . . . To be reared in a workhouse and then to leave a freehold home and land to one's children may not seem much to most people but still out of that my sons can build again. . . . I feel you understand this letter, what is in my heart, and I want to thank you very much for what you have done for me."

Towards the end of September 1932 the League held a meeting to which Gilbert came "as peacemaker." In the course of his speech he remarked that he had often said harsh things of America in the days of her prosperity but that in these days of adversity we might learn much from that country. He instanced the saying he had heard from a business man on his recent visit, "There's nothing for it but to go back to the farm," and noted the fact that America still had this large element of family farms as a basis for recovery. The suggestion that Distributists wanted to turn everybody into peasants had been another point answered in *The Outline*—"What we offer is proportion. We wish to correct the proportions of the modern state." * A considerable

* *Outline of Sanity*, p. 56.

return to the family farm would greatly improve this proportion.

But if he had spoken "harshly" of the United States it was nothing to the way he had talked of the British Empire. Although at moments he saw in imagination the romance of the fact that England had acquired an Empire "absentmindedly" through Englishmen with the solitary spirit of adventure and discovery, yet he had an unfortunate habit of abusing the Dominions. They were the "suburbs" of England (a curious phrase from the man who found suburbs "intoxicating"); we could not learn from them as we could from Europe for they were inferior to us; these and many other hard things he would throw out again and again in his articles. One letter in the *Cockpit* reproached him; from a New Zealander of English descent it asked him whether he really meant that those of his own race were so utterly indifferent to him; whether he really preferred Bohemians and Norwegians to Britons. The letter received no answer.

My husband and I used to wonder with secret smiles whether he was the Australian from whom Gilbert derived the idea of that country as a "raw and remote colony." Belloc also, in a letter extolling the Faith, asked "what else would print civilised stuff in Australasia?" Many years earlier Gilbert had written, in reviewing a book on the Cottages of England, of the inconsistency of the English upper classes who exalt the achievement of the national character in creating the Empire and disparage it concerning the possibility of re-creating the rural life of England. "Their creed contains two great articles: first that the common Englishman can get on anywhere, and second that the common Englishman cannot get on in England." Surely Chesterton had this same inconsistency, as it were, in reverse? The common Englishman was great in England, the common Irishman was great in Ireland, the common Scot was a figure of romance in Scotland, but when these common men created a new country that new country became contemptible.

The Empire took a magnificent revenge, for it was in the "Suburbs of England" that Distributism was first taken seriously and used as practical politics. A far more effectively distributist paper than *The Distributist* appeared in Ceylon under the able editorship of J. P. de Fonseka, in which action was recorded and the movements of Government watched and sometimes affected from the Distributist angle, and Catholic Social thinking formed on Distributist lines. This paper has a considerable effect also in India. But of course the main Distributist impact has been felt in the States, in Canada and in Australia.

There is a double-edged difficulty in talking about the influence of anyone on his times. On the one hand, as Mgr. Knox pointed out, all our generation has grown up under Chesterton's influence so completely that we do not even know when we are thinking Chesterton. One sees unacknowledged (and unconscious) quotations from him in books and articles, one hears them in speeches and sermons. On the other hand into the making of a movement there flow so many streams that it is possible to claim too much for a single influence however powerful. An American Distributist said to me lately that the movement set on foot by Chesterton had reached incredible proportions for one generation. I think this is true but we have also to render thanks (for example) to the suicide of the commercial-capitalist-combine which created the void for our philosophy. That the Distributist League has had much influence I doubt: in the United States the Chesterton spirit is better represented by that admirable paper *Free America* than by the American Distributists—for *Free America* is offering us precisely what the League has for the most part failed to offer—the laboratory test of the Distributist ideal. Every number carries stories of men who have in part-time or whole-time farming, in small shops, in backyard industries tried out Distributism and can tell us how it has worked and *how to work it*. Its editors Herbert Agar, Ralph Borsodi, Canon Ligutti and others, all foremost in the Ruralist movement, acknowledge debt to Chesterton and are carrying on the torch. Monsignor Ligutti's own work in the field of part-time farming, his own periodical and the thoughts that inspire the Catholic Rural Life Movement of America are among the most important manifestations of that universal religious and rural awakening for which Chesterton worked so hard and longed so ardently.

In Canada the Antigonish movement has shown a happy blending of theory and practise. For the University itself has in its Extension Movement and by its organ *The Maritime Co-operator* provided the theory, while up and down the country co-operative groups have built their own houses and canneries, started their own co-operative stores and savings banks, and made the Maritime Provinces a hopeful and property-owning community of small farmers and fisher folk. Several important books have grown out of this movement and at its basis lies the insistence on adult education which shall make ordinary men "Masters of their Destiny." Surely it is the authentic voice of Chesterton when Dr. Tompkins says "Trust the little fellow" or Dr. Coady declares "The people are great and powerful and can do everything."

In Australia Distributism has given a fresh slant to both Labour and Catholic leadership. The direct debt to Chesterton of the *Australian Catholic Worker* is immense, and while the paper also owes much to *The Catholic Worker* of America and to the Jocistes of France and Belgium, we find too that in America, France, and Belgium, Chesterton himself is studied more than any other Catholic Englishman. The Campion Society founded in Melbourne in 1931, the Catholic Guild of Social Studies in Adelaide, the Aquinas Society in Brisbane, the Chesterton Club in Perth and the Campion Society in Sydney have all based their thinking and their action on the Chesterbelloc philosophy. These groups have closely analysed Belloc's *Servile State* and *Restoration of Property* and have applied its principles in their social action in a most interesting fashion. Thus they opposed—and helped to defeat—a scheme for compulsory national insurance chiefly on the ground that "the social services in a modern State were the insurance premiums which capitalism paid on its life policy." With wages high enough to keep families in reasonable comfort and save a little, with well distributed property, national insurance would be rendered unnecessary. Yet on the other hand they supported —and won—national "child endowment" because although fundamentally only a palliative this at least strengthened the family by supplementing wages and helping parents towards ownership and property.

Most important however of all the Australian developments has been the approval of the main Distributist ideal by the Australasian Hierarchy as the aim of Catholic Social Action. This was especially set out in their Statement on Social Justice, issued on occasion of the first Social Justice Sunday in 1940.* The Hierarchy of New Zealand joined with that of Australia in establishing this celebration for the third Sunday after Easter.

Indeed, the social policy of Australian Catholicism has produced the slogan "Property for the People," while the policy has been brought into action both by many scattered individuals in that huge but thinly populated country and in organised fashion by the Rural Life movements with their own organs of expression.

If it is difficult to estimate the impact of mind upon mind it becomes bewilderingly impossible to weigh, in such a movement as Distributism, the actual practical effects. Partly because, while Distributism leads naturally to co-operation (an individual, says Chesterton, is only the Latin word for an atom and to reduce society to individuals is to smash it to atoms), still the movement is essentially local, the groups usually small.

For my own part I have travelled a good deal, always

* Published by the Australian C.T.S.

CHESTERTON DICTATING TO DOROTHY COLLINS—1929

with a primary interest in social developments, and everywhere I have found Chesterton or his derivatives. The numbers in America alone—both in the States and Canada—who are trying out these ideas in big and small communities is amazing. I did begin to make a list of vital movements beginning with the Jocistes and the American Catholic Worker, roving over the world and trying to estimate in each movement I had met the proportion of Chesterton's influence, and again the extent to which one movement is in debt to another—but I gave it up in despair. One can only say that certainly there has been a great stirring of the waters in every country: each has taken and has given to the other: and most of those thus co-operating have been the "little" men whom G.K. loved and in whom Dr. Tompkins tells us to trust. To utter nobly the thoughts of that little man was, Chesterton held, the highest aim that poet or prophet could set before him. Distributism is that little man's philosophy. Chesterton gave it large utterance.

And he could do it the more richly because—as he said many years ago of the religious philosophy that was the basis of his social outlook—"I did not make it. God and humanity made it and it made me."

Meanwhile he himself distributed royally. He gave help to the Catholic Land Movement, to Cecil Houses, to all who asked him for help. He educated several nieces and nephews of Frances and gave money or lent it in considerable sums to old friends in difficulties. If some event—perhaps Judgment Day— should call together all those helped financially by Gilbert and Frances, I think they will be surprised to meet one another and to discover what a lot of them there are. They gave too to the Catholic Church at Beaconsfield, which later became Gilbert's monument, and to which Top Meadow was left after Frances's death. But even Top Meadow was distributed, a small piece being cut off the garden and left to Dorothy Collins. And I think even in a Distributist heaven it must add to Gilbert's happiness to see the seventeen rabbits, the chickens and the beehives—to say nothing of the huge quantities of vegetables produced on this fragment of his property.

For this war like the last, with all its suffering, will, if the Bureaucracy permit it, again energise the people of England into that creative action which is the only soil for the seed of Distributism. It began by distributing the people. And London was no place for a Distributist movement. It is no chance that the growth of this philosophy is among small groups and in the countryside. "On the land," as Father Vincent often says, "you need not waste a moment of time or a scrap of material." This is the fierce and pious thrift that Gilbert saw in his youth as so poetical and in his age as a part of the philosophy of Distributism.

CHAPTER XXVII

Silver Wedding

THE CONSIDERATION OF the Distributist League that flowed out of the foundation of *G.K.'s Weekly* in 1925 has carried us some years ahead of our story. Back then to 1926 when Frances and Gilbert had been married 25 years.

One of the things taught me long ago when I first visited them at Beaconsfield was that it was properly to be called Beckonsfield: that it was *not* named for Disraeli but that he, impertinently, had chosen to be named for it. Gilbert often spelt it Bekonsfield to impress his point. Both in theory and practice he had a lot of local patriotism and a little of that special pride taken by all men in houses built by themselves. But most of his pride went out to the fact that his home was intensely English. He quoted a lover of Sussex who said among the beech trees of Buckinghamshire, "This is really the most English part of England." He felt it "no accident that has called this particular stretch of England the home counties." Public life was so ugly just now, the decay of patriotism under the corroding influence of an evil and cowardly sort of pacifism was hateful to him, but England still remained to re-vitalise the English when the time should come. The oaks that had made our ships could still fill us with "heroic memories; of Nelson dying under the low oaken beams or Collingwood scattering the acorns that they might grow into battleships." Yet if, he said, "I were choosing an entirely English emblem, I should choose the beech-tree." Beaconsfield was, by one theory, named from the beech forests that surrounded it, and while the oaks suggested adventure and the British lion, the beeches suggest rather the pigs that feed upon their mast and villages that grow up in the hollows and slow curves of the hills.

"The return to the real England with real Englishmen would be a return to the beech-woods, which still make this town like a home. At least they did until recently. I shall probably be told tomorrow that several beech forests have been removed to enable a motorist, temporarily deaf and blind, to go from Birmingham to Brighton."

It is at Top Meadow, whither they moved in 1922, that I always see Frances and Gilbert in a memory picture. They were to live there for the rest of their lives, and life there was the quiet background for all the vast mental activity and the journeying over England and Ireland and Europe and America that marked the years that remained.

The house began simply as a huge room or studio built in the field opposite Overroads. At one end was a stage which became the dining room: at the other end a minute study for Gilbert. The roof was high with great beams: at the study end was a musicians' gallery. A wide open fireplace held two rush-bottomed seats on one of which Frances sat in winter. They were the only warm corners, but Gilbert did not feel the cold and certainly could not have fitted into the inglenook. Opposite the fire was a long low window looking into the prettiest garden, where St. Francis stood guardian and preached perpetually to the birds. A pool held water lilies; and the flowers that surrounded the pool and the house were also cut and brought indoors in great quantities. Frances loved to have them in glowing masses against the background of books.

New shelves had to be added every year as the books accumulated. Big as the room was, the wall space was not enough and one large bookcase was built out from the wall near the fireplace into the middle of the room, as in a public library. It looked well there and it screened one from the bitterest blasts. For the place seemed full of air from the four winds of heaven. The rest of the house was built on to this room and looked tiny beside it. Kitchen and servants' quarters, two fair-sized and one very small bedroom, a minute sitting room for Frances where she kept her collection of tiny things—toys and ornaments mostly less than an inch, many far smaller, that were the delight of children. She had not, Gilbert remarked, allowed her taste to guide her in choosing a husband.

A mixture of Gilbert's strong and weak qualities affected his dealings with his dependents. I am not sure he felt certain that it was quite right that he should have a gardener: anyhow, no man was ever paid so highly and allowed to idle so completely as was one gardener I remember there, an exceedingly able gardener when he chose to work. To such trifles as the disappearance of coal or tools, neither Gilbert nor Frances would dream of adverting. And they were entirely at the mercy of a "hard case" story at all times. One man used to call weekly to receive ten shillings—for what service no one was able to form the faintest conception. Should he fail to appear Gilbert mailed the money. He was found one day fighting another man on the doorstep for daring to beg from Mr. Chesterton!

From a conventional point of view the maids were inconceivably casual. Neither Gilbert nor Frances would have thought it right to insist on caps or indeed on any sort of uniform. It is my impression that I have been waited on at dinner by someone garbed in a skirt, a sweater and a pair of bedroom slippers. And the parlor maid took for granted her own presence beside Frances and Dorothy Collins as a chief mourner at Gilbert's funeral.

According to Bernard Shaw, writing of Dickens, marriage between a genius and an ordinary or normal woman could not succeed—the gap was too wide. Dickens had thought he could go through with it, only because he had not measured the gap. In this theory, as in so much else, Gilbert stood violently opposed to Shaw. No doubt he must at times have realised that there was an intellectual gap between himself and the ordinary man or woman, but it was a thing utterly unimportant. Character, love, sanity: these things mattered infinitely more, and he more than once depicts the genius as painfully climbing to reach the ordinary.

His views concerning the sexes were equally at variance with those of Shaw and of most of the moderns. He was quite frankly the old-fashioned man and Frances was the old-fashioned woman. They both agreed that there is one side of life that belongs to man—the side of endless cigars smoked over endless discussions about the universe. Gilbert, in *What's Wrong With the World,* tells us that the voice in which the working woman summons her husband from the tavern is the same voice as that of the hostess who, leaving the men in the dining room, tells her husband not to stay too long over the cigars.

Of this voice he entirely approved so long as it did not ask to stay on in the dining room. He often said that the important thing for a country was that the men should be manly, the women womanly: the thing he hated was the modern hybrid: the woman who gate-crashes the male side of life: no one, he had said in a letter of his engagement time, "takes such a fierce pleasure as I do in things being themselves." And both he and Frances found amusement in that "eternal equality" which Gilbert saw in the sexes so long as they kept their eternal separateness. If everything, he said, is trying to be red some things are redder than others, but there is an eternal and unalterable equality between red and green.

It so happens that in the matter of the wives of great men he had something to say more than once. He longed to hear the point of view of Mrs. Cobbett who "remains in the background of his life in a sort of powerful silence." He combated Shaw's notion that the young poet would repudiate domestic toils for his wife: rather he would idealise them—though this,

Gilbert admits, might at times be hard on the wife. But the matter is best expressed in the love scene in one of his later romances: *Tales of the Long Bow:*

That valley had a quality of repose with a stir of refreshment, as if the west wind had been snared in it and tamed into a summer air. . . .

"What would you say if I turned the world upside down and set my foot upon the sun and the moon?"

"I should say," replied Joan Hardy, still smiling, "that you wanted somebody to look after you."

He stared at her for a moment in an almost abstracted fashion as if he had not fully understood; then he laughed quite suddenly and uncontrollably, like a man who has seen something very close to him that he knows he is a fool not to have seen before. So a man will fall over something in a game of hiding-and-seeking, and get up shaken with laughter.

"What a bump your mother earth gives you when you fall out of an aeroplane," he said. "What a thing is horse-sense, and how much finer really than the poetry of Pegasus! And when there is everything else as well that makes the sky clean and the earth kind, beauty and bravery and the lifting of the head—well, you are right enough, Joan. Will you take care of me?" *

Frances was not especially interesting intellectually although she had much more mind than Joan in the story, but above all she carried with her a "quality of repose with a stir of refreshment."

"Will you take care of me?"

Neither of them probably had measured at first all that that care would mean. Only bit by bit would the full degree of his physical dependence, as we have seen it through the years, become clear to her. The strenuous campaign in the matter of appearances begun during the engagement might alter in direction but had rather to be intensified in degree as he grew older. Shaving, bathing, even dressing were daily problems to him.

* Pp. 89, 119.

"Heat the water," an early secretary at Overroads heard Frances saying to the cook, "Mr. Chesterton is going to have a bath." And "O, need I," came in tones of deepest depression from the study. The thought of that vast form climbing into and out of the bathtub does make one realise how a matter of easy everyday practice to the normal person became to him almost a heroic venture. His tie, his boots, were equally a problem: I remember his appearing once at breakfast in two ties and claiming, when I noticed it, that it proved he paid too much, not too little, attention to dress. Doctors, dentists, oculists were all needed at times, but Gilbert would never discover the need or achieve appointments or the keeping of them. Still more serious was the question of how the two were to live and to do all the acts of generosity that to them both seemed almost more necessary than their own living. Hard as he worked, Dorothy Collins has told me that when she came to them in this year (1926) they had almost nothing saved.

It may be remembered that Gilbert wrote to Frances during their engagement that his only quality as a shopper was ability to get rid of money and that he was not good at "such minor observances" as bringing home what he had bought or even remembering what it was. Through boyhood and into manhood his parents, as we have seen, had never given him money to handle and he certainly never learnt to handle it later in life. "He spent money like water," Belloc told me. Realising his own incapacity he arranged fairly early to have Frances look after their finances, bank the money and draw checks. "When we set up a house, darling," he had said, "I think you will have to do the shopping." All he handled was small sums by way of pocket money—"very playfully regarded by both" Father O'Connor writes, for he had often witnessed the joke that they made of it.

"What could she do," he continues, "when Gilbert went out with £5.18.6 or words to that effect, and came back invariably without a copper, not knowing where his money had gone?"

At a hotel in Warsaw the manager entreated him not to bring every beggar in town around the door. He could never refuse a beggar and the money not given away was probably dropped in the street or in a shop. The solution they hit upon was that of accounts at the shops and hotels for anything that could not simply be brought home by Frances and placed by his side. Father O'Connor wrote to Dorothy Collins of "the loving care with which Frances anticipated all his wishes— never was the cigar box out of date—*you* know this, and it was so long before you came. And his toddle to the Railway Hotel for port or a quart according to climatic conditions. . . . She devised and built the studio for Gilbert to play at and play in. It used to be crowded at receptions, as on the night when Gilbert broke his arm. He had been toying with the tankard that evening, to the detriment of social intercourse, but not much, I thought. We were all in good fettle. The *Ballad of the White Horse* was just going to the printers. That was never penned in Fleet Street. Nor *The Everlasting Man*. He wrote verbosely there in the office. At Beaconsfield he was pulled together, braced."

The studio, become the house, almost certainly cost more than they had planned—building always does—but the two great drains were the benefactions and the paper. Frances signed, as a matter of course, every check Gilbert wanted, but I imagine it was sometimes with a little sigh that she wrote the checks for the endless telephones, telegrams, printers' bills and other expenses that poured out to support a paper which to her seemed chiefly a drain on Gilbert's energies that could not but diminish his creative writing. In the six years 1927–1933, he paid over £3000 into the paper. 1931–2 were the worst years. In them the checks she had to sign totalled £1500.

The last sentences quoted from Father O'Connor touch on

the deepest—perhaps the only deep—problem for them both. For far the hardest thing was the struggle against the real danger that he might again drink too much, as he had before the illness that so nearly killed him in 1915. This struggle was rendered especially hard by two elements in her make-up: Frances wanted always to give Gilbert exactly what *he* wanted, and she hated to admit even to herself anything that could be called a fault in him. She saw the overwork that she was powerless to stop: she could not but be aware how great it made the temptation. It was for her to remember the old illness, to be vigilant without worrying him, to help him against himself.

After the long illness Dr. Pocock had advised total abstinence for some years, largely because, as he told me, Gilbert, unless specially warned, ate and drank absentmindedly anything that happened to be there! He observed this prohibition faithfully until Dr. Pocock left Beaconsfield in 1919. Dr. Bakewell, who succeeded him advised moderation but only occasionally found it necessary to order total abstention. It was the amount of liquid he feared rather than its nature. When he forbade wine he did so because wine increased the general tendency to absorb liquid. For Gilbert was always unslakeably thirsty. Daily he drank several bottles of Vichy Water or Evian, also of claret at what may be called the "open" seasons, and many cups of tea and coffee. Spirits he practically never touched, nor such heavier wines as port and sherry. But even two bottles of claret or Burgundy, although usually appearing to brighten his intellect, might well be a serious strain on the digestion of a man who overworked the mind without exercising the body.

"He loved to sip a glass of wine," Monsignor O'Connor writes, "and to stroll between sips in and out of his study, brooding and jotting, and then the dictation was ready for the morning."

Dorothy Collins once kept a record for a few weeks of the number of words dictated of the book of the moment—usually

thirteen to fourteen thousand, about twenty-one hours weekly
—exclusive of journalism, editing and lecturing. The pressure
was tremendous and increasing, nor was it felt by Gilbert only.
In a letter to Maurice Baring at the time of his conversion he
writes: "For deeper reasons than I could ever explain, my mind
has to turn especially on the thought of my wife, whose life
has been in many ways a very heroic tragedy; and to whom I
am so much in debt of honour that I cannot bear to leave her,
even psychologically, if it be possible by tact and sympathy to
take her with me."

Frances would indeed have been amazed to find herself cast
for such a part. Her life had held two tragic events—Gertrude's
death and the much sadder death of her brother, believed to
have killed himself. With her faith and her profound affections
such an end had stabbed deep. Yet certainly Frances did not
view herself as other than happy: in fact, I think she very seldom thought about herself at all. There was something of
heroism in this very self-forgetfulness. Frances never had good
health and for some years had suffered from arthritis of the
spine. Yet intimate as I was I knew this only after her death.
My husband was saying lately that had he been asked to choose
adjectives to describe Frances he would have chosen "cheerful"
and "well-balanced." Of all the people we have known we felt
she was one of the closest to the norm of sanity and mental
health: quite an achievement for a woman suffering from a
really painful complaint.

Yet I think when Gilbert used the strong phrase "heroic
tragedy" he saw with his great insight that his frail wife, beside
their heavy cross of childlessness, beside the burden of her own
physical and spiritual sufferings, was carrying the weight of his
achievement, and that it was not a light one. Heroic was the
right word but tragedy the wrong, for this life given to her
keeping ended on a note of triumph.

The treatment of a situation of this kind can, of course,

easily be made unreal. In the sort of golden glow cast by the imagination on Fleet Street with its taverns and its drinks, next morning's headache is always omitted: but even the finer, deeper glow of the domestic hearth has its ashy moments. No finite beings can conduct their lives with complete absence of errors and regrets. In any human relationship, however perfect, the people concerned sometimes bore or annoy or even hurt one another. That is one of the main things that sends Catholics week by week or month by month to the Confessional, which brings for everyman something of the renewal and re-creation of daily joy that the genius Gilbert saw when he wrote *Manalive*. In this story the hero is always eloping with his own wife and marrying her again. Flora Finching's "It was not ecstasy it was comfort" is a common enough view of a reasonably successful marriage, but Gilbert wanted to keep and did keep the flashes of ecstasy. When he wrote *Manalive* he had been married eleven years and he used a thought that had inspired a poem to Frances while they were engaged. The heroine in the story keeps changing her second name, but the name is always a colour: in one town the hero runs away with her as Mary Grey, in another as Mary Green. Thus as a girl Gilbert had seen Frances in green and had understood why green trees and fields are beautiful; had seen her in grey and had learnt a new love for grey winter days, and the grey robes of palmers; and in blue—

> Then saw I how the fashioner
> Splashed reckless blue on sky and sea
> And ere 'twas good enough for her
> He tried it on eternity.

When they came back from Jerusalem Gilbert dedicated to Frances *The Ballad of St. Barbara* and we find him again at his old trick: seeing as her throne the great stones of the mediaeval walls, seeing nature as her background. With all apologies to the cynics I am afraid that the judgment of the biographer upon all the evidence must be that after twenty-five years Gilbert not only loved his wife tenderly, but was still ardently in love with her!

A curious prayer of his youth was fulfilled as they celebrated this year their silver wedding.

> A wan new garment of young green,
>   Touched as you turned your soft brown hair;
>   And in me surged the strangest prayer
> Ever in lover's heart hath been.
>
> That I who saw your youth's bright page,
>   A rainbow change from robe to robe,
>   Might see you on this earthly globe,
> Crowned with the silver crown of age.
>
> Your dear hair powdered in strange guise,
>   Your dear face touched with colours pale,
>   And gazing through the mask and veil
> The mirth of your immortal eyes.*

Four years earlier Frances had aided Gilbert in making the decision for which she was not yet herself ready, to do the act which he called "the most difficult of all my acts of freedom." And indeed much of that freedom of full manhood he owed to her.

Now after four years of waiting she was almost ready to join him. She wrote to Father O'Connor:

June 20 [1926]

Dear Padre—

I want now, as soon as I can see a few days clear before me to place myself under instruction to enter the Church. The whole position is full of difficulties and I pray you Padre to tell me the first step to take. I *don't* want my instruction to be here. I don't want to be the talk of Beaconsfield and for people to say I've only followed Gilbert. It isn't true and I've had a hard fight not to let my love for him lead me to the truth. I knew you would not accept me for such

---

* "The Last Masquerade," *Collected Poems,* pp. 348-9.

motives. But I am very tired and very worried. Many things are difficult for me. My health included which makes strenuous attention a bit of a strain. I know you understand—Tell me what I shall do.

Yours affecly

FRANCES CHESTERTON.

Between this letter and the next Gilbert and Frances celebrated their silver wedding.

July 12

MY DEAR PADRE—

We have had such a week of alarums and excitements that I had not even time to thank you for the spoons. They are just what I like and incidentally just what I wanted. I feel so hopeless at getting out of this net of responsibilities in which I am at present enmeshed and to find time for instruction. I feel I have a lot to learn and I think after all I had better go quietly to Father Walker * and talk to him. Gilbert is writing to you himself. I know he thinks I have made myself rather unhappy about things—and he is so involved with the paper (I pray he gives it up) we have not been able to talk over things sensibly. Please be very patient with me, because it is so difficult to get clear. My nephew Peter is very ill and I have to spend a lot of time with my poor sister.

Yrs gratefully

FRANCES CHESTERTON.

[Undated]

DEAR PADRE—

Many grateful thanks. Did you receive your copy of the "Incredulity of Father Brown." It was put aside for you, but I do not know if it was sent off or appropriated by somebody else.

I have written to Father Walker and after having seen him and had a talk I shall know what I ought to do. It is only the mass of work, the paper, my poor Peter and money worries that keep me on the edge from morning till night. I feel the paper must go, it is too much for Gilbert (4 days work always) and consequently too much for me who have to attend to everything else. Trying tc settle an income-tax dispute has nearly brought me to tears.

* The Parish Priest.

You will understand how difficult it is to get time to think and adjust my conclusions.

Yrs affect.

FRANCES CHESTERTON.

This group of letters is for Frances amazingly unreserved. I have never known a happier Catholic than she was once the shivering on the bank was over and the plunge had been taken. One would say she had been in the Church all her life.

This was indeed a year of fulfillment: the year of the completion of their home, for they surprisingly acquired a daughter! I sometimes wondered why Frances and Gilbert had never adopted a child: they lavished much love on nieces, nephews and godchildren, but this was the only fulfillment to their longing until almost old age—and even then their conscious act was merely that of engaging a secretary. They had had many secretaries before, some of whom came with a quite inadequate training. "They learnt on Gilbert," as a friend once put it. It was difficult, too, for the secretaries, since neither Gilbert nor Frances had any idea of hours or of the arrangement of work. It was quite probable that Gilbert would suddenly want to dictate late in the evening or again that Frances would ask the secretary of the moment to run into the village for the fish in the middle of the morning. Hence rather general discomfort. Gilbert dictated straight to the typewriter, so shorthand was not needed. He went very slowly with many pauses. But it is typical of this period that no carbons were kept of letters sent, no files of letters received.

In 1926 came Dorothy Collins. Not only did she bring order out of chaos, but she became first the very dear friend of both Frances and Gilbert and finally all that their own daughter could have been. I remember how Frances talked of her to me when she was hoping Dorothy would become a Catholic (which she did some years later) and again when she herself was left solitary by her husband's death, and how I felt with inward thanksgiving that no child could mean more to her mother. But long before this stage was reached came a great lightening of the burden of living. No longer would Frances cry over income tax returns, no longer would money worry her. Chauffeur as well as secretary Dorothy drove them both to London for engagements and through England and Europe on holidays or lecture tours. She went with them to America and handled the business of their second tour there. Now when friends rang up to make arrangements Frances or Gilbert could say: "Would you ring again when Dorothy comes in. I'm not quite sure. She keeps the engagement book." And while Dorothy sternly warded off the undesirables, it worked out much better for friends as no engagement book had been kept before with any regularity. Now engagements were kept as well as an engagement book. Frances would still deal with the clothing question, but Dorothy handled it if she were unwell, and in every case delivered him punctually and brought him home again. A few of the lectures and debates of these years were: "Is Journalism Justifiable?", "An Aspect of St. Francis of Assisi," "The Problem of Liberty," "Is the House of Commons any Use," "What Poland Is," "Culture and the Coming Peril," "Progress and Old Books," "Americanization," "The Modern Novel," "If I Were a Dictator."

The excitement of Catholics everywhere had been intense when Gilbert came into the church: in England it was almost as great over Frances. Her real wish to remain in the background, her dislike of publicity, were seldom believed in by those who did not know her. I happened to be present at a conversation between the proprietor and the editor of a Catholic paper which had displayed a poster all over London announcing her conversion. One of them had heard that she was annoyed and for a moment both seemed a little dashed. Then said one: "Of course she has to pretend not to like it"—and this was at once accepted by the other: for both took for granted that such publicity could in reality have given her nothing but pleasure.

It was difficult at first for either Frances or Gilbert to see the wood for the trees in their new environment, and it was the greatest good fortune that the year of Frances's reception was also that of the new simplification following upon Dorothy's arrival. For the preceding few years had resembled the hectic period of the lionising of the young Chesterton of 1904. Requests poured in, for lectures, for articles, for introductions to books. "Are there no other Catholics to do things?" Frances asked me rather plaintively. Of these years Monsignor Knox said later, "his health had begun to decline, and he was overworked, partly through our fault."

A dip into the post bag brings up some letters from Father Martindale to Gilbert and Frances passing on various requests, but also realising the difficulty: "I sympathize with all desperately busy men": "I have already protected him by advising small or fussy groups not to invite him now and again." The solitary recollection I have of any interest Gilbert showed in a review of his books is the remark he made to my husband when Father Martindale had said of *The Queen of Seven Swords* "Francis Thompson is here outpassed." Gilbert repeated the phrase and said eagerly: "He wouldn't say it unless he meant it, would he?"

C.C.M., who has himself been caricatured talking on the radio, typing and eating at the same time, as different from G.K.C. as possible in his pale slimness and almost transparent appearance, was no less busy over a thousand activities. It was interesting that he should ask Gilbert's help, especially in that cementing of Catholics throughout the Empire that has always so passionately preoccupied him. In the War he had discovered in military hospitals the ordinary Englishman and above all the ordinary Australian and New Zealander. To them and to the Apostolate of tne Sea he was to aevote primarily all his later life.

Writing therefore to counsel the Chestertons as to which Catholic works should have precedence, we find him wanting an article for a New Zealand paper "the only one of its sort in N.Z., and you may say that it affects the *entire Catholic* community of the two islands," an autographed book for "a hulking devotee of yours and a member of the Australia rugger team, I think eight of them are Catholics." This "would give enormous joy to him" and "would be known in no time throughout Australia. Do try to."

From South Africa he wrote to Frances:

You will be surprised to get a letter from me from a nameless place 50 miles inland from the Nyanga mountains, which you will find (variously spelt) westward from, say Beira on the African east coast. This is the reason—

Recently a boy in a kraal here was found cutting pious pictures from a newspaper that he had somehow got hold of (he was a good little Catholic!). "Why are you cutting out that one?" "Because *this* is a Great Mukuru in the Catholic Church." (Mukuru is Potentate and will serve from St. Joseph right along to the Pope, not to mention the Little Flower. . . .) The Great Mukuru in this case was yourself! So there!

I hope you will smile with pleasure, but not try to answer, as please God I sail on the 31st and ought to be back in London in early Sept., a good deal better, thank God.

Please remember me affectionately to Gilbert. This is the first time a typemachine has clicked just here; its accompaniment, in an otherwise dead silence, is a distant gurgling yodel, so to say—some native feeling happy in the brilliantly hot sunlight, which, all the same, cannot make the thin air hot. I sleep (when possible) under furs, with the occasional insect dropping off the thatch over my head.

Later, planning a meeting for the Apostolate of the Sea at Queen's Hall, he writes to Gilbert:

Similarly Fr. McNabb must be given his head and I have told him he shall be given it. I hope to be purely practical and possibly a little sentimental. . . . The Seaman is everywhere, yet, for us, nowhere. He carries everywhere his child's heart, man's body, hungry unfed soul, unique power of feeding his goodness into others. The all-round (the world) man; the sea-limited man; the man whose life is made up of storms and stars; the most secretive and the most open-hearted man of any. . . . Now *I* will do all the clumsy stuff. *You* pull it all up into the human-sublime divine-humble air.

He has no privacy, and is more lonely than anyone. He has Water, and God; and MUST find Christ walking over the waves towards him. And no ghost.

Father Vincent McNabb who was to be "given his head" at this meeting was not a new friend of Catholic days but a very old one. A friendly critic of my manuscript asks whether he, even more than Belloc or Chesterton, does not merit the title of the Father of Distributism. At least he brings into the movement something none other could bring. He bases his social philosophy closely on the gospels—of which his knowledge is almost unique—and his articles bear such titles as "The Economics of Bethlehem" or "Big Scale Agriculture and the Gospels." Hatred of machinery has combined with love of poverty to sunder him from a typewriter, and these articles are all hand-written in most exquisite and legible script. His letters have always come in old envelopes turned inside out; he walks whenever possible and wears a shabby white habit and broken boots. Both Frances and Gilbert loved him dearly and their rare meetings were red letter days for both. Besides the link of Distributism the two men were united in caring deeply for the re-awakened interest in St. Thomas and his philosophy.

The Benedictine, as well as the Dominican, outlook and history especially appealed to Gilbert, and the friendship with Father Ignatius Rice, which had begun almost with the century, grew steadily. He assisted, as we have seen, at Gilbert's reception into the Church: and whenever they met after that Gilbert would remind him, "We were together on the great day."

High Wycombe was the Chesterton's parish until, largely by

their help, a church could be built at Beaconsfield. At first this church was served by Father Walker, parish priest of High Wycombe. It was he who had prepared Gilbert for his First Communion and he has sent me some of his recollections:

It certainly did not take long to prepare him for he evidently knew as much as I could tell him. Nevertheless, he said I was to treat him as I would any child whom I was teaching. This, knowing the man whom I was instructing, for I had at the time carefully waded through his *Orthodoxy* twice, was, indeed, an undertaking of magnitude. However, I went through the catechism (he was importunate that I should use it as he said all the children made use of it), very meticulously explaining all the details, to which he lent a most vigilant and unswerving attention. For instance, he wanted me to explain the reason of the drop of water being put into the wine at the preparing of the chalice for the Holy Sacrifice.

Father Walker describes Gilbert opening a bazaar and spending lavishly at every stall, afterwards being photographed in his company. Father Walker himself weighed 245 lbs., and the caption was "Giants in the Faith." On his departure, Gilbert presided at the farewell meeting and made a speech which, says Father Walker, "gave me no end of delight." Father (now Monsignor) Smith became the first rector of Beaconsfield as a separate parish. The Chestertons loved the little church there which later became Gilbert's memorial and to which, among other things, they gave a very beautiful statue of Our Lady. But when it had first been dedicated there had been for both Frances and Gilbert a deep disappointment. Curiously enough, neither of them had any devotion to the Little Flower who was chosen as Patron: they had hoped for a dedication to the English Martyrs. Later Gilbert used to tell Dorothy, who loved St. Thérèse, that he could not care for her, "with all apologies to you, Dorothy."

He did not go often to Confession, Dorothy says, but when he did go you could hear him all over the church. Getting up in the morning was always a fearful effort to him, and starting for early Mass he would say to her, "What but religion would bring us to such an evil pass!"

Meanwhile the books went on. In 1926 appeared *The Outline of Sanity*, *The Catholic Church and Conversion*, chiefly concerned with his own mental history, *The Incredulity of Father Brown* and *The Queen of Seven Swords*. In 1927 for the first time his scattered poems were brought into the volume of *Collected Poems*.

St. Augustine asks whether we can praise God before we know Him: Gilbert answered that question when by praise and thanksgiving he came as a boy to the discovery of God, beginning by a passionate desire to thank *someone* for the Universe. There is much praise in the *Collected Poems*. There is the note of hope in an almost hopeless fight in *The Ballad of the White Horse*. There are lovely poems to his wife. Since Browning none has understood the Sacrament of Marriage as well as Gilbert Chesterton.

In 1927 there also appeared, beside a couple of pamphlets:

> The Return of Don Quixote
> Robert Louis Stevenson
> The Secret of Father Brown
> The Judgment of Dr. Johnson

Robert Louis Stevenson took Gilbert back to his boyhood and is by general agreement among the best of his literary studies. But the best thing he ever said apropos of Stevenson came not in this book but in his attack on the "science" of eugenics:

Keats died young; but he had more pleasure in a minute than a Eugenist gets in a month. Stevenson had lung trouble; and it may, for all I know, have been perceptible to the Eugenic eye even a generation before. But who would perform that illegal operation: the stopping of Stevenson? Intercepting a letter bursting with good news, confiscating a hamper full of presents and prizes, pouring torrents of intoxicating wine into the sea, all this is a faint approximation for the Eugenic inaction of the ancestors of Stevenson. This, however, is not the essential point; with Stevenson it is not merely a case of the pleasure we get, but of the pleasure he got. If he had died without writing a line, he would have had more red-hot joy than is given to most men. Shall I say of him, to whom I owe so much, let the day perish wherein he was born? Shall I pray that the stars of the twilight thereof be dark and it be not numbered among the days of the year, because it shut not up the days of his mother's womb? I respectfully decline; like Job, I will put my hand upon my mouth.*

When the *Stevenson* itself appeared, Sir Edmund Gosse wrote:

I have just finished reading the book in which you smite the detractors of R.L.S. hip and thigh. I cannot express without a sort of hyperbole the sentiments which you have awakened; of joy, of satisfaction, of relief, of malicious and vindictive pleasure. We are avenged at last. . . .

It is and always since his death has been impossible for me to write anything which went below the surface of R.L.S. I loved him, and still love him, too tenderly to analyse him. But you, who have the privilege of not being dazzled by having known him, have taken the task into your strong competent hands. You could not have done it better.

The latest survivor, the only survivor, of his little early circle of intimate friends thanks you from the bottom of his heart.

Don Quixote is a fantasia about the future: in which the study of heraldry leads to the discovery of England and the centuries of her happiness and of her faith. Increasingly Gilbert saw the only future for his country in a re-marriage between those divorced three hundred years ago: England and the Catholic Church. *Don Quixote* is among the less good of his books, but like all the works of these years it is saturated with Catholicism. I wondered whether I felt more admiration or amazement

---

* *Eugenics and Other Evils*, p. 57.

when a man once asked us to publish a book on Chesterton saying, "I am an atheist myself but that doesn't matter, as I don't deal with his religion."

As a young man Gilbert had wanted to marry the religion of Dr. Johnson to the Republicanism of Wilkes and in his Catholic faith of today he saw simply the rounding out and the completing of the religion of Dr. Johnson. *The Judgment of Dr. Johnson,* his play about that great man was, like *Magic,* an immense succès d'estime but not a stage success: it was brilliantly acted and appreciatively criticised but could not win a public. Bernard Shaw was still constantly urging Gilbert towards the drama. Belloc too believed he could write a successful play and he and Anstey (author of *Vice Versa*) suggested the dramatising of a Belloc story. But neither the scenario they jointly sketched for Belloc's *Emerald* nor another made by Gilbert alone for his own *Flying Inn* ever reached the stage.

I remember going with the Chestertons to a pre-view of a Father Brown picture. Two of the stories had been cleverly combined, the cast was first rate, including Una O'Connor and Walter Connolly, and I came out feeling convinced that Father Brown would become another Charlie Chan. The stories would adapt so well, abounding as they do in scenes impossible for the stage but perfectly easy for the screen—high walls, windows, ladders, flying harlequins. But the first picture failed (possibly because it was too short) and no more were made. The drama remained the one field in which he had no success.

Shaw's name for Gilbert and Belloc—the Chesterbelloc—had come by the public to be used for the novels in which they collaborated. Belloc wrote the story, Chesterton drew the pictures, and the resulting product was known as the Chesterbelloc. A number of letters from Mr. Belloc beg Gilbert to do the drawings early in order to help the story. "I have already written a number of *situations* which you might care to sketch. I append a list. Your *drawing* makes all the difference to my *thinking:* I see the people in action more clearly." And again, "I can't write till I have the inspiration of your pencil. For the comedy in me is ailing."

Belloc would come over to Beaconsfield for a day or a night and the two men retire into Gilbert's minute study whence hoots of laughter would be heard. At the end of a couple of hours they would emerge with the drawings for a book complete, indeed several more than were needed.

Father Rice asked Gilbert once what he was writing and he replied, "My publishers have demanded a fresh batch of corpses." The little detective-priest ("I am very fond," said one reader to Chesterton, "of that officious little loafer") became a feature in crime anthologies, and when Anthony Berkeley in 1929 wanted to found the Detective Club he wrote that it "would be quite incomplete without the creator of Father Brown."

Gilbert soon became President. "Needless to say," writes Dorothy Sayers, "he read his part of the initiation ceremony with tremendous effect and enormous gusto."

In an article Gilbert wrote about the Club, he called it "a very small and quiet conspiracy, to which I am proud to belong." Meeting in various restaurants its members would "discuss various plots and schemes of crime." Some results of these discussions may be seen in the Initiation ceremonies which he made public in the article "thereby setting a good example to the Mafia, the Ku Klux Klan, the Illuminati . . . and all the other secret societies which now conduct the greater part of public life, in the age of Publicity and Public Opinion."

The Ruler shall say to the Candidate:

M.N. is it your firm desire to become a Member of the Detection Club?

Then the Candidate shall answer in a loud voice:

That is my desire.

Ruler:

Do you promise that your detectives shall well and truly detect the crimes presented to them using those wits which it may please you to bestow upon them and not placing reliance on nor making use of Divine Revelation, Feminine Intuition, Mumbo Jumbo, Jiggery-Pokery, Coincidence or Act of God?

Candidate:

I do.

Ruler:

Do you solemnly swear never to conceal a vital clue from the reader?

Candidate:

I do.

Ruler:

Do you promise to observe a seemly moderation in the use of Gangs, Conspiracies, Death-Rays, Ghosts, Hypnotism, Trap-Doors, Chinamen, Super-Criminals and Lunatics; and utterly and for ever to forswear Mysterious Poisons unknown to Science?

Candidate:

I do.

Ruler:

Will you honour the King's English?

Candidate:

I will.

Then the Ruler shall ask:

M.N. Is there anything you hold sacred?

Then the Candidate having named a Thing which he holds of peculiar sanctity, the Ruler shall ask:

M.N. Do you swear by (*Here the Ruler shall name the Thing which the Candidate has declared to be his Peculiar Sanctity*) to observe faithfully all these promises which you have made, so long as you are a member of the Club?

But if the Candidate is not able to name a Thing which he holds sacred, then the Ruler shall propose the Oath in this manner following:

M.N. Do you, as you hope to increase your Sales, swear to observe faithfully all these promises which you have made. so long as you are a member of the Club?

A book called *The Floating Admiral* was brought out by the Club. Chesterton wrote the introduction and each member produced one chapter. Reading it without inside knowledge I conceived that the idea was for each to clear up the problems created by his predecessor and create fresh ones for his successor. Gilbert tells of the subtler joke underlying the story:

Perhaps the most characteristic thing that the Detection Club ever did was to publish a detective story, which was quite a good detective story, but the best things in which could not possibly be understood by anybody except the gang of criminals that had produced it. It was called *The Floating Admiral*, and was written somewhat uproariously in the manner of one of those "paper games" in which each writer in turn continues a story of which he knows neither head nor tail. It turned out remarkably readable, but the joke of it will never be discovered by the ordinary reader; for the truth is that almost every chapter thus contributed by an amateur detective is a satire on the personal peculiarities of the last amateur detective. This, it will be sternly said, is not the way to become a best-seller. It is a matter of taste; but to my mind there is always a curious tingle of obscure excitement, in the works of this kind which have remained here and there in literary history; the sort of book that it is even more enjoyable to write than to read.

The Floating Admiral was a fair success financially. "We hired a sort of garret," writes Monsignor Knox "with the proceeds, as Club Rooms; and on the night after we all received our keys the premises were burglariously entered; why or by whom is still a mystery, but it was a good joke that it should happen to the Detective Club."

Lord Peter and Father Brown and Monsieur Poirot—how were the mighty fallen!

There is a custom in both English and Scottish universities of electing a Lord Rector with the accompaniment of much undergraduate "ragging" of the choicest kind. The candidates usually each represent a political party but personal popularity has much to say in their success. At the Scottish universities the contests are particularly spirited, and his keen sense of fun made Gilbert ready to accept frequent invitations to stand. At Glasgow in 1925 Austen Chamberlain got 1242 votes, Chesterton 968 and Sidney Webb 285. "What swamped you," wrote Jack Phillimore, always critical of the gentler sex, "was the women, whose simple snobbery cannot get past the top hat and frock coat and Right Honourable . . . Boyle was never kidnapped: others were removed into the mountains."

The last sentence might have been lifted from Sir Walter: it refers to a pleasing habit among Scots undergraduates of kidnapping the supporters of their opponents and keeping them safely concealed till after the election.

Whether or not it was through their simple snobbery, as Professor Phillimore said, it was certainly the women's vote that swamped him: of the 374 votes by which Austen Chamberlain beat Chesterton, the men only accounted for 20, the women for 354. But it must have been some profounder passion that caused one of England's leading women novelists to write to the Secretary of the Glasgow University Liberal Club:

> I fail to see why you should desire to embarrass Liberalism at one of its least happy moments by associating it with that village idiot on a large scale who is responsible for the muddled economics and disagreeable fantastics of "G.K.'s Weekly."

This was the outlook of that official Liberalism which had long made it so difficult for Gilbert to go on calling himself a Liberal. The Servile State was in full swing and official Liberalism asked nothing better than to be allowed to operate it. Whether Belloc and Cecil Chesterton had been right or wrong at an earlier date in seeing the political parties in collusion it is certain that by now an utter bankruptcy in statesmanship had reduced them all to saying the same things while they did nothing. Ten years later, on the day of the last General Election of his life, Gilbert wrote:

The Liberal has formed the opinion that Peace is decidedly preferable to its alternative of War; and that this should be achieved through support of the League of Nations interfering with the ambitions of other nations. The Ministerialist, on the other hand, holds that we should, if possible, employ a machinery called the League of Nations; with the object of securing Peace, to which he is much attached. The Ministerialist demands that strong action should be taken to reduce Unemployment; but the Liberal does not scruple to retort that Unemployment is an evil, against which strong action must be taken. The Liberal thinks that we ought to revive our Trade, thus thwarting and throwing himself across the path of the National Tory, who still insists that our Trade should be revived. Thus the two frowning cohorts confront each other; and I hear the noise of battle even as I write.

In June 1928 he was invited to stand for Edinburgh University. He replied:

I do hope you will forgive me if there has been any delay in acknowledging your exceedingly flattering communication; I have been away from home and moving about a good deal; and have only just returned from London. Certainly there is nothing which I should feel as so great an honour, or one so exciting or so undeserved, as to receive even the invitation to stand for such a position in the great University that has already been so generous to me. If you really think it would be of any service to your cause, I can hardly refuse such a compliment. Of course you understand that it is only in a rather independent sense, though as I think in the right sense, that I shall always call myself a Liberal; indeed, I find it difficult to imagine any real sort of Liberal who is not really an independent Liberal. I am quite certain I am not a Tory or a Socialist.

He was defeated at this election by Winston Churchill who got 864 votes to 593 for G.K. and 332 for Mrs. Sidney Webb. He was again defeated at Aberdeen in 1933, coming second to

Major Elliott, the other candidates being C. M. Grieve and Aldous Huxley. At one stage of the contest the *Daily Express* writes: "The Huxley supporters are smarting under the surprise attack made by the Chestertonians at the Huxley concert at the week-end and are preparing reprisals."

The following letter is G.K.'s reply to the first proposal from the Aberdeen students:

25th October, 1933

I can at least assure you that the delay in acknowledging properly the most flattering compliment which you have paid me was not due to any notion of neglecting it. It was due to the practical necessity at the moment of discovering and deciding on a fact which may, for all I know, save you the trouble of further consideration of the matter; and it is for this reason that I mention the practical difficulty first. I now find that I shall almost certainly be obliged to be out of England (and Scotland) for about three or four months, or conceivably a little more, beginning about the middle of January. I do not know what preliminary formalities would be demanded of me as a candidate, or when the demand for them would arise. But I was so strongly impressed with the honour you have paid me that I thought it my duty to find out the facts on this particular point, so that you might act on it in any way you think right. In any case, if the delay thus involved has placed you in any difficulty, I need not say that I shall fully understand your finding the project unworkable; and I shall be quite content to remember the compliment of the request.

There is another consideration which would help the practical side of the case; and for that I fear I must make the practical enquiries of you, as people understanding the circumstances. You do not mention the Party you represent; and though I am, like most of us, long past attaching a horrid sanctity to the name, I hope you will forgive that much curiosity in a poor bewildered journalist, who has been exhibited in many lights and cross-lights. I was put up as a candidate at Glasgow as a Liberal, which is really quite true; but I think I managed in my election pamphlet to give my own definition of Liberalism. I have also more recently, on a public platform in Glasgow, supported my friend Mr. Compton Mackenzie when he stood as a Scottish Nationalist. Both these positions I am quite prepared to defend; but in the latter, you might naturally prefer a

Nationalist candidate who was not only a quarter of a Scotsman. I may remark that as the quarter is called Keith, and comes from Aberdeen, I am rather thrilled at the name of Marischal College.

There is one other point I think it only right to mention, for your sake as much as my own. You know the local conditions. Do you think it likely that we should be left with one and a half votes, looking a little ridiculous, because the miserable quarter of a Scot happens to have the same religion as Bruce and Mary Stuart? I only ask for information; which you alone could supply. But it may be that the considerations I have already mentioned have disposed of the matter. Believe me, my gratitude is none the less.

Gilbert said of my father that he showed an embarrassing respect for younger men. Surely Gilbert's own tone of respect must here have embarrassed even undergraduates. The uncertainty of success or failure only troubled him as it might affect his supporters. The sporting element in the contest appealed to his undying boyishness.

Perhaps this chapter may find its best conclusion in the vivid memories written down in answer to my request of one of Gilbert's younger friends—Douglas Woodruff—who came to know him in the year of that Silver Wedding which meant so much that I have chosen it for the title of a chapter covering much of Chesterton's Catholic life.

Chesterton devotes a long passage in the Autobiography to the dinner given at the old Adelphi Terrace Hotel to Belloc on his sixtieth birthday, in July 1930. I remember very well the high old fashioned car the Chestertons used to hire in Beaconsfield, for I accompanied him with particular instructions to deliver him safely and on time, as was very necessary for he was in the Chair. We might have lost him, for we went first to the Times Office where I was then working, as I had proofs to correct before disappearing for the rest of the evening, and he was seized with the idea that it would be very good fun for him to enter Printing House Square and have it announced that it was Mr. Chesterton come to write the leaders, having brought the thunder with him under his cloak. Quite early on the drive up he began speculating about who would be at the party, and when he had suggested various figures who were certainly not going to be there he said with a mixture of regret and acceptance, "There is always such a *sundering* quality about Belloc's quarrels." When he rose to propose the toast he said at once that if he or anybody else in the room was remembered at all in the future it would be because they had been associated with the guest of the evening. He meant that. The evening stood out in his memory because it was so unlike the ordinary sort of dinners he knew where he was a principal figure. It delighted him that without any programme or premeditation all the thirty diners in turn made speeches, in the main parody speeches. It was, in short, a party and not a performance.

In the decade when I had the good fortune to know Topmeadow he was still paying the price of a literary fame which he had sought in youth because it meant success in his calling and an income, but which became a barrier he was always meeting and breaking through. Many literary men genuinely enough prefer company in which they are on just the same footing as everyone else to company in which they are little Kings, but Chesterton was exceptional in liking to live in the fullest equality of intercourse not only with all sorts of men but with the lesser practitioners of his own calling. He sought the affection and not the admiration of his fellow men, or, more precisely, he sought neither: what he sought was to do things like discovering the truth in their company. No man more naturally distinguished between a man and his views, or found easier the theological injunction to hate the sin but love the sinner. One of the few occasions on which I recall him as rather hurt was just after he had met Stanley Baldwin, at Taplow, and had not been welcomed as a fellow Englishman sharing immense things like the love of the English country or English letters, but with a cold correctitude from a politician who seemed chiefly conscious he was meeting in G.K. a man who week by week sought to bring political life into hatred, ridicule and contempt.

He was not made by nature for the kind of journalistic tradition which Belloc and Cecil Chesterton established and his loyal affection for them made him adopt. I recall him expounding to the lawyers of the Thomas More Society the absurdity of the legal definition of libel, arguing that of its nature free discussion meant arousing at any rate ridicule and contempt if not hatred against men and measures of which you disapproved. It was ridicule that he preferred to arouse. The lawyers were quite unconvinced, as they generally are when laymen have any complaints about the law, and they soon realized that to Chesterton the whole idea of invoking the law because of arguments and discussions and invective was hitting below the belt.

He could be seen at his happiest in the Mock Trials which were held every summer for the last ten years of his life at the London School of Economics, for the King Edward VII Hospital Fund. He was relied upon year after year to prosecute. One year it was leading actors and actresses, another year sculptors and architects, another year politicians, another Headmasters. He entered completely into the spirit of an entertainment which combined two of his abiding interests, public debate and private theatricals. That was a setting in which he could completely exemplify his favourite recipe for the modern world, that it should be approached in a spirit of intellectual ferocity and personal amiability. But what marked his own contributions to these affairs was the intellectual "ferocity," in the weight and content of his criticism. Most of the eminent men who consented to take part came to play a game for the sake of the Hospitals, and because they rarely unbent like that in public they were wholly facetious and trivial. To Chesterton there was no difficulty or incongruity in combining the fun of acting with the fun of genuine intellectual discussion. When he prosecuted the Headmasters of leading public schools for Destroying Freedom of Thought I came down in a lift with them afterwards and found they were volubly nettled at the drastic and serious case he had made inside the stage setting of burlesque, and seemed to think he had not been playing the game when he wrapped up so much meaning in his speech and examinations. This had never entered his head; it had come perfectly naturally to him to make wholly real and material points even in a mock trial and with a wealth of fun. But he liked being one of a troupe on a stage very much more than being a lonely and eminent figure on a platform, because to him the great attraction of discussion was that it should be a joint quest, a mental walk with an object in view, but also with an eye for everything that might and would turn up on the way.

He laughed his high laugh—like Charlemagne his voice was unequal to his physical scale—at his own jokes because they came

NEW HAVEN, CONN. 1931

CHESTERTON   WILLIAM LYON PHELPS   A. E. (GEORGE RUSSELL)

to him as part of the joint findings of the quest, something he had seen and collected and brought for the pot. When he made jokes about his size as he so commonly did at the outset of a speech, it was to get rid of the elevation of the platform, and to get on to easy equal terms with the audience; "I am not a cat burglar," he began to the Union at Oxford, and had won them. The radio suited him so excellently, precisely because it is a personal sitting down man to man relationship that the successful broadcaster must establish; that was the relationship inside which he naturally thought. His difficulty was that while he had not the faintest desire to be "a Literary Man," and still less a Prophet, the kind of truth he divined was, in fact, on the scale of the prophets. It seemed to me that over the last decade of his life he found himself more and more in the dilemma that in the life of his mind he was living with ideas, the fruit of a contemplative preoccupation with the Incarnation and the Sacraments, which he shrank from talking about, from a natural humility and a clear and grateful understanding of the Catholic tradition of reverence and reticence.

England is full enough of men to whom the distinction between the platform and the pulpit is very unreal; they have a moral message and they do not much mind where they give it. But Chesterton, unlike most public men who deal in general ideas, did not come to the idea of public speaking through the Protestant tradition but through the secular tradition, the freethinker's debate, the political and not the religious side of Hyde Park oratory, where men in knots shout one another down, not where some lonely longhaired prophet declaims conversion. After he became a Catholic he sought to set himself frontiers, the apologetic territory suitable for a layman like himself. But he found himself more and more preoccupied with a territory further inland, penetrating all the time to the deeper meaning of the creed he had embraced. He could look back and see how most of his early books had seized upon some essential part of Catholic doctrine. . . . He had written what he had seen at the time, but he did not stop looking because he had written, and then he always continued to see more, the great contemplative.

He looked out on the universe from a very solid tower of observation because in all but the deepest sense of the word he always had a home. His lasting significance is his pilgrimage, but the spiritual journey was lived out in a warmly rich setting. When he wrote of "the home" he was not dealing with a notion but with a surrounding reality, one on which he had opened his eyes as a baby and which he enjoyed without a break to the end. Frances Chesterton is among the great wives of our literary history. When he said "I can never have enough nothing to do," it was the remark of a man with a house he was generally in, a house full of things.

He loved to produce cigars and wine, but tea also remained an important fixed part of the day, in the Victorian tradition, and when he was told by the doctor he had better drink nothing, he had many alternatives, like detective stories read over tea and buns, which other lovers of wine would perhaps have found no consolation. Other men are secret drinkers, he would confide, I am a secret teetotaller. The first time I had tea with him, in Artillery Mansions in 1926, I was much struck that he brought three detective stories to the teatable. I imagine he always had time for *Jack Redskin on the Trail,* or whatever it might be because he had the gift, to an extent I have never seen elsewhere, of opening a book and as it were pouring the contents down in one draught like a champion German beer drinker. He once seized from my shelves in Lincoln's Inn, Wyndham Lewis's *Apes of God* saying it was a book he had not seen and wanted to see. It is a folio and I suggested he should take it away. But he opened it and stood reading it and here and there, not a process which could be called dipping, but a kind of sucking out of the printed contents, as though he were a vacuum cleaner and you could see the lines of type leaving the pages and being absorbed. When he put it down it was to discuss the thesis and illustrations of the book as a man fully possessed of its whole standpoint. Once he made one of his common confusions and forgot he was addressing the Wiseman Dining Society on the Oxford Movement. In the train from Beaconsfield he said how nice it was that he had not got to speak. Frances Chesterton told him not to be silly, he knew he was speaking on the Oxford Movement. He was visibly disconcerted at the start, for many grave seniors had assembled to hear him; but all went well in the discussion as soon as he was attacked for something he had said about Newman's views. You cannot catch me out about Newman, he said, with joy of battle, and he produced then and there a most detailed account of just where in Newman's writings the points in question were developed. Yet he was curiously content to read what happened to come his way and to rely upon his friends for references and facts, remembering what they might tell him, but not ordering the books which would have greatly strengthened him in the sort of newspaper arguments in which he was so often employed. He had a large collection of books at Topmeadow, but they gave the impression that they had assembled themselves. Masses of them were adventure stories, many were presentation copies from writers. You felt that they had got into the house knowing that it was a hospitable one, if not built for books, and that they would probably be allowed to stay. But he had a study which would barely home him, and the library room he did eventually build was only finished as he died.

I think nothing is more superficial or belittling to him than the idea that while he might have liked the real country he could not like Beaconsfield, as it developed into a dormitory town while he lived there. His sympathies were far too wide. He liked to tell how he had had to complain of the noise made by an adjoining Cinema Company. His secretary had said Mr. Chesterton finds he cannot write; and the Cinema people replied we are well aware of that.

He liked to think of Mr. Garvin near by, "not that I see him very much," he said, "but I like to think that that great factory is steaming away night and day." He had great satisfaction when a friend and I, driving away in the evening, knocked down a white wooden post outside the house in starting the car. He held that he had witnessed just how many a grand old local custom must have originated, in men covering up their mistakes by saying they were fulfilling a ritual which had fallen into neglect. You must say you did it on purpose, he said, say it was a rite too long omitted and it will soon be kept up every year and men will forget its origin, and it will be known as the Bump of Beaconsfield. When a friend of his brought him a two-bladed African spear, he said, as he threw it about the lawn, that it was sad to think how many lawns there were in Beaconsfield and how few weapons were ever thrown on any of them, although all men enjoyed, or would enjoy spear throwing more, he believed, than they enjoyed clock golf. He at any rate was a genuinely free man, who did what it amused and pleased him to do, and did not think he had to choose between the forms of activity or rest currently pursued by his neighbours. Much of the serene atmosphere of his home came from that quiet resolute practice of the liberty of a free mind.

CHAPTER XXVIII

Columbus

He wished to discover America. His gay and thoughtless friends, who could not understand him, pointed out that America had already been discovered, I think they said by Christopher Columbus, some time ago, and that there were big cities of Anglo-Saxon People there already, New York and Boston and so on. But the Admiral explained to them, kindly enough, that this had nothing to do with it. They might have discovered America, but he had not.

From *A Fragment*, in *The Coloured Lands*.

IN THE CHAPTER of his *Autobiography* entitled "The Incomplete Traveller" Chesterton has said "after all, the strangest country I ever visited was England." It was of the very essence of his philosophy that each one of us has to make again the discoveries of our ancestors if we are to be travellers and not trippers. "The traveller sees what he sees; the tripper sees what he has come to see." Thus Chesterton tried to discover each country that he visited and he records that the nearer countries are sometimes harder to discover than the more remote. For Poland is more akin to England than is France: Ireland more mysterious than Italy.

France, Ireland and supremely Palestine brought their contribution to that mental and spiritual development traced in earlier chapters. On Ireland, Rome, Jerusalem and the United States he wrote books. It may really be said that on the States he wrote two books, for in the volume of essays *Sidelights on New London and Newer York* which followed his second visit he showed a much greater understanding than in *What I Saw in*

America. His first visit took place in 1921-22, his second in 1930.

On the first trip Frances kept clippings of almost all their interviews. Gilbert himself said that, while the headlines in American newspapers became obscure in their violent efforts to startle, what was written underneath the headlines was usually good journalism and the press cuttings of this tour bear out his remark. Interviewers report accurately and with a good deal of humour. Sketches of G.K.'s personal appearance abound, and if occasionally they contradict one another in detail they yet contrive to convey a vivid and fairly truthful impression of the "leonine" head, the bulky form, the gestures and mannerisms. That a man of letters and lecturer should choose to wear proudly not one of these titles but that of journalist, was pleasing and flattering to the brotherhood. The atmosphere of the tour is best conveyed by rather copious quotation. A crowd of journalists met him at the boat. One of them writes of

. . . his voluminous figure, quite imposing when he stands up, though not so abundantly Johnsonian as his pictures lead one to expect. He has cascades of grey hair above a pinkly beaming face, a rather straggly blond mustache, and eyes that seem frequently to be taking up infinity in a serious way.

His falsetto laugh, prominent teeth and general aspect are rather Rooseveltian. . . .

Mr. Chesterton, who is accompanied by Mrs. Chesterton, and who will deliver a lecture soon in Boston on the Ignorance of the Educated, said he did not expect to go further west than Chicago, since "having seen both Jerusalem and Chicago, I think I shall have touched on the extremes of civilization."

In the event he visited Omaha and Oklahoma City and went south as far as Nashville, Tennessee.

Possibly Frances had thought she would pass unnoticed but in fact, besides constant photographs of the pair, the lynx eye of the interviewer was upon her as much as upon him. On arrival at New York:

He shook hands with some half-dozen Customs officials who welcomed him to the city on their own behalf. The impression given by Mr. Chesterton as he moved majestically along the pier or on the ship was one of huge bulk. To the ordinary sized people on the pier he seemed to blot out the liner and the river. Mrs. Chesterton was busy with the baggage.

"My wife understands these things," he said with a sweep of his stick, "I don't." . . .

In order to get the two figures into the same picture one of the newspaper photographers requested Mr. Chesterton to sit in a big armchair while his wife stood beside him. When they were settled in the required pose he exclaimed: "I say I don't like this; people will think that I am a German."

Another newspaper remarks: "He was accompanied by his wife, who looked very small beside him. She attended to the baggage examination, opening trunks and bags while her husband delivered a short essay on the equality of men and women in England since the war." This reporter was perhaps not without irony: but if it actually happened like that, G.K. must have seen the joke too for he has a similar situation in the first scene of his play "The Judgement of Dr. Johnson." The same reporter adds that Chesterton speaks in essays, so that his interviewers "received a brief essay instead of a direct reply to a leading question."

We next come upon them in their New York hotel:

I found, with Mrs. Chesterton at the Biltmore, this big, gentle, leonine man of letters six feet of him and 200 odd lbs. There is a delightful story of how an American, driving with him through London, remarked "Everyone seems to know you, Mr. Chesterton."

"Yes," mournfully responded the gargantuan author, "and if they don't they ask."

He really doesn't look anything like as fat as his caricatures make him, however, and he has a head big enough to go with his massive tallness. His eyes are brilliant English blue behind the big rimmed eyeglasses: his wavy hair, steel grey; his heavy mustache, bright yellow. Physically he is the crackling electric spark of the heaven-home-and-mother party, the only man who can give the cleverest radical debaters a Roland for their Cliver.

In subsequent interviews G.K.'s height grew to six foot three and his weight to 300 lbs. (which was surely closer to the mark); his mannerisms were greatly remarked.

Mr. Chesterton speaks clearly, in a rather high-pitched voice. He accompanies his remarks with many nervous little gestures. His hands, at times, stray into his pockets. He leans over the reading desk as if he would like to get down into the audience and make it a sort of heart-to-heart talk.

Mr. Chesterton's right hand spent a restless and rather disturbing evening. It would start from the reading desk at which he stood and fall to the points of that vast waistcoat which inspired the description of him as "a fellow of infinite vest." It would wander aimlessly a moment about his—stomach is a word that is taboo among the polite English—equator, and then shift swiftly to the rear until the thumb found the hip pocket. There the hand would rest a moment, to return again to the reading desk and to describe once more the quarter circle. Once in a while it would twist a ring upon the left hand, once in a while it would be clasped behind the broad back, but only for a moment. To the hip pocket and back again was its sentry-go, and it was a faithful soldier.

Several interviewers remark on the unexpected calibre of his voice. He himself spoke of it as "the mouse that came forth from the mountain."

One would never suspect him of being our leading American best-seller. His accent, mannerisms, and dress are pro-Piccadilly and he likes his Oolong with a lump of sugar. He thinks with his cigar, a black London cheeroot.

He, Gilbert K. Chesterton, was sipping a cup of tea, expertly brewed by Mrs. Chesterton when a reporter yesterday entered his room at the Blackstone [in Chicago]. Before he submitted to interrogation he lighted the cigar.

"My muse," he explained. "A Parnassian pleasure. Tobacco smoke is the Ichor of mental life. Some men write with a pencil, others with a typewriter, I write with my cigar." . . .

Throughout the interview he was profoundly concerned not with the subjects under discussion, but with the black cheeroot. Seven times it went out. Seven times he relighted it. The eighth time he tossed it away.

When asked which of his works he considered the greatest, he said: "I don't consider any of my works in the least great." . . .

"Slang," he said, "is too sacred and precious to be used promiscuously. Its use should be led up to reverently for it expresses what the King's English could not."

"Seeing and hearing a man like Gilbert Keith Chesterton," said a Detroit newspaper, "makes a meal for the imagination that no reading of books by him or about him can accomplish."

He spoke Sunday in Orchestra Hall on The Ignorance of the Educated; it grows more difficult as his tour progresses, he admits, and the Lecture, he insists, grows worse. His thesis is that "the besetting evil of all educated people is that they tend to substitute theories for things." The uneducated man never makes this mistake. He states the simple fact that he sees a German drinking beer: he does not say "there is a Teuton consuming alcohol."

At Toronto the Chairman—a professor of English—thought that there must have been an error in the title as printed, and announced that Mr. Chesterton would speak on The Ignorance of the *Un*educated. Another Detroit newspaper quotes from the lecture:

There is a deeper side to such fallacies. The whole catastrophe of the Great War may be traced to the racial theory. If people had looked at peoples as nations in place of races the intolerable ambition of Prussia might have been stopped before it attained the captaincy of the South German States.

The only other lecture subjects mentioned are "Shall We Abolish the Inevitable" and "The Perils of Health." There are innumerable caricatures. One by Cosmo Hamilton is accompanied with a story of how he once debated with Chesterton. The subject was: "There is no law in England." G.K. made so overwhelming a case that Hamilton decided the only way of making reply possible was to twist the subject making it "there are no laws in England" and "go off at 1000 tangents like a worried terrier."

To hear Chesterton's howl of joy when he twigged how I had slipped out, to see him double himself up in an agony of laughter at my personal insults, to watch the effect of his sportsmanship on a shocked audience who were won to mirth by his intense and pea-hen-like quarks of joy was a sight and a sound for the gods.

Probably Chesterton has forgotten this incident but I haven't and never will, and I carried away from that room a respect and admiration for this tomboy among dictionaries, this philosophical Peter Pan, this humorous Dr. Johnson, this kindly and gallant cherub, this profound student and wise master which has grown steadily ever since.

In the *Daily Sketch*, Hamilton later described G.K. speaking in this debate:

During the whole inspired course of his brilliant reasoning, he caught the little rivulets which ran down his face, and just as they were about to drop from the first of his several chins flicked them generously among the disconcerted people who sat actually at his feet. From time to time, too, unaware of this, he grasped deep into his pockets and rattled coins and keys, going from point to point, from proof to proof, until the Constitution of England was quite devoid of Law and out from under his waistcoat bulged a line of shirt.

It was monstrous, gigantic, amazing, deadly, delicious. Nothing like it has ever been done before or will ever be seen, heard and felt like it again.

A clever caricature depicts Dickens in one corner, his arms full of bricks, hammers and jagged objects, labelled "American Notes." The rest of the picture is an immense drawing of a smiling Chesterton, his arms full of roses, labelled "Kind Words for America." He is pointing at Dickens and saying: "America must have changed a great deal since then."

Not only Gilbert but also Frances was constantly interviewed. "I tell them," one interviewer quotes her as saying, "that I didn't know I was the wife of a great man till I came to America. It never bothered me before."

This, coming from one of those English wives, so popularly portrayed as representing the acme of submission, was delightful. A slight, slim little figure, looking slighter and slimmer in the wake of her overshadowing husband, with an outward appearance of unsurpassed mildness and meekness which her conversation readily dispelled, the wife of this delightful Englishman of letters presented a very intimate Chestertonian paradox.

Frances kept a Diary of which almost the first entry is "So far my feelings towards this country are entirely hostile, but it would be unfair to judge too soon. We have refused all invitations; it's the only thing to do." This idea they must have abandoned, for one paper after Gilbert's death describes him as an immense success socially but "a big bland failure" as a lecturer. As the tour proceeds the entries in the Diary become more favorable but unlike her letters from Poland—where what she liked best was anything really Polish—the Diary shows Frances as singling out for approval those things approximately English —e.g., houses where she stayed in Boston and Philadelphia. She hated hustle, heat and crowds, and the Diary is full of remarks about her exhaustion.

G.K. commented in one interview on the different conception of a Club in England and in America. While groups of men entertained him, Women's Clubs were entertaining his wife. But an English Club "is really a promoter of unsociability. . . . And while the English woman in her Club does not, perhaps, stare into vacancy with the same fervour, fixity and ferocity as the English man, still there is something of the sort, you know." After a lecture in Philadelphia a lady asked him, "Mr. Chesterton, what makes women talk so much?" Heaving himself out of his chair, he answered only "God, Madam."

Two further caricatures were an impression drawn by Will Coyne for the New York *Evening Post* of Chesterton as Porthos of the Pen, and another, drawn for the New York *Herald* by Stewart Davis, of Chesterton supplying "Paradoxygen to the World." This was accompanied by a poem called *Paradoxygen,* by Edward Anthony:

> O Gilbert I know there are many who like
> Your talks on the darkness of light,
> The shortness of length and the weakness of strength
> And the one on the lowness of height.
>
> My neighbour keeps telling me "How I adore
> His legality of the illicit
> And I've also a liking intense for his striking
> Obscurity of the explicit."
>
> But I am unmoved. What's the reason? O, well,
> The same I intend to expound
> Some evening next week, when I'm going to speak
> On the shallowness of the profound.

"Everyone who goes to America for a short time," said G.K., "is expected to write a book; and nearly everybody does." In accordance with this convention he wrote *What I Saw in America.* He did see a great deal. The same imagination that had found the mediaeval aspect of Jerusalem saw many elements missed not only by the ordinary tourist but by the people themselves who live nearest to them. Thus he keenly appreciated the traditional elements in Philadelphia, Boston and Baltimore:

In coming into some of these more stable cities of the States I felt something quite sincerely of that historic emotion which is satisfied in the eternal cities of the Mediterranean. I felt in America what many Americans suppose can only be felt in Europe. I have seldom had that sentiment stirred more simply and directly than when I saw from afar off, above that vast grey labyrinth of Philadelphia, great Penn upon his pinnacle like the graven figure of a god who had fashioned a new world; and remembered that his body lay buried in a field at the turning of a lane, a league from my own door.

In Baltimore the Catholic history appealed to him yet more strongly, and, invited to visit Cardinal Gibbons, he felt himself touching "the end of a living chain." In Boston, "much more beautiful than its name," he companioned again with the Autocrat and recalled how in his own youth English and American literature seemed to be one thing. Indeed he was there reminded even "of English things that have largely vanished from England." Washington he saw both as a beautiful city and an idea—"a sort of paradise of impersonal politics without personal commerce." And in Nashville, Tennessee it was "with a sort of intensity of feeling" that he found himself "before a dim and faded picture; and from the dark canvas looked forth the face of Andrew Jackson, watchful like a white eagle."

The things Chesterton chose for description all have relevance to the main thesis of the book which has often been missed and which emerges most clearly in the first and the last chapters. He insists always that he writes as a foreigner—and indeed repeats frequently that it is by keeping our own distinct nationality that Englishmen and Americans will best understand and like one another—but he writes also as a man not unconscious of history. Thus writing, the older cities represent to him one trend in the States and New York another. I am sorry to say that he does not appreciate New York as he ought, because of his dislike of cosmopolitanism. Its beauty he sees as breath-taking: not solid and abiding but a kind of fairyland. The lights on Broadway evoked from him the exclamation "What a glorious garden of wonders this would be for anyone who was lucky enough to be unable to read," and he imagines a simple peasant who fancies that they must be announcing in letters of fire: "Liberty, Equality, Fraternity," and must be put up on occasion of some great national feast, whereas they are but advertising signs put up to make money.

The Skyline seemed to him most lovely: "vertical lines that suggest a sort of rush upwards, as of great cataracts topsy turvy —the strong daylight finds everywhere the broken edges of things and the sort of hues we see in newly turned earth or the white sections of trees. . . ." He feels the intense "imaginative pleasure of those dizzy turrets and dancing fires." But he ends with the note that really spoilt New York for him: "If those nightmare buildings were really all built for nothing, how noble they would be."

Advertisement, Big Business, Monopoly might have invaded the old traditionary cities of America as they had those of England, but New York existed (he felt) as a new and startling expression of them. They shrieked in every light and from every sky-scraper. The whole question of America was: would the older simpler really great historical tradition win, or would it be defeated by the new and towering evil? He has an interesting chapter on the countryside, finding hope in the considerable extension of small ownership among the farmers and in the houses built from the growing material that wood is, but he is again depressed at the reflection that the culture of the countryside is not its own but imported from the towns—therefore itself largely commercialised.

Roaming over the world in search of his examples Chesterton sees the ideal of the early republicans as dead in the republics of today, and nowhere more dead than in America. It would be useless, he feels, to invoke Jefferson or Lincoln in the modern world against the tyranny of wage-slavery or in favour of racial justice because "the bridge of brotherhood had broken down in the modern mind."

Jefferson the Deist "said the sight of slavery in his country made him tremble, remembering that God is just," but the modern who has lost these absolute standards has "grown dizzy with degree and relativity." Hence came the same terrible peril in both England and America: that in the eyes of the new plutocracy the idea of manhood has gone. "There were different sorts of apes; but there was no doubt that we were the superior sort."

Only in one direction did he see real hope. The new dreams of the 18th century had gone, but the ancient dogmas of the Catholic Church remained. Catholics might forget brotherhood, like their fellows, but "the Catholic type of Christianity had rivetted itself irrevocably to the manhood of all men." "The church would always continue to ordain negroes and canonise beggars and labourers." "Where its faith was fixed by creeds and councils it could not save itself even by surrender. . . . THERE IS NO BASIS FOR DEMOCRACY EXCEPT IN A DOGMA ABOUT THE DIVINE ORIGIN OF MAN."

I have put that final sentence in capitals for it is the climax both of Gilbert's thinking about America and of one of the most important trains of thought that brought him to the home of liberty secured for the human race by dogma—that is to say by revealed truth. He went home to be received into the Catholic Church as I have earlier related.

What I Saw in America is of special importance in relation to later discussions in *G.K.'s Weekly.* While the journalists seemed convinced on his first visit that he had nothing but roses to throw, and compared him favorably to Dickens, a collection of quotations could be made from *G.K.'s Weekly* of a quite opposite kind, yet I do not think he ever attacks America as much as he attacks England. He was himself much amused at finding he was expected to be either "For America" or "Against America," both of which attitudes appeared to him absurd. In that sense he was neither for nor against his own country. He liked Americans, he disliked certain trends in America: because he loved England he disliked the same trends even more in England. Certain things in modern civilisation which he hated he did regard as primarily American. American comfort to him seemed acute discomfort. He thought every American lives in an "airless furnace in the middle of which he sits and eats lumps of ice."

He had a great hatred of intelligence tests which he called the "palpable balderdash of irresponsible Yankee boomsters. . . . It is really one of the maladies of American democracy to be swept by these prairie fires of pseudo-scientific fads, and throw itself into Eugenics or Anthropometric inquiry with the buoyancy of babies." He believed that there was more democracy in America than in England. But he hated what he called the "glare of American Advertisement." He spoke of a "common thief like the American Millionaire" but he certainly did not exclude the English Millionaire from the same indictment. His whole view of advertisement reaches a peak in an article * entitled "If You Have Smiles."

We read the other day an absolutely solemn and almost tender piece of advice, in a leading American magazine, about the preservation of Beauty and Health. It was intended quite seriously. . . . After describing in most complicated detail how the young woman of today (well known to be enamored of all that is natural and free) is to strap up her head and face every night, as if it had to be bandaged after an accident, it proceeds to say with the most refined American accent: "With the face thus fixed in smile formation: . . ." but we have a difficulty about taking this serious advice of American Beauty Business even so seriously as to meditate on its social menace. The prospect of such a world of idiots ought to depress us, but . . . no, it is no good. Our faces are fixed in smile formation when we think of that American.

He repeated often how much he liked the inhabitants of Main Street (grievously wronged by Sinclair Lewis).

American ideals are not nearly so nice as American realities. We lament not so much what Babbitt is as what he is trying to be. What he is is a simple and kindly man . . . what he's trying to be is the abomination of desolation; the Man who made Salesmanship an Art; the Man Who Would Not Stay Down; the Man Who Got the

* *G.K.'s Weekly*, December 10, 1927.

Million Dollar Post After Taking Our Correspondence Course; the Man Who Learned Social Charm in Six Lessons.*

At the time of the depreciation of the franc Belloc's articles in *G.K.'s Weekly*, echoed in the Leaders, pointed to finance, especially American finance, as the criminal that was forcing down the French currency. An American correspondent in the paper attacked these attacks on the ground that they were inspired by British Imperialism! Chesterton felt it a little hard to be at this date confused with Kipling. He replied that his correspondent committed "the blunder of an extravagant and excessive admiration for England." He speaks of

that tremendous procession that passed through Paris, literally an army of cripples. It was a march of all those walking units, those living fragments of humanity that had been left by the long stand of five years upon the French frontiers; a devastated area that passed endlessly like a river . . . they illustrate the main fact that France was in the center of that far-flung fighting line of civilization; that it was upon her that the barbarian quarrel concentrated; and that is an historical fact which the foolish vanity of many Englishmen, as well as of many Americans, is perpetually tempted to deny. Our critic is therefore quite beside the mark if he imagines that I am trying to score off his country out of a cheap jealousy on behalf of my own. My jealousy is for justice and for a large historical understanding of this great passage in history. My own country won glory enough in that and other fields to make it quite unnecessary for any sane Englishman to shut his eyes to Europe in order to brag about England. . . . I have not the faintest doubt what Thomas Jefferson would have said, if he had been told that a few financial oligarchs who happen to live in New York, were beating down the French wealth; and had then seen pass before him that awful panorama of the wrecks of the French Republican Army; heart-shaking, like a resurrection of the dead. . . . I do not admit, therefore, that in supporting the French peasants and soldiers against the money dealers and wire-pullers of the town, I am attacking America or even merely defending France.†

* Jan. 14, 1928.   † *G.K.'s Weekly*, Sept. 1, 1926.

On November 6 and 13, 1926 he writes two articles on "The Yankee and the Chinaman," in which he contrasts the philosophic spirit with the so-called scientific. Like Bishop Barnes in England wanting to analyse the Consecrated Host, Edison was reported in America as having said that he would find out if there was a soul by some scientific test:

Any philosophic Chinaman would know what to think of a man who said, "I have got a new gun that will shoot a hole through your memory of last Monday," or "I have got a saw sharp enough to cut up the cube root of 666," or "I will boil your affection for Aunt Susan until it is quite liquid."

In 1927 Gilbert, Frances and Dorothy spent a month in Poland where immense enthusiasm was shown for the man who had consistently proclaimed Poland's greatness and its true place in Europe.

Invited by the Government, "all the hospitality I received," he says, "was far too much alive to remind me of anything official." One of the multitude of unwritten books of which G.K. dreamed was a book about Poland. The Poles and the English were, he felt, alike in many things but the Englishman had never been given the opportunity to understand the Pole. We knew nothing of their history and did not understand the Resurrection we had helped to bring about. "The nonsense talked in the newspapers when they discuss what they call the Polish Corridor" was only possible from want of realisation of what Poland had been before she was rent in three by Prussia, Austria and Russia. Thus too we did not realise "the self-evident fact that the Poles always have a choice of evils." Pilsudski told him that *of the two* he preferred Germany to Russia, while Dmowski voiced the more general opinion in telling him that *of the two* he preferred Russia to Germany. For the moment at any rate tortured Poland was herself and incredibly happy. Revival in this agricultural country had been amazingly swift.

Peasant proprietors abounded and lived well on twelve acres or so, while even labourers possessed plots of land and a cow or two.

"The P.E.N. Club Dinner," Frances wrote in a letter to her mother, "was, I fancy, considered by the Poles a huge success. If numbers indicate anything, it certainly was. I found it a little embarrassing to have to eat hot kidneys and mushrooms standing about with hundreds of guests, and this was only the preliminary to a long dinner that followed and refreshments that apparently continued until two o'clock in the morning. The speeches were really perfectly marvellous and delivered in English quite colloquial and very witty and showing a detailed knowledge of Gilbert's works which no Englishman of my acquaintance possesses. Gilbert made an excellent, in fact, a very eloquent speech in reply, which drew forth thunders of applause."

Their hosts drove the Chestertons all over the country and showed them home life on the little farms, home industries and arts—brightly woven garments and pottery for use, not for exhibition—and the great historic scenes of Poland's history. With the scene he remembered most vividly, Gilbert's musings on Poland conclude: they were visiting a young nobleman who excused the devastation of his own home by Bolshevik soldiers in the heat of battle but added, "There is only one thing I really resent."

. . . He led us out into a long avenue lined with poplars; and at the end of it was a statue of the Blessed Virgin; with the head and the hands shot off. But the hands had been lifted; and it is a strange thing that the very mutilation seemed to give more meaning to the attitude of intercession; asking mercy for the merciless race of men. *

Karel Capek who had long wanted Chesterton to visit Prague wrote mournfully, "You wrote me that it would be difficult for you to come to Prague this spring. But it was in the newspapers

* *Autobiography,* p. 330.

that you were last month in Warsaw; why in Heaven's sake did you not come to Prague on this occasion? What a pity for us! Now we are waiting for a compensation." Two earlier letters had shown him eager for contributions from Chesterton for a leading review. Another delightful letter is dated December 24th (no year given):

My dear Mr. Chesterton,

It is just Christmas Eve; my friends presented me with some of your books, and I cannot omit to thank you for the consolation and trust I found there as already so many times. Be blessed, Mr. Chesterton.

I wrote you twice without getting any answer; but it is Christian to insist, and so I write you again. Please, would you be so kind to tell me, if it shall be possible for you to come next year to Prague? Our PEN club is anxious to invite you as our guest of honour. If you would like to come next spring, I beg you to be my guest. You are fond of old things: Prague is one. You shall find here so many people who cherish you. I like you myself as no other writer; it's for yours sake that being in London I went to habit in Notting-Hill and it is for yours sake that I liked it. I cannot believe that I should not meet you again. Please, come to Prague.

I wish you a happy New Year, Mr. Chesterton. You must be happy, making your readers happier. You are so good.

Yours sincerely,

Karel Capek.

He never, alas, got to Prague, or to many another country that wanted him. There are letters asking him to lecture in Australia, to lecture again in U.S.A., in South America "to make them aware of English thought and literature." "The Argentine Intelligencia," says Philip Guedalla, "is acutely aware of your writings. Local professors terrified me by asking me on various occasions to explain the precise position which you occupied in our Catholic youth. . . . A visit from you would mean a very great deal to British intellectual prestige in these parts."

No Catholic Englishman was anything like so widely known

in Europe. Books have been written about him in many languages and his works translated into French, German, Dutch, Czech, Russian, Polish, Spanish and Italian. A letter from Russia asks for his photograph for *The Magazine of International Literature* as a writer whose works are well known in the Soviet Union. The Kulturbund in Vienna sends an emissary inviting him there also and, like Prague, the Vienna P.E.N. Club wants him.

"You have a distressing habit," Maude Royden once wrote, "of being the only person one really wants to hear on certain subjects."

A visit to Rome in 1929 produced *The Resurrection of Rome*. Despite brilliant passages the book is disappointing. It bears no comparison with *The New Jerusalem* and gives an impression of being thrown together hastily before the ideas had been thought through to their ultimate conclusions. Perhaps Rome was too big even for Chesterton.

He never loved the Renaissance as he did the Middle Ages, but he saw it not as primarily pagan but as one more example of the immense vitality of a Catholicism which had had so many rebirths that it had buried its own past deeper than the past of paganism. He loved the fountains that threw their water everywhere and he felt about Rome that the greatest monuments might be removed and yet the city's personality would remain. For Rome is greater than her monuments. He wanted to argue with those who cared for Pagan Rome alone and who spent their time despising the "oratory in stone" of the Papal city and gazing only on the Forum. "And it never once occurs to them to remember that the old Romans were Italians, or to ask what a Forum was for."

He was, as usual, constantly invited to lecture—at the English College, the Scots College, the American College, the Beda. At the Holy Child Convent he spoke to a crowded audience on "Thomas More and Humanism." Father Cuthbert, O.S.F.C., thanking him, remarked on the mental resemblance between More and Chesterton, saying that he could quite well imagine them sitting together making jokes, some of them very good and some of them very bad. "Chesterton and More," says Father Vincent McNabb, "were both cockneys." Gilbert's classical insight also seemed to him like the great Chancellor's; "Erasmus says that though More didn't know much Greek, he knew what the words ought to mean."

He interviewed Mussolini and found that Mussolini was interviewing him, so that he talked at some length of Distributism and his own social ideal. Mussolini knew at least some of Gilbert's books. He told Cyril Clemens that he had keenly enjoyed *The Man Who Was Thursday*. He promised at the end of this interview that he would go away and think over what Chesterton had said, and it might have been better for the world had he kept that promise. For what had been said was an outline of the one possible alternative to the growing tyranny of governments.

From his anxiety to be fair to Fascism, Gilbert was often accused of being in favour of it, but, both in this book and in several articles, having given the case for it he went on to give the case against it—a much stronger case than that usually given by its opponents. The case *for* Fascism lay in the breakdown of true democracy and the reign of the tyranny of wealth in the democratic countries. Chesterton would, he said, have been on the side of the Partito Popolare as against the Fascism that succeeded it; in England and America he would "have infinitely preferred that the purgation of our plutocratic politics should have been achieved by Radicals and Republicans. It was they who did not prefer it." It was not that Fascism was not open to attack but "that Liberalism has unfortunately lost the right to attack it."

Those of us who were in Italy at that time will remember the truth of his description of the vitality and happiness that seemed to glow among the people. *Giovinezza, bellezza,* heard everywhere, had then no hollow sound at the heart of it. Italy was radiant with hope.

In Mussolini himself Gilbert saluted a belief in "the civic necessity of Virtue," in the "ideal that public life should be public," in human dignity, in respect for women as mothers, in piety and the honour due to the dead. Yet, summing up the man and the movement, he saw it as primarily the sort of riot that is provoked by the evils of an evil government, only "in the Italy of the twentieth century the rioters have become the rulers." For although Mussolini had in many ways made his rule popular, although in his concessions to modern ideas and inventions he was "rather breathlessly progressive," yet in the true sense of the word Mussolini was a Reactionary. A Reactionary is one who merely reacts against something, or permits "that something to make [him] do something against it. . . . A Reactionary is one in whom weariness itself has become a form of energy. Even when he is right there is always a danger that what was really good in the previous society may be destroyed by what is good in the new one."

Mussolini's reaction was against the Liberalism in which as an idea Chesterton still believed, it was a reaction from democracy to authority. And his weakness, the fundamental weakness of Fascism was that "it appeals to an appetite for authority, without very clearly giving the authority for the appetite. . . . When I try to put the case for it in philosophical terms, there is some doubt about the ultimates of the philosophy." It seemed to Chesterton that there were only two possible fixed and orderly constitutions, hereditary Monarchy or Majority Rule. The demand of the Fascists to hold power as an intelligent and active minority was in fact to invite other intelligent and active minorities to dispute that rule; and then only by tyranny could anarchy be prevented.

"Fascism," he said in summary, "has brought back order into

the State; but this will not be lasting unless it has brought back order into the mind."

The two things in the Roman visit that remain most prominent in Dorothy's memory are Gilbert's loss of a medal of Our Lady that he always wore and his audience with the Holy Father. The loss of the medal seemed to distress him out of all normal proportion. He had the elevator boy looking for it on hands and knees and gave him a huge reward for finding it. Gilbert has left no record of his Papal audience. But, says Dorothy, it excited him so greatly that he did no work for two days before the event or two days after.

Their second visit to America in 1930–31 was far better enjoyed by Gilbert, and also I think by Frances until she got ill, because on it they came much closer to the real people of the country, especially during the period when he was lecturing at the University of Notre Dame, Indiana. They lived at a little house in South Bend and he lectured every night, alternating a course on Victorian Literature with one on the great figures of Victorian history. There were 36 lectures all told, and the average attendance at each lecture was 500.

At Notre Dame and the Sister College of St. Mary's, I felt the best way to get the atmosphere of this visit would be to get together for a talk the people who remembered Gilbert: they would stimulate one another's memories. I invoked the aid of Sister Madeleva and she suggested the two Fathers Leo Ward, Professors Engels and O'Grady, and, best of all Johnnie Mangan the chauffeur. Johnnie is a great institution at Notre Dame. He remembered driving my father nearly thirty years ago and he had specially vivid memories of the Chesterton period. We all sat in a circle in Sister Madeleva's sitting room. I give here the notes I took.

Johnnie Mangan: "It was the hardest job getting him into the car, harder getting him out. He'd walk on the porch and all the children came. He'd talk to the children on the road. Money meant nothing to him: the lady would give me the money saying himself would leave it in the shop if the barber wasn't honest enough to give change.

"He enjoyed everything: when they dedicated the stadium he stayed till the very end. Father O'Donnell introduced him to all the naval officers and he was the last off the ground. He enjoyed talking to all the naval officers. He loved cheer-leading."

Mr. O'Grady: "He spent one evening in Professor Phillips' room after the lecture from 9 to 2.30 A.M. His host was deaf, G.K. learnt later, and he made another date when he found his host had missed most of the fun."

Mr. Engels: "He would sit around consuming home-made ale by the quart; said the head of the philosophy faculty made the best brew in the college. Enjoyed little drives round the countryside. The faculty were a little shy of inviting him."

"In a lecture he got an immense laugh by calling Queen Elizabeth an 'old crock.' He then laughed above all the rest."

Mr. Engels noticed mannerisms: "The constant shifting of his great bulk around," "rotating while he was talking," "flipping his eyeglasses," "lumbering on to the stage, going through all his pockets, finally finding a piece of dirty yellow paper and talking from it as if most laboriously gathered and learned notes. But the paper was only for show. Father Burke saw him get out of the cab, he got on to the stair landing and then saw G.K.'s yellow paper on the ground. He had delivered his whole course with hardly a single note—occasionally looked through material for a quarter of an hour or so before speaking." All thought him a great entertainer as well as an informing talker. "No one enjoyed himself more than he did." Trying to get him for an informal gathering they mentioned they had some Canadian Ales—quite something in Prohibition days.

G.K.: "The ales have it."

Johnnie: "He'd chat all the time he was driving."

Father Leo L. Ward: "The problem of getting G.K. to and fro in a coupe was only solved by backing him in."

They remembered G.K. "in Charley's big chair, his hands barely touching over his great expanse."

They recalled that on receiving his honorary degree he said the last time he received one at Edinburgh they tapped him with John Knox's hat. He did not expect anything so drastic here: perhaps they might tap him with Tom Heflin's sombrero.*

When he had been invited to Notre Dame he was not certain where it was but with a name like that, even if it were in the mountains of the moon, he should feel at home. "If I ever meet anybody who suggests there's something Calvinistic or Puritanical in Catholicism I shall ask, 'Have you ever heard of the University of Notre Dame?'"

Johnnie: "He'd do anything she'd say, or Miss Collins. They certainly had that man by the neck, but they took wonderful care of him."

Mr. O'Grady: "It was a very intelligent arrangement. And did they tidy him."

Johnnie: "Very much so. It was their business every evening."

Sister Madeleva: "Did he walk on the campus and see the students?"

Johnnie: "He didn't walk much only to Charlie Phillips' rooms. He didn't mind being a little late but his lady and Miss Collins loaded him into the car to get him there on time.

"The woman they lodged with used to swear like a trooper. But she (the landlady) cried like a kid when he left. And he and the lady seemed lonesome at leaving her.

"In his spare time at the house he would be drawing some fancy stuff."

"What did he talk to you about?"

Johnnie: "He'd just talk about the country, he'd admire the streams and things like that. I took him to the Virgin Forest and I could hardly get him back. He even got out to notice the trees. He spent almost an hour. The women raved at me and said I must get him back at a certain time. He'd ask me the names of the trees. He loved rivers and would ask me about the fish. At one time Father O'Donnell thought he should drive to Chicago or some big town

* Tom Heflin was the fiercely anti-Catholic Senator from Alabama.

but he didn't care for towns, said they all looked alike to him, so after that we always went to the country."

Someone asked, "Did he ever get grouchy?"

Johnnie: "He always had a smile. Was always calling kids over to talk to him. He'd touch one with his stick to make him look round and play with him, and then he'd laugh himself sick playing with them. The kids were always around him. The ones of four or five years, those were the ones he'd notice the most. He liked to ask them things and then if they gave a good answer he could get a good laugh at it."

Mr. O'Grady: "I know he enjoyed himself here. I met him in Ottawa afterwards. He was autographing a book, the pen was recalcitrant and he shook it over the rug, 'Dear me, I'm always cluttering up people's rugs.' His cousin in Ottawa had him completely surrounded by ash trays but the cigar had ash almost half length and it was falling everywhere."

Father Ward: "Father Miltner one evening in pleasant fall weather found G.K. on the porch. The campus was empty. He got a grunt in return to his greeting, tried three or four times, almost no answer. G.K. looked glum.

" 'Well, you're not very gay this evening.'

" 'One should be given the luxury of a little private grouch once in a while.' "

To Johnnie—"Did he take the lecture business seriously?"

"No. He just wanted five minutes on the porch when he would talk to no one but the kids."

Mr. O'Grady: "He said once, 'What I like about notes is that when once you begin you can completely disregard them.' He stood for the first lecture but mostly he sat. He enjoyed a joke so much, and they enjoyed his enjoyment."

Mr. Engels: "For the first lecture he stood—part of him stood behind a little rostrum, after that he sat at a big table."

Father Leo R. Ward was at Oxford when he debated "That the Law is a Hass" and was amazed at the way the undergraduates adored him. "His opponent begged them not to vote for G.K. at this critical moment in the world's history. They cheered G.K. but voted against him to make the other fellow feel good."

Sister Madeleva: "What did he do for recreation?"

Johnnie: "He did a lot of—sketching I guess you'd call it—and he'd read the papers."

Sister Madeleva: "Did he like the campus?"

Johnnie: "Very much."

"Did he ever go down to the Grotto?"

Johnnie: "He seen it but he never got out of the car."

"Was it hard for him to walk?"

Johnnie: "No, he could walk kinda fast, but it was so hard for him to get in or out of the car."

"Where did he go to church?"

Johnnie: "He came here to Notre Dame. He was close to 400 lbs. but he'd never give it away. He'd break an ordinary scale, I guess. I brought him under the main building, he got stuck in the door of the car. Father O'Donnell tried to help. Mr. Chesterton said it reminded him of an old Irishwoman: 'Why don't you get out sideways?' 'I have no sideways.'"

. . . .

To the debate with Darrow, Frances Taylor Patterson had gone a little uneasy lest Chesterton's arguments "might seem somewhat literary in comparison with the trained scientific mind and rapier tongue of the famous trial lawyer." She found however that both trained mind and rapier tongue were the property of G.K.C.

I have never heard Mr. Darrow alone, but taken relatively, when that relativity is to Chesterton, he appears positively muddle headed.

As Chesterton summed it up, he felt as if Darrow had been arguing all afternoon with his fundamentalist aunt, and simply kept sparring with a dummy of his own mental making. When something went wrong with the microphone, Darrow sat back until it could be fixed. Whereupon G.K.C. jumped up and carried on in his natural voice, "Science you see is not infallible!" . . . Chesterton had the audience with him from the start, and when it was over, everyone just sat there, not wishing to leave. They were loath to let the light die! *

* *Chesterton* by Cyril Clemens, pp. 67–68.

As in England, so also in the States, Gilbert's debating was held to be far better than his straight lecturing. He never missed the opportunity for a quick repartee and yet when he scored the audience felt that he did so with utter kindness. At a debate with Dr. Horace T. Bridges of the Ethical Cultural Society on "Is Psychology a Curse?" Bishop Craig Stewart who presided, describes how:

In his closing remarks Chesterton devastatingly sideswiped his opponent and wound up the occasion in a storm of laughter and applause, "It is clear that I have won the debate, and we are all prepared to acknowledge that psychology is a curse. Let us, however, be magnanimous. Let us allow at least one person in this unhappy world to practice this cursed psychology, and I should like to nominate Dr. Bridges."

The Bishop on another occasion introduced Gilbert at a luncheon in Chicago by quoting Oliver Herford's lines:

> When plain folks such as you and I
> See the sun sinking in the sky,
> We think it is the setting sun:
> But Mr. Gilbert Chesterton
> Is not so easily misled;
> He calmly stands upon his head,
> And upside down obtains a new
> And Chestertonian point of view.
> Observing thus how from his nose
> The sun creeps closer to his toes
> He cries in wonder and delight
> How fine the sunrise is tonight!

The fact that nearly all the headlines he chose sounded like paradoxes, the fact that they did not themselves agree with him, had on Chesterton's opponents and on some members of his audience one curious effect. Dr. Bridges when asked his opinion of his late sparring partner, after paying warm tribute to his brilliance as a critic, his humour and his great personal charm, discovered in his "subconscious" (*Is* Psychology a Curse?) "a certain intellectual recklessness that made him indifferent to truth and reality . . . fundamentally—perhaps I should say subconsciously—he was a thorough-going skeptic and acted upon the principle that, since we cannot really be positive about anything we had better believe what it pleases us to believe."

So too at the British University of Aberystwyth when Chesterton spoke on "Liberty," taking first historically the fights of Barons against despots, yeomen against barons, factory hands against owners, and then giving as a modern instance the fight of the pedestrian to keep the liberty of the highway, we are told that "the Senior History Lecturer and some others were of the opinion that the whole thesis of the address was a gigantic leg-pull."

Chesterton must have seen again the fixed stare on the faces of the Nottingham tradesmen thirty years earlier on the famous occasion when he himself "got up and played with water." But that earlier audience had the intellectual advantage over the university professors that they

> Tried to find out what he meant
> With infinite inquiring.

Gilbert often said that his comic illustrations ought not to have prevented this. But it was really more his inability to resist making himself into a figure of fun. He was funny and the jokes were funny but they did prevent his really being given by all the position given him by so many, of the modern Dr. Johnson.

It is possible, though not easy, to imagine Johnson dragged from the station to his hotel by forty undergraduates of Aberystwyth while members of the O.T.C. secured a footing on the carriage armed with a battle axe (borrowed from the Arts Department), hoes, rakes, spades, etc.—their officers having refused them the privilege of bearing arms on the occasion.

But it is scarcely possible to imagine the Doctor called upon for a speech standing on the steps of the hotel and saying, "You need never be ashamed of the athletic prowess of this College. The Pyramids, we are told, were built by slave labour. But the slaves were not expected to haul the pyramids in one piece!" *

In San Francisco I saw many people who had met Gilbert including a journalist who took him to a "bootleg joint"—which is Western for a Speakeasy. There he asked for "some specialty of the house" and was offered a Mule.

"Six of these babies will put you on your ear," remarked the bartender.

"What did he say about my ear?" Gilbert queried.

He downed three of the potent mixture, in spite of his theory against cocktails and his host remarked his continued poise with admiration while the bartender commented "He can take it," another slang expression that appeared to be new to Gilbert. He told his host, Mr. Williams, that he delighted in meeting such folk as bartenders and all the simpler people whom he saw too seldom. This suggested an idea—would he come out to a school across the bay which could not afford his fees, because it educated the daughters of poorer Catholics. He agreed at once and not only talked to them brilliantly for three quarters of an hour, but also wrote for the children about 50 autographs.

But of course, he had forgotten something—an engagement to attend a big social function. A huge car arrived at the school complete with chauffeur and several agitated ladies. "Mr. Chesterton, you have broken an important engagement." "I have filled an important engagement," he answered, "lecturing to the daughters of the poor."

If it were possible for Gilbert to be better loved anywhere than in England that anywhere was certainly America. From coast to coast I have met his devotees. I have come across only one expression of the opposite feeling—and that from a man who seems

* *Chesterton* by Cyril Clemens, p. 50.

(from his opening sentence) to have been unable to stay away from the lectures he so detested:

I heard Chesterton some six or seven times in this country. His physical make-up repelled me. He looked like a big eater and animalism is repugnant to most of us. His appearance was against him.

Not one of his lectures seemed to me worth the price of admission and some of them were so bad that they seemed contemptuous morsels flung at audiences for whom he adjudged anything good enough.

One of his lectures, at the Academy Brooklyn, was a great disappointment. And he charged $1,000 for it. It was not worth $10 and Chesterton knew it. After the lecture, he remarked to a friend of mine, "I think that was the worst lecture I ever gave." He may have been right. Certainly it was the worst I ever heard him give. But he took the thousand and a bonus of $200 for the extra large crowd in attendance. No: I did not like Chesterton.

What of the money? With his American agent Chesterton had a quite usual arrangement: he received half the fees paid. The agent made engagements, paid travelling expenses and received for this the other half. Out of the half Chesterton received, he paid a further ten per cent to the London agent who had introduced him to the American agent; he also had to pay the expenses of his wife and his secretary and further gave a large present to his secretary for her trouble on the tour: the rest went chiefly into *G.K.'s Weekly*. I doubt if he could have told anyone at what figure the original fee stood for any lecture.

One of the Basilian Fathers, then a novice, remembers Gilbert's appearance in Toronto. The subject of this lecture was "Culture and the Coming Peril." The Coming Peril, he explained, was not Bolshevism (because Bolshevism had now been tried—"The best way to destroy a Utopia is to establish it. The net result of Bolshevism is that the modern world will not imitate it"). Nor by Coming Peril did he mean another great war (the next great war, he added, "would happen when Germany tried to monkey about with the frontiers of Poland"). The Coming Peril was the intellectual, educational, psychological, artistic overproduction which, equally with economic overproduction, threatened the well-being of contemporary civilisation. People were inundated, blinded, deafened, and mentally paralysed by a flood of vulgar and tasteless externals, leaving them no time for leisure, thought, or creation from within themselves.

At question period he was asked:

"Why is Dean Inge gloomy?"

"Because of the advance of the Catholic Church. Next question please."

"How tall are you and what do you weigh?"

"I am six feet two inches, but my weight has never been accurately calculated."

"Is George Bernard Shaw a coming peril?"

"Heavens, no. He is a disappearing pleasure."

For an apparently haphazard collection of essays *Sidelights on New London and Newer York*, published on his return to England from the second visit, has a surprising unity. Blitzed in London and out of print in New York it is now hard to obtain, which is a pity as it is full of good things. Discussing the fashions of today Chesterton attempts "to remove these things from the test of time and subject them to the test of truth," and this rule of an eternal test is the one he tried to apply in all his comments. Obviously nothing human is perfect—and this includes the human judgment, even Chesterton's judgment. Talking of the past or of the present, of England or America, he may often have been wrong and he would certainly have been the last man to claim infallibility for his judgments. His weakness as a critic was perhaps a tendency to get his proportions wrong—to make too much of some things he saw or experienced, too little of others. His qualities were intellectual curiosity and

G. K. CHESTERTON
From photograph by Howard Coster

personal amiability together with the measuring rod of an eternal standard.

This second visit to America only deepened in Gilbert's mind many of the impressions made by the first. Yet the atmosphere of the book is curiously different from that of *What I Saw in America*. Living in the country even a few months had so greatly deepened his understanding. He still preferred the Quakers to the Puritans, "The essential of the Puritan mood is the misdirection of moral anger." He still felt that as a whole the United States had started with "a great political idea, but a small spiritual idea": that it needed a "return to the vision" in politics and sociology. It was the fashion today to laugh at the wish for "great open spaces," yet the "real sociological object in going to America was to find those open spaces. It was *not* to find more engineers and electric batteries and mechanical gadgets in the home. These may have been the result of America: they were not the causes of America." Asked why he admired America yet hated Americanisation, he replied:

I should have thought that I had earned some right to apply this obvious distinction to any foreign country, since I have consistently applied it to my own country. If the egoism is excusable, I am myself an Englishman (which some identify with an egoist) and I have done my best to praise and glorify a number of English things: English inns, English roads, English jokes and jokers; even to the point of praising the roads for being crooked or the humour for being Cockney; but I have invariably written, ever since I have written at all, against the cult of British Imperialism.

And when that perilous power and opportunity, which is given by wealth and worldly success, largely passed from the British Empire to the United States, I have applied exactly the same principle to the United States. I think that Imperialism is none the less Imperialism because it is spread by economic pressure or snobbish fashion rather than by conquest; indeed I have much more respect for the Empire that is spread by fighting than for the Empire that is spread by finance.*

* *Sidelights on New London & Newer York*, p. 178.

He felt that the real causes for admiration, the real greatness of America, could be found partly through facing its incompleteness and defects, partly through contemplating the character of the greatest and most typical of Americans, Abraham Lincoln.

Whilst I was in America, I often lingered in small towns and wayside places; and in a curious and almost creepy fashion the great presence of Abraham Lincoln continually grew upon me. I think it is necessary to linger a little in America, and especially in what many would call the most uninteresting or unpleasing parts of America, before this strong sense of a strange kind of greatness can grow upon the soul. . . . The externals of the Middle West affect an Englishman as ugly, and yet ugliness is not exactly the point. There are things in England that are quite as ugly or even uglier. Rows of red brick villas in the suburbs of a town in the Midlands are, one would suppose, as hideous as human half-wittedness could invent or endure. But they are different. They are complete; they are, in their way, compact; rounded and finished with an effect that may be prim or smug, but is not raw. The surroundings of them are neat, if it be in a niggling fashion. But American ugliness is not complete even as ugliness. It is broken off short; it is ragged at the edges; even its worthy objects have around them a sort of halo of refuse. Somebody said of the rugged and sardonic Dr. Temple, once Archbishop of Canterbury: "There are no polished corners in our Temple." . . .

. . . there are no polished corners even in the great American cities, which are full of fine and stately classical buildings, not unworthy to be compared to temples. Nobody seems to mind the juxtaposition of unsightly things and important things. There is some deep difference of feeling about the need for completeness and harmony, and there is the same thing in the political and ethical life of the great Western nation. It was out of this landscape that the great President came, and one might almost trace a fanciful shadow of his figure in the thin trees and the stiff wooden pillars. A man of any imagination might look down these strange streets, with their frame-houses filled with the latest conveniences and surrounded with the latest litter, till he could see approaching down the long perspective that long ungainly figure, with the preposterous stove-pipe hat and the rustic umbrella and deep melancholy eyes, the humour and the hard patience and the heart that fed upon hope deferred.

That is admiring Abraham Lincoln, and that is admiring America.*

Among the "stately and classical buildings" were those making up the University of Notre Dame where he had been lecturing and which turned his musings in a direction they were ever inclined to take. Founded by a group of Frenchmen a century ago with a capital of four hundred dollars in a small log building on a clearing of ten acres, the University today numbers forty-five buildings on a seventeen hundred acre campus. The gold dome of the Church visible from miles away, the interesting combination of the extraordinary fame of its football team with a keen spiritual life, especially fascinated Gilbert. He wrote a poem dedicated to the University and called "The Arena." In it he pictures first the golden image on "the gilded house of Nero" that stood for all the horrors of the Pagan Amphitheatre. Then comes in contrast another image:

> I have seen, where a strange country
> Opened its secret plains about me,
> One great golden dome stand lonely with its
> golden image, one
> Seen afar, in strange fulfilment,
> Through the sunlit Indian summer
> That Apocalyptic portent that has clothed her
> with the Sun.

The boys shout "Notre Dame" as they watch the fortunes of the fray and Chesterton sees Our Lady presiding fittingly even over a football contest.

> And I saw them shock the whirlwind
> Of the world of dust and dazzle:
> And thrice they stamped, a thunderclap; and
> thrice the sand-wheel swirled;

* *Ibid.,* pp. 168–170.

> And thrice they cried like thunder
> On Our Lady of the Victories,
> The Mother of the Master of the Masterers of
> the World.

He recurs to a favourite thought that the Mother of Sorrows is the cause of human joy:

> Queen of Death and deadly weeping
> Those about to live salute thee,
> Youth untroubled; youth untortured; hateless war
> and harmless mirth
> And the New Lord's larger largesse
> Holier bread and happier circus,
> Since the Queen of Sevenfold Sorrow has brought
> joy upon the earth.

No wonder that, as Johnnie Mangan said, you could not drag him away from the game, if the game meant also a meditation. The "holier bread" came perhaps to his mind from the fact that the average of Daily Communion is unusually high at Notre Dame.

When he desired for Americans a return to their great political vision he desired also an opening of the eyes to that greater spiritual vision which was to him the supreme opportunity of the human spirit. E. S. P. Haynes in *Fritto Misto,* comments on the absence of any reference to universities in *What I Saw in America.* Nor have I anywhere found any discussion by Chesterton of the intellectual quality of Catholic education—any comparison with the secular teaching—either in England or in America. But that the problems of these two countries and of all the world could be solved only by what that golden Dome housed he cried with no uncertain voice. Death is in the world around, Resurrection in the Church of the God who died and rose again.

> Queen of Death and Life undying
> Those about to live salute thee.

CHAPTER XXIX

The Soft Answer

*I have only one virtue that I know of
I could really forgive unto seventy times seven.*
                    The Notebook

O NE OF THE commonest of biographers' problems is the
question of quarrels and broken friendships. At the
distance of time separating a life from its record some of these
look so empty of meaning as to imperil any reputation—yet they
happened, and when they were happening they probably appeared full of significance. Other quarrels involve issues of
importance in which the biographer cannot take wholeheartedly
the side of his hero. Thus my own father, writing *his* father's
life, had to pronounce judgment on Newman's side in the issues
that divided them, yet later, writing Newman's biography, he
had to admit the faults of temper that at least weakened the
Cardinal's case. For only so could he tell an entirely truthful
story.

In Chesterton's life there is no such problem. Attacks on public characters in his paper, attacks on abuses and ideas, absorbed
all his pugnacity. Fellow writers, rival journalists, friends, furnished often enough material for a quarrel; but Chesterton
would never take it up. He excelled in the soft answer—not that
answer which seeming soft subtly provokes to wrath, but the
genuine article. Belloc said of him that he possessed "the two
virtues of humility and charity"—those most royal of all Christian virtues. In the heat of argument he retained a fairness of

mind that saw his opponent's case and would never turn an argument into a quarrel. And most people both liked him and felt that he liked them. While he was having his great controversy with Blatchford back in 1906, it is clear from letters between them that the two men remained on the friendliest terms.

Edward Macdonald writes of his experiences of Chesterton when he was working with him on the paper.

He loved all the jokes about his size. He was the first to see the point and to roar with laughter when Douglas Woodruff introduced him to a meeting as "Mr. Chesterton who has just been looking round in America. . . ."

He came into the office once on Press Day and saw the disordered pile of papers and proofs on my desk. The place was certainly in an awful mess. I wanted to show him a particular letter and shoved my hand into the middle of one pile and was lucky enough to put my hand right on the right document. G.K.C. complimented me on a filing system that demanded a keen memory and then remarked enviously "I wish they'd let me have a desk like that at home."

When Thomas Derrick drew his famous cartoon of G.K.C. milking a cow he hesitated to give it to me for fear that G.K.C. would be offended. I wanted to print it in a special number and telephoned to Beaconsfield.

"Mr. Chesterton, I have here a cartoon of Derrick and would like to put it in the special number. But as you are the subject of the cartoon Derrick is afraid you may not like it."

"I would rather it were not printed," he replied. "I never liked the idea of my name being used in the title of the paper and don't want well-intentioned but embarrassing personalities. Of course, if it were highly satirical, insulting and otherwise unflattering I'd gladly have it on the front-page."

I assured him that it was anything but flattering and on the front-page it went. It was used as the frontispiece of G.K.'s Miscellany.

Many of the obituary writers said that he hated the cinema. In fact he told me once that he had long wished to write a new translation of *Cyrano* and would like to try his hand at a film scenario of the play. His fingers had itched in the first place to retranslate the duel scene in order to restore the strength of the ballade in English.

When he saw the film version of a Father Brown story I asked him what he thought of it. He had liked the film as a film and the acting. He added as an afterthought, "It gave me an idea for a new Father Brown story."

A short-hand note was taken of the famous debate with Bernard Shaw. It was decided to devote four pages of *G.K.'s Weekly* to a report which I tried to compile by avoiding the third person and concentrating on significant quotations. But whereas Shaw put his points in a few words from which elaboration could be cut, G.K.C.'s argument was so closely knit that it was difficult to leave out passages without spoiling the effect. He walked into the room as my pencil went through a fairly long extract from Shaw's speech.

"And whose words are you so gaily murdering?" he asked.

"Shaw's, Mr. Chesterton."

"Very well. Now put them all back and murder mine. I refuse to deny Shaw a full opportunity to state his case in my paper."

As a result Shaw's speech took up a great part of the space allotted and G.K.C. was inadequately reported.

He was always careful if he had reviewed a book in the paper criticising its ideas to take an immediate opportunity to show the author his warm personal friendliness. Middleton Murry, sending him a book of his own, criticised G.K. as "Perverse" for thinking communism and capitalism alike.

Your clean idea [of liberty and property] delights me, I believe, quite as much as it does you. But it is a vision and a dream, in this capitalistic world. . . . The communist is the man who has made up his mind to "go through with" the grim business of capitalism to the bitter end because he knows there is no going back. He makes a choice between following a dream which he *knows* is only a dream, and following a hope which he knows his own devotion may help to make real. Communism is the faith which a man wins through blank and utter despair. . . .

For my own part, if it were possible, I would rather see the world converted to Christianity than to communism. But the world has had its chance of becoming Christian; it will not get it again. . . .

The wrath to come—that is what communism is. And we can flee from it only by repentance. And repentance itself means communism. That is the fact as I see it. I hope, and sometimes dream, that we shall have the communism of repentance, and not the communism of wrath here in England.

Chesterton replied (May 19, 1932):

Thank you so very much for your most interesting and generous letter, which reached me indirectly and was delayed; also for your most interesting and generous book, which I immediately sat down and read at a sitting; which in its turn so stimulated me that I immediately wrote a rapid and rather curt reply for my own little rag. I fear you will find the reply more controversial than I meant it to be; for your book is so packed with challenges that I could not but make my very short article a thing packed with mere repartees. But I do hope you will understand how warm a sympathy I have with very much of what you say and with all the motives with which you say it. Needless to say, I agree with every word you say against Capitalism; but I particularly want to congratulate you on what you say about parasitic Parliamentary Labour. I thought that chapter was quite triumphant.

As for the rest, it is true that it has not shaken me in my conviction that the Catholic Church is larger than you or me, than your moods or mine; and the heroic but destructive mood in which you write is a very good example. You say that Christ set the example of a self-annihilation which seems to me almost nihilist; but I will never deny that Catholics have saluted that mood as the Imitation of Christ. Lately a friend of mine, young, virile, handsome, happily circumstanced, walked straight off and buried himself in a monastery; never, so to speak, to reappear on earth. Why did he do it? Psychologically, I cannot imagine. Not, certainly, from fear of hell or wish to be "rewarded" by heaven. As an instructed Catholic, he knew as well as I do that he could save his soul by normal living. I can only suppose that there is something in what you say; that Christ and others do accept a violent reversal of all normal things. But why do you say that Christ did it and has left no Christians who do it? Our Church has stood in the derision of four hundred years, because there were still Christians who did it. And they did it to *themselves*, as Christ did; you will not misunderstand me if I say that this is different from throwing out a violent theory for other people to follow.

Now for the application. Some of these monks, less cloistered, are to my knowledge, helping the English people to get back to the ownership of their own land; renewing agriculture as they did in the Dark Ages. Why do you say there is no chance for this normal property and liberty? You can only mean to say of our scheme exactly what you yourself admit about the Communist scheme. That it requires awful and almost inhuman sacrifices; that we must turn the mind upside-down; that we must alter the whole psychology of modern Englishmen. We must do that to make them Communists. Why is it an answer to say we must do that to make them Distributists? I could point out many ways in which our ideal is nearer and more native to men; but I will not prolong this debate. I should be very sorry that you should think it is only a debate. I only ask you to believe that we sympathise where we do not agree; but on this we do not agree.

Mr. Murry wrote later of Gilbert: "I liked the man immensely and he was a very honourable opponent of mine, much the most honourable I ever encountered." *

G.K.'s Weekly was of course Gilbert's own platform, so perhaps his care to apologise and his great magnanimity are more remarkable in incidents outside its columns. T. S. Eliot had *his* platform—he edited the *Criterion*. Chesterton on being reproached by him for a hasty article not only apologised but dedicated a book to Mr. Eliot. He had written confusing him with another critic who disapproved of alliteration and had also misquoted a stanza of his poetry. Mr. Eliot had written:

I should like you to know that it was apparently your "sympathetic reviewer," not I, who made the remark about alliteration; to which it seems he added a more general criticism of mine: so that *snob* is not the right corrective. Some of your comments seem to be based on a belief that *I* object to alliteration.

And may I add, as a humble versifier, that I *prefer* my verse to be quoted correctly, if at all.

* Mark Twain Quarterly, Chesterton Memorial No.

Chesterton replied:

I am so very sorry if my nonsense in the *Mercury* had any general air of hostility, to say nothing of any incidental injustices of which I was quite unaware. I meant it to be quite amiable; like the tremulous badinage of the Oldest Inhabitant in the bar parlour, when he has been guyed by the brighter lads of the village. I cannot imagine that I ever said anything about you or any particular person being a snob; for it was quite out of my thoughts and too serious for the whole affair. I certainly did have the impression, from the way the reviewer put it, that you disapproved of my alliteration; I also added that you would be quite right if you did. I certainly did quote you from memory, and even quote from a quotation; I also mentioned that I was doing so casual a thing. Of course, on the strictest principles, all quotations should be verified; and I should certainly have done so if I had in any way resented anything you said, or been myself writing in a spirit of resentment. If you think a letter to the *Mercury* clearing up these points would be fairer to everybody, of course I should be delighted to write one.

This attitude of the "oldest inhabitant" was the Chestertonian fashion of accepting the youthful demand for something new. When a young writer in *Colosseum* alluded to him as out of date he took it with the utmost placidity. "Good," he said to Edward Macdonald. "I like to see people refusing to accept the opinions of others before they've examined them themselves. They're perfectly entitled to say that I'm not a literary lion but a Landseer lion." Mr. Eliot's answer was a request to Gilbert to write in the *Criterion* and an explanation that he had felt in a false position since he rather liked alliteration than otherwise.

Thus too when Chesterton had answered a newspaper report of a speech made by C. E. M. Joad, the latter complained that it was a criticism "not of anything that I think, but of a garbled newspaper caricature of a few of the things I think, taken out of their context and falsified."

He added that he had not said science would destroy religion but that at its present rate of decline the *Church of England* would become a dead letter in a hundred and fifty years. Next, that science "has no bearing upon the spiritual truths of religion," but

has been presented, at any rate by the Church of England, in a texture of obsolete ideas about the nature of the physical universe and the behaviour of physical things which science has shown to be untrue.

Finally that religion is vital but it is in Mysticism that the core of religion lies for me, and mystical experience, as I understand it, does not want organizing.

I may be wrong in all this, but I hope that this explanation, such as it is, will lead you to think that I am not such an arrogant fool as your article suggests.

Chesterton replied (May 4, 1930):

I hope you will forgive my delay in thanking you for your very valuable and reasonable letter; but I have been away from home; and for various reasons my correspondence has accumulated very heavily. I am extremely glad to remember that, even before receiving your letter, I was careful to say in my article that my quarrel was not personally with you, but with the newspapers which had used what you said as a part of a stupid stunt against organised religion. I am even more glad to learn that they had misused your name and used what you did not say. I ought to have known, by this time, that they are quite capable of it; and I entirely agree that the correction you make in the report makes all the difference in the world. I do not think I ever meant or said that you were an arrogant fool or anything like it; but most certainly it is one thing to say that religion will die in a century (as the report stated) and quite another to say that the Church of England will experience a certain rate of decline, whether the prediction be true or no. I shall certainly take some opportunity to correct my statement prominently in the *Illustrated London News*; I hope I should do so in any case; but in this case it supports my main actual contention; that there is in the press a very vulgar and unscrupulous attack on the historic Christian Church.

The four points you raise are so interesting that I feel I ought to touch on them; though you will forgive me if I do so rather rapidly. With the first I have already dealt; and in that matter I can only apologise, both for myself and my unfortunate profession; and touching the second I do not suppose we should greatly disagree; I merely used it as one example of the futility of fatalistic prophecies such as the one attributed by the newspapers to you. But a thorough debate between us, if there were time for it, touching the third and fourth points, might possibly remove our differences, but would certainly reveal them.

In the third paragraph you say something that has been said many times, and doubtless means something; but I can say quite honestly that I have never been quite certain of what it means. Naturally I hold no brief for the Church of England as such; indeed I am inclined to congratulate you on having found any one positive set of "ideas," obsolete or not, which that Church is solidly agreed in "presenting." But I have been a member of that Church myself, and in justice to it, I must say that neither then nor now did I see clearly what are these things "about the nature of the physical universe, which science has shown to be untrue." I was not required as an Anglican, any more than as a Catholic, to believe that God had two hands and ten fingers to mould Adam from clay; but even if I had been, it would be rather difficult to define the scientific discovery that makes it impossible. I should like to see the defined Christian dogma written down and the final scientific discovery written against it. I have never seen this yet. What I have seen is that even the greatest scientific dogmas are not final. We have just this moment agreed that the ideas of the physical universe, which are really and truly "obsolete," are the very ideas taught by physicists thirty years ago. What I think you mean is that science has shown *miracles* to be untrue. But miracles are not ideas about the nature of the physical universe. They are ideas about the nature of a power capable of breaking through the nature of the physical universe. And science has not shown *that* to be untrue, for anybody who can think.

Lastly, you say that it is indeed necessary that Religion should exist, but that its essence is Mysticism; and this does not need to be organised. I should answer that nothing on earth needs to be organised so much as Mysticism. You say that man tends naturally to religion; he does indeed; often in the form of human sacrifice or the temples of Sodom. Almost all extreme evil of that kind is mystical. The only way of keeping it healthy is to have some rules, some responsibilities, some definitions of dogma and moral function. That at least, as you yourself put it, is what I think; and I hope you will not blame me for saying so. But as to what I said, in that particular article, it was quite clearly written upon wrong information and it will give me great pleasure to do my best to publish the fact.

In any such argument Gilbert was never, in the words of the Gospel, "willing to justify himself." He only wanted to justify certain ideas, and the thought of having misrepresented anyone else was distressing to him.

Even the hardened controversialist Coulton wrote in the course of one of their arguments:

If I speak very plainly of your historical methods, it is not that I do not fully respect your conversion. I have more sympathy with your Catholicity than (partly no doubt by my own fault) you may be inclined to think; I believe you to have made a sacrifice of the sort that is never altogether vain; it is therefore part of my faith that you are near to that which I also am trying to approach; and, if this belief does little or nothing to colour my criticisms in this particular discussion, that is because I believe true Catholicism, like true Protestantism, can only gain by the explosion of historical falsehoods, if indeed they be false, with the least possible delay. If (on the other hand) they are truths then you may be trusted to make out the best possible case for them, and my words will recoil upon myself.

The dispute was about Puritanism and Catholicism. It was republished as a pamphlet. It is the only case I have found in which Chesterton wrote several versions of one letter (to the *Cambridge Review*). In its final form he omitted one illuminating illustration. Coulton had maintained that the mediaevals condemned dancing as much as the Puritans and had dug up various mouldy theologians who classed it as a mortal sin. Father Lopez retorted by a quotation from St. Thomas saying it was quite right to dance at weddings and on such like occasions, provided the dancing was of a decent kind.

Chesterton comments:

We have already travelled very far from the first vision of Mr. Coulton, of Dark Ages full of one monotonous wail over the mortal sin of dancing. To class it seriously as a mortal sin is to class it with adultery or theft or murder. It is interesting to imagine St. Thomas and the moderate moralists saying: "You may murder at weddings; you may commit adultery to celebrate your release from prison; you may steal if you do not do it with immodest gestures," and so on. The calm tone of St. Thomas about the whole thing is alone evidence of a social atmosphere different from that described.

The rest of his analysis of Coulton's method of dealing with a historical document and distorting it is in the published version. A valuable part of Chesterton's line is also interesting as a comment on his own historical work. The expert he says is so occupied with detail that he overlooks the broad facts that anyone could see. On this point the review of Coulton's Mediaeval History in the *Church Times* is illuminating. The reviewer noted that in the index under the word "Church" occurred such notes as: "soldiers sleeping in," "horses stabled in," and other allusions to extraordinary happenings. But nowhere, he said, could he find any mention of the normal use of a church—that men prayed in it.

With H. G. Wells several interchanges of letters have shown in earlier chapters how the soft answer turned aside a wrath easily aroused, but also easily dissipated. Another exchange of letters only three years before Gilbert's death must be given. The third letter is undated and I am not sure if it belongs here or refers to another of Gilbert's reviews of a book of Wells.

47 Chiltern Court, N.W.I.
Dec. 10, 1933

DEAR OLD G.K.C.

An *Illustrated London News* Xmas cutting comes like the season's greetings. If after all my Atheology turns out wrong and your

Theology right I feel I shall always be able to pass into Heaven (if I want to) as a friend of G.K.C.'s. Bless you.

My warmest good wishes to you and Mrs. G.K.C.

H.G.

MY DEAR H.G.,

I do hope my secretary let you know that at the moment when I got your most welcome note I was temporarily laid out in bed and able to appreciate it, but not to acknowledge it. As to the fine point of theology you raise—I am content to answer (with the subtle and exquisite irony of the Yanks) I should worry. If I turn out to be right, you will triumph, not by being a friend of mine, but by being a friend of Man, by having done a thousand things for men like me in every way from imagination to criticism. The thought of the vast variety of that work, and how it ranges from towering visions to tiny pricks of humour, overwhelmed me suddenly in retrospect: and I felt we had none of us ever said enough. Also your words, apart from their generosity, please me as the first words I have heard for a long time of the old Agnosticism of my boyhood when my brother Cecil and my friend Bentley almost worshipped old Huxley like a god. I think I have nothing to complain of except the fact that the other side often forget that we began as free-thinkers as much as they did: and there was no earthly power but thinking to drive us on the way we went. Thanking you again a thousand times for your letter . . . and everything else.

Yours always
G. K. CHESTERTON.

MY DEAR CHESTERTON:

You write wonderful praise and it leaves me all aquiver. My warmest thanks for it. But indeed that wonderful fairness of mind is very largely a kind of funk in me—I know the creature from the inside—funk and something worse, a kind of deep, complex cunning. Well anyhow you take the superficial merit with infinite charity—and it has inflated me and just for a time I am an air balloon over the heads of my fellow creatures.

Yours ever
H. G. WELLS.

Gilbert loved to praise his fellows in the field of letters even when their philosophy differed from his own. In the obituaries in *G.K.'s Weekly* this is especially noticeable. Of two men of letters who died in 1928, he wrote with respect and admiration although with a mind divided between pure literary appreciation and those principles whereby he instinctively measured all things. Of Sir Edmund Gosse he wrote "The men from whom we would consent to learn are dying." G.K. felt he could never himself appreciate without judging, but he could learn from Gosse a uniquely "sensitive impartiality." With him "there passes away a great and delicate spirit which might in some sense be called the spirit of the eighteenth century; which might indeed be very rightly called the spirit of reason and civilisation." *

"These are the things we hoped would stay and they are going," he quoted from Swinburne, and of him and of Hardy, who died in 1928, and in whom he saluted "an honourable dignity and simplicity" he felt that though they had stated something false about the universe—that all the good things are fugitive and only the bad things unchanged—yet ". . . something rather like it might be a half truth about the world. I mean about the modern world. . . ." These poets lamented the passing of roses and sunbeams, but in the modern world

it is rather as if, in some inverted witchcraft the rose tree withered and faded from sight, and the rose leaves remained hovering in empty air. It is as if there could be sunbeams when there was no more sun. It is not only the better but the bigger and stronger part of a thing that is sacrificed to the small and secondary part. The real evil in the change that has been passing over Society is the fact that it has sapped foundations and, worse still, has not shaken the palaces and spires. It is as if there was a disease in the world that only devours the bones. We have not weakened the gilded parody of marriage, we have only weakened the marriage: . . . we have not abolished the House of Lords because it was not democratic. We have merely preserved the aristocracy, on condition that it shall not be aristocratic. . . . We have not yet even disestablished the

* May 26th, 1928.

Church; but there is a very pressing proposal that we should turn out of it the only people who really believe it is the Church. . . . There is now in the minds of nearly all Capitalists a sort of corrupt communism. . . . The Bank remains, The Fund remains, The Foreign Financier remains, Parliamentary Procedure remains, Jix remains. These are the things we hoped would go; but they are staying.

Sixteen years earlier Chesterton had in *The Victorian Age in Literature* characterised Hardy's novels as "the village atheist brooding and blaspheming over the village idiot." Yet Cyril Clemens has told me that Hardy recited to him some of Chesterton's poetry, and I think this obituary links with that fact in showing that a profound difference in their philosophy of life did not prevent a mutual appreciation and even admiration.

Gilbert Chesterton entered the last years of his life having made no enemies in the exceedingly sensitive literary world to which he primarily belonged. Whether he had made any in the world of politics I do not know, but he certainly felt no enmities. He said once it was impossible to hate anything except an idea, and to him I think it was. Against one politician who died in 1930 he had many years ago launched his strongest bit of ironical writing—Lord Birkenhead, then F. E. Smith, who had spoken of the Welsh Disestablishment Bill as having "shocked the conscience of every Christian community in Europe."—The last lines of Chesterton's mordant answer ran

> For your legal cause or civil
>   You fight well and get your fee;
> For your God or dream or devil
>   You will answer, not to me.
> Talk about the pews and steeples
>   And the cash that goes therewith:
> But the souls of Christian peoples . . .
>   Chuck it, Smith.

Later, Smith had stood with Sir Edward Carson against Cecil Chesterton at the Old Bailey. Now he was dead and many who had feared him in his lifetime were blackening his memory with subtle sneers and innuendo. Gilbert refused to join in this and he wrote in his paper: "In him we were confronted by and fought, not a set of principles but a man. . . . Lord Birkenhead was a great fighter! with one more pagan virtue—Pride—he would have been a great pagan."

Lord Balfour died in the same year. With him neither the paper nor its editor had fought personally, but upon almost all his policies had stood in opposition. Yet few better appreciations of him appeared than the article entitled by Chesterton "A Man of Distinction."

The English squire was an unconscious aristocrat; the Scotch laird was a conscious aristocrat; and Lord Balfour with all his social grace and graciousness, was conscious and even self-conscious. But this was only another way of saying that he had a mind which mirrored everything, including himself; and that, whatever else he did, he did not act blindly or in the dark. He was sometimes quite wrong; but his errors were purely patriotic; both in the narrow sense of nationalism and in the larger sense of loyalty and disinterestedness.

He instances Balfour's policies in Ireland and Egypt and continues:

In some ways he seems to me to have been too good a Stoic to be entirely a good Christian; or rather (to put it more correctly) to feel, like the rest of us, that he was a bad Christian. . . . There was much more in him of the Scotch Puritan than of the English Cavalier.

It is supremely characteristic of the present Parliamentary atmosphere that everybody accused Lord Balfour of incomprehensible compromise and vagueness, because he was completely logical and absolutely clear. Clarity does look like a cloud of confusion to people whose minds live in confusion twice confounded. . . .

. . . People said his distinctions were fine distinctions; and so they were; very fine indeed. A fine distinction is like a fine painting or a fine poem or anything else fine; a triumph of the human mind

. . . the great power of distinction; by which a man becomes in the true sense distinguished.*

The distinction Mr. Swinnerton draws † between Belloc and Chesterton may be a little too absolute, but substantially it is right. "One reason for the love of Chesterton was that while he fought he sang lays of chivalry and in spite of all his seriousness warred against wickedness rather than a fleshly opponent, while Belloc sang only after the battle and warred against men as well as ideas."

Did the tendency to find good in his opponents, did Chesterton's universal charity deaden, as Belloc believes, the effect of his writing?

He wounded none, but thus also he failed to provide weapons wherewith one may wound and kill folly. Now without wounding and killing, there is no battle; and thus, in this life, no victory; but also no peril to the soul through hatred.‡

In various controversies during the final years of *G.K.'s Weekly* the very opposite opinion is expressed. Hoffman Nickerson writes of the "subversive" nature of Chesterton's work, of his giving weapons to Communism and doing his bit towards starting "a very nasty class war" in America. Mr. Nickerson was allowed to develop this theme in a series of articles in Chesterton's own paper. Correspondents too complained often enough in the paper of its attacks on vested interests and on other schools of thought than its own.

In the course of a controversy with Mr. Penty, in which I think G.K. most distinctly misunderstood his opponent but in which both men kept the friendliest tone, Penty says that Chesterton treats as a drive much that he himself would call a drift: that the mind is more in fault than the will of mankind in

* March 29, 1930.   † *Georgian Scene*, p. 88.
‡ *The Place of Chesterton in English Letters*, p. 81.

getting the world into its present mess. With this diagnosis Chesterton certainly agreed for the greater part of mankind. He spoke often of a "madness in the modern mind." Psychology meant "the mind studying itself instead of studying the truth" and it was part of what had destroyed the mind. "Advertisements often tell us to Watch this Blank Space. I confess I do watch that blank space, the modern mind, not so much for what will appear in it, as for what has already disappeared from it."

Thus too when the Rev. Dick Shepherd remarrying a divorced woman—i.e., encouraging her to take again the solemn vow she had already broken—said that he heard the voice of Christ: "Go in peace," it was not for impiety that Chesterton condemned him. He wrote with restraint "There is scarcely a shade of difference left between meaning well and meaning nothing."

Was Penty still right in thinking he saw a drive where he ought to see a drift and Nickerson in thinking he was dangerously subversive in his attitude to the rich? And anyhow what about Belloc?

I incline to think that the truth was that while G.K. could never hate an individual he could hate a group. If he suddenly remembered an individual in that group he hastily excepted him from the group in order to leave the objects of his hatred entirely impersonal. Thus he hated politicians but found real difficulty in hating *a* politician. He hated what he called the plutocracy, but no individual rich man. I do think however that while believing firmly in original sin he was somewhat inclined to see it as operative more especially in the well-to-do classes. His championship of the poor was in no way impersonal. His burning love and pity went out to every beggar. He tended to love all men but the poor he loved with an undivided heart, and when he thought of them his thoughts grew harsh towards the rich who were collectively their oppressors.

I doubt if he allowed enough for the degree of stupidity required to amass a fortune. He would have agreed that love of money narrowed the mind: I doubt if he fully grasped that only a mind already narrow can love money so exclusively as to pursue it successfully. And I am pretty sure he did not allow enough for the fact that rich like poor are caught today in the machinery they have created. He saw the bewildered, confused labourer who has lost his liberty: he failed to see the politician also bewildered, the millionaire also confused, afraid to let go for fear he might be submerged. And yet at moments he did see it. He wrote in the paper a short series of articles on men of the nineteenth century who had created the confusion of today; on Malthus, Adam Smith and Darwin. Far from its being true that supernatural religion had first been destroyed and morality lost in consequence, it had been the Christian morality that was first destroyed in the mind. G.K. summarised Adam Smith's teachings as: "God so made the world that He could achieve the good if men were sufficiently greedy for the goods." Thus the man of today "Whenever he is tempted to be selfish half remembers Smith and self-interest. Whenever he would harden his heart against a beggar, he half remembers Malthus and a book about population; whenever he has scruples about crushing a rival he half remembers Darwin and his scruples become unscientific." Because none of these theories were in their own day seen as heresies and denounced as heresies they have lived on vaguely to poison the atmosphere and the mind of today.

English Conservatives had been shocked when Chesterton began: Mr. Nickerson was shocked when he was ending: because he demanded a revolution. Surely, Mr. Nickerson said, if he looked at Communism closely he would prefer Capitalism. He not only would, he constantly said he did. But he wanted a Revolution from both: he preferred that it should not be "nasty" for what he wanted was the Christian Revolution. Like all revolutions however it must begin in the mind and he felt less and less hopeful as he watched that blank space.

But I do not believe that Chesterton failed because he had not at his command the weapon of hatred. Here Belloc surely makes the same mistake that Swift (whom he instances) made and for the same reason. The Frenchman and the Irishman understand the rapier of biting satire as does not the Englishman: for direct abuse of anyone, no matter how richly merited, nearly always puts the Englishman on the side of the man who is being abused. What happened to Swift's Gulliver—that most fierce attack upon the human race? The English people drew its sting and turned it into a nursery book that has delighted their children ever since. There are more ways than one of winning a battle: you can win the man instead of the argument and Chesterton won many men. Or you can take a weapon that once belonged chiefly to the enemy but which Chesterton wrested from him; a very useful weapon: the laugh.

Orthodoxy, doctrinal and moral, was a lawful object of amusement to Voltaire and his followers but now the laugh has passed to the other side and Chesterton was (with Belloc himself) the first to seize this powerful weapon. Thus when Bishop Barnes of Birmingham said that St. Francis was dirty and probably had fleas many Catholics were furious and spoke in solemn wrath. Chesterton wrote the simple verse

A Broad-minded Bishop Rebukes the Verminous Saint Francis

If Brother Francis pardoned Brother Flea
There still seems need of such strange charity
Seeing he is, for all his gay goodwill
Bitten by funny little creatures still.

I shall never forget going to hear Chesterton debate on Birth Control with some Advanced Woman or other. Outside the hall were numbers of her satellites offering their literature. I was just about to say something unpleasant to one of them when a verse flashed into my mind:

If I had been a Heathen,
I'd have crowned Neaera's curls,
And filled my life with love affairs,
My house with dancing girls!
But Higgins is a Heathen
And to lecture-rooms is forced
Where his aunts who are not married
Demand to be divorced.

The rebuke died on my lips: why get angry with the poor old aunts of Higgins demanding the destruction of their unconceived and inconceivable babies?

Swinburne had mocked at Christian virtue but the Dolores of Chesterton replied to him:

I am sorry old dear if I hurt you,
No doubt it is all very nice,
With the lilies and languors of virtue
And the raptures and roses of vice.
But the notion impels me to anger
That vice is all rapture for me,
And if you think virtue is languor
Just try it and see.

But in fact G.K. did not merely use laughter as a weapon: he was often simply amused—and did not conceal it. He told Desmond Gleeson that he remembered reading Renan's Christ "while I was standing in the queue waiting to see 'Charley's Aunt.' But it is obvious which is the better farce for 'Charley's Aunt' is still running." No wonder that Eileen Duggan when she pictured him as a modern St. George saw him "shouting gleefully 'Bring on your dragons.'" Even dragons may be bothered by the unexpected. And it may well be that when the rapier of anger has been blunted against the armour of some accustomed fighter he will be driven off the field by gales of Chestertonian laughter.

CHAPTER XXX

Our Lady's Tumbler

I hate to be influenced. I like to be commanded or to be free. In both of these my own soul can take a clear and conscious part: for when I am free it must be for something that I really like, and not something that I am persuaded to pretend to like: and when I am commanded, it must be by something I know, like the Ten Commandments. But the thing called Pressure, of which the polite name is Persuasion, I always feel to be a hidden enemy. It is all a part of that worship of formlessness, and flowing tendencies, which is really the drift of cosmos back into chaos. I remember how I suddenly recoiled in youth from the influence of Matthew Arnold (who said many things very well worth saying) when he told me that God was "a stream of tendency." Since then I have hated tendencies: and liked to know where I was going and go there—or refuse.

G.K.'s Weekly, Aug. 18, 1928.

IN 1932, WHEN Gilbert had been in the Church just ten years and Frances six, my husband and I met them at the Eucharistic Congress in Dublin. They were staying at the Vice-Regal Lodge and were very happy in that gathering of the Catholic world brought about by the Congress. It was this thought of the potential of the faith for a unity the League of Nations could not achieve—only dogma is strong enough to unite mankind—that gave its title to the book *Christendom in Dublin*.

In the crowd that thronged to that great gathering he saw Democracy. Its orderliness was more than a mere organisation: it was Self-Determination of the People. "A whole mob, what many would call a whole rabble, was doing exactly what it wanted; and what it wanted was to be Christian." The mind of that crowd was stretched over the centuries as the faint sound of St. Patrick's bell that had been silent so many centuries was heard in Phoenix Park at the Consecration of the Mass: it was stretched over the earth as the people of the earth gathered into one place which had become for the time Rome or the Christian Centre.

During the Congress an Eastern priest accosted G.K. with praise of his writings. His own mind full of the great ideas of Christendom and the Faith, he felt a huge disproportion in the allusion to himself. And when later the priest asked to be photographed at his side it flashed through G.K.'s mind that he had heard in the East that an idiot was supposed to bring luck. This sort of humorous yet sincere intellectual humility startles us in the same kind of way as does the spiritual humility of the saints. We have to accept it in the same kind of way—without in the least understanding it, but simply because we cannot fail to see it.

But the world could fail even to see it. It could and did fail in imagining a mind so absorbed in the contemplation of Infinite Greatness that its own pin-point littleness became an axiom: rather it seemed an affectation—none the less an affectation and much the less pardonable because the laughter was directed against others as well as against himself.

There is an old mediaeval story of a tumbler who, converted and become a monk, found himself inapt at the offices of Choir and Scriptorium so he went before a statue of Our Lady and there played all his tricks. Quite exhausted at last he looked up at the statue and said, "Lady, this is a choice performance." There is more than a touch of Our Lady's tumbler in Gilbert. He knew he could give in his own fashion a choice performance, but meeting a priest come from a far land where he had reconciled a hitherto schismatic group with the great body of the Catholic Church, who could forgive sins and offer the Holy Sacrifice, he truly felt "something disproportionate in finding one's own trivial trade, or tricks of the trade, amid the far-reaching revelations of such a trysting-place of all the tribes of men." *

His awe and reverence for priests was, says Father Rice, enormous. "He would carefully weigh their opinion however fatuous." His comment on the bad statues and fripperies which so many Catholics find a trial was: "It shows the wisdom of the Church. The whole thing is so terrific that if people did not have these let-downs they would go mad."

Yet it may have been a fear of excess of this special let-down that made him reluctant to go to Lourdes. Lisieux he never liked but he was, Dorothy says, fascinated by Lourdes when she persuaded him to go. He went several times to the torchlight procession and he said as he had said in Dublin, "This is the only real League of Nations."

The thing he liked best in Dublin was the spontaneous outburst of little altars and amateur decorations in the poorest quarters of the city. The story he loved to tell was that of the old woman who said when on the last day the clouds looked threatening: "Well, if it rains now He will have brought it on Himself."

The year of the Congress two other books were published: *Sidelights on New London and Newer York,* already discussed, and *Chaucer.* The books contrast agreeably: one throwing the ideal against the real of his own day, the other evoking his ideal from the past. The *Chaucer* was much criticised—chiefly because he was not a Chaucer scholar. As a matter of fact the notion of his writing this book did not originate with Chesterton but with Richard de la Mare who had projected a series of essays called "The Poets on the Poets." This developed, still at his suggestion, into a literary biography of Chaucer. But in any event G.K. had all his life combatted the notion that only a scholar should write on such themes. He stood resolutely for the rights of the amateur: yet I think the scholar might well start off with

* *Christendom in Dublin,* p. 35.

some exasperation on reading that if Chaucer had been called the Father of English poetry, so had "an obscure Anglo-Saxon like Caedmon," whose writing was "not in that sense poetry and not in any sense English." It is a curious example of one of the faults Chesterton himself most hated—overlooking something because it was too big: something too that he had realised in an earlier work—for Caedmon spoke the language of Alfred the Great.

In a brilliant garnering of the fruits of her scholarship—*Word Hoard*—Margaret Williams has quoted Chesterton's Alfred as a stirring expression of the significance of the spiritual conquest of England by Christianity. In the same book she shows how superficial is the view which believes that the English language was a creation of the Norman Conquest. The struggle, she says "between the English and French tongues lasted for some three hundred years, until the two finally blended into a unified language, basically Teutonic, richly romantic. The English spirit emerged predominant by a moral victory over its conqueror. . . ." *

No one would wish that Chesterton should have ignored the immense debt owed by our language to the French tributary that so enriched its main stream, but it seems strange that in his hospitable mind, in which Alfred's England held so large a place, he should not have found room for an appreciation of the Saxon structure of Chaucer and for all that makes him unmistakably one in a line of which Caedmon was the first great poet. In this book, only his debt to France is stressed, because England is to be thought of as part of Europe—and the part she is a part of is apparently France!

Yet what excellent things there are in the book:

The great poet exists to show the small man how great he is. . . .
The great poet is alone strong enough to measure that broken strength we call the weakness of man.

* *Word Hoard* by Margaret Williams, p. 4.

The real vice of the Victorians was that they regarded history as a story that ended well because it ended with the Victorians. They turned all human records into one three-volume novel; and were quite sure that they themselves were the third volume.

He quotes Troilus and Cressida on "The Christian majesty of the mystery of marriage":

Any man who really understands it does not see a Greek King sitting on an ivory throne, nor a feudal lord sitting on a faldstool but God in a primordial garden, granting the most gigantic of the joys of the children of men.

When we talk of wild poetry, we sometimes forget the parallel of wild flowers. They exist to show that a thing may be more modest and delicate for being wild.

Romance was a strange by-product of Religion; all the more because Religion, through some of its representatives may have regretted having produced it. . . . Even the Church, as imperfectly represented on its human side, contrived to inspire even what it had denounced, and transformed even what it had abandoned.

The best chapter is the last: The Moral of the Story—and that moral is: "That no man should desert that [Catholic] civilisation. It can cure itself but those who leave it cannot cure it. Not Nestorius, nor Mahomet, nor Calvin, nor Lenin have cured, nor will cure the real evils of Christendom; for the severed hand does not heal the whole body."

Healing must come from a recovery of the norm, of the balance, of the equilibrium that mediaeval philosophy and culture were always seeking. "The meaning of Aquinas is that mediaevalism was always seeking a centre of gravity. The meaning of Chaucer is that, when found, it was always a centre of gaiety. . . ."

The name of Aquinas thus introduced on almost the last page of this book shows Chesterton's mind already busy on the next and perhaps most important book of his life: *St. Thomas Aquinas.*

"Great news this," wrote Shaw to Frances, "about the Divine Doctor. I have been preaching for years that intellect is a passion that will finally become the most ecstatic of all the passions; and I have cherished Thomas as a most praiseworthy creature for being my forerunner on this point."

When we were told that Gilbert was writing a book on St. Thomas and that we might have the American rights, my husband felt a faint quiver of apprehension. Was Chesterton for once undertaking a task beyond his knowledge? Such masses of research had recently been done on St. Thomas by experts of such high standing and he could not possibly have read it all. Nor should we have been entirely reassured had we heard what Dorothy Collins told us later concerning the writing of it.

He began by rapidly dictating to Dorothy about half the book. So far he had consulted no authorities but at this stage he said to her:

"I want you to go to London and get me some books."

"What books?" asked Dorothy.

"I don't know," said G.K.

She wrote therefore to Father O'Connor and from him got a list of classic and more recent books on St. Thomas. G.K. "flipped them rapidly through," which is, says Dorothy, the only way she ever saw him read, and then dictated to her the rest of his own book without referring to them again. There are no marks on any of them except a little sketch of St. Thomas which was drawn in the margin opposite a description of the affair, which G.K. so vividly dramatises, of Siger of Brabant.

Had we known all this we should have been asking ourselves even more definitely: What will the experts say? Of the verdict of the greatest of them we were not long left in doubt. Etienne Gilson, who has given two of the most famous of philosophical lecture series—the Gifford Lectures at Aberdeen and the William James Lectures at Harvard—had begun his admiration for Chesterton with *Greybeards at Play* and had thought *Orthodoxy* "the best piece of apologetic the century had produced." When *St. Thomas* appeared he said to a friend of mine "Chesterton makes one despair. I have been studying St. Thomas all my life and I could never have written such a book." After Gilbert's death, asked to give an appreciation, he returned to the same topic—

I consider it as being without possible comparison the best book ever written on St. Thomas. Nothing short of genius can account for such an achievement. Everybody will no doubt admit that it is a "clever" book, but the few readers who have spent twenty or thirty years in studying St. Thomas Aquinas, and who, perhaps, have themselves published two or three volumes on the subject, cannot fail to perceive that the so-called "wit" of Chesterton has put their scholarship to shame. He has guessed all that which they had tried to demonstrate, and he has said all that which they were more or less clumsily attempting to express in academic formulas. Chesterton was one of the deepest thinkers who ever existed; he was deep because he was right; and he could not help being right; but he could not either help being modest and charitable, so he left it to those who could understand him to know that he was right, and deep; to the others, he apologized for being right, and he made up for being deep by being witty. That is all they can see of him.*

In joining the Church Chesterton had found like all converts, from St. Paul to Cardinal Newman, that he had come into the land of liberty and especially of intellectual liberty. "Conversion," he said, "calls on a man to stretch his mind, as a man awakening from sleep may stretch his arms and legs." †

I suppose one of the reasons why the surrounding world finds it hard to receive this statement from a convert is that he has only to look around him to see so many Catholics wrapped in slumbers as placid as the next man's. To this very real difficulty,

---

* *Chesterton*, by Cyril Clemens, pp. 150–151.
† *Well and Shallows*, p. 130.

and to all its implications, Chesterton unfortunately seldom adverted. To the scandal wrought by evil Catholics, historical or contemporary, he was not blind—he summarised one element in the Reformation conflict:

> Bad men who had no right to their right reason
> Good men who had good reason to be wrong.

But I wish that with his rare insight into minds he had analysed us average Catholics. He might have startled us awake by explaining to non-Catholics *how* those who know such Truths and feed upon such Food can yet appear so dull and lifeless. Anyhow, whether the fault lie in part with us or entirely with the world at large, certain it is that in that world a convert is always expected to justify not merely his beliefs but his sincerity in continuing to hold them. I wonder if the Pharisees said of St. Paul that they were sure he really wanted to return to his old allegiance as some said it of Newman, or spoke as Arnold Bennett did when he accused Chesterton of being Modernist in his secret thoughts? Were St. Paul's epistles an Apologia pro Vita Sua?

An Apologia does not of course mean an apology but a justification, and the ground on which justification was sometimes demanded amused Gilbert rather than annoying him. Playing the Parlour Game which consists of guessing at what point in an article on hydraulics, elegiacs or neo-Platonism Dean Inge will burst into his daily attack on the Church, he wrote:

The Dean of St. Paul's got to business, in a paragraph in the second half of his article, in which he unveiled to his readers all the horrors of a quotation from Newman; a very shocking and shameful passage in which the degraded apostate says that he is happy in his religion, and in being surrounded by the things of his religion; that he likes to have objects that have been blessed by the holy and beloved, that there is a sense of being protected by prayers, sacramentals and so on; and that happiness of this sort satisfies the soul.

The Dean, having given us this one ghastly glimpse of the Cardinal's spiritual condition, drops the curtain with a groan and says it is Paganism. How different from the Christian orthodoxy of Plotinus!*

This playful, not to say frivolous, tone was fresh cause of annoyance to those who were apt to be annoyed. It is easier to understand their objection than the opposite one: that he became dull and prosy after he joined the Church (or alternatively after he left Fleet Street for Beaconsfield). The only real difficulty about his later work arises from the riot of his high spirits. In his own style I must say there are moments when even I want to read the Riot Act. And those who admire him less feel this more keenly. Bad puns, they say, wild and sometimes ill-mannered jokes are perhaps pardonable in youth but in middle age they are inexcusable. The complainants against *The Thing* are in substance the complainants against *Orthodoxy* grown more vehement with the passage of years.

The idea had been adumbrated of calling one of his books: *Joking Apart* and only rejected because of the fear that if he said he was *not* joking everyone would be quite certain that he was. This greatly amused G.K. and he began the book (it actually appeared as *The Well and the Shallows*) with "An Apology for Buffoons." After defending the human instinct of punning he remarked that "many moderns suffer from the disease of the suppressed pun." They are actuated even in their thinking by merely verbal association.

I for one greatly prefer the sort of frivolity that is thrown to the surface like froth to the sort of frivolity that festers under the surface like slime. To pelt an enemy with a foolish pun or two will never do him any grave injustice; the firework is obviously a firework and not a deadly fire. It may be playing to the gallery, but even the gallery knows it is only playing.†

* *The Thing*, pp. 156-7.   † *Well and Shallows*, pp. 11-12.

CHESTERTON AT THE MICROPHONE—1935

Such playing was a necessity if the gallery, i.e. all the people, were to be made to listen: if the things you were thinking about were important to them as well as to yourself: if the ideas were more important than the dignity or reputation of the person who uttered them. In this book Gilbert sketched briefly one side of his reason for feeling these ideas of paramount importance for everybody. "My Six Conversions" concerned reasons given him by the world that would have made him become a Catholic if he were not one already.

He had been brought up to treasure liberty and in his boyhood the world had seemed freer than the Church. Today in a world of Fascism, Communism and Bureaucracy the Church alone offered a reasoned liberty. He had been brought up to reverence certain ideals of purity: today they were laughed at everywhere but in the Church. The "sure conclusions" of Science that had stood foursquare in his boyhood had become like a dissolving view. Liberalism had abdicated when the people of Spain freely chose the Church and English Liberals defended the forcing upon them of a minority rule. "There are no Fascists; there are no Socialists; there are no Liberals; there are no Parliamentarians. There is the one supremely inspiring and irritating institution in the world and there are its enemies." Above all, he felt increasingly, as time went on that those who left the Faith did not get Freedom but merely Fashion; that there was something ironic in the name the atheists chose when they called themselves Secularists. By definition they had tied themselves to the fashion of this world that passeth away.

These six conversions then were what the world would have forced upon him: the Church as an alternative to a continually worsening civilisation. While he hated the Utopias of the Futurists and while he accepted the Christian view of life as a probation he felt too that life today was abnormally degraded and unhappy.

There is a sense in which men may be made normally happy; but there is another sense in which we may truly say, without undue paradox, that what they want is to get back to their normal unhappiness. At present they are suffering from an utterly abnormal unhappiness. They have got all the tragic elements essential to the human lot to contend with; time and death and bereavement and unrequited affection and dissatisfaction with themselves. But they have not got the elements of consolation and encouragement that ought normally to renew their hopes or restore their self-respect. They have not got vision or conviction, or the mastery of their work, or the loyalty of their household, or any form of human dignity. Even the latest Utopians, the last lingering representatives of that fated and unfortunate race, do not really promise the modern man that he shall do anything, or own anything, or in any effectual fashion be anything. They only promise that, if he keeps his eyes open, he will see something; he will see the Universal Trust or the World State or Lord Melchett coming in the clouds in glory. But the modern man cannot even keep his eyes open. He is too weary with toil and a long succession of unsuccessful Utopias. He has fallen asleep.*

Chesterton demanded urgently that the worldlings who had failed to make the world workable should abdicate. "The organic thing called religion has in fact the organs that take hold on life. It can feed where the fastidious doubter finds no food; it can reproduce where the solitary sceptic boasts of being barren." In short, in religion alone was Darwin justified, for Catholicism was the "spiritual Survival of the Fittest." †

If these Six Conversions are read without the balancing of something deeper they have the superficial look that belongs of necessity to Apologetics. Some essays in *The Well and the Shallows,* most of *The Thing, Christendom in Dublin,* and above all, *The Queen of Seven Swords* give us that deeper quieter thinking when the mind is meditating upon the great mysteries of the faith.

---

* *G.K.'s Weekly,* October 20, 1928.
† *Well and Shallows,* p. 82.

Only very occasionally is it possible to glimpse beneath Gilbert's reserve, but such glimpses are illuminating. Father Walker, who prepared him for his First Communion, writes, "It was one of the most happy duties I had ever to perform. . . . That he was perfectly well aware of the immensity of the Real Presence on the morning of his First Communion, can be gathered from the fact that he was covered with perspiration when he actually received Our Lord. When I was congratulating him he said, 'I have spent the happiest hour of my life.'"

Yet he went but seldom to Holy Communion, and an unfinished letter to Father Walker gives the reason. "The trouble with me is that I am much too frightened of that tremendous Reality on the altar. I have not grown up with it and it is too much for me. I think I am morbid; but I want to be told so by authority."

And in *Christendom in Dublin,* he says: "The word Eucharist is but a verbal symbol, we might say a vague verbal mask, for something so tremendous that the assertion and the denial of it have alike seemed a blasphemy; a blasphemy that has shaken the world with the earthquake of two thousand years."

I have heard it said that in these later years Gilbert's writing became obscure, and I think it is partly true. Only partly, for the old clarity is still there except when he is dealing with matters almost too deep for human speech. He wrote in *The Thing*:

A thinking man can think himself deeper and deeper into Catholicism . . . the great mysteries like the Blessed Trinity or the Blessed Sacrament are the starting-point for trains of thought . . . stimulating, subtle and even individual. . . . To accept the Logos as a truth is to be in the atmosphere of the absolute, not only with St. John the Evangelist, but with Plato and all the great mystics of the world. . . . To exalt the Mass is to enter into a magnificent world of metaphysical ideas, illuminating all the relations of matter and mind, of flesh and spirit, of the most impersonal abstractions as well as the most personal affections. . . . Even what are called the fine doctrinal distinctions are not dull. They are like the finest operations of surgery; separating nerve from nerve but giving life. It is easy enough to flatten out everything around for miles with dynamite if our only object is to give death. But just as the physiologist is dealing with living tissues so the theologian is dealing with living ideas; and if he draws a line between them it is naturally a very fine line.

If there appears a contradiction in the picture of Chesterton the philosopher pondering on the Logos and Chesterton the child offering trinkets to Our Lady, we may remember the Eternal Wisdom "playing in the world, playing before God always" whose delight is to be with the children of men.

Chapter XXXI

The Living Voice

CHESTERTON SPOKE ONCE of the keen joy for the intellect of discovering the causes of things, but he was not greatly interested in science. He would have said that although the physical sciences did represent an advance in the grasp of truth it was, in the words of Browning, only the "very superficial truth." He desired a knowledge of causes that did not dwell simply on what was secondary but led back to the First and Final Cause. To the mediaeval thinker, science was fascinating as Philosophy's little sister: it was to Philosophy what Nature was to man. Nature had been to St. Francis a little lovely, dancing sister. Science had been to St. Thomas the handmaid of philosophy. The modern world thought these proportions fantastic. Huxley used Nature as a word for God. Physical Science had ousted Philosophy.

An American friend lately told me of a girl who, asked if she believed in God replied, "Sure, I believe in God, but I'm not nuts about Him." Gilbert was not "nuts" about Science: therefore in a world that saw nothing else to be "nuts" about he was called its enemy. And as with other things taken more solemnly by most moderns he preferred to get fun out of the inventions of the age.

He wrote in a fairly early number of *G.K.'s Weekly*:

ESKIMO SONG

. . . So that the audience in Chicago will have the advantage of hearing Eskimos singing. (Or words to that effect.)

—*Wireless Programme.*

Oh who would not want such a wonderful thing
As the pleasure of hearing the Eskimos sing?
I wish I had Eskimos out on the lawn,
Or perched on the window to wake me at dawn:
With Eskimos singing in every tree
Oh that would be glory, be glory for me!

Oh list to the song that the Eskimos sing,
When the penguin would be if he could on the wing,
Would soar to the sun if he could, like the lark,
But for most of the time it is totally dark.

Or hark to the bacchanal songs that resound
When they're making a night of it half the year round,
And carousing for months till the morning is pale,
Go home with the milk of the walrus and whale.

Oh list to the sweet serenades that are hers,
Who expensively gowned in most elegant furs,
Leans forth from the lattice delighted to know
That her heart is like ice and her hand is like snow.

God bless all the dear little people who roam
And hail in the icebergs the hills of their home;
For I might not object to be listening in
If I hadn't to hear the whole programme begin.
And the President preach international peace,
And Parricide show an alarming increase,
And a Justice at Bootle excuse the police,
And how to clean trousers when spotted with grease,
And a pianist biting his wife from caprice,
And an eminent Baptist's arrival at Nice,
And a banker's regrettably painless decease,
And the new quarantine for the plucking of geese,
And a mad millionaire's unobtrusive release,
And a marquis divorced by a usurer's niece—
If all of these items could suddenly cease
And leave me with one satisfactory thing
I really *should* like to hear Eskimos sing.

This was hardly the expression of an attitude to science, but he did have such an attitude. Life was to him a story told by God: the people in it the characters in that story. But since the story was told by God it was, quite literally, a magic story, a fairy story, a story full of wonders created by a divine will. As a child a toy telephone rigged up by his father from the house to the end of the garden had breathed that magic quality more than the Transatlantic Cable could reveal it in later life. It did not need mechanical inventions to make him see life as marvellous. His over-ruling interest was not in mechanics but in Will: the will of God had created the laws of nature and could supersede them: the will of Man could discover these laws and harness them to its purposes. Gold is where you find it and the value of science depends on the will of man: a position which may not sound so absurd in the light of the harnessing of science to the purposes of destruction. When discussing machines "we sometimes tend," said Chesterton in *Sidelights,* "to overlook the quiet and even bashful presence of the machine gun."

There was an impishness in Gilbert, especially in his youth, that encouraged the idea of his enmity to science. Where he saw a long white beard he felt like tweaking it: an enquiring nose simply asked to be pulled. It was only in (comparatively) sober age that he bothered in *The Everlasting Man* to explain "I am not at issue in this book with sincere and genuine scholars, but with a vast and vague public opinion which has been prematurely spread from certain imperfect investigations." * That "vast and vague public opinion" certainly suspected him of irreverence even towards sincere and genuine scholars. Yet it was by his use of the most marvelous of modern inventions that he won in the end the widest hearing among that public that he had ever known.

It is not so many years ago that we donned earphones in a doubtful hope of being able to hear something over the radio.

* *The Everlasting Man,* p. 67.

It is the less surprising that it was only in the last few years of his life that Gilbert became first interested in the invention and presently one of the broadcasters most in request by the B.B.C. He felt about the radio as he did about most modern inventions: that they were splendid opportunities that were not being taken—or else were being taken to the harm of humanity by the wrong people. What was the use of "calling all countries" if you had nothing to say to them.

"What much modern science fails to realise," he wrote, "is that there is little use in knowing without thinking."

And again, writing about the amazing discoveries of the day: "Nobody is taking the smallest trouble to consider who in the future will be in command of the electricity and capable of giving us the shocks. With all the shouting about the new marvels, hardly anybody utters a word or even a whisper about how they are to be prevented from turning into the old abuses. . . . People sometimes wonder why we not infrequently refer to the old scandal covered by the word Marconi. It is precisely because all these things are really covered by that word. There could not be a shorter statement of the contradiction than in men howling that word as a discovery and hushing it up as a story." *

For the thing that really frightened him about the radio was its possibilities as a new instrument of tyranny. The British Broadcasting Company holds in England a monopoly and is to a considerable extent under Government control. It is possible to forbid advertising programmes because the costs are met by a tax of 10 sh. a year levied on the possession of a radio set.

In an article called "The Unseen Catastrophe" (January 28, 1928) Gilbert wrote:

Suppose you had told some of the old Whigs, let alone Liberals, that there was an entirely new type of printing press, eclipsing all others; and that as this was to be given to the King, all printing would henceforth be government printing. They would be roaring

* *G.K.'s Weekly*, Aug. 15, 1925.

like rebels, or even regicides, yet that is exactly what we have done with the whole new invention of wireless. Suppose it were proposed that the king's officers should search all private houses to make sure there were no printing presses, they would be ready for a new revolution. Yet that is exactly what is proposed for the protection of the government monopoly of broadcasting. . . . There is really no protection against propaganda . . . being entirely in the hands of the government; except indeed, the incredible empty-headedness of those who govern. . . . On that sort of thing at least, we are all Socialists now. It is wicked to nationalize mines or railroads; but we lose no time in nationalizing tongues and talk . . . we might once have used, and we shall now never use, the twentieth century science against the nineteenth century hypocrisy. It was prevented by a swift, sweeping and intolerant State monopoly; a monster suddenly swallowing all rivals, alternatives, discussions, or delays, with one snap of its gigantic jaws. That is what I mean by saying, "We cannot see the monsters that overcome us." But I suppose that even Jonah, when once he was swallowed, could not see the whale.

In the autumn of 1932 Gilbert was first asked to undertake a series of radio talks for the B.B.C. Every one seems agreed that he was an extraordinary success. Letters from Broadcasting House are full of such remarks as: "You do it admirably," "quite superb at the microphone." In one his work is called "unique." Radio was now added to all his other activities during the four years he still had to live. Dorothy kept a diary in which she noted in one year the giving of as many as forty lectures, and entered reminders of engagements of the most varying kinds all over England: from the King's Garden Party to the Aylesbury Education Committee and the Oxford Union: to Scotland for Rectorial Campaigns: dinners at the Inner Temple and the Philosophical Society: Detection Club dinners and Mock Trials, at one of which he was Defendant on the charge of "perversely preferring the past to the present."

Besides the books discussed in the last chapter, the Dickens' *Introductions* and the *Collected Foems* were republished in 1933. Other books were planned, including one on Shakespeare.

That same year Gilbert's mother died. During her last illness Frances was torn between London and Beaconsfield, for her own mother was dying in a Nursing Home at Beaconsfield, her mother-in-law at Warwick Gardens. Once I drove with her between the two and she told me how she suffered at the difficulty of giving help to two dying Agnostics. She told me on that drive how she knew her mother-in-law had not liked her but had lately made her very happy by saying she realised now that she had been the right wife for Gilbert. To a cousin, Nora Grosjean, Frances spoke too of how she and Mrs. Edward had drawn together in those last days and she added, "No mother ever thinks any woman good enough for her son." Nora Grosjean also reports, "Aunt Marie said to me more than once, 'I always respect Frances—she kept Gilbert out of debt.'"

Warwick Gardens had been their home so long that vast accumulations of papers had piled up there. "Mister Ed." too had been in a sort keeper of the family archives. Gilbert glanced at the mass and, as I mentioned at the beginning of this book, told the dustman to carry it off. Half had already gone when Dorothy Collins arrived and saved the remainder. She piled it into her car and drove back to Beaconsfield, Gilbert keeping up a running commentary all the way on "the hoarding habits of women."

The money that came to Gilbert and Frances after Mrs. Edward's death made it possible for them to plan legacies not only for friends and relatives but also for the Catholic Church in Beaconsfield with which they had increasingly identified their lives and their interests. Their special dream was that Top Meadow itself should be a convent—best of all a school—and in this hope they bequeathed it to the Church.

A year later another family event, this time a joyful one, took Gilbert back to his youth; Mollie Kidd, daughter of Annie Firmin, became engaged to be married. She was a rather special young cousin to Gilbert both because of the old affection for her mother and because she had played hostess to him in Canada when her mother was ill. He wrote

Postmark. Aug. 28, 1934

MY DEAR MOLLIE,

I am afraid that chronologically, or by the clock, I am relatively late in sending you my most warm congratulations—and yet I do assure you that I write as one still thrilled and almost throbbing with good news. It would take pages to tell you all I feel about it: beginning with my first memory of your mother, when she was astonishingly like you, except that she had yellow plaits of hair down her back. I do not absolutely insist that you should now imitate her in this: but you would not be far wrong if you imitate her in anything. And so on—till we come to the superb rhetorical passage about You and the right fulfilment of Youth. It would take pages: and that is why the pages are never written. We bad correspondents, we vile non-writers of letters, have a sort of secret excuse, that no one will ever listen to till the Day of Judgment, when all infinite patience will have to listen to so much. It is often because we think so much about our friends that we do not write to them—the letters would be too long. Especially in the case of wretched writing men like me, who feel in their spare time that writing is loathsome and thinking about their friends pleasant. In the course of turning out about ten articles, on Hitler, on Humanism, on Determinism, on Distributism, on Dollfuss and Darwin and the Devil knows what, there really are thoughts about real people that cross my mind suddenly and make me really happy in a real way: and one of them is the news of your engagement. Please believe, dear Mollie, that I am writing the truth, though I am a journalist: and give my congratulations to everyone involved.

Yours with love,

G. K. CHESTERTON.

And in that year came two bits of public recognition of rather different kinds. He was elected to the Athenaeum Club under Rule II—Honoris causa; and he and Belloc were given by the Pope the title of Knight Commander of St. Gregory with Star.

During these years the paper had gone steadily on "at some considerable inconvenience" because, he said, he still felt it had a part to play. At home and abroad the scene had been steadily darkening. In July 1930, three years before Hitler came to the Chancellorship, we find the following among the notes of the Week:

When we are told that the ancient Marshal Hindenburg is now Dictator of Germany we suspect a note of exaggeration . . . Hindenburg never was the dictator of anything and never will be. He is, however the man who keeps the seat warm for a Dictator to come. Hindenburg has led us back to Frederick the Great. . . . Hindenburg has now given rein to the extreme Nationalists, with the delivered provinces to support him in the flush of patriotism. And the extreme Nationalists have only one policy: to reconstitute the unjust frontiers of Germany, which Europe fought to amend.

In 1931 had come the Customs Union between Germany and Austria, the obvious impotence of the League of Nations to restrain Japan, the "National" Government and falling sterling in England. Less than two years later Hitler was Chancellor of Germany, and in 1934 came the murder of Dollfuss. Chesterton wrote of the tragedy whereby the name Germany was taken from Austria and given to Prussia. With Dollfuss fell all that was left of the Holy Roman Empire: the barbarians had invaded the center of our civilisation and like the Turks besieging Vienna had struck at its heart. He regarded Hitler merely as the tool of Prussianism. The new Paganism was the logical outcome of the old Prussianism: it was too the apotheosis of tyranny. "In the Pagan State, in antiquity or modernity, you cannot appeal from Tyranny to God; because the Tyranny is the God."

Belloc solemnly warned our country that we were making inevitable "the death in great pain of innumerable young Englishmen now boys. . . . It may be in two years or in five or in ten the blow will fall." (November 8, 1934.)

Yet even this seemed less terrible to Chesterton than the

state of mind then prevailing: the mood—nay the fever—of pacifism that demanded the isolation of England from Europe's peril. He called it "Mafficking for peace": a sort of Imperialism that forgot that the Atlantic is wider than the Straits of Dover and allowed Lord Beaverbrook to regard England as a part of Canada. "Englishmen who have felt that fever will one day look back on it with shame." "This most noble and generous nation," he wrote with a note of agony, "which lost its religion in the seventeenth century has lost its morals in the twentieth."

The League of Nations had, G. K. held, been thought at first to be a kind of Pentecost but had in reality "come together to rebuild the Tower of Babel." And this because it had no common basis in religion. "Humanitarianism does not unite humanity. For even one isolated man is half divine." But today man had despaired of man. "Hope for the superman is another name for despair of man."

Reading a recent commentary in a review, I suddenly saw that politics and economics were not what mattered most in the paper. The commentary in question was to the effect that *G.K.'s Weekly* was inferior to the *New Witness* because G.K. had "only" general principles and ideas and no detailed inside knowledge of how the world of finance and politics was going. Looking again through the articles I had marked as most characteristically his, I saw that they were not only chiefly about ideas and principles but also that they were mostly pure poetry. Chesterton was, I believe, greatest and most permanently effective when he was moved, not by a passing irritation with the things that pass, but by the great emotions evoked by the Eternal, emotions which in Eternity alone will find full fruition.

There are in the paper articles in which, appearing to speak out of his own knowledge, he is merely repeating information given him by Belloc. And it was quite out of Chesterton's character to write with certainty about what he did not know with certainty. Hence this writing is his weakest. But the paper has, too, some of his strongest work and his mind as he drew to the end of life lingered on thoughts that had haunted him in its beginning.

Before the Boer War had introduced me to politics, or worse still to politicians [he wrote in a Christmas article in 1934], I had some vague and groping ideas of my own about a general view or vision of existence. It was a long time before I had anything worth calling a religion; what I had was not even sufficiently coherent to be called a philosophy. But it was, in a sense, a view of life; I had it in the beginning; and I am more and more coming back to it in the end. . . . my original and almost mystical conviction of the miracle of all existence and the essential excitement of all experience.*

This he felt must be the profound philosophy by which Distributism should succeed and whereby he tested the modern world and found it wanting—

something of which Christmas is the best traditional symbol. It was then no more than a notion about the point at which extremes meet, and the most common thing becomes a cosmic and mystical thing. I did not want so much to alter the place and use of things as to weight them with a new dimension; to deepen them by going down to the potential nothing; to lift them to infinity by measuring from zero.

The most logical form of this is in thanks to a Creator; but at every stage I felt that such praises could never rise too high; because they could not even reach the height of our own thanks for unthinkable existence, or horror of more unthinkable non-existence. And the commonest things, as much as the most complex, could thus leap up like fountains of praise. . . .

We shall need a sort of Distributist psychology, as well as a Distributist philosophy. That is partly why I am not content with plausible solutions about credit or corporative rule. We need a new (or old) theory and practice of pleasure. The vulgar school of panem et circenses only gives people circuses; it does not even tell them how to enjoy circuses. But we have not merely to tell them how to enjoy circuses. We have to tell them how to enjoy enjoyment.†

* December 6, 1934.   † December 13, 1934.

In attacking a special abuse, Chesterton was most successful when he took the thought to a deeper depth. The following Christmas (1935) he wrote:

We live in a terrible time, of war and rumour of war. . . . International idealism in its effort to hold the world together . . . is admittedly weakened and often disappointed. I should say simply that it does not go deep enough. . . . If we really wish to make vivid the horrors of destruction and mere disciplined murder we must see them more simply as attacks on the hearth and the human family; and feel about Hitler as men felt about Herod.

The modern world tended to gild pure gold and then try to scrape the gilt off the gingerbread, to paint the lily and then complain of its gaudiness. Thus it had vulgarised Christmas and now demanded the abolition of Christmas because it was vulgar. It was the truth he had emphasised years ago in contrast with Shaw: the world had spoilt the ideas but it was the Christian ideas the world needed, if only in order to recover the human ideas. He went on—

If we want to talk about poverty, we must talk about it as the hunger of a human being. . . . We must say first of the beggar, not that there is insufficient housing accommodation, but that he has not where to lay his head . . . we must talk of the human family in language as plain and practical and positive as that in which mystics used to talk of the Holy Family. We must learn again to use the naked words that describe a natural thing. . . . Then we shall draw on the driving force of many thousand years, and call up a real humanitarianism out of the depths of humanity.

I should like to collect all the essays and poems on Christmas; he wrote several every year, yet each is different, each goes to the heart of his thought. As Christopher Morley says: "One of the simple greatnesses of G.K.C. shows in this, that we think of him instinctively toward Christmas time." * Some men, it may be, are best moved to reform by hate, but Chesterton was best moved

* *Mark Twain Quarterly*, Spring, 1937.

by love and nowhere does that love shine more clearly than in all he wrote about Christmas. It will be for this philosophy, this charity, this poetry that men will turn over the pages of *G.K.'s Weekly* a century hence if the world still lasts. It is for us who are his followers to see that they are truly creative. Destruction of evil is a great work but if it leaves only a vacuum, nature abhors that vacuum. Creation is what matters for the future and Chesterton's writing is creative.

So too with the radio. In this new medium his mind was alert to present his new-old ideas, his fundamental philosophy of life after some fresh fashion. A letter from Broadcasting House (Nov. 2, 1932) after his first talk records the delight of all who heard it:

The building rings with your praises! I knew I was not alone in my delight over your first talk. I think even you in your modesty will find some pleasure in hearing what widespread interest there is in what you are doing. You bring us something very rare to the microphone. I am most anxious that you should be with us till after Christmas. You will have a vast public by Christmas and it is good that they should hear you. Would you undertake six further fortnightly talks from January 16th onwards?

He was asked to submit a manuscript but promised he should not be kept to the letter of it. "We should like you to make variations as these occur to you as you speak at the microphone. Only so can the talk have a real show of spontaneity about it." "You will forgive me," one official writes, "if I insist on speaking to you personally. That is how I think of our relations." G.K. was unique and they told him so.

A lot of reading was necessary for these talks—each one dealing with from four to ten books—and also a principle of selection. The principle Gilbert chose for one series was historical: "Literature lives by history. Otherwise it exists: like trigonometry." In the fifth talk of the Autumn series of 1934, he gives a general idea of what he has been attempting.

This is the hardest job I have had in all these wireless talks; and I confront you in a spirit of hatred because of the toils I have endured on your behalf; but, after all, what are my sufferings compared to yours? Incredible as it may seem to anybody who has heard these talks, they had originally a certain consistent plan. I dealt first with heroic and half-legendary stories, touched upon medieval chivalry, then on the party-heroes of Elizabethan or Puritan times; then on the eighteenth century and then the nineteenth. In this address I had meant to face the twentieth century; but I find it almost faceless, largely featureless; and, anyhow, very bewildering. I had meant to take books typical of the twentieth century as a book on Steele is typical of the eighteenth or a book on Rossetti of the nineteenth. And I have collected a number of most interesting twentieth century books, claiming to declare a twentieth-century philosophy; they really have a common quality; but I rather hesitate to define it. Suppose I said that the main mark of the twentieth century in ethics as in economics, is bankruptcy. I fear you might think I was a little hostile in my criticism. Suppose I said that all these books are marked by a brilliant futility. You might almost fancy that I was not entirely friendly to them. You would be mistaken. All of them are good; some of them are very good indeed. But the question does recur; what is the good of being good in that way? . . .

Mr. Geoffrey West's curious "Post War Credo" has one Commandment. He does say, he does shout, we might say, he does yell, that there must be No War . . . but he cannot impose his view because authority has gone; and he cannot prove his view; because reason has gone. So again it all comes back to taste. And I have enjoyed the banquet of these excellent books; but it leaves a bad taste in my mouth.

The peculiar half-official half-private direction of Broadcasting House is based on a theory of strict impartiality towards all opinions and an attempt simply to give the public the programmes that the public wants. Whether it is possible to maintain such a position is another question: that this is the theory there is no doubt—and one result is an abiding uncertainty of mind in most of the officials.

Broadcasting House hangs suspended in the air of public

opinion and that fickle breath leaves them in no security as to any of their artists. The resulting sensitiveness became soothed as the months passed on and they got as near to trusting Chesterton as they ever come with any one. True, letters came attacking him, but far more enthusiastically approving of him. And the attacks he answered often by private letters that turned the critic into a friend.

Some of his suggestions were not acceptable. He was warned off a proposed humorous talk about Dean Inge and Bishop Barnes in a series called "Speeches that never happened"— ("Subject too serious," "avoid religion"). But he was later asked to talk in a series on Freedom *as* a Catholic and also to debate with Bertrand Russell on "Who should bring up our children." In this debate he was especially brilliant, says Maurice Baring; and another friend wrote "I have just been listening not without joy to your putting it across Mr. Bertrand Russell. . . .

"*Afterthought*: What a Mincer! It struck me very much, having read much of his writing with interest. It just shows that the spoken word still has something that the written one can't convey. Is there a Mincing Mind, of which a mincing voice is the outward and visible warning?"

It was interesting that the last few years of Gilbert's life should have furnished this unique opportunity of contact through the spoken word between him and the English people. His voice on the radio had none of the defects that marred it in a hall: his material was far better arranged, his delivery perfect. He seemed to be there beside the listener, talking in amity and exchanging confidences. The morning after his death Edward Macdonald passed a barber's shop off Chancery Lane. The man was lathering a customer's face but recognising Mr. Macdonald, left the customer and ran out brush in hand.

"I just want to say I was sorry to hear the news," he said. "He was a grand man."

Mr. Macdonald asked him if he knew Chesterton well.

"Never read a word he wrote," the barber answered. "But I always listened to him on the wireless. He seemed to be sitting beside me in the room."

"That man," Edward Macdonald comments, "emphasised what I still think: that G.K.C. in another year or so would have become the dominating voice from Broadcasting House."

In 1934 Gilbert had jaundice and on his recovery he started with Frances and Dorothy on one of those trips that were his greatest pleasure. They went to Rome—it was Holy Year—and thence to Sicily, intending to go on to Palestine. At Syracuse, however, Gilbert became really ill with inflammation of the nerves of the neck and shoulders. They stayed five weeks in Syracuse, gave up the trip to Palestine and returned home by Malta. Gilbert and Frances were to have dined at Admiralty House but he was too unwell to dine out and only came up one afternoon. Lady Fisher remembers going to see them at the Osborne Hotel. Gilbert was sitting on a rickety basket chair, obviously in pain and talking a good deal in order to hide it. She sympathised with him for the cold weather, his obvious physical misery, and the discomfort of his chair.

"You must never sympathise with me," Gilbert answered, "for I can always turn every chair into a story."

The next year they motored in France and Italy and Gilbert records in the *Autobiography* an experience in a French café when he felt a rare thrill—not in talking on the radio but in listening—on a day that "was dateless, even for my dateless life; for I had forgotten time and had no notion of anything anywhere, when in a small French town I strolled into a café noisy with French talk. Wireless songs wailed unnoted; which is not surprising, for French talk is much better than wireless. And then, unaccountably, I heard a voice speaking in English; and a voice I had heard before. For I heard the words, '. . . wherever you are, my dear people, whether in this country or beyond the sea,' and I remembered Monarchy and an ancient cry; for it was the King; and that is how I kept the Jubilee."

After he got home I remember how delightedly Gilbert quoted the captions on two banners hung in the heart of the London slums. One read, "Down with Capitalism—God Save the King." The other read, "Lousy but loyal." He knew that it was true and it served to increase the passionate quality of his pity. Patient he could be for himself, but the lot of the poor aroused in him a terrible anger—and in a broadcast on Liberty he gave that anger vent. For worse than the presence of lice in our slums was the absence of liberty. He would gladly, he said, have spoken merely as an Englishman but he had been asked to speak as a Catholic, and therefore, "I am going to point out that Catholicism created English liberty; that the freedom has re-mained exactly in so far as the faith has remained; and that where it is true that all our Faith has gone, all our freedom is going. If I do this, I cannot ask most of you to agree with me; if I did anything else, I could not ask any of you to respect me."

Other speakers in the series had dwelt on the liberty secured to Englishmen by our Parliamentary and Juridical system, both, he noted of Catholic origin. But in his eyes even that liberty was being imperilled today where it was not lost, while the most important freedom of all—freedom to handle oneself and one's daily life—had disappeared for the mass of the people. The liberty so widely praised that followed the Reformation

has been a limited liberty because it was only a literary liberty. . . . You always talked about verbal liberty; you hardly ever talked about vital liberty . . . the faddist was free to preach his fads; but the free man was no longer free to protect his freedom. . . . Monarchy, aristocracy, democracy, responsible forms of rule, have collapsed under plutocracy, which is irresponsible rule. And this has come upon us because we departed from the old morality in three essential points. First, we supported notions against normal customs. Second, we made the State top-heavy with a new and secretive tyranny of wealth. And third, we forgot that there is no faith in freedom with-

out faith in free will. A servile fatalism dogs the creed of materialism; because nothing, as Dante said, less than the generosity of God
could give to Man, after all ordinary orderly gifts, the noblest of all
things, which is Liberty.

The thoughts that had thronged and pressed on him for half
a century found final expression in these broadcasts. Most of all
in two talks: one given only three months before his death in a
series entitled "The Spice of Life," the other two years earlier
in one called "Seven Days Hard." He was haunted by the ingratitude of humanity. As in his boyhood, he saw the wonder
of the world that God has given to the children of men and he
saw them unconscious of that wonder. What did a week mean
for most of them? Seven dull days. What did it really mean?
"What has really happened during the last seven days and
nights? Seven times we have been dissolved into darkness as we
shall be dissolved into dust; our very selves, so far as we know,
have been wiped out of the world of living things; and
seven times we have been raised alive like Lazarus, and found
all our limbs and senses unaltered, with the coming of the
day."

Seven days of human life, the meaning of the phrase, "the
spice of life," both brought the same recurring motif that "a
great many people are at this moment paying rather too much
attention to the spice of life, and rather too little attention to
life." Not in any "distraction from life is the secret we are all
seeking, the secret of enjoying life. I am perfectly certain that
all our world will end in despair unless there is some way of
making the mind itself, the ordinary thoughts we have at
ordinary times, more healthy and more happy than they seem to
be just now, to judge by most modern novels and poems. . . ."

A week had never been for Chesterton just seven days hard,
although he had worked hard enough. He had enjoyed the spice
of life, he had liked Beer and Skittles and the distractions of
life and its high points of achievement.

But it is much more important to remember that I have been intensely and imaginatively happy in the queerest because the quietest places. I have been filled with life from within in a cold waiting-room, in a deserted railway-junction. I have been completely alive sitting on an iron seat under an ugly lamp-post at a third rate watering place. In short, I have experienced the mere excitement of existence in places that would commonly be called as dull as ditchwater. And, by the way, is ditchwater dull? Naturalists with microscopes have told me that it teems with quiet fun.

The younger generation were despairing of life in the face of life's manifold gifts. Chesterton as a youth had revolted against the pessimism of his elders, now he revolted as an old man against a young generation corroded by a yet more poisonous pessimism. "The Hollow Men" T. S. Eliot had called a poem and in it came the lines

> This is the way the world ends
> This is the way the world ends
> This is the way the world ends
> Not with a bang but a whimper.

Forgive me if I say in my old world fashion, that I'm damned if I ever felt like that . . . I knew that the world was perishable and would end, but I did not think it would end with a whimper, but, if anything, with a trump of doom . . . I will even be so indecently frivolous as to burst into song, and say to the young pessimists:

> Some sneer; some snigger; some simper;
> In the youth where we laughed, and sang.
> And *they* may end with a whimper
> But *we* will end with a bang.

His last message for this generation was the sound of a trumpet calling us to Resurrection. A dead world must find life again, must go back to the meaning of the book of Genesis at which it had learnt to sneer: must realise a week once more with—"the grandeur of that conception, by which a week has become a wonderful and mystical thing in which Man imitates God in his labour and in his rest."

Through his call sounds a note of most solemn warning.

Unless we can bring men back to enjoying the daily life which moderns call a dull life, our whole civilisation will be in ruins in about fifteen years. Whenever anybody proposes anything really practical, to solve the economic evil today, the answer always is that the solution would not work, because the modern town populations would think life dull. That is because they are entirely unacquainted with life. They know nothing but distractions from life; dreams which may be found in the cinema; that is, brief oblivions of life. . . . Unless we can make daybreak and daily bread and the creative secrets of labour interesting in themselves, there will fall on all our civilisation a fatigue which is the one disease from which civilisations do not recover. So died the great Pagan Civilisation; of bread and circuses and forgetfulness of the household gods.*

This splendid world that God has given us, and the furniture of it as the writer of Genesis saw it in his vision, has in it the material of happiness in labour and in the true end of labour. "For the true end of all creation is completion; and the true end of all completion is contemplation."

* *The Listener*, January 31, 1934.

CHAPTER XXXII

Last Days

DOROTHY TOLD ME one day in 1935 that Gilbert had written
the beginning of an autobiography some years before but
had laid it aside. She had, she said, a superstitious feeling about
urging him to get on with it—as though the survey of his life and
the end of his life would somehow be tied together. I urged her to
get over this feeling because of all the book would mean to the
world. After this talk she got out the manuscript and laid it on
Gilbert's desk. He read what he had written and immediately set
about dictating the rest of the book.

Early in 1936 he told a group of friends that the book was
finished. One of them said "Nunc dimittis" and Edward Macdonald, who was present, commented: "The words were chill-
ing, though he seemed to be in fairly good health. But certainly
he was tired. . . ."

The book showed no sign of fatigue. High-spirited and intensely amusing, it seemed to promise many more—for into
almost old age he had carried the imagination and energy in
which as a very young man we saw his resemblance to the
youthful Dickens.

Reviewing his life with the thread of thanksgiving that had
been his clue throughout, he looked back on it as "indefensibly
happy" and it was in truth a rich and full human existence. Yet
Father Vincent, who knew him intimately, speaks of him in
these last years as heartbroken by public events, as suffering
with the pains of creation. "He was crucified to his thought.

Like St. Thomas he was never away from his thought. A fellow friar had to care for Thomas, to feed him 'sicut nutrix' because of his absorption in his thought." Thus Father Vincent saw Frances cherishing Gilbert both mind and body.

A friend, protesting vehemently against the phrase "crucified to his thought" says, "It was his life-long beatitude to observe and ponder and conclude."

Of his own so-called paradoxes Gilbert was wont to maintain that it was God not he, who made them, and here we have surely one of the paradoxes of human life. Intense vitality, joy in living, vigor of creative thought bring to their owners immense happiness *and* acute suffering.

Is it not a part of the most fundamental of all antinomies— the greatness and the littleness of man? Created for eternity and prisoned in time, we have no perfect joy in this world, and the reaching upward and outward of the mind is at once the keenest joy and the fiercest pain—rather as we talk of growing pains. Only Gilbert loved to grow so much that he would not think of the pain. "You must never pity me," he said to Lady Fisher, and all through his life he was saying and meaning "You must never pity me."

But while he was writing the *Autobiography* and giving thanks for his life, its last months were shadowed by trials especially heavy for a man of his imagination and temperament. For now more than ever his thought was not allowed to concentrate on those realities where the joy of contemplation overpowers the pain of growth.

He loved Italy—even more than France he says in one letter— yet he could not but condemn the invasion of Abyssinia. The shadow of the Spanish war loomed on the horizon and behind it a darker shadow. In his political thinking Chesterton was haunted by the present war. Then too, while public controversy did not trouble him at all, he hated any breach of the peace within the ranks of his own small army. The fights among the staff of the paper about Distributism had been as nothing compared with those about Abyssiania. There are leading articles taking one line and letters in the Cockpit in violent opposition. Maurice Reckitt writes in *As it Happened*:

In the last autumn of his life I wrote to him privately in distress at the line which the *Weekly* was taking on Abyssinia, and saying that I felt that I ought to leave the board, as I was so much out of sympathy with this. I received this reply, from which I have deleted only some personal references:

"Top Meadow, Beaconsfield
19th September 1935.

"My dear Mr. Maurice Reckitt,

"I do hope you will forgive me for the delay in answering your most important letter, involving as it does tragic dooms of separation which I hope need not be fulfilled. . . . I should like to ask you to defer your decision at least until you have seen the next week's number of the paper, in which I expand further the argument I have used in the current number and bring it, I think, rather nearer to your natural and justifiable point of view. Between ourselves, and without prejudice to anybody, I do think myself that there ought to have been a more definite condemnation of the attack on Abyssinia. The whole thing happened while I was having a holiday. . . .

"Very shortly, the mortal danger, to me, is the rehabilitation of Capitalism, in spite of the slump, which will certainly take the form of a hypocritical patriotism and glorification of England, at the expense of Italy or anybody else. For the moment I only want you to understand that this is the mountainous peril that towers in my own mind.

"Yours always,

"G. K. Chesterton."

Three months later in *G.K.'s Weekly* he wrote about the whole matter in an article in which he treated the question as largely one of proportion. Not enough was being said in England of her own or the League's position about Japan's attack on China: too much (in proportion) about Italy in Abyssinia. "If the League of Nations really were an impartial judicial authority; and if (what is about as probable) I were one of the judges; and if the Abyssinian Case were brought before me, I should decide instantly against Italy. I have again and again in this place stated in the strongest words the particular case against Italy." He was against Italy in Abyssinia as he had been against England in South Africa. But "I should not be bound to rejoice at the Prussians riding into Paris because it might prevent the British riding into Pretoria."

"Tragic dooms of separation" on public issues were not the only trouble with *G.K.'s Weekly*: the staff were also engaged in violent personal quarrels about which Gilbert was asked to take sides—was even bitterly reproached by one for supposedly favouring another. It would be hard today to say what it was all about, but two of the contestants have told me since that had they had the least notion how ill he was getting they would have died rather than so distress him. For it was a real and a very deep distress.

It may be remembered that Miss Dunham noted how Gilbert used to make a mysterious sign in the air as he lit his cigar. That sign, says Dorothy, was the sign of the cross. Long ago he had written of human life as something not grey and drab but shot through with strong and even violent colours that took the pattern of the Cross. He saw the Cross signed by God on the trees as their branches spread to right and left: he saw it signed by man as he shaped a paling or a door post. The habit grew upon him of making it constantly: in the air with his match, as he lit his cigar, over a cup of coffee. As he entered a room he would make on the door the sign of our Redemption. No, we must never pity him even when his life was pressed upon by that sign which stands for joy through pain.

Those nearest to him grew anxious quite early in 1936. He was overtired and working with the weary insistence that over-fatigue can bring. The remedy so often successful of a trip to the continent was tried. They went to Lourdes and Lisieux and he seemed better and sang a good deal in his tuneless voice as Dorothy drove them through the lanes of France. From Lisieux he wrote a pencilled letter, long and almost illegible "under the shadow of the shrine"—trying to reconcile the disputants with himself and with one another.

The summer was cold and bleak and the tour was all too short. Home again his mind seemed not to grip as well as usual and he began to fall asleep during his long hours of work. The doctor was called and thought very seriously of the state of his heart—that heart which many years ago another doctor had called too small for his enormous frame. The thought of a Chesterton whose heart was too small presents a paradox in his own best manner.

To Edward Macdonald who had missed a message that he was too ill to be visited, Gilbert talked in his old fashion and promised a poem he had just thought of for the paper—on St. Martin of Tours. "The point is that he was a true Distributist. He gave *half* his cloak to the beggar."

Soon after this he fell into a sort of reverie from which awaking he said:

"The issue is now quite clear. It is between light and darkness and every one must choose his side."

Frances and he had both thought his recovery in 1916 was a miracle. "I did not dare," said Frances, "to pray for another miracle."

Monsignor Smith anointed him and then Father Vincent arrived in response to a message from Frances which he thought meant she wanted him to see Gilbert for the last time. Taken to the sick room he sang over the dying man the Salve Regina. This hymn to Our Lady is sung in the Dominican Order over every dying friar and it was surely fitting for the biographer of St. Thomas and the ardent suppliant of Our Lady:

"Salve Regina, mater misericordiae, vita dulcedo et spes

nostra salve. . . . Et Jesum benedictum fructum ventris tui nobis post hoc exsilium ostende. . . ."

Gilbert's pen lay on the table beside his bed and Father Vincent picked it up and kissed it.

It was June 14, 1936, the Sunday within the Octave of Corpus Christi, the same Feast as his reception into the Church fourteen years earlier. The Introit for that day's Mass was printed on his Memorial card, so that, as Father Ignatius Rice noted with a smile, even his Memorial card had a joke about his size:

The Lord became my protector and he brought me forth into a large place. He saved me because he was well pleased with me. I will love Thee O Lord my strength. The Lord is my firmament and my refuge and my deliverer.

To these words from the Mass, Frances added Walter de la Mare's tribute:

> Knight of the Holy Ghost, he goes his way
> Wisdom his motley, Truth his loving jest;
> The mills of Satan keep his lance in play,
> Pity and innocence his heart at rest.

The day of the funeral was one of blazing sunshine. "One of your days," Gilbert would have said to Frances. Grey days were his, when nature's colours he said were brightest against her more sombre background, sunny days were hers for she loved a blue blazing sky. The little church near the railway was filled to overflowing by his friends from London, from all over England, from France even and from America. All Beaconsfield wanted to honour him, so the funeral procession instead of taking the direct route passed through the old town where he had so often sat in the barber's shop and chatted with his fellow citizens. At Top Meadow we gathered to talk. Frances a few of us saw for a little while in her own room. With that utter self-forgetfulness that was hers she said to her sister-in-law, "It was so much worse for you. You had Cecil for such a short time."

Later Mgr. Knox preached in Westminster Cathedral to a crowd far vaster. Both Frances and Cardinal Hinsley received telegrams from Cardinal Pacelli (now Pope Pius XII). To Cardinal Hinsley he cabled "Holy Father deeply grieved death Mr. Gilbert Keith Chesterton devoted son Holy Church gifted Defender of the Catholic Faith. His Holiness offers paternal sympathy people of England assures prayers dear departed, bestows Apostolic Benediction." This telegram was read to the vast crowd in the Cathedral and found an echo in the hearts of his fellow countrymen.

Hugh Kingsmill wrote to Cyril Clemens: "My friend Hesketh Pearson was staying with me when I read of Chesterton's death. I told him of it through the bathroom door, and he sent up a hollow groan which must have echoed that morning all over England." It was with reason that the Pope offered his sympathy not to Catholics alone, but to all the people of England. To the policeman who said at the funeral, "We'd all have been here if we could have got off duty. He was a grand man." To the man at the *Times* office who broke in on the announcement of his death, "Good God. That isn't *our* Chesterton, is it?" To the barber who had to leave his customer unshaved that he might talk to Edward Macdonald. To all of us, his friends, on whom the loss lay almost unbearably heavy. To those for whom his presence would have pierced and lightened even the dark shadow of the war. To all the people of England.

Once more a Pope had bestowed upon an Englishman the title Defender of the Faith. The first man to receive it had been Henry VIII and the words are still engraved on the coins of England. The secular press would not print the telegram in full because it bestowed upon a subject a royal title.

After Gilbert's death Frances tried to take up life again. She visited her cousins in Germany, a university professor and his

English wife, who were undergoing the persecution of the Swastika. She was deeply moved by their suffering and the peril they stood in.

Home again she surrounded herself more than ever with children, taking a Catechism class and encouraging her small scholars to come to Top Meadow where her garden also helped her towards a difficult peace and serenity, rendered harder by the struggle with ill health. Soon we began to realise that the physical weakness, which all her courage could not overcome, was more than merely her old malady. "What did Frances die of?" Bernard Shaw wrote to me. "Was it of widowhood?"

In fact it was a most painful cancer heroically endured. She was cared for by Dorothy and presently by the nuns of the Bon Secours. Her friends visited her as they were allowed. Father Vincent McNabb, after a talk of almost an hour, noted how never once did she speak of herself or of her suffering.

Her concerns were for Dorothy, for the Church, and for Gilbert's memory; Eric Gill's monument, the biography, the permanence of his own writing. She survived him little more than two years. Near the end, from the face of a dying woman shrunken with pain, we still could see those "great heavenly eyes that seem to make the truth at the heart of things almost too terribly simple and naked for the sons of flesh." *

* Letter from Gilbert, see p. 99.

Appendices

Appendix A

An Earlier Chesterton

BOTH THE *Autobiography* and *Prison Life* of George Laval Chesterton are worth reading. There is conscious humour: we feel it might be our own Chesterton when we hear the Captain describing himself as "laughing immoderately" because he had made a fool of himself and others were laughing at him. There is unconscious humour, especially in the astonishing style, full of such phrases as "I was the most obnoxious to peril," or "something not far removed from impunity stalked abroad."

Captain Chesterton started life as a soldier. During the Peninsular War his regiment was stationed at Cartagena. "It was a subject of deep mortification to most of us to be thus supinely occupied in this lone garrison," thereby being "debarred from the Peninsular medal, and hence a widespread disaffection on that most tender subject which no reasoning has been equal to dispel." However, later he saw a good deal of active service, being in the War of 1812, in the course of which the battle of Bladensburg was fought and Washington fell to the British arms. "The astonished slaves," he says, describing the advance on Washington, "rested from their work in the fields contiguous; and the awe-struck peasants and yeomen of this portion of America beheld with perturbation the tremendous preparations to devastate their blooming country."

To the smaller professional armies of that day peace was a misfortune, and in his quaint style Captain Chesterton describes the demonstrations of joy on the part of himself and his fellow officers at the escape of Napoleon from Elba, foreseeing, as he frankly observes, "a scope for further adventure and hope of personal advancement." This hope was short-lived and we next see him fighting in the British Legion of a rebel South American army against Spain. The general mismanagement of this expedition, and the fact that the Republicans killed all their prisoners "was a death blow to all my past enthusiasm in the Republican cause." Many British officers "participating with me in the detestation for cold-blooded butchery, conspired from that moment to elude this detested service. . . . Mark ye who delight in transcendant liberalism . . . the cruel exigencies of such a warfare."

In his acceptance of "transcendant liberalism," yet his determination to see truly what passed before his eyes and when needful to change his standpoint, this earlier Chesterton was much like the later. He had not the genius of Gilbert, he could not see so far, but he shared his refusal to be blinded by custom, theory or even patriotism. In his accounts of army life he had commented fearlessly on the cruelty of the punishments and described his fellow officers as made ill by seeing a private receive five hundred lashes. He had noted corruption in the "Train Service" which "was consequently divested of its genuine claim to honour." Fêted by the planters of Jamaica, he had yet spoken with horror of their slave ownership.

Now he was appointed governor of a prison in England and here began the great work of his life in a frontal attack on the corruptions he discovered. The yardsmen did a secret traffic in all the goods forbidden in the prison, there were caches of tobacco, spirits and such things under the pavements, the weaker prisoners were robbed by the stronger. The women's and men's quarters were so arranged that by connivance of the jailors frequent meetings took place. On one of these occasions Captain Chesterton himself appeared:

My hands were seized with tender empressement, and I was addressed as "my love," "my darling," "my dear creature:" and all the conventional endearments of the pavé were showered upon me. I had to struggle for enlargement, and beat a hasty retreat, quite confounded by my initiation into "prison discipline." And the consternation occasioned by this discovery became perfectly electric.*

Attempts to bribe him were followed by attempts to kill him, but he stood firm. Mrs. Fry invoked his aid to improve the home conditions to which the prisoners had to return. Chesterton turned to Dickens and to Dickens's friend, Miss Coutts, in defiance of a narrow-minded magistrate

who perversely insisted (as was by cynical interpretation literally too true) that Miss Coutts had no right to confer with prisoners within those walls, nor was it "to be tolerated that Mr. Charles Dickens should walk into the prison whenever he pleased." †

From Cold Bath Fields the reforms begun by Captain Chesterton and warmly seconded by Dickens spread to other prisons, "Although (he declares) I consented to forego pecuniary advantage, I cling the more tenaciously to the credit of my past exertions; when, beset with fraud, ferocity, and moral pollution, I achieved a triumph fraught with civilizing influences." ‡

* *Revelations of Prison Life*, pp. 84–85.
† *Ibid.*, p. 186.
‡ *Ibid.*, p. v.

Prize Poem Written at St. Paul's

This is the only version I have been able to find. Across the top is written in another hand: "This is not exactly the same as given in the prize poem." The difference is probably slight.

ST. FRANCIS XAVIER
The Apostle of the Indies

He left his dust, by all the myriad tread
Of yon dense millions trampled to the strand,
Or 'neath some cross forgotten lays his head
Where dark seas whiten on a lonely land:
He left his work, what all his life had planned,
A waning flame to flicker and to fall,
Mid the huge myths his toil could scarce withstand,
And the light died in temple and in hall,
And the old twilight sank and settled over all.

He left his name, a murmur in the East,
That dies to silence amid older creeds,
With which he strove in vain: the fiery priest
Of faiths less fitted to their ruder needs:
As some lone pilgrim, with his staff and beads,
Mid forest-brutes whom ignorance makes tame,
He dwelt, and sowed an Eastern Church's seeds
He reigned a teacher and a priest of fame:
He died and dying left a murmur and a name.

He died: and she, the Church that bade him go,
Yon dim Enchantress with her mystic claim,
Has ringed his forehead with her aureole-glow,
And monkish myths, and all the whispered fame
Of miracle, has clung about his name:

So Rome has said: but we, what answer we
Who in grim Indian gods and rites of shame
O'er all the East the teacher's failure see,
His eastern church a dream, his toil a vanity.

This then we say: as Time's dark face at last
Moveth its lips of thunder to decree
The doom that grew through all the murmuring past
To be the canon of the times to be:
"No child of truth or priest of progress he
Yet not the less a hero of his wars
Striving to quench the light he could not see,
And God, who knoweth all that makes and mars,
Judges his soul unseen which throbs among the stars.

God only knows, man failing in his choice,
How far apparent failure may succeed,
God only knows what echo of His voice
Lives in the cant of many a fallen creed,
God only gives the labourer his meed
For all the lingering influence widely spread
Broad branching into many a word and deed
When dim oblivion veils the fountain-head;
So lives and lingers on the spirit of the dead.

This then we say: let all things further rest
And this brave life, with many thousands more
Be gathered up in the eternal's breast
In that dim past his Love is bending o'er
Healing all shattered hopes and failure sore:
Since he had bravely looked on death and pain
For what he chose to worship and adore
Cast boldly down his life for loss or gain
In the eternal lottery: not to be in vain.

The Chestertons

The composition of *The Chestertons* is not without interest for the student of legendary literature. By a curious paradox the book had to be strikingly untrue to be accepted as true, since the jokes about sisters-in-law are legion, so that mere commonplace shafts of what is called "feminine spite" would have gained little credence. Yet on the other hand, Mrs. Cecil Chesterton was able (to quote *The Mikado*) to get from her husband a good deal of "corroborative detail designed to give verisimilitude to an otherwise bald and unconvincing narrative." Of these details some are true, some false, all arranged to support the main untruth of Frances and Gilbert's relation to one another. The thesis of the book is that Gilbert was an unhappy and frustrated man (a) because Frances shrank from consummating their marriage, and (b) because she dragged him away from his London life and friends to bury him in a middle class suburb.

I confess that I am Victorian enough heartily to dislike writing this appendix. Yet it is necessary, for many who read *The Chestertons* have supposed that a story told by so near a connection must be true.

The ground was laid for the introduction of the Legend by the Tale of the Red Haired Phantom, if I may describe it in the terms of a ghost story. That ghost was easy to lay (see Introduction). Next comes the odd account of Gilbert and Frances' honeymoon and of the years that followed. It is of course possible that the first night of their marriage was not happy—especially in the Victorian days of reticence which left wife and even possibly husband unprepared for life together: (though this did not normally prevent a happy marriage and a pack of children afterwards). But I find it impossible to imagine Cecil Chesterton, like the bridesmaid on the honeymoon, receiving and passing on such a story as that of Gilbert "quivering with self-reproach" so that after the first night he "dared not even contemplate a repetition. . . . Gilbert, young and vital, was condemned to a pseudo-monastic life, in which he lived with a woman but never enjoyed one." (p. 282)

There is a psychological reason for thinking this story especially improbable and a physical reason for dismissing it as actually impossible.

A white horse had from his childhood been for Gilbert the supreme sign of romance, and he had chosen to spend the first night of his honeymoon at the White Horse Inn. From his honeymoon he wrote home that he had "a wife, a piece of string, a pencil and a knife. What more can any man want?" Ten years later he wrote *The Ballad of the White Horse* and dedicated it to Frances, saying,

> "O go you onward, where you are
> Shall honour and laughter be.
> Past purpled forest and pearled foam,
> God's winged pavilion free to roam,
> Your face, that is a wandering home,
> A flying home for me."

And over thirty years later he wrote again of beginning his honeymoon under the shadow of the White Horse, and compared it to a trip to fairyland.

Can any human being read the record of this recurrent motif and reconcile it with Mrs. Cecil's picture?

Let me refer again to *The Ballad of the White Horse*. Is it conceivable that any man should write after ten years of frustration and unhappiness:

Up through an empty house of stars
Being what heart you are,
Up the inhuman steeps of space
As on a staircase go in grace
Carrying the firelight on your facc
Beyond the loneliest star.

This is not the way a man writes to a neurotic cold-hearted woman who has made a hermit of him!

Mrs. Cecil was of course never in the intimacy of the family. She only married Cecil in 1917—by which date Gilbert and Frances had been married sixteen years—and before that she was merely an acquaintance. But Frances's intimates could have told her how absurd her story was, for by a rare good fortune the operation Frances underwent to enable her to bear children is itself evidence one could hardly have hoped for in a matter which civilized people are not much given to discussing. Frances talked of the operation to Monsignor O'Connor, to Dorothy Collins and to Annie Firmin, and I have quoted the doctor's letter about it (see above, page 244). It was an abiding tragedy for both husband and wife that it was unsuccessful. Frances would have shrunk from no suffering in her passionate wish for a child.

There is another curiosity in the Legend: Gilbert, despite this story, was apparently perfectly happy in London during the *first eight years of marriage*: it was only after the removal to Beaconsfield and in almost middle life that he began to be "frustrated."

Poor Frances: what a picture of her had been proposed for posterity: so powerful she could waft Gilbert away from London and from his friends, could force him to make her his banker and reduce him to a "bounty" strictly limited to half-a-crown, yet so powerless that "she had to sign" the cheques for *G. K.'s Weekly*, much as she hated it. Her poetry (described as "quite charming") is spoken of as appearing in "little Parish Magazines"—

the only papers she cared to read owing to her implacable hatred for Fleet Street. It is hard to picture Frances with an implacable hatred for anything, and it will be remembered that she actually begged Father O'Connor to leave Gilbert to be "a jolly journalist." The periodicals in which her poems appeared were *The Observer, The Sunday Times, The Daily Chronicle, The Westminster Gazette* and *The New Witness.* Personally I have never much admired Frances's verse, but a professional journalist might have been quite pleased at "making" all these papers. Not one poem ever appeared in a Parish Magazine so far as either Dorothy or I have been able to ascertain. The point is not a very important one but the sneer is symptomatic.

A curious magic pervades *The Chestertons:* succulent sausages appear in the kitchen at Overstrand Mansions, and flowing torrents of beer, so that Gilbert can steal away from an unsympathetic wife to consume them with his Fleet Street friends. A studio materialises in a meadow at Beaconsfield. Can we imagine Gilbert cooking or even ordering sausages, getting beer to the flat, designing or discovering the studio? Anyone thinking about what really happened would realise that Frances ordered the beer and sausages, Frances built the studio. But that is not the sort of thought we are to think about Frances.

About her we are told: that she always wore the wrong colors: that she gave Gilbert insufficient and indigestible food: that she did not know what work meant: that Mrs. Belloc thought Gilbert ought to beat her: that she kept the journalists away when Gilbert was dying (in point of fact both telephone and door bell were so near the sick room that the use of both had to be avoided): that she did not give her guests enough to eat at his funeral: that she actually sought the quiet of her own room instead of staying downstairs to receive condolences when her husband's coffin had just been lowered into the grave.

With all this spate of detail, we are not told that Frances left £1000 to Mrs. Cecil plus £500 for her Cecil Houses.

Even if I could have ignored the attack on Frances, I should be obliged as his biographer to deal with the attack on Gilbert—more subtly but no less certainly made. The story of the marriage affects Gilbert as much as Frances, and the book culminates in the final assertion that his drinking killed him. Here are the comments (sent to me by Dorothy) of the doctor who attended Gilbert and Frances from 1919 until they died:

"Today Dr. Bakewell came in and answered the questions about the book which we asked him.

(1) He says that the idea that G.K. was better when drinking in Fleet Street because the stimulus of conversation would eat up effects of the alcohol is absolute nonsense. It would have just as bad an effect under any conditions. Dr. Bakewell said that G.K. was his patient for nearly twenty years and during that time he never treated him for alcoholism or saw any trace of it, though in an absentminded way he was always liable to drink too much of anything if it were there—even water.

Without the 'understanding, loving, tactful care' of Frances he would have died twenty years before. Certainly if he had racketted around Fleet Street any longer.

Dr. Bakewell said Gilbert was 'perfectly happy in Beaconsfield and not in any way frustrated. There was no frustration of any kind and no longing for London life or friends.' He was very intimate with Gilbert and would have known if there had been.

(2) The doctor says that Gilbert died of a failing heart owing to fatty degeneration, leading to dropsy.

(3) Frances had arthritis of the spine. (Not curvature as stated by Mrs. Cecil.)

The doctor said that he put him on the water wagon several times and when this was done Gilbert observed the rule most meticulously. Dr. Bakewell said that he did not do it very often because he did not consider that drink was in any way affecting Gilbert's health during the greater part of the time he knew him."

In a later conversation he added that when he did forbid alcohol at certain periods it was simply to make liquid less attractive, as too much of even water was bad for Gilbert.

The statement made by Mrs. Cecil that drinking in London was not so serious because the talk and excitement among friends would carry off the effects, is thought by doctors almost comic. Dr. Bakewell denies it absolutely: Dr. Pocock who, it will be remembered, attended Gilbert during his illness of 1914–15 says, "Absolute nonsense: would probably have been worse in London." He adds also, "I cannot understand why such an attack was made upon G.K. From my personal observation he owed a very great deal to Mrs. G.K. who greatly helped his restoration to health."

One can get one's pen'orth of fun out of the chapter on the Exile of Beaconsfield when one remembers the true story of those years: Rome, Jerusalem, U.S.A., Poland, France, Spain, Malta, lectures all over England, lively contests for the Lord Rectorship of three universities, London again and again—for editing, mock trials, debates and Distributist Beanos—and frequently in furnished flats which Frances would take for the winter months. One can only suppose that Mrs. Cecil was so little intimate with them that she did not realise all this.

And then Beaconsfield itself—parties in the Studio; people down from London, visitors from Poland, France, America, Italy, Holland and other countries; the Eric Gills, the Bernard Shaws, the Garvins, the Emile Cammaerts and others living in the neighborhood; the guest room always occupied by some intimate. Meanwhile the books poured out of the little study. Mrs. Cecil thinks Gilbert hardly ever again wrote a masterpiece after leaving Battersea, yet in support of this idea she lists as masterpieces *The Ball and the Cross* (written at Beaconsfield), *Lepanto* (written at Beaconsfield), *Magic* (written at Beaconsfield), *Stevenson* (written at Beaconsfield) and *The Ballad of the White Horse* (mainly written at Beaconsfield). Of all the books she mentions in this connection only three were written in London! And she admits that the world at large did not share her view of the sterilizing effect of Beaconsfield, for she writes,

"Meanwhile his fame grew wider, his sales greater. In exile he ruled a literary world." *

Gilbert left to Mrs. Cecil Chesterton sums equal to those later left to her by Frances—£1000 for herself and £500 for Cecil Houses.

The ingratitude that omitted all mention of these benefactions struck the imagination of several of the Chesterton family as the worst feature in the book. But to Gilbert and Frances the giving of money even in their own lifetime was a slight matter. They had given something far greater.

Why is the memory of Cecil Chesterton alive today? Because of his brother's labors. Why is it possible for Mrs. Cecil to declare that he was the greater editor, to imply that he was the greater man? Because Gilbert kept saying so. Never has such devotion been shown by one brother to the memory of another: never has the greater man exalted the lesser to such a pedestal.

We are told in *The Chestertons* that Frances sacrificed both Gilbert and herself on the altar of her family. Truly there was much self-sacrifice in the lives of both to family, friends and causes. They did not feel it as self-sacrifice to enrich the lives of others even at cost to themselves.

But the heaviest cost they paid lay in the years of a toil that was literally killing Gilbert while Frances watched him growing old too soon and straining his heart with work crushingly heavy: and if there was a single altar for that supreme sacrifice it was no other than the altar of Cecil's memory.

* P. 83.

Acknowledgments

I am exceedingly grateful to the following publishers for permission to quote from these books:

DODD, MEAD & CO.:
The Man Who Was Thursday; Orthodoxy; The Napoleon of Notting Hill; Heretics; George Bernard Shaw; The Ball and the Cross; The Poet and the Lunatic; Alarms and Discursions; The Ballad of the White Horse; What's Wrong with the World; Manalive; Sidelights on New London and Newer York; The Uses of Diversity; The History of England; Irish Impressions; Collected Poems; The Queen of Seven Swords; The Everlasting Man; Cobbett; Outline of Sanity; Tales of the Long Bow; What I Saw in America; The Thing; The Defendant; The Barbarism of Berlin: or The Appetite of Tyranny; Eugenics and Other Evils; Collected Poems; G. K. Chesterton, A Criticism (by Cecil Chesterton).

DOUBLEDAY DORAN:
St. Francis of Assisi; The Years Between.

E. P. DUTTON & CO., INC.:
Criticisms and Appreciations of the Works of Charles Dickens.

FARRAR & RINEHART:
Chaucer.

THE MACMILLAN COMPANY:
Robert Browning; The Catholic Church and Conversion.

OXFORD UNIVERSITY PRESS:
The Victorian Age in Literature.

G. P. PUTNAM'S SONS:
Rufus Isaacs, First Marquess of Reading.

UNIVERSITY OF NOTRE DAME:
The Arena.

669

Bibliography

In this list I have given dates of earliest publication. In some cases publication in England preceded that in the United States.

1900. *Greybeards at Play.* R. B. Johnson. Reprinted 1930.
The Wild Knight and Other Poems. Included in *Collected Poems.*
1901. *The Defendant.*
1902. *G. F. Watts.*
Twelve Types.
1903. *Robert Browning.*
1904. *The Napoleon of Notting Hill.*
1905. *The Club of Queer Trades.*
Heretics.
1906. *Charles Dickens.*
1907. *The Man Who Was Thursday.*
1908. *Orthodoxy.*
All Things Considered.
1909. *George Bernard Shaw.*
The Ball and the Cross.
Tremendous Trifles.
Defence of Nonsense.
1910. *What's Wrong with the World?*
William Blake.
Alarms and Discursions.
Five Types.
1911. *The Innocence of Father Brown.*
Appreciations and Criticisms of the Works of Charles Dickens.
The Ballad of the White Horse.
1912. *Manalive.*
A Miscellany of Men.
Simplicity of Tolstoy.
The Victorian Age in Literature.
1913. *Magic. A Play.*

1914. *The Wisdom of Father Brown.*
The Flying Inn.
The Barbarism of Berlin.
1915. *Poems.*
Wine, Water, and Song. Reprint of poems from *The Flying Inn.*
The Crimes of England.
Letters to an Old Garibaldian.
1916. *A Shilling for my Thoughts.*
1917. *A Short History of England.*
Utopia of Usurers.
1919. *Irish Impressions.*
1920. *The Uses of Diversity.*
The New Jerusalem.
The Superstition of Divorce.
1922. *Eugenics and Other Evils.*
The Man Who Knew Too Much.
What I Saw in America.
The Ballad of St. Barbara. In *Collected Poems.*
1923. *Fancies versus Fads.*
St. Francis of Assisi.
1924. *The End of the Roman Road.* Preface by St. John Adcock.
1925. *The Everlasting Man.*
Tales of the Long Bow.
William Cobbett.
The Superstitions of the Sceptic.
1926. *The Incredulity of Father Brown.*
The Outline of Sanity.
A Gleaming Cohort.
The Queen of Seven Swords. Poems. Not included in *Collected Poems.*
The Catholic Church and Conversion.
Culture and the Coming Peril. University of London Publication.
Social Reform and Birth Control. Pamphlet—Simpkin Kent & Co., League of National Life.
1927. *Collected Poems.*
The Return of Don Quixote.
Robert Louis Stevenson.
The Secret of Father Brown.

The Judgment of Dr. Johnson. A Play.

Gloria in Profundis. Short Poem.

1928. *Generally Speaking.*

Essays of To-day and Yesterday Series.

Short Stories of To-day and Yesterday Series. Reprinted from other volumes.

The Sword of Wood. Short Story. Edition de Luxe, Signed. Reprinted in Everyman Edition.

1929. *The Poet and the Lunatics.*

Omnibus Volume—Father Brown Stories.

Ubi Ecclesia. Short Poem.

The Thing. Catholic Essays.

G.K.C. as M.C. Collection of Introductions.

The Turkey and the Turk. Christmas Play. Ill. by Thomas Derrick.

1930. *The Grave of Arthur.* Short Poem. Ariel Poem Series.

Come to Think of It. Essays. Edited by E. V. Lucas.

The Resurrection of Rome.

1931. *All is Grist.* Essays edited by E. V. Lucas.

1932. *Chaucer.* A Study.

Sidelights on New London and Newer York. Essays.

Christendom in Dublin. Essays on Eucharistic Congress, Dublin.

1933. *All I Survey.* Essays. Edited by E. V. Lucas.

St. Thomas Aquinas.

Collected Poems. Republished

Collected Prefaces to Charles Dickens's Works. Reprinted.

Methuen's Library of Humour. 1 vol.

1934. *Avowals and Denials.* Essays.

1935. *The Scandal of Father Brown.*

George Bernard Shaw. New edition with additional chapter. The Later Phases.

The Well and the Shallows.

1936. *As I Was Saying.* Essays. Edited by E. V. Lucas.

POSTHUMOUS PUBLICATIONS

1936. *Autobiography.*

1937. *The Paradoxes of Mr. Pond.*

1938. *The Colored Lands.*

1940. *The End of the Armistice.*

PREFACES TO OTHER AUTHORS' BOOKS

1902. Carlyle, *Past and Present.*
      Nonsense Rhymes, by W. C. Monkhouse.
      R.L.S., in Bookman Booklets.
      Tolstoy, in Bookman Booklets.
1903. *Boswell. Life of Johnson Extracts.*
1904. O. W. Holmes, *Autocrat of the Breakfast Table.* Red Letter
         Library.
      Carlyle, *Sartor Resartus.* National Library.
      Bunyan, *Pilgrim's Progress.* National Library.
1905. Maxim Gorky, *Creatures That Once Were Men.*
1906. *Dickens* in Everyman Library. Prefaces to all volumes.
      Matthew Arnold. Everyman Library.
      Elsie Lang. Literary London.
      Characteristics of R.L.S. Little Books for Bookmen.
      Tennyson as an Intellectual Force. Little Books for Bookmen.
1907. *The Book of Job.*
      George Haw, *From Workhouse to Westminster: Will Crooks.*
1908. Ruskin, *Poems.* Muses Library.
      W. W. Crotch, *The Cottage Homes of England.*
1909. Darrell Figgis. *A Vision of Life.*
      Margaret Arndt, *Meadows of Play.*
1910. *Thackeray, Selection.* Masters of Literature Series.
      Eyes of Youth, Anthology.
1911. *Johnson, Extracts.* Ed. Alice Meynell.
      Thackeray, *The Book of Snobs.* Red Letter Library.
1912. *Famous Paintings, Reproduced in Colour.*
      A. V. Baverstock, *English Agricultural Labourer.*
      Aesop's Fables. Translated by Vernon Jones.
1913. Dickens, *The Christmas Carol.* Waverley Dickens.
1915. *Bohemia's Claim for Freedom.* London, Czech Committee.
1916. C. C. Mendell and E. Shanks, *Hilaire Belloc.*
      Cobbett, *Cottage Economy.*
      Harewranath Maitra, *Hinduism.*
1917. S. Nordentoft, *Practical Pacifism and Its Adversaries.*
1918. Sybil Bristowe, *Provocations.*
      William Dyson, *Australia at War.*
      Leonard Merrick, *House of Lynch.*
1919. Cecil Chesterton, *History of the U. S. A.*
      Bernard Capes, *The Skeleton Key.*

1920. M. E. Jones, *Life in Old Cambridge.*
1921. Vivienne Dayrell, *Little Wings.*
H. M. Bateman, *A Book of Drawings.*
1922. Jane Austen, *Love and Friendship.*
1923. Irene Hernaman, *Child Mediums.*
O. R. Vassall Phillips, *The Mustard Tree.*
1924. O. F. Dudley, *Will Men Be Like Gods.*
Greville Macdonald, *George MacDonald and His Wife.*
Catholic Who's Who.
P. M. Wright, *Purple Hours.*
1925. Fulton Sheen, *God and Intelligence.*
Alexander Arnoux, *Abishag.* Trans. Joyce Davis.
1926. A. H. Godwin, *Gilbert and Sullivan.*
Johnson, *Rasselas.*
Catholic Who's Who.
L. G. Sieveking, *Bats in the Belfry.*
The Man Who Was Thursday, Dramatized Version.
W. S. Masterman, *The Wrong Letter.*
Royal Society of Literature, Essays, Vol. vi.
1927. E. Turner, *Grandmamma's Book of Rhymes.*
G. C. Heseltine, *The Change.* Essays on the Land.
H. Massis, *Defence of the West.*
Forster's Life of Dickens. Everyman Library,
1928. Mary Webb, *The Golden Arrow.*
1929. H. Ghéon, *The Secret of the Cure D'ars,* trans. F. Sheed.
W. R. Titterton, *Drinking Songs.*
1930. Miss C. Noran, *Book on Spanish History.*
King Lear. De Luxe Edition. Illustrated Yunge.
Introduction to *Vanity Fair,* Thackeray. Limited Edition
Club, New York.
1931. *Giotto's Frescoes at Assisi Reproduced.*
John Gibbons, *Through Unknown Portugal.*
F. Goetel, *The Messenger of the Snow.*
Francis Thompson, *The Hound of Heaven.*
A. A. Thomas, *The Burns We Love.*
J. P. de Fonseka, *Serendipitry.*
Daniel O'Grady, *Cosmology.*
1932. Gleeson, *Essays.*
Essays of the Year, Argonaut Press.
Six Centuries of English Literature, Vol. vi. Meredith to
Rupert Brooke.

Mrs. Homewood, *Reminiscences.*
Penn Country Book.
1933. *Life of Sydney Smith.* Hesketh Pearson.
Tale of Two Cities.
1934. *Peregrine Pickle.* First Edition Club, U. S. A.
Pamphlet on *Nazi Germany* for Friends of Europe publication, edited by Lord Tyrrell.
G.K.'s Miscellany.
1935. Fr. Dowsell, *The Betrayal: A Passion Play.*
Fr. Vincent McNabb, *Book of Essays.*
Detective Stories. Collection from Hutchinson.
1936. F. A. MacNutt, *A Papal Chamberlain.*
1935. Letterpress to *Stations of the Cross,* by F. Brangwyn.

I doubt whether the list of introductions is complete but Dorothy Collins has done her best to make it so. Of the books and essays about Chesterton there is no end. Those I have used in writing this book are

Father Brown on Chesterton, Monsignor O'Connor.
G. K. Chesterton, a Criticism, Cecil Chesterton.
The Place of Chesterton in English Literature, Hilaire Belloc.
The Laughing Prophet, Emile Cammaerts.
G. K. Chesterton, Cyril Clemens.

For the chapters on Sociology I have consulted the invaluable series on the English Labourer by the Hammonds, C. S. Orpen's *Open Fields,* Trevelyan's *Social History of England,* Cobbett's *Rural Rides and Cottage Economy* and Haas' *English Labourer.*

For the Marconi Chapter I have used the Reports of the Parliamentary Commission and of the trial of Cecil Chesterton, C. F. G. Masterman's *Life* and that of Lord Reading, and contemporary press accounts.

Throughout I have made use of the files of *The Eyewitness, The New Witness* and *G.K.'s Weekly.*

Index